212261-cb5
China
195.00
132.50
AF769286

Rising China in the Changing World Economy

China's rapid and sustained growth over the last 30 years has propelled it to become the world's second largest economy today and potentially the largest in the foreseeable future. As one of the first major economies pulling out of recession and the last remaining major socialist country in the world today, China presents a challenge to established thinking on the essential primacy of global capitalism and the settled nature of the world system – as China becomes more integrated into the world economy and the international system, both are themselves potentially transformed as a result of China's involvement. This book explores a wide range of issues connected with the impact of China on the global economy and the prevailing international system. Subjects covered include China's multinationals, international acquisitions, the exchange rate, research and development and technology transfer, China's emerging major business groupings, and small and medium-size enterprises.

Liming Wang is Director of the Irish Institute for Chinese Studies in University College, Dublin; Director of the Confucius Institute for Ireland; the Secretary General of the Chinese Economic Association (Europe); and a Board Director of the Institute of International Trade of Ireland. He is co-author of *Doing Business in China: The Irish experience* and *China's Grain Economy: The challenge of feeding more than a billion.*

Routledge studies on the Chinese economy

Series editor

Peter Nolan, Sinyi Professor, *Judge Business School*, and Chair, *Development Studies, University of Cambridge*

Founding series editors

Peter Nolan, *University of Cambridge and*
Dong Fureng, *Beijing University*

The aim of this series is to publish original, high-quality, research-level work by both new and established scholars in the West and the East, on all aspects of the Chinese economy, including studies of business and economic history.

1 **The Growth of Market Relations in Post-reform Rural China**
A micro-analysis of peasants, migrants and peasant entrepreneurs
Hiroshi Sato

2 **The Chinese Coal Industry**
An economic history
Elspeth Thomson

3 **Sustaining China's Economic Growth in the Twenty-First Century**
Edited by Shujie Yao and Xiaming Liu

4 **China's Poor Regions**
Rural–urban migration, poverty, economic reform and urbanisation
Mei Zhang

5 **China's Large Enterprises and the Challenge of Late Industrialization**
Dylan Sutherland

6 **China's Economic Growth**
Yanrui Wu

7 **The Employment Impact of China's World Trade Organisation Accession**
A.S. Bhalla and S. Qiu

8 **Catch-Up and Competitiveness in China**
The case of large firms in the oil industry
Jin Zhang

9 **Corporate Governance in China**
Jian Chen

10 **The Theory of the Firm and Chinese Enterprise Reform**
The case of China International Trust and Investment Corporation
Qin Xiao

11 **Globalisation, Transition and Development in China**
The case of the coal industry
Huaichuan Rui

12 **China Along the Yellow River**
Reflections on rural society
Cao Jinqing, translated by Nicky Harman and Huang Ruhua

13 **Economic Growth, Income Distribution and Poverty Reduction in Contemporary China**
Shujie Yao

14 **China's Economic Relations with the West and Japan, 1949–79**
Grain, trade and diplomacy
Chad J. Mitcham

15 **China's Industrial Policy and the Global Business Revolution**
The case of the domestic appliance industry
Ling Liu

16 **Managers and Mandarins in Contemporary China**
The building of an international business alliance
Jie Tang

17 **The Chinese Model of Modern Development**
Edited by Tian Yu Cao

18 **Chinese Citizenship**
Views from the margins
Edited by Vanessa L. Fong and Rachel Murphy

19 **Unemployment, Inequality and Poverty in Urban China**
Edited by Shi Li and Hiroshi Sato

20 **Globalisation, Competition and Growth in China**
Edited by Jian Chen and Shujie Yao

21 **The Chinese Communist Party in Reform**
Edited by Kjeld Erik Brodsgaard and Zheng Yongnian

22 **Poverty and Inequality among Chinese Minorities**
A.S. Bhalla and Shufang Qiu

23 **Economic and Social Transformation in China**
Challenges and opportunities
Angang Hu

24 **Global Big Business and the Chinese Brewing Industry**
Yuantao Guo

25 **Peasants and Revolution in Rural China**
Rural political change in the North China Plain and the Yangzi Delta, 1850–1949
Chang Liu

26 **The Chinese Banking Industry**
Lessons from history for today's challenges
Yuanyuan Peng

27 **Informal Institutions and Rural Development in China**
Biliang Hu

28 **The Political Future of Hong Kong**
Democracy within communist China
Kit Poon

29 **China's Post-Reform Economy – Achieving Harmony, Sustaining Growth**
Edited by Richard Sanders and Chen Yang

30 **Eliminating Poverty Through Development in China**
China Development Research Foundation

31 **Good Governance in China – A Way Towards Social Harmony**
Case studies by China's rising leaders
Edited by Wang Mengkui

32 **China in the Wake of Asia's Financial Crisis**
Edited by Wang Mengkui

33 **Multinationals, Globalisation and Indigenous Firms in China**
Chunhang Liu

34 **Economic Convergence in Greater China**
Mainland China, Hong Kong, Macau and Taiwan
Chun Kwok Lei and Shujie Yao

35 **Financial Sector Reform and the International Integration of China**
Zhongmin Wu

36 **China in the World Economy**
Zhongmin Wu

37 **China's Three Decades of Economic Reforms**
Edited by Xiaohui Liu and Wei Zhang

38 **China's Development Challenges**
Economic vulnerability and public sector reform
Richard Schiere

39 **China's Rural Financial System**
Households' demand for credit and recent reforms
Yuepeng Zhao

40 **Sustainable Reform and Development in Post-Olympic China**
Edited by Shujie Yao, Bin Wu, Stephen Morgan and Dylan Sutherland

41 **Constructing a Developmental Social Welfare System for All**
China Development Research Foundation

42 **China's Road to Peaceful Rise**
Observations on its cause, basis, connotation and prospect
Zheng Bijian

43 **China as the Workshop of the World**
An analysis at the national and industry level of China in the International division of labor
Yuning Gao

44 China's Role in Global Economic Recovery
Xiaolan Fu

45 The Political Economy of the Chinese Coal Industry
Black gold and blood-stained coal
Tim Wright

46 Rising China in the Changing World Economy
Edited by Liming Wang

47 Thirty Years of China's Reform
Edited by Wang Mengkui

Routledge studies on the Chinese economy – Chinese economists on economic reform

1 Chinese Economists on Economic Reform – Collected Works of Xue Muqiao
Xue Muqiao, edited by China Development Research Foundation

2 Chinese Economists on Economic Reform – Collected Works of Guo Shuqing
Guo Shuqing, edited by China Development Research Foundation

Rising China in the Changing World Economy

Edited by Liming Wang

Routledge
Taylor & Francis Group
LONDON AND NEW YORK

This edition published 2012
by Routledge
2 Park Square, Milton Park, Abingdon, Oxon, OX14 4RN

Simultaneously published in the USA and Canada
by Routledge
711 Third Avenue, New York, NY 10017

Routledge is an imprint of the Taylor & Francis Group, an informa business

© 2012 Liming Wang for selection and editorial material. Individual chapters, the contributors.

The right of the editor to be identified as the author of the editorial material, and of the authors for their individual chapters, has been asserted in accordance with sections 77 and 78 of the Copyright, Designs and Patents Act 1988.

All rights reserved. No part of this book may be reprinted or reproduced or utilised in any form or by any electronic, mechanical, or other means, now known or hereafter invented, including photocopying and recording, or in any information storage or retrieval system, without permission in writing from the publishers.

British Library Cataloguing in Publication Data
A catalogue record for this book is available from the British Library

Library of Congress Cataloging-in-Publication Data
A catalog record has been requested for this book

ISBN: 978-0-415-61095-7 (hbk)
ISBN: 978-0-203-14459-6 (ebk)

Typeset in Times New Roman
by Sunrise Setting Ltd, Torquay, UK

Contents

Figures

Tables

Preface

In the early twenty-first century, irrespective of globalization and its implicit corollary of economic interdependence, human beings still live in nation states that can be seen to both cooperate and compete with each other. Any state that contains a fifth of the human race will inevitably attract serious attention, and deservedly so. China's rise can be immediately understood as the increasing realization of its vast economic potential. Breathtaking as it may be to witness, the swift ascent of China is quite in keeping with the country's size and reform process. Taking a longer term historical perspective, what we are actually witnessing is a proportionate resumption of Chinese economic predominance. On the other hand, China faces very serious challenges and constraints. Economists caution that action needs to be taken to tackle major problems such as environmental damage, income inequality, a real estate bubble and growth patterns affecting the functioning and structure of the Chinese economic system caused by a huge and unprecedented government stimulus through bank loans.

China may provide a textbook case of a mixed economy that synchronizes the virtues of capitalism with those of socialism and complements private initiative with public control. China was the first of the major economies to pull clear of the global recession. In the aftermath of the international financial crisis, the relative success of China's 'socialist market economy' challenges existing critical thought, in particular regarding theory on transitional economies. It now seems imperative to raise the question of valid alternative conceptualizations that can explain the changing landscape of the world economy. In the context of the global recession, rising China and its economic integration with the rest of the world is prompting no less than a serious reconsideration of global capitalism as an ideology. It is also challenging the 'world order' or 'world system' as a fixed and accepted reality.

Integration with the world economy has also been transforming the nature and structure of the Chinese economy. China seems to have acquired the kind of experience and skills that are needed to manage an economy in the process of reform and opening up to the outside world. Its mode of development has recently become increasingly attractive to developing countries in economic transition. The growing importance of China's economy and its potential as a centre for business and institutional innovation is also affecting the way that industrialized nations think about the current world economic order.

While economic inequality has increased during the period of China's sustained high economic growth, it is very important not to ignore the scale of China's achievement in lifting hundreds of millions of its people out of poverty during the last three decades. Huge income inequalities persist throughout the developed world and poverty rates are worsening. Meanwhile, China is rapidly creating the largest middle class in the world, paving the way for long-term economic growth based on domestic consumer demand.

Having experienced the tumultuous years of the 'Cultural Revolution', China's decision to join the western economic system was based on a broad domestic consensus and on globally shared values regarding national development, individual freedom and world peace. Since economic reform and opening up, China has benefited enormously from trade and international technology spill-over. Economic development and integration into the global economic system have made China the world's most influential emerging market. China's rapid industrialization is changing the landscape of the world economy and has brought forward new dynamics in international relations.

A two day International Conference on the theme of 'China and the Changing Landscape of the World Economy' was jointly organized by the Chinese Economic Association (Europe/UK) and the Irish Institute for Chinese Studies at University College Dublin in July 2009. A follow-up conference with the theme of 'China and the Changing Landscape of the World Economy: Confucianism and Financial Crisis Management' was held in Renmin University of China in September 2009. The two conferences were attended by over 200 high-level delegates and over 140 papers were presented. This volume includes the highest quality 16 papers selected from the conferences. Collectively, the papers in this volume provide a comprehensive analysis of important issues concerning China's economic development and its international economic integration with the changing world.

This volume contains contributions that seek to explore the inter-relationship between rising China and its integration with the world economy and the impact of the dynamics of that inter-relationship on various aspects of the Chinese economy. The questions that arise from this inter-relationship include, for example, the extent to which traditional western economic theory can successfully explain the development of the Chinese economy and whether economic theory now needs to be reframed to explain the emergence of a transformed China in a global economy. The contributions in this volume are used to address these and other emerging questions faced by different sectors of the Chinese economy.

Liming Wang
Dublin, March 2011

Contributors

David H. Brown is Chair of Strategy and Information Systems and Director of the China Management Centre at Lancaster University Management School, UK. His research interests have two separate but linked strands. First, strategic studies, including strategic information systems, and second the application of these strands internationally, including developing economies. The majority of his work is strongly based around the operation of organizations, including SMEs, and has work has been published widely.

Alan Butt-Philip is an Honorary Jean Monnet Reader in European Integration in the School of Management, University of Bath (UK) and a Visiting Professor at the Charles University in Prague. He has published widely on the EU single market and has held visiting professorships at the Universities of Virginia and Richmond, and at ESCP-EAP in Paris.

Xi Chen is a PhD Candidate in the Charles Dyson School of Applied Economics and Management at Cornell University. His research interests lie in relativity, inequality and well-being. Both of his BSc and MSc were obtained from Nanjing Agricultural University.

Gregory C. Chow is a Professor of Economics and Class of 1913 Professor of Political Economy, Emeritus, at Princeton University. He was Director of the Econometric Research Program at Princeton from 1970 to 1997, and the Program was renamed the Gregory C. Chow Econometric Research Program in 2001 in his honour. He is author of 14 books and over 200 articles in the fields of econometrics, applied economics, dynamic economics and the Chinese economy, and he has advised top government officials of the People's Republic of China on economic reform and the economics of education.

Yizhe Dong is a Post Doctoral Fellow in Accounting and Finance at Durham University. His research interests include efficiency and productivity analysis using stochastic frontier econometrics and mathematical programming, the structure and competition of banking markets, and the design of banking regulation.

Gaston Fornes, is a Teaching Fellow at the School of Sociology, Politics and International Studies at the University of Bristol (UK), and Associate Professor at ESIC Business and Marketing School (Spain). Dr Gaston Fornes worked in industry for around ten years in the United States, Argentina and Chile before starting his career in academia. He received the Liupan Mountain Friendship Award from the Ningxia Government (China) in 2010 and is Fellow of the UK Higher Education Academy. His main research interest is management in emerging economies.

Giuseppe Gabusi is a Lecturer in International Political Economy and Political Economy of East Asia at the University of Turin and the Catholic University, Brescia. He is the Head of Research at the Torino World Affairs Institute (T.wai), and is co-editor of the website www.thechinacompanion.eu. He obtained his masters degree in Political Economy and International Relations at ASERI, Milan and his PhD from the Catholic University of Milan.

Stefan Gravemeyer has been a researcher at the Center for International Economics, University of Paderborn in Germany since 2006. His recent research and publications focus around the areas of income inequality, poverty and migration in urban China.

Thomas Gries is a Professor for Economics at the Centre for International Economics, University of Paderborn in Germany. His research interests are international growth and development, both at the micro and macro level. In recent publications he has focused on developments in Asia and China.

Youwei Li is a Senior Lecturer in Finance at the School of Management, Queen's University, Belfast. His research interests include financial econometrics, quantitative finance, and agent-based modelling of financial markets.

Siyue Liu is an Associate Professor, Associate Director of Finance Department, Economics and Management School, Wuhan University, China. His research interests are mainly in capital operation, commercial bank risk management, foreign exchange risk management and exchange rate theories and policies.

Donal McKillop is a Professor of Financial Services at Queen's University Management School, Belfast. His subject specialisms are financial theory, financial derivatives and financial regulation.

Lutao Ning is a Lecturer in International Business at Durham Business School, Durham University, and holds a PhD degree from the University of Cambridge. His multidisciplinary research background ranges from international business and management, to law, political economy and development studies.

Sangaralingam Ramesh is a Teaching Fellow in Economics at University College, London, and a part-time tutor with the Department of Continuing Education at Oxford University. Dr Ramesh graduated with a PhD in Economics from SOAS in 2009 and taught a variety of undergraduate courses there from 2007–2010.

Dylan Sutherland is a lecturer at the School of Contemporary Chinese Studies, University of Nottingham. Prior to this he worked at Trinity College, Dublin (Department of Economics) and Cambridge University (Development Studies). His current research considers the internationalization of Chinese business.

Xuebing Tang is an Assistant Professor in the Department of Economics, Huazhong Normal University in Wuhan, (since July 2009). He gained his PhD in Economics from Renmin University of China in June 2009. His research focuses on using economic theory and empirical tools to analyze regional economic problems and public economic policy.

Da Teng is a Lecturer in Strategic Management at the Strategy and Applied Management Group of Coventry University Business School, Coventry University. Much of his work deals with Chinese economic development and corporate governance in state-owned enterprises. He is currently engaged in research projects on entrepreneurship, and small and medium enterprises.

Jing Wang is a research student in the School of Economics, Zhejiang University.

Lei Wang is a PhD student of Business Economics and Management at the University of Lugano, Switzerland (since 2006) and a researcher at Bern University of Applied Science (since 2009). Her research interests cover mergers and acquisitions, corporation management, foreign direct investment, energy and environmental economics.

Liming Wang is the director of the Irish Institute for Chinese Studies at University College, Dublin and UCD Confucius Institute for Ireland. His research interests include comparative studies between Chinese and European economies, China's financial market and international trade, China's rural development and grain economy.

Qi Wang holds two Master's Degrees with Distinction – in Information Technology, and Management and Human Resources – from Lancaster University, UK, where she is a Research Associate. An experienced software project coordinator, she has worked in outsourcing, systems development and training. She joined her present company Xi'an Telenavsoftware Inc in 2009 and is focusing on collaborative US–China projects.

Yanbing Wu is an Associate Professor of the Institute of Economics, Chinese Academy of Social Sciences (CASS). He received a PhD in Economics from the Graduate School of CASS in 2006 and was a visiting scholar at the University of California, Berkeley, from 2010–11. His current research focuses on Research and Development, innovation and economic development.

Wei Xia is a PhD candidate in the Michael Smurfit Business School & Law School of University College, Dublin. Her current interests mainly focus on agricultural trade between EU and China, China's rural development and food safety crisis in China.

Jinjun Xue is a Professor at the Economic Research Center, the Graduate School of Economics, Nagoya University, Japan. He has written many publications in English, Japanese and Chinese, and was main author and chief editor of *Inequality in China*, Nippon Hyoron-sha, 2008 (Japanese version), and Social Science Academic Press, 2008 (Chinese version).

Min Ye is a PhD candidate, sponsored by China Scholarship Council, at Michael Smurfit Graduate Business School, University College, Dublin. Her current research interests are mainly in international finance, and specifically in foreign exchange exposure. She earned her BSc and MA degrees from Wuhan University, China.

Ren Zhang is a PhD candidate at the School of Management at Queen's University, Belfast. She currently focuses on the distributional characteristics, price movement, and behaviour of volatility and trading activity on China's futures markets.

Abbreviations

ADL	Activities of Daily Living
AI	Ageing Index
AIC	Akaike's Information Criteria
AMCs	Asset Management Corporations
ARCH	Autoregressive Conditional Heteroskedasticity
ARMA	Autoregressive Moving Average
B-C	Bureaucrats-turned-capitalists
BCC	Banker Charnes Cooper model
BEER	Department for Business, Enterprise and Regulatory Reform
BIC	Bayesian Information Criterion
Big Four	Big four state-owned commercial banks
BPS	Basic Public Services
BRIC	Brazil, Russia, India and China
CAAS	Chinese Academy of Agricultural Sciences
CAD	Computer-aided Design
CAM	Computer-aided Manufacturing
CAPM	Chinese Academy of Preventative Medicine
CAS	Chinese Accounting Standards
CASS	Chinese Academy of Social Sciences
CBOT	Chicago Board Of Trade
CCBs	City Commercial Banks
CCDCP	Chinese Center for Disease Control and Prevention
CCI	Continuous Commodity Index
CCP	Chinese Communist Party (also, Communist Party of China)
CEA	Chinese Economic Association
CEC	China Electronics Corporation
CHIP	Children's Hospital Informatics Program
CHIPS	Chinese Household Income Project Survey
CHNS	China Health and Nutrition Survey
CIO	Chief Information Executive
CITIC	China International Trust and Investment Corporation
CMS	Collective Medical System

COFCO	China National Cereals, Oils and Foodstuffs Corporation
COSCO	China Ocean Shipping Company
COSTIND	State Commission on Science and Technology for National Defence
CPC	Collaborative Product Commerce
CPI	Consumer Price Index
CRB	Commodity Research Bureau
CRM	Customer Relationship Management
C-school	Convergence School
CSAs	Country-specific Advantages
CSY	*China Statistical Yearbook*
CVRD	Companhia Vale do Rio Doce
CZCE	China Zhengzhou Commodity Exchange
DCE	Dalian Commodity Exchange
DEA	Data Envelopment Analysis
EBPS	Equalization of Basic Public Services
EDR	Elderly Dependency Ratio
EE	Emerging Economies
EPB	Environmental Protection Bureau
ERP	Enterprise Resource Planning
EGLS	General Least Squares Estimates
E-school	Experimentalist School
EU	European Union
FAI	Fixed Asset Investment
FDH	Free Disposal Hull
FDI	Foreign Direct Investment
FPE	Final Prediction Error
FSA	Firm-specific Advantages
FTA	Free Trade Agreement
GARCH	Generalized Autoregressive Conditional Heteroskedasticity
GBP	UK Pound
GDP	Gross Domestic Product
GICS	Global Industry Classification Standard
GLS	Generalized Least Squares
GNI	Gross National Income
GOVC	Gross Output Value of Construction
HHI	Herfindahl–Hirschman Index
HKD	Hong Kong Dollar
IAIA	International Association for Impact Assessment
IASB	International Accounting Standards Board
IB	International Business
IC	Income per Capita
ICP	World Bank's International Comparison Program
ICT	Information and Communications Technology
IEA	International Energy Agency

IFPRI	International Food Policy Research Institute
IMF	International Monetary Fund
IMS	Information Management System
IPF	Institutional Possibility Frontier
IRFs	Impulse Response Functions
IT	Information Technology
IV	Instrumental Variables
JPY	Japanese Yen
JSCBs	Joint Stock Commercial Banks
JV	Joint Venture
KOSPI	Korea Composite Stock Price Index
LA	Latin America
LDC	Less Developed Country
LLL	Linkage, Leveraging, and Learning
LIBOR	London Inter-bank Offered Rate
LM test	Lagrange Multiplier test
M&As	Mergers and Acquisitions
MDH	Mixture of Distributions Hypothesis
MII	Ministry of Information Industry
MIS	Management Information System
MOA	Ministry of Agriculture
MoH	Ministry of Health
MOST	Ministry of Science and Technology
MNC	Multinational Corporation
MNE	Multinational Enterprise
NBS	National Bureau of Statistics
NC	Non-capitalists
NHTIDZ	New High Technology Industrial Development Zone
NICs/NIEs	New Industrialized Countries/Economies
NIDL	New International Division of Labour
NIEs	New Institutional Economics
NSMEGTP	National SME Galaxy Training Project
OECD	Organization for Economic Co-operation and Development
OEM	Original equipment Manufacture
ODI	Outward Direct Investments
OIS	Overnight Indexed Swap
OLI	Ownership, Location, and Internalization
OLS	Ordinary Least Squares
PDVSA	Petró leos de Venezuela
P-C	Politicians-turned-capitalists
PF	Physical Functions
PMI	Purchasing Managers' Index
PPs	Primary Products
PP	Property Price
PPP	Purchasing Power Parity

RCRE	Research Center for Rural Economy
R&D	Research and Development
REER	Real Effective Exchange Rate
RHS	Rural Household Survey
RMB	Renminbi – Official currency of China
ROA	Return on Asset
RSESS	Rural Social and Economic Survey Service of the NBS
RSS	Residual Sum of Square
SASAC	State-owned Assets Supervision and Administration Commission
SC	Schwarz Information Criterion
SDC	Securities Data Company
SEGC	Shanghai Electric Group Corporation
SEPA	State Environmental Protection Administration
SEZ	Special Economic Zone
SFA	Stochastic Frontier Analysis
SHFE	Shanghai Futures Exchange
SIC	Standard Industrial Classification
SOE	State-owned Enterprise
SME	Small and Medium-sized Enterprise
SP	Stochastic Process
SRHS	Self-reported Health Status
TCE	Total Coal Equivalent
TFP	Total Factor Productivity
TVE	Township and Village Enterprise
UHS	Urban Household Survey
UK	United Kingdom
UNC	University of North Carolina
UNCTAD	United Nations Conference on Trade and Development
UNDESA	United Nations Department of Economic and Social Affairs
UNDP	United Nations Development Programme
US$	United States Dollars
VAR	Vector Autoregression
VDC	Variance Decomposition
VE	Volatility of Real Effective Exchange Rate
WEO	World Economic Outlook
WHO	World Health Organization
WTO	World Trade Organization

Acknowledgements

This book is the result of collaborative research and hard work by the chapters' contributors. Without their valuable contribution and great expertise, the publication of this book would not be possible. The Confucius Institute Headquarters, Beijing, and University College, Dublin provided financial support for the 2009 Dublin International Conference on 'China and the Changing Landscape of the World Economy', that was organized by the Chinese Economic Association (Europe/UK), and I would like to take this opportunity to express my sincere thanks to these organizations for their generous support.

I am greatly indebted to Francis Kane, Ningyue Liu and Jinghai Zheng, who have kindly provided me with invaluable suggestions and editorial assistance in my preparation of this book. I would like to thank Jian Ke, Beibei Dong, Jing Li, Jingjing Wang and Lin Frazer for their devotion and efforts in the preparation of the typescript. Thanks are due also to the editor at Routledge, Peter Sowden, and his assistant, Jillian Morrison, for their patience and support throughout the editorial process. Finally, my deepest gratitude goes to my wife, Lan Li, for her understanding and unwavering support.

1 Rising China and its integration with the changing world economy[1]

Wei Xia and Liming Wang

The words attributed to Napoleon Bonaparte, as he cast his eye over a map of the world in 1803, provide some insight into European perceptions of China at the dawn of the Industrial Revolution, a time when the balance of the global economy was about to undergo a dramatic shift westwards. Pointing to China, the ambitious young leader of a rising France is said to have declared: "There is a sleeping giant. Let him sleep. When he awakes, the world will shake." While the metaphor of a slumbering China can be overstated and is hardly an accurate reflection of centuries of highly eventful political, social and economic history, it carries some currency in the way it captures the sense, in China's past, of relative detachment from the changing world outside.

The awakening of China in modern times can be traced back to the dramatic moment on October 1, 1949 when Chairman Mao, in proclaiming the People's Republic of China, told a cheering crowd in Tiananmen Square that "the 475 million people of China have stood up." In terms of China's economic resurgence and growing integration with the global economy, a further awakening came almost 30 years later, two years after Mao's death. China's economic reform, launched by Deng Xiaoping in 1978, has had a huge impact both domestically and globally. Over the past three decades since the reform process began, China has undergone a dramatic transformation from a poor and isolated nation to an economic powerhouse of the world economy (Sanders and Chen 2006). China's rapid and consistent growth over last 30 years has propelled it to become the world's second largest economy today and potentially the largest in the foreseeable future. This development has also positioned China as a major driving force not only of economic recovery from global recession, but also of the process of further globalization itself (Woo 2008, 2010).

The recent global recession, for its speed, scale and severity, represents the most serious economic crisis in contemporary history (Strauss-Kahn 2010). The financial crisis started from the subprime mortgage crisis in the United Sates in 2007, but its shocks are spreading worldwide, in both financial and real economy terms (Sheng 2009). In a new century marked by the twin symbols of globalization and marketization, people's faith in "pure" capitalist free market economics has been shaken. Attention has increasingly been drawn to the emerging economies and their ability to maintain growth in spite of the crisis (Kennedy 2010). China is the prime example. It achieved a 9.2 percent growth in its gross domestic product (GDP) in the full-blown global recession year of 2009 and 10.3 percent in 2010, while also becoming the world's second largest economy after the United States and overtaking Germany as the largest exporting country. Two years on, China has confirmed it is on a course of continuing growth and recovery from the financial crisis (Garnaut 2009; Woo and Zhang 2010). Western-dominated world capitalist models, which served as a reference for civil society development during the last century, seem to have lost much of their previous global attractiveness (Schmidt 2008). Although the Cold War lasted little more than four decades and the former Soviet Union never came close to overtaking the United States economically, Ferguson (2011) sees the current rise of China as an historically pivotal development: "What we are living through now is the end of 500 years of Western predominance. This time the Eastern challenger is for real, both economically and geopolitically." The claim that "Europe was the past, the US is the present and a China-dominated Asia the future of the global economy" (Wolf 2003) has been restated to such an extent in recent years that it has almost entered common parlance, achieving the status of a widely accepted and repeated truism of our times.

Whatever the implications of a rising China are for the rest of the world, China's increasing engagement with the world continues apace, especially after its accession to the World Trade Organization (WTO) in 2001 (Dauderstädt and Stetten 2005; Pei 2006; Srinivasan 2006). Furthermore, whether China eventually becomes the world's largest economy or not, its rise is clearly changing the balance of power in the world economic order (Schmidt 2008). Taking an historical perspective on the rise of economically powerful nations, China's emergence can be seen as something of an exception; the developed economies of Britain, Germany, America, Japan and the like were all protectionist before their domestic industries reached a stage where they could compete with foreign competitors (Wade 2004), whereas China has opened its markets at a much earlier development stage. Since the early 1980s, the phenomenon of marketization has become a global trend, and globalization itself has been driven by market forces and rules (Ngok 2007). Due to globalization, countries now have to face the challenges presented by marketization and compete for development (Sheng 2009). The Chinese government is not an outlier in this sense – it is under persistent pressure to adapt successfully and navigate the dynamic changes brought about by globalization and global trends in economic, cultural and political values. However, as Jacques (2009) argues, it would be a leap too far to assume that China will be integrated smoothly into a liberal, capitalist and democratic world system. China is not only the next economic superpower, but the world order under its construction will look very different from what we have had under American leadership (Woo 2008; Rodrik 2010). The prediction by the liberalist school in the 1990s, that China will converge to the standard institutions, practices and social values of advanced Western liberal democracies by deeper integration into the global economy, is in stark contrast with the observable reality that such a convergence has not happened (Peerenboom 2007). Dissection of the Chinese economic reform process offers a means of examining and evaluating how China's pattern of development, including its transition and integration with the world economy, has been evolving.

This chapter presents a fresh four-stage analysis and overview of the reform process, which has been so instrumental in China's rise. If vast China, home to a fifth of all humanity, was once conspicuous by its virtual absence from the integrating world economy, its return to the centre of the global economic stage is startling and unique. The key question of the ultimate goal and future direction of ongoing reform in a changing China is addressed from various perspectives throughout the following sections. The stark contrast between recession and rapid growth within the changing world economy of recent years turns this chapter's attention to the emerging economies of the East, questioning perceptions that over-collectivize Asian experiences while at the same time acknowledging China's commonalities with its near neighbors. Finally, major challenges that lie ahead for the Chinese economy are scrutinized. These include successfully effecting a change in the economic growth pattern, reversing the widening gap between rich and poor, dealing with the effects of an ageing society, achieving environmental sustainability, and ensuring good governance.

Rising China: from a planning to a market system

China's economy from a historical perspective

It was about 500 years ago that Europe began to overtake China as the world's most advanced civilization (Pomeranz 2001). For many centuries before then, Chinese science and technology were the world's best and Chinese productivity and incomes the world's highest. Over the next 500 years, and especially during the last two centuries, as the West grew rich and strong, China at first lay stagnated and then, for most of the first half of the last century, was convulsed by violent conflict and famine. After communist China was established in 1949, the Chinese economy could be characterized as a faithful performer to Stalinist principles of central planning, state ownership and import substitution. Under such a centrally planned system, prices were determined by administrative rather than market mechanisms and resources were allocated by central planners rather than the forces of supply and demand (Pyle 1997). In the period before 1978, several economic disasters befell the country, most notably the incongruously named Great Leap Forward and the decade of anarchy, known as the Cultural Revolution, from 1966 to 1976. As a result, by the late 1970s, China was dealing with a legacy of severe, pervasive rural poverty. China's share of world GDP had declined to its historically lowest point of 4.9 percent in 1978 (see Table 1.1).

At the end of 1978, China launched several economic reforms, beginning with agricultural reform, which led to the abolition of the people's commune system in rural China. Reform then spread to urban areas. The focus of reform in cities was on state-owned enterprises (SOEs), aiming to increase efficiency and improve management in the economy. The strategies and principles of the reforms can be summarized as decentralization, market-orientation, privatization and opening up to the outside world. Since the economic reforms, the world has witnessed

Table 1.1 China regaining its predominance. Share of world GDP in purchasing power parity, 1700–2008 (%)

Country/region	*1700*	*1820*	*1890*	*1952*	*1978*	*1998*	*2003*	*2008*
China	22.3	32.9	13.2	5.2	4.9	11.5	15.1	17.5
India	24.3	16.0	11.0	4.0	3.3	5.0	5.5	6.7
Japan	4.1	3.0	2.5	3.4	7.6	7.7	6.6	6.0
Europe	24.9	26.6	40.3	29.3	27.8	24.0	21.1	19.3
United States	0.1	1.8	13.8	27.5	21.6	21.9	20.6	18.6
USSR	4.4	5.4	6.3	9.2	9.0	5.8	3.8	4.4

Data sources: Maddison (2007, 2010).

Notes: The data for 1700–2003 are derived from Maddison's research report to the OECD. The data in 2008 were from Maddison's statistics datasheet (2010). Europe includes 30 west and ten east European countries (Turkey is excluded). The figures for India do not include Bangladesh and Pakistan from 1952.

China's extraordinary growth and the continuing process of regaining its predominant position in the global economy (see Table 1.1). The mercurial rise of China as a major economic power within a time span of only 30 years is often described by economists as the "China Miracle," one of the greatest economic success stories in modern times (Lin *et al.* 2003).

Economic reform: a four-stage process

China's period of transition towards a market economy exceeds in length the time span dominated by Maoist socialism (Naughton 2007). But although its emergence as an influential economic and political power is widely recognized, the *process* by which China has achieved this position is far less clear (Guthrie 2009). The whole transition has had much continuity, but it is also possible to identify different turning points for the whole reform process. The transition has commonly been viewed as a two-phase evolution process, but different turning points have been put forward for the division, such as the year 1984 (Wang 1994; Raby 2001), 1992 (Naughton 2007) and 1993 (Qian and Wu 2000). We tend to agree with Naughton's (2007) view that 1992 was the watershed, as it was the first time the market economy was officially introduced into the formal congressional decision of the Chinese Communist Party (CCP) and set as the primary goal of reform. Based on Shi's (1998) three-stage work, this chapter proposes a four-stage framework for understanding the transition from planning to market economy in accordance with the evolutionary establishment of a market system and the crucial role of a free price mechanism.

The initiating stage, between 1978 and 1984, was dominated by the planning mechanism with the free market only at the margins. The reform had no predesigned blueprint and was launched to solve urgent problems in the economic system and seek instant welfare improvement (Zhang and Yi 1996; Cai and Wang 2010). Since China was poor and most of the population were largely peasants, the initial stage of the reform mainly focused on the rural economy with very limited experiments in urban areas (Shi 1998; Naughton 2007). The most important characteristic of this stage was "aiming to improve the planned economy with an incentive mechanism" by introducing a "dual track system." The key feature of the dual-track system was not a mixture of planning and market tracks, but rather that the market track was allowed at the margin to parallel the planning track (Zhang and Yi 1996). Reform policies such as the rural household responsibility system, township and village enterprises, and foreign investment in special economic zones, were seen to foster economic growth and development without threatening either existing stakeholders or the central government's ability to command. Scholars such as Naughton (2007) have criticized the reform at this stage for not solving or eliminating existing distortions. However, the big success of the pioneering household responsibility system played an important role in pushing the economic reform and transition forward.[2] First, agricultural outputs surged to meet national demands. By the end of 1984, grain output was as much as 407 million metric tons, about 1.3 times that of 1978 (Naughton 2007). Second, improvement in grain productivity encouraged more labor shift to non-grain and non-agricultural business, especially with regard to the township and village enterprises (TVEs), which were recognized as the most active economic element up to the 1990s. Third, though the goal of price reform at this stage was merely to "improve the planning price system," a market-oriented price system had already formed for some agricultural products when the *Household Responsibility System* spread. Fourth, the national success in rural China in 1978–1984 gave credibility to both the market reforms and the Party leaders who encouraged these reforms (Perkins 1994), resulting in an acceleration of urban reforms.

The second stage, from 1985 to 1991, combined both planning and market mechanisms. At the end of 1984, the *Decisions by the CCP Central Committee on Economic System Reform* in the third Plenary of the Twelfth Central Committee of the CCP defined the socialist economy as a "planned commodity economy on the basis of public ownership" (People's Daily 2008). The reform at this stage mainly focused on three aspects: price system, contract and responsibility system in state-owned enterprises (SOEs), and finance and banking system.[3] These three reforms together pushed SOEs into internal and external competition, reduced the role of central government in resource allocation,[4] and also created incentives for further market development. As a consequence, despite controversy over interpretation of the "planning nature" or the "commodity nature" of reform objectives in the official statement, the market-based portion of the economy grew increasingly prosperous while the planning parts became less and less important. Hence, the major characteristic of this period is the combination of the planning and market mechanism both in ideology and methodology (Qian and Wu 2003; Yuan and Dong 2008).

The third stage lasted from 1992 to 2000 and was dominated by the market mechanism, with planning playing a supplementary role in resource allocation. In 1992, a decisive ideological transition occurred when the party embraced Deng Xiaoping's wisdoms from his southern tour. At the Fourteenth National Congress of CCP, it was declared that the mission of economic transformation was to establish a "socialist market economy" and thus reform was pushed to a new stage (Bell *et al.* 1993). In 1993 the Third Plenum of the Fourteenth Congress of the CCP gave further clarification to this objective by affirming that "the socialist market economy means making the market the fundamental mechanism for resource allocation with national macroeconomic control" (CCP Congress 1993). It also provided a comprehensive blueprint for constructing a new economic structure involving a series of institutional transitions and innovations (Suliman 1998; Qian 2003). The new paradigm was certainly an important breakthrough as it was the first time the goal was set of transforming to a market economy (Qian and Wu 2003) and, essentially, eliminating the concerns of ideological ambivalence in taking more thorough and comprehensive reforms (Bell *et al.* 1993). To achieve economic stability and further growth, the reform was forced to address some intrinsically sensitive parts of the economy, such as the tax and fiscal system, the financial system, and the performance of SOE. From here on, it was unavoidable that the reform would generate losers as well as winners. The most important feature of this period is thus rapid and powerfully comprehensive fiscal and financial reform under the premiership of Zhu Rongji. The initial socialist market was by and large completed during this stage.

The fourth stage, from 2001 onward, has seen the realization and ongoing development of the socialist market economy. Before gaining WTO membership, China was still below the optimal degree of marketization, but since 2001 the accession to the WTO has significantly deepened the formation of a mature market economy and integration with world economy (Woo 2001). For a market economy to function well, a range of elements are considered necessary to be in place, but the most important and difficult of these is the need for a firm entrenchment of a market-supporting institutional framework[5] (Perkins 1994; Woo 2001). Membership of the WTO, on the one hand, provides much of the justification for promoting prototype WTO-specified institutions, including various kinds of government function systems, law and regulations, property rights and modern firm systems, and so forth (Bell *et al.* 1993; Ngok 2007). On the other hand, it also improves nation-wide efficiency by exposing the domestic market, especially the SOEs, to global competition (Tian *et al.* 2002). With development and integration into the world market, Chinese and world market prices are slowly converging with the result that China has become a more integral part of the world market (Dauderstädt and Stetten 2005). Thus, this period is a new era of improving the socialist market economy and initializing "steady and vigorous" market-compatible institutional reform.

Reform strategy: gradualism or big bang?

While there is relatively broad agreement that economic reform is beneficial and desirable, there is less agreement on which approach to adopt or how the transition should be managed and the transformation achieved.[6] So far, China and Vietnam's transition processes have been characterized as gradual and incremental, reflecting a "gradualism" approach to reform. This is in contrast with what has become known as the "big bang" strategy, exemplified by the economic "shock therapy" undergone in Eastern Europe and the former Soviet Union. Since the European big bang was a version of the Washington Consensus, whose strategies focused on three pillars: liberalization, privatization and fiscal austerity (Lin *et al.* 2003; Stiglitz 2004),[7] the debate surrounding these two types of strategies to a great extent reflects different positions of agreement or disagreement with the Washington Consensus. Dissenters put forward new versions of reform strategy such as the Post Washington Consensus[8] (Stiglitz 2002) or the Beijing Consensus[9] (Ramo 2004).

Much has been written on the comparative advantages or disadvantages of these two opposing approaches (Woo 1994; Pyle 1997; Feltenstein and Nsouli 2003; Pei 2006; Chen 2009). In favor of gradualism, the main arguments can be summarized by the following five points. First, a gradualism approach can be Pareto-improving without creating losers (Lau *et al.* 2000). While a beneficial reform introduced in a sudden big bang approach may meet resistance by stakeholders and/or the majority, gradualism may allow such a reform to achieve political viability. Second, gradualism can split and spread transitional costs (on the government budget) and resistance forces over a long period, to guarantee the sustainability and stability of economic transition (Zhang and Yi 1996; Lin *et al.* 2003). Third, it facilitates trial and error dynamic adjustment. Fourth, it helps the government and elites to establish credibility and win support from ordinary people. Finally, the gradual reform process not only can create new market rules and norms but can cultivate and develop them (Lin *et al.* 2003). In sum, gradualism was successful "creative destruction" and provided a path-dependent solution for China to complete dual transitions within a complex historical context (Sanders and Chen 2006; Chen 2009).

However, the big bang approach has had no shortage of supporting theorists. They have cautioned that China may obtain short-term benefits but experience ultimate failure in the long run (Blanchard and Shleifer 2001; Sachs *et al.* 2002; Pei 2006). They suggest, as in the French Revolution and American Civil War, a big bang approach would foster significantly positive economic growth over a relatively long period, merely at the cost of the old generation (Sachs *et al.* 2002; Huang and Zhao 2009).[10] Systematic stability can be achieved through big bang when the regime in the political sphere (political decentralization) is compatible with the regime in the economic sphere (market-orientated economy). There exist potential pitfalls for "gradual" and "incremental" reform including a fall in output (Murphy *et al.* 1992), a distorted market mechanism (Kornai 1992; Pei 2006), increasing disparity of welfare improvements between urban and rural areas (Feltenstein and Nsouli 2003), stalling of reform by its opponents (Pei 2006), and rent-seeking and new distortions when segmental distortions are removed (Young 2000; Pei 2006).

The successful cases of China and Vietnam have led an increasing number of researchers to perceive gradualism as more successful in practice (Murrell 1992; Perkins 1994; Dewatripont and Roland 1995; Zhang and Yi 1996; Wei 1997;

Rawski 1999; Roland 2002; Stiglitz 2002), even though it was once suspected to be intrinsically flawed (Murphy *et al.* 1992). Nonetheless, if gradual transition is so superior, questions arise as to why it did not work well in other contexts such as Poland and Hungary, for example, which also tried gradualist reforms in 1980s. Some researchers point out those comparative studies of transition processes and their relationship to performance run into several problems given the complexity of the issues involved in the reforms (Bouin *et al.* 1998; Feltenstein and Nsouli 2003). The uniqueness of China's economic and political context at the very start of the reform process must be considered to be of the utmost importance in this regard (Perkins 1994; Rawski 1995; Pyle 1997; Wei 1997; Bouin *et al.* 1998; Chen 2008), with particular features highlighted such as: the huge agricultural population (Sachs and Woo 2000; Chen 2008), the influence of Maoist Cultural Revolution (Olson 2000), communist leaders who would not let go (Murrell 1992), the ratio between government revenue and total output (Chen 2008), political centralization (Cai 2007), and ties with Hong Kong, Taiwan and Singapore. Yet, as Von Hayek (1945) notes, "the economic problem of society is mainly one of rapid adaption to changes in the particular circumstances of time and place," so decisions on speed and mode of reform are ultimately best left to those who are familiar with their own practical and particular set of circumstances rather than attempting to apply a "one size fits all" theoretical approach. It was probably "as much by luck as by design, that China stumbled on a strategy that has proved remarkably successful" from a planning economy to an economy governed largely by market forces (Perkins 1994). Conclusive evidence that the gradualist approach would deliver long-term benefits was simply not available 20 years ago, and some scholars wondered whether an eventual shift to a big bang approach would emerge in the following decades (McMillan and Naughton 1992). While there is certainly room for more theoretical innovation, it now seems safe to conclude, two decades later, that gradual transition has been better suited to Chinese circumstances.

Ultimate goal of reform: socialist or capitalist?

Almost all the former socialist countries are moving from central planning economies towards market capitalism (Stiglitz 2002; Guthrie 2009). Nevertheless, the assumption that market capitalism alone is the pinnacle of an advanced economic system risks a degree of complacency if it fails to entertain any possibility of alternative and more nuanced goals of transition. Given that the ideas of socialism and capitalism were both the products of western economic theory advocates (Ma 2002; Wang and Zheng 2010), China apparently rejects adopting a copy of Western capitalism in full, instead demonstrating a will and ability to develop its own path, the so-called "socialism with Chinese characteristics," at least officially (Hoffmann 2008). It seems to have already created "a counterexample to the findings in law, institutions, finance and economic growth literatures" (Allen *et al.* 2005). The Chinese context naturally invites questions as to what exactly is meant by Chinese characteristics, whether there is such a phenomenon as the

"China model," and whether China is indeed a socialist nation or rather a de facto capitalist system that is misleadingly labelled "socialist."

Generally speaking, two schools of thought have emerged in regard to the future of China's reform: the experimentalist school and the convergence school. The experimentalists, represented by Stiglitz (2004), Naughton (1995, 2007) and Ramo (2004), for example, capture the major features of China's reform as an evolutionary, experimental and incremental approach and attribute China's rapid growth to these factors. The scholars in this school highlight "institutional innovation" and are advocators of the "China model," pointing out that "China is evolving towards a unique set of economic institutions" (quoted in Sachs and Woo 2000), without putting all elements of western market economy in place (Zhang 2009). The convergence school, in contrast, takes China's success in economic growth as the fruits of harmonizing its economic institutions as a prototype WTO market economy. Such a view sees no special formula or unique set of secrets that apply only to China, but rather compares China's transition with the experiences of previously emerging Asian economies: market-based, labor-intensive, export-led economies with strong inflows of foreign direct investment. According to this school, there is no "China model." The "institutional innovations" solely reflect temporal responses to China's old political circumstances and the future nature of "institutional innovations" are clear in the long run, as they can be found in the existing advanced market economies (Sachs and Woo 2000).

These two schools actually demonstrate different opinions both on the ultimate desired destination and the means of getting there. What scholars have achieved is merely a variety of starting points from which to begin building a new economic theory for transition (Pickles and Smith 1998). The concerns about democracy, liberalization and privatization of the convergence school, as recognized by Woo (2001), are set against the fact that "a prototype WTO market economy accommodates a variety of institutional forms,"[11] and it is reasonable to expect China to evolve a totally new institutional form of market economy (Hoffmann 2008) with planning and market, socialism and capitalism, coexisting peacefully with each other, like a form of the Chinese paradigm "Yin and Yang" (Wang and Zheng 2010). Instead of a sole product of free market economy, China's success wouldn't be possible without its particular socialist legacy (Wen 2007). Four major reasons underpin this argument. First, the uniqueness of initial economic conditions at the start of the transition should not be neglected. Second, it is necessary to take account of specific Chinese culture, geography, economic, and social structure characteristics. Third, the Party-State is the most important institution in China, involved as it is in microeconomic supervision and shaping the organization and quality of other institutions. Fourth, ideology has lost much of its appeal in the modern China. Instead, internationalism and nationalism are fostered hand in hand as the real driving force behind political and economic trends, and the influence of communalism is ever weakening. Thus, it can be expected that China will not simply follow the path suggested by the "foreign" models of either capitalism or socialism.

The changing global economy

Globalization and recession

Globalization has been the most important characteristic of the world economy over the past two decades[12] (Rodrik 1997; Fidrmuc and Korhonen 2010). The growth rate of world trade is higher than that of world production (Bräuninger and Vöpel 2010), a gap that can be interpreted as evidence of an ongoing process of trade driven globalization. The importance of open trade to the economy has strong philosophical backing: Adam Smith's absolute advantage theory, Richardian's comparative advantage theory, and Krugman's return to scale and imperfect competition theory all suggest that free trade is the optimal choice both for productive efficiency and welfare improvement (Tian *et al.* 2002). Nations are integrated into the world economy network through trade, foreign direct investment, capital flows, migration and the spread of technology (Bhagwati 2004), which have changed the world permanently for both the better and the worse (Friedman 2006). Globalization has been driven by two processes: free global trade in goods and services, and liberalization and integration of global financial system (Woo 2009). The consequences of globalization have not always been benign or beneficial, with increasing income disparity between South and North, environmental deterioration, instability in the global economy (Rodrik 1997; Stiglitz 2002; Adams 1996) and "for the majority of countries the globalization story is one of divergence and marginalization" (UNDP 2005). The ongoing financial crisis of recent years triggered such widespread recession that it poses a fundamental challenge to the future mode of globalization.

Financial turbulence and distress characterized much of the world economy in the 1990s and 2000s (Sheng 2009). A decade ago, the Asian financial crisis raised criticism of the growth model of Asian capital markets and the IMF prescribed an American-style remedy but its limited efficacy cast doubt on the American model of financial liberalization which was once believed to be a successful example for the world (Stiglitz 2002). The "Big Five" crises in modern history, summarized by Reinhart and Rogoff (2008), all left deep impacts on the countries involved in each crisis, most notably Japan's "lost decade."[13] The Japanese experience, from strong growth and innovation to long-lasting stagnation, inflation and fiscal deficit, is one that the crisis-hit economies of today must seek to avoid.

Various culprits have been named as the causes of financial crisis both before and since the current crisis. According to Radelet and Sachs (2000), there are five categories of financial crisis: macroeconomic policy-induced crisis, financial panic, bubble collapse, moral hazard crisis and disorderly workout. A causal linkage between financial liberalization and financial crisis has been put forward (Radelet and Sachs 2000; Stiglitz 2002; Stiglitz 2004);[14] crisis has also been attributed to institutional failure: macroeconomic imbalance, low transparency of credit system, weak cooperate governance and corruption (Radelet and Sachs 2000). The long-running large government budget deficits in major western countries such as the United States and UK, which already exceed 10 percent of their GDP, draw serious criticism (De Grauwe 2009). A global imbalance caused by

China's "inordinately mercantilist currency policies" has been blamed by some, while others attribute the global crisis to basic flaws in capitalism and/or free marketism; others again see a decoupling between the business cycles of western countries and emerging Asian economies (Fidrmuc and Korhonen 2010). Koo and Kiser (2001) contended that all these causes can fall into two categories: weak-fundamentals view and financial panic view. The former suggested a slow recovery by prompt structural reform and recapitalization of financial sector, while the latter predicted a quick recovery from one equilibrium to another by restoring social confidence. However, it seems that neither of these two theories can effectively address the current crisis. BRIC countries have recovered before implementation of major financial reforms, which didn't fit the weak-fundamentals view, while the EU sovereign debt crisis casts many doubts on the financial panic view of simply focusing on restoring public confidence.

No matter how the current downturn is accounted for, isolation and reversal of globalization is neither feasible nor desirable. The problem is not globalization, but how it is managed and turned to the economic benefit of the world's people. A major current issue concerns the role of international cooperation in tackling the worsening situation of sovereign debt crises in European countries. Though the Excessive Deficit Procedure and Stability and Growth Pact agreed by EU members aim to provide a rule-based framework to prevent a debt crisis by emphasizing low government deficit (less than 3 percent of GDP) and low public debt ratio (less than 60 percent of GDP), such measures appear to be insufficient. In 2009, four EU economies ran a fiscal deficit of more than 10 percent of their GDPs: Greece (15.4 percent), Ireland (14.4 percent), Spain (11.1 percent) and the UK (11.4 percent) (EUROSTAT 2010). Greece and Ireland have subsequently been forced to request bail-outs from the European Union (EU) and International Monetary Fund (IMF). There is major concern whether the crisis will spread to other euro zone countries, such as Portugal, Spain and Italy, which are facing similar fiscal deficit problems.[15]

While many economists, drawing on Keynes, would theoretically counsel that expanding fiscal and monetary policies and decreasing tax rates will stimulate aggregate demand and counter economic stagnation and/or crisis, it can also be acknowledged that the complexity of reality may present other less desirable outcomes. Serious problems may be induced, such as sovereign debt crises caused by excessive government deficits. This problem may be worsened in a monetary union context as opposed to a national monetary regime due to the absence of individual monetary policy autonomy (Gianviti *et al.* 2010).[16] Why have China's expansionary monetary policy and stimulatory fiscal policies worked well while the EU was trapped into deeper government crises and economic recession? The answer may lie in the government revenue surplus or deficit. EU member states have only one way to moderate the macro economy in the face of crisis – adjusting fiscal policy, either expanding or tightening it, which easily leads to inflation, deteriorating government deficits and rising unemployment rate.[17] Furthermore, a strong currency hampers efforts to grow exports as a rescue method, especially given the lower production costs of competitors in emerging economies. It has to be concluded that poor coordination between the monetary and fiscal machineries is more likely to deepen an economic crisis than alleviate it.

Though various corrective actions are proposed, including fiscal discipline, structural reform, sovereign debt reconstruction and default of government debt (Gianviti *et al.* 2010),[18] such responses are reactive and temporary, and do not provide a sufficient longer term basis for dealing with future debt crisis.[19] The more fundamental causes of the current crisis may lie in the very economic and social composition of many European countries. It is becoming apparent in the context of an ageing population and an integrated global economy that high welfare spending can no longer be sustained by economic growth, particularly the slow pace of growth which has persisted in Europe for decades. Kaufmann and Kraay (2002) postulated that countries with a government budget surplus can, in general, be expected to achieve more rapid economic growth in comparison with those that incur a deficit. While it is clearly necessary to moderate government deficits, the more fundamental causes of long lasting stagflation need to be addressed. Low economic growth rates in Europe have deep-rooted causes such as muted incentives for technological innovation and entrepreneurship, possibly linked to the high compensation costs of labor,[20] intensive tax rates, low investment in research, and a loss of attractiveness to foreign direct investment.

However, this is not to say that the current crisis can be oversimplified as stemming from the entire Western civil framework. Two hundred years ago, the Industrial Revolution was spreading from Britain to elsewhere in the Western hemisphere. Before long, the West began to economically surpass the East and dominate the world. Such success has fostered heated scholarly interest in the "Western Miracle" and "European exceptionalism" (Needham 1969; Wong 1997; Pomeranz 2001; Mokyr 2002; Jones 2003; Lin 2007). Recently, the economic power's centre of gravity has begun to swing eastwards, and this, second to globalization itself, is another major characteristic of the new world economy (Schmidt 2008). In seeking to understand what lies behind this tide of change and evaluate its prospects, the crisis and ensuing recession that hit the developed economies of the Western world harder than elsewhere only accounts for part of the explanation. It is also necessary to scrutinize the emerging Asian economic miracle economies, particularly China, to identify the roots of economic growth and development of a new global age.

Globalization and the growth of the East

During the gradual process of globalization, emerging Asian economies have increased in economic importance and have had more influence on powering the global economy (Fidrmuc and Korhonen 2010). They are interpreted as "success stories" of marketization and globalization (Stiglitz 1996; Ghosh 2010). From the 1960s, four Asian new industrialized economies (NIEs) maintained average annual growth rates of 10 percent and double digit export growth rates for almost three decades. Such growth has completely changed the poor and backward position of these countries (Lin 2007). Two of the world's four largest economies are now in East Asia. While Japan's position has slipped from second to third, China, as the second largest economy on the planet, is the most dominant emerging economy today. However, China is not alone in this remarkable Asian transformation. India, Thailand, and Indonesia have also instigated market reforms, as have others, and the trend is continuing (Schmidt 2008; Fidrmuc and Korhonen 2010).

For decades after East Asia's takeoff it was widely held that market-orientated reforms, export-driven catching-up strategy, and embodied technological spillovers from Foreign Direct Investment (FDI), were the keys to the growth (Krugman 1994; Haggard 1996; Yusuf and Nabeshima 2006; Lin 2007; Vietor 2007). Asserting the uniqueness of East Asia, the "Miracle School" of thought arose, basing its ideas on the particular nature of East Asian experience, emphasizing the influence of Confucian culture, geographic convenience, distinctive geostrategic position after the Cold War, and state economy (Stiglitz 1996). Nonetheless, the "Miracle School" has been criticized for overlooking China's performance (Peerenboom 2007) or overstating the degree of differences in reasons for development success among societies, as well as inhibiting further research for *common* determinants of economic growth and broader lessons from East Asian experiences[21] (Haggard 1996; Garnaut 2001; Acemoglu *et al.* 2005; Kennedy 2010).

Neoclassical economic theories explained the difference in per capita income growth in terms of the different path of factor accumulation and technological innovation (Solow 1956; Cass 1966; Garnaut 2001). It has been argued that these factors fail to provide a fundamental explanation for growth, however, as they are growth and endogenous themselves (North and Thomas 1973; Lin 2007; Acemoglu 2008). Luck,[22] geography, trade, culture and institutions, on the other hand, are thought to be some of the fundamental determinants of economic performance (Rodrik 2003; Lin 2007; Acemoglu 2008). Luck seems an implausible major factor, as it cannot explain clearly why some countries could not move from low equilibrium to other steady state equilibrium (Lin *et al.* 2003; Acemoglu 2008). Geography is the only entirely exogenous variable, playing an obviously important role in shaping natural resources, human resources and integration (Pomeranz 2001; Jones 2003), but its stable nature is at odds with a logical explanation for the sudden nature of the take offs which occurred in the East Asian Economies. The trade explanation for growth has plausibility, and is supported by Heckscher-Ohlin trade theory from the perspective of specialization and anti-diminishing returns.

Culture is viewed as "a key determinant of the values, preferences, beliefs and therefore behavior of individuals and societies," and hence has a crucial role in determining economic equilibrium outcomes (Acemoglu *et al.* 2005). Culture in a globalizing world becomes an issue of considerable interest, but the degree to which it influences economic outcomes and the manner of its influence present empirical difficulties. For the West, some explanations focus on stable and traditional cultural legacies such as the Protestant Ethic[23] (Weber 2002) and the Enlightenment (Mokyr 1999, 2002), while, conversely, "Asian values" are expounded for the East Asian economies (Adams and Vernon 2007). Others emphasize the evolutionary process of culture in world integration, especially influenced by American values. To modernize successfully, countries may well ask to what extent they should abandon their traditional cultures and adopt more Western ways, observing how well they appear to work. Japan, Singapore, Taiwan, Hong Kong, South Korea and China have already proposed an answer: each has modernized and industrialized without becoming a Western society (Huntington 1996). Interaction and learning between civilizations have been frequent in human history. While Asian countries have adopted much of their rule of law, civil society, democracy, spirit of innovation and entrepreneurship from the Western world since the last century, they also provide much that Westerners could learn and benefit from, such as good saving habits, responsibility and obedience to an organization (e.g. family, group, company, government), and an intense desire for harmony and stability.[24]

Nevertheless, if culture is to be cited as a major explanation for the phenomenon of rapid growth, so it follows that an explanation for its role in stagnation or recession must also be found, and this is where the culture explanation becomes problematic. Asian culture alone cannot explain the lack of economic miracle in North Korea or China under Mao, nor does it account for the Asian crisis of 1997. Instead, there is overwhelming support for institutions as essential preconditions and determinants of economic development rather than other alternative explanations (North and Thomas 1973; Rodrik 2003; Acemoglu *et al.* 2005). The structure of a country's institutions, including its banking system, the quality and independence of the judiciary, police, and military, and the rule of law, has proved to be critical for efficient market function by shaping people's incentives for investment, consumption and trade (Rodrik 2003; Acemoglu *et al.* 2005; Dam 2006; Vietor 2007; Acemoglu 2008). Nonetheless, the presence (or creation) of institutions alone cannot address how Eastern Asian economies can escape the inferior Pareto equilibrium trap suddenly without changing their imperfect institutions with deficient corporate governance and poor shareholder protection.[25]

Authoritarian governments have been playing a critically important role in East Asia's development process, though their effects are perceived controversial.[26] In China, for example, criticism of the party-state authority system has cited: an absence of limits on the Communist party, a lack of voice, accountability, human rights, and transparency, as well as the persistence of widespread corruption. On the other hand, Montinola *et al.* (1995) and Jin *et al.* (2005) argue that China has evolved a new political system, *federalism, Chinese style*, which provides an important set of limits on the behavior of government at all levels and strong incentives for local government to encourage entrepreneurship. This in turn may explain China's sustained economic growth because entrepreneurship is essential for value creation and social prosperity, though the property rights and contract enforcement are protected partially by the local government and social custom (Schumpeter 1934; Ebner 2006) rather than by the law and legislation. There is no consensus that China has formed a third path or created its own unique set of institutions different from the "common sense" of Washington Consensus; but the rationale of Qian (2003) and Rodrik (2003) that "transitional institutions" for "best practice," and designed for a country's specific circumstances, are much more economically and politically feasible for developing countries, seems clear.

At different stages, different aspects of good governance are of different importance for growth or economic development (Quibria 2006). In the earlier stages of the "Asian Miracle," in Japan, the four Asian tigers, in China and Vietnam, good governance focused more on the capacity of the government to "design, formulate and implement" appropriate economic policies relating to political stability, effectiveness in governance and regulatory quality rather than those relating to voice and accountability and control of corruption (Quibria 2006). The contrasting performance of the Philippines, whose institutions and policies best fit conventional wisdom (Washington Consensus) and Vietnam, whose institutions have many heterodox elements like China, invite a rethink of which institutional model is best. The former has virtually stagnated while the latter is already "booming out of a poverty trap" (Pritchett 2003). Since the government resides at the heart of all institutions, economic performance depends greatly on how the government and its policies provide incentives for economic activity by individuals and organizations, especially with regard to entrepreneurship (Stiglitz 1996, 2002; Chen 2009). It was thought that high saving rates are a cultural feature and that this plays an important role in East Asian sustained economic growth, but savings and growth are not solely cultural phenomena, they are also promoted or managed by governments (Stiglitz 1996; Vietor 2007). East Asian governments' success – in encouraging high national savings, export activity, foreign direct investment and fostering high technology industries through strong economic policies – exemplify how governance can work in coordinating investments and technical "catch up" so as to approach the nationwide technical capability frontier (Stiglitz 1996; Wade 2004; Vietor 2007; Chen 2009).

Major challenges ahead

The two-sided story of overall global economic recession contrasted with growth in emerging Asian economies demonstrates that the interdependent effects of marketization and globalization impose dual challenges on the future development of the world economy. China, as both a driving force and beneficiary of economic globalization, has achieved impressive growth over the last 30 years, but is now facing the fundamental question of sustainable growth. According to Lin (2007), "the stage of China's development today is very similar to that of Japan in the early 1960s" based on all major indicators (export growth, the proportion of primary sector in GDP, life expectancy, infant mortality), and it would be reasonable to assume a giant potential exists as did in Japan in 1960s. However, Overholt (2010) compares China under transition and globalization to a man being chased by a tiger. On the one hand, one is impressed by the extraordinary performance of the economic reform (the man), but on the other one is frightened by the sheer scale of problems facing China (the tiger). This is echoed in Chinese Premier Wen Jiabao's statement from his report to the Fourth Session of the Eleventh National People's Congress (NPC) in March 2011. Wen said that China still faces an extremely complex situation in respect of development: the prices of major commodities and the exchange rates of major currencies have become more volatile in the international market, asset bubbles and inflationary pressure have grown in emerging markets, protectionism continues to heat up, competition in the international market is becoming more intense, and there are still many uncertain factors. The most serious problem with China's economy is that the growth is unstable, unbalanced, uncoordinated and unsustainable (Wen 2011). Generated by the reform itself, some major challenges facing the Chinese economy remain inherent from the old system, and some arise from the changing global economy. These major challenges are related and include the economic growth pattern, income disparity and inequality, the aging society, growing resource and environmental constraints, and political governance.

Transformation of economic growth pattern

According to the Twelfth Five-Year Plan for National Economic and Social Development, China will increase its GDP by around 8 percent in 2011 and achieve a target of 7 percent annual economic growth between 2011 and 2015 (Wen 2011). However, the growth pattern of relying heavily on foreign markets, low added value exports, and cheap labor is no longer sustainable[27] (Saich 2009; Ghosh 2010; Garnaut 2011). While China did not suffer from the same liquidity problems European countries experienced, it is not immune from the external downturn (Fu 2009; Woo and Zhang 2010). According to the World Bank, China's exports value dropped by 16 percent in 2009 in nominal terms[28] (WTO 2010). Even before the outbreak of the current crisis, there were massive doubts about the sustainability of China's export-led growth strategy (Fu 2009; Guo and N'Diaya 2009; Woo 2008, 2009). According to Guo and N'Diaye (2009), between 2001 and 2008, net exports and investment related to tradable sectors accounted for over 60 percent of China's growth,[29] much larger than the average rates of other economic bodies, such as the group of seven industrialized countries (G7) (16 percent), Euro Area (30 percent), and the rest of Asia (35 percent). This in turn has led to a substantial expansion of China's global market share (9.2 percent in 2010)[30] and huge foreign exchange reserves (US$2,650 billion by February 2011).

China's export-oriented growth, however, is thus far not unprecedented either in its scope or its speed, when seen in the light of the early experience of Japan and the newly industrialized economies of Asia (Rumbaugh and Blancher 2004). Guo and N'Diaye (2009) cautioned that long run gains for China's export in the world market are quite conditional, even in danger. The maintenance of high export growth could prove even more daunting as the economic recovery of the whole world seems to be far slower than first anticipated (Morrison 2009). Although economists have predicted that the world economy will probably recover in two to five years based on previous experience, the strains before returning to the path could be quite severe (Reinhart and Rogoff 2008). There is also the possibility that increasing protectionism will be introduced in major export markets. Under these conditions, aggressive exporting, pushed by China on its partners, is likely to meet strong resistance and encounter trade conflicts (Akyüz 2010). In order to enjoy sustainable economic growth in the long term, China has to redirect export-and-investment economic growth towards domestic private consumption as its future development strategy (Saich 2008; Fu 2009). The Chinese government has already realized that the transformation of the economic growth pattern and restructuring will be critical for China's economic development in the future. As Wen (2011) pointed out in his report, China will adhere to the strategy of expanding domestic consumption and achieve economic growth driven by a new balanced mix of consumer spending, investment and exports. To accelerate this transformation, China will strive to fully integrate informationization with industrialization, upgrading the manufacturing industry while fostering and developing strategic emerging industries.[31]

Income disparity and inequality

The key determinants for China, as it undergoes the projected transformation of its growth pattern as discussed above, are how increases in deposable household income can be achieved for the whole of the country, and how to spread purchasing power equitably. China is still a relatively poor country in terms of GDP per capita. In 2009, its nominal income per capita was only US$3,650, which represents 7.8 percent of that in the United States, 9.6 percent of that in Japan, and even only 50 percent of that in Malaysia. While China's GDP growth has been recording close to double digit rates for a generation, the proportion of the household consumption expenditure out of GDP has been failing from 48.8 percent in 1990 to 35.1 percent in 2009, according to the data from *China Statistical Yearbook* (2010). During the same period, the proportion of gross fixed capital formation rose from 25 percent to 45.4 percent. State revenues have also increased sharply from 2,937 billion yuan in 1990 to 68,518 billion yuan in 2009, but only a small part of government expenditure had been used to balance income disparities. For quite a long time, growth of household income has lagged behind those of national GDP, productivity, state revenue and enterprise profits.

Income disparity in China is multi-dimensional and complex (Yao 2010). Over the last 30 years, income disparity between the urban rich and the rural poor has widened, though income per capita for both urban and rural residents have increased substantially (Yao *et al.* 2004) (see Figure 1.1). The widening economic gaps, especially between urban and rural households, represent a potential obstacle to further economic growth (Sutherland and Yao 2011). According to Akyüz (2010), furthermore, income disparity is the biggest growing challenge facing China, and is criticized as a major cause of the disparity between consumption and investment and the consequent dependence on foreign markets, together with external imbalances (Wang and Fan 2009). China is now a "rich country with many impoverished people" and the first "poor superpower" in contemporary history. According to World Factbook statistics, China's GDP per capita was estimated at US$7,400 in 2010, ranking 94 in the world, and 150 million Chinese people were living below the international poverty line set by the World Bank in 2009.[32] The

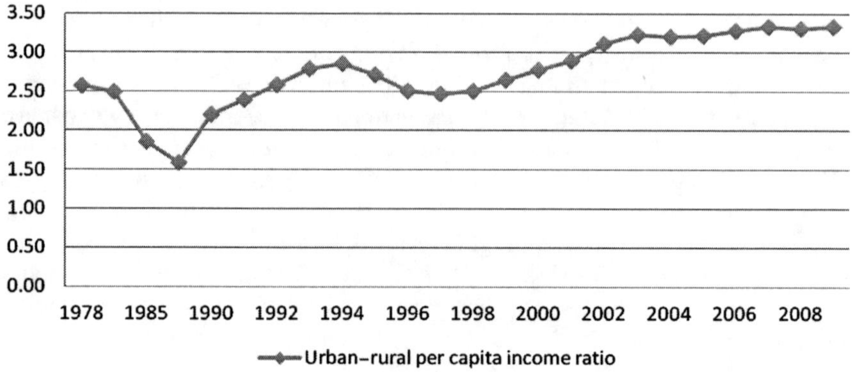

Figure 1.1 Ratio of urban–rural per capita income, 1978–2009.

Source: *China Statistical Yearbook* (2010).

Gini coefficient in China has risen to an internationally alarming level (Sutherland and Yao 2011), 0.47 in year 2010, the highest in the last 60 years (Chen 2010). It indicates one percent of Chinese families own 41.4 percent of national wealth, while urban incomes are almost four times those of rural areas.

It has been cautioned that extreme poverty and income disparity could spark widespread social unrest and even revolution, and become a major risk to China's modernization and continued growth (Yusuf and Nabeshima 2006; Enright 2008; Garnaut *et al.* 2009). Various analyses of income disparities exist in the literature. These include dual sector economy (Lewis 1954), an inverse U-shape relationship between income disparity and economic growth (Kuznets 1955), unbalanced urban–rural and regional development priorities by central government (Chang 2002), emerging rich entrepreneurs, historical socio-geographic factors (such as family business in Zhejiang province), trade openness with skill-biased technological upgrading (Feenstra and Hanson 1996; Xu 2003; Lee and Vivarelli 2004; Meschi and Vivarelli 2007), and corruption or illegal incomes by government officials and their associates. Some suggest that income disparity is the natural product of fast economic development during modernization, but that economic boom is the only way to reduce income disparities (Rogowski and Han 2010). Korea and Taiwan are good examples of balancing growth with equity (Rao 1978; Gosling 2008). Studies also suggest that the provision of democracy, education, health, social security and infrastructure are practical intervention tools for governments to solve the income disparity problem with growth (Haggard 1996; Fields and Yoo 2000). In order to reduce income disparity in China, an effective policy requires significantly greater government transfers to households, particularly in rural areas. Such transfers are the only approach that has lasting effects in reducing income disparities compared with other policies (Adelman and Robinson 1978). Moreover, according to analysis by Abrami *et al.* (2008), the divergent path of China and Vietnam in income disparity within the one-party political framework is caused by the percentage of government budget devoted to transfers. Greater public spending on health, social security, education and career training would not only improve social welfare but also increase households' purchasing power and human capital in the long run (Yusuf and Nabeshima 2006).

Population ageing, resource constraints and environmental degradation

According to the United Nations (UN) Department for Economic and Social Affairs (2009), population ageing is unprecedented, without parallel in human history – and the twenty-first century will witness even more rapid ageing than did the century just past. The economic challenge faced by China and the many other ageing societies of the world economy centers around how to offset and adapt to increases in old-age economic dependency. China's dependency ratio has recently shifted from a steady fall to a new flattening out period as the steep rise in old age dependency is balanced by a correspondingly sharp fall in young age dependency. However, the previous steady fall in the dependency ratio that until very recently accompanied the reform process constituted a "sweet spot" in China's demographic history, and has been cited as a contributing factor in the rapid economic growth of corresponding decades (Bloom *et al.* 2006). But inevitably the bubble of younger working-age people has moved through time to become a bubble of older, retired people, leaving in its wake a much smaller generational wave that cannot replace the previous numbers. China's increasing old age dependency ratio is predicted to eventually outstrip the fall in young age dependency, leading to an eventual rise in overall dependency in the coming decades. Like most societies of the twenty-first century, China is challenged with the task of developing an economy that fits its new and changing demographic structure.

Land and water are the main resource constraints on China's agriculture and food security. To feed its 1.3 billion population, equal to 22 percent of world's population with only 7.8 percent of the world's cultivated land, China is already facing a great food security challenge (Chen 2007). It is predicted that the country will need about 500 to 600 million tons of grain per year for its projected 1.5 billion people (Heilig *et al.* 2000). However, the situation has been worsening over the past two decades due to the interplay of "anthropogenic, sociopolitical and policy factors," including the sheer size of newly increased population, accelerated urbanization and industrialization, land and water scarcity, changes in diet, environmental pollution, and disturbance of world food markets (Heilig *et al.* 2000; Cann *et al.* 2005; Khan *et al.* 2009).

China's cultivated land is shrinking at a rather shocking rate (Cann *et al.* 2005). According to latest data from the *China Statistical Yearbook*, China's cultivated lands were reduced by an average of 1 million hectares per year from the start of 1997 to the end of 2008, resulting in a total amount of approximately 121.7 million hectares at present. China's enormous population renders such growing scarcity of land extremely significant. The area of cultivated land per capita stood at only 0.09 hectares, which was only about 40 percent of the world average. Meanwhile, the country is also confronted with a serious water shortage to irrigate its farmland. China is listed by the United Nations as one of 13 countries most short of water. Total water consumption volume increased from 541×10^9 m^3 in 2003 to 593×10^9 m^3 in 2009 (NBSC 2010). Water supply in agriculture is hampered by a range of severe problems, such as uneven distribution in time and space, low efficiency of irrigation system, conflicts with other types of uses (e.g. urban and industrial uses), climate change, and water pollution (Brown 2011). It is notable that irrigation's share of total water consumption dropped to 54.1 percent in 2010 from 62.6 percent in 2001 (Xu and Li 2010). Li (2003) projected that the water demand from industry is expected to reach 190×10^9 m^3 in 2030, approximately three times as much as that in 2000, which will lead to conflicts with agricultural uses. The continuing shortage of land and water resources acts as an important constraint on China's sustainable growth and its influence will grow more acute as demand for both land and water resources increases among non-farm users.

China, as an emerging manufacturing and trading powerhouse, is certain to magnify its impact on world resources and energy markets in the coming decades. China's phenomenal economic growth is driving a hunt for natural and mineral resources to fuel its prosperity (Woo 2009). China has become the world's top consumer of a wide variety of natural resources and primary commodities, from coal to steel. According to the International Association for Impact Assessment (IAIA) (2010), China has surpassed the United States to become the world's largest energy consumer in 2010 rather than 2025 as the International Energy Agency (IEA) had predicted in 2007 (IEA 2007). China's total energy consumption in 2010 was estimated as 3.25 billion tons coal equivalent (TCE), 5.9 percent higher than in 2009. Coal, crude oil and electricity consumption in 2010 increased by 5.3 percent, 12.9 percent and 13.1 percent respectively (Xinhua 2011). China is the second largest natural oil user and importer. In 2010, China imported 239 million tons of crude oil, approximately 33 percent higher than in 2008 according to estimates by China's National Development and Reform Commission. It is clear that even at 7 percent growth in GDP growth, China's giant economy will still require a huge amount of new energy resources. It is projected that China's total energy consumption will consume 4–6.7 billion TCE in 2030, adding mounting pressure to the world energy market and raising potential insecurity problems for China's further development (Li 2010; Wang *et al.* 2010). The Chinese government has been determined to diversify its energy supply, especially in favor of renewable sources. Currently, hydroelectric sources (6 percent), natural gas (3 percent), nuclear power (1 percent), and other renewables (0.2 percent) account for relatively small amounts of China's energy consumption mix (Energy Information Administration 2010). According to China's Twelfth Five-Year Plan for 2011–2015, non-fossil fuels will be expanded to take up 11.4 percent of primary energy consumption by 2015. However, an absolute increase in China's fossil fuel energy consumption is expected in the coming ten years,[33] but the country cannot duplicate the Western model of environmental pollution (Zeng *et al.* 2008). Therefore, the key challenge facing China in the next two decades is how to make efficient rather than sufficient growth. In addition, in China's Twelfth Five-Year Plan, the construction of more than 50 new nuclear reactor powerhouses, adding 50 GW new capacities towards a greener energy supply, is planned. The recent nuclear crisis in Japan, however, has raised some doubt on China's movement in this direction.

The environmental consequences of rising use of energy and natural resources present huge challenges to China's sustainable development (Zhang 2000; Garnaut *et al.* 2008). Water and air pollution are burdening its economy, endangering the health of its population and tensions with the rest of world. China, according to PBL Netherlands Environmental Assessment Agency, overtook the United States as world's biggest carbon dioxide emitter in 2006.[34] In 2009, China produced 7,706 Million Metric Tons (MMT) of carbon dioxide emissions, about one-quarter of the world's total, 39.8 percent more than in 2005 (Energy Information Administration 2009). China's CO_2 emissions almost tripled from 1990 to 2009 (International Energy Agency 2010). Without remedy, emissions are projected to be more than twice the current level in 2030.[35] China's actions on environmental protection are critically vital to global climate prospects (Garnaut *et al.* 2008; Leggett *et al.* 2008). Environmental concerns, especially those related to climate change and energy, are given priority in China's economic strategy as set out in the Twelfth Five-Year Plan which was endorsed by National People's Congress on March 14, 2011. It is not the first time a Five-Year Plan has made a mandatory commitment to gradually reduce environment pollution with detailed targets and measures to be implemented, but it is the first time a market mechanism to control carbon pollution has been introduced (Australian Government 2011). Moreover, under the United Nations climate change agreement, China is committed to lower carbon intensity by 40–45 percent by 2020 compared to 2005. Between 2006 and 2010, the country has successfully achieved a 19.1 percent decrease and set an ambitious new goal of 16 percent further reduction for 2011–2015. What is uncertain is how much such a big country's compliance with emission targets in such a short timeframe will cost it, given China's reliance on coal (McKibbin *et al.* 2008; Lin *et al.* 2008). To reconcile the goals of economic growth, energy and environmental quality, China will require effective governance capacity to not only design proper incentives for environmental protection through legal systems and national policies, but also to monitor and enforce compliance with laws (Dasgupta *et al.* 2002; Aden and Sinton 2006; Ho and Vermeer 2006).

Political governance and rule of law

Mass socioeconomic transformation has changed the economic conditions of Chinese society and reshaped the parameters of its political governance (Saich 2001).[36] While it is true that the Communist Party of China has carried out some political reform, these changes are seen as limited and insufficient to cope with the challenges presented by: the deepening market economy, further international integration, monopoly of political power, rising corruption, and social protests (Saich 2001; Zhao 2003; Pei 2006; Garnaut 2010). The pressure for political reform is again being felt inside China, and occupies the CCP's agenda. Chinese

Premier Wen Jiabao (2011) has declared that China will actively yet prudently advance political restructuring, expand socialist democracy, and improve the socialist legal system in the next five years. The process of China's economic integration with the world economy attracts wide anticipation and approval of a more democratic, just, and harmonious civil society which is organized under the rule of law. Acemoglu and Robinson (2008) suggest that democratic institution reforms should preferably take place simultaneously. However, political problems and proposed political reform place more serious risk and uncertainty on the sustainability of China's growth than any other economic problems (Srinivasan 2006). Hence, to great extent, the key constraints for further economic development are political (White 1994; Pyle 1997; Pei 2006; Enright 2008).

As discussed in the second section institutional factors are essential to economic development and the achievement of a society's objectives. This is particularly relevant to good governance. As the economy develops, the demand for an effective, efficient and just legal system is rising. Therefore, how China goes about successfully transforming its governmental institutions so that they are compatible with a market-oriented economy becomes of crucial importance. The World Bank uses six indicators to measure the quality of governance: voice and accountability, political stability, government effectiveness, regulatory quality, rule of law, and control of corruption. Therefore, good governance requires accountability, transparency, participation, legal and judicial framework (Rule of Law), and combating corruption (Agere 2000; OECD 2005). While these constitute the ideal target for all societies, it is clear that failures in governance caused by corruption, abuse of the law, political scandals and the triggering of social protest are not solely features of developing countries, but also happen in the developed democratic nations of the world.

At the centre of governance, and the most important, should be the rule of law, which provides the foundation of all social activities (Friedman 2002). Fareed Zakaria (1997) quotes Alan Greenspan's statement on the link between rights and free market economics: "The guiding mechanism of a free market economy . . . is a bill of rights, enforced by an impartial judiciary." China has put great effort into implementing a comprehensive legal system in terms of "a transplant deduced from a pre-given foreign model" in a top-down approach by the central government so as to regulate market behaviour. However, the process of the whole society committing to the rule of law is much more complex than the process of marketization alone, due to a particular set of obstacles and constraints found in East Asian countries, especially China (Perkins 2006; Peerenboom 2007). Future reform in terms of rule of law will aim at regulation of power and responsibility, and election of political leaders, government, and the Communist Party in a more democratic and transparent manner involving the participation and surveillance of the public, where the role of the courts is independent, just and authoritative. Resolution of these issues would inevitably weaken the rule of the Communist Party as well as the status quo of vested interest stakeholders and hence faces powerful resistance. However, unless these fundamental issues are addressed, substantial progress in the rule of law and government efficiency will remain elusive. While much Western criticism holds political ideology and the non-democratic system of rule as the main obstacles to establishing liberal democracy and rule of law in China, the more substantial obstacle should rather be the weak institutional capacity involved in every aspect of China's society (Peerenboom 2007). Should further reforms and social welfare improvements be blocked by one or all of China's elites, both reformers and the public, particularly the new middle classes, will continue to find ways to protect their interests which include social justice. This may eventually put further pressure on the current political system to change.

If China has to democratize, the question is: in which direction and with what consequences? Liberally and competitively, electoral democracy is taken as the first step towards, and the most important and minimum criterion of, democracy (Schumpeter 1934), but the new democratic countries in the third wave have found it difficult to depart from authoritarian governments except for their periodic elections (Peerenboom 2007). Chinese leaders and people welcome the democratic ideas of the Western world, but are more likely to favour civil liberty that embraces freer press and media, effective rule of law, and separation of power, rather than truly multi-party competitive elections (Pan 2003). Chinese people themselves believe that China will never follow a "Western" model of democracy (Peerenboom 2007; Li 2008) and there is a common view that "a general election would cause social chaos and disorder," given China's huge population, weak rule of law, geographic politics, and historical and cultural influences (Pan 2003; He and Feng 2008). China's neighbours, including Japan, Taiwan and South Korea, which are normally thought to have met the criteria for real democracy, have differed significantly from the democratic states prevalent in the West in terms of freedom of speech, free press, and the relative maturity of their election systems (Huntington 1991). Overtime they moved from autocracy to liberalizing autocracy or liberalizing semi-democracy. The political systems in these countries pay more attention to social stability and moral consensus, as well as to the strength of the state (and a strong state), than to truly liberal democracy. Democracy in China is most likely to be the result of evolution rather than revolution (White 1994; Peerenboom 2007). The histories of state-of-the-art democratic countries like the United Kingdom, France, Germany, Japan and the recent "four tigers" in East Asia all testify that political democratization emerged gradually and always lagged behind economic changes (White 1994).[37] A handful of studies suggest that premature democracy at a low economic level is unstable and causes pressing social chaos as well as a slowdown in economic development (Zakaria 1997; Pan 2003).[38] According to Przeworsky *et al.* (1996), there is an ideal "democratic transition zone" – states may transit from authoritarian to democratic at any level of per capita income, but they can sustain democracy only with an annual level of Gross National Income (GNI) per capita above US$6,000. China does not meet this standard, with a nominal (GNI) per capita income at US$3,650 in 2009 according to the World Bank.[39] Meanwhile, the rapid implosion of the former Soviet Union and long-term stagnation of many East European countries has had lessons for China. In the light of the history of East Asia, it could be seen that the CCP was to some extent correct to emphasize consolidating the rule of law in the first place, followed by political liberalization, before reaching liberal democracy (Zakaria 1997; Zhao 2003). It is reasonable to believe that China is on its way to becoming a democratic country but may follow or extenuate from its neighbors' experience to postpone or slow down the democratization process for a relatively long period.[40] Moreover, it is inappropriate to assume western electoral democracy is the only form of democracy countenanced. Democracy has to "give a central place to guaranteeing free public discussion and deliberative interactions in political thought and practice – not just through elections nor just for elections" (Sen 2003). In China, the resulting political system could be dominated by a single party co-existing with elements of institutionalized liberal politics (White 1994). Democracy of this kind can be realized by various means through the National People's Congress, National Committee of the Chinese People's Political Consultative Conference, and direct elections at county level. China is expected to evolve some form of democracy in its own style, just as its economic institutions have evolved in a unique way (Zhao 2003).

In sum, a variety of factors cohere to form an urgent need for significant political reform at this stage, and how the leadership manages the next phase of reform will be crucial (Saich 2009). However, it is necessary to step rather than leap forward with political reform in the next decade, and the one-party political structure will stay in place for the foreseeable future. The most immediate tasks for China are to sustain economic growth and solve urgent problems such as unemployment, income disparity and corruption. The most important step for China to pave the way for democracy at present is to establish rule of law that guarantees basic civil and economic rights. It is possible that the changing balance of power between state and society may in turn generate political impetus for further democratization[41] (Chen 2009). It seems the proper way to build up good governance starts in three directions. First, the rule of law should on the one hand protect the basic civil and economic rights of society and on the other hand provide a redefinition of the position, responsibility, and political check of the Communist Party and its relationship with other state institutions. Second, the political system should be opened up to diverse groups and interests in various ways. China's reform has achieved much in terms of the transparency of its government, particularly at the local level, but more attention should be paid to making the system more accountable (Abrami *et al.* 2008). In addition to widened access and participation in the National People's Congress and Chinese People's Political Consultative Conference, direct elections would be another milestone in the progress of democratization. Direct elections may spread from the village and town level to some small cities. But the effectiveness and efficiency of these access and participation processes depends on the first point – the role, responsibility and boundary of the Party. Third, it is time to release control of public communication and information channels. The most important part of democracy is providing the public with open access to information, and empowering the public to participate in the discussion, reasoning and decision making of policies and institutions (Sen 2003). In fact, the information era has changed the political landscape dramatically – rapid internet in China enables its people to express and share their opinions, access up-to-date information on the latest events, uncover facts and reality beyond media control, and act as a watchdog who can protect people's rights and influence the behaviours and decisions of government and business (Yang 2009).

Concluding remarks

China has been undertaking unprecedented social experimentations on a massive scale: some have worked, some have failed (Hoffmann 2008). History has confounded both optimists and pessimists in regard to China's development path. The future will probably do the same. As Broadfoot (2008) argues, China has various futures in different scenarios, based on four general uncertainties: the ability of China to maintain rapid growth, the cohesiveness of its society, the state's relations with Taiwan, and national relations with the world's other great powers. Rather than inaccurately predicting what the future holds for China in precise terms, this review has primarily sought to provide a comprehensive and deeper understanding of what has happened over the past 30 years in China. What is known and what we do not yet know about China's economic development has been discussed. If we are to assess China's future in the age of globalization and marketization, we can offer the following prediction: China is driving on a one-way street to an unpredictable and dangerous, but also promising, future, with no way back to the socialist past.

The twentieth century saw a gradual transition from the United States as a sole superpower to a more complicated system in which several powers have influence (Grant and Barysch 2008). The United States is likely to remain the leading power in a global sense for several decades, but with the rise of China the role America plays will be profoundly different from its past (Stanzel 2007). "When the day comes that China can shake the world, it will hopefully do so along with, rather than against the West."[42] The world faces crucial challenges to achieving sustainable global economic development (Garnaut 2009). When, how and to what degree it recovers depends greatly on multilateral cooperation among countries (Adams 2006; Sheng 2009). For sustainable growth, China has to harmonize itself with the rest of the world (Woo 2009). China's relations with the great powers of the West, the United States and the EU in particular, represent critical challenges and uncertainties for China and international society (Broadfoot 2008; Woo 2008; Garnaut 2009).

The US–China relationship should be the most influential bilateral relationship in world political affairs at present and in the future (Grant and Barysch 2008). The financial crisis has, on the one hand, called for tighter cooperation between the United States and China, but on the other hand, has also led to deep division in how to dance with the other giant partner, both within China and the United States (Saich 2009). As a whole, the relationship between China and the United States is characterized by one word – complexity (Choucri and North 1975; Friedberg 2005; Scalapino 2008).[43] Given the increasing interdependence in promoting economic growth with trade and investment, a positive relationship between these two leading countries is in the interest of the whole world. Their cooperation could increase global economic prosperity, peaceful resolution of regional disputes, and the successful management of pressing global challenges such as battling recession (Friedberg 2005; Woo 2008). Relations between China and the United States will on balance remain largely positive in the years ahead as their respective leaderships will, beyond doubt, be motivated to curb and contain any rising tensions or conflicts (Scalapino 2008). Nonetheless, recent events demonstrate how difficult it can be to settle conflicts or achieve agreement between these two countries. Recent causes of discord in the relationship include the Sanctions Bill on Chinese currency *yuan*, the United States' large trade deficits with China, China's cooperation with Iran in oil processing, and issues related to Tibet and Taiwan.

The EU is the largest export destination for China and China is the EU's second largest trade partner, just behind the United States (EC 2010). Both the EU and China intend to play a greater role in international affairs to counterbalance America's superpower (Gill and Murphy 2008), in which they have great room for cooperation to maintain international peace and security,[44] but so far Europe–China relations have been mainly commercial rather than strategic (Möller 2002; Gill and Murphy 2008; Grant and Barysch 2008).[45] The current global financial crisis and sovereign debt crisis in Europe have created new opportunities for these two sides to work together. In 2008, they established the EU–China High-Level Economic and Trade Dialogue to address issues of mutual concern in trade. On the one hand, Asian countries, and China in particular, played an increasing role in tackling the euro-area debt crisis by buying government bonds of first Greece, then Ireland, followed by Spain and Italy. Multimillion Euro business and trade contracts – in terms of shipping, tourism, telecommunications and agricultural products with Greece, Spain, United Kingdom and Germany – were sealed during recent visits of top Chinese leaders to Europe (Smith 2010). Nevertheless, there has been considerable uncertainty about the future of the "strategic partnership" of EU–China (Möller 2002; Stanzel 2007; Grant and Barysch 2008; Allen and Smith 2010). China's relations with the EU and the G8 are thought to share some of the same challenges as those with the United States (Scalapino 2008). The EU's trade deficit with China reached 169 billion Euros in 2010, only slightly smaller than the US–China deficit (EC 2011). While EU countries have attributed rising deficit to an undervalued *yuan*, unfair prices, violation of intellectual property rights and unsustainable production behavior, and have expressed concerns over food safety and environmental protection (Grant and Barysch 2008), China on the other end, has complained that the EU is becoming more protectionist against China's exports (Men 2008). Moreover, what makes bilateral cooperation between EU and China more complicated than America and China is that, as a regional organization, the EU aims to adopt a single position towards China in economic and political issues, but member states may have different national commercial interests and different political positions concerning China's military and human rights problems (Algieri 2007; Fox and Godement 2008; Grant and Barysch 2008; Men 2008).[46] Such intra-EU division to some extent places obstacles for real "strategic cooperation." A productive EU–China relationship in the next decade calls for more fundamental reforms to solve internal imbalances, and deeper cooperation-oriented dialogue to achieve win-to-win economic development and improvements in social welfare (Algieri 2007; Fox and Godement 2008).

The new global equilibrium could be a win–win game for the world but the process of achieving such outcome is a painful one (Woo 2009). It is the system that matters, if what the world needs now is "sustainable globalization" and ways to realize it (Berchtold 2009). It provokes two critical questions: what's wrong with the capital free-market economy in the developed countries? How to benefit from globalization and control cross-border risks? For a relatively long period, neoclassical economic theories have held that government's intervention is harmful to the free market, provided it works well; government intervention is necessary only when market failure takes place. The Washington Consensus held that the core issue of good economic performance requires liberalized trade, macroeconomic stability, and a free price system with "a minimalist role" for the government (Stiglitz 2002). The dynamic market power of the United States, Japan, and the Euro Area appeared to have fully established a liberal capitalist model for the world for centuries (Bremmer 2009). However, the current global crisis and economic recession have cast doubt on these traditional ideas of non-intervention state and state involvement only as an ex post facto remedy (Bremmer 2009). The Asian Miracle has helped initialize this suspect, but China's successful experience in dealing with global crisis seems to give additional impetus to further discussion on the government's role (Kennedy 2010). The ultimate source of growth is productivity improvement. The free market theories strongly encourage innovation and liberalization. But the recent global crisis initialized from developed countries indicates growth from financial innovation and the housing market are economic bubbles. So where is the additional resource of further productivity growth in the post-industrial era (Fu 2009)? It is the time to encourage "creatively destructive" entrepreneurship and technological innovation instead of "destructively creative" financial innovation. The financial crisis in 1990s and 2000s proved that unfettered finance leads to uncontrollable instability and destruction (Sheng 2009). The financial system itself will not do a very good job due to the problems of incomplete information, incomplete markets, incomplete contracts, and incomplete cooperate governance (Stiglitz 1998), despite its essential "brain"-like role in the economic system (domestically and internationally). This personal rational behaviour of capital investment has led to disastrous impacts on the whole economy, which spread at an amazing speed due to contemporary globalization (Adams 2006; Sandbrook 2007). "Bad things often happen, even to rational people" (Olson 2000).

It would appear that the only way to recover from the global crisis and realize sustainable economic development is to combine the mechanisms of both market and planning so that they converge on one target: making the economy more efficient and sustainable. On the one hand, government should avoid excessive and direct intervention and leave room for market forces; on the other hand, it should strengthen its capacity to provide effective support, guidance, and regulation to avoid market failure and ensure social justice. The role of government power has been misconceived or misused in the past. Global integration has controversial effects on the government's power. On the one hand, market liberalization limits government's autonomy to design its own institutions and policies at variance with international dogma; on the other hand, domestic pressure from global competition calls for "big government" to provide protection and social welfare (Rodrik 1997; Sandbrook 2007). Macroeconomic policies are within country borders, while capital flows are freely moving worldwide. Even if a government once can successfully manage a financial crisis within the national border, it doesn't guarantee the government would do the same good job in front of borderless world shocks of unfettered finance (Sheng 2009). However, just like Hirst and Thompson (1999) contended that "there are still opportunities for the development of governance mechanism at the level of the international economy that neither undermine national governance nor hinder the creation of national strategies for international control." Government could devise interventions as a complementation to the imperfect market that improves efficiency and makes every one better off, even within the context of imperfect information and underdeveloped market (Greenwald and Stiglitz 1986; Stiglitz 1996).

This combined approach gives a more active and crucial role to government in repairing market failure, something also emphasized by Stiglitz (1996, 2002, 2004) and Vietor (2007). Appropriate regulation (planning) can help the market to maintain a balance between opportunities and risks, as well as the costs and benefits of globalization (Bräuninger and Vöpel 2010). The central problem therefore lies in the balance between government and market so that it is neither too weak nor too instructive. The Asian financial crisis in 1997 was a test of the Asian governance, which had great influence on their government's financial budget – from a net borrower to a net saver; the current financial crisis is also a test for the global governance and governance of all nations (Sheng 2009). For China, government has successfully played and will continue to play an immensely important role in national development (Hoffmann 2008). Unfortunately there is no standard answer, and China's good experience may have adverse effects in another country (Stiglitz 1996). It is a changing, dynamic, completive, closely linked world, which embraces all forms of innovation (Adams 2006). Finding the best balance largely depends on the particular circumstances of political and economic development (Stiglitz 2002, 2004). However, echoing the conclusions of China's vice-premier Li Keqiang, it is clear that China's development will not be possible without the world – and world development needs China (Li 2011). China must therefore, in its own interests, help to promote globalization by strengthening its role in international economic and politic engagement (Woo 2009).

Notes

1 We are extremely grateful to Mr Francis Kane of the University of Ulster for his lengthy discussion, constructive ideas and detailed comments on an earlier draft of this chapter.
2 It became almost universal by the end of 1983, as noted by Naughton (2007, p. 89).
3 The state-owned enterprises paid taxes instead of all profits to the central government, which provided stronger incentives for the directors or managers and the workers to maximize their profits.

4 Since 1984 material-allocation by the central government had been fully committed in absolute terms by the planners.
5 Economists believe that institutions are the fundamental determinant of economic performance and long-run growth in a country, which provide incentives of the whole society (Acemoglu *et al.* 2005). Perkins (1994) identified five elements evolving a functioning market economy: (1) achieve macro stability; (2) make inputs and outputs available for the producers and consumers for free exchange; (3) free price system; (4) remove entry barriers to market; (5) market-supporting institutional framework.
6 Gradualism refers to implementing various reform programs in a sequential, evolutionary fashion, whereas "big bang" style reform implements these reforms at a stroke.
7 The Washington Consensus was a term first coined by John Williamson (1989) which consists of ten basic prescriptions for "standard" economic reform. The fiscal austerity is also called macro-stability.
8 This package of ideas is against the neo-liberal market economy approach by Washington Consensus and favours a more sustainable egalitarian and democratic development with a balance between government and market. Moreover, leading supporter Stiglitz (2002, 2004) called for the role and capacity of government rather than solely the size.
9 Ramo (2004), the most influential holder of "Beijing Consensus," argued a new development model like China is forming. Compared with Washington Consensus, Beijing Consensus is different in three aspects: (1) pragmatic and innovative without any rigid prescription for market formation; (2) not taking per capita GDP as the ends or major measurement for economic development; (3) self-determination and independence of outer powers or wills, emphasizing the idea that "Countries can plan their own development without having to accept the unfavorable terms of the Washington Consensus" (Gresh 2008).
10 However, Stiglitz (2002, p. 122) criticized this argument and pointed out "An economy which has a deep recession may grow faster as it recovers, but it never makes up for the lost time."
11 Stiglitz (2002, p. 217) also argued that the Japanese version of the market system is strikingly different from those of Germany, Sweden and America – "there is not just one market model."
12 But authors like Rosenau (1996) and Van Der Bly (2005) argued that globalization is both an ambiguous and complex concept, which are interpreted differently by people. For detailed information, refer to Van Der Bly (2005).
13 These five big crises were Spain (1977), Norway (1987), Finland (1991), Sweden (1991) and Japan (1992). In Vietor (2007, p. 38), Japan's miracle was forced to end due to America's competition strategy by ending the Bretton Woods Exchange Rate System and imposing import restrictions.
14 Stiglitz (2004) also attributed the openness of capital markets to the volatility of global financial market as an important factor in the debt crisis of 1997–1998.
15 The European Commission and International Monetary Fund (IMF) provided 110 billion Euros to Greece, spread over three years, and 85 billion Euros for Ireland, with requirements of sharp cuts in government spending and increases in tax rates.
16 Before the Greek crisis, banks in European countries exposed themselves massively to foreign governments' debt because they assumed that government debt, like Greek debt, was essentially risk-free. But this assumption was wrong, as governments could not print money to pay off their debts under monetary union regulations.
17 On the other side, the European Central Bank paid more attention to the control of inflation rather than the financial balance of the member countries.
18 Gianviti *et al.* (2010) argued these solutions should be taken under a new framework– a permanent European Crisis Resolution Mechanism which can handle the default of governments.

19 Researchers argued that the causes of the Irish sovereign crisis are the unsustainable debt accumulation by the private sector (real estate bubble) while the Greek crisis was caused by the public sector, that is, excessive borrowing, tax evasion and false national statistics.

20 In 2008, the average hourly compensation cost in manufacturing in EU-15 countries was US$40.31, while it was only US$32.26 in America, US$16.27 in Japan, US$8.68 in Taiwan, and 4.04 in Mexico. China's compensation cost is not compatible with other data, but was €1.36 in 2008. Data available from United States Department of Labor: http://www.bls.gov/ilc/#compensation.

21 Paul Krugman (1994) criticized that the growth of Asian countries in the 1990s were "paper tiger," as these countries just benefited from taking advantage of resources rather than improving efficiency and technology. He also argued "If there is a secret to Asian growth, it is simply deferred gratification, the willingness to sacrifice current satisfaction for future gain." Generally speaking, he is strongly against the "Asian Miracle" school.

22 Luck that leads a nation to escape a poor equilibrium with identical preferences, opportunities and market structure.

23 Protestantism led to a set of religious beliefs emphasizing hard work, thrift, discipline and individualism, which fostered the rise of capitalism (Weber 1930).

24 Confucian culture is thought to apply broadly to East Asian countries and is summarized by six characters: strong responsibilities, guanxi relationship in doing business, a top-down control, acceptance of authorial system, intensive desire of stability and harmony, and strong tradition of self-improvement and education (Adams and Vernon 2007).

25 Acemoglu (1995, 1997) and Acemoglu *et al.* (2005) argued that the market can not deliver the coordinated activities required for getting a country out of the poverty trap.

26 The intervention of government in Asian countries is raised by the likes of Stiglitz (1992, 1996, 2002), Wade (1990) and Garnaut (2009) but criticized by the likes of Krugman (1994) and Pei (2006).

27 Adams *et al.* (2006) show that despite the quantities of traditional low-tech goods export, high-tech exports from China have been growing much more rapidly. Such changes in the range of export products are indicative of the shifting trend in development strategy that is taking place.

28 According to WTO statistics, the change in China's exports and imports were −16 percent and −11 percent in nominal value terms and −11.1 percent and +2.8 percent in volume terms.

29 It is estimated by Akyüz (2010) that around 40 percent of Chinese growth before the crisis came from exports.

30 According to WTO (2011) data, China's export value of world's share in 2010 was 9.24 percent if intra-EU trade were included and 11.91 percent if intra-EU were not.

31 However, Woo and Zhang (2010) cautioned against adopting new growth drivers when the fiscal-monetary mix is unsustainable.

32 With consistent work on poverty, China has made progress during the past 30 years. At the onset of reforms, more than 650 million Chinese were living on less than US$1 a day (Yusuf and Nabeshima 2006). According the World Bank, people who are living below the international poverty line dropped from 10.3 percent in 2004 to 4 percent in 2007 (Zhang 2010).

33 Coal will still account for about 43 percent of total energy consumption in 2020, even with increasing share of other renewable resources, according to Wang, Gu and Zhang (2010).

34 According to IEA (2010, p. 24), China overtook the United States as the biggest emitter of CO_2 gas in 2007.

35 Garnaut (2008, 2011) argues that China will account for over one-third of total global emission by 2030.

36 The political and economic reforms are best seen as two simultaneous aspects of a single process, where the political ones can either undergird or undermine the economic ones.

37 Gordon (1994) argued the United States is "unusual among Western nations in being a 'lucky country' able to start out with a relative political babula rasa in the late eighteenth century" and can't serve as the targeted example for China. It was born in a revolutionary-against-state authority and the political institutions are deliberately designed to avoid accumulation of power and weaken state power (Zakaria 1997; Fukuyama 2004).

38 Peerenboom (2007) provides a list of examples in unsuccessful transition from authoritarian to democratic regimes, including India, Philippians, and Argentina. Pen (2003) initiated a framework for the rule of law and democracy for a transitional country: democracy without the rule of law, rule of law without democracy, both of rule of law and democracy, and neither rule of law nor democracy. He proposed that the first case induces the worst outcomes, and that a "consultative rule of law regime" is the Chinese ideal for democracy, like Singapore and Hong Kong, which is a rule of law with supplement of democracy.

39 However, China may have entered the democratic transition zone in 2009 judging by per capita GNI on purchase power parity basis.

40 However, Pei Minxin (2008) argued gradual transition from communist regimes to democracy may be infeasible and democratic China would be most likely to occur as a result of a sudden collapse in regime.

41 Chen (2009) suggested the authoritarianism is a matter of fact and a kind of means rather than the ends, and therefore "authoritarianism is opposed by authoritarianism," which eventually gradually transformed into a democracy nation, like South Korea and Taiwan.

42 Anonymous, available as teaching materials of Columbia University via: http://www.columbia.edu/itc/sipa/U6800/Question_3.pdf.

43 For more detailed discussion about the pessimist, optimist and constructionist, see Friedberg (2005).

44 For further discussion from various studies, please refer to Crossick and Reuter (2007), Shambaugh, Sandschneider and Zhou (2007), Grant and Barysch (2008) and Wiessala, Wilson and Taneja (2009).

45 Grant and Barysch (2008) argued that "strategic cooperation" should focus on long-term rather than short-term problems, and focus on the most dominating issues rather than all aspects. One of the three major reasons for the "non strategic relation" between the EU and China given by them was that the relationship has so far focused on economic issues. Meanwhile, Möller Kay (2002) pointed out that "the EU has been strongest on the economy, weakest in the region and wavering on world order," which is quite different from the status of the United States; further, the EU doesn't form a strategy towards China, whose policies seem to be driven by events.

46 For more information about division of EU member countries in relation with China, please refer to Page 4 in research by Fox and Godement (2008).

References

Abrami, R., Malesky, E. and Zheng, Y. (2008) 'Accountability and Inequality in Single-Party Regimes: A Comparative Analysis of Vietnam and China,' Online. Available at: http://www.wcfia.harvard.edu/sites/default/files/Abrami_Accountability.pdf (accessed January 12, 2011).

Acemoglu, D. (2008) *Introduction to Modern Economic Growth*, Princeton: Princeton University Press.

Acemoglu, D., Johnson, S. and Robinson, J. A. (2005) 'Institutions as a Fundamental Cause of Long-run Growth,' *Handbook of Economic Growth*, 1: 385–472.

Adams, F. G. (2006) *East Asia, Globalization and the New Economy*, London and New York: Routledge, 1–31, 72–80, 95–114.

Adams, F. G. and Vernon, H. (2007) 'Cultural Considerations of Business and Economic Development in East Asia,' in Henry Wai-Chung Yeung (eds), *Handbook of Research on Asian business*, Cheltenham: Edward Elgar, 335–54.

Adams, F. G., Gangnes, B. and Shachmurove, Y. (2006), 'Why is China so Competitive? Measuring and Explaining China's Competitiveness,' *The World Economy*, 29 (2), 95–122.

Adelman, I. and Robinson, S. (1978) *Income Distribution Policy in Developing Countries: A Case Study of Korea*, Palo Alto: Stanford University Press.

Aden, N. T. and Sinton, J. E. (2006) 'Environmental Implications of Energy Policy in China,' *Environmental Politics*, 15 (2): 248–270.

Agere, S. (2000) *Promoting Good Governance: Principles, Practices and Perspectives*, London: Commonwealth Secretariat.

Akyüz, Y. (2010) 'Export Dependence and Sustainability of Growth in China and the East Asian Production Network,' research papers, South Center.

Algieri, F. (2007) 'It is the System that Matters: Institutionalization and Making of EU Policy Toward China,' in D. L. Shambaugh, E. Sandschneider and H. Zhou (eds) *China–Europe Relations: Perceptions, Policies and Prospects*, Stockholm: Taylor & Francis, 65–83.

Allen, D. and Smith, M. (2010) 'Relations with the Rest of the World,' *Journal of Common Market Studies*, 48: 205–223.

Allen, F., Qian, J. and Qian M. J. (2005) 'Law, Finance, and Economic Growth in China,' *Journal of Financial Economics*, 77 (1): 57–116.

Australian Government (2011) 'Climate Change in China's 12th Five Year Plan'. Government document, Department of Climate Change and Energy Efficiency. Online. Available at: http://www.climatechange.gov.au/government/inter-national/global-action-facts-and-fiction/~/media/publications/international/china-fact-sheet.pdf (accessed September 22, 2010).

Bell, M. W., Khor, H. E. and Kochhar, K. (1993) *China at the Threshold of a Market Economy*, Washington: IMF.

Berchtold, G. (2009) 'Sustainable Globalization,' course lecture, School of Environmental and Waste Management, UCNIP.

Bhagwati, J. (2004) *In Defense of Globalization*, New York, NY: Oxford University Press.

Blanchard, O. and Shleifer, A. (2001) 'Federalism With and Without Political Centralization: China Versus Russia,' IMF staff papers, 171–179.

Bloom, D., Canning, D., Hu, L., Liu, Y., Ajay, M. and Winnie, Y. (2006) 'Why Has China's Economy Taken off Faster than India's?' Paper presented in *Population Association of America 2007 Annual Meeting Program*, March 29–31, 2007. New York, USA. Online. Available at: http://paa2007.princeton.edu/download.aspx?submissionld=70281 (accessed October 22, 2010).

Bouin, O., Coricelli, F. and Lemoine, F. (1998) *Different Paths to a Market Economy: China and European Economies in Transition*, Organization for Economic Cooperation & Development, OECD Publishing.

Bräuninger, M. and Vöpel, H. (2010) 'Globalization and Growth: A Macroeconomic Perspective,' *Globalization* 2.0: 5–19.

Bremmer, I. (2009) 'State Capitalism and the Crisis,' *McKinsey Quarterly*. Online. Available at: http://www.buec.udel.edu/sullivad/Handouts%20Directory/GB%20Readings/State%20capitalism%20and%20the%20crisis.pdf (accessed June 22, 2011).

Broadfoot, R. C. (2008) 'Different Futures for China,' in W. J. Hoffmann and M. J. Enright (eds), *China into Future: Making Sense of the World's Most Dynamic Economy*, Singapore: John Wiley & Sons, 267–311.

Brown, L. R. (2011) *World on the Edge: How to Prevent Environmental and Economic Collapse*, New York: W W Norton & Co Inc.

Cai, F. and M. Wang (2010) 'Growth and Structural Changes in Employment in Transition China,' *Journal of Comparative Economics*, 38 (1): 71–81.

Cann, C. W., Cann, M. C. and Gao S. Q. (2005) 'China's Road to Sustainable Development: An Overview,' in A. Day Kristen (ed.) *China Environment and the Challenge of Sustainable Development*, Armonk, NY: ME Sharpe, 11

Cass, D. (1966) 'Optimum Growth in an Aggregative Model of Capital Accumulation: A Turnpike Theorem,' *Econometrica: Journal of the Econometric Society*, 34 (4): 833–850.

Chang, G. H. (2002) 'The Cause and Cure of China's Widening Income Disparity,' *China Economic Review*, 13 (4): 335–340.

Chen, J. (2007) 'Rapid Urbanization in China: A Real Challenge to Soil Protection and Food Security,' *CATENA*, 69: 1–15.

Chen, J. (2010) 'Country's Wealth Divide Past Warning Level,' *China Daily*, May 20, Beijing. Online. Available at: http://www.chinadaily.com.cn/china/2010-05/12/content_9837073.htm (accessed September 22, 2010).

Chen, Q. (2008) 'Rent Seeking and Economic Liberalization: Why are China and Vietnam Different from Eastern Europe?,' *Journal of the Asia Pacific Economy*, 13 (2): 168–179.

Chen, Y. (2009) *Transition and Development in China: Towards Shared Growth*, Surrey: Ashgate Publishing, 59–116, 293–383.

Choucri, N. and North, R. (1975) *Nations in Conflict: National Growth and International Violence*, San Francisco: WH Freeman.

CPC Congress (1993) 'Some Issues Concerning the Establishment of a Socialist Market Economic System' (in Chinese), Communist Party of China. Online. Available at: http://www.people.com.cn/GB/shizheng/1024/2145119.html (accessed June 22, 2011).

Crompton, P. and Wu, Y. (2005), 'Energy Consumption in China: Past Trends and Future Directions,' *Energy Economics*, 27 (1), 195–208.

Dam, W. K. (2006) *The Law-growth Nexus: The Rule of Law and Economic Development*, Washington, DC: Brookings Institution Press.

Dasgupta, S., Laplante, B., Wang, H. and Wheeler, D. (2002) 'Confronting the Environmental Kuznets Curve,' *Journal of Economic Perspectives*, 16 (1): 147–168.

Dauderstädt, M. and J. Stetten (2005) 'China and Globalisation,' *Intereconomics*, 40 (4): 226–234.

De Grauwe, P. (2009) 'Economics in Crisis: It is Time for a Profound Revamp,' *Financial Times*, July 21. Online. Available at: http://www.ft.com/cms/s/0/478de136-762b-11de-9e59-00144feabdc0.html#axzz1KdywJPIb (accessed October 20, 2010).

Dewatripont, M. and Roland, G. (1995) 'The Design of Reform Packages Under Uncertainty,' *American Economic Review*, 85 (5): 1207–1223.

Ebner, A. (2003), 'Institutions, Entrepreneurship and the Rationale of Government: An Outline of the Schumpeterian Theory of the State,' *Journal of Economic Behaviour and Organisation*, 59 (4), 497–515.

EC (2010) 'China'. Department of Trade, European Commision. Online. Available at: http://ec.europa.eu/trade/creating-opportunities/bilateral-relations/countries/china/ (accessed June 22, 2011).

EC (2011) 'EU Bilateral Trade and Trade With The World: China,' European Commission. Online. Available at: http://trade.ec.europa.eu/doclib/docs/2006/september/tradoc_113366.pdf (accessed December 10, 2011).

Energy Information Administration (2009) *International Energy Statistics*, U.S. Energy Information Administration.

Energy Information Administration (2010) *China Energy Data, Stastics and Analysis. Country Analysis Briefs*, Energy Information Administration. Online. Available at: http://www.eia.doe.gov/cabs/china/pdf.pdf (accessed June 22, 2011).

Enright, M. J. (2008) 'China's Economy into the Future,' W. J. Hoffmann and M. J. Enright (eds) *China into Future: Making Sense of the World's Most Dynamic Economy*, Singapore: John Wiley & Sons, 52–58.

Feenstra, R. C. and Hanson, G. H. (1996) 'Globalization, Outsourcing, and Wage Inequality,' *The American Economic Review*, 86 (2): 240–245.

Feltenstein, A. and Nsouli, S. M. (2003) '"Big Bang" versus Gradualism in Economic Reforms,' *IMF Staff Papers*, 50 (3): 458–480.

Ferguson, N. (2011) *Civilization: The West and the Rest*, London: Penguin Books Press.

Fidrmuc, J. and Korhonen, I. (2010) 'The Impact of the Global Financial Crisis on Business Cycles in Asian Emerging Economies,' *Journal of Asian Economics*, 21 (3): 293–303.

Fields, G. S. and Yoo, G. (2000) 'Falling Labor Income Inequality in Korea's Economic Growth: Patterns and Underlying Causes,' *Review of Income and Wealth*, 46 (2): 139–159.

Fox, J. and Godement, F. (2008) *A Power Audit of EU–China Relations*, London: European Council on Foreign Relations. Online. Available at: http://ecfr.3cdn.net/532cd91d0b5c9699ad_ozm6b9bz4.pdf (accessed December 12, 2010).

Friedberg, A. L. (2005) 'The Future of U.S.–China Relations: Is Conflict Inevitable?,' *International Security*, 30 (2): 7–45.

Friedman, M. (2002) 'Economic Freedom behind the Scenes,' in J. Gwartney and R. Lawson (eds) *Economic Freedom of the World Report: 2002 Annual Report*, The Fraser Institute, 17–21.

Friedman, T. (2006) *The World is Flat: A Brief History of the Twenty-first Century*, New York, NY: Farrar Straus & Giroux.

Fu, J. (2009) 'World Economic Downturn and Challenges for China,' paper presented at *Money and Banking Conference*: *Lessons and Challenges for Emerging Countries during the Crisis*, Buenos Aires, Argentina.

Garnaut, R. (2001) 'Twenty Years of Economic Reform and Structural Change in the Chinese Economy,' in R. Garnaut and Y. Huang (eds) *Growth Without Miracles: Readings on the Chinese Economy in the Era of Reform*, Oxford: Oxford University Press, 1–18.

Garnaut, R. (2009) 'China's New Place in a World in Crisis: Economic, Geopolitical and Environmental Dimensions,' in Garnaut, R., Song, L. and Woo, W. (eds) *China's New Place in a World in Crisis Economic, Geopolitical and Environmental Dimensions*, Canberra: ANU E Press, 1–14

Garnaut, R. (2011) 'Thirty Years of Chinese Reform and Economic Growth: Challenges and How it Has Changed World Development' in Y. Yao and H. Wu (eds) *Reform and Development in China: What Can China Offer the Developing World?*, Abingdon: Routledge, 82–98.

Garnaut, R., Jotzo, F. and Sheehan, P. (2008) 'China's Rapid Emissions Growth and Global Climate Change Policy,' in L. Song and W. T. Woo (eds) *China's Dilemma: Economic Growth, the Environment and Climate Change*, Washington, DC: Brookings Institution Press, 170.

Ghosh, J. (2010) 'Poverty Reduction in China and India: Policy Implications of Recent Trends,' DESA working paper, No. 92, ST/ESA/2010/DWP/92. Online. Available at: http://www.un.org/esa/desa/papers/2010/wp92_2010.pdf (accessed June 24, 2011).

Gianviti, F., Krueger, A. O., Pisani-Ferry, J., Sapir A. and Hagen, J. (2010) 'A European Mechanism for Sovereign Debt Crisis Resolution: A Proposal,' Bruegel. Online. Available at: http://aei.pitt.edu/15123/1/101109_BP_Debt_resolution_BP_clean_01.pdf (accessed December 12, 2010).

Gill, B. and Murphy, M. (2008) *China–Europe Relations: Implications and Policy Responses for the United States*, Washington, DC: Center for Strategic and International Studies.
Gosling, M. (2008) 'A Better Balance Between the Supply and Demand of Skills: Addressing Income Inequality in China and India,' CSD working paper series, City & Guilds Centre for Skills Development.
Grant, C. and Barysch, K. (2008) *Can Europe and China Shape a New World Order?*, London: Center for European Reform.
Greenwald, B. and Stiglitz, J. E. (1986) 'Externalities in Economies with Imperfect Information and Incomplete Markets,' *The Quarterly Journal of Economics*, 101 (2): 229–264.
Gresh, A. (2008) 'Understanding the Beijing Consensus,' *Le Monde Diplomatique*. Online. Available at: http://www.bresserpereira.org.br/Terceiros/08.12.Beijing.pdf (accessed October 20, 2010).
Guo, K. and N'Diaya, P. (2009) 'Is China's Export-Oriented Growth Sustainable?,' IMF working paper, International Monetary Foundation.
Guthrie, D. (2009) *China and Globalization: The Social, Economic and Political Transformation of Chinese Society (Global Realities)*, New York: Routledge, Taylor & Francis.
Haggard, S. (1996) 'Lessons from Successful Reformers: Korea and Taiwan,' *Economic Reform Today, Constructing a Market Economy*, 2: 16–20.
He, K. and Feng, H. (2008) 'Path to Democracy: In Search of China's Democratization Model,' *Asian Perspective*, 32 (3): 139–169.
Heilig, G. K., Fischer, G. and Velthuizen, H (2000) 'Can China Feed Itself? An Analysis of China's Food Prospects with Special Reference to Water Resources,' *International Journal of Sustainable Development and World Ecology*, 7 (3): 153–172.
Hirst, P. and Thompson, G. (1999) *Globalization in Question: The International Economy and the Possibilities of Governance*, Oxford: Polity Press.
Ho, P. and Vermeer, E. B. (2006), 'China's Limits to Growth? The Difference Between Absolute, Relative and Precautionary Limits,' *Development and Change*, 37 (1), 255–71.
Hoffmann, W. J. (2008) 'China into Future,' in W. J. Hoffmann and M. J. Enright (eds) ,*China into Future: Making Sense of the World's Most Dynamic Economy*, Singapore: John Wiley & Sons, 8–11.
Huang, S. and Zhao, J. (2009) 'Unbalanced System Change and Economic Growth: A Rent-seeking Model' (in Chinese), *Economic Research Journal*, 12: 80–92.
Huntington, S. (1991) 'Democracy's Third Wave,' *Journal of Democracy*, 2 (2): 12–34.
Huntington, S. (1996) 'The West Unique, not Universal,' *Foreign Affairs*, 75 (6): 28–46.
International Energy Agency (2010) *CO_2 Emissions From Fuel Combustion: Highlights*, Paris, OECD.
Jones, E. L. (2003) *The European Miracle: Environments, Economies, and Geopolitics in the History of Europe and Asia*, Cambridge: Cambridge University Press.
Kennedy, S. (2010) 'The Myth of the Beijing Consensus,' *Journal of Contemporary China*, 19 (65): 461–477.
Khan, S., Hanjra, M. A. and Mu, J. (2009) 'Water Management and Crop Production for Food Security in China: A Review,' *Agricultural Water Management*, 96 (3): 349–360.
Koo, J. and Kiser, S. L. (2001) 'Recovery from a Financial Crisis: The Case of South Korea,' *Economic and Financial Review*, Q(IV): 24–36.
Kornai, J. (1992) *The Socialist System: The Political Economy of Communism*, Oxford: Oxford University Press.
Krugman, P. (1994) 'The Myth of Asia's Miracle,' *Foreign Affairs*, 73 (6): 62–78.
Kuznets, S. (1955) 'Economic Growth and Income Inequality,' *The American Economic Review*, 45 (1): 1–28.
Lau, L., Qian, Y. and Roland, G. (2000) 'Reform Without Losers: An Interpretation of China's Dual-track Approach to Transition,' *Journal of Political Economy*, 108 (1): 120–143.

Lee, E. and Vivarelli, M. (eds) (2004) *Understanding Globalization, Employment, and Poverty Reduction*, Basingstoke: Palgrave Macmillan.

Leggett, J. A., Logan, J. and Mackey A. (2008) *China's Greenhouse Gas Emissions and Mitigation Policies*, CRS Report for Congress, Congressional Research Service.

Lewis, W. A. (1954) 'Economic Development with Unlimited Supplies of Labour,' *Manchester School of Economics and Social Studies*, 22 (2): 139–191.

Li, C. (2008) 'After Hu, Who?: The Rising Stars of China's Fifth Generation,' in W. J. Hoffmann and M. J. Enright (eds) *China into Future: Making Sense of the World's Most Dynamic Economy*, Singapore: John Wiley & Sons.

Li, K. (2011) 'The World Should not Fear a Growing China,' *Financial Times*, January 10.

Li, Z. F. (2010) 'Quantitative Analysis of Sustainable Energy Strategies in China,' *Energy Policy*, 28: 2149–2160.

Li, X. (2003) 'Pressure of Water Shortage on Agriculture in Arid Region of China,' *Chinese Geographical Science*, 13 (2): 124–129.

Lin, J. (2007) 'Needham Puzzle, Weber Question and China's Miracle: Long Term Performance since the Song Dynasty,' *Journal of Peking University (Philosophy and Social Sciences)*, 4: 93.

Lin, J. Y. (2007) 'Development and Transition – Idea, Strategy, and Viability,' Development Economics working papers, China Center for Economic Research, No. E2007007.

Lin, J. Y., Cai, F. and Zhou, L. (2003) *The China Miracle: Development Strategy and Economic Reform*, Hong Kong: The Chinese University Press.

Lin, J., Zhou, N., Levine, M. and Fridley, D. (2008) 'Taking Out 1 Billion Tons of CO_2: The Magic of China's 11th Five-Year Plan?,' *Energy Policy*, 36: 954–970.

Ma, L. J. C. (2002) 'Urban Transformation in China, 1949–2000: A Review and Research Agenda,' *Environment and Planning A*, 34 (11): 1545–1569.

Maddison, A. (2007), *Chinese Economic Performance in the Long Run* (Second edn.), Development Centre Studies: OECD, 44.

Maddison, A. (2010) 'Statistics on World Population, GDP and Per Capita GDP, 1-2008 AD,' Groningen Growth and Development Center. Online. Available at: http://www.ggdc.net/MADDISON/oriindex.htm (accessed September 22, 2011).

McKibbin, W. J., Wilcoxen, P. J. and Woo, W. (2008) 'China Can Grow and Still Help Prevent the Tragedy of the CO_2 Commons,' in L. Song and W. T. Woo (eds) *China's Dilemma: Economic Growth, the Environment and Climate Change*, Washington, DC: Brookings Institution Press, 190.

McMillan, J. and Naughton, B. (1992) 'How to Reform a Planned Economy: Lessons From China,' *Oxford Review of Economic Policy*, 8 (1): 130.

Men, J. (2008) 'EU–China Relations: From Engagement to Marriage?,' EU Diplomacy Paper, Bruges, College of Europe.

Meschi, E. and Vivarelli, M. (2007) 'Trade Openness and Income Inequality in Developing Countries,' CSGR Working Paper Series. Online. Available at: http://www2.warwick.ac.uk/fac/soc/csgr/research/workingpapers/2007/wp23207.pdf (accessed June 15, 2010).

Mokyr, J. (1999) 'The British Industrial Revolution,' *Nake Nieuws*, 11 (3): 5–13.

Mokyr, J. (2002) 'The Enduring Riddle of the European Miracle: the Enlightenment and the Industrial Revolution,' draft presented to the Conference on *Convergence and Divergence in Historical Perspective: The Origins of Wealth and Persistence of Poverty in the Modern World*, Riverside.

Möller, K. (2002) 'Diplomatic Relations and Mutual Strategic Perceptions: China and the European Union,' *The China Quarterly*, 169: 10–32.

Morrison, W. M. (2009) *China and the Global Financial Crisis: Implications for the United States*, CRS Report for Congress, Congressional Research Service.

Murphy, K., Shleifer, A. and Vishny, R. W. (1992) 'The Transition to a Market Economy: Pitfalls of Partial Reform,' *The Quarterly Journal of Economics*, 107 (3): 889–906.

Murrell, P. (1992) 'Evolutionary and Radical Approaches to Economic Reform,' *Economics of Planning*, 25 (1): 79–95.
Naughton, B. (2007) *The Chinese Economy: Transitions and Growth*, Cambridge: The MIT Press.
Needham, J. (1969) *The Grand Transition: Science and Society in East and West*, London: George Allen & Unwin.
Ngok, K. (2007) 'Marketization, Globalization and Administrative Reform in China: A Zigzag Road to a Promising Future,' *International Review of Administrative Sciences*, 73 (2): 217.
North, D. and Thomas, R. (1973) *The Rise of the Western World: a New Economic History*, Cambridge: Cambridge University Press.
OECD (2005) *China in the Global Economy, Governance in China*, Organization for Economic Co-operation and Development.
Olson, M. (2000) *Power and Prosperity: Outgrowing Communist and Capitalist Dictatorships*, New York: Basic Books.
Pan, W. (2003) 'Toward a Consultative Rule of Law Regime in China,' *Journal of Contemporary China*, 12 (34): 3–43.
Peerenboom, R. (2007) *China Modernizes: Threat to the West or Model for the Rest?* New York: Oxford University Press.
Pei, M. (2006) *China's Trapped Transition: The Limits of Developmental Autocracy*, Cambridge, Mass.: Harvard University Press.
People's Daily (2007) 'Keyword: Establishing a Socialist Market Economy.' Online. Available at: http://english.cpcnews.cn/92460/6285873.html (accessed October 20, 2010).
Perkins, D. (1994) 'Completing China's Move to the Market,' *The Journal of Economic Perspectives*, 8 (2): 23–46.
Perkins, D. (2006) 'China's Recent Economic Performance and Future Prospects,' *Asian Economic Policy Review*, 1(1): 15–40.
Pickles, J. and Smith, A. (1998) *Theorising Transition: The Political Economy of Post-Communist Transformations*, London and New York: Routledge.
Pomeranz, K. (2001) *The Great Divergence: China, Europe, and the Making of the Modern World Economy*, New Jersey: Princeton University Press.
Porter, M. E. (1990) *The Competitive Advantage of Nations*, New York: The Free Press.
Pritchett, L. (2003) 'A Toy Collection, a Socialist Star and a Democratic Dud: Growth Theory, Vietnam, and the Philippines,' in D. Rodrik (ed.) *In Search of Prosperity: Analytical Narratives on Economic Growth*, Princeton: Princeton University Press, 123–151.
Pyle, D. J. (1997) *China's Economy: From Revolution to Reform*, New York: St. Martin's Press.
Qian, Y. (2003) 'How Reform Worked in China,' in D. Rodrik (ed.) *In Search of Prosperity: Analytic Narratives on Economic Growth*, Princeton: Princeton University Press, 297–333.
Qian, Y. and Wu, J. L. (2000) 'China's Transition to a Market Economy: How Far Across the River?,' paper prepared for the Conference on Policy Reform in China at the Center for Research on Economic Development and Policy Reform (CEDPR), Stanford University, 31.
Quibria, M. (2006) 'Does Governance Matter? Yes, No or Maybe: Some Evidence From Developing Asia,' *Kyklos*, 59 (1): 99–114.
Raby, G. (2001) 'The "Neither This Nor That" Economy,' in R. Garnaut and Y. Huang (eds) *Growth Without Miracles: Readings on the Chinese Economy in the Era of Reform* Oxford: Oxford University Press, 19–35.
Radelet, S. and Sachs, J. (2000) 'The Onset of the East Asian Financial Crisis,' in P. R. Krugman (ed.) *Currency Crises*, Chicago: The University of Chicago Press, 105–162.
Ramo, J. (2004) *The Beijing Consensus*, London: Foreign Policy Centre.

Rao, D. (1978) 'Economic Growth and Equity in the Republic of Korea,' *World Development*, 6 (3): 383–396.
Rawski, G. T. (1999) 'Reforming China's Economy: What Have We Learned?,' *The China Journal*, 139–156.
Rawski, T. (1995) 'Implications of China's Reform Experience,' *The China Quarterly*, 144: 1150–1173.
Reinhart, C. M. and K. S. Rogoff (2008) 'Is the 2007 US Sub-prime Financial Crisis so Different? An International Historical Comparison,' *American Economic Review*, 98 (2): 339–344.
Rodrik, D. (1997) *Has Globalization Gone Too Far?*, Washington DC: Peterson Institute.
Rodrik, D. (2003) 'Introduction: What Do We Learn from Country Narratives?,' in D. Rodrik (ed.) *In Search of Prosperity: Analytic Narratives on Economic Growth*, Princeton: Princeton University Press, 1–19.
Rogowski, R. and Han, K. J. (2010) 'Do Hard Times Reduce Inequality?,' paper presented at a Conference in honor of Peter Gourevitch.
Roland, G. (2002) 'Transition and Economics. Politics, Markets, and Firms,' *Economics of Transition*, 10 (2): 513–523.
Rumbaugh, T. and Blancher, N. (2004) 'International Trade and the Challenges of WTO Accession,' in E. Prasad (ed.) *China's Growth and Integration into the World Economy: Prospects and Challenges*, Washington, DC: International Monetary Fund.
Sachs, J. and Woo, W. (2000) 'Understanding China's Economic Performance,' *Journal of Economic Policy Reform*, 4 (1): 1–50.
Sachs, J., Woo, W. and Yang, X. (2002) 'Economic Reforms and Constitutional Transition,' in T. V. Hoa (ed.) *Economic Crisis Management: Theory, Practice, Outcomes and Prospects*, Cheltenham: Edward Elgar Publishing Limited, 28–85.
Saich, T. (2001) 'China on the Threshold of a Market Economy,' Harvard University. Online. Available at: http://www.hks.harvard.edu/m-rcbg/research/a.saich_cbg_china.threshold.pdf (accessed October 20, 2010).
Saich, T. (2008) 'China: Socio-Political Issues', in W. J. Hoffmann and M. J. Enright (eds) *China into Future: Making Sense of the World's Most Dynamic Economy*, Singapore: John Wiley & Sons, 137–162.
Saich, T. (2009) 'Web Up-date for Governance and Politics of China'. Online. Available at: http://www.palgrave.com/politics/saich/docs/update1.pdf (accessed June 12, 2011).
Sandbrook, R. (2007), *Social Democracy in the Global Periphery: Origins, Challenges, Prospects*, New York: Cambridge University Press, 32–34, 212–231.
Sanders, R. and Chen, Y. (2006) 'Crossing Which River and Feeling Which Stones? China's Transition to the New Economy,' in J. Chen and S. Yao (eds) *Globalization, Competition and Growth in China*, London: Routledge, 308–332.
Scalapino, R. A. (2008) 'China Confronts Globalization: Achievements and Challenges,' W. J. Hoffmann and M. J. Enright (eds) *China into Future: Making Sense of the World's Most Dynamic Economy*, Singapore: John Wiley & Sons, 107–135.
Schmidt, V. (2008) 'Limits to Growth? China's Rise and its Implications for Europe'. Online. Available at: https://ap3.fas.nus.edu.sg/fass/socvhs/research/Limits%20to%20Growth.%20Chinas%20Rise%20and%20its%20-Implications%20for%20Europe.pdf (accessed April 12, 2011).
Schumpeter, J. (1934) *The Theory of Economic Development*, Cambridge: Harvard University Press.
Sen, A. (2003) 'Why Democratization is Not the Same as Westernization?,' *The New Repubic Online*(4). Online. Available at: http://hdrnet.org/462/1/Democracy_Global_ Roots.pdf (accessed April 12, 2011).
Sheng, A. (2009) *From Asian to Global Financial Crisis: An Asian Regulator's View of Unfettered Finance in the 1990s and 2000s*, New York: Cambridge University Press, 1–18, 278–302.

Shi, Z.-l. (1998) 'Review and Experience of Economic Structure reform in China,' in O. Suliman (ed.) *China's Transition to a Socialist Market Economy*, Westport: Greenwood Press, 3–20.

Smith, H. (2010) 'Debt-ridden Greece Gets Vote of Confidence from China,' Online. Available at: http://www.guardian.co.uk/business/2010/jun/15/greece-china-contracts-signed (accessed January 21, 2011).

Solow, R. (1956) 'A Contribution to the Theory of Economic Growth,' *The Quarterly Journal of Economics*, 70 (1): 65–94.

Srinivasan, T. N. (2006) 'China, India and the World Economy,' *Economic and Political Weekly*, 41 (34): 3716.

Stanzel, V. (2007) 'The EU and China in the Global System,' in D. L. Shambaugh, E. Sandschneider and H. Zhou (eds) *China–Europe Relations: Perceptions, Policies and Prospects*, London: Taylor & Francis, 251–269.

Stiglitz, J. (1996) 'Some Lessons from the East Asian Miracle,' *World Bank Research Observer*, 11(2): 157–177.

Stiglitz, J. (1998) 'More Instruments and Broader Goals: Moving Toward the Post-Washington Consensus,' Volume 2 of WIDER annual lectures, The World Bank Group.

Stiglitz, J. (2002) *Globalization and its Discontents*, London: Penguin Books, 91–99, 122.

Stiglitz, J. (2004). 'The Post Washington Consensus Consensus,' in *The Initiative for Policy Dialogue*, Columbia University. Online. Available at: http://policydialogue.org/files/events/Stiglitz_Post_Washington_Consensus_Paper.pdf (accessed January 20, 2011).

Stiglitz, J. (2007). *Making Globalization Work*, New York: W.W. Norton & Company.

Strauss-Kahn, D.(2010) 'Message from the Managing Director and Chair of the Executive Board' in IMF (eds) *International Annual Report 2009: Fighting the Global Crisis*, Washington, DC: International Monetary Fund, 4–5.

Suliman, M. O. (ed.) (1998) *China's Transition to a Socialist Market Economy*, Westport CT: Greenwood Publishing Group.

Sutherland, D. and Yao, S. (2011) 'Income Inequality in China Over 30 years of Reforms,' *Cambridge Journal of Regions, Economy and Society*, 4 (1): 91.

Tian, G., Yuan, Y. and Zhou, X. (2002) 'Economic Globalization, Marketization Reform and Economic Development in China,' *American Review of China Studies*, 3: 1–16.

Turin, D. R. (2010) 'China and the Beijing Consensus: An Alternative Model for Development,' *Student Pulse Academic Journal*, 2 (1): 1–13.

UN's Department for Economic and Social Affairs (2009) 'World Population Aging 2009,' Online. Available at: http://www.un.org/esa/population/publications/WPA2009/ WPA2009-report.pdf (accessed October 20, 2010).

UNDP (2005) 'International Cooperation at a Crossroads: Aid, Trade and Security in an Unequal World,' *Human Development Report 2005*, K. Watkins.

Vietor, R. (2007) *How Countries Compete: Strategy, Structure, and Government in the Global Economy*, Boston, MA: Harvard Business Press.

Von Hayek, F. A. (1945) 'The Use of Knowledge in Society,' *American Economic Review*, 35 (4): 519–530.

Wade, R. (2004) *Governing the Market: Economic Theory and the Role of Government in East Asian Industrialization*, Princeton, New Jersey: Princeton University Press.

Wang, H. (1994) *The Gradual Revolution: China's Economic Reform Movement*, New Brunswick, NJ: Transaction Publishers.

Wang, L. and Zheng, J. (2010) 'China and the Changing Landscape of the World Economy,' *Journal of Chinese Economic and Business Studies*, 8 (3): 203–214.

Wang, X. and Fan, G. (2009) 'Economic Crisis, Keynesianism and Structural Imbalance in China' in Garnaut, R. Song, L. and Woo, W. (eds) *China's New Place in a World in Crisis: Economic, Geopolitical and Environmental Dimensions*, ANU E Press and Brookings Institution Press, Canberra and Washington, DC, 137–154.

Wang, Y., Gu, A. and Zhang, A. (2010) 'Recent Development of Energy Supply and Demand in China and Energy Sector Prospects through 2030,' *Energy Policy* (in press).

Weber, M. (2002) *The Protestant Ethic and the Spirit of Capitalism: And Other Writings*, P. Baehr (ed.), Penguin Group Publishing.

Wei, S.-J. (1997) 'Gradualism Versus Big Bang: speed and Sustainability of Reforms,' *The Canadian Journal of Economics*, 30 (4b): 1234–1247.

White, G. (1994) 'Democratization and Economic Reform in China,' *The Australian Journal of Chinese Affairs*, 31 (Jan.): 73–92.

Wong, R. B. (1997) *China Transformed: Historical Change and the Limits of European Experience*, New York: Cornell University Press.

Woo, W. T. (1994) 'The Art of Reforming Centrally Planned Economies: Comparing China, Poland, and Russia,' *Journal of Comparative Economics*, 18 (3): 276–308.

Woo, W. T. (2001) 'Recent Claims of China's Economic Exceptionalism – Reflections Inspired by WTO Accession,' *China Economic Review*, 12 (2–3): 107–136.

Woo, W. T. (2008) 'The Re-Emergence of China: The Valid Concerns and the Opportunities for All,' conference paper of *Markets and Models: Policy Frontiers in the AWH Phillips Tradition*, Wellington, New Zealand, July 9–11.

Woo, W. T. (2009) 'China and International Financial Reform,' in R. Garnaut, L. Song and W. Woo (eds) *China's New Place in a World in Crisis: Economic, Geopolitical and Environmental Dimensions*, ANU E Press, 15–32.

Woo, W. T. (2009) 'Updating China's International Economic Policy after 30 Years of Reform and Opening: What Position on Regional and Global Economic Architecture?,' *Journal of Chinese Economic and Business Studies*, 7 (2): 139–166.

Woo, W. T. and Zhang, W. (2010) 'Time for China to Move from Macro-stability to Macro-sustainability: Making Macro-stimulus Work and Maintaining its Effects,' *Journal of the Asia Pacific Economy*, 15 (4): 349–368.

WTO (2010) *World Trade 2009, Prospects for 2010*, Geneva: World Trade Organization, 7.

Xinhua (2011) 'China's 2010 Energy Consumption per Unit of GDP Drops 4%,' Chinese Government Official Website, *China Daily*, February 28, 2011 Online. Available at: http://www.chinadaily.com.cn/china/2011-02/28/content_12090709.htm (accessed April 15, 2011).

Xu, B. (2003) 'Trade Liberalization, Wage Inequality, and Endogenously Determined Nontraded Goods,' *Journal of International Economics*, 60 (2): 417–431.

Xu, Z. and Li, J. (2010). 'Sustainable Water Resource Management in China: A Great Challenge,' in K. Fukushi, Hassan, K. M., Honga, R. and Sumi, A. (eds) *Sustainability in Food and Water: An Asian Perspective*, London & New York: Springer, 3–10.

Yang, G. (2009) *The Power of the Internet in China: Citizen Activism Online*, New York, NY: Columbia University Press.

Yao, S. (2010) 'Economic Growth and Income Inequality in China over 30 Years of Reforms,' in S. Yao and H. Wu (eds) *Reform and Development in China: What Can China Offer the Developing World*, 101–125.

Yao, S., Zhang, Z. and Hanmer, L. (2004) 'Growing Inequality and Poverty in China,' *China Economic Review*, 15 (2): 145–163.

Young, A. (2000) 'The Razor's Edge: Distortions and Incremental Reform in the People's Republic of China,' *Quarterly Journal of Economics*, 115 (4): 1091–1135.

Yuan, Y. and Dong, R. (2008) 'Outlook: Running the Countries in Thirty Years with all Previous Third Plenaries in Chinese Communist Party,' *Outlook Weekly*, Beijing: Xinhua News Agency.

Yusuf, S. and Nabeshima, K. (2006) *China's Development Priorities. Directions in Development: Countries and Regions*, Washington, DC: The World Bank.

Zakaria, F. (1997) 'The Rise of Illiberal Democracy,' *Foreign Affairs*, 76 (6): 22–43.

Zeng, N., Ding, Y., Pan, J., Wang, H. and Gregg, J. (2008) 'Climate Change – The Chinese Challenge,' *Science*, 319 (5864): 730–731.

Zhang, J. (2009) 'Assessing China's Economic Transformation and Growth since 1978,' in A. Sweetman and J. Zhang (eds) *Economic Transitions with Chinese Characteristics: Thirty Years of Reform and Opening Up*, Montreal and Kingston: McGrill-Queen's University Press, 11–42.

Zhang, W. and Yi, G. (1996) 'China's Gradual Reform: Historical Perspective,' *Technical Report*, Asia-Pacific Financial & Forecasting Research Center.

Zhang, Z. (2000) 'Decoupling China's Carbon Emissions Increase from Economic Growth: An Economic Analysis and Policy Implications,' *World Development*, 28 (4): 739–752.

Zhao, S. (2003) 'Political Liberalization without Democratization: Pan Wei's Proposal for Political Reform,' *Journal of Contemporary China*, 12 (35): 333–355.

Zhu, J. (2010) 'China to Raise Its Poverty Line,' *China Daily*. Online. Available at: http://www.chinadaily.com.cn/china/2010-10/28/content_11467561.htm (accessed December 13, 2010).

2 Rising China

Its strength and problems

Gregory C. Chow

Introduction

The rise of China is a major event in world history at the turn of the twenty-first century. China's rapid economic growth is not only recorded in statistics that show a 9.4 percent annual growth in its real gross domestic product from 1978 to 2000 and a slightly higher rate after 2001, but can be witnessed by tourists travelling to China who are invariably impressed by its level of economic development, especially in the coastal cities.

In this chapter we will first point out the major factors contributing to China's successful economic development and then discuss some of the problems in its economic system.

Factors contributing to rapid economic growth in China

In my books *China's Economic Transformation* (Chow 2007a) and *Knowing China* (Chow 2004) I pointed out three fundamental economic factors that have contributed to China's rapid economic growth. These are the abundance of high-quality human capital, a set of workable market institutions, and the technological gap between China and the most developed economies.

On China's human capital I include both its labor force and potential entrepreneurs. The Chinese labor force is highly skilled and has good working habits. Such qualities are derived from Chinese culture beginning several thousand years ago. Witness the bronze vessels made in the Shang Dynasty over three thousand years ago that are exhibited in museums. They were skillfully crafted using advanced technology at the time. In more recent years the Chinese porcelain (or china) also demonstrates the skill of the labor force. This is the same labor force that is employed to make computer chips and other modern industrial products. A free market existed in China at least in the Han Dynasty as it was ably described by the Chinese historian Sima Qian (as quoted on p. 13 of Chow 2007a, second edition). In about 1,100 AD, the Song Dynasty had a well-functioning market economy, as described in a well-known painting at the time, "Along the River in a Spring Festival," that shows various economic activities of production, transportation, trading, and leisure enjoyment. Chinese entrepreneurship has been on show in several South-Eastern Asian countries during the last 150 years where Chinese immigrants became very successful entrepreneurs.

The high-quality of Chinese human capital has been demonstrated again since economic reform started in 1978. The Chinese labor force produces much of the industrial products distributed all around the world. Many Chinese have started successful business enterprises in China and have become rich in the process. Millions of Chinese have accumulated financial assets worth more than US$1 million. A number of domestic private enterprises or joint ventures are in the process of becoming international corporations, with a few listed in the Fortune 500. All this should be attributed to the Chinese culture, which has nurtured both skilled labors and able entrepreneurs.

The second factor is market institutions, which have been developed under the government's economic reform policies. The high-quality Chinese human capital could not be effectively utilized under central planning, within which economic decisions were made by the government and the Chinese people had no way to receive an appropriate reward for their efforts. The new market institutions include: private farming introduced under the household responsibility system, the dynamic township and village enterprises and rapidly growing private enterprises which began in the early 1980s, a corporate structure for state-owned enterprises in the late 1990s, stock markets introduced in Shenzhen and Shanghai in the 1992, and a commercial banking system formally introduced in the 1980s but beginning to function as modern commercial banks especially after China joined the World Trade Organization in 2002. There are many imperfections in China's market institutions such as the lack of transparency of Chinese corporations. Despite this they are good enough to support rapid economic growth, as demonstrated by the actual growth experience in the last three decades.

The most important feature of China's market institutions is free entry for all. It is true that all successful Chinese businessmen or businesswomen need the cooperation of government bureaucrats and that some bureaucrats get rich mainly from their positions rather than their talents. Yet there is free entry for all Chinese. If an able Chinese entrepreneur finds some small business opportunity he or she can borrow a small amount of capital from friends or relatives as well as using his own savings to get the business started. When his business becomes successful, he can expand it with the approval and help of some government officials. These are the rules of the game. Most government officials are intelligent enough to give support to the more able entrepreneurs because doing so will yield a higher return for them. Hence able and talented entrepreneurs flourish in the Chinese market economy. Because of this important role of bureaucrats I have called the Chinese economy a bureaucratic market economy in Chow (2004).

Regarding the third factor, the technological gap between China and the most advanced economies, China has been able to adopt the most advanced technology and managerial systems, which others took a long time to develop. The use of cell phones and up-to-date personal computers is more widespread in major Chinese coastal cities than in American cities. Large proportions of the buildings in Chinese cities are new. China has skipped many steps in its development process and could do this rapidly. As the technological gap becomes narrower in the course of China's economic development the speed of growth will eventually slow down, but we are still one or two decades away from that time because many parts of China's interior are still undeveloped.

This leads us to answer the question when will this rapid growth in the Chinese economy slow down? As long as the above three fundamental factors remain in force China's growth will continue at a rapid rate. The third factor of having a technological gap may be weakened gradually in the course of time but this negative effect will not take place in the next ten to 15 years. Thus China's annual growth rate will remain at 8 percent or above during this period. The rapid growth of China has been called an economic miracle. It is not really a miracle because it follows from the economic law that the above mentioned three factors are sufficient to propel a high rate of growth. This law was also demonstrated by the economic development of Japan before and after World War II, and of Hong Kong, Singapore, Taiwan and South Korea in the 1960s and 1970s.

Another interesting question is when China will surpass the United States in total output. According to the World Bank China's GDP was half that of the United States in 1998 in terms of purchasing power parity (PPP). PPP treats a basket of goods produced in China valued in RMB (units of the Chinese currency) as equivalent to the same basket of goods produced in the United States valued in US dollars, and converts the output in China valued in RMB to the value in US dollars by an exchange rate that satisfies the above condition. Such an exchange rate is close to two RMB for one dollar and much different from the official exchange rate of 8.3 RMB to one dollar in 1998. Given this starting point, if China's total economic output was to grow from 1998 onwards at a mere 6.6 percent and the US output at three percent, the Chinese output would surpass the US output by 2020. One might question the PPP calculation of the World Bank and use a PPP exchange of 3:1, for example. We will still reach the same conclusion by raising the Chinese hypothetical growth rate to eight percent or below. Of course, since the Chinese population is about 4.5 times that of the United States, when China's total output reaches that of the United States, per capita output of China will only be about 1/4.5 of the United States per capita output. On the other hand in terms of economic influence in the world economy total output may be a more relevant measure than per capita output.

Problems in the Chinese economic system

I will discuss the following five problems facing the Chinese economic system: corruption, income disparity, education, healthcare, and environmental degradation.

Corruption

Corruption in China is widespread and has gotten worse in the last decade. By corruption I mean government officials taking advantage of their economic power to obtain illegitimate personal gains from the public, private institutions or from government organizations. Their economic power is derived from the economic assets under their control such as financial assets of state-owned banks or land, or from their authority in granting economic assets such as licenses or permits.

Corruption has increased in the course of China's economic development because both the demand for it and supply of it has increased. Demand has increased because more people need government approval to establish and operate their expanding businesses and products, and international trading need licenses and permits. Supply has increased because the bureaucracy has expanded to deal with a growing economy and the bureaucrats have more tasks to perform in operating government enterprises and in approving new products and granting licenses.

The Communist Party leadership and the central government of China have tried very hard to control corruption. We often read in the newspapers that a certain corrupt official received a death sentence. Such effort has not reduced corruption because the fundamental economic reason for its existence still remains. From an economic point of view, one can imagine trying to reduce corruption by treating its root, namely reducing the economic power of government officials. First, one could streamline the procedures for the establishment and operation of businesses by reducing the number of approvals and inspections required. This is not easy to achieve because of the vested interests of the officials who benefit from such power. Second, one can also think of reducing the steps for the approval of new drugs. In traditional China, producing herbal medicine required no license and was not protected by patents. People were free to reproduce drugs if they could discover the way. Some economists question the usefulness of the modern Western system of patents as justified by the necessity to encourage research. Patents have two serious disadvantages. Consumers lose the benefits of getting new medicine early and at a lower cost. Other potential inventors are hindered in their research for fear of infringing on existing patents. In the Chinese case officials receive bribes in millions of RMB for the approval of drugs to be sold in the market. Third, a most important source of corruption is in the approval of land for urban development. Since land is publicly owned under the Chinese Constitution, it is in fact controlled by government bureaucrats. In their term of office these bureaucrats may attempt to approve the land under their control for development to receive benefits, rather than keeping most of it undeveloped to wait for future opportunities as in the case of private ownership. However, due to political implications, changing the public ownership of land is almost impossible.

In sum, we can say that corruption is rooted in the economic power of the bureaucrats. Hence to reduce corruption we need to reduce that economic power. In the three important sources of economic power that we have discussed the political feasibility of reducing the power is nil. Thus corruption is expected to last for sometime to come. Corruption has created social discontent but is not serious enough to generate major social instability because most Chinese have learned to live with it while they are getting rich under the current system.

Income disparity and rural poverty

In China the income disparity between the urban rich and the rural poor has widened in the last 15 years. The per capita income of the urban population has been growing at an annual rate of 7.5 percent while that of the rural population has been growing at 5.5 percent. Arithmetic shows that this created a widening of the income gap between the two groups. Note, however, that the livelihood of rural population has been advancing at a rapid rate also, although not as rapidly as the urban population.

There are three major components of the rural poverty problem. First, as pointed out, the rural population has experienced a widening income gap in comparison with the urban rich. This is not a serious problem because the rural population has also been getting rich. The percentage of the rural population below the poverty line defined as per capita income below 600 Yuan in 2003 prices was reduced from 12 percent in 1985, to 9 percent in 1990 and dropped further to 3.5 percent in 2003.

The second component is the unfavorable treatment of rural residents by the central government when compared with urban residents. The government has spent less on infrastructure investment in rural areas. It invested only a limited amount to improve agricultural productivity. It provided less welfare benefits including education and healthcare subsidies to rural residents. Migrant workers who travel from rural to urban areas do not receive the same educational and medical care benefits as urban residents. The procurement prices for farm products paid by the government were often below market prices while the farmers were not allowed to sell their products in the market. Note, however, that under the "Three-farm program" initiated in 2001 and dedicated to the improvement of farming, the government has started to increase its spending to improve rural education, healthcare, and infrastructure. It also abolished all taxes on farmers in 2005.

The third and most serious component of the rural poverty problem is the mistreatment of the rural population by village Communist Party secretaries who have power to control the population in their village. There have been illegal levies for road construction and for the building or maintenance of local schools where there was no need. More importantly there have been frequent seizures of land that was legally assigned to farmers without adequate compensation. Thousands of demonstrations have taken place in recent years without being reported in newspapers. Although the right to keep the land assigned to farmers under contract is protected by law, this law is often violated in practice. This has generated much discontent among the rural population but the central government is not able to control the behavior of local party officials who are protected by officials above them. I once suggested that the media be given more freedom to expose the offenders, but the degree of freedom given to the press is an important matter in China, subject to significant influence of the leadership of the Communist Party.

Education

Two aspects of the problem of income disparity are the inadequate education and healthcare provisions received by poor residents in rural areas. Although China has an official policy of providing compulsory education for nine years, in reality many children of school age do not receive it. This is because the financial burden for the provision of this policy is left entirely to local governments. These local governments, particularly in poorer villages, do not have enough financial resources to provide free compulsory education. As a result many poor families spend a large fraction of their income to pay for tuition and fees for their children attending local schools. In China there are many private schools at all levels because the government allows and even encourages these "people-operated" schools to flourish to supplement the public schools, but most poor families cannot afford to send their children to these schools. Over 40 percent of total education expenditure in China is financed by non-government sources including the payment of tuition fees. This illustrates the problem of inadequate financing of education for the children of poor families.

The inequality of education opportunities between the rich and the poor is a most serious part of the income disparity problem discussed in the last section. It affects income inequality for future generations and also hinders the selection of the most able young people in China for personal development. The national government has received revenues that have grown at an even higher rate than GDP because of improvements in the tax collection system. Total education expenditure by the central government has kept up with the increase in revenue but much of it is spent on higher education, still leaving the responsibility of financing primary school education to local governments and individuals. Although in the last few years the central government has increased its subsidy to local government for education, inequality of education opportunities still persists and the children of very poor families do not get educated. In many rural families the oldest child, particularly if a girl, is not supported by her family to go to school beyond the primary school and is asked to go to work to support her younger siblings so that they will have a better education.

Healthcare

Like education, healthcare is the responsibility of the central government but most of this financial burden is left to local governments; the central government has devoted more resources to providing healthcare to the urban population than the rural population.

In rural China before economic reform, healthcare provision was good given the low level of income. Under the commune system healthcare was provided under a three-tier system with barefoot doctors taking care of minor illnesses which occurred most often, local clinics taking care of patients that the barefoot doctors could not treat, and hospitals taking care of more serious illnesses. This was an economically efficient way of utilizing medical resources. As a result the death rate in China was reduced from 17 per thousand in 1952 to 6.34 in 1980, and life expectancy was increased from 40.8 years in the early 1950s, to 49.5 in the early 1960s, and 65.3 in the late 1970s. After economic reform, with the introduction of private farming and the disintegration of the communes, the financing and provision of healthcare have been left to market forces. Healthcare is paid for privately. The rural population in some poor areas cannot afford to pay for medical care, and often do not go to get treatment when they fall sick. The government is trying to establish a Collective Medical System (CMS) as a form of collective insurance for each rural resident to pay for medical expenses. A policy announced in 2005 was to have each individual insured for 50 Yuan per year, with the central government paying 20 Yuan, the local government paying 20 Yuan and the rural family itself paying the remaining 10 Yuan. As of the middle of 2006 only about 30 percent of the rural families had joined the CMS. One reason for this is that many rural residents do not trust the government's promise to pay 40 Yuan for the stated purpose because of their experience in past dealings with local government officials. In 2006 the government introduced a policy of achieving 80 percent participation of the CMS program but the degree of actual participation as of mid-2007 is still below this goal.

Healthcare for the urban population has gotten better since economic reform. Previously employers provided healthcare for their employees. Due to the fact that reform of industrial enterprises was a slow process, unlike the collapse of the commune system, most employees remained protected for many years. In the meantime, the government introduced an insurance system with the employer and the employee each paying 6 percent of the salary. In addition the hospitals of the employing units like state enterprises and universities remain in operation, unlike the barefoot doctors who went into private practice and the local clinics which were no longer financed under the commune system.

Healthcare is considered a major problem in China because its price has been rising at the rate of about 12 percent per year in the last ten years and quality of service has deteriorated with long waiting lines in good hospitals. The reason for the rapid rise in the price of medical care is that the quantity supplied per person has remained about constant since 1995 but the demand for healthcare has increased rapidly because of the increase in per capita real income. The reason for supply per capita to have been constant is the policy of public supply of healthcare under which the local governments are given the responsibility to provide healthcare. We can measure the quantity supplied by the total national expenditure on healthcare divided by a price index of healthcare, and further divided by population to convert it to a per capita quantity, using statistics given in the *China Statistical Yearbook*. We can also measure it by the number of hospital beds per 10,000 population or the number of doctors per 10,000 population. Using all of these statistics the quantity of medical care supplied has been constant since 1995 – while the quantities of all other consumer goods and services have increased. This is because local governments do not have sufficient funds to provide healthcare in line with the growth of the local economy; they would rather use the funds for economic development. A simple solution to the shortage of supply is to allow or even encourage the entry of private hospitals, which should be subject to the same regulations on standards that govern the existing public hospitals. Unlike education where private schools are allowed or even encouraged, the Chinese government still maintains the notion that healthcare should be publicly supplied. The entry of private hospitals would increase supply while providing competition to public hospitals to lower the prices and improve the quality of their services.

In mid 2007 there were signs that the central government may change its policy to allow for competition. There was a debate in China among expert consultants appointed by the Chinese government to examine whether the government should spend its healthcare expenditures by giving it to the public hospitals or to the individuals in the form of additional insurance coverage so that they can choose the hospital for treatment, whether public or private. The debate is framed in terms of whether to finance the demand side or the supply side of healthcare. There came an executive order from the State Council issued in mid July 2007 to establish several experimental stations for financing the demand side and even allowing for some private hospitals. This is an encouraging development for someone like the author who has championed the establishment of private hospitals in the last two years through communications with top government leaders. The arguments for supporting the demand side are the same as those favoring the use of school vouchers to allow parents to choose schools rather than financing public schools directly to supply public education.

Energy and environment

The problem of environmental degradation is common to all developing countri-esthat try to increase output and consumption because production and consumption require the use of energy, and the use of energy affects the environment. The effects are air pollution, water pollution, and the emission of CO_2 that causes global warming. Furthermore the use of energy from exhaustible resources can create energy shortages in the future.

The air and water in China, especially in urban areas, are among the most polluted in the world. According to a report by the World Health Organization (WHO) in 1998, of the ten most polluted cities in the world, seven can be found in China. China's water is polluted by the disposal of waste. Water beds of several important cities including Beijing and Shanghai are low, causing shortage of supply of well water. Supply of water from rivers including the Yellow River and the Yangtze River are running short because of diversion to agricultural production and electricity generation. In terms of energy use, China's energy intensity in 1990 as measured by thousand British Thermal Units per US dollar of output was high, reaching 36,000, as compared with 21,000 for Indonesia, 13,000 for South Korea, 4,000 for Japan and 11,000 for the United States. This was because of the differences in output mix among these countries and in energy intensities in producing the same products.

Carbon dioxide emissions result in changes in the climate, which are affecting the world's physical and biological systems. As of 2001 China accounted for 13 percent of the world's energy related carbon emissions, whereas the same measure for Western Europe was 16 percent and the United States was 24 percent. By 2007 China had overtaken the United States for the first time as the world's top producer of greenhouse gases. China's environmental policies are aimed at cutting energy costs and reducing local pollution, rather than reducing carbon emissions, the effects of which are not felt at present.

The Chinese central government has been aware of the environmental problems and has made serious attempts to protect and improve China's environment. The 1982 Constitution included important environmental protection provisions. Article 26 of the Constitution requires that "the state protects and improves the environment in which people live and the ecological environment. It prevents and controls pollution and other public hazards." This article formed the basis of the Water Pollution Prevention and Control Law of 1984, the Air Pollution Prevention and Control Law of 1987, the Water and Soil Conservation Law of 1991, the Solid Waste Law of 1995, the Energy Conservation Law of 1997 and several important international agreements including the Kyoto and Montreal Protocol.

China's environmental protection policies include: (1) restricting the quantity of outputs, especially those that are environmentally polluting and high-energy consuming, by tightening land use and credit supply; (2) setting environmental standards for production, especially in new projects; (3) improving methods of production to make it environmentally friendly, including the promotion of the use of hydropower, wind and atomic energy; (4) imposing heavy penalties on emissions of sulfur dioxide and encouraging the building of equipment to capture sulfur dioxide; (5) imposing a tax on high-sulfur coals to reduce the use of coal and to encourage a switch to cleaner burning fuels; (6) experimenting in some cities with a system of emissions trading for sulfur dioxide, similar to that used in the United States; and (7) introducing technologies that will treat wastewater, prevent air pollution and improve environmental monitoring systems.

The most serious problem for China's well-intended environmental policies is the failure in implementation. As an illustration, on Friday May 8, 2007, Premier Wen Jiabao made a speech stating that the current macro-control policy must focus on energy conservation and emission reduction in order to develop the economy while protecting the environment. The Chinese government has set a target for reducing energy consumption by 20 percent for every 10,000 Yuan (US$1,298) of GDP by 2010 (or four percent per year), while pollutant discharge should decrease by 10 percent. However, this policy was not successfully implemented, with the actual rate of reduction being 1.6 percent instead of the targeted four percent in 2006.

The implementation of environmental policies especially in pollution control fails mainly because local government officials often do not cooperate in law enforcement as they are interested in increasing output of their own regions. Central government needs to establish and monitor a set of clear-cut environmental standards and severely punish the provincial governor for serious violations in his province to the extent of removing him from office. If so the provincial governor would apply the same policy to enforce environmental standards in cities and counties in his province by similarly punishing the officials below him. However the Communist Party leadership may not have such a strong resolve and thus China's environmental laws will not be effectively enforced for some time to come. In the meantime central government can try to protect the environment by reducing energy intensity in production and increasing the use of clean energy through the provision of economic incentives for energy saving and reduction of the relative price of clean energy. How to design a set of incentives to achieve this in practice remains a very challenging problem for the government. The end result is that the quality of China's environment will continue to deteriorate in the near future until the country is rich enough and the government is determined enough to spend more resources on environmental protection.

A second important problem is to achieve a multinational agreement to limit the emission of CO_2. If the level of carbon dioxide reaches twice the level existing before the Industrial Revolution great climate instability will occur. How to achieve an international consensus to reduce the rate of increase with each country taking its fair share so as not to exceed the critical level is a most pressing problem today, but a politically feasible solution is difficult to achieve.

Conclusion

I have discussed three fundamental economic factors contributing to the rapid economic growth in China that also contributed to the rapid growth in other Asian countries. To the extent that these factors remain in force, China's rapid growth will continue. Among the problems affecting the functioning of the Chinese economic system I have discussed corruption, income disparity and rural poverty, education, healthcare and environmental protection. All these problems are characteristic of a rapidly developing economy where the government has not been able to control the undesirable consequences of economic growth. Corruption, and to a lesser extent exploitation of peasants by local Party officials and the violation of environmental protection laws, are political problems that are difficult to resolve. Education and healthcare problems require simple changes in economic policies that can be easily achieved if central government is willing. Fortunately for China, these problems will not do sufficient harm to create serious social instability that would impede further growth. In other words, the rising China will keep on rising.

References

Chow, G. C. (2004) *Knowing China*, Singapore: World Scientific.

Chow, G. C. (2006a) 'An Economic Analysis of Healthcare in China', Princeton University: Center for Economic Policy Studies Working Paper, No. 132.

Chow, G. C. (2006b) 'Demand for Education in China', *International Economic Journal*, 20 (2): 129–147.

Chow, G. C. (2006c) 'Rural Poverty in China: Problem and Policy', Princeton University: Center for Economic Policy Studies Working Paper, No. 134.

Chow, G. C. (2007a) *China's Economic Transformation*, 2nd edn, Oxford: Blackwell.

Chow, G. C. (2007b) 'Corruption from an Economic Point of View', *Hong Kong Economic Journal Monthly*, 364: 62–63.

Chow, G. C. (2008) 'China's Energy and Environmental Problems and Policies', *Asia-Pacific Journal of Accounting and Economics*, Vol. 15, April, 2008, 55–70

3 Evolution after revolution

The Chinese 'claiming state' between history and textbook economics

Giuseppe Gabusi

Deng's China: experiment or convergence?

When Mao started his revolution in China nobody could imagine that one day his Chinese Communist Party (CCP) and the regime he founded would be championed as models of pragmatism and evolutionary and non-ideological change. After abandoning the revolutionary mayhem of the Cultural Revolution the leadership introduced marginal incentives which gradually changed the economic landscape in agriculture, in rural and in urban industry, and in international trade and investment issues. This change set off a process of growth that is still in action at present. How was that possible? If 'institutions matter',[1] why did China develop despite the absence of the 'right institutions' recommended by the *post-Washington consensus* (consensus hereinafter: post-Washington consensus)?[2] And – if China's economy is so successful – does it mean that the Chinese invented a new (state-led) 'model' of economic development that international development agencies should recommend to developing countries?

First of all, not everyone in the literature thinks that the Chinese experience should be viewed in such a positive light. In fact, Woo (1999: 116) draws a distinction between 'the Experimentalist school (the E-school)', represented by authors like Gary Jefferson, Thomas Rawski, Barry Naughton and Peter Nolan, and 'the Convergence school (the C-school)', represented mainly by himself and Jeffrey Sachs,[3] even though I would now add Yasheng Huang as a member of the same group of scholars.[4]

While the E-school claims that 'China's seemingly disparate reforms have generated high growth because incremental experimentation has unleashed an unintended virtuous cycle'[5] (Woo 1999: 116–17), the C-school 'rejects Naughton's and Rawski's "*ex-post* coherence" as a fallacy, and as guilty of a '*post hoc, ergo propter hoc* argument' (Woo 1999: 117). Thus, the C-school posits that China's economic success has occurred 'despite gradualism' and that 'China's experiments in non-capitalist institutions' are 'unsuccessful' (Woo 1999: 118). In fact, in support of this thesis, it is shown that collective rural industry was being *de facto* privatized, State-Owned Enterprises (SOEs) were being corporatized, and the country was accepting in full the international trade regime. Significantly,

Huang (2008: 10) talks about China's 'directional liberalism' in the 1980s. In this sense, the C-school thinks that China's experience is not different from that of the East Asian countries, where 'increasing liberalization, internationalization, and privatization of economic activities' (Woo 1999: 116) are deemed to be the factors behind a not-so-evident 'miracle'. In other words, by not even pointing to the institutional specificities of the Asian Newly-Industrialized Countries (NICs), the C-school is more similar to Paul Krugman's (1994) position than to the one endorsed by the World Bank in its 1993 *The East Asian Miracle*:

> The ... central argument is that little institutional experimentation is needed or desirable, in that the long-run goals of institutional change are clear, and are found in the economic models of existing market-based economies.[6]
>
> (Woo 1999: 118)

Furthermore, the C-school (Sachs and Woo 1994a, b, 1997; Woo 1999) points to China's peculiar economic structure as the fundamental explanation of the different economic performances of China and post-Soviet Russia. Unlike Russia, China had a vast pool of surplus labour in the countryside, which would be easily employed in a growing non-state industrial sector, conforming to the 'Lewis model' of development.[7] On the contrary, the Soviet Union was much more industrialized and the figures excluded the mere possibility of following the same path.[8] Therefore, a more radical approach could easily have been adopted, like – according to the C-school – it effectively had been adopted in the case of the introduction of the household responsibility system in agriculture,[9] but gradualism prevented this option from being implemented. In turn, gradualism was not an economic necessity, but the result of 'political deadlock and compromises within the CCP between conservative reformers and liberal reformers'[10] (Woo 1999: 123). In this approach, even the 'grasp the large' policy towards SOEs is regarded as a political appeasement to the conservative faction, while all SOE profits were indeed 'disappearing' (Woo 1999: 126). The E-school considers – as factors driving this loss of SOE profitability – the increasing competition of the non-state sector and 'the failure of the SOEs to improve their efficiency despite the new profit incentives' (Woo 1999: 126).

While considering the first factor, the E-school falsifies 'the empirical validity' of the latter factor and, above all, totally overlooks a third factor – namely, 'the over-compensation of SOE personnel' (Woo 1999: 126). In opposition, the C-school sees SOE losses as 'the result of embezzlement of profits and asset-stripping by managers and employees'[11] (Woo 1999: 126). Actually, incentives introduced by reforms would make even things worse, as profit incentives also became incentives to steal.[12] As far as Township and Village Enterprises (TVEs) are concerned, the C-school regards some formally collective ownership frameworks in rural industry as a 'cover for an evolving ownership pattern' towards 'partnerships between local officials and private entrepreneurs' and 'privately-financed and privately-operated enterprises' (Woo 1999: 130). In other words, the collective label would conceal – especially after the path followed by rural industry in the 1990s – the informal private nature of the most efficient rural firms. The absence of well-defined property rights, in particular, was making it difficult 'to get outsiders to invest in a TVE' (Woo 1999: 132).

On the contrary, outsiders *did* invest hugely in TVEs. Woo's sentence is plausible only if the benchmark is the take-over process as observed in Anglo-Saxon capitalist economies. Nobody of course went to village leaders launching offers to buy a 'share' in local firms. Investors and local leaders found a way to accommodate their reciprocal interests, but it was certainly not the unclear definition of property rights which could prevent for instance Hong Kong capital from moving into mainland China and doing business with the collective sector of the economy. Furthermore, efficiency was not the main concern, neither for investors nor for localities. Anyway, the C-school sets itself in opposition to the E-school observation that it is hard to conceive faster and higher rates of growth for Deng's China,[13] and believes that faster growth would be produced by 'faster privatization of SOEs and TVEs in a transparent and equitable manner and [by] more sweeping industrial and trade regulation' (Woo 1999: 137). However, the debate between the two schools should not be limited to a 'slow-fast debate' (Woo 1999: 136), as such a definition would '[miss] the fact that instant convergence to all the institutions of a private market economy is not technically achievable' (Woo 1999: 136). Even though in this way the C-school tries to defuse the accusation of 'market fundamentalism', it cannot escape from the conclusion that while the E-school probably committed a sin of 'rationalization *ex-post*', it symmetrically can be charged with 'justification *ex-ante*'. Let us admit for a moment that convergence to private markets is the desirable goal of every economy: nonetheless, the C-school does not say anything about the transition costs – in Khan's (1995) terms[14] – that development processes require – or about who is the likely subject to bear these costs.

The evolutionary path followed by China under the dual-track system seems precisely to address this issue. According to Lau *et al.* (2000), the co-existence of market and plan during transition was both Pareto-improving and politically acceptable. In fact, under the market track prices were working at the margin and making economic actors 'better off', whereas under the plan track 'status quo rents' were 'compensat[ing] potential losers'[15] (Lau *et al.* 2000: 122). Thus,

> the dual-track full market liberalization provides a useful way to implement a reform without creating losers while simultaneously achieving efficiency under the same conditions . . . Because of its Pareto-improving property, the dual-track approach minimizes political opposition to reform ex ante and maximizes political opposition to reversal of reform ex post.
>
> (Lau *et al.* 2000: 122)

Both the single-track and the dual-track approach are deemed to be efficient,[16] but in 'distributional' terms the dual-track approach is ostensibly different (Lau *et al.* 2000: 124). Some reasons are given to show how plan track enforcement was made possible (Lau *et al.* 2000: 133). For the government it was 'informationally much less demanding' to implement an already-drafted plan than to design an entirely new one. Also, by introducing a market track, what mattered in the plan were 'plan-mandated interenterprise deliveries' rather than 'total enterprise productions' as was traditionally the case under the pre-reform planned economic regime. In other words, the dual track reduced information costs by introducing prices and by making enterprises themselves monitoring agents. Of course, the success of the plan track required that all actors' 'expectations of the credibility of state enforcement' were met (Lau *et al.* 2000: 134).

With this observation Lau *et al.* (2000) bring institutions back in, and have to recognize that the dual-track efficiency was based on incentives 'which may depend on the ownership and governance structure' (Lau *et al.* 2000: 135). Then, the authors find that most of the conditions set out for making the dual track work were present in China. In fact, the continued credibility of institutions in enforcing the plan was not 'an issue' (Lau *et al.* 2000: 135). Profit-maximization depended on 'circumstances' and it was certainly a fulfilled condition in agriculture and in rural industry, although less so in urban state industry (Lau *et al.* 2000: 136). Finally, in product market almost 'full market liberalization' was achieved as 'resales, subcontracting, and purchases for redelivery' were all permitted[17] (Lau *et al.* 2000: 136). Even in the labour market a new type of flexible contract was introduced for new employees, while keeping 'permanent employment status' for pre-existing state workers (Lau *et al.* 2000: 140). Several forms of both standard and non-standard social safety nets were utilized.[18] In conclusion, Lau *et al.* (2000) vision is not fundamentally dissimilar from that of Naughton (1995b), as both think ultimately that growth made the plan track increasingly residual and unimportant for political and economic agents alike, even though it is true that Lau and others put a slightly heavier accent on political compensation costs.[19]

According to this logic, the dual-track approach reduced transaction costs, and made the plan track irrelevant in the end. But if production costs are taken into account, the logic might well be reversed, pointing to state capacity in enforcing production: 'It is unclear . . . why transaction costs should be more important than production costs for development, especially when production costs usually include costs of coordination and distribution' (Amsden 1997: 473). Once again, Amsden (1997: 473–74) refers especially to the experience of late industrializers, where 'business-government collaboration' and 'the grey area of public-cum-private money' were the observed rules, not the exceptions.[20] If the focus is then shifted to 'investment in productive capacity', 'the notion that industrialization is a process of moving toward increasingly perfect markets is palpably false' (Amsden 1997: 477).

The transition from the plan track to the market track should anyway be seen also as 'a process of learning' how markets work: 'Learning by experimentation' and 'structured learning' are the best ways to learn, because transition is an incremental process where mistakes can be corrected without causing disruption of the economic and institutional systems and without the need to overcome 'information overload'[21] (Qian and Stiglitz 1996: 187–88). In a similar fashion,

Susan Shirk (1993: 341) argues that Chinese gradualism – which was necessary to build political consensus – allowed 'the reorientation of the preferences of officials, managers, and even workers in state-owned industry'. In her vision, this reorientation was a consequence of increasing competition.[22]

Chinese institutions between disorder and dictatorship

Another option which can be found in the literature is that of moving the attention away from perfect markets to perfect institutions (Djankov *et al.* 2003). Simeon Djankov's paper is credited with the attempt to classify a 'new comparative economics' (Djankov *et al.* 2003: 1) after the collapse of socialist economic systems in Europe. The authors see the comparison of 'alternative capitalist models' as the new object of the discipline (Djankov *et al.* 2003: 1) and – making reference to Murrell (1995) – stress 'the effectiveness of the newly created institutions' (Djankov *et al.* 2003: 4). Their theory is based on a 'tradeoff between dictatorship and disorder' (Djankov *et al.* 2003: 5) and is portrayed, for our purposes, in Figure 3.1. On the x-axis, dictatorship is measured as 'social losses due to state expropriation', while on the y-axis disorder is defined as 'social losses due to private expropriation'. Both variables are defined 'relative to a perfect property rights benchmark'. Then, a curve is drawn, which is called 'the Institutional Possibility Frontier (IPF)' for a society. The IPF is 'convex to the origin',[23] and points on the IPF represent single institutions (Djankov *et al.* 2003: 7).

The first problem that arises is to determine 'the shape and the location of the IPF', which are different for different societies as well as 'within a society'[24] (Djankov *et al.* 2003: 9). The paper resolves the issue by defining location as the product of 'civic capital': the more such capital in societies, the closer the IPF to the origin (i.e., to the perfection) and the more co-operative capability among members of the society (Djankov *et al.* 2003: 10). For determinants of 'civic capital', the authors make explicit references to the relevant literature and list among the best candidates 'culture' (Landes 1998), 'ethnic heterogeneity' (Alesina *et al.* 1999), 'factor endowment and physical environment' (Engerman and Sokoloff 1997, 2002), 'mortality of European settlers' (Acemoglu *et al.* 2001), and co-operation 'in the production of public goods' (Putnam 1993). Then, other factors are introduced – namely, 'technology of production', 'technology of government repression', and 'the level of human capital' (Djankov *et al.* 2003: 10–11). The concept of 'civic capital' is the weakest element in this otherwise fascinating theory, and in fact – after admitting that it is 'somewhat vague' – its relevance is dismissed by considering it a given constraint (Djankov *et al.* 2003: 11). By so doing, the risk again – as in Acemoglu *et al.* (2001) – is to become either deterministic or somewhat racist. There is instead the possibility that the location is neither determined by 'civic capital', nor is its shift irrelevant and exogenously-determined. Putting aside this critique for the moment (in fact, the rest of the chapter will build on it), the purpose is to develop Djankov's framework by looking at China, compared with the process of economic transition in Russia and in Eastern Europe, which is one of the four case studies analysed in the paper.[25]

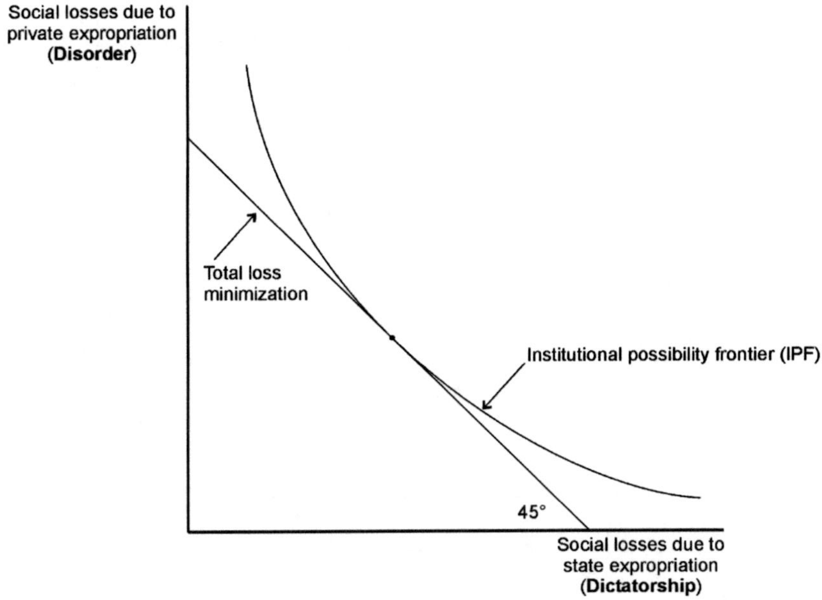

Figure 3.1 The Institutional Possibility Frontier (IPF).

Source: Djankov *et al.* (2003: 8).

Figure 3.2 shows Russia's and Eastern Europe's IPFs. That of Russia and the former Soviet Union is deemed to be 'less attractive' than that of Eastern Europe, for the reasons stated above (i.e., Eastern Europe possessing relatively more civic capital) (Djankov *et al.* 2003: 24). In the 1990s, Russia and the Eastern European countries moved upwards on their respective IPF, but Russia moved farther because in this country both the 'decline in dictatorship' and the 'rise in disorder' were much more significant (Djankov *et al.* 2003: 24).

Then, I utilize Djankov's reference to Kornai (1992), who underlines the relevance of the communist party as 'the critical mechanism of keeping economic, political, and social order in socialist countries' (Djankov *et al.* 2003: 24) and I insert China's curve in Figure 3.3. In fact, China's communist authoritarianism has always been more fragmented and decentralized than that of the Soviet Union. If the idea of 'civic capital' were taken for good (and it is not), it could anyway be stated plausibly that China was even better endowed in this sense, in terms for example of ethnic homogeneity and of historical length of communist rule.[26] Therefore, by analogy with Figure 3.2, China's curve is placed beneath Russia's, but considered to be above Eastern Europe's, since China has never been exposed successfully to liberal values in the same way as the periphery of Europe was.[27]

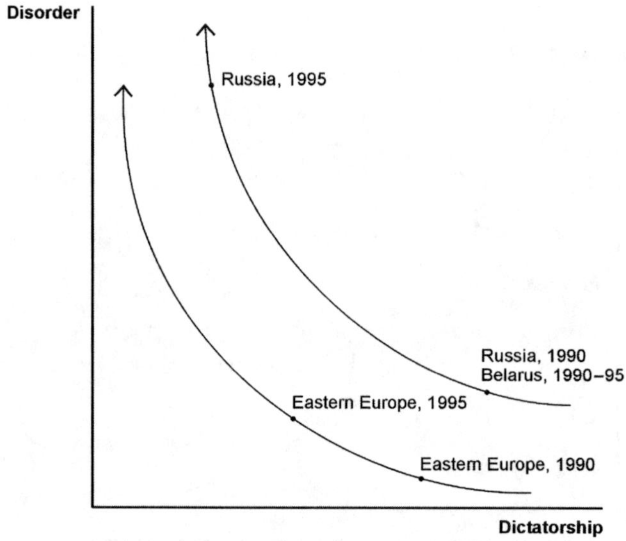

Figure 3.2 The IPF, Russia and Eastern Europe.

Source: Djankov *et al.* (2003: 25).

Communist rule in China was most effective in the 1950s and in the early 1960s when the Party, after the revolutionary success, was firmly in control of the country. Land reform and collectivization of agriculture were completed in 1957–58, and in the same years industry was benefiting from Soviet technology and technical support. Even during the Great Leap Forward (1958–60) Maoist policies were effectively implemented, in spite of their economic irrationality and catastrophic outcomes. During the Cultural Revolution (1966–76), while apparently the dictatorial grip on power became stronger, in terms of trade-offs between dictatorship and disorder China definitively experienced a shift towards disorder, as Red Guards were closing schools and universities, forcing people to leave their jobs and to move to the countryside in unknown and often hostile environments and causing stagnation in urban industries.[28] Mao himself in the end had to rein in the forces he had unleashed due to internal power struggles within the Party.[29] As a result, in Figure 3.3 China moved upward. In the reform period Deng restored order and tried to make Party rule more effective, returning also to an increasing professionalization of the bureaucracy. But at the same time, reforms were moving China towards the origin – namely, the marginal amount of dictatorship required to reduce disorder was diminishing as the Cultural Revolution's turmoil became a more distant past. Property rights were also being horizontally clarified, as the role of the private economy was gradually increasing in the late 1980s. Therefore, in Figure 3.3, Deng's China is placed in a position indicating less disorder and more control, but at the same time requiring a comparatively lower degree

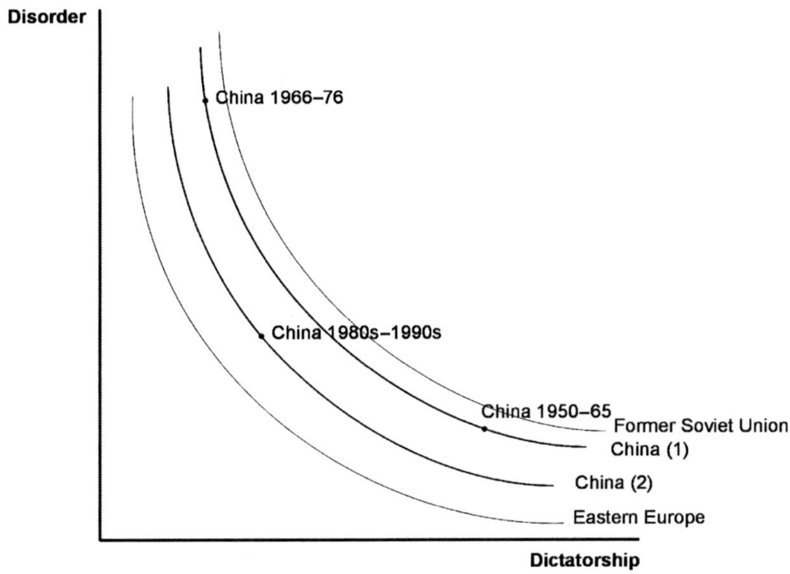

Figure 3.3 The IPF and China.

Source: The author, drawing upon Djankov *et al.* (2003: 25).

of dictatorship. China's curve shifts from (1) to (2). Paradoxically, Deng's 'evolutionary' success could well be rooted in Mao's 'revolutionary' successes and failures, in line with Kohli's (1994) idea that high-growth political economies in the global periphery might come from a distant past.

Djankov's position is to be welcomed for the acceptance of the importance of flexibility[30] and for the adoption of a historical approach, for its re-evaluation of the function of politics,[31] and for putting forward the idea that dictatorships can be efficient too. However, by relying too confidently on neoclassical tools, it overlooks the political economy framework's role in shaping and locating the IPF and consequently has to recourse to a concept (that of 'civic capital') that it is unable to define properly. Therefore, the question of what ultimately drives IPF changes remains unanswered. If the idea that civic capital is ultimately 'the ability to cooperate' (Djankov *et al.* 2003: 37) were to be accepted, then it would hardly be possible to explain China's economic failures during Mao's last decade, when co-operation for the advancement of socialism was an ideological commandment, duly enforced in revolutionary ways. In conclusion, then, Djankov and others cannot hide a bias towards deregulation, which is a typical expression of the Washington consensus more than of the post-Washington consensus.[32]

The view that neoclassical approaches to institutions just shift the discourse from perfect markets to perfect institutions is stressed by Lo (2004), who points out how Djankov and others' framework is based on the idea that there exists a utopian state 'free of "social losses"', thereby making the room for institutional diversity very limited[33] (Lo 2004: 7). His paper argues that institutional analysis in the neoclassical tradition brings us to 'dead ends', while approaches like the 'comparative institutional analysis' – which combine 'collective as well as individualistic rationality' – are more 'promising' (Lo 2004: 3): 'rationality cannot solely determine institutional change but must rather interact with objectified institutions and paradigmised technology' (Lo 2004: 3). Reliance on individual rationality alone cannot explain market failure, because it postulates that the market alone is the mechanism that, in 'institutional formation', brings about 'the equilibrium of individualistic rational choice' (Lo 2004: 9). In other words, where alternative visions stress that institutions are 'the joint product of individualistic and collective learning'[34] (Lo 2004: 9), neoclassical theories of efficient institutions 'must assume, in a very restrictive way, that sources of productivity improvement are marketable, or at least potentially exchangeable between individuals' (Lo 2004: 11).

As an alternative Lo (2004) proposes an examination of classical economy, and of Marxian economics within it, which – with the term 'social force of production' – views 'the social and technical aspects of the labour process as integrals of a unified whole' (Lo 2004: 12). As Amsden (1997) would say, this observation has the merit of bringing production 'back in' to institutional discourse. Techno-economic paradigms underline how capitalism is not a natural, but a historical process,[35] in contrast with neoclassical theories that frame 'general theories of efficient institutions on the basis of some universal characteristics of human nature' (Lo 2004: 13). His paper then analyses how techno-economic paradigms can explain the relationship between globalization and development. More interesting, for Lo, are such theories like the 'new international division of labour' (NIDL) (Fröbel *et al.* 1980), and its idea that specialization of developing countries on 'low skill/technology industrial activities' would force the developing world into a 'development trap' (Lo 2004: 15). As a response to these price constraints, given the objective working of the dynamics of world capitalism, states can build either 'flexible' or 'rigid, long-term' institutions – the former giving in to international forces requiring low skills and incomes, the latter showing 'behavioural flexibility' due to 'collective learning and horizontal co-ordination' in order to turn globalization into a developmental opportunity (Lo 2004: 16). Specifically, China escaped the acceptance of the "'low skill/technology, low income" model' and adopted the "'high skill/technology, high income" model' (Lo 2004: 16):

> It is the ability of the Chinese state to resist the demands of the international political-economic establishment that has enabled it to escape the indicated development trap as well as the type of financial and economic crisis that engulfed East Asia in the closing years of the century.
>
> (Lo 2004: 17–18)

Moreover, 'disorder' and 'dictatorship' are two limited concepts which do not give evidence of the social forces that were at work in China:

> In the case of China, meanwhile, a higher degree of mass participation in economic and social affairs was coupled with a similar 'developmental state' to largely account for the record of sustained rapid growth. The existence of these 'anti-systemic conditions'..., then, while being interpreted as producing no more than undesirable disorder and dictatorship, are arguably necessary for late development in the context of capitalist globalisation.
>
> (Lo 2004: 19)

Thus, the explicative power of Djankov *et al.* (2003) framework is limited by the sterilized concept of 'civic capital', which misses out on the complex socio-economic and political dynamics of developing countries. In order to explain what causes the shift from China's curve (1) to China's curve (2), for example, reference could be made to Rawski's (1995) critique on textbook economics: 'marginal analysis is a powerful tool for investigating the consequences of incremental change against a stable institutional backdrop, but it is not intended for studying systems in the midst of massive socio-economic change' (Rawski 1995: 1158).

Thus, Rawski (1995) underlines the necessity to look at initial historical conditions, and – in line with the main tenets of the post-Washington consensus and Douglass North's main findings – he stresses how China's 'process of becoming'[36] shows that 'bargaining and experimentation' give birth to new alternatives, whose feedback creates institutional choices: 'the "market for institutions" resembles commodity and asset markets in that chaotic appearances conceal important regularities' (Rawski 1995: 1161).

Thomas Rawski refuses the leadership argument in the development debate,[37] stresses that development is a path-dependent process, and also rejects market fundamentalism *à la* Sachs and Woo,[38] but fails to recognize that no 'market for institutions' was developing in China. Power was more important than choice when – for instance – 'private' entrepreneurs were wearing 'red hats' and registering as collectives. Although he sees that bureaucracy's 'manipulative participation' (Rawski 1995: 1663) in the reform process was fundamental, he falls short of looking into the details of this political process.[39] Thus, Rawski's main positive lesson remains that if a country has a unique history, this does not mean that analogies and general principles cannot be drawn from it:

> Chinese initial conditions are different. They may be so different that Chinese-style reform cannot generate favourable outcomes elsewhere. But any such conclusion must rest on sustained comparison between Chinese reform mechanisms and corresponding possibilities elsewhere.
>
> (Rawski 1995: 1163)

The experience and results of reforms in China challenge the widely-shared view that Leninist regimes cannot be reformed gradually but need a complete institutional overhaul, because in socialist regimes – encompassing monolithically politics, economics and civic society – changes in one institution inevitably imply changes in another.[40] Behind the common façade of ideological paraphernalia and under the common formal state structures of 'democratic centralism', Leninist regimes can hide deep differences in the informal rules governing the dynamic interplay between state, markets and society at large.[41] These differences can be deeply rooted in the historical past, where legacies cannot be disregarded when analysing development options and outcomes.

China as a 'claiming state' and the party as a political economy residual claimant

As far as the nature of the Chinese state is concerned, it has been argued that:

> neither the term 'developmental state' nor 'entrepreneurial state'[42] is adequate to capture the complex web of interests that now connect government and emerging big businesses in China. Whatever the name one chooses to give it, it is clear that a new institutional form is being born.
>
> (Nolan 2004a: 169)

However, China – after 30 years of market-oriented reforms – could not easily be defined as 'an aspiring developmental state' (Sutherland 2003: 66). Indeed, there was something more at work in reforming China that could shed light on development dynamics in general.

In truth, by sharing some aspects of both the developmental and the entrepreneurial state, reformed China can be defined as a claiming state. The claiming state is a state which requests – formally and informally, at all levels of public administration and society[43] – from all economic actors, the delivery of results in terms of output, profit and trade because it firmly believes that it is within its rights to do so and as long as the process does not put into question its political legitimacy. The claiming state is more concerned with profit and technology than with ownership issues.[44] This preference is of crucial importance for development since, for economic actors within an embryonic capitalist system, profit is indeed more important than ownership.[45] The definition of the claiming state also blurs the distinction between the developmental state as 'plan rational' and the socialist state as 'plan ideological',[46] because the claiming state – while gradually diluting ideology in the political discourse and moving towards market rationality – keeps an ideology which combines the remains of socialism with the needs of the market as the basis of its political legitimacy. In the end, it is the threat to the state's political legitimacy that sets the boundaries of what power and markets are allowed to achieve.[47] Furthermore – on the positive side – economic growth has the effect of strengthening the political legitimacy of claimants at all levels.[48]

Central to the working of the claiming state is clientelism, defined in particular in socialist states as 'a type of elite-mass linkage through which the state and the party exercise control at the local level, and through which individuals participate in the political system' (Oi 1985: 238). This view of clientelism is different from both the totalitarian model and the interest group model developed in the literature. In the former, the party is a means to control passive, non-elite masses, whereas the second stresses the room left for particular groups to influence the process of policy through inputs which percolate through the interstices of the regime structure.[49] What Oi (1985: 238–39) disputes is that, in developing countries, 'informal networks' created by individuals 'upon personal ties' are more important than groups that weakly articulate their interests through 'formal channels'. Thus, the clientelist model's attention shifts to patron–client relationships, considering therefore 'the political behaviour of *individuals* in dyads... [and] the myriad ways in which non-elites try to affect the policy *implementation* process and to further their particular interests' (Oi 1985: 240).

In this model, patrons have 'monopolistic' access to 'opportunities, goods and various other resources', and through control over their 'allocation' they exercise power (Oi 1985). Although the focus of Oi's article is on the situation in rural China from the 1950s to the 1970s – before the reforms, then – his article outlines some general principles that are still valid in communist China.[50] Writing in the middle of the 1980s, Oi anticipated the reality that the market in China has not negated clientelism, even though clientelist patterns have become 'more complex and dispersed', actually resembling those of pre-revolutionary China[51] (Oi 1985: 265). The reason for this historical continuity is that the 'structural circumstances' (Oi 1985: 265) under which clientelism thrives in China still exist to a varying degree. In particular, it is arguable now that reforms just reinforced two of the features that are present in socialist systems – namely, 'unequal access to and personalized control over the distribution of basic goods and income opportunities' and 'the fusion of economic and political authority'.[52] In fact, reforms multiplied opportunities and brought wealth to a significant part of the population, but the system of control over new economic resources remained basically the same: for instance, the study of Zweig (2002) shows clearly how trade bureaucrats held the key to valuable internationalization channels, managing rents and financial flows in pursuit of their interests and those of their clients. A particular feature of communist clientelism is that every political actor is at the same time both patron and client,[53] since 'power and (unequal) opportunities in a socialist clientelist system are based on *position* within the communist bureaucracy' (Oi 1985: 263).

The Party and its agents are the key elements of patronage in China.[54] Power of cadres over resources depends on their rank in the administrative hierarchy.[55] As Shirk (1993) would certainly say in this context, what you *have to allocate* depends on where you sit.[56] 'Loyalty and trust' are the basis of the patron–client relationship[57] (Oi 1985: 257). Since a patron derives his power from the state, and his tenure is a function of his capacity to deliver results, 'socialist clientelism is one of the more unstable varieties of patron–client relationships' (Oi 1985: 255–56).

Without clear and uniform legal rules, and within this (unreformed) political framework, economic reforms have just increased instability and forced all cadres to jump on the development train (to use the railway image made famous in Coase 1960) in their own interest and in the interest of the organization they were in charge of – in other words, strategies pursued by patrons and clients are 'interest-maximizing' (Oi 1985: 263). In a sense, property rights were being destabilized, and new patrons and clients were emerging, but this change was occurring within the same institutional pattern of patronage. In other words, the clientelist model confirms that the Party was acting as the *political economy residual claimant* behind the claiming state, with the task of maximizing the country's output.

The concept of residual claimant has been defined by Alchian and Demsetz (1972), who analyze property rights within the context of a capitalist economy. According to them these rights are defined as rights to hire and fire labour and to work with assets. The modern means of production is characterized by team production,[58] where marginal product is a myth[59] and only team output matters. This way of organizing the firm creates an incentive for workers to cheat, and therefore a monitor is needed. The monitor is to be the 'residual claimant', i.e. the one who gets the profits (the surplus, in Marxian terms). In fact, he is the capitalist.[60]

Drawing upon Alchian and Demsetz (1972), the *political economy residual claimant* can be defined as the entity that has:

(i) The right to political residuals (in terms of power legitimacy) and to economic residuals (in terms of the material benefits of growth).
(ii) The monopoly of violence as expression of the monitoring power – i.e., the threat to use force should economic incentives move in a direction that does not coincide with its interests.

After 1978, the CCP based its legitimacy on the capacity to deliver economic growth, and – especially after the collapse of the Soviet Union – the Marxism–Leninism–Mao Zedong-thought pillars enshrined in the Constitution as the founding principles of the People's Republic no longer represented the operational guidelines behind government strategies, but were not deleted from the statute books.[61] Party cadres benefited personally from economic growth in terms of power and wealth, but the Party used its power both in a positive way – 'governing the market' (Wade 1990) – and in a negative sense – preventing the birth of a competing economic elite and monitoring the behaviours of economic actors.[62] New entrepreneurs and managers were socially connected to the dominant elite to such a high degree that the Chinese economy is sometimes referred to as 'the princelings' economy'.[63] 'New conservatism' is the term used to define this mixture of class collaboration and defence of the old elite's positions.[64] The corporatist strategy was obviously an important – if not the main – component of the actual translation into practice of 'new conservatism': constrained co-operation became the rule governing relationships between different actors.[65]

Once again, it was the Party which was at the apex of the principal-agents chains and which ultimately would pull the strings. The Party nurtured a '*nomenklatura* system' which 'functions like mucilage' and ensures overall coherence

(McNally 2007b: 117). Each actor knew in his mind how far he could go and the consequences he would face in the event of not-confirming behaviours.[66] This is precisely the logic which drove many individuals to wear 'red hats' and to register as collectives their *de facto* individual companies, or which motivated SOEs to open 'collective' subsidiaries. In fact – paradoxically – as reforms were transferring downwards rights over residuals to localities, enterprises, farmers and managers, on the cognitive side officials' power grew in importance: 'peasants and workers understand that their livelihoods depend considerably upon the decisions of officials directly above them, and they are able to see more clearly the relationship between cadre decisions and their incomes' (Walder 1994: 13–14).

Although Walder (1994) makes his point in relation to a possible birth of a civic conscience against cadre arbitrariness, his observation can work also in the opposite direction – namely, peasants and workers can measure the distance between Pareto-improving opportunities and power concerns, and act accordingly. It seems also that this logic is widely accepted by Chinese individuals and groups who

> do not seek autonomy but rather closer embeddedness with the state. They recognize that to be autonomous is to be 'outside the system' (*tizhiwai*), and therefore powerless. Instead they seek to be part of the system (*tizhinei*) in order to better pursue their interests and maximize their leverage.
>
> (Dickson 2003: 19)

However, it is not possible to give a cultural explanation of this co-operative, Confucian-like attitude for the reason that Confucian culture was presumably present in the Chinese mind even during the Maoist era. Neither do I want to say that Chinese people do not desire a freer environment to live in. Dickson's point is a mere observation of the fact that in authoritarian states there is no such a thing as the possibility to freely choose who to do business with and which property to own. Contrary then to the post-Washington consensus position on this matter, which views civic society as a powerful – and efficiency-improving – counterweight to the state's arbitrariness and interference in the private sphere of citizens' life, when analysing China 'we need to use a nuanced notion of civil society, one that acknowledges that civil society is not necessarily antagonistic toward the state'[67] (Dickson 2003: 19).

Again, recalling the famous Coasian example, the Party would have been in a position to stop the train from running through the valley – if the passage of the train had run against their interests – and peasants would have had to return to the fields. For example, local cadres – given local conditions – knew what actions central Party authorities would tolerate and what they would not. Private individuals were conscious of the conditions under which they could defy local authorities and of the conditions when not even large bribes could buy them off. Centrally, the Party has always been firmly in control. On the 'action' side, through the Organization Department, it controlled the appointment of key Party and government positions at the provincial, prefecture and 'central economic cities' levels (Chung 2001: 60). On the 'repression' side, when there presented situations where some outsiders were trying to shift political and economic residuals in their favour, the Party did not hesitate to use force to crash the outsiders' ambition.[68] It happens at a macro level – the Tiananmen revolt is an obvious example,[69] when students were physically eliminated and liberal Party leaders were ousted from office – but also it occurs at micro level whenever the Party-state for instance orders the execution of local leaders, whose serious corruption or gross authoritarianism threatens a dangerous shift of power legitimacy away from the Party. In a sense, the reforms gave the Party 'even more control over society' (Goodman 2001: 135).

The economic benefits of ownership were shared in various ways between (often overlapping) patrons and clients, but the Party's power worked in such a way as to make sure that this profit-sharing remained within the boundaries of the socialist institutional system, which masked a well-defined clientelist order. Clientelism based on informal networks is all the more important in China, where an informal power structure exists in parallel with the formal institutional framework enshrined in the constitution of the Party and of the state. In this sense, Lieberthal (1995: 183–218) offers a 'view from the inside' as opposed to a 'view from the outside'. The inside view – which best explains how the Chinese institutional system works – is necessarily based on 'a distinction between "organizations" and "institutions", for the Chinese system is strewn with organizations that have not become institutions'[70] (Lieberthal 1995: 183).

In the 1980s and in the 1990s China was governed by the Party's top elite comprising 'twenty-five to thirty-five leaders' (Lieberthal 1995: 184) divided among the elders,[71] the key generalists,[72] the bridge leaders,[73] and the specialized leaders.[74] Although the system has become less personalized with the passing of the second-generation of elders,[75] it has not been fully institutionalized, as shown in Nathan and Gilley (2003). Personalization in Chinese politics is also reflected by the fact that all top leaders have personal assistants, and, within this group, 'secretaries' (*mishu*s) whose influence and political power should not be underrated (Lieberthal 1995: 189–92). In fact, *mishu*s are 'a vehicle of factional politics',[76] since their fortune or misfortune depends on the political career of their patron, and since in turn they can become patrons for other clients[77] (Lieberthal 1995: 190). In sum, *mishu*s are used to build precisely the loyalty and trust which is at the operational core of patron–client relationships.[78] Then, the organization of power is centred on the concepts of *kou* ('gateways') and *xitong* (Lieberthal 1995: 192–94). *Kou*s are 'major functional areas' which broadly correspond – even if the number of *kou*s is not fixed – to 'party affairs, government work, state security, and foreign affairs' (Lieberthal 1995: 192). *Xitongs* are 'groupings of bureaucracies' each in charge of a specific policy issue: the party affairs *xitong*, the organization and personnel *xitong*, and the propaganda and education *xitong* all belong to the party affairs *kou*, whereas the political and legal affairs *xitong* and the military *xitong* fall under the jurisdiction of state security *kou*. Finally, the finance and economics *xitong* is situated within the government work *kou*. For our purposes, it suffices to focus the attention only on party affairs and on the finance and economics *xitongs*. The party affairs *xitong* is the key to territorial political control[79]: in fact, although

> [territorial Party committees] do not have absolute power – each of the other *xitongs* slices into virtually every locality in China [–,]. . . the top party secretaries of the territorial party committees and the party committees themselves bear a special responsibility for making sure that things in their area work well.
>
> (Lieberthal 1995: 195)

In other words, the claiming state in China devoted administrative resources for 'getting things to work well', which in the reform period essentially meant producing, making profits, and trading. The Finance and Economics *xitong* is the central bureaucratic stage for development, since its concern is growth in the urban economy.[80] It has been both a loser and a beneficiary from reforms (Lieberthal 1995: 203–04). In fact, as the economy was growing and development became the overall final goal of policy strategies, more financial resources were available for this *xitong*, and bureaucrats working in these sectors found new opportunities for rent-seeking activities, both legal and illegal. As the plan track was gradually abandoned or re-shaped in favour of markets, this *xitong* lost a great deal of its original power and function. Within the Finance and Economics *xitong*, bargaining was particularly 'clear and prevalent', and relative bargaining strength relied upon 'a group of loyal followers' engaged in 'ongoing exchanges of resources and benefits" (Lieberthal 1995: 214). Consequently, each cadre had to develop a relationship with both patrons and clients in order to pursue a three-pronged strategy:

> obtaining access to scarce resources that he can distribute to individuals in his own organization; protecting his organization from the uncertainties of an external environment in which top leaders can act capriciously and bureaucratic authority is fragmented; and developing goods and services within his organization that he can use to strike his bargains with the external environment.
>
> (Lieberthal 1995: 215)

This is a crucial aspect to understanding China's economic reforms. Market incentives offered new opportunities which were made compatible with the existing domestic political economy framework. New channels of internationalization, new production ventures, and new jobs did not directly change patron/client patterns – they simply empowered new actors, forcing them sometimes to wear 'red hats', within the same power structure. Sometimes these new incentives forced internal changes, with bureaucrats obliged to build new patron/client relationships in order to keep their power intact. It is precisely the mix of new market incentives and old patronage patterns which in my application of Djankov *et al.* (2003) model depicted in Figure 3.3 causes China's curve to shift from position (1) to position (2). 'Civic capital' – the concept that supposedly determines the location of the curves in Djankov's theory – was basically the same in the 1970s and in the 1980s, but the release of market forces enlarged bureaucratic boundaries, reduced the need of administrative control, and the system required less 'dictatorship' to be governed. For instance, as the role of the plan track was increasingly reduced, the bureaucratic apparatus in charge of it – i.e., the Finance and Economics *xitong* – was not dismantled, but to maintain its *raison d'etre* it had to take on new functions compatible with the fact that capitalism was being imported through the internationalization of large sectors of the economy. Contrary to the idea that government intervention beyond the minimum is conducive to economic failure (Krueger 1990), China's economic take-off shows that personal and (state) organizational interests combined with economic incentives and caused growth – even in absence of 'good governance' and in the presence of large pockets of waste,[81] corruption and rent-seeking activities.[82]

At this point it is useful to recall Khan's (1995) concept of political transaction costs, determined as the costs of organizing collective action (Olson 1965) within a similar class, group or faction, or within the same pattern of patron–client relationships. Clearly enough, the group that needs to be investigated in China, in relation to the application of Khan's idea, is represented by the Party and its multi-faceted and pervasive organizational system. Political transaction costs are a function of patron–client networks (Khan 1998a, b), which in turn depend on different social structures in different countries. The logic behind Khan's reasoning is that non-capitalist groups can exploit patron–client networks in order to prevent capitalist change from occurring. On the other hand, if intermediate classes find that it is in their interest to protect and nurture a nascent capitalist class, they will support change. If the basis of patron–client exchanges is basically the transfer from 'politicians' to 'non-capitalist clients', the system will not undergo capitalist change, even if this change might in theory mean the extraction of 'bigger bribes'[83] (Khan 1998b: 118). In this way, Khan's transaction costs look beyond the assumption of economic rationality of bureaucrats – namely, the idea that bureaucrats will support change if their pockets are lined as a result – and brings to the fore political power considerations that are no less important than economic issues in developing societies facing a redistribution of assets, benefits, and property rights (Knight 1992). Relative gains matter more than absolute gains, and how they are distributed is the key to understanding how transition institutions work.[84]

In developing countries there is no 'civil society' to defend capitalism against state interference[85] – that is why Zhu and Elbern's (2002) idea that peasants were asking for individual property rights in rural industry, while all they got from the state was a stake in TVEs, is profoundly misleading. Civil society in China was not necessarily in accordance with the preferences of reformist state leaders. Not even in the Party were opponents of reforms absent or weak, as the existence of cycles of reforms dependent upon shifts in the balance of power between reformers and conservatives shows (Howell 1993).

As a result, Khan's (1998a, b, 2004b) powerful insights into patron–client networks as agents of change in developing countries appear to be appropriate to China, a socialist country with all the characteristics of developing economies.

Khan argues that

> in a context where the emerging capitalist system does not enjoy political stability and general acceptance, where the state is not strong enough to enforce order by force and where civil society is failing to create the ideological support for the emergence of capitalism, patron–client networks which organise payoffs to the most vociferous opponents of the system are an effective if costly way of maintaining political stability.
>
> (Khan 1998b: 115)

In fact, Deng's China satisfied all three conditions laid down by Khan, albeit to a varying degree. Emerging capitalists were not protected by law, and new and old property rights were unstable; China at the end of the 1970s was not a failing state and the Party was in firm command, but certainly it had been seriously weakened by the anarchy of the Cultural Revolution, and Deng had to strive to restore order (see Figure 3.3); and finally, ideological support for capitalism is still a political taboo, and 'market socialism with Chinese characteristics' is still the official label put on the economic system. Drawing upon Khan's (1998b) model, Figure 3.4 indicates the exchange pattern between patrons and clients in Deng's China.

Even though China is a highly bureaucratized country and almost every politician is a bureaucrat, I place Khan's division of institutional actors into two parallel hierarchies, that of the bureaucracy (B) and that of politicians (P), only grouping members of the Party's top elite into the political hierarchy. Then – always sticking to Khan's model – two social groups are considered: capitalists (C) and non-capitalists (NC). These terms, however, must be understood in the context of a socialist economy in transition, which only accepted businessmen and entrepreneurs into the Party's ranks in 2002, when the Sixteenth Party Congress endorsed this policy as a corollary of Jiang Zemin's theory of 'The Three Represents'. Therefore, we place all 'would-be capitalists' under the label 'capitalist', for example private entrepreneurs wearing 'red hats', managers of

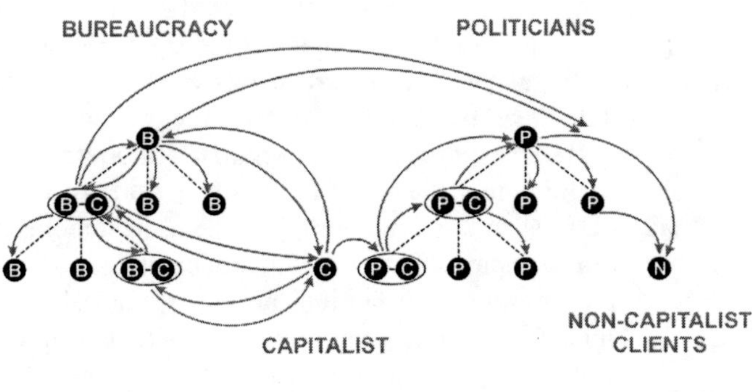

Figure 3.4 Exchanges between patrons and clients in Deng's China.

Source: The author, drawing upon Khan (1998b).

SOEs who enjoyed greater autonomy in conducting business for their firm, and foreign managers of joint-ventures: their drive to profits was *de facto* capitalist. 'Non-capitalists' in China were the (largely residual) groups (outside the bureaucracy) who had something to lose from the restructuring of the economy, such as, for instance, peasants in the poorest regions or workers in SOEs. Finally, we introduce the concept of bureaucrats-turned-capitalists (B-C) and of politicians-turned-capitalists (P-C), since both bureaucrats and politicians were ready to 'wear two hats' and to grasp the new entrepreneurial possibilities offered by reforms.[86]

Following Khan's (1998b) model, each echelon of the hierarchy is a patron for actors at lower levels and a client for higher-ranked subjects. Arrows express flows of pay-offs between patrons and clients. Payoffs can be either legal or illegal, in the form of subsidies, quotas, access to financial resources, and tariff protection, or in the form of bribes, exactions, or discretionary taxes. Payoffs between non-capitalists and politicians are not shown, since they consist of political payoffs 'in the form of quiescence or support' (Khan 1998b: 118). The key innovation in Deng's China is represented by the gradual emergence of a group of capitalists who were totally absent in the pre-reform period. Their presence was a consequence of new incentives introduced into the economy. However, their action was only a necessary but not sufficient condition for economic take-off. In fact, their activities and profits could well have been exploited in a non-productive way by bureaucrats, politicians and non-capitalists alike. Instead, as the economy was growing 'out of the plan' (Naughton 1995b) but not out of the bureaucracy, capitalists were largely co-opted within an existing pattern of patronage as it is described in Oi (1985). Capitalists had to exchange payoffs with bureaucrats, receiving protection and services in return. As fiscal reforms made local administrations dependent for revenue on local firms, bureaucrats were increasingly interested in management of enterprises' output, profit and trade. Bureaucrats developed their entrepreneurial skills, whereas capitalists acted under the protective umbrella of bureaucracy. If capitalists did not deliver economic results and/or did not meet political loyalty expectations (for instances they went too far in practising corruption), they easily could be left to their own devices, with the prospect of being pushed out of the system, sometimes even violently and with coercion. Exchanges occurred mainly from lower-to-next or higher-to-next levels, although in the informal dynamics of the *xitong* structure, skipping a level in the exchange was not impossible, albeit riskier for political careers. As bureaucrats were witnessing the success of B-Cs, who were taking profit from the fruits of 'segmented deregulation' (Zweig 2002), they started to embrace new capitalist attitudes. In turn, through fiscal contracting with the centre (the highest level of P), successful localities which met their 'payoff quota' to the centre enjoyed greater autonomy and entrepreneurial 'freedom'. Similarly, pay-offs were sent from capitalists to politicians, who in their turn set up – through their families and offspring – their own business undertakings. The logic of the system marginalized non-capitalist groups, which did receive pay-offs from politicians – in terms of social safety-nets, or the possibility of a 'return to the land' should a peasant remain jobless in the cities – but were not strong enough to hijack the reform process, contrary to what has happened for decades in South Asia according to Khan (1998b). Sometimes their concerns found support in conservative politicians, but the logic at work in the bureaucratic hierarchy was more pressing and ultimately prevailed. Political transaction costs continued to be high, but a premium was granted to those actors who started to cultivate capitalist clients, as this was the only change that mattered. It must also be remembered that a potential group of non-capitalists formed by intellectuals and urban workers had also been seriously weakened by the Cultural Revolution, thereby reducing transition costs faced by reformers.

In conclusion, the patronage pattern in China explains why and how state and markets worked in symbiosis during the take-off stage and well into the reform age. Non-capitalists were facing high political transaction costs in buying off other groups as potential allies in their eventual struggle against change. In a sense, China has followed the path of low transition costs/high transaction costs already traced by the East Asian NICs (Khan 1995). The difference between pre-1978 China and Deng's China is not cultural, but lies in the institutional reception of new incentive-led dynamics into old patron/client frameworks.[87] In other words, it is not 'civic capital' but a change of the nature of actors and payoffs within the patron/client patronage framework which is responsible for the shift of China's curve from location (1) to location (2) in Figure 3.3. Ultimately, in this play with so many actors on the stage, the Party worked as the director and managed to keep them singing the same tune, even though with many voices and occasional dissonances.

Capitalism as it is, not a Chinese economic 'model'

The debate on economic development and institutions that gave birth to the post-Washington consensus has gone a long way to show that development is better seen as a process of evolutionary change (Qian 2002). Nevertheless, the determinants of change and innovation are profoundly misunderstood in the consensus. Three critiques are worth considering in this respect. First, new institutions and new policies in developing countries are not the subject of bargaining within the context of supposedly existing 'markets for institutions',[88] contrary to the logic of New Institutional Economics (NIEs) (see for instance North 1990). In Deng's China, there was no bargaining between the different factions of the Party, or between bureaucrats and peasants. New institutions emerged from old power considerations and strategies.

Second, the Chinese case adds strength to the observation that the consensus is misleading on the succession of stages within the development process. Following the regression line found in relevant econometric studies, the consensus would like to see developing countries move from low growth/bad governance patterns straight to high growth/good governance patterns which are fairly typical of developed countries. Of course, the key to this path is the implementation of the post-Washington consensus policies. Instead, the observed historical path of economic development has followed a different trajectory: countries have first grown in a situation of 'bad governance', and only in a subsequent stage they have adopted 'good governance' institutions (Khan 2004: 173). In other words, developing countries which enjoyed rapid transition to capitalism did not move from a situation characterized by high transition costs/high political transaction costs into a nineteenth century Anglo-Saxon world of low transition costs/low political transaction costs.[89] Rather, successful countries managed to reduce transition costs but they did not necessarily reduce or did not have to reduce political transaction costs (Khan 2004: 183). In this sense, China – a country ridden with corruption and unclear property rights – seems to be no exception to history, as for instance only in the late 1990s has a clarification of the horizontal dimension of property rights in industry been observed, while political transaction costs within the regime were still high.

Third, leadership cannot be regarded as the crucial factor behind change, because history demonstrates that the same leadership – even in authoritarian states – can change if the socio-political setting changes too. For instance, moving from the mainland to the island of Taiwan, Chiang Kai-Shek led a Leninist party that shifted from predatory behaviours to developmental policies[90] (Khan 2004: 184). It is true that the beginning of reforms in China coincided with an important change of leadership, but Deng Xiaoping was not a newcomer and – above all – he had dutifully implemented Mao's policies for years.[91] Furthermore, neither the personnel at lower levels of bureaucracy changed much, even though in due time Deng promoted cadre professionalization and de-ideologization, and the administrative structure of the state was rationalized (Zheng 2004). In the 1980s, for instance, village Party secretaries were the same people who had served under Mao and had received primary education only.

In conclusion, there is no such a thing as a linear path of development, either in negotiating actors' behaviours, or on leaders' minds, or in international agencies' projects. Revolutions of all kinds and colours have failed because of this rationalization mistake, and effectively even the 'neo-liberal' revolutionary policies that Russia implemented under International Monetary Fund (IMF) suggestions in the early 1990s were a complete failure and led to Yeltsin's period of corruption, disorder and slow growth which had to be reversed by Putin's return to authoritarianism. On the contrary, institutional evolution is more in line with historical patterns of experimentation and it allows for mistakes and errors to be corrected and re-addressed. Evolution allows building on existing institutions, with clear informational cost-savings (Qian and Stiglitz 1996). Furthermore, with evolution learning processes might be easier, and the gradual implementation of reforms can even buy off social dissent by using existing institutions as social safety nets (Lau *et al.* 2000). 'Experimentation, competition and innovation' are well-used concepts in the consensus language (World Bank 2002), but they fail to recognize that experiments must be understood within a broad context of socio-political change which is an essential feature of all development processes. Evolution is something that takes place in historical environments. Institutional experimentation is not the fruit of negotiations.[92] The impact of developed countries' world expansion on the rest of the world left a legacy of conflicts, wars and revolutions that changed profoundly and forever societies in the developing world.

Therefore, it is not a paradox at all that evolution has revolutionary roots that must be dealt with if economic change is to be encouraged in the right direction. China's evolutionary reforms succeeded in a social and institutional landscape that had been tarnished by the Cultural Revolution and that was far from being settled and contention-free.[93] As a result, they might not have worked in a different context.[94]

Teaching the international community of donors some lessons derived from their own experience might be tempting for China. However, Chinese reformers should avoid an obvious mistake regarding to the development debate. If there is an overall lesson that the development debate can give to China it might be an appropriate issue to conclude this chapter with: *there is nothing like a 'Chinese model' of economic development.*

The fact that Chinese reforms enhanced growth and afforded an economic take-off, without applying the tenets of the post-Washington consensus, are not an excuse to substitute one ideologically-framed universal principle with another one of the same but opposite sort – perhaps renamed the 'Beijing consensus' – to be adopted by developing countries.[95] Nolan (2004b: 174) argues that China is pursuing 'its own Third Way' as it has been doing for centuries,[96] but the reality is that 'the inter-relationship between state and market' is not a feature of a supposed 'Third Way', but it is a historical constituent of capitalism, which is characterized by three elements: 'A distinctive drive to extract and accumulate capital', 'the structuring role of markets' and state elites which '[see] it in their interest to support the expansion of capital-oriented classes' (McNally 2007a: 21, drawing on Heilbroner 1985, 1993). All these features are present in China's transition, as well in all societies undergoing a similar process of industrialization. That is why there is no reason for China to escape the incompleteness of the post-Washington consensus in order to fall victim of its own legitimate success and ambitions and to claim originality.[97] In three decades of reforms, the Chinese economic system has simply learnt the historical lesson of capitalism and how state and capital (i.e. political rulers and merchants) historically competed and collaborated while giving birth to capitalism (Weiss and Hobson 1995; McNally 2007b).[98]

The Chinese experience – which is in line with developmental success stories of some of China's neighbours and relied on forms of 'coordinated capitalism' and 'network capitalism' (McNally 2007b: 108) – is nothing exceptional – if not for the fast pace of change in such a large country. What is worth saying is that this 'no exception excuse' is valid in both directions – namely, both as a critique of the consensus incapacity to explain China and as a warning to those who think (or fear[99]) that the Chinese success legitimates the formulation of a new 'model' of development. After spilling so much ink and spreading so many words for the acceptance of concepts like 'history matters' and 'one size does not fit all', it would be ironical indeed if one day the literature on development had once again to face the consequence of the transposition of conceptualized, sterilized and rationalized Chinese reforms into different contexts. For example, reforms that did work in authoritarian China will not necessarily work in authoritarian Myanmar. Once again, Khan's lesson about the need to match institutions and institutional capacity in the context of patron/client patterns indicates its explanatory power in development issues. This lesson is valid also for the future path of Chinese reforms.

Conclusion: China in search of a direction

In fact, Chinese rulers must surely know by now the historical lesson that 'primitive accumulation' cannot last forever.[100] China's breakneck industrial growth in the last 30 years is not endless. Capitalism changes societies, and the costs of change become apparent at some point and have to be tackled. Economic growth in China had some negative effects. Uneven territorial development has meant that inequalities between cities and the countryside, and between the rich and the poor, have increased – reaching alarming Latin-American style figures; pollution and waste have seriously deteriorated the environment;[101] the economy depends too much on exports, and too little on domestic consumption; the demand for energy is apparently insatiable; the number of labour migrants deprived of rights has mushroomed; and finally, the social costs of corruption and land-grabbing have been causing serious social unrest, dutifully suppressed.[102] GDP growth is not everything in people's life.[103] The government in Beijing is well aware that all these issues must be dealt with, and both policies of pursuing a 'scientific development' while building a 'harmonious society' – first aired in 2003–4 and officially adopted by the Party Central Committee in 2006 – are a right step in this direction. In October 2010, the Fifth Plenum of the Seventeenth CPC Central Committee approved the guidelines of the twelfth Five-Year Plan (2011–2016), based on the concept of 'inclusive growth', stressing 'the "people first" principle, paying more attention to comprehensive, sustainable development and overall planning and coordination, and putting more emphasis on securing and improving people's livelihood to promote social equality and justice' and 'harmonious labour relations'.[104]

However, the implementation of these policies could face a crucial obstacle. In fact, the patronage system that developed in reformed China supports a vicious circle or a 'growth trap' (Pei 2006). Growth creates negative side effects, but 'the only way to prevent these problems from galvanizing into deeper unrest or from becoming a significant challenge to the central authorities is to promote continued economic growth' (Halper 2010: 138). When in the 1990s Jiang Zemin was at the helm of the country, he presided over a period of strong capital-intensive urban growth which did not necessarily improve ordinary citizens' welfare. In fact, Huang (2008) shows – drawing on a huge quantity of empirical data – that China's growth was of real benefit to people in the 1980s, when rural entrepreneurial spirits were finally set free to engage in economic activities which were *de facto* privately owned. On the contrary, he points out that in the 1990s there was a comeback of political support for state-owned (restructured) enterprises, accompanied by new policies favouring capital over labour, large-scale infrastructures over small-scale entrepreneurial ventures, cities over countryside and public intervention over private initiative and private property rights. Thus, GDP growth – sustained by the explosion of the real estate industry which dramatically changed the landscape of cities like Shanghai – did not automatically mean that citizens were better off than in the 1980s – i.e., growth was not 'without losers'. Indeed, in the last decade of the twentieth century, productivity growth slowed down (Huang 2008: 288). The difficulties Hu Jintao and Wen Jiabao encountered in implementing policies aimed at redressing domestic economic imbalances – for instance, shifting the emphasis onto peasants and rural China[105] – might precisely stem from this dilemma. After nurturing a patron–client system that made CCP power legitimacy dependent on growth at all costs, how is it now possible for the 'claiming state' to frame and implement a new development strategy – which would in turn require a new patronage system – without losing political legitimacy? In other words, the leadership has changed 'policy *goals*', but not 'policy *methods*', relying on 'heavy interventionism of the government' (Huang 2008: 297) precisely because changing patterns of behaviour would mean breaking a well-entrenched socio-political mechanism. In Figure 3.3, China – instead of moving towards the origin of the axes as it ought to, according to convergence theory – could well slowly move down the slope, forced to accept more dictatorship in order to avoid more disorder. Clearly, the continuously and rapidly evolving relationship between the centre and the provinces and the localities is crucial in this regard:

> Strong and privileged interest groups and commercialized local governments are blocking equal distribution of the benefits of economic growth throughout society, thereby rendering futile the CCP's strategy of trading economic growth for people's consent to its absolute rule.
>
> (Yang 2010)

When 'local governments in China simply pursue economic gain' (Yang 2010), because 'CCP incentives have generated a "growth-above-all-else" mentality among local cadres' (McNally 2007b: 118), attempts at economic strategy reform face inevitable deadlock. Looking at China's periphery is of the utmost importance, because it is at local levels that 'the two processes of state-led development from above and network-based development from below meet', resembling political economy patterns of the Song to late Qing dynasties (McNally 2007b: 120–21). It has also been argued that the CCP is acting as an 'organizational emperor', reproducing patterns of power similar to those of imperial China and adapting itself to rapidly-evolving socio-economic changes (Zheng 2010). Again, 'history matters'.

The take-off stage in China might well have been over by the end of the twentieth century, and it might be symbolically marked by China's World Trade Organization (WTO) entry in 2001. With the country fully integrated into the global trade system, it will be more difficult for China to build the indigenous technology it seriously needs for its industrial policy,[106] just when entrepreneurs are keener on cultivating political ties than working on much-needed innovation (Huang 2008: 292). Moreover, the government will seriously have to consider the necessity of abandoning the remains of the plan and of playing more of a role of market regulator. This, of course, should not mean that China will embrace that kind of unfettered, unrestricted and free-market ideology so popular, and internationally acclaimed, at the beginning of the 1990s following the dissolution of the Soviet Union. That model is in full demise now, especially after the collapse of the Washington consensus into the 'Washington confusion' (Rodrik 2006)[107] has been reinvigorated by the Great Recession, which is forcing even developed countries to elaborate new ideas on the relationship between states and markets. As Halper (2010: 251) recalls, a popular joke among Western elites is that '*Capitalism saved China in 1989; China saved capitalism in 2009*'. Moreover, the ongoing financial and economic crisis – depriving China of exports to American and European markets – simply exacerbated China's imbalance, making the need for reforms even more urgent (Overholt 2010). China's financial strength is affording the country a new prominence among those called upon to build a new global order: if China now sneezes, the world will get a serious flu.

In the end, the background in all discourses on China's political economy is the question of the likelihood of China becoming a democracy in the future. Here is a general lesson from China: rather than exporting democracy and creating weak states, the community of international donors should let developing countries import capitalism, bearing in mind that capitalism has historically been no stranger to state and politics, and certainly it is not that sort of caricature of itself that is portrayed in the consensus. However, at one point, successful capitalist transitions bring about 'the bifurcation of secular authority', meaning 'the rise of capitalists to both economic and political prominence' (McNally 2007a: 23–4). In truth, this socio-political change has not happened in China yet. Entrepreneurs and professionals can – after the official adoption of Jiang Zemin's 'Three Represents' (*san ge daibiao*) theory – join the Party, but they do not claim an alternative and competitive political role, as when kings and merchants fought over power in modern Europe. On the other hand, the leadership is aware – in Li Changchun's words (building on Jiang Zemin's notion of 'guidance of public opinion')[108] – of the 'three closeness' (*san ge tiejin*) that policies must pursue: 'To be close to reality, close to the people and close to life' (Ramo 2004: 30). As a solution to the dilemma facing the Party, Yang (2010) states that 'there is no alternative to greater democratization if the CCP wishes to encourage economic growth and maintain social stability', thereby unmasking the myth of 'China's model of authoritarian growth' and signalling the premature 'end of the Beijing Consensus'.

Nevertheless, the parallel story is that neither democracy is an empty slogan: if capitalism is replicating itself in the Middle Kingdom, China will one day – can it be dared to say in two generations or is it yet too short a period?[109] – be more democratic than it is now (as today's authoritarian China is more democratic than in the 1970s), but at that point democracy in the Western world will have changed too, since slowly but steadily it is finally leaving behind the mass-party ideologies of the twentieth century and adapting itself – while chartering into unknown territories – to a future with new historical challenges from the developing world. Voices like those of Yu Keping (2009, 2010), who speaks of 'orderly democracy' (*yongxu minzhu*) and 'incremental democracy' and of Li Junru, (who talks about 'consultative democracy' (*xieshang minzhu*) (Shambaugh 2008) are in fact efforts to look beyond the Western liberal tradition without denying the value of democracy *per se*. That is why works like that of Gilley (2004) do not have much predictive value: They are based on the liberal model of Western democracies in the nineteenth and twentieth centuries which is deeply changing even in today's Europe and America.[110] In other words, they can rather be seen as 'wishful thinking' for Western public opinion. The Chinese 'claiming state' will probably never fully conform to the Anglo-Saxon archetype of a two political groups alternatively in charge of power with all constitutional guarantees for election losers in the opposition.[111] But this is really a story that would not be written here without adding to the present chapter enough material for at least another dissertation, if not for a full book.

Notes

1 Burki and Perry (1998).

2 The World Bank Report *Building Institutions for Markets* marked the definitive official recognition that institutions *do* play a role in economic development, and that different institutions *can* lead countries to different patterns of growth (or stagnation): historical conditions matter and 'one size does not fit all' (World Bank 2002). Institutions are defined as 'rules, enforcement mechanisms, and organizations... by which agents interact' (World Bank 2002: 6). Basically, the Report is about the formation process of market-supporting institutions, and about the incentives that can be put in place in order to make it successful. Drawing on the literature which explores how inadequate information and incomplete definition of property rights give rise to transaction costs which hinder economic development (North 1981, 1990; Stiglitz 1994), the Report suggests *what kind of institutions* promote market-driven growth. Effective institutions are those which are 'incentive compatible' and thereby reduce transaction costs, which permit an adequate flow of information to be widely shared, which define clear property rights and make them enforceable and stable, and which dismantle existing barriers to competition of ideas on institution-building.

3 Gradualism is criticized also by Yeh (1996: 54).

4

> The successes of the Chinese economy are a function of conventional sources – private-sector development, financial liberalization, and property rights security.... A second and related idea in this argument is that Chinese economic success is a result of a movement toward *manifestly and explicitly* efficient policies and institutions, not just a result of *functionally* efficient policies and institutions.
>
> (Huang 2008: 30)

5 Rawski (1995: 1152–54) summarizes well the succession of steps that – according to his school – makes gradual transition successful:

> Government initiates partial reform measures; ... Partial reform destabilizes outcomes and intensifies competition; ... Competition reduces profitability; ... Enterprises respond to financial pressures; ... Governments react to financial pressures and enterprise lobbying; ... Feedback effects accelerate the impact of reform ... [and] experience reforms attitudes and expectations as well as behaviour.

Within this process, a 'mix' of 'top-down initiative' (mainly in the 1990s) and 'bottom-up reaction' (more relevant in the 1980s) was 'itself a variable element' (Rawski 1995: 1155).

6 Neither the 2002 World Bank's *Building Institution for Markets*, with its emphasis on 'innovation and experimentation', would agree with this passage.

7 Even for non-members of the C-school like Peter Nolan, in the Pearl River Delta

> the political economy is firmly that of the "Lewis model", with vibrant capital accumulation for Hong Kong capitalists made possible by an unlimited supply of labour to their factories in the Pearl River Delta at a constant, or possibly even declining, real wage for unskilled labour.
>
> (Nolan 2004b: 63)

8 In fact,

> while only 18 per cent of China's workers were employed in State-owned enterprises at the start of Deng's reforms in 1978, the share in Russia was effectively 99 per cent at the start of Gorbachev's reforms in 1985 and 91 per cent at the start of Yeltsin's reforms in 1991. This makes clear that the Soviet Union ... had no reserves of labour outside the SOE sector that could provide the engine of growth for a new non-state sector.
>
> (Woo 1999: 120)

Transition in China was also easier because, whereas 'the Soviet Union extended its social safety net to the entire urban and rural labour force, ... in China it cover[ed] only some 20 per cent, primarily in the urban state sector' (Walder 1995: 971). By contrast, Nolan and Ash (1995: 996) stress the Soviet Union's and China's 'important similarities at the start of their reform programmes', like 'the existence of large reservoirs of entrepreneurial skills [,] the basic framework of planning within a command system... [and] large amounts of capital and technical expertise locked up in their military sectors'. They also point that the two economies were 'massively under-performing relative to the productive potential of existing stocks of physical and human capital' (Nolan and Ash 1995: 997). In conclusion, they argue that 'differences in policy choice' were at the origin of the opposite performance of reformed Russia and Deng's China (Nolan and Ash 1995: 997).

9 This point in Sachs and Woo (1994a) is best summarized by Walder (1995: 965):

> China's leaders... in fact implemented a bold and unprecedented "big bang" in agriculture early on, dismantling all forms of collective agriculture in favour of a system of family smallholding.... This rural "big bang", not China's gradualism, is what gave the economy a burst of growth at the outset.

On the contrary, Sicular (1995) posits that, far from being the result of a 'big bang' approach, reforms in agriculture – while undoubtedly introducing significant and far-reaching market elements – did not diminish state control: '... the state continues to play an important role in the commercial sphere. State commercial agencies still handle a significant share of commercial transactions, and for certain products they dominate the market' (Sicular 1995: 1020–21). Neither the idea of the agriculture reform as a 'big bang' is shared by Ash (1996: 64):

> The institutional thrust of agricultural strategy during the 1990s was summed up in the advocacy of the creation of a "two-tier operational system" (*shuangceng jingying tizhi*), which would integrate decentralized, household-based farming with a collectively-organized "socialized service system" (*shehuihua fuwu tixi*)'. Of course,

this does not mean to deny that 'the demise of collective agriculture... had a profound effect in releasing peasant initiative.

(Ash 1996: 56)

10 Conservative reformers accepted Chen Yun's

doctrine of a "bird cage economy"': the central plan is the cage and the bird is the economy. The premise is that without central planning, production would be in chaos – i.e., without the cage the bird will fly away: 'the amount of market activity that is to be tolerated to keep the economy working is analogous to the amount that the cage needs to be swung to create the illusion of greater space so as to keep the bird happy.

(Woo 1999: 123)

Reform feasibility and people support were indeed a strong government concern. One of Zhao Ziyang's chief economic advisers said: 'We try to protect everyone's vested interests. This has negative as well as positive consequences. It means it's slow. As a rule, we have two years of fermentation for every reform policy. But it means people support the reform' (quoted in Shirk 1993: 130).

11 Woo's observation, though, comes 'with the qualification that the erosion of profits in China's small SOEs was exacerbated by competition from TVEs' (Woo 1999: 126).

12 According to Woo, ideology mattered as well: 'The reduction in the state's monitoring ability combined with the steady reduction in discrimination against the private sector also made it easier for the managers illicitly to transfer state assets to themselves' (Woo 1999: 127).

13 For example, Woo (1999: 137) quotes Putterman (1995: 1064) affirming: 'it is doubtful that a more economically liberal regime could have produced a significantly better overall record of growth, especially if social equity and stability are accorded any weight'.

14 'The transition cost is the political cost faced by initiators of new institutions. It depends on the change attempted, the gainers and losers from that change and the balance of power in that society' (Khan 1995: 81). These political costs are deemed to be 'the relevant cost of institutional change' (Khan 1995: 86).

15 Shirk (1993: 137) too thinks that reforms were '*compromises designed to leave no one worse off than before*'.

16 In fact, since for lack of incentives in the planned economy production was often 'deep inside the production possibility frontier . . . , once some incentives [were] provided [by the market track], new resources [could] be released for production and the scope for Pareto improvement [could] be substantial' (Lau *et al.* 2000: 133). On the other hand, 'as the compensatory transfers are inframarginal and thus lump-sum in nature, the dual-track approach can be efficient too' (Lau *et al.* 2000: 122). However, efficiency of the dual-track path requires 'additional conditions of profit and utility maximization, perfect competition, and full liberalization of the market track' (Lau *et al.* 2000: 134), as these assumptions 'ensure that enterprises and households will have the right incentives' (Lau *et al.* 2000: 135).

17 Quoting Xu (1988: 292) and China Reform and Development Report (1992–93) (1994: 54), it has been pointed out that 'the share of transactions at plan prices, in terms of output value, fell from 100 per cent before the reform to 64 per cent in 1985 and further to 45 per cent in 1990' (Lau *et al.* 2000: 138). The accent in this case is on plan effectiveness as the other side of Naughton's (1995b) 'growing out of the plan': 'This provides evidence of the decline of the plan track relative to the market track but also of the relatively effective enforcement by the state of the plan delivery obligations (otherwise the share would have declined to zero)' (Lau *et al.* 2000: 138).

18 For instance,

> schemes used for protecting workers' preexisting rents are *xiagang* ("stepping down from one's post") and *zaijiuye* ("reemployment"). *Xiagang* workers continue to receive a partial salary, housing, health care, and other benefits from their enterprises. Many furloughed workers were retrained through *zaijiuye* projects and later found jobs in the nonstate sector. By the end of 1996, out of the 8.91 million *xiagang* workers, 3.57 million had found jobs, 2.34 million had decided to stay home, and 3 million were still looking for jobs (Cao *et al.* 1999).
>
> (Lau *et al.* 2000: 142)

19 The following sentence can be presented as evidence: 'Moreover, with rapid growth, the plan track becomes, in no time, a matter of little consequence to most potential losers, which in turn reduces the cost required for compensating them' (Lau *et al.* 2000: 142).
20 The idea that the East Asia miracle (World Bank 1993) relied on 'getting the basics right' is also challenged (Amsden 1997: 477).
21 Several advantages of structured learning are outlined:

> at the individual level, people learn, first, what the market prices are; second, where the profit opportunities are; third, how to maximize profits, given the constraints; and fourth, how to increase profits by relaxing constraints. At the institutional level, the government learns, first, what kinds of decisions can be decentralized without disruptive costs; second, who should carry out what types of experiments; and third, what new institutions should be selected and promoted.
>
> (Qian and Stiglitz 1996:187–88)

22 'During the decade of transition, people in state-owned industry learned that market competition offered them rewards as well as risks. As a result, they no longer opposed market reform and even demanded more market freedoms for themselves' (Shirk 1993: 341).
23 In fact, the IPF measures 'how much disorder can be reduced with an incremental increase in the power of the state' (Djankov *et al.* 2003: 7).
24 Quite intuitively but also quite generally, 'the institutional possibilities of modern Sweden, or even China, are far superior to those of Albania or Congo' (Djankov *et al.* 2003: 9).
25 The other three case studies are the different legal origins of civil law and common law systems, the rise of the regulatory state in the U.S., and the transplantation of legal systems in the colonies.
26 'For China, the socialist phase was briefer than for the Soviet Union. . . . This simple fact means that there are many more people still alive who were socialized in, and had personal experience with, a petty capitalist environment' (Whyte 1995: 1007).
27 Of course, the elitarian attempt of Sun Yat-Sen's republic in 1911–12 was short-lived and was ultimately a failure.
28 In fact, by 1969

> the CCP itself and much of the state apparatus had been paralyzed, with a large percentage of leading figures at all levels humiliated, stripped of power, and forced to do manual labour or to suffer a worse fate. The economy largely stagnated because of disruptions in transportation, decline in worker discipline, and virtual destruction of the central economic statistical apparatus. Worse yet, technological innovation stagnated almost completely, as the nativist impulses in the country surged to the fore. The PLA assumed control over administration of economic, governmental, police, and social units, but this in turn raised tensions and political conflicts at all levels of the military.
>
> (Lieberthal 1995: 116)

Even the police and military apparatus nearly collapsed while observing the country descending into anarchy:

> Red Guard groups [i.e., urban students called by Mao to attack the Party and the political conservatism attached to it] quickly launched a reign of terror in most big cities.... The Red Guards... took to the street to, in the slogan of the day, 'destroy the four olds'. This translated into destroying old culture by raiding houses, burning books and antiques, beating and humiliating people who seemed not to be in the spirit of things, and killing those who tried to resist. In all these instances, the police stood back and let the youths wreak havoc. In addition to causing general mayhem, the Red Guards also attacked officials at all levels of the political system. Through the end of 1966, the military and police permitted this to unfold virtually without interference.
>
> (Lieberthal 1995: 113)

29 When Mao realized that 'things had gone too far', 'a substantial delegation and decentralization of power had taken place, probably unintentionally' (Roberts 1999: 719).

30 In essence, 'reforms in any country should be evaluated to its own institutional opportunities, rather than some idealized benchmark free of dictatorship and disorder' (Djankov *et al.* 2003: 38).

31 However, in NIE tradition, politics is viewed only as a strong 'force toward institutional efficiency', in North's and Coase's sense, with the inevitable result to stress politics as a mechanism of democratic choice and to portrait the Anglo-Saxon model as the perfect institutional model: 'The tendency of democratic states to seek efficiency is well illustrated by the adoption of that great American invention for balancing dictatorship and disorder – a rigid constitution with checks and balances (Brennen and Buchanan 1980)' (Djankov *et al.* 2003: 35). Then, the authors feel obliged to concede that 'not all efficiency-enhancing bargains have the sweet smell of the Magna Carta or the U.S. Constitution, but they may still improve welfare' (Djankov *et al.* 2003: 36).

32 In this sense, Djankov and others' position risks losing the sight of politics by embracing ideology: 'regulation is nearly universally associated with poor outcomes because public officials abuse their powers over private agents. Deregulation is likely to diminish the problems of dictatorship without a significant increase in disorder' (Djankov *et al.* 2003: 32).

33

> The slope of the IFP, that is, the level of development of the market relative to that of the government ... [determines] the scope allowed for institutional diversity. But, note that, in the figure both the vertical and horizontal axes are defined in a negative way, as distances from a state that is free of 'social losses'. And this state refers to a world with perfect property rights, which defines institutional uniformity.
>
> (Lo 2004: 7)

34 Lo (2004: 9) is pointing here to Aoki (2001), which is summarized in the following way:

> An institution ... can be conceptualised as a system of self-sustaining shared beliefs of the players about the structure of the game that they actually play. It is the joint product of individualistic and collective learning, or, the equilibrium of the co-evolution of the traits of individuals and the convention of behaviour. In this way, an institution is both endogenously created and existing objectively. And an efficient institution corresponds not to individualistic rationality per se, but rather to some particular combination of individualistic rational choices – that is, collective rationality.

35 Harvey (1982: 27) is here quoted: 'The relation between capital and labour has no "natural" basis – it arises as the result of a specific historical process' (Lo 2004: 13).
36 China's experience has been defined as 'reform amid confusion' (Rawski 1995: 1159).
37 In fact, 'China's approach to institutional change... represents a historical outcome that was neither anticipated nor welcomed by China's central leaders' (Rawski 1995: 1162).
38 'Reform means improvement, not perfection' (Rawski 1995: 1167).
39 Instead, the accent is put on the influence of a change of incentives on bureaucrats' behaviours (Rawski 1995: 1163).
40 We refer here to the 'assumption that Soviet-style systems are, by their very nature, incompatible with the assumptions of systemic reform – namely, the gradual and incremental transformation of economic and political systems by leaders who "use and build upon the existing structures of society"' (Goldstein 1995: 1105, quoting Oksenberg and Dickson 1991). This is the general explanation why market reforms in socialist countries, especially in Hungary, did not work (Kornai 1986: 1729):

> Such efforts, János Kornai contended, created a situation of 'dual dependence' whereby firms looked to both the market and the state authorities. The latter, because of their great power, took precedence and weakened the effectiveness of market mechanisms. Kornai thus identified the 'stubborn inner contradiction in the whole reform process': gaining the participation of the very people who will lose a part of their power if the process is successful.
>
> (Goldstein 1995: 1107)

As we will see in the following pages, the key instead is to let these people *change* the basis of their power without losing the grip on that.
41 It has been remarked that

> unlike the Communist Party in Eastern Europe and the former Soviet Union, the Chinese Communist Party has a tradition of being able to adapt to changing environments. In the past, cadres have been screened and trained to adapt to political movements, like the Great Leap Forward and Cultural Revolution. Now they adapt quickly to another environment: fast growth in the market economy.
>
> (Qian and Stiglitz 1996: 180)

42 Blecher (1991) makes the distinction between the 'developmental state' (e.g., Japan) and the 'entrepreneurial state' (e.g., Korea and Taiwan). In the former, the government firmly dictates conditions and puts pressure on markets, but in addition in the latter the state is directly in charge of managing companies, especially in heavy industry. See also Nolan (2004a: 147–49).
43 One Chinese economist interviewed in Shirk (1993: 335) defines the meaning of Chinese reforms as 'transferring power to lower levels and allowing lower levels to gain more profits'.
44 'In a township or village, the immediate question facing the community is how to make more profit and what technology to use. The ownership problem is postponed to be solved later' (Qian and Stiglitz 1996: 184).
45 The drive to profits was sometimes the only thing joint-venture (public) partners had in common: see the story of a company like Zhuhai Asia Simulation & Control System Engineering Co. Ltd., told by Qian and Stiglitz 1996: 184.
46 'Plan ideological' states 'defin[e] their mission in terms of Marxian, class, and other objectives divorced from questions of economic efficiency per se'. On the contrary, the 'plan rational' state 'pursu[e] not blind ideological goals but enhanced competitiveness' (Pempel 1999: 139–40). In the same pages, Pempel points out that even though the distinction was developed by Johnson (1982), due credit must be given to Ralf Dahrendorf (1968), who first noted it.

47 This aspect of state tolerance was clear in rural industry, and also in corruption issues: 'One check on unacceptable corruption is the party: duplication of the functions of government and the party sometimes serves as part of a system of checks and balances' (Qian and Stiglitz 1996: 193).

48 In China's case, the observed behaviour was not different in the pre-reform and in the transition periods: 'as in the past, local officials strove for high growth rates to promote their careers by demonstrating that they were enthusiastically and competently carrying out the center's policies' (Shirk 1993: 183).

49 Oi (1985: 239).

50 If for instance the following passage is considered and compared to the picture that emerged in Deng's China, it will be easily noted how the political logic in the countryside was still the same:

> The premise is that the political behaviour of peasants is closely tied to the economic realities of their daily lives. The economic environment of the village, which centers on the distribution of private and collective goods, is the basis of political authority and forms the core of the clientelist politics.
>
> (Oi 1985: 241)

51 Therefore, Oi (1985: 265) can conclude that 'the institutional structure of a communist state does not so much eliminate traditional patterns of clientelism as it reshapes them'.

52 The other two circumstances outlined by Oi (1985: 265) are 'centralized distribution systems' and 'scarcity of goods'. Undoubtedly, both situations were less and less common as the Chinese economic system was increasingly marketized, but they have not disappeared, especially in agriculture and in the poorest regions.

53 Within the commune system, where the team leader was the powerful patron of the village's peasants, Oi (1985: 255) observes that 'a team leader's power derives from his position in the administrative hierarchy and is granted to him by the state', thereby depending for his power 'both on the state and on his members'. What was true for team members in Maoist China can be indeed generalized for communist cadres under Deng.

54 Institutionally, in communist states 'one party and its agents control access to all essential goods – including food, work, and income opportunities' (Oi 1985: 263).

55 In this way, socialist clientelism is different from traditional patronage (like, for instance, that of a landlord) which 'is based on personal ownership of the wealth or property that he uses for patronage' (Oi 1985: 255).

56 'Where You Stand Is Where You Sit' (Shirk 1993: 98).

57 As a matter of fact, 'in the long run, each must honor the mutual obligations of being patron and client. The patron is obliged to give his client favored treatment. In return, he has certain expectations regarding the benefits he will receive' (Oi 1985: 257).

58 Team production is defined as a 'production in which (1) several types of resources are used and (2) the product is not a sum of separable outputs of each cooperating resource' and '(3) not all resources used in team production belong to one person' (Alchian and Demsetz 1972: 779). The team production concept is important because it can partially account for the fact that – contrary to neoclassical assumptions – neither firms are 'black boxes', since they 'perform a variety of operations, not all of which are identical among those firms that seem to produce the same commodity' (Barzel 1997: 66).

59 In fact, 'with team production it is difficult, solely by observing total output, to either define or determine each individual's contribution to this output of the cooperating inputs' (Alchian and Demsetz 1972: 779).

60

> It is this entire bundle of rights: (1) to be a residual claimant; (2) to observe input behaviour; (3) to be the central party common to all contracts with inputs; (4) to alter

> the membership of the team; and (5) to sell these rights, that defines the ownership (or the employer) of the classical (capitalist, free-enterprise) firm.
>
> (Alchian and Demsetz 1972: 783)

The residual claimant's task, therefore, is precisely the maximization of team output value.

61 One of the results of the intellectual reflection after the end of the Soviet Union in 1991 was the document called 'Realistic responses and strategic options for China after the Soviet coup', quoted in Xin and Kelly (1994: 224). The document was a summary of a discussion among 'young intellectuals associated with the theoretical department of *China Youth Daily*' and is also known as a 'manifesto of the princes' party (*taizidang*)' (Fewsmith 2001: 98). It basically criticized 'utopian socialism' of the revolutionary kind and 'utopian capitalism' of the radical type and advocated 'social stability and gradual reform' drawing on 'Western rationalism... and Chinese tradition' (Fewsmith 2001: 99).

62 It must be kept in mind that 'the capacity to monitor and sanction economic and social behaviour are key elements of a Leninist system' (Dickson 2003: 15).

63 For instance, a study on Shanxi has found that '47 per cent of private entrepreneurs, 43 per cent of joint venture managers, 40 per cent of owner-operators, and 45 per cent of the private enterprise managers had a parent who had been a member of the party-state' and that 'a substantial portion of the economic elite ... had been involved in the party-state even before reform' (Goodman 2001: 141, 144). Also, the local political and economic elites'... established close communities of mutual interest where county and section-level cadres on the one hand, and rural entrepreneurs, private entrepreneurs, and owner-operators on the other, all worked together. Politically, most of the local economic elite were members of the CCP' (Goodman 2001: 149).

64 In fact, new conservatism has been seen as 'a broad principle of class collaboration in a post-Deng world' which 'may offer a *modus vivendi* between an array of new elite groups' like 'the widening circle of "nomenklatura" capitalists' and 'the ruling circle in Beijing, a grouping of princelings ruling in the name of an essentially developmentalist ideological charter... The *modus vivendi* between these groups would be explicitly non-Marxist and developmentalist' (Xin and Kelly 1994: 230).

65 The 1998 Organization Law stated that 'every organization must register with the government and have a party or government unit as its supervisory organization, responsible for its daily affair' (Dickson 2003: 25).

66 For example, it must not be forgotten that in state industry the Party, through its Organization Department, had the power to appoint and dismiss managers. It is true that with greater space for the market the carrot of political promotion to higher levels of bureaucracy 'becomes less attractive than before', but reforms accrued wealth to manager, so that 'disciplinary dismissal by the Party will cause severe damage to managers because of the removal of the rents associated with the position' (Qian 1996: 435). Furthermore, profit-sharing schemes produced what Nee and Su (1996) call individual 'informal property rights' which were made conditional on performance:

> as long as the firm provides a reliable revenue stream to local government, the manager can expect to retain his or her post and any informal rights over the use of the firm's resources established through mutual understanding.... If a manager or entrepreneur fails to meet the performance standards of local government, his or her informal rights can be withdrawn.
>
> (Nee and Su 1996: 117)

67 Actually, it has been observed that 'intellectuals in modern China... are more likely to be reformers trying to improve both the efficiency and the responsiveness of the state than to offer a dramatic alternative to the status quo' and that emerging groups

of 'entrepreneurs, professionals [and] high tech specialists... [are] apolitical, even anti-political' (Dickson 2003: 21).

68 In effect, in the post-Mao era the relationship between the centre and the localities is more complex to manage and compliance is never to be regarded as given, but it is clear that 'the center may possess more patience with local discretion and deviations in economic issue areas as long as they promote growth at the system level' (Chung 2001: 65).

69 It is important to note that the reaction of entrepreneurs to the Tiananmen revolt was largely negative: 'Most private businessmen did not support the 1989 demonstrations; many of those who did later regretted doing so because it led to a temporary retreat from Deng's reform and opening policies and damaged the business environment in China' (Dickson 2003: 22). After all, China's entrepreneurial class is quite new and 'with a precarious identity and poorly protected property rights'. Therefore it is the weak that seeks the protection offered by the strong: 'Private entrepreneurs are more likely to be partners with the state, rather than adversaries of it' (Dickson 2003: 23), thereby confirming Weiss and Hobson's (1995) argument on capitalism as a result of the competition/cooperation between strong states and weak societies.

70 Lieberthal (1995: 183) offers the following version of the distinction between institutions and organizations: '"Organizations" are coherent, internally interdependent administrative or functional structures. "Institutions", by contrast, are "practices, relationships, and organizations *that have developed sufficient regularity and perceived importance to shape the behaviours of their members*"'.

71 The elders in those two decades 'have decided all important issues themselves' and 'like a corporate board, they set the major directions of the enterprise, and those in daily charge of the enterprise serve only as long as they maintain the elders' confidence' (Lieberthal 1995: 188).

72 Within a supposed 'PRC, Inc.', key generalists would be 'the chief executive officer or president of a major corporation' (Lieberthal 1995: 188). The General Secretary of the Party and the Prime Minister are included in this category.

73 'To continue our metaphor of "PRC, Inc.", these bridge leaders are vice presidents in charge of major function', since they are 'responsible for helping to develop policy within a certain sphere' (Lieberthal 1995: 188–89).

74 'In corporate terms, these are the individuals in charge of top-level departments (strategic planning, finance, etc.) and the heads of the most important operating divisions of the firm' (Lieberthal 1995: 189). They are for example ministries, heads of state commissions, and heads of provincial bodies.

75 The ascendancy of Hu Jintao at the Sixteenth CCP Congress in 2002 marked the accession to power of the fourth generation of leaders, after those of Mao Zedong, Deng Xiaoping and Jiang Zemin.

76 The ability of leaders to dispatch right *mishus* to right administrative positions can help leaders themselves to build their 'political base at the Center and in the provinces' (Lieberthal 1995: 190).

77 In fact, 'when [*mishus*] leave the personal office of their patron, and if their patron is still in good standing and they themselves have not made an error – they assume very important positions' (Lieberthal 1995: 190).

78 For instance, 'via the *mishu* system, leaders cement their ties with each other by employing the offspring of their colleagues and then placing them into official positions' (Lieberthal 1995: 190).

79 In truth, it should be said that the Party affairs *xitong* is the key to overall control, since '*all* positions of real importance in China fall under the CCP's nomenklatura' (Lieberthal 1995: 209).

80 By mid-90s, the Finance and Economics *xitong* included 'the planning commission, the major production ministries, the finance ministry, the banking system, the subordinate organs of these bodies, and the state enterprises' (Lieberthal 1995: 204).

81 Inefficiencies were widespread: 'enterprises were steadily and increasingly losing money during the 1980s', although 'state-operated enterprises... accounted for 76.9 per cent of all losses' (Field 1996: 107). For a definitively more optimistic assessment of the state sector, though, see Lo (1997).

82 Administrative decentralization and unclear property rights just reinforced these aspects (Putterman 1995: 1052).

83 It might be useful to recall here that Korea, Malaysia and Thailand are considered by Khan to be examples of the first (successful) model, whereas the Indian sub-continent is given as evidence of the second (unsuccessful) pattern.

84 The following passage is crystal clear on this issue: 'The transitional institutions are not created solely for increasing the size of a pie, they are also created to reflect the distributional concerns of how the enlarged pie is divided and the political concerns of how the interests of those in power are served' (Qian 2002: 11).

85 This is plausibly what happens in developed countries:

> modern liberal democratic theories treat civil society as an abstract 'good thing'. It is implicitly an agglomeration of interest and pressure groups which have a collective stake in the capitalist system and can moreover monitor and keep in check the self-seeking state, which is also assumed.
>
> (Khan 1998b: 114)

86 It is useful to recall here that Dickson (2003: 5) makes the distinction between two groups of China's 'red capitalists': those who left 'jobs in the party, government, or state-owned enterprises to go into the private sector' and 'those who were co-opted into the party after demonstrating their entrepreneurial skills and business success'.

87 This means that it is necessary to go beyond the observation that 'it is the political coalition backing growth that was new in China after the 1980s' (Khan 2004: 179). However, Khan is perfectly right on continuities in communist China's economic history: 'The state's ability to restructure property rights in line with its changing objectives is not [new], and has been demonstrated time and again since 1949' (Khan 2004: 179).

88 In fact, 'human history... is certainly not a history of negotiated institutional change' (Khan 1995: 82).

89 Khan (1995) acknowledges that there is a relationship between transition costs and (political) transaction costs. Following 'the logic of political survival' (Khan 1998b: 125), transition costs measure the resistance to changes furthered by groups proposing growth. Political transaction costs are referred to collective action costs within a same class, group and faction or within the same pattern of patron–client relationship. While high transition costs result always in low transition, this can be even slower if dominant groups meet low political transaction costs in buying off allies for their reaction against change. On the contrary, low transition costs are conducive to rapid transition, in presence of both low and high transaction costs – the United States and UK experiences and the East Asian and Chinese ones respectively being given as examples showing different levels of political transaction costs (Khan 1995: 83–84).

90 The social picture of unstable mainland China and formerly Japanese-ruled Taiwan was undoubtedly different:

> In pre-1949 China, the relative weakness of the Kuomintang and its failure to control competing warlords led the Chiang Kai Shek regime to follow highly predatory policies, but in post-1949 Taiwan (China), the same party and leader organized an exemplary developing state, largely because the balance of power between state and society in Taiwan (China) allowed the state to engage in effective enforcement of transformation strategies.
>
> (Khan 2004: 184)

91 Naughton (1995a) and Shambaugh (1995).
92 The historical importance of evolution resides precisely in those discontinuities that would not effectively have existed, if the NIE logic had been at work: 'Real-world institutional change involves path changes. These are discontinuous breaks in the paths that would have been negotiated through compensation' (Khan 1995: 82).
93 The Cultural Revolution represented a supply side shock on the urban economy, which 'created shortages that the rural entrepreneurs rose to fulfill', thereby sowing the seeds of 'the post-reform takeoff of rural entrepreneurship' (Huang 2008: 61).
94 On the importance of Deng's ability 'to recognize that Mao's mantle, in terms of economic policies and institutions, should not be dismantled overnight in favour of any shock therapy', see Kueh (2008: 39).
95 Ramo (2004: 11–12) defines the Beijing Consensus as

> simply three theorems about how to organise the place of a developing country in the world ... The first theorem is about using innovation to reduce the friction-losses of reform. [The] second theorem demands a development model where sustainability and equality become first considerations ... Finally, the Beijing Consensus contains a theory of self-determination....

See also: 'Wrong model, right continent', *The Economist*, 28 October 2006, 16–18; Peerenboom (2007); Halper (2010). According to Ravallion (2009), there are in particular two lessons that Africa should learn from the Chinese experience, namely the importance of productivity growth in agriculture – due to right microincentives and public support – and the necessity of a strong leadership heading a capable public administration. Instead, Thornton (2007) thinks that the supposed Chinese 'model' is just the revival of a neoliberist movement supported by the alliance between political power and multinationals, resulting in a reduction of democratic space.
96 According to Nolan, in this sense China's third way

> was a complete philosophy that combined comprehensive thought about concrete ways of both stimulating and controlling the market, with a deeply elaborated system of morality for rulers, bureaucrats and ordinary people.... It is a complete misunderstanding (not least, by Karl Marx) to view the traditional Chinese state as a stagnant 'Oriental despotism'.
>
> (Nolan 2004b: 174)

97 As far as ambition is concerned, Chinese rulers should remember Lao Zi's suggestion for ambitious superpowers: 'Win the war, but do not boast; win the war, but do not show arrogance; whatever it is in its prime is bound to decline, for, being in the prime goes against the *Dao*; whatever goes against the *Dao* will come to an early end' (Lao Zi 1995: 149–51, quoted in Nolan 2004b: 26).
98 In this sense, China did not necessarily have to imitate acritically the Western world: 'Chinese history has deep lessons, not only for China itself, but also for the wider world, about the nature of the relationship between the state and economy and society' (Nolan 2004b: 112). In fact, 'the central preoccupation of Chinese political practice over... thousands of years has been the attempt to find a function for the state, and nurture a social ethic that enables the economy and society to operate in a way that serves that whole social interest' (Nolan 2004b: 154). In other words, China could be 'us[ing] the past to serve the present (*gu wei jin yong*)' (Nolan 2004b: Chapter 3, making reference to a passage in Jiang Zemin's speech of 1 July 2001 for the celebration of the eightieth birthday of the CCP).
99 For instance, it has been argued that 'the expanding appeal of China's governing model is shrinking the West – making our notions of society and government less relevant – and

will do more to alter the quality of life for Americans and the West in the twenty-first century than any other development' (Halper 2010: 252).

100 In fact, 'primitive accumulation' is 'nothing else than the historical process of divorcing the producer from the means of production' (Marx 1887: 714, quoted in Nolan 2004b: 61).

101 On China's environmental disaster see for instance Economy (2005).

102 See for instance Wang (2003). Apparently, the leadership knows that corruption and income gaps are serious problem that have to be resolved. In fact, in a speech in December 2002, Party Secretary Hu Jintao – who became also China's President in March 2003, making reference to Mao's (1944) slogan 'Serve the people', stated:

> Our population's standard of living has, generally speaking, attained the level of 'small comfort'. . . .We can have no reason for being satisfied with the present situation, and forgetting the need to forge ahead. . . .If we cast aside the work style of plain living and hard struggle, and covet material comforts, if we are unwilling to carry on with hard work, if we are indifferent to the masses' sickness and suffering, if we turn a deaf ear to the cries of the masses, then we will inevitably be separated from the masses.
>
> (Hu 2003, quoted in Nolan 2004b: 169–70)

Actually, in the tradition that requires each General Secretary of the Party to contribute to Chinese communist thought with an 'original' theory, it seems that Hu Jintao wants to be remembered as the one who put forward the idea of a 'socialist harmonious society', adopted by the Party's Central Committee on 11 October 2006:

> The. . . document. . . prescribes many ways to make China harmonious. They include promoting political reform (how is not said) and cracking down on domestic and foreign "hostile forces". Another element. . . is creating a "new socialist countryside", as distinct from the present one where corruption is rampant, health care and education are becoming prohibitively expensive and incomes are falling ever further behind those in the booming cities.
>
> ('Dreaming of harmony', *The Economist*, 21 October 2006: 66–7)

See also Woo (2006).

103 In this respect, Smith (1761), widely and intelligently quoted in Nolan (2004b: 151–53), invites us to distinguish between wealth and happiness, and warns against the chaos brought about by a profoundly unjust society. It is not by chance then that Prime Minister Wen Jiabao told the *Financial Times* in 2009 that he was travelling with a copy of Adam Smith's *The Theory of Moral Sentiments* in his suitcase. The interview is available online at http://www.chinaconsulatesf.org/eng/xw/t535971.htm (accessed 29 September 2010).

104 See 'Full text of Communique of the Fifth Plenum of the Seventeenth CPC Central Committee', available online at http://news.xinhuanet.com/english2010/china/2010-10/18/c_13563388_4.htm (accessed 12 November 2011). The term 'inclusive growth' comes from a 2007 Asian Development Bank (ADB) paper, and is defined – in typical international organizations' jargon – as

> growth with equal opportunities. . . [which] focuses on both creating opportunities and making the opportunities accessible to all. Growth is inclusive when it allows all members of a society to participate in and contribute to the growth process on an equal basis regardless of their individual circumstances.
>
> (Ali and Zhuang 2007: 10)

105 As a result of this policy shift, 'the average growth of rural household per capita income between 2003 and 2005 was 5.8 percent, compared with 3.9 per cent during the Jiang Zemin era' (Huang 2008: 293).

106 See for instance Nolan (2001).

107 Rodrik (2006).

108 Li Changchun's speech was formulated in January 2003 with regard to state policy on media control.

109 Nolan (2004b) notes that authoritarianism in Korea and Taiwan lasted during the 'Lewis phase' of economic development. The difference with China is that it is a much larger country with a more vast pool of surplus labour to be absorbed in a much longer time, and if the observation is true, 'then China would face the prospect of an exceptionally long period under such a structure' (Nolan 2004b: 69), similarly to what happened in 'Britain from 1750 until the mid-nineteenth century and [in] the Meiji Period in Japan' (Nolan 2004b: 63). See also Wang (2003) and Zheng (2004).

110 Actually, Gilley (2004) frames a kind of democratic and federalist structure for China, by dividing for instance the legislature in provincial and national congresses, assigning seats to every province according to their population. Reading Gilley (2004) one has the clear sensation of an American-inspired model of government which does not exist even in continental Europe and which is – not convincingly – advocated for China's future. He disregards 'the age-old preoccupation of Chinese political thought: system stability' (Nolan 2004b: 73) and falls in the same trap that captured also Marx, who viewed 'the violent intrusion of Western colonialism in a positive light, liberating Asian peoples from "Oriental despotism"' (Nolan 2004b: 72).

111 In democratic Asia, Japan experienced the first alternation to power of political parties only in 2009 – in fact, the Liberal Party had incessantly governed the country for more than 50 years, with ramifications at all levels of society – and within a 'societal-corporatist patronage structure' (Unger and Chan 1996: 113) – of those kinds described for instance by Evans (1995) or Aoki *et al.* (1996).

References

Acemoglu, D., Johnson, S. and Robinson, J. A. (2001) 'The Colonial Origins of Comparative Development: An Empirical Investigation', *American Economic Review*, 91: 1369–1401.

Alchian, A. A. and Demsetz, H. (1972) 'Production, Information Costs, and Economic Organization', *American Economic Review*, 62: 777–95.

Alesina, A., Baqir, R. and Easterly, W. (1999) 'Public Goods and Ethnic Divisions', *Quarterly Journal of Economics*, 114: 1243–84.

Ali, I. and Zhuang, J. (2007) 'Inclusive Growth toward a Prosperous Asia: Policy Implications', ERD working paper No. 97, Manila: Asian Development Bank. Online. Available at: www.adb.org/Documents/ERD/Working_Papers/WP097.pdf (accessed 12 November 2010).

Amsden, A. H. (1989) *Asia's Next Giant*, New York, NY: Oxford University Press.

Amsden, A. H. (1997) 'Bringing Production Back in: Understanding Government's Economic Role in Late Industrialization', *World Development*, 25: 469–80.

Aoki, M. (2001) *Towards a Comparative Institutional Analysis*, Cambridge, MA: MIT Press.

Aoki, M., Murdock, K. and Okuno-Fujiwara, M. (1996) 'Beyond the East Asian Miracle: Introducing the Market-Enhancing View', in M. Aoki, H.-K. Kim and M. Okuno-Fujiwara (eds) *The Role of Government in East Asian Economic Development: Comparative Institutional Analysis*, Oxford: Clarendon Press, 1–35.

Ash, R. F. (1996) 'Agricultural Development in China since 1978', in R. F. Ash and Y. Y. Kueh (eds) *The Chinese Economy Under Deng Xiaoping*, New York, NY: Oxford University Press, 55–87.

Barzel, Y. (1997) *Economic Analysis of Property Rights*, Cambridge: Cambridge University Press.

Baum, R. (1994) *Burying Mao: Chinese Politics in the Era of Deng Xiaoping*, Princeton, NJ: Princeton University Press.

Brennan, G. and Buchanan, J. (1980) *The Power to Tax: Analytical Foundations of the Fiscal Constitution*, Cambridge: Cambridge University Press.

Blecher, M. (1991) 'Developmental State, Entrepreneurial State: The Political Economy of Socialist Reform in Xinju Municipality and Guanghan County', in G. White (ed.) *The Chinese State in the Era of Economic Reform: The Road to a Crisis*, Basingstoke: Macmillan, 265–90.

Burki, S. J. and Perry, G. E. (1998) *Beyond the Washington Consensus: Institutions Matter*, Washington, DC: World Bank.

Cao, Y., Qian, Y. and Weingast, B. R. (1999) 'From Federalism, Chinese Style, to Privatization, Chinese Style', *Economics of Transition*, 7: 103–31.

China Reform and Development Report (1992–93) (1994) Beijing: China Far East Publishing House.

Chung, J. H. (2001) 'Reappraising Central-local Relations in Deng's China: Decentralization, Dilemmas of Control, and Diluted Effects of Reform', in C. Chao and B. J. Dickson (eds) *Remaking the Chinese State: Strategies, Society, and Security*, London: Routledge, 46–75.

Coase, R. H. (1960) 'The Problem of Social Cost', *Journal of Law & Economics*, 3: 1–44.

Dahrendorf, R. (1968) 'Market and Plan: Two Types of Rationality', in R. Dahrendorf (ed.) *Essays in the Theory of Society*, London: Routledge and Kegan Paul, 215–31.

Dickson, B. J. (2003) *Red Capitalists in China: The Party, Private Enterpreneurs, and Prospects for Political Change*, Cambridge: Cambridge University Press.

Djankov, S., Glaeser, E. L., La Porta, R., Lopez-de-Silanes, F. and Shleifer, A. (2003) 'The New Comparative Economics', Cambridge, MA: NBER working paper 9608; reprinted in *Journal of Comparative Economics*, 31: 595–619 A similar version Online. Available at: http://mba.tuck.dartmouth.edu/pages/faculty/rafael.laporta/publications/LaPorta%20PDF%20Papers-ALL/New%20Comparative%20Economics.pdf (accessed 22 September 2010).

Economy, E. C. (2005) *The River Runs Black. The Environmental Challenge to China's Future*, Ithaca, NY: Cornell University Press.

Engermann, S. L. and Sokoloff, K. L. (1997) 'Factor Endowments, Institutions, and Differential Paths of Growth among New World Economies', in S. Haber (ed.) *How Latin America Fell Behind: Essays on the Economic Histories of Brazil and Mexico, 1800–1914*, Stanford, CA: Stanford University Press, 260–96.

Engermann, S. L. and Sokoloff, K. L. (2002) 'Factor Endowments, Inequality, and Paths of Development among New World Economies', Cambridge, MA: NBER working paper 9259.

Evans, P. B. (1995) *Embedded Autonomy: States and Industrial Transformation*, Princeton, NJ: Princeton University Press.

Fewsmith, J. (2001; 2nd edn 2008) *China Since Tiananmen: The Politics of Transition*, Cambridge: Cambridge University Press.

Field, R. M. (1996) 'China's Industrial Performance Since 1978', in R. F. Ash and Y. Y. Kueh (eds) *The Chinese Economy Under Deng Xiaoping*, New York, NY: Oxford University Press, 88–125.

Fröbel, F., Heinrichs, J. and Kreye, O. (1980) *The New International Division of Labour: Structural Unemployment in Industrialised Countries and Industrialisation in Developing Countries*, Cambridge: Cambridge University Press.

Gilley, B. (2004) *China's Democratic Future: How It Will Happen and Where It Will Lead*, New York, NY: Columbia University Press.

Goldstein, S. M. (1995) 'China in Transition: The Political Foundations of Incremental Reform', *China Quarterly*, 144: 1105–31.

Goodman, D. S. G. (2001) 'The Interdependence of State and Society: The Political Sociology of Local Leadership', in C. Chao and B. J. Dickson (eds) *Remaking the Chinese State: Strategies, Society, and Security*, London: Routledge, 132–56.

Halper, S. (2010) *The Beijing Consensus. How China's Authoritarian Model Will Dominate the Twenty-First Century*, New York, NY: Basic Books.

Harvey, D. (1982) *The Limits to Capital*, Oxford: Basil Blackwell.

Heilbroner, R. L. (1985) *The Nature and Logic of Capitalism*, New York, NY and London: W.W. Norton.

Heilbroner, R. L. (1993) *21st Century Capitalism*, New York, NY and London: W.W. Norton.

Howell, J. (1993) *China Opens Its Doors: The Politics of Economic Transition*, Hemel Hempstead: Harvester Wheatshef.

Hu, J. (2003) 'Hu Jintao's speech at the Xibaipo study meeting: Carry out the fine work style of "plain living and hard struggle" (*jianku fendou*); strive to achieve the great objective of all-roundedly establishing a small comfort (*xiaokang*) society', *Renmin ribao (People's Daily)*, 2 January.

Huang, Y. (2008) *Capitalism with Chinese Characteristics: Entrepreneurship and the State*, New York, NY: Cambridge University Press.

Johnson, C. (1982) *MITI and the Japanese Miracle*, Palo Alto, CA: Stanford University Press.

Khan, M. H. (1995) 'State Failure in Weak States: A Critique of New Institutionalist Explanations', in J. Harris, J. Hunter and C.M. Lewis (eds) *The New Institutional Economics and Third World Development*, London and New York, NY: Routledge, 71–86 Online. Available at: http://mercury.soas.ac.uk/users/mk17/Docs/State%20Failure%20in%20Weak%20States%20NIE.pdf (accessed 22 September 2010).

Khan, M. H. (1998a) 'Patron–Client Networks and the Economics Effects of Corruption in Asia', *European Journal of Development Research*, 10: 15–39 Online. Available at: http://mercury.soas.ac.uk/users/mk17/Docs/Corruption%20EJDR.pdf (accessed 22 September 2010).

Khan, M. H. (1998b) 'The Role of Civil Society and Patron–client Networks in the Analysis of Corruption' in OECD/UNDP (ed.) *Corruption and Integrity Improvement Initiatives in Developing Countries*, New York, NY: UNDP, Management Development and Governance Division, 111–27 Online. Available at: http://www.u4.no/document/literature/Khan-1998-the-role-of-civil-society.pdf (accessed 22 September 2010).

Khan, M. H. (2004) 'State Failure in Developing Countries and Institutional Reform Strategies', in B. Tungodden, N. Stern and I. Kolstad (eds) *Toward Pro-Poor Policies: Aid Institutions and Globalization,* Proceedings of Annual World Bank Conference on Development Economics, Oxford: Oxford University Press and World Bank, 165–95 Online. Available at: http://www0.gsb.columbia.edu/ipd//pub/Controversies_Role_of_State_Khan.pdf (accessed 22 September 2010).

Khan, M. H. (2005) 'What is a "Good Investment Climate"?', in G. Kochendorfer-Lucius and B. Pleskovic (eds) *Investment Climate, Growth, and Poverty*, Washington, DC: World Bank, 77–83 Online. Available at: http://mercury.soas.ac.uk/users/mk17/ . . . /120%20Berlin%20Khan%201st%20pg.pdf (accessed 22 September 2010).

Knight, J. (1992) *Institutions and Social Conflict*, Cambridge: Cambridge University Press.

Kornai, J. (1986) 'The Hungarian Reform Process: Visions, Hopes, and Reality', *Journal of Economic Literature*, 24: 1687–1738.

Kornai, J. (1992) *The Socialist System: The Political Economy of Communism*, Oxford: Oxford University Press.

Krugman, P. (1994) 'The Myth of Asia's Miracle', *Foreign Affairs*, 73: 62–78 Online. Available at: http://www.foreignaffairs.com/articles/50550/paul-krugman/the-myth-of-asias-miracle (accessed 22 September 2010).

Kueh, Y. Y. (2008) *China's New Industrialization Strategy: Was Chairman Mao Really Necessary?*, Cheltenham: Edward Elgar.

Landes, D. S. (1998) *The Wealth and Poverty of Nations: Why Some Are So Rich and Some So Poor*, New York, NY and London: W.W. Norton & Company.

Lau, L. J., Qian, Y. and Roland, G. (2000) 'Reform Without Losers: An Interpretation of China's Dual-track Approach to Transition', *Journal of Political Economy*, 108: 120–43 Online. Available at: http://deepblue.lib.umich.edu/bitstream/2027.42/39527/3/wp137.pdf (accessed 22 September 2010).

Lieberthal, K. (1995; 2nd edn 2004) *Governing China*, New York, NY: W.W. Norton & Company.

Lo, D. (1997) *Market and Institutional Regulation in Chinese Industrialization, 1978–94*, New York, NY: St. Martin's Press.

Lo, D. (2004) 'Globalisation and Comparative Economics: of Efficiency, Efficient Institutions, and Late Development', Department Of Economics working paper No. 137, London: School of Oriental and African Studies. Online. Available at: http://www.soas.ac.uk/economics/research/workingpapers/file28842.pdf (accessed 22 September 2010).

McNally, C. A. (2007a) 'Reflections on Capitalism and China's Emergent Political Economy', in C. A. McNally (ed.) *China's Emergent Political Economy: Capitalism in the Dragon's Lair*, London: Routledge, 17–35.

McNally, C. A. (2007b) 'The Institutional Contours of China's Emergent Capitalism', in C. A. McNally (ed.) *China's Emergent Political Economy: Capitalism in the Dragon's Lair*, London: Routledge, 105–25.

Mao, Z. (1965) [1944] 'Serve the People', in *Selected Works of Mao Tse-tung*, Vol. III, Beijing: Foreign Language Press.

Marx, K. (1967) [1887] *Capital, Vol. 1*, New York, NY: International Publishers.

Murrell, P. (1995) 'The Transition According to Cambridge, Mass.', *Journal of Economic Literature*, 33: 164–78 Online. Available at: http://econweb.umd.edu/~murrell/articles/The%20transition%20according%20to%20Cambridge,%20Mass.pdf (accessed 22 September 2010).

Nathan, A. J. and Gilley, B. (2003) *China's New Rulers: The Secret Files*, New York, NY: The New York Review of Books.

Naughton, B. (1995a) 'Deng Xiaoping: The Economist', in D. Shambaugh (ed.) *Deng Xiaoping: Portrait of a Chinese Statesman*, New York, NY: Oxford University Press, 83–106.

Naughton, B. (1995b) *Growing Out of the Plan: Chinese Economic Reform, 1978–1993*, Cambridge: Cambridge University Press.

Naughton, B. (2007) *The Chinese Economy: Transition and Growth*, Cambridge, MA and London: MIT Press.

Nee, V. and Su, S. (1996) 'Institutions, Social Ties, and Commitment in China's Corporatist Transformation', in J. McMillan and B. Naughton (eds) *Reforming Asian Socialism: The Growth of Market Institutions*, Ann Arbor, MI: University of Michigan Press, 111–34.

Nolan, P. (2004a) *Transforming China*, London: Anthem Press.

Nolan, P. (2004b) *China at the Crossroads*, Cambridge: Polity Press.

Nolan, P. and Ash, R. F. (1995) 'China's Economy on the Eve of Reform', *China Quarterly*, 144: 980–98.

North, D. C. (1981) *Structure and Change in Economic History*, New York, NY: W.W. Norton & Company.

North, D. C. (1990) *Institutions, Institutional Change and Economic Performance*, Cambridge: Cambridge University Press.

Oi, J. C. (1985) 'Communism and Clientelism: Rural Politics in China', *World Politics*, 37: 238–66.

Oksenberg, M. and Dickson, B. J. (1991) 'The Origins, Processes, and Outcomes of Great Political Reform: A Framework of Analysis', in D. A. Rustow and K. P. Erikson (eds) *Comparative Political Dynamics: Global Research Perspectives*, New York, NY: Harper Collins, 235–62.

Overholt, W. H. (2010) 'China in the Global Financial Crisis: Rising Influence, Rising Challenges', *Washington Quarterly*, 33: 21–34. Online. Available at: http://www.twq.com/10january/docs/10jan_Overholt.pdf (accessed 24 September 2010).

Peerenboom, R. (2007) *China Modernizes: Threat to the West or Model for the Rest?*, New York, NY: Oxford University Press.

Pei, M. (2006) *China's Trapped Transition: The Limits of Developmental Autocracy*, Boston, MA: Harvard University Press.

Pempel, T. J. (1999) 'The Developmental Regime in a Changing World Economy', in M. Woo-Cumings (ed.) *The Developmental State*, Ithaca, NY: Cornell University Press, 137–81.

Putnam, R. D. (1993) *Making Democracy Work: Civic Traditions in Modern Italy*, Princeton, NJ: Princeton University Press.

Putterman, L. (1995) 'The Role of Ownership and Property Rights in China's Economic Transition', *China Quarterly*, 144: 1047–64.

Qian, Y. (1996) 'Enterprise Reform in China: Agency Problems and Political Control', *Economics of Transition*, 4: 427–47. Online. Available at: http://elsa.berkeley.edu/~yqian/94-2.pdf> (accessed 22 September 2010).

Qian, Y. (2002) *How Reform Worked in China*, CEPR discussion paper No. 3447, Berkeley, CA: University of California.

Qian, Y. and Stiglitz, J. (1996) 'Institutional Innovations and the Role of Local Government in Transition Economies: The case of Guangdong Province of China', in J. McMillan and B. Naughton (eds) *Reforming Asian Socialism: The Growth of Market Institutions*, Ann Arbor, MI: University of Michigan Press, 175 –94.

Ramo, J. C. (2004) *The Beijing Consensus*, London: Foreign Policy Centre.

Ravallion, R. (2009) 'Are There Lessons for Africa from China's Success Against Poverty?', *World Development*, 37: 303–13.

Rawski, T. G. (1995) 'Implications of China's Reform Experience', *China Quarterly*, 144: 1150–73.

Roberts, J. M. (1999) *The Penguin History of the Twentieth Century*, London: Penguin Books.

Rodrik, D. (2006) 'Goodbye Washington Consensus, Hello Washington Confusion? A Review of the World Bank's Economic Growth in the 1990s. Learning from a Decade of Reform', *Journal of Economic Literature*, 44: 973–87. Online. Available at: http://www.wcfia.harvard.edu/sites/default/files/Rodrick_Goodbye.pdf (accessed 22 September 2010).

Sachs, J. D. and Woo, W. T. (1994a) 'Structural Factors in the Economic Reforms of China, Eastern Europe and the Former Soviet Union', *Economic Policy*, 9: 101–46 Online. Available at: http://team.univparis1.fr/teamperso/DEA/Cursus/M1/DocChine/Sachs%20and%20Woo%20structural%20reforms.pdf (accessed 22 September 2010).

Sachs, J. D. and Woo, W. T. (1994b) 'Understanding the Reform Experiences of China, Eastern Europe and Russia', in C. H. Lee and H. Reisen (eds), *From Reform to Growth: China and Other Countries in Transition in Asia and Central and Eastern Europe*, Paris: OECD, 23–48.

Sachs, J. D. and Woo, W. T. (1997) *Understanding China's Economic Performance*, Cambridge, MA: NBER working paper No. 5935.

Shambaugh, D. (1995) 'Deng Xiaoping: The Politician', in D. Shambaugh (ed.) *Deng Xiaoping: Portrait of a Chinese Statesman*, New York, NY: Oxford University Press, 49–82.

Shambaugh, D. (2008) *China's Communist Party: Atrophy and Adaption*, Washington, DC: Woodrow Wilson Center Press.

Shirk, S. L. (1993) *The Political Logic of Economic Reform in China*, Berkeley and Los Angeles, CA: University of California Press.

Sicular, T. (1995) 'Redefining State, Plan and Market: China's Reforms in Agricultural Commerce', *China Quarterly*, 144: 1020–46.

Smith, A. (1982; 1st edn 1761) *The Theory of Moral Sentiments*, Indianapolis, IN: Liberty Classics edition.

Stiglitz, J. E. (1994) *Whither Socialism*, Cambridge, MA: MIT Press.

Sutherland, D. (2003) *China's Large Enterprises and the Challenge of Late Industrialisation*, London: Routledge Curzon.

Thornton, W. A. (2007) 'Sino-globalization: Politics of the CCP/tnc Symbiosis', *New Political Science*, 29: 211–35.

Unger, J. and Chan, A. (1996) 'Corporatism in China: A Developmental State in an East Asian context', in B. L. McCormick and J. Unger (eds) *China After Socialism: In the Footsteps of Eastern Europe or East Asia?*, Armonk, NY: M.E. Sharpe, 95–129.

Wade, R. (1990) *Governing the Market: Economic Theory and the Role of the Government in East Asian Industrialisation*, Princeton, NJ: Princeton University Press.

Walder, A. G. (1994) 'Evolving Property Rights and Their Political Consequences', in D. S. G. Goodman and B. Hopper (eds) *China's Quiet Revolution*, New York, NY: St. Martin's Press, 3–18.

Walder, A. G. (1995) 'China's Transitional Economy: Interpreting its Significance', *China Quarterly*, 144: 963–79.

Wang, H. (ed. T. Huters) (2003) *China's New Order: Society, Politics and Economy in Transition*, Cambridge, MA: Harvard University Press.

Wang, Y. (2003) *China's Economic Development and Democratization*, Aldershot: Ashgate.

Weiss, L. and Hobson, J. M. (1995) *States and Economic Development: A Comparative Historical Analysis*, Cambridge: Polity Press.

Whyte, M. K. (1995) 'The Social Roots of China's Economic Development', *China Quarterly*, 144: 999–1019.

Woo, W. T. (1999) 'The Real Reasons for China's Growth', *China Journal*, 41: 115–37.

Woo, W. T. (2006) 'A Harmonious Socialist Society or Bust: China's Quest for Sustainable Development', in *Reframing China Policy: The Carnegie Debates.*, Washington, DC: Carnegie Endowment for International Peace. Online. Available at: http://www.brookings.edu/~/media/ Files/ rc/ papers/ 2006/ 1201globaleconomics_woo/ 20061206woo.pdf (accessed 22 September 2010).

World Bank (1993) *World Development Report, the East Asian Miracle: Economic Growth and Public Policy*, Washington, DC: Oxford University Press. Online. Available at: http://www.wds.worldbank.org/external/default/WDSContentServer/IW3P/IB/1993/09/01/000009265_3970716142516/Rendered/PDF/multi_page.pdf (accessed 22 September 2010).

World Bank (2002) *World Development Report, Building Institutions for Markets*, Washington, DC: Oxford University Press. Online. Available at: http://web.worldbank.org/WBSITE/EXTERNAL/EXTDEC/EXTRESEARCH/EXTWDRS/0,contentMDK:22295291~pagePK:478093~piPK:477627~theSitePK:477624,00.html#fulltext (accessed 22 September 2010).

World Bank (2005) *World Development Report, Economic Growth in the 1990s: Learning from a Decade of Reform*, Washington, DC: Oxford University Press. Online. Available at: http://www1.worldbank.org/prem/lessons1990s/ (accessed 22 September 2010).

Xin, G. and Kelly, D. (1994) 'New Conservatism: Intermediate Ideology of A "New Elite"', in D.S.G. Goodman and B. Hopper (eds) *China's Quiet Revolution*, New York, NY: St Martin's Press, 219–33.
Xu, Q. (1988) *China's Economic System Reform*, Beijing: China Fiscal and Economic Publishing House.
Yang, Y. (2010) 'The End of the Beijing Consensus. Can China's Model of Authoritarian Growth Survive?', *Foreign Affairs*. Online. Available at: http://www.foreignaffairs.com/articles/65947/the-end-of-the-beijing-consensus (accessed 22 September 2010).
Yeh, K. C. (1996) 'Macroeconomic Issues in China in the 1990s', in R. F. Ash, and Y. Y. Kueh (eds) *The Chinese Economy Under Deng Xiaoping*, New York, NY: Oxford University Press, 159–216.
Yu, K. (2009) *Democracy is a Good Thing. Essays on Politics, Society, and Culture in Contemporary China*, Washington, DC: Brookings Institution Press.
Yu, K. (2010) *Democracy and the Rule of Law in China*, Leiden: Koninkljike Brill NV.
Zheng, D. (2004) *Will China Become Democratic?*, Singapore: Eastern University Press.
Zheng, Y. (2004) *Globalization and State Transformation in China*, Cambridge: Cambridge University Press.
Zheng, Y. (2010) *The Chinese Communist Party as Organizational Emperor. Culture, Reproduction and Transformation*, Oxford: Routledge.
Zhu, Q. and Elbern, S. (2002) 'Economic Institutional Evolution and Further Needs for Adjustments: Township Village Enterprises in China', ZEF Discussion Paper on Development Policy no. 56, Bonn. Online. Available at: http://www.zef.de/fileadmin/webfiles/downloads/zef_dp/zef_dp56.pdf (accessed 22 September 2002).
Zweig, D. (2002) *Internationalizing China: Domestic Interests and Global Linkages*, Ithaca, NY: Cornell University Press.

4 Continental drift

China and the global economic crisis

Sangaralingam Ramesh

Introduction

The economic prosperity associated with the Coastal regions of China has not 'trickled' down to the Western and Central regions sufficiently enough to eliminate the disparities in income between the regions. Indeed, the disparities between China's Coastal regions and its other regions continue to deepen. In the Mao period central planners held the mistaken belief that investment in the railways and development of heavy industry in the interior parts of China would bring prosperity. In the reform period and beyond the focus of economic development in China has been to take advantage of China's low labour costs. In the earlier part of the reform era the focus of economic reforms centred on the development of Special Economic Zones (SEZ's). In the second phase of reform policies were centred on the High Technology Development Zones. A characteristic feature of both SEZ's and the New High Technology Industrial Development Zone (NHTIDZ's) is that they represent a concentration of infrastructure within a predefined spatial area.

The current global economic crisis has presented China with a unique opportunity to deepen the economic transformation of the Coastal regions by shifting the focus of economic development to its interior regions. Indeed, the government's efforts to stave off the effects of the global crisis on the Chinese economy, by attempting to maintain economic growth above 8 per cent through an expansive fiscal stimulus, has had the effect of initiating a transformation of the interior Chinese economy. This then represents China's third stage of economic development since 1949. This chapter will examine the factors leading to China's third stage of economic development originating from the global economic crisis – the Continental drift in the economic development of China.

China's post-1949 economic development was characterized by central planning, heavy industry in the style of the Soviet Union, and political episodes such as the Great Leap Forward and the Cultural Revolution. However, a change of leadership in 1977, and the realization that unless China reformed its economy Chinese people would not be exposed to market forces which allowed citizens in the developed world to accumulate wealth, led to the post-1978 economic reforms. These reforms focused on the development of China's Coastal regions under the slogan of 'let us have some prosperity first'; and the focused concentration of infrastructure in specifically designated areas which had free market properties. These specially designated areas were the SEZ's of the Coastal regions – the islands of capitalism in a sea of central planning. However, the ensuing prosperity of the Coastal regions meant that the post-1978 economic reforms, which were also related to education and research and development (R&D), became more deeply embedded in China's Coastal regions than in its Central and Western regions. This derived from a lack of connectivity[1] in China's Central and Western provinces, and an increase in the heterogeneity of the population of these provinces. The combination of tougher labour legislation, tougher enforcement of environmental protection by the Chinese government, and the deeper embedding of the fruits of educational and R&D reforms in China's Coastal regions has two implications. First, the higher cost of production in the Coastal regions implies that manufacturing will shift further inland or overseas, spurring the economic development of China's interior regions or shifting economic development opportunities elsewhere.

Second, China's Coastal regions will be transformed into a pole of economic development through knowledge creation. The catalyst for this divergence in the nature of economic development between China's regions, Coastal and interior, emanates from the current global economic crisis emanating from the sub-prime lending crisis in the United States. It will be this crisis which will accentuate the economic development of China's Western and Central provinces. The global economic crisis has resulted in China engaging in 'stimulus spending' in four key areas, wealth redistribution, market integration, sustainable development and institutional development, to boost domestic consumption and counteract the effects of collapsing global demand for Chinese exports. This chapter will seek to evaluate the factors responsible for the movement in China's economic development from East to West, the so called 'Continental Drift'.

The Chinese economy

Neo-classical theory suggests that the production process involves the creation of a certain level of output for a given level of labour and capital, assuming that technology is freely available to all firms but with no mention of the environment or how it may impact on labour. China produces agricultural and manufacturing goods as well as engaging in the extraction of natural resources. The factor common to all three activities is that there may be one or more input or output in the production process which emerges and circulates into the air, water or soil, which either kills or maims living things. In this way the production process not only impacts on the environment but also affects labour in a number of ways, depending on how exploitation of labour is prevented. Modern industries which have substantial foreign investment, such as the manufacture of automobiles and fuels, are very efficient. However, Chinese industries which are locally financed, such as coal mining, cement, and paper manufacturing, tend to be inefficient and use technologies which pollute.[2] Another feature of Chinese industry is its structure, with Town and Village Enterprises (TVE) which have on average six employees, accounting for 50 per cent of Chinese exports, but contributing a much greater amount to environmental damage through pollution.[3] It is worthwhile at this stage to point out that pollution and China are not new to each other. Both became acquainted after the 1949 revolution through deforestation, the impact of the Great Leap Forward which saw a fourfold increase in the number of factories and further deforestation, as well as the 'Third Line' program during which many factories were located to the interior of China.[4] A discussion of Labour Legislation, Environmental Protection, the Global Financial Crisis, and finally, Continental Drift follows.

Labour legislation

China's post 1978 economic growth was fuelled by the manufacture and export of consumer goods to consumers in developed countries. China in effect became the manufacturing workhouse of the world. The post-1978 economic boom required workers to operate machines which were to produce goods for export. These workers were to be found in China's vast interior region, and were required to migrate to Coastal areas such as Guangdong and Shenzhen where manufacturing firms had become established following the government's reform policies. However, once the workers became employed by firms in the Coastal region many were simply at their employer's mercy, due to the fact that the relationship between worker and employer had no legal status in China. The increasing demand for workers by firms in China's Coastal regions placed an upward pressure on wages in those regions.

This phenomenon can be clearly seen in Figure 4.1 which shows the total remuneration for employees in the provinces of Henan, Hubei, Hunan and Guangdong for successive quarters between 2003 and 2009. The first three provinces are in central China and the last is a Coastal province bordering both Shenzhen and Hong Kong. It illustrates that total remuneration of workers in Guangdong is significantly higher than in the other three provinces in all quarters from 2003 to 2009.

The lack of transparent contractual obligations between worker and employer meant that employers could do as they liked to remain profitable. Indeed, 'given the seemingly endless labour supply from China's rural areas, workers who complained about wages or working conditions ran the risk of losing their jobs to others who were more compliant'.[5] Nevertheless, according to Wang *et al.* (2009) the combined effects of falling birth rates and increased demand for labour and technology led to workers gaining an upper hand over employers. These factors also led foreign firms to seek safer havens for their centres of manufacture in countries such as Vietnam. There was thus a need for government intervention which materialized with China's new labour contract law, passed into legislation in 2008. The purpose of establishing the rights of workers, through a legally binding contract, was to make them answerable to the law. The main provisions of the new labour contract law are:[6]

(a) the requirement for the employer to enter into an employment contract with the employee within one month of starting employment;

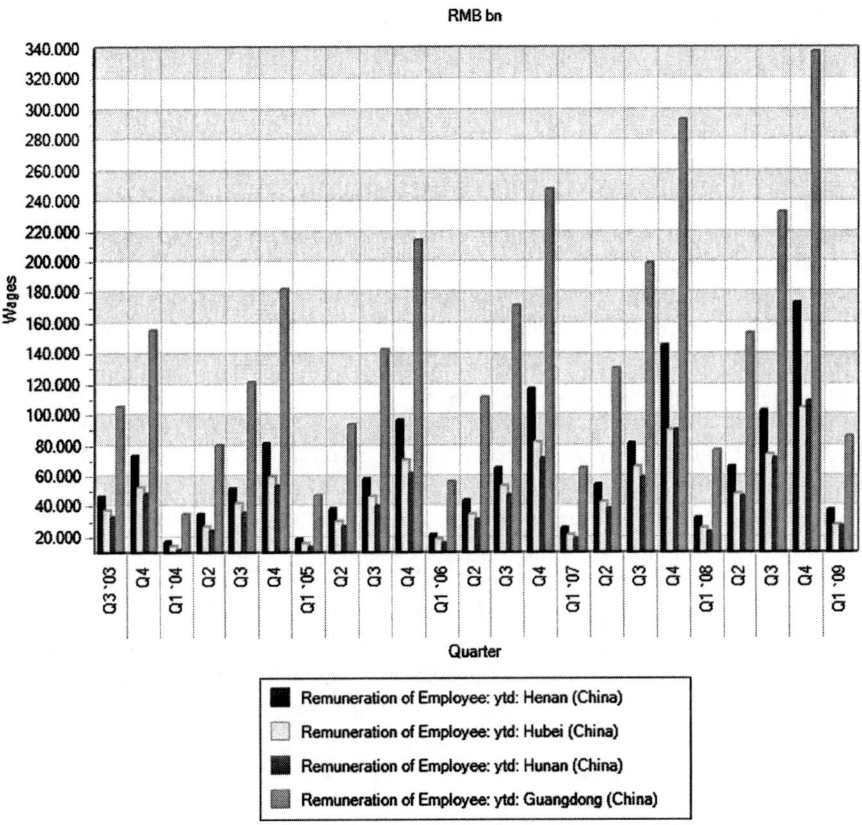

Figure 4.1 Total remuneration of employees by region.

Source: www.ceicdata.com.

(b) the requirment for non-fixed term contracts if the employee has been employed for at least ten consecutive years;
(c) enhanced powers for trade unions to enter into collective agreements with employers on behalf of workers, to increase safety and hygiene at work for example;
(d) the regulation of part-time work, outsourcing and overtime.

The introduction of these new measures increased the variable costs for employers operating in China's Coastal regions due to higher wages. It is intuitive to believe that these regulations will increase the variable costs of firms due to the introduction of inflexible mechanisms into the production process. However, although employers have found ways to sidestep the regulations,[7] it is far easier for firms to relocate operations to an interior province in China or move to another country such as Vietnam.

Environmental protection

Environmental protection and sustainable development have increassed in importance since the launch of economic reforms in 1978, from which time high economic growth has been at the expense of damage to the environment. This is because pollution reduces GDP due to associated costs. Specifically, these costs relate to the healthcare issues associated with treating victims of pollution-related illnesses, and economic losses arising from damage to the environment and loss of worker productivity. In 2004, pollution costs amounted to 3.05 per cent of China's GDP.[8] Indeed, 'rapid growth has brought with it substantial environmental damage that in some cases has slowed economic development, boosted domestic dissatisfaction, and contributed to instability within the country'.[9] The Green GDP project, which would have given a clearer indication of the economic cost of pollution and its impact on GDP, was stopped in 2007 due to pressure from local officials. It is clear that central government environmental policies are not effectively enforced at the local level as the local objective of maximizing economic growth is at the expense of environmental degradation.[10] However, the level of enforcement of central legislation varies with the degree of state capacity, defined as a combination of human capital, reach/responsiveness and fiscal strength.[11] Schwartz (2003) has shown that a relationship exists between provincial capacity and the level of provincial compliance with central government legislation regarding environmental protection. It was found that high capacity provinces, such as Liaoning, Jiangsu, Heilongjiang and Guangdong, demonstrate high levels of compliance with environmental legislation, compared to low capacity provinces, such as Shandong, Henan, Hunan, Guangxi and Yunnan, which display low levels of compliance. Of the high capacity/high compliance provinces two [Jiangsu and Guangdong] are Coastal provinces; and of the low capacity/low compliance provinces at least three are central provinces. These circumstances lend evidence towards a hypothesis that the Coastal provinces have benefited most from the post-1978 economic reforms (i.e. higher levels of human capital and higher fiscal strength). Moreover, Coastal leadership realized the economic and social costs of environmental degradation and adopted a lead role in enforcing environmental protection legislation. This approach may reflect the fact that without provincial environmental safeguards foreign investors will be wary of investing money at provincial level, instead favoring provinces which have a high commitment and capacity to enforce central environmental legislation.[12] With regards to Jiangsu, 'central government pressure has resulted in Jiangsu provincial government efforts to enforce environmental policies'.[13] This in turn incentivized Enviromental Protection Bureau [EPB] officials to adopt actions to protect the environment as they know that they have the backing of provincial, municipal and central authorities. However, in a majority of the least developed provinces this may not be the case. In these provinces, provincial and municipal authorities may be unwilling to support the actions of local EPB officials in protecting the environment from the impact of economic development. Moreover, Schwartz (2003) points out that 'the lack of commitment often found among officials opens the door to an important aspect of low commitment contributing to ineffective enforcement – corruption'. Intuitively, this may be a reason why manufacturing firms in the Coastal regions are relocating to sites further inland – they are free to pollute as long as they make profits and bring wealth to provincial coffers.

Environmental issues facing China today relate to industrial pollution, soil erosion and river damage, water and air pollution. In 1973 the first government institution to focus on enviromental protection was formed, transforming into the National Environmental Protection Agency in 1988, and then into the State Environmental Protection Administration [SEPA] in 1998. The latter became the Ministry of Environmental Protection in March 2008. The Chinese Ministry of Health (MoH), although playing no part in the prevention of diseases caused by pollution, 'tend to deal primarily with the consequences of environmental pollution on health, rather than taking a more proactive and preventative position'.[14] In February 2007, the MoH and SEPA started an inter-agency mechanism aimed at generating better data and providing for education and training. The MoH and SEPA share their duties for environmental issues with the Ministry of Construction which deals with waste management issues. This results in a conflict of interests.

Environmental protection became a national principle in 1983, a policy for sustainable development being instituted in 1994, with the first environmental protection regulations enshrined within the Ninth Five-Year plan in 1996.[15] Environmental protection regulations were rolled out in the Tenth Five-Year plan (2001–2005). With regards to enterprises the most significant regulation was that the authorities could collect fees from those polluting enterprises, and use those fees for environmental protection.[16] These fees represented a type of environmental protection tax, in effect forming a market for the externality of pollution. In China's Eleventh Five-Year plan (2006–2010) there were several objectives referring to environmental protection. The main objective regarding environmental protection was to reduce energy consumption per unit of GDP by 20 per cent and pollutant discharges by 10 per cent by 2010.[17] There were other aspects of the plan relevant to environmental protection.[18] First, economic restructuring which moulded environmental protection into industrialization. Second, an improvement in all aspects of law enforcement relating to pollution. Third, the utilization of technology and innovation to meet the needs of Environmental Protection (i.e. clean coal technologies). Fourth, improving the use of environmental education to inform the public about environmental damage. And, finally, an improvement in the cooperation between local and national government to make Environmental Protection more effective. An initiative was also started in the latter part of 2007 which focused solely on research and regulatory responses to environmental health issues arising from air, water and solid waste pollution.[19] As of March 2009, the Chinese government invited bids to conduct research into various aspects of environmental protection to be implemented in the Twelfth Five-Year plan.[20]

Global financial crisis

The roots of the financial crisis, which surfaced in July 2007 and became worldwide following the collpase of Lehman Brothers in September 2008, lay in the sub-prime mortgage market in the United States. Between 2001 to 2003 mortgage lending in the United States rose dramatically and this trend continued until 2006.[21] The main problem was that home loans were made to borrowers who would be unable to continue their repayments in the event of unemployment or if interest rates increased.

In the period 2004–2006, US$1.4 trillion were securitized, representing 79.3 per cent of all sub-prime mortgages. According to Lapavitsas (2009) 'securitisation involved parcelling mortgages into small amounts, placing them into larger composites, and selling the lots as new securities held by financial institutions across the world'. As interest rates began to rise, after 2004, mortgage foreclosures increased. The result of the latter was that the underlying securities became unsaleable. This in turn raised questions about the solvency of banks that preferred to hoard liquid assets instead of continuing to extend credit to the market. The resulting liquidity shortage was epitomized by the movement between the 3 month London Inter-bank offered rate (LIBOR) or interbank lending rate and the 3 month Overnight Indexed Swap (OIS) rate, with the former exceding the latter after August 2007, reaching a peak in Sept/Oct 2008.[22] Thus, liquidity dried up with banks unwilling to lend to each other, and consequently to firms and consumers. The impact of this was reduced consumption, increasing unemployment and an overall contraction in the economies of developed countries whose consumers had created the demand for Chinese exports. As demand from western consumers dried up the export capacity of Chinese firms began to contract resulting in the unemployment of millions of Chinese workers in the Coastal provinces, who had to return to their homes in China's interior provinces. While this level of unemployment may cause rural unrest, it may also support the economic development of China's interior provinces. The mechanism for this economic development rests with the skills of returning workers and the November 2008 fiscal stimulus by the Chinese government instituted to mitigate the impact of the global financial crisis on China's economy.

An interesting aspect of Chinese overseas investments post September, 2009 was that holdings of US treasury bonds by the Chinese government continued to expand as indicated in Figure 4.2. As exports collapsed, leaving millions unemployed in exporting regions such as Guangdong and Shenzhen, the Chinese government announced a stimulus package which involved increased spending in ten key areas:[23]

(a) housing
(b) rural infrastructure
(c) transportation
(d) health and education
(e) environment
(f) industry

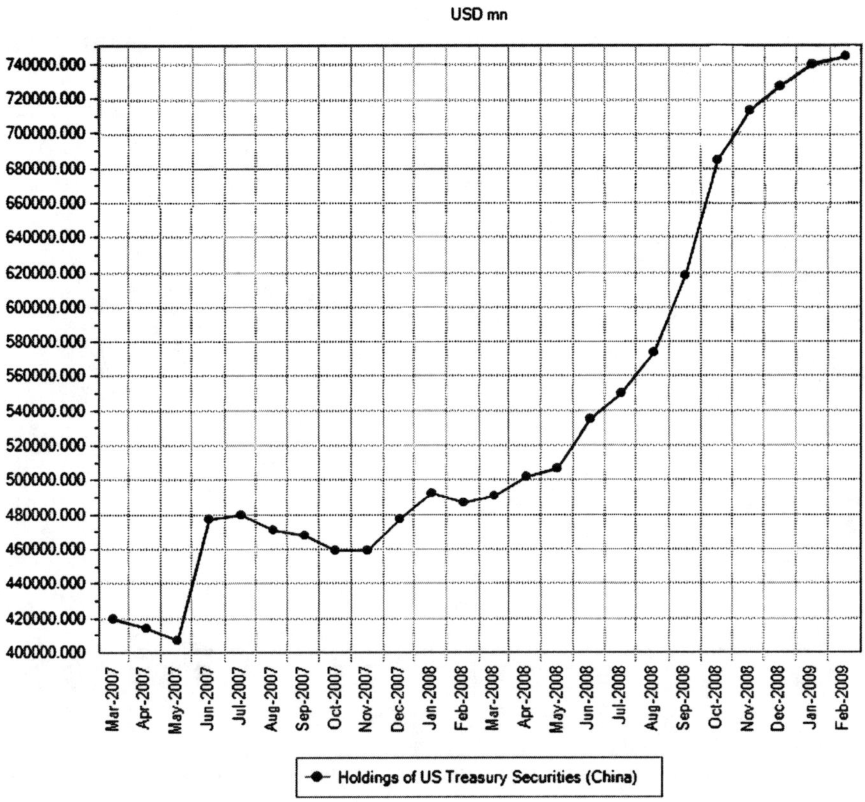

Figure 4.2 China's holdings of US treasury securities May 2007 to February 2009.

Source: www.ceicdata.com

(g) disaster rebuilding
(h) incomes
(i) taxes
(j) finance.

In relation to economic development these categories of spending may be more specifically defined. For example, housing, health and education, and disaster rebuilding may be defined in terms of the redistribution of wealth. Rural infrastructure and transportation may be defined in terms of the integration of China's economy, easing the distinction between Coastal, Central, Western, rural, and urban economies. The fiscal stimuli addressing the environment may be related to sustainable development, while incomes, taxes, and finances may be related to institutional development. In short, the fiscal stimulus of November 2008 is facilitating China's economic growth through the redistribution of wealth, market integration, and sustainable and institutional development.

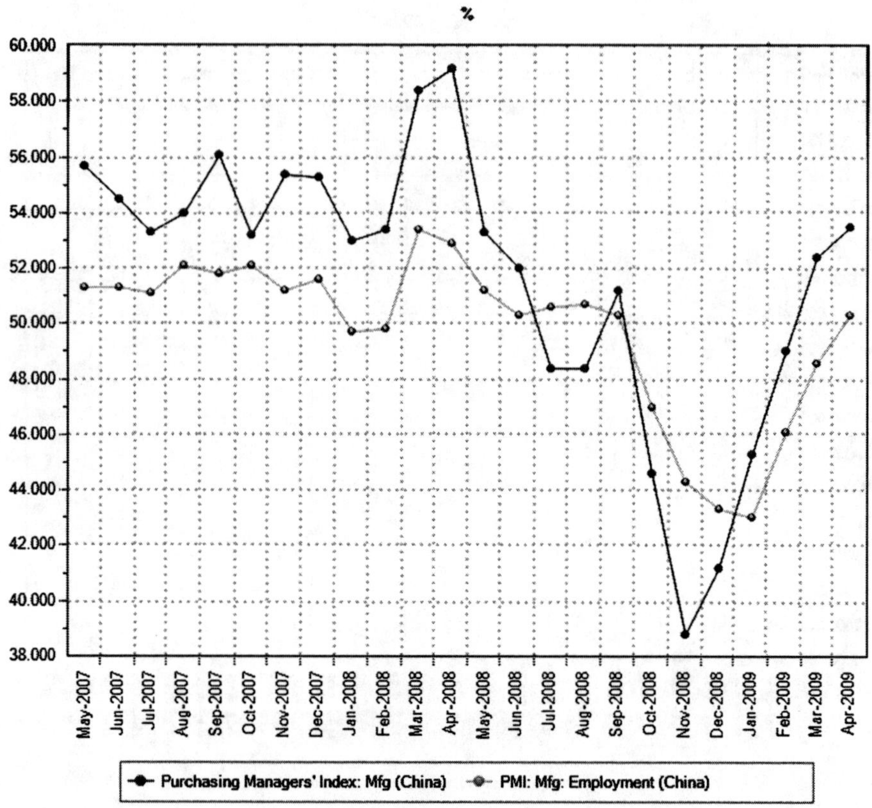

Figure 4.3 Purchasing managers' index (China) – manufacturing and employment.

Source: www.ceicdata.com.

One clearly discernible measure of economic activity in the Chinese economy is the changes in the Purchasing Managers' Index. The result of stimulus spending by the government resulted in increased economic activity evidenced by changes in the Purchasing Managers Index, and illustrated in Figure 4.3 above. Both indices for manufacturing and employment began to fall in March 2008, indicating decreased economic activity. However, having hit a trough in November 2008, both indicies have risen since then, suggesting increased economic activity and thus expansion in the Chinese economy. This may be due to the impact of the November 2008 economic stimulus.

It must be emphasized that despite the problems associated with bad corporate and individual debts facing Western banks, Chinese banks are in better shape. This is due mainly to three reasons: First, the Chinese government took early steps to remove non-performing loans from the books of Chinese banks. Second, Chinese banks sought larger deposits to support home loans than did their western

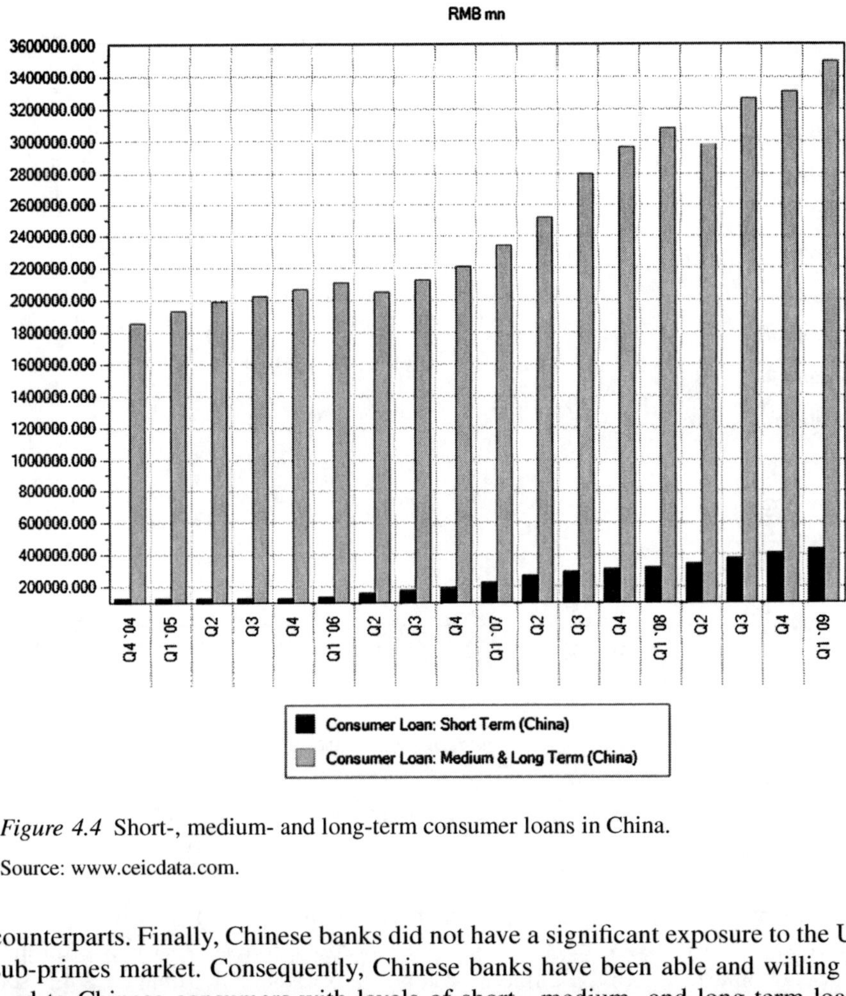

Figure 4.4 Short-, medium- and long-term consumer loans in China.

Source: www.ceicdata.com.

counterparts. Finally, Chinese banks did not have a significant exposure to the US sub-primes market. Consequently, Chinese banks have been able and willing to lend to Chinese consumers with levels of short-, medium- and long-term loans increasing. This is demonstrated in Figure 4.4 above, and is in sharp contrast to the liquidity problems experienced by Western banks.

It is clear from Figure 4.4 that, from the first quarter of 2006 to the first quarter of 2009, the levels of short-, medium- and long-term consumer loans have shown steady increases. Short-term loans may be for goods such as cars, whereas medium- and long-term loans may be for the purchase of items with a higher capital value, such as an apartment. This consumer loan facet of the Chinese economy is indicative that bank lending to consumers in China is elastic, suggesting that Chinese consumer demand is not only buoyant but also increasing.

Yet another feature of China's economy, which indicates its relative health compared to other economies, is the upward trend on the current account balance of payments, as shown in Figure 4.5. In addition to the increase in consumer loans,

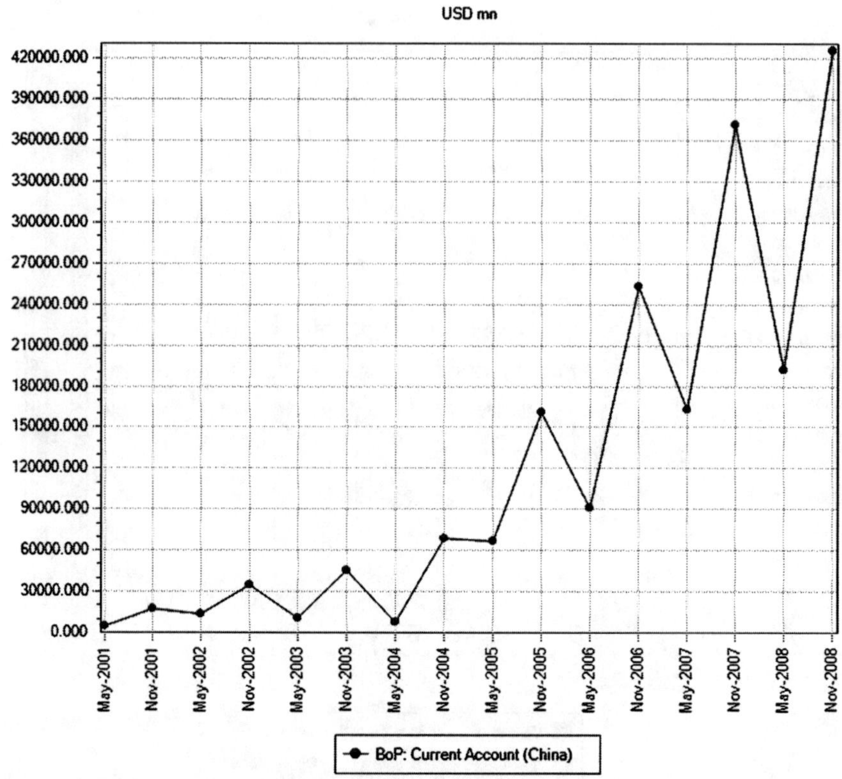

Figure 4.5 China's current account balance of payments.

Source: www.ceicdata.com.

this bodes well for China's economic growth which many pundits have suggested will only grow by a maximum of 6 per cent in 2009. However, evidence on the macroeconomic health of the Chinese economy, presented in this chapter, suggests that Chinese economic growth in 2009 should reach 6 per cent, and perhaps also exceed it, even without the support of the former levels of exports. Therefore, a combination of the global economic crisis and tougher labour and environmental legislation may be the catalyst which affords increased economic development in China's interior provinces. It may be the case that economic prosperity emanating from the post-1978 economic reforms, which has locked itself into China's Coastal regions for the past 30 years, may finally have started to move westward, demonstrating the continental drift of China's economic development.

Continental drift

A number of regional development theories portray how economic development spreads from one region of a country to another. However, these theories are generalizations and none give a clear image of the specific mechanisms influencing the continental drift of economic development. It is the contention of this study that a combination of enhanced labour legislation, environmental protection in the Coastal regions, and the global economic crisis, are driving the drift in economic development from China's Coastal regions to its interior. The specific causes are increased labour costs, tougher enforcement of environmental protection by provincial governments in the Coastal provinces, and a government fiscal stimulus focused on the redistribution of wealth, market integration, and sustainable and instititutional development.

China's post-1978 economic development was regionally based with the Coastal provinces and their SEZ's and open coastal cities taking a lead role. The SEZ's facilitated economic growth through the manufacture of exports. Indeed, regional economics depend largely on locational theory and international trade theory,[24] and has often been associated with the regional policy pursued by a sovereign state in pursuit of national economic growth. Indeed a specific regional policy has formed the development strategy of many developing countries. In China regional policy in the post-1978 reform years was one of urban bias and development of the Coastal regions. It was anticipated that prosperity from the Coastal regions would trickle into the Chinese hinterland. In terms of location, this policy meant that one region was favourably discriminated in terms of the allocation of resources and power.[25] The Coastal regions of China received a very large developmental impulse as government policy meant that they received a high proportion of Foreign Direct Investment (FDI) as many of the initial economic reforms were focused on opening up the Coastal regions to international markets. In addition, enterprises in the Coastal regions had easy access to world markets for manufactured goods and incentives to import capital goods. The costs associated with moving goods, people and information have been identified as a key variable in regional economics.[26]

Some of the key theorists in regional development theory include Myrdal and Friedmann. Myrdal (1957) argues that once a particular region experiences development then this will have a momentum of its own drawing in resources, labour and capital from poorer surrounding areas. Indeed the greater the mobility of labour, capital, resources and trade, then the greater will be what Myrdal (1957) calls the 'backwash' effects. These backwash effects relate to peripheral regions losing labour, through migration to richer regions, and capital, due to greater investment returns in richer regions. These backwash effects are akin to negative externalities i.e. pollution. In the case of China, since economic reform was started in 1979, there has been a net migration of labour from the rural sector in the hinterland regions to the booming regions on the Coast. Furthermore, Myrdal (1957) defines the positive effects of development as spread effects. For example, the building of an army base in a town may result in infrastructure being built. Myrdal (1957) argues that spread effects are greater in developed countries than in developing countries. On the other hand, Friedmann (1966) argues that once a centre-periphery relationship is established market forces dictate that there will be a divergence in the economic growth rate of centre and periphery. The centre will grow much faster than the periphery leading to an income disparity between the two. In the domestic Chinese economy, if one considers the centre to be the Coastal regions of China and the periphery to be the Central and Western regions, then in terms of income disparities between centre and periphery, reality is as theory indictates. Furthermore, in the context of the global economy, the Coastal region of China may be considered to be a periphery to the international market as the centre.

It is due to the weakness of market forces to bring about a convergence in the incomes of centre and periphery that, Friedmann (1966) argues, there is a role for government economic policy to ensure such convergence occurs. In an attempt to balance the growth of the Western and Central regions with that of the Coastal region, the 2000–2005 [Tenth] Five-Year plan focuses on investing in infrastructure in the Western regions of China. Thus, by attempting to reduce and eliminate income disparities between regions, government regional policy seeks to reconfigure the spatial distribution of factors and units of production so that there is an equal distribution of productive assets in the spatial economy. In essence, the distinction between periphery and centre disappears and fragmented markets become fully integrated. Furthermore, the combination of tougher labour and environmental legislation, in conjunction with the government's fiscal stimulus [09/08 and the Western Development plan], is blurring the distinction between the core Coastal region and the periphery interior and Western regions.

These mechanisms of homogeneous economic growth form an effective regional policy, which has two characteristics.[27] The first is that interconnected urban regions replace the periphery. The second is that the fragmented markets in the spatial economy are integrated into one market. This integration is best implemented through a programme of investment in infrastructure. Due to the building of roads, bridges and railways, fragmented markets will be connected leading to the transmission of information, market signals, resources and goods from one market to another. However, Gore (1984) argues that spatial equilibrium may not be Pareto optimal for two reasons. The first is that an activity may generate externalities [pollution and the exploitation of labour] which may not be measurable in terms of cost or price, and is generally characterized by market failure. The free market mechanism cannot effectively allocate resources in the presence of externalities. There is thus a case for government intervention with the implementation of environmental protection laws and enhanced labour legislation. The second reason that spatial equilibrium may not be Pareto optimal is that competition will not be perfect due to the existence of transport costs between locations. Thus, in the presence of market imperfections such as externalities and transports costs the implication is that in spatial terms general equilibrium cannot be Pareto optimal. If perfect competition is not possible across spatial points then general equilibrium theory and the spatial economy are incompatible.[28] The locational interdependence of firms is further exhibited by what are called agglomeration economies. This is a type of externality which causes other firms to save costs in a market due to the presence of increasing returns to scale to one firm in the market.

Chinese economic development has been uneven because the Coastal regions have received the biggest stimulus for economic growth through the implementation of favourable government economic policies. This resulted in a spatial pattern of productive units characterized by a concentration of those units in the Coastal regions. This may not be the spatial pattern that optimally maximizes the national growth rate or that facilitates an equal distribution of income throughout society. The Western Development policy favours investment in the Western regions at the expense of investment in the Coastal regions. The type of investment the government is promoting in the Western regions is investment in 'core infrastructure', i.e. the building of roads, bridges and railways. Where inter-regional income inequity is addressed by dispersing industry, as was done under the 'Third Front' program, then in the short run this can be seen as a trade off between a higher national growth rate and greater inter-regional income equity.[29] In the long run, structural transformation in the spatial economy, i.e. greater investment in core infrastructure, will bring about sustained economic growth and greater interregional income equality. Hirschmann (1958) sees disparities in regional income as the inevitable consequence of economic growth. Indeed, government policies designed to address imbalances in spatial development patterns within a country by promoting growth in poorer regions may lead to greater disparities between regions.[30]

The Coastal regions of China have experienced rapid economic growth over the last 25 years. Accompanying this rapid economic growth has been the rapid urbanization of China's Coastal cities and towns. This rapid urbanization has brought with it the migration of millions of rural people to urban centres, seeking work and a share of the prosperity. However, the paradox is that the Hukou system acts to prevent the movement of peoples from one region of the country to another. Nevertheless, this system has not had the intended effect on the movement of labour in China due the actual migration of labour from the hinterland to Coastal regions. The effects of the rapid urbanization of Coastal regions have been an increase in the demand for housing, infrastructure capacity, social services, and greater levels of crime. However, due to existing infrastructure, such as ports, railways and roads, firms will be able to benefit from investments they themselves have not made. These are termed agglomeration economies and the formation which are fundamental to Krugman (1991) and his 'New Geographical Economics'.

Friedmann (1972) developed a general theory of polarized development. Central to Friedmann's theory is that impulses of innovation are transmitted from the core regions to the periphery regions, and that the domination of the periphery by the core causes conflict between those in positions of authority in the core and the periphery. Thus, Friedmann (1972) adds a political dimension to regional development analysis. The process occurs in three stages. First, the core region imposes on the periphery region what Gore (1984) terms a state of 'organised dependency'. Second, the core region reinforces the state of 'organised dependency' through six feedback effects of core region growth. These effects include the dominance, information, psychological, modernization, linkage and production effects. Third, core region growth will result in the flow of information to the periphery because of the introduction of core region innovations into the dominated periphery. This results in unforeseen side effects of core region dominance.[31] If the periphery region successfully challenges the independence of the dominating core region, then the probability of information exchange and the probability of innovation will increase over the whole spatial economy. This will induce Myrdal spread effects, a weakening of the core order of political hierarchy, establishment of new core regions, and gradual integration of the dominated periphery regions with core regions. Therefore, fragmented markets will become integrated in the spatial economy to a single homogenous market. However, Friedmann's theory is deficient as it ignores the role of infrastructure. Without infrastructure the third stage is muted, if not negated.

The New Economic Geography seeks to explain the formation of economic agglomerations in the spatial economy under a general equilibrium framework. At one end of the spectrum lies the global core–periphery structure represented, in the main, by the three trading blocks of Europe, North America and East Asia. At the other edge of the spectrum are the regional income disparities that occur within the spatial economy of the nation state, as in the case of China where regional income disparities occur between the Western, Central and Coastal regions. Furthermore, regional and urban agglomerations are reflected by the existence of a number of cities where various industries are nested. Within the cities, industrial activities tend to agglomerate within certain areas and service industries within their own areas.

The distribution of economic activity in the city spatial economy is highly dependent on local geographical topography, but the distribution of economic activity is not difficult to explain within the context of competitive economic theory.[32] However, the same framework cannot be used to explain why the dispersion of industries occurs. In this regard the mechanisms for the dispersion of industry from China's Coastal regions to the interior elucidated in this chapter provides an insight on the specific factors which may cause industry to disperse during the course of economic development, and thus provide for balanced regional development. The picture of economic activity within China can be assessed by evaluating monthly data for Fixed Asset Investment [FAI], Property Price [PP], Gross Output Value of Construction [GOVC] and provincial Income per Capita [IC]. In Figure 4.6, the monthly FAI for Guangzhou, Shenzhen, Chengdu and Xian can be seen. Chengdu has the largest FAI from February 2008. It must be noted that the Sichuan Earthquake did not strike until August 2008. From May to November 2008 FAI in Xian is greater than that in Guangzhou. The FAI in Shenzhen has shown a lower trajectory of growth since January 2008. This is the portrait of economic activity, presented by FAI data, after the implementation of environmental protection legislation and employment legislation but before the fiscal stimulus of November 2008. It is possible to infer that the first two mechanisms in the dispersion of economic activity were already having a significant impact on continental drift even before the government's four pillars of economic stimulus [wealth redistribution, market integration, sustainable development and institutional development] became active. Monthly data relating to Provincial IC is also

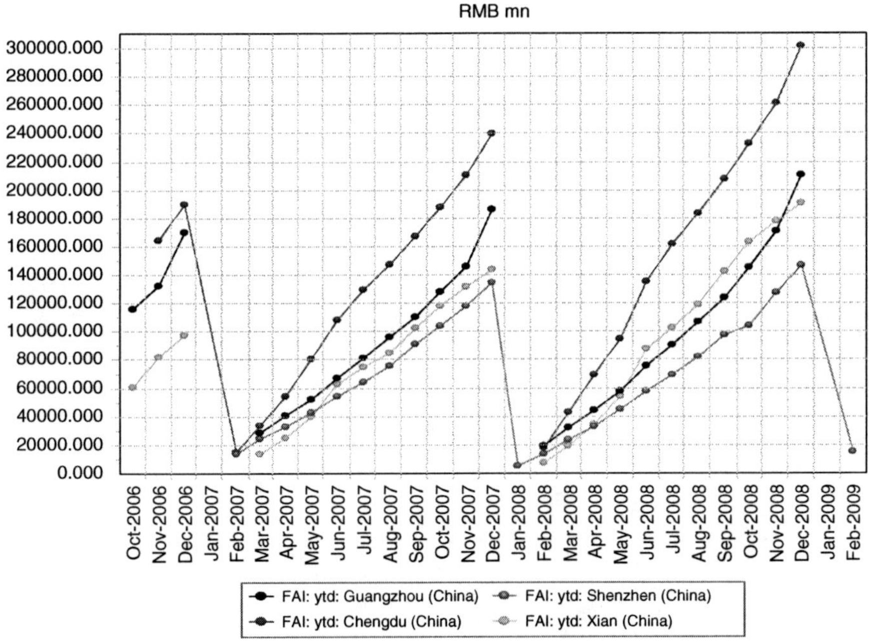

Figure 4.6 Fixed Asset Investment: Guangzhou, Shenzhen, Chengdu and Xian.

Source: www.ceicdata.com.

a good indicator of the strength of economic activity. This is reflected in Figure 4.7 which shows the Income per Capita from the first quarter of 2007 to the fourth quarter of 2008 for Changsha, Hefei, Lanzhou, Xining, Yinchuan and Urumqi. The IC for Changsha and Hefei, both in Central China, is higher in all quarters compared to the other provinces, of which three are in Western China. However, it is not possible to discern whether the higher IC of the Central provinces can be explained by a 'trickle-down' effect of prosperity from the Coastal provinces or tougher environmental protection in the Coastal provinces forcing firms to move further inland. The impact of tougher labour legislation would not have impacted on firms until after January 2008 when the November 2008 fiscal stimulus had not yet been proposed.

Changes in property prices reflect changes in the demand for property and is in itself a sign of the stability of provincial economic activity. Figure 4.8 below, shows the monthly property prices for the whole of China and the provincial cities of Hefei, Nanchang, Xian, Urumqi, Changsha and Xining. The data for the whole of China suggests that property prices, whilst indicating an upward trend, have been relatively stable since April 2007. Moreover, monthly property price data for Hefei shows an upward trend, while the data for Changsha illustrates an

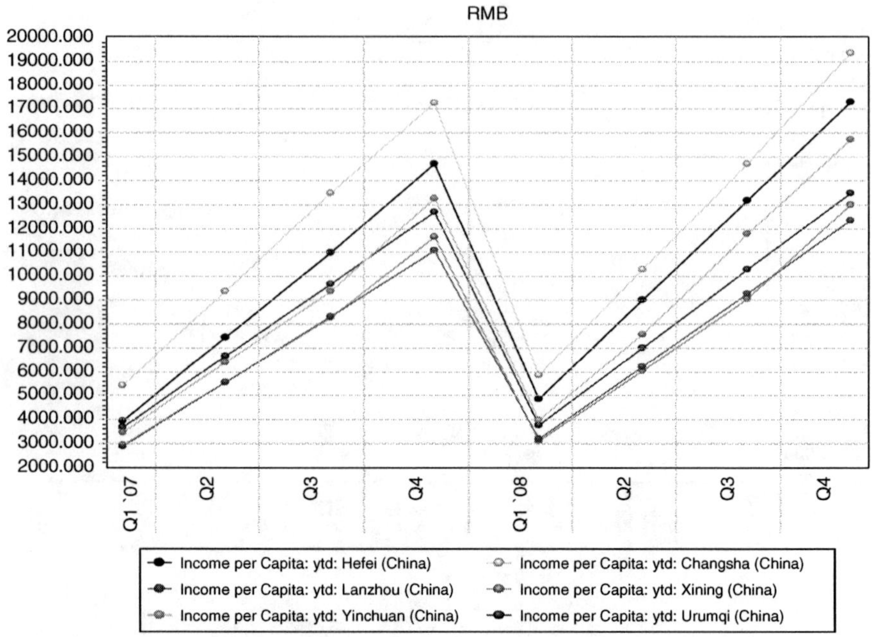

Figure 4.7 Income per capita: Hefei, Changsha, Lanzhou, Yinchuan, Xining and Urumqi.

Source: www.ceicdata.com.

upward trend since April 2008. This may reflect a movement of economic activity from other parts of China, perhaps from the Coastal regions where firms and people have shifted from one region to another, perhaps due to tougher environmental protection as this was prevalent prior to tougher labour legislation and the government's fiscal stimulus.

As of 1 August 2008, China's GOVC was up for the first half of 2008 by 24.4 per cent, compared to the first half of 2007.[33] At the provincial level, Figure 4.9, below, shows quarterly data for the GOVC for Jiangsu, Anhui, Henan, Hubei, Hunan and Guangdong, from the last quarter of 2005 to the last quarter of 2008. The GOVC includes the value of projects relating to the installation of equipment and the value of construction of buildings, as well as the value of repair to buildings.[34] It can be clearly seen from Figure 4.9 that Coastal provinces such as Guangdong and Jiangsu have the largest GOVC in every quarter. Nevertheless, the central provinces such as Henan, Hubei and Hunan follow with the next largest set of GOVC. This observation appears to be at odds with the notion that tougher environmental and labour legislation are driving firms further inland. However, this paradox may be solved by arguing that perhaps it is due to tougher environmental protection enforcement that firms and Multi National Corporations [MNC] are upgrading their facilities or building environmentally

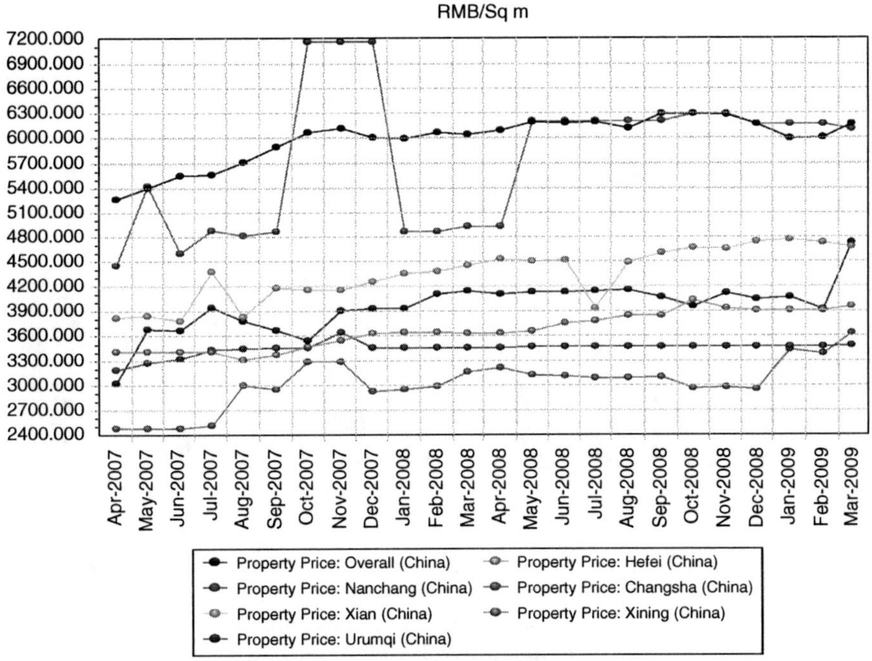

Figure 4.8 Property prices: China, Hefei, Nanchang, Xian, Urumqi, Hefei, Changsha and Xining.

Source: www.ceicdata.com.

compliant factories from scratch. Due to a lack of data it is not possible to discern whether this alternate argument is water tight in supporting the continental drift of economic development.

Conclusion

This chapter advanced the concept of a continental drift of economic development from China's Coastal regions to its interior, influenced by tougher environmental protection enforcement in China's Coastal provinces, increased labour costs for firms in the Coastal regions due to enhanced labour legislation, and the economic stimulus proposed by the Chinese government in November 2008. Due to the fact that exports to America and Europe from China fell as a result of the global economic crisis, the only way in which China's economy can grow at rates at or above 6 per cent is to light the fires of domestic consumption. This can happen if tougher enforcement of environmental protection legislation in the Coastal provinces and the increased costs associated with improved legal protection of workers makes firms move away from China's Coastal provinces to the interior. Firms moving

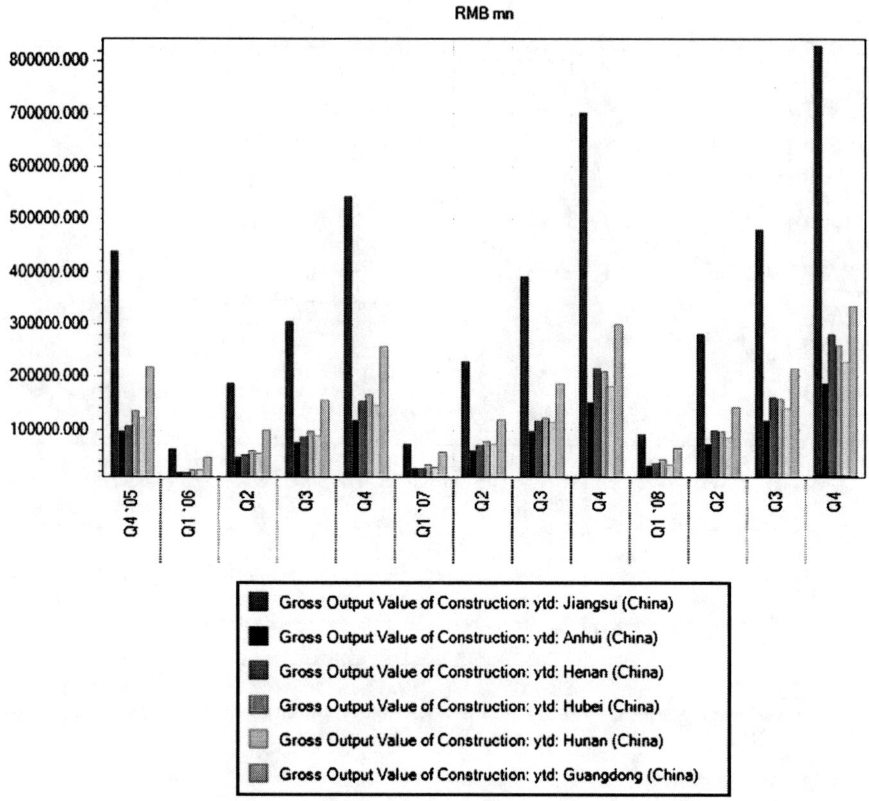

Figure 4.9 Gross output value of construction: Jiangsu, Anhui, Henan, Hubei, Hunan and Guangdong.

Source: www.ceicdata.com.

to China's interior would increase employment among workers in the interior and hence their incomes. Increased incomes would give workers a higher disposable income which may be used for consumption. However, firms can also move production to countries such as Vietnam. If firms move into China then this will surely act as a boost to the domestic economy by creating jobs in places which have not experienced the kind of prosperity seen in the Coastal provinces. Moreover, the fiscal boost of November 2008 will also boost domestic Chinese consumption through its four pillars – wealth redistribution, the effects of market integration, sustainable development and institutional development.

It might be argued that the data analysed in this chapter is not sufficiently robust to support the notion of continental drift. However, there is sufficient evidence that economic activity in China is robust and that perhaps tougher enforcement of environmental protection in China's Coastal provinces has had a greater impact on continental drift than tougher labour legislation or the fiscal stimulus of November 2008 (the impact of which is demonstrated by movements in the Purchasing Managers Index in Figure 4.3). Nevertheless, it is suggested that further research, such as the use of surveys to determine the impact of tougher enforcement of environmental protection legislation, and enhanced labour legislation, on firms and their intentions, should provide robust evidence in favour of continental drift.

Notes

1 This refers to a lack of infrastructure in the interior provinces. A concentrated investment in infrastructure as in the SEZ's of the coastal provinces would lead to a higher rate of return than if the infrastructural investment had been more sparsely spread in China's interior regions.
2 Liu, X. and Diamond, B. (2005), 'China's Environment in a Globalising World: How China and the rest of the world affect each other?' *Nature* Volume 435/30, June 2005.
3 Ibid.
4 Ibid.
5 Wang, H. *et al.* (2009), 'China's New Labour Contract Law: Is China moving towards increased Power for Workers?' *Third World Quarterly*, Vol. 30, No. 3, 2009, pp. 485–501.
6 Ibid.
7 Ibid.
8 Liu, X. and Gill, B. (2007), '*Assessing China's Response to the Challenges of Environmental Health*', Woodrow Wilson International Center for Scholars.
9 Schwartz. (2003), 'The impact of State Capacity on Enforcement of Environmental Policies: The Case of China', *Journal of Environment and Development*, Vol. 12, No. 1, March 2003, pp. 50–81.
10 Ibid.
11 Ibid.
12 Clarke, S. and Thomas, F. (1997), '*Pollution Control in the PRC: An Investors Guide*', London, Environmental Resources Management.
13 Ibid.
14 Liu, X. and Gill, B. (2007), '*Assessing China's Response to the Challenges of Environmental Health*', Woodrow Wilson International Center for Scholars.
15 Liu, J. and Diamond, J. (2005), 'China's Environment in a Globalising World: How China and the rest of the world affect each other?', *Nature* Volume 435/30, June 2005.
16 http://english.peopledaily.com.cn/200201/12/eng20020112_88510.shtml.
17 Xinhua News Agency, (2007), http://www.china.org.cn/english/government/225976.htm.
18 Ibid.
19 Liu, X. and Gill, B. (2007), '*Assessing China's Response to the Challenges of Environmental Health*', Woodrow Wilson International Center for Scholars.
20 http://www.chinaenvironmentallaw.com/2009/03/04/chinas-environmental-protection-12th-five-year-plan/.
21 Lapavitsas, C. (2009), '*Financialised Capitalism:Crisis and Financial Expropriation*', Research on Money & Finance, Discussion Paper 1, SOAS.
22 Ibid.
23 http://news.xinhuanet.com/english/2008-11/09/content_10332422.htm, downloaded 10 May 2009.
24 Gore, C. (1984). '*Regions in Question: Space, Development Theory and Regional Policy*', Methuen, London.
25 Ibid.
26 Ibid.

27 Ibid.
28 Richardson, H. W. (1969). '*Regional Economics: Location Theory, Urban Structure and Regional Change*'. New York, Praeger.
29 Ibid.
30 Barkin, D. (1972). 'A Case Study of the Beneficiaries of Regional Development'. *International Social Development Review* **4**: 84–94.
31 Ibid.
32 Fujita, M. and Mori, T. (2005). '*Frontiers of the New Economic Geography*'. Institute of Developing Economies Discussion Paper (27).
33 http://www.chinadaily.com.cn/bizchina/2008-08/01/content-6897589.htm.
34 Ibid.

References

Baran, P. (1957) *The Political Economy of Growth*, New York: Monthly Review Press.

Barkin, D. (1972) 'A Case Study of the Beneficiaries of Regional Development', *International Social Development Review*, 4: 84–94.

Clarke, S. and Thomas, F. (1997) *Pollution Control in the PRC: An Investor's Guide*, London: Environmental Resources Management.

Friedmann, J. (1966) *Regional Development Policy: A Case Study of Venezuela*, Cambridge: MIT Press.

Fujita, M. and Mori, T (2005) 'Frontiers of the New Economic Geography', Institute of Developing Economies Discussion Paper (27).

Gore, C. (1984) *Regions in Question: Space, Development Theory and Regional Policy*, London: Methuen.

Hirschmann, A. O. (1958) The *Strategy of Economic Development*, New Haven: Yale University Press.

http://www.chinadaily.com.cn/bizchina/2008-08/01/content-6897589.htm (accessed 10 May 2009).

http://www.chinaenvironmentallaw.com/2009/03/04/chinas-environmental-protection-12th-five-year-plan/ (accessed 10 May 2009).

http://english.peopledaily.com.cn/200201/12/eng20020112_88510.shtml (accessed 10 May 2009).

http://news.xinhuanet.com/english/2008-11/09/content_10332422.htm (accessed 10 May 2009).

Johnson, E. A. J. (1970) *The Organisation of Space in Developing Countries*, Cambridge, Mass: Harvard University Press.

Koopmans, T. C. and Beckmann, M. J. (1957) 'Assignment Problems and the Location of Economic Activity', *Econometrica*, 25: 53–76.

Krugman, P. (1991) 'Increasing Returns and Economic Geography', *The Journal of Political Economy*, 99 (3): 483–499.

Lapavitsas, C. (2009) 'Financialised Capitalism: Crisis and Financial Expropriation', Research on Money & Finance, Discussion Paper 1, SOAS.

Liu, J. and Diamond, J. (2005) 'China's Environment in a Globalising World: How China and the rest of the world affect each other?' *Nature*, 435 (30).

Liu, X. and Gill, B. (2007) 'Assessing China's Response to the Challenges of Environmental Health', Woodrow Wilson International Center for Scholars.

Myrdal, G. (1957) *Economic Theory and Underdeveloped Regions*, London: Duckworth.

Richardson, H. W. (1969) *Regional Economics: Location Theory, Urban Structure and Regional Change*, New York: Praeger.

Schwartz, J. (2003) 'The Impact of State Capacity on Enforcement of Environmental Policies: The Case of China', *Journal of Environment and Development*, 12 (1): 50–81.

Wang, H., Appelbaum, R. P. and Degiuli, F. (2009) 'China's New Labour Contract Law: Is China Moving Towards Increased Power for Workers?', *Third World Quarterly*, 30 (3): 485–501.

Xinhua News Agency (2007), Online. Available at: http://www.china.org.cn/english/government/225976.htm (accessed 16 May 2009).

5 Chinese MNCs in Latin America[1]

Gaston Fornes and Alan Butt-Philip

Introduction

The Chinese economy has become the world's fourth largest and, by some estimates, "could be the world's largest by 2025 in terms of purchasing power parity" (IADB 2004: 1). Although the Chinese domestic market is still far from mature many Chinese companies have started to look for opportunities abroad. It has been suggested that this international expansion is aimed at acquiring resources from Western economies in the form of knowledge, products, technology or even strategic positioning to secure the supply of raw materials. It has also been suggested that the Chinese outward internationalization process differs from patterns seen in other countries (Boisot and Child 1996; Buckley *et al.* 2007; Child and Rodrigues 2005; Child and Tse 2001).

Most Chinese investments in Latin American emerging countries have been made by state-owned enterprises (SOEs) or by private companies with support from China's government (Blazquez-Lidoy *et al.* 2006; La Tercera 2007b, c; Sanchez Ancochea 2006; Santiso 2006, 2007), apparently with weaker competitive capabilities compared to their Western competitors (Boisot 2004; Guthrie 2005; Rugman and Li 2007). The Chinese government seems to have taken a direct role in developing relationships with the most important Latin American countries (Argentina, Brazil, Chile, Ecuador, Peru and Venezuela) and strengthening their economic and political ties by signing investment and trade agreements.

It is in this context that the internationalization of Chinese companies in Latin American emerging countries is worth studying. First, because the support from the government, and second, the apparently weak competitive capabilities are increasingly referred to in the literature on China's outward internationalization to developed countries (Buckley *et al.* 2007; Child and Rodrigues 2005; Peng *et al.* 2008); the presence of these two factors in the investments in Latin America (LA) raises questions about the nature of the internationalization process for Chinese firms in emerging markets, as well as common areas (if any) with the internationalization process in developed countries.

The explosion (in both directions) of trade between China and LA may suggest a future wave of Chinese investments as companies currently selling products to Latin American markets take the next steps in the internationalization process in the short to medium term (going from exporting to contracting, and then foreign direct investment). In fact, a new strong axis of trade and investment between China and LA seems to be developing as flows of trade and investment exceed US$50 billion (ECLAC 2008, 2010), a figure similar to the value of trade between the European Union (EU) and Japan at the end of 1990s. Furthermore, this growth in the trade flows between China and LA appears to be different from other Chinese investments in developing countries, e.g. in Africa where trade growth is mainly in China's direction. It also tends to diverge from what might be expected in terms of current major Chinese investments in extractive industries and infrastructure in LA where this growth is mainly in the trade flow to China.

This chapter will review and analyse the literature on the internationalization process for Chinese companies in emerging economies, in particular in LA. In order to achieve this aim, the chapter is divided into four main sections. The first section will present a review of the literature on the internationalization process adopted by Chinese Multi National Corporations (MNCs), the main characteristics found in Chinese international firms, and the conceptual frameworks discussed in different studies. The second section will indicate the contextual framework for the analysis, while the third will discuss and analyse three main areas analysed in detail: the competitive capabilities of Chinese firms, supports provided by the Chinese government, and the possible consequences of the explosion in trade between China and LA. Finally, the fourth section will present the summary and conclusions relating to the main issues presented.

Literature review on the internationalization of Chinese MNCs

Previous works have found that

> the Chinese Communist Party retain[s] full control of the country's affairs and remain[s] firmly committed to many of socialism's key tenets... State agencies provid[e] most of the country's still-limited financial services.... Indeed, the state – and the Party – [are] central players in nearly all aspects of China's economy, guiding a development trajectory often labelled as capitalism with social characteristics.
>
> (Spar and Oi 2006: 1)

For example, "many of its MNEs remain in state hands, even though corporatised... which means that these firms still align their operations, whether at home or abroad, with the five-year plans and national imperatives" (Buckley *et al.* 2007). In addition, "China's developing capitalism is not solidly based on law, respect for property rights and free markets" (Blazquez-Lidoy *et al.* 2006: 10).

It is in this context that China's economy embarked on an outward internationalization process (Cai 1999; Tseng 1994) "after the Chinese government initiated its open-door policy at the end of the 1970s" (Cai 1999: 859). In this process it is possible to identify three main stages: a first mainly experimental stage up to the 1990s, characterized by strong supervision from the Government; a second stage during the 1990s which saw a large increase in the number of Chinese subsidiaries abroad, many of which reported losses, and with little evidence of strategic focus (Cai 1999; Quan 2001; Warner *et al.* 2004; Zhang and Van Den Bulcke 1996). Finally, the third stage commenced recently with China's accession to the World Trade Organization (WTO) when a number of leading Chinese firms went international "with a view to becoming global players in international markets" (Child and Rodrigues 2005).

In this context, Child and Rodrigues (2005) identified three routes adopted by Chinese companies in the internationalization process, namely: "(i) the partnership route, via original equipment manufacture (OEM) or joint venturing (JV), (ii) the acquisition route, and (iii) the organic expansion route" (p. 389). The first route, although regarded as inward internationalization, has been seen as a means of transferring knowledge from the international partner, which should eventually improve the Chinese firms' competitiveness. The second route is supported by an international shopping spree by Chinese firms – US$2.85 billion in 2003, roughly US$5.55 billion in 2004, US$12.2 billion in 2005, US$21.1 billion in 2006, and US$22.4 in 2007 (Business Week 2004; Santiso 2006; WTO 2008), with similar trends in 2008 and 2009 (ECLAC 2010; MOFCOM 2008). The third route is characterized by the "greenfield establishment of subsidiaries and facilities within targeted markets. It is initially aimed at securing differentiation advantages in terms, for example, of adjustment to local market needs and tastes" (p. 394).

Chinese MNCs: some characteristics

Different works have shown that Chinese firms operating overseas tend to lean on ethnic and other similar networks for business opportunities, relations with local authorities, and management of labor (Brown 1995; Buckley *et al.* 2007; Lecraw 1993; Yeung and Olds 2000). In this context, Rauch and Trindade (2002) found that "ethnic Chinese networks have a quantitatively important impact on bilateral trade through mechanisms of market information and matching and referral services, in addition to their effect through community enforcement of sanctions that deter opportunistic behaviour" (p. 129). Boisot and Child (1996) stated that Chinese managers use these networks to reduce transaction costs and explore new business opportunities.

Buckley *et al.* (2007) highlighted the apparent market imperfections where Chinese companies operate. These imperfections can be seen in: (i) some SOEs with capital available at below-market rates, (ii) subsidized or soft loans from banks influenced or owned by the government, (iii) an inefficient internal capital market that may encourage cross-subsidies in conglomerates, and (iv) cheap capital from family firms to fund international expansion. In this sense, Cai (1999) and Child and Rodrigues (2005) added that the influence of central and local governments seems to have directed many of the outward Foreign Direct Investment (FDI) processes to promote exports and secure raw materials abroad, although some SOEs also used FDI to acquire technology and skills.

Nolan (2001) argued that "the competitive capability of China's large firms after two decades of reform is still painfully weak in relation to the global giants" (p. 187) mainly in the areas of R&D, marketing ability, development of brands, and restrictions from the authorities. Nolan suggested that this is probably the result of the government's protection of the domestic market, advantageous funding conditions, protection of distribution channels and procurement from the government (for both state-owned and non-state enterprises).

Nevertheless, Zeng and Williamson (2003) claimed to have found a "new breed of Chinese companies that have already succeeded in capturing some foreign markets." These firms can be grouped as follows: (i) national champions, companies using their domestic strength to compete abroad, (ii) dedicated exporters, enterprises aiming at acquiring market share in international markets to strengthen their economies of scale, (iii) competitive networks, groups of companies that "have taken on world markets by bringing together small, specialized companies that operate in close proximity," and (iv) technology start-ups, firms exploiting technology developed by government-run research institutes (pp. 3–4).

Finally, Edwards (2007: 10) added that China's foreign exchange reserves, at more than US$1,000 billion, along with continuing "deregulation and integration into the global economy" will help Chinese companies to "gain new markets, technologies and control over resources." In this context, Mallet found that "China Development Bank... has begun to deploy some of its capital abroad, particularly to help Chinese energy and mineral companies working in developing countries" (2006).

The internationalization of Chinese MNCs: conceptual frameworks

The main question seems to be "whether FDI from emerging economies, and specifically from China, requires a special theory nested within the general theory" (Buckley *et al.* 2007). Most of the literature on the internationalization process for companies from emerging economies is based on mainstream theory developed in Western economies, based on their MNCs and adapted to the specific characteristics of developing countries, for example, Lecraw (1993) and Wells (1983). However, China's case it has been suggested that an extended theoretical framework may be required due to its newly developed capitalist system, its culture, and its different market institutions (Boisot and Child 1996; Child and Rodrigues 2005; Child and Tse 2001). After all, "China is different from other less developed countries in terms of market size, as well as cultural connections, and may not fall into a regular LDC [less developed country] category" (Makino *et al.* 2002: 412) and "is already a much more open economy than most emerging markets" (Blazquez-Lidoy *et al.* 2006). Santiso (2005a, b) also suggested that the Chinese internationalization process has presented a particular "cognitive effect" as it has been very pragmatic and the result of balanced efforts between markets and government intervention.

In this context, Child and Rodrigues (2005: 384–385) claimed that the specific characteristics of the Chinese outward internationalization process need to be analysed on their own merits. The first point supporting their claim is that China's emergence as an industrial power falls within the late development thesis (also applied to other East Asian countries), as China's companies need to catch up in terms of technology, know-how, and in the development of competitive business environments. Their argument in this area is based on Chinese firms' need to use outward FDI to close the gap with Western MNCs through the acquisition of assets and resources rather than by the exploitation of prior competitive advantages, the latter being the main assumption in mainstream theory (Buckley and Casson 1976; Dunning 1977).

Their second point concerns the Chinese government's role in the internationalization process, as many firms have received financial support and protection from the authorities to reduce their late-comer disadvantage.

The third point is a counterpart of the second: the companies receiving support and aid as described "could be weakened by the way they remain beholden to administrative approval and bear a legacy of institutional dependence" which may suggest that their strategic options are limited by the Chinese institutional environment.

The fourth point supporting their claim concerns Chinese culture and institutions including, for example, a reliance on close personal relationships and management styles, which may increase psychic distance (Johanson and Wiedersheim-Paul 1975). This liability of foreignness could eventually jeopardize the effectiveness of a strategy of acquiring resources abroad.

Mathews (2006) added three more characteristics: very rapid internationalization, an internationalization achieved through organizational innovations (rather than based on technological innovations), and the development of strategic innovations that enabled "them to exploit their latecomer and peripheral status to advantage" (p. 13).

Based on these characteristics, Mathews proposed an extension of the OLI (Ownership, Location, and Internalization) paradigm (Dunning 1977) as this traditional model uses "a 'push-oriented' concept" from Western MNEs where a firm's internationalization "is propelled by some strategic objectives" rather than by a pull and push process that seems to be the reality for most Asian Pacific companies (Mathews 2006: 16). This extended model, LLL (Linkage, Leveraging, and Learning), is also supported by the idea that the internationalization of "EE [emerging economies]-based firms is not necessarily based on the possession of overwhelming assets, but rather on a firm's ability to leverage its capability in organizational learning" (Yamakawa *et al.* 2008: 68).

Nevertheless, these views are contrasted with previous findings from Cai (1999) who suggested that "the motives for Chinese outward FDI are generally similar to those for FDI from other developing and developed market economies," even if the links with the authorities are visible. In this sense Cai listed the following motives for outward FDI: (i) "to seek, maintain or expand export markets", (ii) "to acquire a stable supply of resources", (iii) "to obtain foreign technology and management skills", (iv) "to raise capital, primarily in Hong Kong, for domestic use", and (v) for "political considerations" (pp. 867–874). Wong and Chan (2003) added two elements to this list: (vi) saturation in the home market, and (vii) avoidance of non-tariff barriers. Furthermore, Wong and Chan (2003), and Cai (1999) agreed that "China lacks personnel who possess international management skills and who have sufficient knowledge about market conditions of host countries... and a good understanding of the intricacies of international [business,] largely as a result of its long-time isolation from the world economy" (Cai 1999: 874).

Finally, in one of the first works modelling Chinese outward direct investments (ODI), Buckley *et al.* (2007) found that, on the one hand, the determinants of these ODI are market size, natural resource endowments, the institutional environment, policy liberalization/home country institutions and cultural proximity. On the other hand, they also found that "Chinese ODI is attracted, rather than deterred, by political risk," that China's capital market imperfections play an important role (especially in the measurement of risks), that state ownership can be considered as a firm-specific advantage, and that these factors combined "may have equipped Chinese MNEs with the special ownership advantages needed to be competitive in other emerging economies." They concluded by arguing that "for the present, Chinese outward investors clearly present marked contrasts from the conventional model in key aspects." In other words, these investments have "both a conventional and an idiosyncratic dimension" (pp. 513–514).

The internationalization of Chinese MNCs in Latin America: contextual framework

Trade between China and LA has increased more than ten-fold since 1995, due mainly to the Chinese demand for raw materials such as soya, iron ore and copper, and also because LA appears to be one of the most complementary trade partners for China (Lapper 2007; Santiso 2006).

An analysis of trade flows indicates that Mexico and Central America have growing deficits with China (ECLAC 2008, 2010). In fact, the Asian country has displaced Mexico as the United States' main trading partner, mainly due to the fact that Mexico and other Central American countries seem to have a similar export basket to China in low and intermediate technology manufacturing, as well as in textiles and apparel (ECLAC 2006: 43).

However, South American countries post trade surpluses through their supply of raw materials, food products, and energy products to fuel China's rapid growth. In fact, China has become a major trading partner for Brazil, Chile, Argentina and Peru. In addition, in South America China finds a favourable market for its exports as it has obtained the market economy status from many of its countries (ECLAC 2006: 41).

Table 5.1 represents LA and the Caribbean's trade structure with China by category, and indicates how this has changed between primary products (PPs) and manufacturing over the last 12 years. It is also possible to identify trade trends with the whole of LA, with the Mercosur countries and with other large South American countries.

Besides the increasing trade, "in 2004, 50 percent of Chinese FDI went towards LA (more than the 30 percent that went towards Asia)" (Blazquez-Lidoy *et al.* 2006: 35). In 2005 LA was the destination for 53 percent of all Chinese foreign investments; in 2006 the region received US$8.45 billion (40 percent of all

Table 5.1 Latin America and the Caribbean's structure of merchandise trade with China, by category

	Total Latin America				*Mercosur*				*Other South American countries*			
	Primary products	*%*	*Manufactures*	*%*	*Primary products*	*%*	*Manufactures*	*%*	*Primary products*	*%*	*Manufactures*	*%*
Exports from Latin America to China												
1996	569,123	20	2,339,183	80	296,377	16	1,540,808	84	235,097	27	632,250	73
1998	975,375	37	1,686,896	63	625,234	38	1,037,494	62	322,181	42	448,628	58
2000	1,780,767	47	1,993,374	53	1,289,937	65	688,242	35	457,250	31	1,013,822	69
2002	2,643,347	42	3,590,273	58	2,098,741	56	1,625,831	44	531,153	27	1,431,564	73
2004	6,410,593	46	7,373,034	53	4,682,442	57	3,541,854	43	1,654,489	34	3,230,328	66
2006	13,256,841	58	9,483,191	42	8,726,536	72	3,343,927	28	3,667,329	49	3,791,148	51
2008	25,196,800	62	15,443,200	38	17,368,000	76	5,614,000	24	7,039,000	50	7,056,000	50
Imports from China to Latin America												
1996	203,183	5	3,504,569	94	105,015	5	1,888,828	94	39,283	5	807,672	95
1998	283,683	5	5,230,959	94	142,909	6	2,235,832	94	47,293	4	1,247,108	96
2000	327,850	4	7,942,359	95	128,246	5	2,645,445	95	64,264	3	1,846,245	97
2002	511,887	4	11,243,492	95	279,813	12	2,034,586	88	49,073	2	2,577,520	98
2004	778,259	3	25,134,704	96	487,835	8	5,621,378	92	64,165	1	5,019,721	99
2006	569,900	1	49,925,673	98	210,216	2	12,725,867	98	90,330	1	8,859,689	98
2008	872,840	1	86,411,160	99	326,000	1	30,196,000	99	144,000	1	18,133,000	99

Source: Authors' calculations with data from (ECLAC 2008, 2010).

Note: Other South American countries: Bolivia, Chile, Colombia, Ecuador, Peru, Venezuela.

Chinese FDI for the period (MOFCOM 2007)), and a similar trend is apparent in 2008 (MOFCOM 2008). However, Chinese investment only represents around 1.5 percent of total FDI received by LA since 2005 (ECLAC 2006, 2008).

It is in this context that Santiso (2006: 96) claimed that "the expanding link between Asia and LA is symbolic of the economic shakeout going on worldwide." This situation is evident in the flows of trade and investment between China and LA exceeding US$50 billion (ECLAC 2008, 2010), a figure similar to the trade from the EU to Japan in the late 1990s, thus indicating a new commercial "axis" between these emerging countries.

The trade flows can be seen in Table 5.1 and are the result, among other things, of investment and trade agreements signed between China and Argentina, Brazil, Chile and Peru in 2004, with Venezuela in 2006, a Free Trade Agreement (FTA) between Chile and China signed in 2005 (Bravo 2006), an FTA signed between Peru and China (La Tercera 2007a; MOFCOM 2009), and China's membership of the Inter-American Development Bank (Lapper 2007). In addition, China has committed investments of around US$100 billion to the region by 2015 (Sanchez Ancochea 2006), probably with the aim of "controlling assets and exerting political influence" (Lapper 2005).

Discussion

From a review of the literature and the analysis of available data presented above, three main areas for discussion have been identified, namely, the competitive capability of Chinese MNCs, support from the government, and the possible consequences of an explosion in trade between China and LA. These will be further elaborated below.

Competitive capability of Chinese MNCs

Part of the debate on a suitable conceptual framework for the study of Chinese MNCs relates to the existence of prior competitive advantages (Porter 1980), whether firm-specific advantages (FSA) (Rugman *et al.* 2006), or ownership-specific advantages (Dunning 1977) by Chinese firms, and their ability to exploit these abroad (Buckley and Casson 1976), the latter reflecting the main assumption in mainstream internationalization theory. This debate is necessary in the context of China's integration into the world economy, and especially in the study of the competition that Chinese MNCs bring to developed countries.

This has been the focus of many works, for example Guthrie (2005) suggested that Chinese companies internationalize to acquire competitive advantages and complement their current strengths in the domestic market, such as low wages and production improvements resulting from international joint ventures or partnerships as well as government support. Boisot (2004) also stated that "many Chinese firms will not be moving abroad to exploit a competitive advantage that was developed in the domestic market, but to avoid a number of competitive disadvantages incurred by operating exclusively in the domestic market" (p. 6).

In addition, Rugman and Li's (2007) study of three acquisitions by Chinese MNCs in the United States, the UK and France added that they "mainly reflect China's country-specific advantages (CSAs) rather than FSAs" (p. 71). The authors also maintain that Chinese "MNEs are likely to develop by exploiting China's CSAs in cheap, unskilled, and skilled labor [as] it is highly unlikely that Chinese MNEs will go abroad in any significant numbers over the next five to ten years on the basis of FSAs" (p. 79).

These studies tend to question the value of some Chinese firms' existing internal strengths (FSAs) and their ability to use these strengths to internationalize their operations in developed economies. However, Wright *et al.* suggested that this debate, in the context of companies from less developed countries, should adopt a different perspective, and they argue that emerging markets are "a new context in which to understand the relative strengths and weaknesses of the different [conceptual] perspectives" used in conventional theory (p. 2).

In this sense, Wright *et al.* (2005: 7) added that "domestic firms competing within emerging economies face a 'high velocity' environment of rapid political, economic, and institutional changes that are accompanied by relatively underdeveloped factor and product markets." This changing environment presents different challenges for firms operating in these countries which have been widely documented in the literature (see for example (Filatotchev *et al.* 2003; Fornes 2008; Fornes 2009; Fornes and Cardoza 2009; Guillen 2000; Hoskisson *et al.* 2000; Khanna and Palepu 1997; Khanna and Palepu 2000; Peng 2003)). Most of these works on firms in emerging markets suggest that MNCs from these countries develop a set of specific advantages needed to cope with a changing environment and the relatively low development of the markets. These specific advantages can help companies successfully exploit opportunities in other emerging markets, or create a framework to develop the necessary resources to acquire, as well as to manage, assets in other countries.

For example, Wells (1981, 1983) found that companies from emerging economies successfully compete in other less developed countries as they can use advantages developed in the home market to cope with the uncertainty of the host market (mainly poor information on the value of local assets and weak distribution networks), and to deal with the weak legal framework protecting their technological knowledge. In addition, studies on asset-seeking FDI in less developed countries from Asia indicated that companies use this strategy to reinforce their price competitiveness, but also to strengthen their non-price competitiveness when investing in developed countries (Chen and Chen 1998; Kumar 1998).

In the case of Chinese companies in LA, the fact that they have displaced Mexico as the United States' main trading partner (ECLAC 2008) suggests that firms from China possess some advantages that they are applying abroad, particularly in the low and intermediate technology manufacturing sectors in countries with competing export baskets. The figures in Table 5.1, especially the growth in manufacturing exports from China, apparently confirm this advantage. Total exports from LA to China grew 14-fold between 1996 and 2008, with PPs exports expanding 44-fold and manufacturing only showing a seven-fold increase. PPs exports to China from the Mercosur grew more than 40 times during the same period (manufacturing growth was limited to only four times), while PPs from other South American countries grew 30-fold and manufacturing only displayed an 11-fold increase. On the other side, total exports from China during the same period increased 23 times, with manufacturing the largest element and PPs showing a more modest, four-fold, growth. Manufacturing imports by Mercosur increased 16 times, while other South American countries experienced a 22-fold increase (compared to PPs growth for each region of three and four times respectively). Some of the increase in PPs exports can be explained by a price effect, as most of the commodities exported by LA, especially in the Mercosur region, experienced a substantial price increase (two, three, or four times in many cases). This apparently greater competitiveness relative to Latin American companies can partly be explained by country-specific advantages, such as: (i) a higher rivalry in the domestic market (Porter 1998), where China "is already a much more open economy than most emerging markets" (Blazquez-Lidoy *et al.* 2006) and particularly more open than most Latin American countries (perhaps with the exception of Chile), (ii) access to state-supported research (Child and Rodrigues 2005; Zeng and Williamson 2003), (iii) domestic cost advantages (Rugman and Li 2007), (iv) institutional factors (Buckley *et al.* 2007), and/or (v) economies of scale from a large domestic economy and market (Rui and Yip 2007; Zeng and Williamson 2003).

Nevertheless, the question regarding firm-specific advantages remains. Trade figures and the industries/products (low and intermediate technology manufacturing) in which Chinese companies are gaining market share, suggest that the competitive capabilities of these firms are stronger than those of Latin American companies. Some of these advantages have probably been transferred to Chinese firms through OEM agreements or JVs (Guthrie 2005), and now Chinese enterprises are using this enhanced competitiveness to enter new markets in other emerging economies (Chen and Chen 1998). Latin American companies have also participated in arrangements similar to OEMs or JVs (maquiladoras, for example). However, the data in Table 5.1 suggests that firms from LA are losing out to Chinese competition. Therefore, it is possible to say that China's MNCs already possess some competitive capabilities that, although not yet completely developed and consolidated to compete against companies in developed countries, allow them to successfully compete in Latin American markets. Rugman and Li phrase it differently: "in general, China lacks firms with FSAs . . . in comparison to Western MNEs in the world's top 500" (2007: 79) but LA has fewer companies in this list. If this is eventually confirmed (when more data becomes available), it will have important implications for the conceptual frameworks used to analyse the internationalization of Chinese companies, as discussed.

This sub-section has attempted to analyse the literature and evidence on the relative competitive capabilities of Chinese firms compared to their Latin American counterparts. This analysis is relevant in the context of this study as previous works suggested that the competitive capabilities of Chinese firms is relatively weak comparative to those possessed by MNEs from developed countries. The results tend to indicate that, first, Chinese companies enjoy a set of CSAs that allow them to compete successfully against Latin American companies in specific sectors (low and intermediate technology manufacturing, textiles, and apparel, for example). Previous works reached similar conclusions (Blazquez-Lidoy *et al.* 2006; Rugman and Li 2007; Rui and Yip 2007; Zeng and Williamson 2003). Second, the results suggest that firms from China are in possession of firm-specific advantages that are strong enough to allow them to successfully compete in Latin American emerging economies. This differs from previous works in industrialized economies indicating that Chinese firms' FSAs are still relatively weak compared to their Western counterparts (Nolan 2001; Rugman and Li 2007). The latter conclusion may be biased by the trade and investment agreements described in the contextual framework, therefore this will be studied under the "Possible consequences of the explosion in the trade..." section below.

This section also indicated that too much emphasis was devoted to China's outward internationalization in developed countries, while little attention was paid to the country's trade and investment relations with less developed countries, particularly LA which has received around half of the funds invested abroad by China (Blazquez-Lidoy *et al.* 2006; MOFCOM 2007, 2008; Sanchez Ancochea 2006; Santiso 2006). Another issue is that the methods adopted in the majority of studies of China's MNCs tend to be static (utilizing case studies and analysing qualitative data). Therefore comparative studies and other methods based on quantitative information are needed to develop an understanding of this phenomenon, especially the relative value of Chinese firms' FSAs. Finally, the need for longitudinal research is evident in the many questions raised by different research studies on Chinese MNCs, especially those on the sustainability of investment returns once the first wave of FSAs, probably acquired from OEMs or JVs, had been exhausted. Unfortunately, the data required for this kind of study is not readily available for the period prior to 2000 and also some sources are not completely reliable.

Support from the government

The committed Chinese investment in LA (by 2007) can be divided into (the percentage represents roughly the number of companies in each category):[2] (i) state-owned companies investing relatively large amounts of money in extractive industries (46 percent), (ii) relatively large investments in infrastructure projects agreed between the Chinese government and the host country (27 percent), (iii) medium-sized companies investing relatively small amounts of money in natural resources (19 percent), and (iv) large private companies aiming for a share of the domestic markets (7 percent). This list indicates that the majority of Chinese investments are either extractive industries or infrastructural projects, presumably to improve the transportation of raw materials to China, with the former investments largely involving SOEs and the latter presumably funded by state-owned banks.

Chinese government support is evident in the LA investments outlined above, a characteristic also identified in previous research on investments in developed countries (Cai 1999; Child and Rodrigues 2005). Buckley *et al.* (2007), for example, found that this support is visible in some SOEs providing capital at below-market rates and in subsidized or soft loans from banks influenced or owned by the government.

However, there seems to be a difference in the case of LA as the Chinese government has adopted a more direct participation, with most of the investments committed to by China's government (La Nación, 2004a, b, c, d) rather than by a group of SOEs/MNEs as is the case in most developed countries. This direct participation in initiatives beyond China's borders suggests a different pattern of supports than those identified in previous works (Buckley *et al.* 2007; Child and Rodrigues 2005; Peng *et al.* 2008) where this support has been mainly in the home country.

This support outside the country is also evidenced by the Chinese government actively pursuing the signing of treaties and trade and investment agreements with Latin American and other emerging economies (ECLAC 2007). For example, by 2006, China had signed agreements with 32 countries or groups of countries in Africa, Asia, LA, and the southern Pacific, representing 25 percent of the country's total trade in 2005 (Bin 2006). In fact, it has been suggested that China is using trade and investment agreements, among other things, to ensure recognition of its market status economy by its counterpart countries (ECLAC 2005, 2007). So far, most of the states that have recognized China as a market status economy are developing countries. The ECLAC (2007) stated that many of these agreements do not include sensitive products or sectors such as the protection of intellectual property, the liberalization of sectors, or issues related to labor or the environment (the latter may explain why China is pursuing agreements with developing countries (ECLAC 2007), as it will probably find a limited reception with industrialized countries if, for example, these sensitive areas were not included in the agreements.

This framework raises questions about the literature on the internationalization of Chinese firms in other emerging markets, in particular LA. For example, most of the investments made by Chinese SOEs are taking the form of JVs with other SOEs in LA (e.g., with Brazil's Petrobras and Companhia Vale do Rio Doce (CVRD), with Chile's Codelco and with Venezuela's Petró leos de Venezuela (PDVSA)) in contrast to the generic, and usually sequential, strategies (exporting, contracting, and FDI) followed by most Western companies when internationalizing (Buckley and Casson 1998; Buckley and Ghauri 1993; Root 1994). This implies that the entry mode of Chinese companies in LA is an area in need of future research.

In addition, this JV strategy, where Chinese firms appear to be providing most of the funding (La Tercera 2007c), may expose Chinese companies to the potential discretion of host governments, and therefore may have negative implications for relationships between the countries. The potential risks and/or gains presented by this strategy involve a relatively complex situation that is worth studying, as Chinese investments in natural resources could create a potential overdependence on Latin American countries. Also, LA's infamous political and economic instability could be an issue, given the current early stage of internationalization by Chinese companies. This offers limited options to offset, via investments in other regions, any potential negative consequences of changes in the business environment.

In any case, the Chinese government's support for the internationalization of Chinese companies in emerging markets raises a similar question to that posed by Buckley *et al.* (2007) about "whether FDI from emerging economies and, specifically, from China requires a special theory nested within the general theory." In other words, are China's institutional conditions adequately recognized in existing theories? For example, theory suggests that the internationalization of Chinese MNEs in emerging economies, in this case LA, is driven by both FSAs and CSAs (Rugman *et al.* 2006), and that the distinction between the two is blurred.

If this is eventually verified, when more data is available, it will reinforce the conclusions from the previous section: Chinese MNCs' current capabilities, together with the active participation of the government in emerging markets, appears to equip Chinese firms with a competitive edge relative to companies in host countries. However, as the extent of the government's participation and influence in industrialized countries is relatively less, this edge seems to remain weak comparative to the competitive capabilities present in most Western MNCs, as recognized in previous works (Nolan 2001; Rugman and Li 2007). These types of combinations have not been widely discussed in mainstream internationalization theories, a conclusion supported by other authors, for example (Buckley *et al.* 2007; Child and Rodrigues 2005; Child and Tse 2001). This appears to be another challenging area for future research.

Possible consequences of the explosion in trade between China and LA: market-seeking FDI?

As described in the contextual framework above, a new commercial axis between China and LA is developing, with flows of trade and investment in excess of US$50 billion (ECLAC 2008, 2010; IADB 2004). The potential business opportunities of this new axis render this growing commercial relationship worth studying.

The explosion in trade between China and LA seems to be based on their complementary export baskets (Santiso 2006). On the one hand China demands raw materials and food products where Latin American countries have comparative and competitive advantages, and, on the other hand, Latin American consumers are demanding products that are now accessible to the mass market thanks to Chinese low manufacturing costs. In fact, the trade agreements signed between the countries (discussed above) do not appear to have played a major role in this explosion in trade as they were signed in 2004, and some of them became operative in 2005, while most of the growth in trade started many years earlier (see Table 5.1). Moreover, the trade agreements will probably speed up and facilitate the growth in trade between the countries from now on. Also, as the growth in trade has been relatively uniform across Latin American countries, it does not seem to be indicative of a country-specific bias.

In the context of this work, trade (Table 5.1) and investment trends (Blazquez-Lidoy *et al.* 2006; Sanchez Ancochea 2006; Santiso 2006, 2007) hint that, in the medium term, Chinese MNCs may acquire strategic assets and capabilities extending their value chains to LA through, for example, the acquisition of local brands, distribution channels, or retail services to market their products. In other words, Chinese investments in LA up to 2007 were mainly resource-seeking FDI, but current trade and investment trends between the countries imply that market-seeking FDI (Dunning 1993) can be expected in the near future. Buckley *et al.* (2007) found that Chinese companies are already seeking markets in Organization for Economic Co-operation and Development (OECD) countries to invest in. After all, SOEs' projects, investments in infrastructure, and trade agreements can serve not only to feed China's need for raw materials and food from LA, but also to improve access to Latin American markets for Chinese products.

In addition, the growth in Chinese exports is most likely the result of efforts made by small, medium and large companies in the manufacturing sector successfully selling their products to Latin American markets. These companies will probably take the next steps in their internationalization process in the short and medium term, moving from exporting to contracting, and then FDI (Buckley and Casson 1998; Buckley and Ghauri 1993; Root 1994). If this eventually materializes, this phenomenon presents another area for future research into the internationalization of Chinese MNCs in emerging economies, in particular LA, as: (i) they tend to rely on ethnic Chinese networks (Brown 1995; Buckley *et al.* 2007; Lecraw 1993; Rauch and Trindade 2002; Yeung and Olds 2000) but they will be operating in a region where the prevalence of such networks is still low (South America may be one of the few places in the world where it is very difficult to find a Chinatown!), (ii) LA presents an important psychic distance, (iii) trade and investment is geographically dispersed in a large continent where communications are not easy, (iv) Chinese companies tend to operate in a relatively more centralized fashion (Cai 1999) which could eventually prevent them from making decisions locally and adapting smoothly to changes in the business environment, and (v) one of the weaknesses identified by previous works is such firms' lack of experience in international business (Cai 1999; Wong and Chan 2003). These points are especially relevant in the context of investments in LA as it has been documented that this region presents a challenging environment for business (Fornes 2008, 2009), and that its changing nature has affected the performance of large foreign investors (Fornes and Cardoza 2009).

Perhaps more important, in terms of areas for future research, is how the internationalization by Chinese companies into Latin American emerging economies fits with existing theories. In this sense, questions worth pursuing may be the ability of Chinese MNCs to take advantage of a combination of positive factors, including: (i) domestic cost advantages, (ii) economies of scale, (iii) institutional factors, (iv) access to capital at below-market rates, (v) the government's direct participation, (vi) the ability to exploit known technologies rather than innovating capabilities. In conventional models these factors (especially (i) to (iv)) indicate that exports will be favoured over FDI, but factors (v) and (vi), along with current Chinese investment trends in LA, suggest that FDI will be the next step adopted by Chinese firms. This is apparently a consequence of the relatively important weight of factors (v) and (vi) in the success of Chinese MNCs in LA (as discussed in previous sections). The existing literature does not seem to accommodate this adequately; and similar conclusions have been reached throughout this work, as well as in previous papers (Buckley *et al.* 2007; Child and Rodrigues 2005; Child and Tse 2001).

Summary and conclusions

This chapter presented a review and analysis of the literature on the internationalization of Chinese companies in emerging economies, in particular LA. As suggested at the beginning, this article was divided into four main sections: the first set out a review of the literature on the internationalization process adopted by Chinese MNCs, the main characteristics of Chinese international firms, and the conceptual frameworks discussed in different works; the second outlined the contextual framework for the analysis; the third section described the three areas identified as relevant in the first section, namely the competitive capabilities of China's firms, the support from the Chinese government, and the possible consequences of the growth in trade between China and LA.

This fourth and final section presents the conclusions where, from what has been shown in this chapter, the first point to highlight is that the vast majority of academic literature relates to the characteristics of Chinese MNCs in relation to their expansion into developed countries, and to conceptual frameworks needed to understand the international expansion of Chinese companies.

The second point is that the internationalization of Chinese companies in LA requires more attention, as both trade and investment between these regions shows a clear upward trend. This relatively new phenomenon – companies from emerging markets entering other emerging markets – has been described as a different context which may challenge traditional international business concepts (Wright *et al.* 2005). In this framework, further studies are needed, in particular with regard to the relative value of Chinese companies' existing advantages comparative to Latin American companies. The available evidence tends to suggest that Chinese MNCs already possess some competitive capabilities that, although not yet completely developed and consolidated to compete against companies in developed countries, allow them to successfully compete in Latin American markets. In order to eventually confirm this, research on the sustainability of the existing advantages is recommended, together with the use of research methods based on quantitative and comparative data to complement the qualitative works and case studies published recently.

Third, previous studies have shown that the Chinese government has supported, mainly through mechanisms in the home country (access to capital at below-market rates, capital market imperfections, political considerations, etc), the internationalization of its indigenous firms to developed countries. In the case of investments in Latin American emerging markets, this support is also present in the investments committed to the region. This work has indicated that further research is needed on the implications of the entry mode chosen by Chinese SOEs (JVs also with SOEs from the host country) on relationships between countries and on the management of risk exposure of Chinese firms.

Fourth, the evidence presented in this work indicates that support from the government in the case of investments in Latin American emerging economies took a different format than support for investments in developed countries. The main difference was that the government participated directly by committing most of the investments itself, and also by signing treaties and trade and investment agreements with more than 20 developing countries. This finding suggests that China's institutional conditions are not adequately recognized within the general theory and therefore indicates the need for further research.

Fifth, the current trade and investment figures hint that, in the medium term, Chinese MNCs may be involved in market-seeking FDI in LA, similar to what Buckley *et al.* (2007) found in OECD countries. The analysis of this likely phenomenon questions the fit of Chinese MNCs' characteristics with the Latin American reality. It also questions the fit of existing theories with the reality for Chinese firms, as the current literature does not seem to accommodate adequately the combination of factors present in Asian companies investing in LA.

Sixth, a point not discussed before in this study but considered relevant in the broader context of this work: China and Latin American countries are net and large recipients of FDI from developed countries. For example, China received around US$83.5 billion and LA and the Caribbean US$126.2 billion in FDI in 2007 (WTO 2008). In these countries, foreign investments stocks represent between 15 percent and 30 percent of the countries' GDP (as an average between 1995 and 2006), with cases like Chile where foreign funds represent around 50 percent (Fornes 2009; UNCTAD 2007). Within this context, it seems worth asking, given the relative importance of foreign investors from developed countries in China and LA, and in the context of their growing commercial relationship if MNCs from industrialized economies operating in these emerging countries will be impacted in any way (some evidence of this is starting to appear (Morán 2008)).

All in all, it seems that, regarding LA, Chinese internationalization involves a combination of resource-seeking and market-seeking, with the Chinese government playing a role in paving the way for a market-seeking movement at a later stage. In this case, there seems to be interesting complementarities between the Chinese state and firms in the internationalization process.

Finally, and more broadly, internationalization of companies from emerging countries into other emerging markets presents interesting routes for developing the International Business (IB) agenda. In this sense, Buckley (2002) suggested that one of the potential areas for IB research in the future is the identification of trends towards and away from globalization, to which Peng (2004) added that future studies need to have a focus on the factors affecting the success and failure of firms in international markets. From what this article has presented it is possible to argue that the internationalization of Chinese companies in other emerging markets, along with the growing trade and investment relations between China and LA, are trends towards globalization that affect international firms' performance in ways which have yet to be understood.

Notes

1 A previous version of this chapter was published in 2011 in the *International Journal of Emerging Markets*, 6 (2).
2 Sources: (Santiso 2007), Brazil's External Affairs Ministry, Chile's Foreign Investments Committee, Argentina's Ministry of Economy and Production.

References

Bin, S. (2006) 'The political economy of an Asian Pacific trade area: a China perspective', in C. E. Morrison and E. Pedrosa (eds) *An APEC Trade Agenda? The Political Economy of a Free Trade Area of the Asia Pacific, Singapore*, The Pacific Economic Cooperation Council/The APEC Business Advisory Board.

Blazquez-Lidoy, J., Rodriguez, J. and Santiso, J. (2006) 'Angel or devil? China's trade impact on Latin American emerging markets', Paris, OECD Development Centre.

Boisot, M. (2004) 'Notes on the internationalization of Chinese firms', unpublished paper, Open University of Catalonia, Barcelona, Spain.

Boisot, M. and Child, J. (1996) 'From fiefs to clans and network capitalism: Explaining China's emerging economic order', *Administrative Science Quarterly*, 41: 600–28.

Bravo, X., 'China se convirtió en noviembre en el mayor destino de envíos chilenos', *La Tercera*, 20/12/2006.

Brown, R. (1995) *Chinese Business Enterprise in Asia*, London: Routledge.

Buckley, P. (2002) 'Is the international business research agenda running out of steam?', *Journal of International Business Studies*, 33 (2): 365–374.

Buckley, P. and Casson, M. (1976) *The Future of the Multinational Enterprise*, London: Macmillan.

Buckley, P. and Casson, M. C. (1998) 'Analysing foreign market entry strategies: extending the internationalisation approach', *Journal of International Business Studies*, 29 (3): 539–562.

Buckley, P. and Ghauri, P. (1993) 'Introduction and overview', in P. Buckley and P. Ghauri (eds) *The Internationalization of the Firm: A Reader*, London: Academic Press.

Buckley, P., Clegg, J., Cross, A., Liu, X., Voss, H. and Zheng, P. (2007) 'The determinants of Chinese outward foreign direct investment', *Journal of International Business Studies*, 38 (4): 499–518.

Cai, K. (1999) 'Outward foreign direct investment: a novel dimension of China's integration into the regional and global economy', *China Quarterly*, 160: 836–80.

Chen, H. and Chen, T. (1998) 'Network linkages and location choice in foreign direct investment', *Journal of International Business Studies*, 29 (3): 445–467.

Child, J. and Rodrigues, S. (2005) 'The internationalization of Chinese firms: a case for theoretical extension?', *Management and Organization Review*, 1 (3): 381–410.

Child, J. and Tse, D. (2001) 'China's transition and its implications for international business', *Journal of International Business Studies*, 32: 5–21.

'China goes shopping', *Business Week*, 20/12/04.

Dunning, J. (1977) 'Trade, location of economic activity, and the MNE: a search for an ecletic approach', in B. Ohlin, P. O. Hesselborn and P. M. Wijkman (eds) *The International Allocation of Economic Activity*, London: Macmillan.

Dunning, J. (1993) *Multinational Enterprises and the Global Economy*, New York: Addison-Wesley.
ECLAC (2005) *Latin America and the Caribbean in the World Economy, 2004*, Santiago de Chile, Economic Commission for Latin America and the Caribbean.
ECLAC (2006) *Foreign Investment in Latin America and the Caribbean, 2005*, Santiago de Chile, Economic Commission for Latin America and the Caribbean.
ECLAC (2007) *Latin America and the Caribbean in the World Economy, 2006–2007*, Santiago de Chile, Economic Commission for Latin America and the Caribbean.
ECLAC (2008) *Latin America and the Caribbean in the World Economy, 2007–2008*, Santiago de Chile, Economic Commission for Latin America and the Caribbean.
ECLAC (2010) Interactive Graphic System of International Trade Data. Online. Available at: http://www.eclac.org/cgibin/getprod.asp?xml=/comercio/noticias/paginas/9/33539/P33539.xml&xsl=/comercio/tpl-i/p18f.xsl&base=/comercio/tpl-i/top-bottom.xsl (accessed January 15, 2010).
Edwards, J. (2007) 'We must prepare for the march of China's giants', *Financial Times*, January 16.
Filatotchev, I., Wright, M., Hoskisson, R., Uhlenbruck, K. and Tihanyi, L. (2003) 'Governance, organizational capabilities, and restructuring in transition economies', *Journal of World Business*, 38: 331–47.
Fornes, G. (2008) 'Foreign exchange exposure in emerging markets. A holistic approach to minimising its effects on multinational enterprises', Academy of Management Conference Best Paper Proceedings Conference, Anaheim.
Fornes, G. (2009) *Foreign Exchange Exposure in Emerging Markets. How Companies Can Minimize It*, Basingstoke: Palgrave Macmillan.
Fornes, G. and Cardoza, G. (2009) 'Foreign exchange exposure in emerging markets. a study of Spanish companies in Latin America', *International Journal of Emerging Markets*, 4 (1): 6–25.
Guillen, M. F. (2000) 'Business groups in emerging economies: a resource-based view', *Academy of Management Journal*, 43 (3): 362–380.
Guthrie, D. (2005) 'Organizational learning and productivity: State structure and foreign investment in the rise of the Chinese corporation', *Management and Organization Review*, 1: 165–95.
Hoskisson, R. E., Eden, L., Lau, C. M. and Wright, M. (2000) 'Strategy in emerging economies', *Academy of Management Journal*, 43 (3): 249–267.
IADB (2004) 'The emergence of China: opportunities and challenges for Latin America and the Caribbean', Washington, Inter-American Development Bank.
Johanson, J. and Wiedersheim-Paul, F. (1975) 'The internationalization of the firm. Four Swedish cases', *Journal of Management Studies*, 12: 305–22.
Khanna, T. and Palepu, K. (1997) 'Why focused strategies may be wrong for emerging markets', *Harvard Business Review*, 4 (75): 3–10.
Khanna, T. and Palepu, K. (2000) 'The future of business groups in emerging markets: long-run evidence from Chile', *Academy of Management Journal*, 43 (3): 268–285.
Kumar, N. (1998) *Globalization, Foreign Direct Investment and Technology Transfers: Impacts on and Prospects for Developing Countries*, New York: Routledge.
La Nación (2004a) 'China prevé invertir US$100.000 millones en América Latina', *La Nación*, November 13.
La Nación (2004b) 'China prometió que invertirá US$8000 millones en Brasil', *La Nación*, November 16.
La Nación (2004c) 'Hu quiere una "asociación estratégica"', *La Nación*, November 18.
La Nación (2004d) 'Kichner y Hu Jintao firmaron convenios', *La Nación*, November 16.
La Tercera (2007a) 'China y Perú iniciarán conversaciones hacia TLC en los próximos días', *La Tercera*, March 18.
La Tercera (2007b) 'Pekin estimulará la inversión exterior en cuatro sectores', *La Tercera*, May 16.

La Tercera (2007c) 'Venezuela quintuplicara los envíos petroleros a China', *La Tercera*, March 27.

Lapper, R. (2005) 'Beijing's growing profile in Latin America', *Financial Times*, March 9.

Lapper, R. (2007) 'US agrees to China joining IADB', *Financial Times*, March 18.

Lecraw, D. (1993) 'Outward direct investment by Indonesian firms: Motivation and effects, *Journal of International Business Studies*, 24: 589–600.

Makino, S., Chung-Ming, L. and Rhy-Song, Y. (2002) 'Asset-exploitation versus asset-seeking: implications for location choice of foreign direct investment from newly industrialized economies', *Journal of International Business Studies*, 33 (3): 403–421.

Mallet, V. (2006) 'Overseas investments: hunt for resources in the developing world', *Financial Times*, December 12.

Mathews, J. (2006) 'Dragon Multinationals: new players in 21st century globalization', *Asia Pacific Journal of Management*, 23 (1): 5–27.

MOFCOM (2007) 'Statistical Bulletin of China's Outward Foreign Direct Investment', Beijing, Ministry of Commerce the People's Republic of China.

MOFCOM (2008) 'Statistical Bulletin of China's Outward Foreign Direct Investment', Beijing, Ministry of Commerce the People's Republic of China.

MOFCOM (2009) 'China and Peru signed free trade agreement', Online. Available at: http://english.mofcom.gov.cn/aarticle/newsrelease/significantnews/200905/20090506231332.html (accessed May 8, 2009).

Morán, C. (2008) 'Los gigantes chinos de construcción se fijan en el mercado español', *Expansión*, September 23.

Nolan, P. (2001) *China and the Global Economy*, Basingstoke: Palgrave.

Peng, M. (2003) 'Institutional transitions and strategic choices', *Academy of Management Review*, 28: 275–96.

Peng, M. (2004) 'Identifying the big question in international business research', *Journal of International Business Studies*, 35 (2): 99–108.

Peng, M., Wang, D. and Jiang, Y. (2008) 'An Institution-based view of international business strategy: a focus on emerging economies', *Journal of International Business Studies*, 39: 920–936.

Porter, M. (1980) *Competitive Strategy*. New York: Free Press.

Porter, M. (1998) 'Competing accross locations: Enhancing competitive advantage through a global strategy', in M. Porter (ed.) *On Competition*, Boston: Harvard Business School Press.

Quan, Y. (2001) 'Access to the WTO and internationalization strategy of Chinese companies', *Enterprise Studies*, 8: 12–24.

Rauch, J. and Trindade, V. (2002) 'Ethnic Chinese networks in international trade', *The Review of Economics and Statistics*, February: 116–130.

Root, F. (1994) *Entry Strategies for International Markets*, San Francisco: Jossey-Bass.

Rugman, A. and Li, J. (2007) 'Will China's multinationals succeed globally or regionally?', *European Management Journal*, 25 (5): 333–343.

Rugman, A., Collinson, S. and Hodgetts, R. (2006) *International Business*, Harlow: Pearson.

Rui, H. and Yip, G. (2007) 'Foreign acquisitions by Chinese firms: theoretical implications', Academy of International Business UK and Ireland Chapter Conference, London.

Sanchez Ancochea, D. (2006) 'El impacto de China en América Latina:? 'oportunidad o amenaza?', *ARI – Real Instituto Elcano*, 2006 (38): 4–8.

Santiso, J. (2005a) 'America Latina y Asia: bailando con los tigres y los dragones asiaticos', *Anuario Elcano: America Latina*, 2004–2005: 275–298.

Santiso, J. (2005b) 'La emergencia de China y su impacto en America Latina', *Politica Exterior*, 19 (107): 97–112.

Santiso, J. (2006) 'Of dragons & elephants', *LatinFinance*, September.

Santiso, J. (ed.) (2007) *The Visible Hand of China in Latin America*, Paris, OECD Development Centre Studies.

Spar, D. and Oi, J. (2006) 'China: building "capitalism with socialist characteristics" ', *Harvard Business School Cases*, 9706–041.

Tseng, W. (1994) 'The process of internationalisation of PRC multinationals', in H. Schultte (ed.) *The Global Competitiveness of the Asian Firm*, Basingstoke: Macmillan.

UNCTAD (2007) 'World Investment Report', Geneva, United Nations.

Warner, M., Ng, S.-H. and Xu, X. (2004) ' "Late development" experience and the evolution of transnational firms in the People's Republic of China', *Asia Pacific Business Review*, 10: 324–45.

Wells, L. (1981) 'Foreign investors from the Third World', in K. Kumar and M. McLeod (eds) *Multinational from Developing Countries*, Lexington, MA: Health and Company, 23–36.

Wells, L. (1983) *Third World Multinationals: The Rise of Foreign Direct Investment from Developing Countries*, Cambridge, MA: MIT Press.

Wong, J. and Chan, S. (2003) 'China's outward direct investment: expanding worldwide', *China: An International Journal*, 1 (2): 273–301.

Wright, M., Filatotchev, I., Hoskisson, R. E. and Peng, M. W. (2005) 'Strategy research in emerging economies: Challenging the conventional wisdom', *Journal of Management Studies*, 42 (1): 1–33.

WTO (2008) 'World Investment Report', Geneva, World Trade Organization.

Yamakawa, Y., Peng, M. and Deeds, D. (2008) 'What drives new ventures to internationalize from emerging to developed economies?', *Entrepreneurship Theory and Practice*, 32 (1): 59–82.

Yeung, H. and Olds, K. (eds) (2000) *Globalization of Chinese Business Firms*, New York: St. Martin's Press.

Zeng, M. and Williamson, J. (2003) 'The hidden dragons', *Harvard Business Review*, October: 92–99.

Zhang, J. and Van Den Bulcke, D. (1996) 'International management strategies of Chinese multinational firms', in J. Child and Y. Lu (eds) *Management Issues in China: International Enterprises*, London: Routledge.

6 An exploration of pyramidal business groups in China

Dylan Sutherland, Lutao Ning and Jing Wang

Introduction

Business groups, as opposed to free-standing firms, have played prominent roles in the economic development of many developing economies. This is particularly true for the economies of East Asia and especially so for China today.[1] By the end of 2008 there were 2,971 officially recognized business groups in China with 30,164 first-tier majority owned subsidiaries, employing around 33 million people directly (SSB 2009).[2] Beneath this first-tier, moreover, many further tiers of participating firms existed within further subsidiaries and associated firms. Indeed, the full extent of group membership in China is still unknown but it is likely to be very large. As such, the influence and reach of China's business groups is very important, and their role in the Chinese economy going forward is only likely to become more so. Yet, despite this, academic research on Chinese groups is still in its infancy. Very few studies, moreover, have directly investigated the question of whether pyramidal structures are forming in Chinese groups, though many look at more general business group related questions (Morck and Nakamura 2007; Morck *et al.* 2005; Yiu *et al.* 2005; Keister 2000).

A recent summary of the business group literature asks whether business groups are 'paragons' or 'parasites' (Khanna and Yafeh 2007). While there are some reasons why groups may be thought of as paragons, there are also reasons for believing such groups may play a negative and harmful role in economic development. Of special relevance, in this regard, is the impact certain types of business group structures may have on the corporate governance of member firms. Pyramidal type structures have been picked out as having particularly negative consequences for economic performance (Morck *et al.* 2005). The economies of East Asia and South Korea, in particular, have also been cited as examples where pyramidal structures have been especially harmful. Despite this, to date there is comparatively little research on the extent to which China's business groups have evolved pyramidal type structures. The main purpose of this chapter is to examine this question. We also speculate as to the reasons why pyramidal groups may be forming and possible consequences.

First, we introduce the concept of the pyramidal business group, provide a background summary of China's groups and review relevant research findings on pyramidal groups in China. Second, we further outline our research questions and then outline the different approaches and methods used. Third, we report our results, illustrating them using several examples from both state-owned and private sectors. Finally, the implications of our findings are discussed.

Background

We briefly consider literature on business groups in general and then review what we already know about pyramidal structures in China's groups and literature on Chinese groups.

Pyramidal business groups

A concern of the business group literature has been to ask whether business groups play positive or negative roles (Khanna and Yafeh 2007). Among the benefits of group formation, it has been hypothesized that groups may fill the institutional voids that are common in emerging markets (and transition economies in particular). By compensating for imperfect or under developed markets in finance, labour and products, it is argued that groups help facilitate exchanges that could not otherwise happen through markets. Further, groups have been hypothesized to play an important role in technology acquisition, particularly via their expertise in acquiring 'project execution capabilities' – un-packaging and assimilating new technologies, at which they become experts (Amsden and Hikino 1994). The negative traits associated with business groups include those related to their monopoly powers, engagement in rent-seeking activities and association with crony capitalism, moral hazard and excessive and inefficient investment. Moreover, one of the most discussed negative traits concerns the pyramidal structures that groups often develop (La Porta *et al.* 1999; Morck *et al.* 2005). Such 'control pyramids' allow a firm (often family-owned, but also quite often state-owned, which is relevant to note for our examination of the Chinese case) to control several listed companies, each of which may in turn control yet more listed companies, and so on. Under such conditions an apex firm may come to control numerous other firms. Critically, it can do so without making commensurate capital investments. Morck and Nakamura (2005) provide a simple stylized example in which a first tier listed firm is 49 per cent financed by outside shareholders and 51 per cent by a single controlling shareholder (in reality, however, far lower stakes – as little as 10 per cent – are needed to lock-in control). In lower tiers a similar relationship holds, so as we move down the tiers of the pyramid at each new tier new firms will be increasingly financed by outside shareholders, while control still lies at the apex firm. To illustrate:

> Those in the second tier are 49% directly financed by outside shareholders and 51% financed by first tier firms, which are also 49% financed by outside shareholders. The net result is that second tier firms are 74% financed by outside shareholders. Firms in the third tier are 85.25% financed by outside

> shareholders, and those in the fourth tier are 92.25% financed by outside shareholders. Lower tier firms are successively more thoroughly financed by public shareholders. Despite this, every firm is still controlled by the apex firm's controlling shareholder.
>
> (Morck and Nakamura 2007: 3)

In such situations it is argued that 'apex firm value maximization is unlikely to coincide with shareholder value maximization in any individual lower tier firm' (Morck and Nakamura 2007: 40). Indeed, the controlling shareholder is likely to be biased towards firms higher in the pyramid, moving resources from lower tiers up the pyramid. Pyramidal type ownership structures in business groups, therefore, have the potential to destroy value.

Why do pyramidal groups form and are they common? While cross-shareholdings and super voting rights may also be used to bolster the control power of the apex, La Porta *et al.* (1999) find pyramidal structures are the most common mechanism of increasing divergences between ownership and control. Clearly, such structures provide many benefits for the ultimate controlling shareholders. As a direct result of the large divergences between control and ownership, the elites that control pyramidal groups required only relatively limited supplies of capital to expand their power bases. Historically, powerful families or state actors have been among the elites using such ownership structures to harness enormous economic influence over vast corporate empires. Because at each level, moreover, new corporate entities are formed with limited liabilities, the controlling elites are shielded from heavy losses should one or more firms in their pyramids fail. These complex corporate structures may also be used to minimize tax bills (Morck 2007). Unsurprisingly, such pyramidal structures have proved popular among their elite owners. They are common throughout the world. In fact, widely held firms, according to La Porta *et al.* (1999), may be thought of as the 'the rarest of curiosities' in most countries. This is with the exception of the United Kingdom and United States. By the 1920s, according to Morck (2007: 16), large pyramidal corporate groups 'were probably the dominant form of large organization throughout the world'. They remain important today.

In summary, much recent discussion of business groups has focused on the question of whether they may be seen as paragons or parasites (Khanna and Yafeh 2007). Their parasitical tendencies, in particular, have dwelled upon their propensity to form pyramidal features and tunnel resources from minority shareholders. Pyramidal groups may, so doing, also vastly inflate the power of their controlling elites which may in turn have economy-wide ramifications. As La Porta *et al.* (1999) have noted, if pyramidal structures are common and widely held ownership scarce, the Berle and Means (1932) image of the modern corporation, with diffuse owners attempting to control managers, may need replacing. Instead, a key question becomes: who keeps controlling shareholders from expropriating minority shareholders? This, of course, may be especially pertinent in countries with weak legal protection, such as China.

Chinese business groups

The rapid development of China's business groups raises numerous questions. A number of papers have employed quantitative approaches to examine, among other things, whether and under what conditions companies may benefit from group membership in China and, more generally, what groups can do to affect affiliated firms' performance. Keister (1998, 2000), for example, examines the performance of 40 of China's largest groups between 1988 and 1990 using a panel data set. She finds that internal finance companies (facilitating internal financial markets) and interlocking directorates (which promote information exchange between group members) are associated with improved performance.[3] Yiu *et al.* (2005) examine the profitability of 224 business groups (including all subsidiaries) to find out how groups acquire resources and capabilities so that they can become successful agents in promoting economic transformation and growth. They find that group profitability is negatively related to what they call 'endowed resources' (including such things as the age of the group, the extent of government ownership and the prevalence of management with government links) but positively related to what they call 'acquired resources'. Such resources, they argue, are acquired through actions such as acquisitions, internal capability development and international diversification (Yiu *et al.* 2005). Ma *et al.* (2006), on the other hand, look to examine how business groups fill 'ownership voids' by serving as the direct owners of state-owned enterprises in the absence of other private actors. They find that the combination of business group affiliation and state ownership has a positive effect on subsidiary performance. Therefore, as well as substituting for imperfect markets, they argue that business group affiliation and state ownership may also play an important role in ownership reforms, a point to which we later return. Guest and Sutherland (2010) use a large panel data set of China's listed firms and identify listed subsidiaries of the preferred national team trial groups (those referred to in Table 6.1) to examine their financial performance *vis-a-vis* non trial group subsidiaries. They argue that large trial groups are more likely to be genuine business groups (with function internal capital markets organized around a financial company, labour market functions, research and technology centres capable of transferring technologies, and so on). As such, we might expect these subsidiaries to outperform non-affiliated businesses. Their findings do find outperformance, though they caution of the difficulties of inferring causality.

Carney *et al.* (2009) address the question of institutional voids. Does affiliation with a business group improve a firm's performance in circumstances of poor-quality institutions and extensive market failures? They speculate that the positive effects of group affiliation may decline in China as the quality of market institutions improves. They also consider how state and private ownership impact on affiliation to a group. As with Sutherland Guest (2010), they use data on publicly listed firms (476 in total), but for two specific periods (1999 and 2004). They find support for the idea that affiliation to a business group improves performance. However, they also find that the value of group affiliation declines over time. As well as this, they find support for the idea that high levels of state ownership initially enhanced the worth of group affiliation, but that this affect quickly disappeared (by 2004). They argue, therefore, that their results suggest the institutional and market infrastructure conducive to entry by unaffiliated, freestanding firms, is now developing in China.

He *et al.* (2010) look at whether China's groups facilitate internal capital markets. They also look at how institutional factors, including the ultimate ownership of the group and level of market development, affect Chinese business groups. They find groups do help member firms overcome constraints in raising external capital. They also find internal capital markets more likely to be an alternative financing channel among state-owned than private firms. The internal capital market, however, is more likely to help those affiliated firms that are private or local government owned relative to those owned by central government, or located in regions with a well-developed institutional environment (He *et al.* 2010).

Chinese pyramidal business groups

Despite the emerging number of studies, particularly empirical ones, on Chinese groups, none have really considered the question of whether pyramids are forming. Away from research directed specifically at China's business groups, a body of work on Chinese corporate governance has looked at the question of pyramidal structures. The particular definition of what constitutes a 'pyramid' used in this work, however, is not the same as La Porta *et al.*'s (1999) definition. Liu and Pei (2005), examine how many studies measuring performance of private firms against state firms have been misled by China's complex scheme of ownership classifications. These do not identify the ultimate controlling shareholder. Liu and Pei (2005), however, relax the rule that two or more listed companies are required in the control chain. Fan *et al.* (2005) discuss the reasons for the emergence of what could more accurately be described as control chains. They note the packaging of good assets of state-owned enterprises for listing, and the way in which these firms can be controlled and owned directly by a state asset management agency or, alternatively, through several intermediate companies. They note, however, that the intermediate 'pyramidal layers' are in fact nearly always 'non-publicly traded State-Owned Enterprises (SOEs) solely owned by the local government or jointly owned by local government and other government agencies' (Fan *et al.* 2005: 6). In their definition, therefore, they do not require publicly listed companies. As such, research to date does not use any one single definition of what a pyramidal group may be.

Sutherland and Ning (forthcoming) undertake one of the few studies in Western literature on Chinese pyramids using La Porta *et al.*'s (1999) definition. They provide a useful breakdown of the growth in Chinese groups, as well as how affiliated firms are contributing to their overall development. Table 6.1, based on data taken from the *Yearbook of China's Large Enterprise Groups*, shows China's group grew at around 26 per cent per annum in real terms (sales and assets) over the period in question – much faster than the national economy as a whole. There is little sign that this growth is abating. As firms continue to join these groups (Table 6.2) they

Table 6.1 The growth of China's business groups

	1997	*1998*	*1999*	*2000*	*2001*	*2002*	*2003*	*2004*	*2005*	*2006*	*2007*	*2008*	*Year 2008/1997*
Total number of groups	2,369	2,472	2,757	2,655	2,710	2,627	2,692	2,764	2,845	2,856	2,926	2,971	1.3
Number of state-owned groups	1,455	1,667	1,808	1,735	1,786	1,684	1,619	1,546	1,446	1,364	1,315	1,293	0.9
Number of trial groups	119	121	126	119	119	116	113	111	110	104	101	98	0.8
Number of private groups	...	...	...	...	...	...	...	...	...	1,089	1,212	1,290	...
Total assets	5,035	6,699	8,732	10,698	12,805	14,254	17,017	19,478	23,076	27,121	34,355	41,131	8.2
Total profits	122	109	172	290	321	417	555	829	1,039	1,307	1,881	1,458	12
Total R&D expenditures	15.5	21.4	35.5	48	66.9	80.7	90.5	119.9	150.5	205.5	251.9	319.1	20.6
Number of employees	18.5	20.9	23.4	22.8	25.2	25.2	25.9	26.7	28.3	30.1	32.39	32.85	1.8
Total exports	258	269	359	458	540	629	754	999	1,180	1,474	1,707	1,793	6.9
Outward FDI	...	...	...	...	...	...	...	...	...	360	529	541	...
Profits/GDP	1.5	1.3	1.9	2.9	2.9	3.5	4.1	5.2	5.6	6.2	7.3	4.8	3.2
Exports/ total exports	17	17.6	22.2	22.2	24.5	23.3	20.8	20.3	18.8	19	18.3	17.9	1.1

Source: *Yearbook of Large Enterprise Groups*, various years.

Notes: All figures billion RMB except where otherwise specified, number of employees are counted in millions.

Table 6.2 Contribution of subsidiaries to China's business groups by ownership registration (numbers, assets and profits in 100 million RMB)

	Numbers			*Assets*			*Profits*		
	2002	*2008*	*Change (%)*	*2002*	*2008*	*Change (%)*	*2002*	*2008*	*Change (%)*
Panel A									
SOEs	7,234	4,969	−31.3	43,529	94,168	116.3	4,367	2,831	−35.2
State invested companies	2,281	2,816	23.5	14,207	36,949	160.1	150	769	412.7
Other limited liability companies	9,060	16,562	82.8	17,858	93,026	420.9	408	2,855	599.8
Stock limited companies	1,618	1,781	10.1	21,994	117,958	436.3	3,411	6,065	77.8
Foreign joint ventures	1,338	1,598	19.4	1,302	12,680	873.9	268	735	174.3
Foreign listed companies	...	243	...	...	1,913	...	...	112	...
HK, Taiwan, Macao joint venture companies	719	681	−5.3	502	2,992	496.0	87	175	101.1
HK, Taiwan, Macao listed companies	...	59	...	...	1,625	...	...	−84.59	...
Other	2,266	1,451	−36.0	4,091	6,473	58.2	224	297	32.6
Subsidiaries	24,523	30,164	23.0	106,610	367,859	245.1	8,915	13,759	54.3
Mother companies	2,627	2,971	13.1	84,392	155,936	84.8	5,353	4,891	−8.6
Total	27,150	33,135	22.0	191,002	523,795	174.2	14,268	18,650	30.7

Table 6.2 Continued

	Numbers			*Assets*			*Profits*		
	2002	*2008*	*Change (%)*	*2002*	*2008*	*Change (%)*	*2002*	*2008*	*Change (%)*
	Shares (%) of total								
Panel B									
SOEs	26.6	15.0		22.8	18.0		30.6	15.2	
State invested companies	8.4	8.5		7.4	7.1		1.1	4.1	
Other limited liability companies	33.4	50.0		9.3	17.8		2.9	15.3	
Stock limited company	6	5.4		11.5	22.5		23.9	32.5	
Foreign joint venture	4.9	4.8		0.7	2.4		1.9	3.9	
Foreign listed companies	0	0.7		0	0.4		0	0.6	
Hong Kong, Taiwan, Macao joint venture company	2.6	2.1		0.3	0.6		0.6	0.9	
HK, Taiwan, Macao listed companies	0	0.2		0	0.3		0	0.0	
Other	8.3	4.4		2.1	1.2		1.6	1.6	
Subsidiaries	90.3	91.0		55.8	70.2		62.5	73.8	
Mother companies	9.7	9.0		44.2	29.8		37.5	26.2	
Total	100	100		100	100		100	100	

Source: SSB (2003–2008).

Notes: The shares show the percentage of the national business group total (i.e. including parent and first-tier subsidiaries).

are likely to continue to grow. Although there are now large numbers of business groups (and an increasing number of privately registered groups, around 1,000), a small number of very large state-owned groups remain of paramount importance. Around half of all assets, sales, R&D expenditures and profits of China's groups were concentrated in a batch of trial enterprise overseen by the State Council.

Sutherland and Ning (forthcoming) also show that there have also been considerable changes in the ownership structure within China's groups at all levels, owing to the corporatization processes that have been unfolding in recent years. In particular, the emergence of limited liability and shareholding companies among the 30,000 subsidiaries, facilitating the entrance of new owners, means the ownership structure and organization within these groups has become very complex.

Table 6.2 looks at the composition by ownership of China's 2,971 officially recognized business groups and, perhaps more interestingly, the 30,164 first-tier subsidiaries. It looks at the evolution over the period 2002 and 2008 using two panels. First, it is noteworthy for our investigation of pyramids that the number and type of firms participating within China's business groups has grown quickly. The total number of first tier subsidiaries increased from 24,523 to 30,164 (from about ten to 11 first-tier subsidiaries per group). Their share of all business group assets also increased, to around 70 per cent of the total in 2008 (SSB 2008). The type of subsidiaries, as they are registered, has also changed greatly (Table 6.2). Specifically, shareholding companies (*gufen gongsi*) are becoming more important to the groups. By 2008 the most important type of subsidiary in terms of numbers was limited liability companies. The number and share of such companies had increased rapidly, from 9,060 (33 per cent) to 16,562 (50 per cent) of a total 30,164 subsidiaries. Limited liability companies are typically smaller than shareholding companies and were a product of the 1994 company law.[4] As such their share of total group assets was relatively small, increasing from around nine to 18 per cent of the total (Table 6.2). By 2008, however, the most important type of company among the business groups in terms of assets and profits, not numbers, were limited liability *shareholding* companies (*youxian ziren gufen gongsi*). Importantly, their contribution to the business groups was also growing faster than other types of company. In terms of numbers, however, these companies were far fewer (only 1,781 in 2008, 5.4 per cent of the total) meaning their average asset size was 6.6 billion RMB, compared with only around 400 million RMB. For the smaller limited liability companies. These joint-stock companies may raise funds through initial public offering and stock market listing. As such they may reflect the extent to which the stock market is being used to raise capital to develop business groups and also, following from this, also develop pyramidal structures.

Ownership transformation, at least in the simple terms of the registration of corporations, is clearly taking place at speed within these groups. Three main points emerge from Table 6.2 (Sutherland and Ning forthcoming). Subsidiaries are becoming more important in terms of contribution to groups. Their ownership is changing rapidly introducing more kinds of investors, possibly firm insiders, as important new owners. Finally, in aggregate it also seems publicly-owned shareholding corporations are becoming more important within the groups – that they are increasingly raising capital using stock markets. What this points to is the growing potential for pyramidal type structures to form.

Understanding Chinese pyramids: four case studies

Much research on Chinese business groups has focused on how groups may or may not affect performance using quantitative methods and samples taken from China's listed companies (for which there is good data). As with all studies of this type, however, there are challenges in undertaking meaningful econometric estimations. Here, we address a slightly different question, but one that we believe to be of fundamental importance. Are pyramidal groups forming in China? If so, what is their nature and why might they be forming? Given their prevalence in other countries, and apparent centrality in precipitating economic crises, this seems an important question. Despite the widespread condemnation of such groups, there is still a great paucity of information on their actual numbers, whereabouts and nature (Khanna and Yafeh 2007). In this chapter we follow the definition of La Porta *et al.* (1999) in our identification of pyramids. They make it clear that listed firms in pyramids require 'at least one publicly traded company between it and the ultimate owner in the chain. . . . Pyramids require publicly traded intermediate companies' (La Porta *et al.* 1999: 480). This condition is important, as it allows large numbers of outside public investors to participate via equity holding in firms over which they have little actual control, thus creating the divergences between ownership and control needed to create incentives for tunnelling.

La Porta *et al.* (1999) use data on the ownership structures of large corporations in 27 wealthy economies and look to identify the ultimate controlling shareholders of these firms. They examine, among other things, the top 20 firms ranked by market capitalization of common equity at the end of 1995. They exclude financial organizations. They look, among other things, for all shareholders who control more than 10 per cent of the votes. Often the main shareholders are corporate entities and financial institutions. In such cases they try to find the major shareholders in these entities, then the major shareholders in the major shareholders, and so on, until they find the 'ultimate controllers of the votes'. Detailed investigation of individually listed firms and their business groups is therefore needed to ascertain whether pyramidal business groups exist in China. However, this is a time consuming and arduous process and, as mentioned, to date few studies have undertaken such work. Sutherland and Ning (forthcoming), however, do examine around 100 of China's largest groups for evidence of pyramids. They follow La Porta *et al.*'s (1999) ownership thresholds. As most small shareholders do not vote at annual meetings, they argue voting stakes in the 10 to 20 per cent range are adequate to lock in control. They therefore look for subsidiaries in which the 10 per cent or more ownership share is directly or indirectly held (though they actually find that in nearly all cases it is far higher than this). Interestingly, they find evidence that pyramids are forming, particularly within the largest top 50 groups. According to their research, undertaken in 2008, 17 of the largest 50 business groups, many controlled by State-owned Assets Supervision and Administration Commission (SASAC), have already developed pyramidal structures. This includes: Sinopec (1st), Sinochem corporation (7th), Bao Steel Group (8th), Dongfeng Motor Corporation (12th), China State Construction Engineering Corporation (13th), China Minmetals (16th), China Ocean Shipping Company (COSCO) (18th), Haier (20th), Aluminium Corporation of China (21st), China Resources National Corporation (22nd), China Unicom (25th), China Huaneng Group (26th), China International Trust and Investment Corporation (CITIC) Group (29th), China National Cereals, Oils and Foodstuffs Corporation (COFCO) Group (31st), China National Chemical Corporation (35th), China Shipping Group Company (40th), China Electronics Corporation (41st), China Guodian Group (43rd) and Shanghai Electric Group (47th). These results, in terms of numbers, are corroborated to some extent by Liu and Pei (2006). By the end of 2001 they report that 30 of China's listed firms met La Porta's definition (Liu and Pei 2005: 47).

Building from the finding that pyramids are developing in China, we further explore some of these pyramidal groups in greater detail so as to further illustrate their features and why they may be forming. We look at China Electronics Corporation (CEC), CITIC, Shanghai Electric Group and Fosun Group. Each is a large business group and has a pyramidal form (following the LaPorta definition). As well as this, each has a different type of ultimate controlling shareholder (CITIC owned by the Ministry of Finance, CEC owned by SASAC and Fosun is private). They are also engaged in different types of businesses. First we introduce the four groups and explain the nature of their pyramidal structures. We then consider why these structures may be forming, including specifically the issue of tunnelling.

China Electronics Corporation

China Electronics Corp is a state-owned group under SASAC. It is the largest state-owned IT Company in China. It has hundreds of affiliates and subsidiaries and is presently in the process of consolidating many units. It produces across five major areas, including integrated circuits and electronic components, software, computers and key components, mobile communication terminals and E-commerce. It employs around 10 million people, making it an exceptionally large group. By 2008 its total assets stood at around 73.4 billion RMB and its sales were nearly 68.5 billion RMB (CEC 2009). As it is such a large group it has 14 listed subsidiaries in total (see Figure 6.1, the companies in italic are listed). It also has several companies that are held through pyramidal ownership chains (Figure 6.1). This includes Chinasoft International, Shenzhen SED Industry, China Great Wall Computer, Shen Zhen Kaifa Technology and TPV Technology Ltd. A number of these listed companies are also incorporated in Hong Kong.

CITIC Group

The CITIC Group is organized into eight major areas, including financial services, investment holding, real estate and civil infrastructure, engineering contracting,

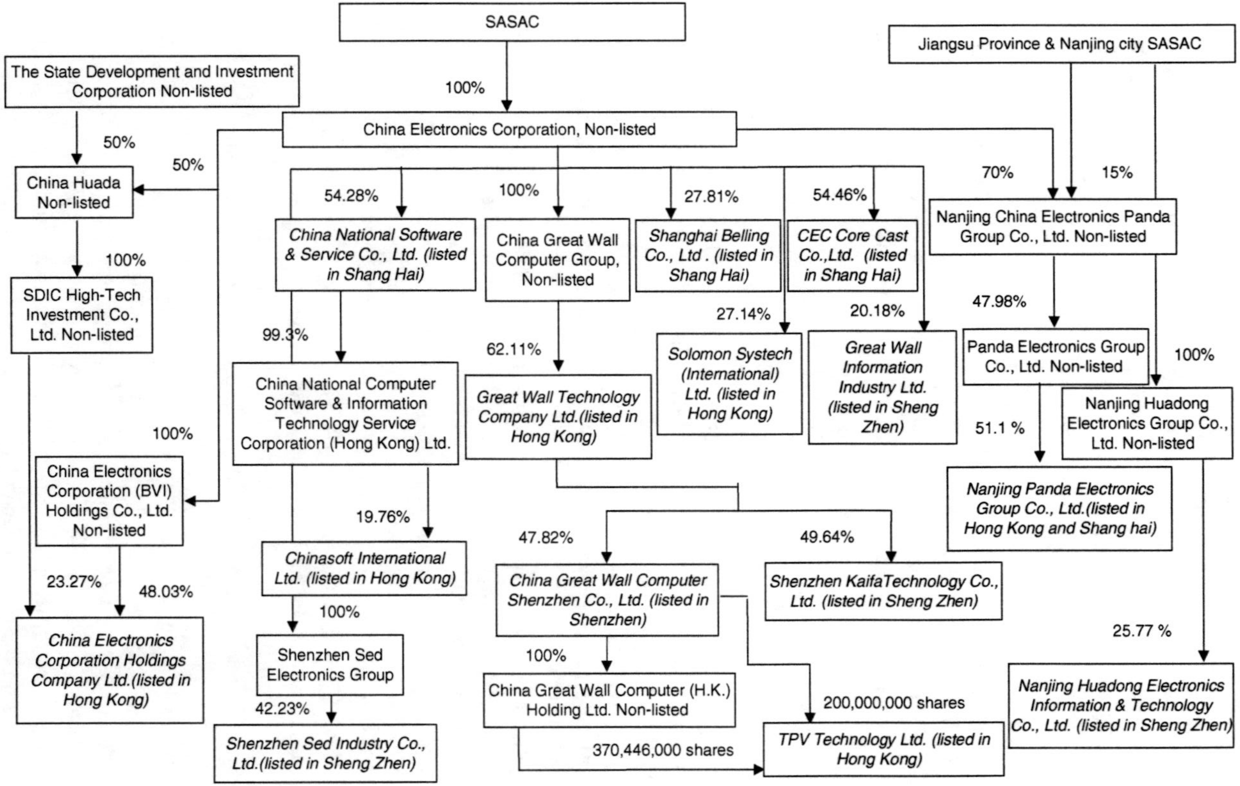

Figure 6.1 China Electronics Corporation.

Source: Annual reports.

Notes: Figures in italics are listed.

energy and resources, manufacturing, information technology, and trade and services. Its subsidiaries across these major business areas are themselves each part of separate groups (see Figure 6.2). In 1994 the State Council designated CITIC as a pilot for modern enterprise reform. In 2000 it became a state-authorized investment institution, and established China's first financial holding company. The group has grown very quickly and is also a role model, having pioneered a number of early trial reforms. By 2007 its assets stood at around 1.3 billion RMB (CITIC 2009). CITIC Group has ten listed subsidiaries within the group.[5] Compared with other groups, it has more international listings, particularly in Hong Kong. However, it also has four domestically listed subsidiaries. Within the group, CITIC 1616 Holdings Limited is held in part through CITIC Pacific (52.6 per cent). Therefore, there are examples of subsidiaries in which the cash flow to the parent, CITIC Group, are less than the control rights. The ownership structure in the group, therefore, can be defined as pyramidal.

Fosun Group

Fosun Group, unlike CITIC and CEC, is controlled by private entrepreneurs. It is one of the largest private companies in China. Established in 1992, Fosun has grown rapidly. In 2007, Fosun International, the holding company of Fosun Group, was listed on the main board of the Hong Kong Stock Exchange. Its business operations cover five main areas, including pharmaceuticals, property development, steel, mining, retail, services and strategic investments. Fosun's principal businesses have benefitted from China's growing consumer demand and sustained urbanization. After nearly 18 years of development it considers that it has developed three core capabilities, suited for the Chinese market. These include: the capability to explore and capture investment opportunities in high growth areas; the capability to continuously improve its management efficiency, and, finally the capability to optimize financing from multiple sources, including listing companies. In 2009, Fosun International had revenues of RMB 34.855 billion and a net profit of RMB 4.647 billion (Fosun 2010). Fosun retains its position among the Top 100 Chinese enterprises and has been one of the largest taxpayers among China's private enterprises. In 2009, Fosun ranked 81 in terms of its net profits among Top 500 Chinese enterprises and 91 in terms of revenue among Top 500 Chinese enterprises (Fosun 2010).

Owing to the listing of the parent company, Fosun Group has a number of listed companies that are held in pyramidal chains (Figure 6.3) – Zhejiang Crystal-OpTech, Shanghai Fosun Pharmaceutical Group, Tongjitang Chinese Medicines, Shanghai Forte Land, Shanghai Shanghai Yuyuan Tourist Mart, Zhaojin Mining Industry. In this last example, Zhaojin is held in a chain with three publicly listed companies, increasing the divergence between cash-flow and control rights.

Shanghai Electric Group

A final example we use is that of Shanghai Electric Group (Figure 6.4). The Group operates in ten major industries and has around 92,000 employees (assets

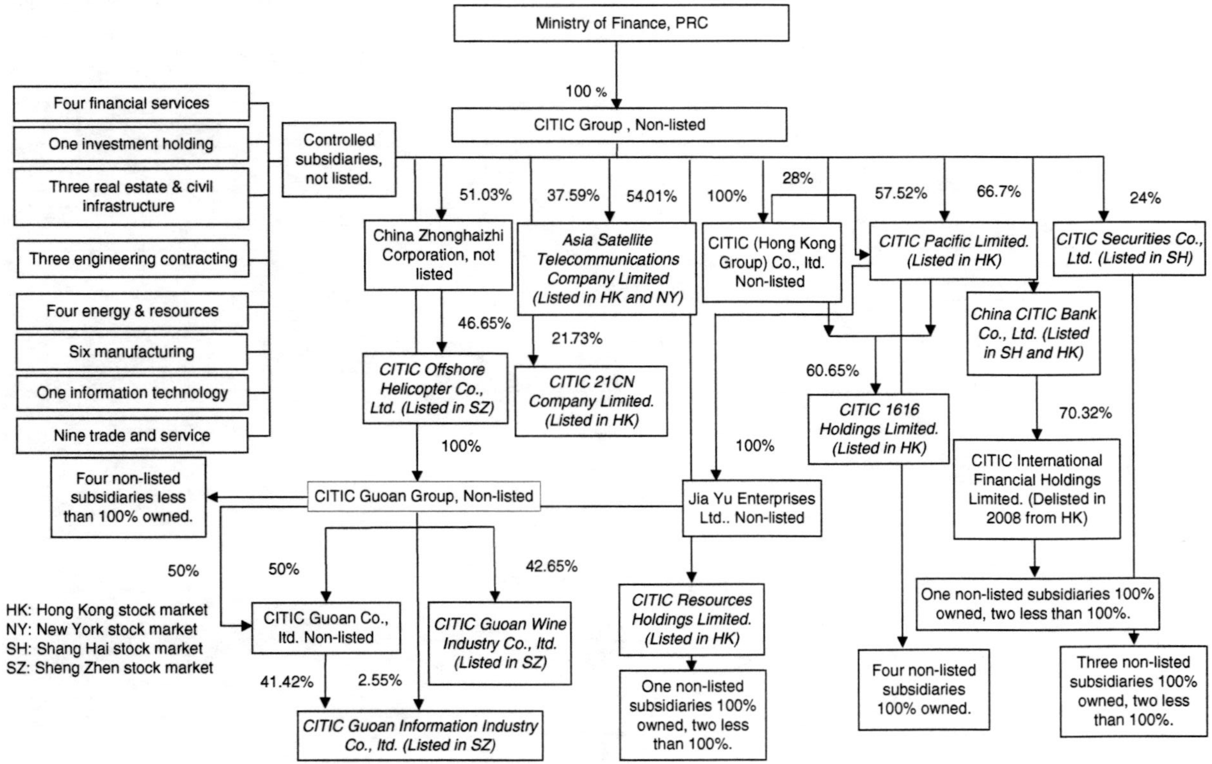

Figure 6.2 CITIC Group.

Source: Annual reports.

Notes: Listed companies in italics.

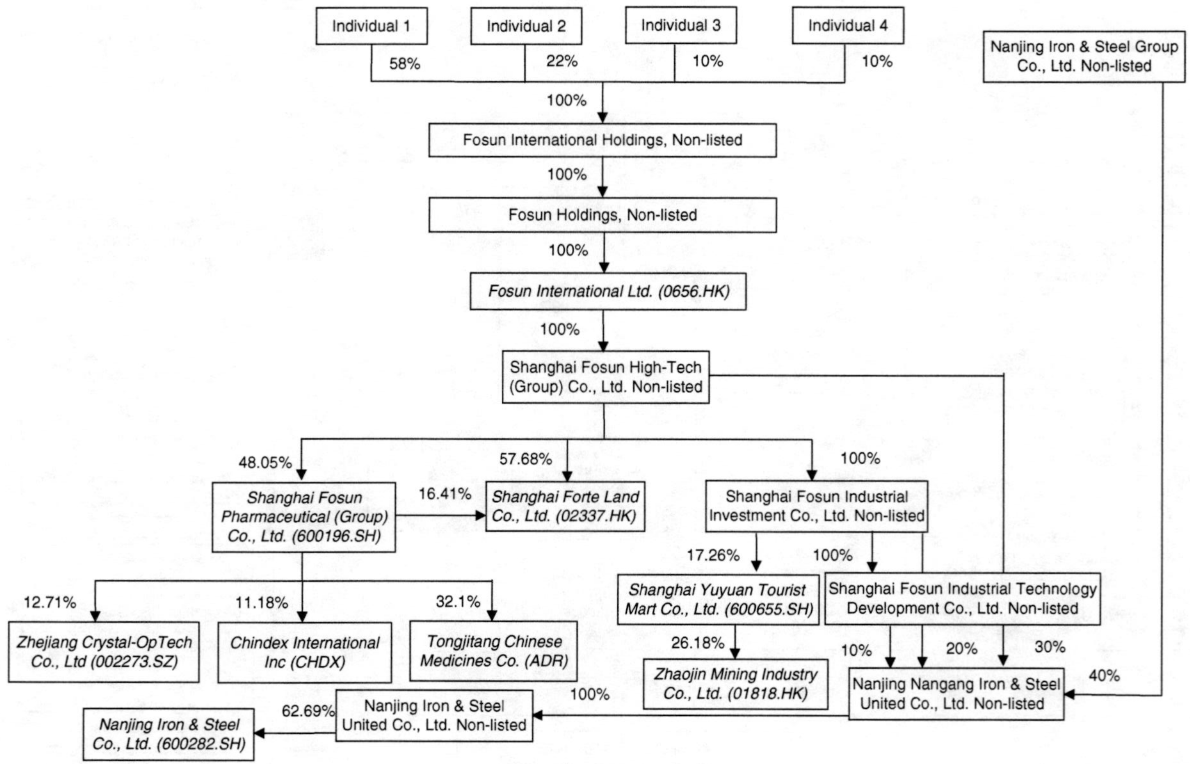

Figure 6.3 Fosun Group.

Source: Annual reports.

Notes: Listed companies in italics.

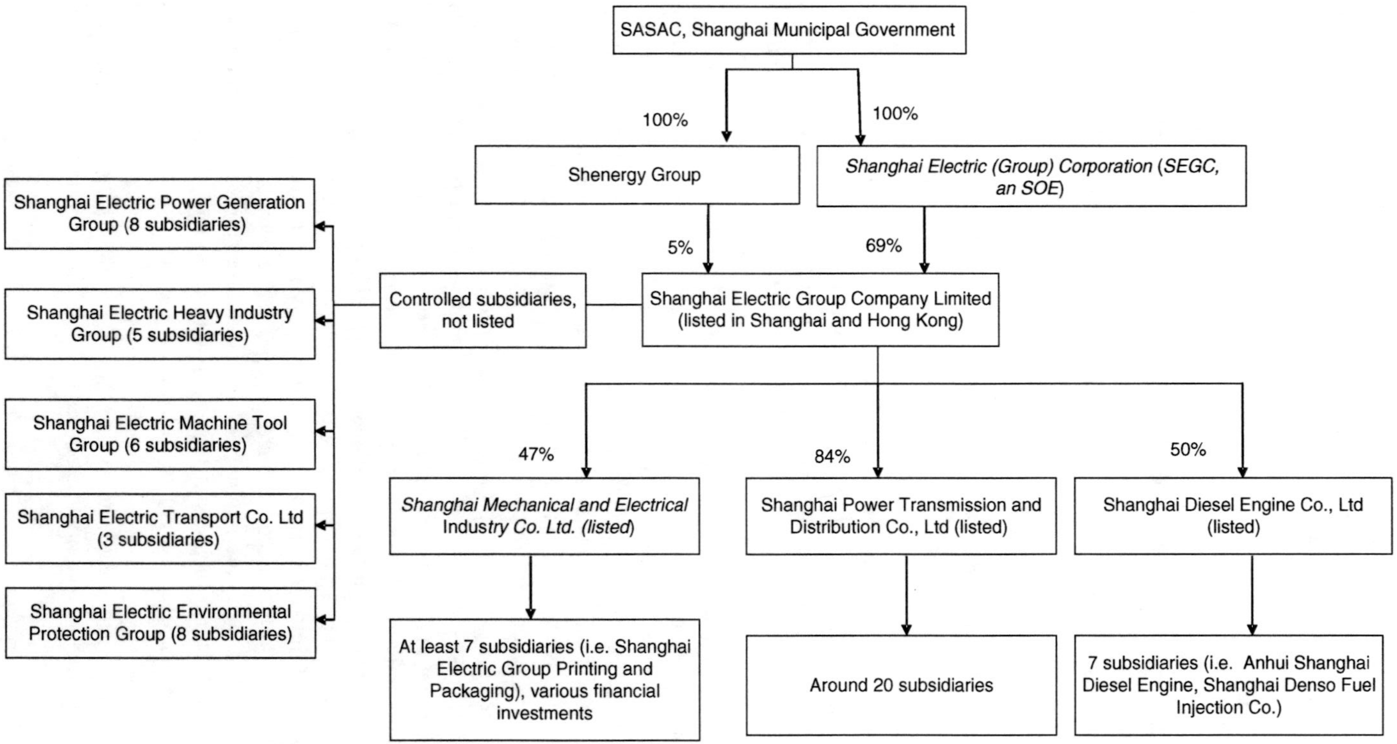

Figure 6.4 Shanghai Electric Group.

Source: Annual reports.

Notes: Listed companies in italics.

of 95.7 billion RMB). The group has grown quickly. The major business areas themselves each consist of separate groups (see Figure 6.4; Shanghai Electric 2006). Among the first-tier of subsidiaries there are three listed first-tier subsidiaries beneath a listed apex company, Shanghai Electric Group Company (listed in Shanghai and Hong Kong). Above this listed firm in turn stands the rather opaque Shanghai Electric (Group) Corporation (an SOE), which is its major shareholder (along with another smaller shareholder, Shenergy Group). Both of these two entities are in turn owned by Shanghai's SASAC. The ownership structure in the group leads to the classic divergence between cash flow and control rights. As of the end of 2006 the listed apex firm had varying ownerships shares in three listed subsidiaries (Shanghai Mechanical & Electrical Industry Co., Ltd. (47 per cent), Shanghai Power Transmission and Distribution Co., Ltd. (84 per cent) and Shanghai Diesel Engine Co., Ltd. (50 per cent) which were all listed on the Shanghai Stock Exchange.

Explaining China's pyramidal groups

To answer why pyramidal groups exist we may also ask the related question: in whose interests is it to form pyramids? We know that control pyramids 'concentrate a country's corporate decision making in remarkably few hands', magnifying the 'political and economic clout of the controlling shareholder' (Morck *et al.* 2005: 666). In the case of SOE related groups, therefore, their formation could, theoretically, be a deliberately coordinated plan by the controlling shareholders – the state/Communist Party. In doing so these groups could facilitate ownership diversification (by increasing the participation of the general public as shareholders) while maintaining control at the apex – in the hands of Party bureaucrats – a desirable option for those accustomed to power. Indeed, pyramidal control structures provide a neat solution for the state, allowing it to effectively socialize the risk of their business group expansion plans. Policy documents related to business group formation, however, provide little support for this argument. In the case of private groups, the incentives for pyramidal business group formation remain similar to those seen elsewhere in the world – enriching elites and enlarging their corporate empires – if one is cynical. From a more positive perspective, such methods also allow the most successful groups to expand at speeds they would otherwise not be able to achieve, as they allow the large-scale tapping of private investors to fund their business group expansion (i.e. like Fosun Group, which has used the capital it has raised to expand its operations at high speed).

It is also interesting to ask what other parties may benefit through formation of pyramids, particularly for state-owned groups, where pyramids appear to be more common. Recent research suggests current enterprise reforms in the state sector have favoured firm *insiders* at the expense of *outsiders* (such as the ultimate shareholders i.e. SASAC in many of the groups we consider). Lee and Hahn (2004), for example, show that insider control has become more dominant in business groups in recent years. They go so far as to suggest their formation is a direct result of insiders wishing to tunnel resources for their own private use (i.e. a form of corruption). Indeed, in many instances *de facto* privatization to insiders has already extended into *de jure* privatization through management buyouts (there are now around 1,000 private business groups in China). Our investigation of China's largest state groups shows how rather opaque 'group corporations' usually exist between the ultimate controlling shareholder and lower tiers of firms. These, in reality, are the corporations that determine the overall group strategy (though their exact nature and governance mechanisms are not very transparent, so we know less about them). These pyramidal structures, particularly when combined with the vast sea of other participating member firms (again, see Table 6.2), may provide opportunities for the controllers of these groups to expropriate minority shareholders (via, for example, transfer to other limited liability companies they may indirectly have interests in). Alternatively, if not for direct personal gain, the expropriation of minority shareholders at lower tiers of the pyramid may serve the more general targets that these group corporations wish to achieve (i.e. maintaining employment, providing social services and so on). In this sense the rationale for pyramids may be no different to some of the more nefarious original rationales for publicly listing firms. Key among these was the raising of capital on highly favourable terms. Pyramidal chains, of course, are even more efficient than the conventional method as they increase the divergence between ownership and control. The emergence of pyramids in China, therefore, may be part of an entrenchment process of certain corporate elites – mainly controllers of the non-listed group corporations – looking to enrich themselves personally as well as elevate themselves politically. In the Chinese case it may well be incumbent managers as opposed to the ultimate controlling shareholders (often SASAC, local and central) that have the greatest incentives to create pyramidal structures.

These pyramidal structures, of course, also go some way to appeasing the ultimate controlling shareholders (SASACs) and, ultimately, central policy makers (such as the State Council and related bodies) as well as insiders. This is because, as discussed, pyramids allow groups to expand very quickly with limited capital (as they draw from public investors). Government policy has looked to develop larger internationally competitive groups. This policy, at times, has emphasized size, as opposed to other firm-level indicators of success (i.e. good corporate governance). State Council directives issued in 1991 and 1997, for example, explicitly recognized the need to develop large-scale groups that could reap economies of scale, invest heavily in research and development, undertake overseas investment and, ultimately, compete internationally as modern transnational corporations. This policy has accelerated in recent years (Table 6.1, for example, captures the speed of growth among the groups). In this regard it is also interesting to note that until recently dividends from group subsidiaries have not been paid to the ultimate controlling shareholders, but instead to the parent group companies. This has also left these parent companies as 'cash cows' with large profits available for reinvestment to further help their expansion. The creation of pyramidal structures also facilitates this rapid expansion as at lower tiers within the pyramid the controlling shareholder commits smaller volumes of capital. Pyramidal structures may be a useful tool for inside controllers of groups to rapidly expand their size, so appeasing demands of their ultimate controlling shareholders, while also providing opportunities for personal gains.

During our investigation of China's largest groups we were struck by the extent of related business transactions ongoing among parent and subsidiary companies reported in the annual reports of the listed companies within these business groups. To give an impression of how insiders may use pyramidal structures to control group wide resources, reconsider again the example of CEC Group (Figure 6.1). In 2009, for example, China Great Wall Computer Shenzhen (listed in Shenzhen) sold some of the equity of Great Wall Computer Software and Systems Limited (valued more than 45 million RMB) to China National Software & Service Co., Ltd. (also listed in Shanghai) (China Great Wall Computer 2009; China Great Wall Computer Shenzhen 2010). This is an example of a lower tier company, held in a pyramidal chain, undertaking a transaction with a company higher up in the pyramid. While, as with most of these transactions, they are ostensibly considered to be undertaken at arm's length (i.e. market prices), there are clear conflicts of interest, particularly given the number of transactions taking place within the pyramidal groups between lower and higher tier firms. For example, there are also records of China Great Wall Computer also providing services and products to numerous other first tier subsidiaries (China Great Wall Computer 2009: 18). Again, such transactions may be subject to transfer pricing, and may be a means of tunneling resources from lower tier subsidiaries to those higher up in the group (with larger cash-flows to the parent company). Numerous other related party transactions exist within this group.

In CITIC Group, our second pyramidal business group example, the extent of pyramidal chains appears to be less dramatic. In fact, owing to the recent delisting of CITIC International Financial Holdings (Figure 6.2), the number of such companies held in chains appears to be decreasing. However, there are still numerous related party transactions ongoing between different companies in the group. CITIC 1616 Holdings, for example, which is held through CITIC Pacific Limited and CITIC (Hong Kong) Group, has entered into a number of recurring transactions with CITIC Pacific (a company higher up in the pyramid). For example, it has provided telecommunication services to CITIC Pacific (totaling around US$60 million) while at the same time it has paid CITIC Pacific a range of professional fees, including operating lease charges, building management fees and 'professional fees' (totaling around US$25 million) (CITIC 1616 Holdings 2009; CITIC 2009). Clearly, such transactions may be prone to agency problems in pyramidal business groups.

Turning to Fosun Group, as a private business group example, it also has a surprising number of listed companies held in pyramidal chains. This is particularly so because the parent of the group, Fosun International, has recently itself been listed. Moreover, the group as a whole has used the global financial crisis as an opportunity to buy up other listed Chinese companies. In particular, it has acquired large shares in some successful Chinese companies listed in the United States (Tongjitang Chinese Medicines, for example), whose valuations have been hit by the crisis. As such, it appears to be rapidly developing pyramidal ownership chains and expanding by using public shareholders to fund its investments. There are, unsurprisingly, a number of examples of ongoing related party transactions between member firms. Furthermore, a large number of these appear to be driven by the financial relationship between the parent and its subsidiaries. Typically, it seems, the parent has acted as the financier to other members of the group, giving rise to numerous transactions that have the potential for tunneling activities. Shanghai Forte Land, for example, had received large loans and loan guarantees from Fosun International. In total Fosun International has loaned around 1.5 billion RMB to other members of its group, repayable at an interest rate well above that set by the People's Bank of China (Shanghai Forte Land 2009). Clearly, it is one possibility that such financial relationships may facilitate tunneling.

Finally, Shanghai Electric Group also has a considerable number and variety of 'connected transactions' between the state-owned group corporation and listed firms in the lower tiers of the pyramid. For example, according to an earlier 2006 annual report of Shanghai Electric Group Company (listed in Hong Kong and Shanghai) these included purchasing agreements, financial services agreements, as well as the purchasing of companies from the SOE parent company Shanghai Electric Group Corporation (SEGC) (Shanghai Electric 2006). In a framework purchase agreement a first-tier listed group company, for example, agreed to buy raw materials and component parts from SEGC. In 2006, for example, the listed group's purchases from SEGC amounted to around 100 million dollars (Shanghai Electric 2006: 33).[6] This listed company also entered into financial services agreements with SEGC through Shanghai Electric Group Finance Co., Ltd., a subsidiary and the listed group's finance company.

As well as financial transactions, a range of asset transfers took place between SEGC and the first-tier listed firm. In 2006, for example, the listed group company acquired a 51 per cent equity interest in a firm belonging to SEGC.[7] The only real oversight, moreover, was provided by the supervisory committee: 'The Supervisory Committee has monitored the Company's connected transactions and is not aware of any act detrimental to the interests of the Company and shareholders in regard to the connected transactions in the reporting period'. Despite these assurances a number of irregularities existed in the governance of Shanghai Electric Group. Of which the most glaring of all was that in 2007 it emerged that the general manager of the *second tier listed company* (Shanghai Mechanical and Electric, see Figure 6.1) was concurrently the vice president of SEGC (contravening rule 27 of the company law: 'a listed company's business shall be completely independent from that of its controlling shareholders'). As the general manager of the second-tier listed arm, this individual was in the ideal position to tunnel resources back to SEGC. Indeed, according to the annual report of Shanghai Mechanical and Electric in 2006, it transferred ownership of one firm back to the parent company (apparently because it was losing money). Being a second-tier listed firm, owned through the listed group company (Figure 6.1), a wider divergence between ownership and control existed and incentives to tunnel from this firm were greater than from the apex firm. Of course, it is also possible to transfer resources to other limited liability companies in the group, in which managers may indirectly have interests in. If we return back to our earlier aggregate description (Table 6.2) it is fascinating to note just how rapidly limited liability companies have grown within these groups, opening up possibilities for such abuses.

Conclusion

We can still only speculate as to the exact reasons for the formation of pyramids in China and the implications of their formation. In other countries, such as Japan's pre-war *zaibatsu* and more recently South Korea's *chaebols*, however, pyramids allowed groups to grow rapidly and also led to elites controlling vast economic empires. In the Chinese case, they may also afford similar opportunities, as well as allowing insiders to personally benefit at the same time. If this is correct we might conclude that pyramidal structures may, ultimately, be highly damaging for minority shareholders and investors as a whole. This is because pyramidal type groups may end up further undermining the confidence of public investors. The increased perception of risk in undertaking investments, in the end, may drive up the cost of capital for Chinese firms. Morck *et al.* (2005) further believe that pyramidal structures' effects on corporate governance 'might well be especially injurious in countries that provide public shareholders ineffective legal rights against malfeasance by corporate insiders' (Morck *et al.* 2005: 693). This description would seem to fit China quite well. They further argue that the macroeconomic impact of such pyramids will also depend on their share of national corporate assets. In China the share of its business groups is large and has been growing quickly. As we know, by the end of 2008 there were around 3,000 officially recorded large enterprise groups with around 30,000 direct subsidiaries, employing in the region of 30 million people (SSB 2009). They have grown, on average, at around 20 per cent per year in real terms with regards to a number of indicators (assets, profits, research and development expenditures), so becoming relatively more important to the Chinese economy. If pyramids are forming, this could potentially become a serious corporate governance issue.

At the same time, it is significant that subsidiary growth has become a driver behind business group expansion, raising the question of how these groups are organized and what types of firms are now participating in them. One question of great relevance concerns whether pyramidal structures, considered by many to have a number of negative traits, are emerging. It is interesting to note, moreover, that although pyramidal ownership structures still remain common outside the United States and UK, this was actually not well recognized until quite recently (La Porta *et al.* 1999). In fact it has been shown that most large corporations in the world have controlling owners and that these owners most commonly use pyramidal structures to 'amass control over not just a single firm, or even just a few firms, but over large groups of corporations' (Morck *et al.* 2005: 659). This is particularly true of the East Asian economies where business groups have played a pivotal role in their development. Building on these observations we looked to ascertain the extent to which pyramidal structures are emerging among China's large groups, a question ignored to date. We have identified that pyramidal groups are forming in China – but are they common? Claessens *et al.* (2000) have found that the top 15 family controlled pyramids held corporate assets worth considerable shares of their GDP: 84 per cent in Hong Kong, 76.2 per cent, in Malaysia, around 50 per cent in Singapore and the Philippines and 40 per cent in Thailand. They argue that 'a relatively small number of families effectively control most East Asian economies' (quoted in Morck *et al.* 2005: 667). In an East Asian perspective then, extended hierarchical pyramidal business groups are still comparatively rare in China. What is more, our examples have found that in most cases the length of chains involved in the pyramids are comparatively short. Morck and Nakamura (2007), for example, report that as many as ten layers existed even by the 1920s in some pyramids in the United States. Longer chains increase differences between cash-flow rights and ownerships rights, exacerbating corporate governance issues. Given the short history of China's market economy and SOE transformation, however, the fact that we find any pyramids at all might be considered surprising.

Explaining why such group structures are emerging is not straightforward. Our case studies point towards some possible explanations. The withdrawal of the state's role to that of shareholder, to some extent, has possibly further opened the door to insider control. The formation of pyramids, therefore, may not be directly driven by the ultimate controlling shareholders, as it has been in other nations and at other periods of history, though it may also be looked upon positively by them. This is because it allows the groups to quickly grow in size by drawing ever greater volumes of capital from public investors (reflected in our aggregate data). The creation of larger corporate empires meets the aspirations and vision of the ultimate shareholders (local and central SASACs) in the case of state-owned groups. These owners (and policy makers) ultimately hope to transform their groups into internationally competitive groups, which many equate with size alone. Pyramidal groups, by allowing them to raise capital to fund new subsidiaries without forsaking control, therefore may help insiders meet these objectives. At the same time, the complex structure of these pyramidal groups may also help facilitate tunneling for direct private benefit to insiders. This is now far easier to accomplish given the transformation of other participating business group firms – the thousands of subsidiaries involved in related transactions – into limited liability firms through management buyouts and other mechanisms. In the case of private groups, the motivations for their formation may well be similar to those seen elsewhere in the world.

A striking feature of the groups we investigated were the significant number of mechanisms and high volume of transactions between related parties taking place within the groups. Such transactions may be undertaken for the wider benefit of the group (i.e. for all firms within the group, subsidizing certain loss making subsidiaries for the overall benefit of the group), but also clearly provide opportunities for private benefit. It may still be too early to say exactly why pyramids are forming. It is interesting, however, to note that as of yet there is limited discussion of these structures among policy makers. This is surprising, as the broader economic impacts of such ownership structures could be significant. If large segments of an economy are controlled in this way, some argue corporate governance problems can attain macroeconomic importance. These in turn might affect rates of innovation, economy wide resource allocation, and economic growth. This has been referred to as 'economic entrenchment' and occurs as a result of the political influence of these entrenched elites:

> If political influence depends on what one controls, rather than what one owns, the controlling owners of pyramids have greatly amplified political influence relative to their actual wealth. This influence can distort public policy regarding property rights protection, capital markets, and other institutions. We denote this phenomenon economic entrenchment, and posit a relationship between the distribution of corporate control and institutional development that generates and preserves economic entrenchment as one possible equilibrium.
>
> (Morck *et al.* 2005: 655)

What are the policy implications? Pyramidal ownership structures seem to evolve organically in most economies as there are strong incentives for elites to create them (even if these are not to the benefit of minority shareholders). By the 1920s, 'they were a preferred structure for big businesses throughout the world' (Morck and Nakamura 2007). Historically, the dismantling of business groups required concerted efforts on the part of regulators. In the United States, after the Great Depression, for example, inter-corporate dividend taxes were introduced, which led to their break up. In the UK, more stringent stock market listing rules were introduced in the 1970s with similar results (Morck 2007). In East Asia, Japan's *zaibatsu* were forcibly pulled apart in the aftermath of the second-world war. More recently, South Korea's *chaebols* and their pyramidal structures have been radically restructured in response to the Asian financial crisis and the perceived harmful role of these groups. If current trends continue it is possible China in future may face similar problems. At the very least, greater awareness and discussion of the possible problems such groups may pose, which has been very limited to date, is required.

Notes

1 According to one definition, business groups may be thought of as collections of independent firms with both formal and informal ties, the tendency to operate in numerous industries and often with the participation of outside investors (though to varying degrees) (Khanna and Yafeh 2007: 331).

2 The definition of the business group used by China's State Statistical Bureau includes all groups with sales or assets of over 500 million RMB. Firms are considered business group members in this data if over 50 per cent of their equity is owned by the parent company (referred to as *mu gongsi*, or literally 'Mother Company').

3 Keister's study, while very thorough, relegates the question of causality in her estimations to a single footnote. She therefore attributes the good performance of groups to internal institutional features (finance companies and so on) as opposed to the better

groups forming such institutions (i.e. the direction of causality reversed). Some of the other quantitative papers suffer from similar problems.

4 Under this law such companies require a minimum registered capital of 100,000 RMB and a minimum of two shareholders.

5 About 30 per cent of its investments in subsidiaries were in listed companies according to the annual report (p. 91). This is a proportion rather close to the national average (see Table 6.2).

6 It is stated that transacting prices are stipulated

> by the PRC Government (if any); and if there are no such stipulated prices, – prices not exceeding any pricing guidelines or pricing recommendations set by the PRC Government (if any); and if there are no such pricing guidelines or recommendations, – prices not exceeding market prices for a particular product.
>
> (annual report, p. 32)

Clearly these could be open to manipulation and in turn tunnelling through transfer pricing.

7 Shanghai Ship-use Crankshaft Co., Ltd. from SE Corporation for RMB 71.4 million. It also acquired Magine Machine Tool Co., Ltd. from SE Corporation for 252.4 million RMB.

References

Amsden, A. and Hikino, T. (1994) 'Project Execution Capability, Organizational Know-how and Conglomerate Corporate Growth in Late Industrialization', *Industrial and Corporate Change*, 3 (1): 111–148.

Carney, M., Shapiro, D. and Tang, Y. (2009) 'Business Group Performance in China: Ownership and Temporal Considerations', *Management and Organization Review*, 5 (2): 167–193.

CEC (2009) 'China Electronics Corporation Annual Reports', Online. Available at: http://www.cec.com.cn/ (accessed 11 September 2010).

China Great Wall Computer (2009) 'Annual Report', Online. Available at: http://www.greatwall.com.cn/ (accessed 8 September 2010).

China Great Wall Computer Shenzhen Co., Ltd (2010). 'Interim Report', Online. Available at: http:// www.cninfo.com.cn/ (accessed 27 August 2010).

CITIC (2009) 'CITIC Annual Report', Online. Available at: http://www.citic.com/ (accessed 8 September 2010).

CITIC 1616 Holdings Limited (2009) 'Annual Report', Online. Available at: http://www.citic1616.com/ (accessed 11 February 2010).

Claessens, S., Djankov S. and Lang, L. (2000) 'The Separation of Ownership and Control in East Asian Corporations', *Journal of Financial Economics*, 58 (1–2): 81–112.

Fan, P. H., Wong, T. J. and Zhang, T. (2006) 'The Emergence of Corporate Pyramids in China', *CESifo Economic Studies*, 52 (2): 415–453.

Fosun (2010) 'Fosun Annual Report'. Online. Available at: http:www.fosun.com (accessed 14 September 2010).

Granovetter, M. (1995) 'Coase Revisited: Business groups in the Modern Economy', *Industrial and Corporate Change*, 4 (1): 93–130.

Guest, P. and Sutherland, D. (2010) 'The impact of business group affiliation on performance: evidence from China's "national champions"', *Cambridge Journal of Economics*, 34 (4): 617–631.

He, J., Rui, O. M. and Zha, X. (2010) 'Business Groups in China', Online. Available at: http://www.fma.org/NY/Papers/financialconstraintandbusinessgroup.pdf (accessed 16 September 2010).

Keister, L. (1998) 'Engineering Growth: Business Group Structure and Firm Performance in China's Transition Economy', *American Journal of Sociology*, 104: 404–440.
Keister, L. (2000) *The Structure and Impact of Interfirm Relations during Economic Development*, Oxford: Oxford University Press.
Khanna, T. (2000) 'Business Groups and Social Welfare in Emerging Markets: Existing Evidence and Unanswered Questions', *European Economic Review*, 44: 748–761.
Khanna, T. and Yafeh, Y. (2007) 'Business Groups in Emerging Markets: Paragons or Parasites?', *Journal of Economic Literature*, XLV: 331–372.
La Porta, R., Lopez-de-Silanes, F. and Shleifer, A. (1999) 'Corporate Ownership around the World', *Journal of Finance*, 54 (2): 471–517.
Lee, K. and Hahn, D. (2004) 'From Insider–Outsider Collusion to Insider Control in China's SOEs', *Issues and Studies*, 40 (2): 1–45.
Leff, N. (1978) 'Industrial Organisation and Entrepreneurship in the Developing Countries: the Economic Groups', *Economic Development and Cultural Change*, 78: 661–674.
Liu, G. and Pei, S. (2005) 'The Class of Shareholdings and its Impacts on Corporate Performance: A Case of State Shareholding Composition in Chinese Public Corporations', *Corporate Governance*, 13 (1): 46–59.
Ma, X., Yao, X. and Xi, Y. (2006) 'Business Group Affiliation and Firm Performance in a Transition Economy: A Focus on Ownership Voids', *Asia Pacific Journal of Management*, 23: 467–483.
Morck, R. (2004) 'How to Eliminate Pyramidal Business Groups – The Double Taxation of Inter-corporate Dividends and other Decisive Policies', NBER Working Paper No. 10944.
Morck, R. and Nakamura, M. (2007) 'Business Groups and the Big Push: Meiji Japan's Mass Privatisation and Subsequent Growth', NBER Working Paper No. 13171.
Morck, R., Wolfenzon, D. and Yeung, B. (2005) 'Corporate Governance, Economic, Entrenchment, and Growth', *Journal of Economic Literature*, XLIII: 655–720
SEGC (Shanghai Electric Group) (2006) 'Annual Report', Online. Available at: http://www.shanghai-electric.com/en/.
Shanghai Forte Land Co., Ltd. (2009) 'Annual Report', Online. Available at: http://www.forte.com.cn/ (accessed 15 March 2010).
Smyth, R. (2000) 'Should China be Promoting Large-scale Enterprises and Enterprise Groups?', *World Development*, 28: 721–737.
SSB (State Statistical Bureau). (2002–2009) *China's Large Business Group Yearbook*, Beijing: China Statistical Press.
Sutherland and Ning, L. (forthcoming) *The Emergence and Evolution of Chinese Business Groups: Are Pyramidal Groups Forming? In China's State Capitalism: Growth and Crisis*, in B. Naughton and K. Tsai (eds.) Cambridge: Cambridge University Press.
World Bank (2005) 'SOE Dividends: How Much and to Whom?', *World Bank Policy Note*, World Bank, Beijing Office.
Yiu, D. Bruton G. D. and Yuan L. (2005) 'Understanding Business Group Performance in an Emerging Economy: Acquiring Resources and Capabilities in Order to Prosper', *Journal of Management Studies*, 42 (1): 183–206.
Zhang, L.Y. (2004), The Roles of Corporatization and Stock Market Listing in Reforming China's State Industry, *World Development*, 32 (12): 2031–2047.

7 Sustaining the growth of China's SMEs through ICT

Recent experience of policy initiatives and their implementation

David H. Brown and Qi Wang

Introduction

In the narrative of China's three decades of growth the importance of the non-state sector enterprises, comprising collective and private enterprises, including Township and Village Enterprises (TVE), is well documented. Until recently there was considerable confusion over the classification of enterprises but taking the broadest definition the non-state sector now contributes some 70 per cent of the economy, up from 20 per cent in 1980. This sector is dominated by privately registered enterprises. In 2006, excluding the 38 million private household enterprises, there were 4.3 million small and medium enterprises (SMEs) registered under the Administration of Industry and Commerce Department (China SME Online 2009). The ability of China to achieve sustainable growth of 8 per cent – the figure widely recognized as necessary to achieve a harmonious society and economy – is crucially dependent on this sector and the policy context within which it operates.

Despite the central role of SMEs in the economy the historic growth in these enterprises has come with little improvement in efficiency (total factor productivity), but in future this will need to change as the competitive environment becomes more challenging. The Government recognizes this and productivity increases from improved technology, especially the role of information and communications technology (ICT) or 'informatization', is a central strand of their policy for the promotion of SMEs.

It is in this context that the chapter explores Chinese Government ICT policy initiatives for SMEs and the reality of their implementation. Following this introduction the paper is structured into four parts. The first part is a short introduction to SMEs including their development in China. Part two discusses China's ICT policies and plans especially in relation to SMEs. In part three some selected theories are reviewed which inform the empirical work and the interpretation of the findings. Part four describes the case based research approach and a case study of implementing one aspect of ICT policy namely specialized ICT training for SMEs. Finally, part five discusses the findings and draws some conclusions and policy implications.

Background and China's SME

In virtually all economies SMEs play a critical role. They are the main source of new employment opportunities and are a major factor in innovation. The UK is a typical example of Western economies. In 2007 SMEs including sole proprietorships accounted for 59.2 per cent of employment and 51.5 per cent of private sector turnover. Employment growth was 1.5 per cent over 2006 underlining SMEs role in job creation (BERR 2009). In the European union (EU) overall there are 23 million SMEs representing 99 per cent of all enterprises and provide over 100 million jobs, and in some sectors account for more than three-quarters of all jobs (EU 2009).

Not surprisingly given this central importance there has been an increased policy focus on SMEs in Europe aimed at strengthening the sector. China's is no different. This point was made in the 2009 China Quarterly Update by the World Bank Country Director, who advocated that China should give more support to SMEs because future growth will come from the service sector and the SMEs that dominate this sector (World Bank 2009).

The first attempt to categorize small enterprises was made in 1988 and revised in 1992. However, the major policy framework for SMEs was laid out in the SME Promotion Law of the Peoples Republic of China, and adopted at the ninth session of the National People's Congress (NPC) in 2002 (China Online 2007). This wide ranging law under the State Council aimed to guide, regulate and develop the SME sector. It defined the general principles for national and local government above county level in respect of finance, enterprise, technical, market and social factors.

Although often described and referred to in the literature as a single sector SMEs are highly heterogeneous and comparisons are problematic not only within countries but between them. In the EU the main criteria for SMEs is number of employees (micro 0–9; small 10–49; medium 50–250). Turnover is a second but less used criterion (micro n/a; small $\geq$7 million euros; medium $\geq$40 million euros). In the Organization for Economic Co-operation and Development (OECD) the employee range is extended up to a maximum of 299 and in the United States up to 500 (Levy and Powell 2005). China is significantly different. Table 7.1 summarizes the categorization. The main differences are twofold. First, the number of employees varies between sectors so that small firms in China's classification would be medium elsewhere, and second China has a category of SME enterprise which is effectively 'large–medium' and is outside of the Western classifications for SMEs. These differences mean that direct comparisons with China need careful interpretation.

Notwithstanding these differences China's increased policy focus on SMEs reflects their role in job creation and innovation, as in the West. The initiatives announced at the Ninth National People's Congress (NPC) included the setting up of a National SME Development Fund arranged through a central fiscal budget and an explicit undertaking to increase technological innovation in SMEs including the use of information technology (IT) (Levy and Powell 2005). During the recent international financial crisis Minister Li Yizhong of the Ministry of Industry and

Table 7.1 China SME categories adapted by authors from www.sme.gov (*authors nomenclature for this category of enterprise)

Sector/size	*No of employees*	*Annual revenue (million RMB)*	*Assets (million RMB)*
Industrial			
large–medium*	≤2,000	≤300	≤400
medium	≥300	≥30	≥40
small	≤300	≤30	≤40
Construction			
large–medium	≤3,000	≤300	≤400
medium	≥600	≥30	≥40
small	≤600	≤30	≤40
Wholesale and retail			
large–medium (retail/wholesale)	≤500/≤200	≤150/≤300	n/a
medium (retail/wholesale)	≥100/≥100	≥10/≥30	n/a
small (retail/wholesale)	≤100/≤100	≤10/≤30	n/a
Transportation and post			
large–medium (trans/post)	≤3,000/ ≤1,000	≤300/≤300	n/a
medium (trans/post)	≥500/≥400	≥30/≥30	n/a
small (trans/post)	≤500/≤400	≤30/≤30	n/a
Hotels and restaurants			
large–medium	≤800	≤150	n/a
medium	≥400	≥30	n/a
small	≤400	≤30	n/a

Information Technology recognized the fragile position of many SMEs in terms of their finances and announced a doubling of funds for the SME Development Fund in 2009–10 from 3.9 to 9.6 billion RMB and that the 20 billion RMB in discounted loans for technology transformation would be steered towards SMEs (Li Yizhong 2009). A similar position in response to the need to improve the development environment for SMEs was recently introduced by the Sichuan Provincial Government (Sichuan SME Bureau 2009). In summary the central role of China's SMEs in growing the economy is well recognized and national and local policies reflect this, especially the need to improve SMEs products and performance through technology innovations. In the next part we look at the China's ICT sector including usage by SMEs.

China's ICT plans and informatization

China's policy setting bodies are the Ministry of Information Industry (MII), the Ministry of Science and Technology (MOST), and the State Commission on Science and Technology for National Defence (COSTIND). For ICT related industries and applications the most important is MII. The route to informatization started with the goal to achieve self sufficiency in IT early in the 1980s but had changed to emphasizing the use of IT in all sectors and by developing production capacity through joint ventures with foreign enterprises by the end of the decade (Kraemer and Dedrick 1995). Throughout and into the 1990s this was supported by a number of policy initiatives. They included: High-Tech Research and Development Plan, including an ICT theme (1986); Torch Programme for high-tech products, industrial development zones and ICT-based management and operating systems (1988); Golden Projects to develop an information economy and build administrative capability in key areas such as communications, cards and tax (1996) (Lovelock *et al.* 1996; National ICT Policies 2002). In addition to these national initiatives there were many other programmes linked to high-tech zones including five-year tax breaks for start-ups.

Since 2000 there have been several guiding policy instruments, notably the First National ICT Plan 2002, the National Plan for Science and Technology 2006–20, which includes the informatization development strategy, and the E-Business Eleventh Five-Year Plan 2006. These have been complemented by directives (e.g. for electronic signatures and online trading), 732 national standards and technical specifications for enterprise informatization (e.g. for Enterprise Resource Planning (ERP), Customer Relationship Management (CRM) and Collaborative Product Commerce (CPC)) (China SME Informatization Development Report 2007).

Under this dual Ministry structure China has made remarkable progress since the mid-1990s, and in 2004 overtook the United States as the world's leading exporter of information technology goods. In the period 1996–2004 the value of China's exports grew nine fold from US$19–180 billion (Kroeber 2007). But there are issues if this momentum is to be maintained for the next ten years and beyond. In a detailed study the World Bank has identified ICT as vital to managing China's unprecedented growth challenges but highlighted the low end of the value chain where the ICT industry is positioned. An illustration of this is that currently software products account for just 1–2 per cent of China's total IT industry exports – reflecting China's comparative strength in IT manufacturing and weakness in software development. Two further linked issues identified in the report, and central to this chapter, are the lack of skilled ICT workers (only 16 per cent of teachers in China have ICT training) and the relative low level of ICT application – *informatization* – in all Chinese firms (World Bank 2007).

In the specific context of SMEs informatization has also been problematic. The process has been both planned and emergent, over four stages (China Online 2008):

- Stage 1. 1980–2000: non-networked applications in office administration, production including Computer-aided Design (CAD)/Computer-aided Manufacturing (CAM), and Management Information System (MIS).
- Stage 2. 2000–2007: the 'Enterprise Informatization Program' through networked applications to do business and to improve the management.

- Stage 3. 2008–2015: popularization and deepening period to implement informatization of core businesses. Coverage of ERP related applications to reach 60–80 per cent.
- Stage 4. 2016-onwards: advanced period linking production, supply chain and customer relationships to achieve coverage of 80–90 per cent.

In reality China is still in Stage 2. Around 80 per cent of SMEs are connected to the internet but the percentage of SMEs that utilize Internet technologies and ERP/CRM 'complex type' applications is very low, probably less than five per cent. Only 10 per cent of enterprises have ICT trained staff and few of these are enterprise leaders. There is an acknowledgment in government that informatization in SMEs has different characteristics than in large enterprises. Specific problems include the gap between SMEs' informatization needs and current provision, the imbalance between developed and undeveloped regions and the relationship between informatization and enterprise size.

In this situation the focus is on tackling issues that constrain SME informatization by the provision of policy guidance, environment construction, organizing and coordination and service provision and the training of personnel (Ping Cui 2008). The World Bank summarized the position in their 2007 report and recommended:

> Many SMEs that do not have the means to access ICT applications or expertise can be aided by government – sponsored incubation ... Most of China SMEs are still in the early stages of deploying ICT applications. Firms that want to pursue e-commerce but do not have the means to do so can be assisted through government-sponsored e-platforms. Such initiatives could be coupled with promotional programs and e-commerce trade shows that demonstrate how e-commerce works.
>
> (World Bank 2007: 8)

In this chapter we describe a case which fits the above and took the form of a training initiative to increase awareness of e-commerce by SMEs in Shaanxi Province. But first in the next section we look at a theory framework for interpreting the case experience.

Theory perspectives

The discussion of theory and concepts is briefly summarized and centres on two selected areas. First, the role of government in the diffusion of technology (ICT) from the perspective of institutional theories, including an ICT policies review framework (*UNCTAD Information Economy Report* 2006); second, the implementation of policy at the enterprise level.

Institutional theories on ICT adoption and diffusion

Many previous studies of ICT adoption and diffusion focus more on the firm level, which regard diffusion as driven primarily by characteristics of the technology or users' perception of the technology. However, the adoption and diffusion of ICT may be influenced as much or more by the institutional environment in which the firm is embedded (Gibbs and Kraemer 2004). According to King *et al.* (1994, pp. 148), the institution can be defined as 'any standing social entity that exerts influence and regulation over other social entities'. The influence and regulation can be exerted by government authorities, international agencies, research-oriented high education institutions, etc. All may create barriers or incentives to the diffusion and adoption of ICT. The institutions might intervene in IT innovation and diffusion through influence and regulation which can play different roles depending on the 'supply–push' or 'demand–pull' forces driving the innovation. The supply–push force for technological innovation derives from the production of an innovative product or the process itself. Intervention can concentrate more on stimulating the production and application of factors that go into innovating, such as a growing support of scientific and technical knowledge. Demand–pull force arises from the willingness of potential users to use the innovation. For example, the e-commerce approach in Denmark focuses on ensuring rapid adaptation, implementation and exploitation of e-commerce. The Government draws attention to this through their own actions by requiring the use of e-technology in the public sector's own daily transactions. This is effectively a 'carrot and stick' approach and is combined with the Government's public information initiatives to motivate the private sector and consumers to participate (Andersen *et al.* 2003).

Institutional theory emphasizes the importance of institutional environments on the processes that shape organizational structures and actions and argues that organizational decisions are not driven purely by rational goals of efficiency but also the social and cultural factors and concerns for legitimacy (DiMaggio and Powell 1983; Gibbs and Kraemer 2004; Andersen *et al.* 2003). The theory pointed out that firms become more similar because of isomorphic pressures and pressures for legitimacy. Isomorphic pressures mean that firms in the same field tend to look like each other over time because they need to get legitimacy from competitors and customers through copying industry leaders. For example, instead of making decisions to adopt e-commence purely on internal driving forces to improve efficiency, firms are more likely to be induced to adopt and use e-commerce by external isomorphic pressures from competitors, trading partners, customers and government (Gibbs and Kraemer 2004). DiMaggio and Powell (1983) identified three mechanisms through which isomorphic change occurs, including (1) *coercive isomorphism* that results from formal and informal pressures by other organizations upon which they are dependent and by cultural expectations in the society (i.e. the existence of a common legal environment affects many aspects of an organization's behaviour and structure); (2) *mimetic processes* when uncertainty becomes a powerful force that encourages imitation (i.e. organizations may model themselves on other organizations when organizational technologies are poorly understood, when goals are ambiguous or when the environment creates symbolic uncertainty); (3) *normative pressures* that stem primarily from professionalization which is defined as 'the collective struggle of members of an occupation to define the conditions and methods of their work, to control "the production of producers" and to establish a cognitive base and legitimacy for their occupational autonomy' (i.e. Chief Information Executive-CIO) (DiMaggio and Powell 1983, pp. 152).

Government as a powerful institutional force

Among various institutions that exert their forces on the diffusion of ICTs, governments can be very significant:

> Many countries have designed and are implementing national ICT policies to reach overall development goals, recognizing the potential of new technologies in fostering economic and social development.
>
> (UNCTAD Information Economy Report 2006: 133)

However, the role of government as an institutional factor influencing the ICT diffusion is contested with researchers arguing for and against (Kraemer *et al.* 1992; King *et al.* 1994; Land 1990; Freeman 1988; Andersen *et al.* 2003; Scupola 2003). The opponents of government intervention in the diffusion of technologies invoke neoclassical economic philosophy of *laissez-faire*, which advocates the free spirit of innovation in the private sphere (Kraemer and King 1978, in King *et al.* 1994). It is argued that government intervention in the processes of innovation could distort the market for new ideas or mislead the private initiative, thereby damaging the underlying capabilities of technological innovation in the long run (Stiglitz 1987 in Kraemer *et al.* 1992). The governments policies derived from this model are dominated by three imperatives: (1) deregulation to remove the obstacles, (2) fostering competition and preventing the formation of monopolistic tendencies, (3) providing the individual with as much choice as is compatible with necessary safety, health and minimum moral standards (Land 1990: 8).

On the other hand, there are groups advocating government policies that support both domestic production and the use of computing technology. These proponents argue that the government could play a critical role in the process of technologies innovation. In the context of developing economies three different types of government policy have been in evidence addressing different sectors. There are *cross-cutting policies* relating to telecommunications infrastructure, awareness creation, training and education etc among all the sectors; *E-business policies* relating to the business environment, enterprise development (especially for SMEs) and ICT industry; *E-society and e-government policies* relating to areas as well as government services and customs (UNTAD Ecommerce and Development Report 2003). Recognizing that elements and priorities of national ICT strategies might differ between developed and developing countries UNCTAD introduced a model framework for the review and formulation of a national ICT strategy which focuses on the special concerns of developing countries and

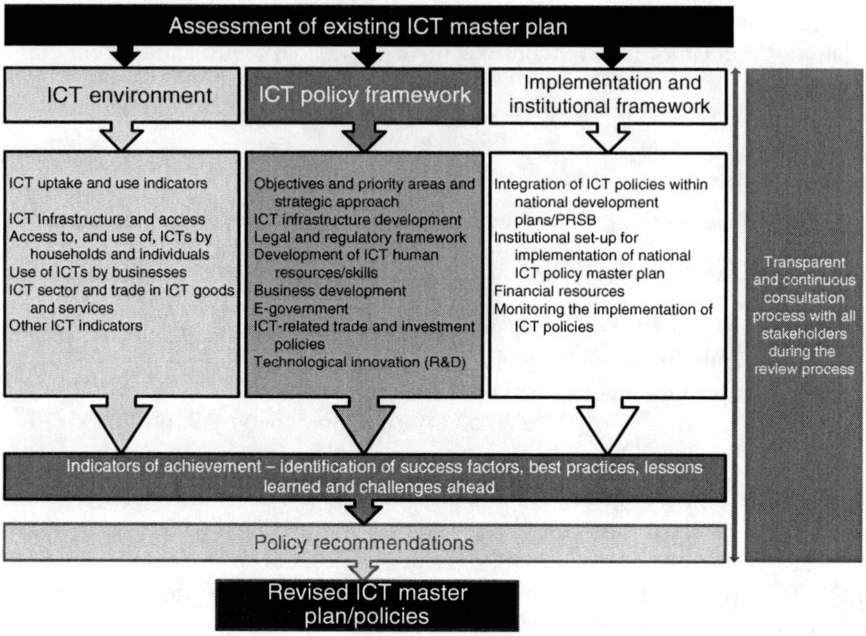

Figure 7.1 UNCTAD based ICT policy review model.

highlights three elements: environment; policy framework; and implementation and institutional framework (UNCTAD Information Economy Report 2006: 135).

In this chapter the emphasis is on the implementation mechanism and institutional framework which we discuss below.

Policy implementation

From the discussion in the second section above on China's ICT plans, direct government intervention and facilitation will play a role in ICT diffusion, including support for SMEs. It is also clear, however, that government or national ICT plans cannot guarantee the results of ICT application. The experience of western developed countries indicates that classical state-centred hard' policy-instruments such as legislation and economic support have been replaced by the more 'soft' action such as 'dialogues', 'governing through vision'; 'bench-marks and best practice' (Hall and Løfgren 2004: 150). Therefore, the effect of government intervention based on national ICT policies is greatly dependent on how it is implemented.

It is argued in the governance literature that central government is no longer capable (neither financially or in terms of expertise) of managing all the complex issues of modern society, and has to, to a certain extent, either entrust its capability to other actors (i.e. local government, trans-national bodies, social movements or the market), or to rely on networks of co-governing arrangements with a plurality of actors and institutions (Newman 2001, in Hall and Løfgren 2004). Policies are normally enacted through programmes and raise implementation issues arising from these co-governing arrangements (Locke 2006). Policy intervention, however, is an on-going, socially constructed and negotiated process and public agents and intermediaries exercise considerable influence. In this situation policies tend to be made as much at the *street level* by public agencies, as by the heads of policy agencies (Vega *et al.* 2008: 112; Lipsky 1980). In the following part we describe a specific policy initiative and its implementation from national to local level, which forms the basis of the case. In our final part the case description provides the basis for the discussion and our conclusions.

Case: National SMEs Informatization Promoting Project

In 2003 the National Development and Reform Commission (NRDC) launched the National SME Galaxy Training Project (NSMEGTP), which included provision for online training of SMEs under the Information Management System (IMS) initiative. In August 2005 the Chinese SMEs informatization alliance was established with the aims of establishing alliance of hardware, software, system services among SMEs, ICT providers and vendors and government. At the same time the MII, National Council Information Office and the Department of SMEs under NRDC jointly announced and implemented the '*National SMEs Informatization Promoting Project*'. The project was targeted at the problems of ICT diffusion and application by SMEs by providing ICT support and service to SMEs through the informatization alliance. The content included: SMEs informatization survey; selection of typical cases; free training by intermediaries to 10,000 SMEs on ICT application in different areas (training materials and limited number of funds provided by NRDC); promotion of one million SMEs online; holding SMEs information technology exhibition etc. Among the various actions, the priority was given to the initiatives for the free ICT training program for 10,000 SMEs and to get one million SMEs online (SMEonline 2006). It was this training initiative which became the focus of the case and in particular the experience of implementing the policy in Shaanxi Province.

Research approach and data collection

The overarching methodology is interpretive case study using primary and secondary data collected through multiple methods in the Shaanxi Province and centred on Xian. Case study research is particularly appropriate for problems in their formative stages when the experiences of actors and context are important and critical (Benbasat *et al.* 1987). The data collection, over a three-month period, is summarized below.

1. Secondary data collection: ICT policies, SME development, initiatives via online, papers, reports.
2. Primary data collection semi-structured interviews (ten): SME Info Service Co Ltd; Shaanxi SME Promotion Bureau; participating companies.
3. Primary data collection participant observation: Attendance at training conference.

Case narrative: stakeholder framework for service provision

At the central government level the main actors were NRDC (SMEs department), MII, State Council and others such as the National Council Information Office. Together they designed the overall plan for the SMEs Informatization Promotion Project, including purpose, content, possible process, participation and general instructions for the local governments relating to finance or resources. Contributing to this process there are also important intermediary companies including large IT enterprises and Beijing Online Co. Ltd. (founded by NRDC and responsible for China SME online), which offers online applications.

At the Shaanxi Government level the implementation was in the hands of Shaanxi SMEs Promotion Bureau (responsible for regulations and supervising the development of SMEs in the province and formed in 2006), and the Information Statistics Department with responsibilities for SME statistics and the promotion of ICT applications by SMEs. As with the central government there are important intermediaries notably Shaanxi SME Info Service Co. Ltd. This was founded under the Director of NRDC and the Shaanxi Government and since the start of the SME Informatization Promotion Programme has played a key implementation role. In discussion with the Shaanxi officials they felt that the Shaanxi government was on a learning curve. They indicated their current emphasis was to build awareness by SMEs of ICT applications and to help them get online for promoting their services. They specifically wanted to assist with computer usage and with building web sites and there was little consideration of complex applications. In Shaanxi Province they felt that few SMEs had the financial and human resources to utilize ICT in their businesses.

The final stakeholders in the delivery of the programme were the large IT enterprises. They were invited or persuaded by the Shaanxi government to sponsor the SME Informatization Project through funding and inputs. In return they were able to promote products and services as part of their input.

The intermediary companies at central and provincial levels receive financial aid from government as service-providers to government and also to SMEs directly. This reflects the requirement for professional knowledge of both technologies and management for ICT promotion. In this way intermediary service companies play a vital role in the process of implementing various initiatives. In 2006 and 2007, ten conferences or similar events were held but delays were experienced as a result of the approval process between the intermediaries and the government agencies. The events covered conferences, visits to example companies and fact finding seminars. The conference events were the preferred activity for policy implementation by Shaanxi.

Case narrative: training conference event

The targeted training conference was the high profile '10,000 SMEs Informatization Training – Xi'an Training Conference'. This was a national initiative under the NRDC centred on local Shaanxi companies. It was implemented by Shaanxi SMEs Promoting Bureau mainly through Shaanxi SME Online (Shaanxi SME Info Service Co. Ltd) and China SMEs Online (Beijing SME online Co. Ltd). Since this training was mainly for the manufactory companies, Machinery Industry Information Center China (http://www.miic.com.cn/) participated. Besides these government related stakeholders, commercial IT suppliers played a vital role. They were also the sponsors for the conference, Shaanxi SME Info Service Co. Ltd. The local organizer reported that most of the expense for the conference was met by the commercial IT suppliers since it gave them promotion opportunities. Because of the involvement of these suppliers, the training conference had a commercial air.

The training event had two key processes – *selection,* and *procedures and content*. Each is described below.

Selection: About 260 companies from different areas of Shaanxi province attended the conference. Most of them were manufacturing companies. From interviews with the officials and the participating managers there was no fixed process of choosing companies. In general, there were main four ways that companies were selected to attend the training.

- The online documentation on the government website gave an explanation about the content of the training, the subject, the time and the venues etc. Since the training was for the whole Shaanxi province, there was also a quota of companies assigned to different cities and towns. Companies could apply to their supervisory authority to be one of these.
- Besides the online publication, 'red-tile' documents were also sent to the subordinate local government authorities to invite companies to come. These were usually SMEs that had close relationships with city or township government. In some cases, in order to complete the quota of companies in a specific area, some companies would be asked to come by the government, even though they had low interest.
- The Shaanxi SME Info Service Company had online members for web services and some were invited.
- Commercial suppliers supporting the conference could issue invitations.

In summary, invitations were through multiple channels. Since the aim of most training was to build ICT awareness and popularize the concept, the willingness to attend, as well as suitability, were the main selection factors.

Procedures and content: The format for the conference followed a consistent pattern:

- Companies registered and received training materials about ICT applications for business, together with flyers from suppliers. Companies also received a password to become a member of the China SMEs Online, where companies could put their information online and enjoy some service provided for free (SMEonline 2006). The training book was produced centrally by the national intermediaries. The book used a simple and easy way to introduce various applications of ICT by SMEs such as enterprise website, management information system or research engine.

- Representatives from government (Shaanxi SME Promoting Bureau), intermediary services companies (Beijing SME online Co. Ltd and Shaanxi SME Info Service Co. Ltd) and commercial suppliers gave welcome speeches to indicate the importance the ICT application for SMEs with an emphasis on national policies but with special reference to SMEs in Shaanxi province and the manufacturing industry.
- Three lectures from the commercial IT sponsors. Each supplier introduced the importance and benefits of ICT for the enterprise but also introduced their products to the companies as well, indicating how these technologies can be applied to the business for SMEs. Since these suppliers were leading companies in their areas, the content they provided was up-to-date.
- One academic lecture that was generally thought to be too difficult.
- One lecture given by an enterprise about their approach to applying ICT, and the benefits and changes that happened to their enterprise. The General Manager of this company used clear statistics to present the dramatic change and shared the stories of both success and failure during the whole process. This was the most well received input.

For the researchers as participant observers the content of the training was quite disappointing. There is no clear connection between the different lectures. This also seemed to be the general view of the participants interviewed. A lot of information was too advanced to be really useful. For example, ERP (Enterprise Resource Planning) featured strongly in the training lectures and was recommended. However, it was quite impractical for the most of the 260 companies present since a large number of enterprises were informally managed with manual data. These companies were at the beginning of ICT usage. The academic input was out of date and did not relate to the current situation of most SMEs.

The total training conference lasted a full day of inputs with little opportunity for the participating companies to discuss the issues or express their opinions. There was no formal process for the feedback.

Discussion and conclusions

The Shaanxi case provides an insight into the mechanism of ICT policy implementation at the central and local levels and offers an opportunity to reflect on the likely extent to which the government's goal of *informatization* is being served by the '*ICT training for 10,000 SMEs*' initiative. The case can be discussed from two perspectives – policy and local implementation practice – and can be linked to the theory frames introduced in part three.

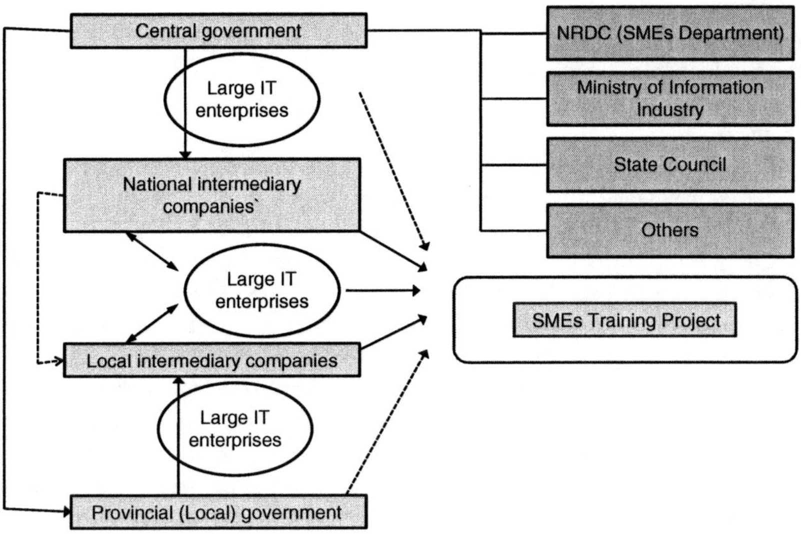

Figure 7.2 Stakeholder involvement in the National Informatization Promoting Project.

Policy and stakeholders

According to the e-business framework developed by the United Nations Conference on Trade and Development (UNCTAD), the lack of efficient institutional framework and consultations with all stakeholders are the major bottlenecks for a limited implementation of ICT programmes (UNCTAD Information Economy Report 2006, pp. 148). The communication and cooperation among various stakeholders becomes significantly important in the whole process of implementation. In the context of China, the implementation involves an array of stakeholders and these are shown in Figure 7.2.

Overall the position in China is clearly one of a government as a powerful institutional force. It decides policy, identifies and plans the major policy initiatives (projects) and provides significant funds. Informing these activities is a variety of stakeholders and expertise. As can be seen in the figure there are no direct links (bold) between central or local government and the training project. Instead they influence implementation indirectly (dotted line) through intermediaries. Of particular interest are the large commercial IT companies who are present centrally and at the local level. At the central level they influence policy and plans and at the local level their involvement in the detailed activities is very significant. They provide resources, both financial and training inputs, and in return promote products and services. Implementation via this network of stakeholders presents a communication challenge as signalled in the UNCTAD report. The direct evidence in this research is that bottlenecks did occur and delays followed as a result of poor links between the local intermediary companies, and local and central government for funding approvals.

The extent of the IT suppliers involvement in such a high profile policy initiative is strong evidence of China's policy of supply–push to promote the ICT diffusion among SMEs (King *et al.* 1994). In the process of implementing ICT policies, the government's focus is on popularizing the concept of ICT applications by SMEs. Large IT enterprises come to explain what their products can do for SMEs but from our research in Shaanxi there is little prior investigation into the specific needs of the SMEs by these companies. The government anticipates that SMEs will introduce ICT into their processes as a result of the inputs and product promotion of the large suppliers. Some SMEs clearly do appreciate the advantages from ICT and have in place the resources to implement. Others are being influenced to do so even if, as was suggested by several of the participants, their businesses are not ready. Additionally, many of the applications promoted during the training such as Enterprise Resource Planning (ERP) software are derived from western business and organizational models and are not suited to local SME arrangements.

This supply–push emphasis is relevant to the concept of isomorphic pressures on enterprises suggested in institutional theory (DiMaggio and Powell 1983). In the context of the training project coercive isomorphism is clearly present resulting from the formal and informal pressures, including expectations set by the alliance of stakeholders. The selection process embodies this with the requirement for many firms to attend the training. Similarly, the follow up processes through SME online Ltd reinforce the expectations. Mimetic pressures are more subtle and arise from the best practice examples and from the difficult economic position for many SMEs which makes them more susceptible to adopt the technologies.

Beyond the training project coercive isomorphism for ICT usage within SMEs is evidenced in other ways. The government's huge commitment to develop official web sites as the preferred channel of communication and influence extends to the SME sector. New regulations and laws provide the legal framework for the e-business. Intermediaries maintain the web sites for SME ICT services and provide services directly to SMEs. Encouraged by the government, there are also different ICT alliances depending on location and industry sector. Finally, the government SME Development Funds favouring ICT is yet another pressure. With the above evidence it is clear that the mimetic pressure has emerged as a powerful force for the promotion of ICT diffusion in Chinese SMEs.

Local implementation

There have been a number of studies looking at policy and e-business adoption by SMEs including Taylor and Murphy (2004), Gengatheran *et al.* (2005), Brown and Lockett (2004) and Locke (2006). What is striking here in a broader context is the prescience of Lipsky (1980) with the concept of *street-level bureaucracy*. The SME Training Project provides powerful evidence of the way in which the intermediaries influence and impact on the policy intent at the final implementation stage. It occurs at the selection stage when different stakeholders invite SMEs.

An example is the invitation to unsuitable firms to fill quotas, or invitations to prospective clients by suppliers. It also occurs in the training content through the emphasis by suppliers on selected ICT applications such as ERP. These are complex applications that are relevant to a relatively small number of the 260 firms in the training project, but these are potential clients. In this way the government's central policy aim of raising ICT awareness within small firms through the training conferences is undermined by local agendas. The comments from participants support this conclusion with their doubts about the complexity of the material.

Summary

SMES are crucial to China's economy – they are important sources of new employment and innovation. Part of this innovation is technology independent but increasingly ICT is a driver of innovation not just in product terms but in processes within the firm and to access markets. In this respect the ICT readiness of China's SMEs, like many western economies, is poor. The government's policy of supply–push is a significant response to this and the '*ICT training for 10,000 SMEs*' is a major project within this policy. The findings above illustrate two difficulties of implementing technology-based policy to SMEs. First, SMEs are highly heterogeneous and this is difficult to accommodate in the design of projects. Not only are they at different stages of readiness in terms of financial and human resources, but they are also in different sectors. This training conference in Shaanxi was exclusively for the manufacturing sector and to date in Shaanxi no equivalent conference for the retail and service sectors has been available. Second, there are 4.3 million SMEs and many of these are potential beneficiaries of ICT. This combination of scale and technical expertise means that the government must implement through a complex network of intermediaries to act at the local level. In doing so policy intent and local delivery can diverge as was the case here. Managing intermediaries emerges from this research as an important challenge for the China government.

From the above evidence and analysis there are doubts about the rate at which Chinese SMEs can be *informatized* and this will adversely influence their rate of growth – the starting point of this chapter. This is a key link from this chapter to the theme of the book. Our view on rising China and its role in the global economy are informed by recent history, but herein lies a difficulty. Future growth will require improved productivity and much of this will come from more effective use of ICT within SMEs. In respect of push–pull policies whilst it is the case that western economies have tended to innovate through market pull mechanisms this hasn't been entirely successful for ICT and SMEs. In this chapter we have shown how push based ICT policies in China for improving productivity in SMEs have been introduced but that policy implementation remains a challenge. It is a challenge that China will need to resolve to achieve sustainable growth in SME performance and in doing so would offer insights into the role of government intervention for enhancing ICT in SMEs in many economies.

References

Andersen, K. V., Bjørn-Andersen, N. and Dedrick, J. (2003) 'Governance Initiatives Creating a Demand-Driven E-Commerce Approach: The Case of Denmark', *The Information Society*, 19 (1): 95–105.

Benbasat, L., Goldstein, D. K. and Mead, M. (1987) 'The Case Research Strategy in Studies of Information Systems', *MIS Quarterly*, September, 369–386.

Berr (2007) 'Department of Business and Regulatory Reform SME Statistics for 2007', Online. Available at: http://stats.berr.gov.uk/ (accessed 21 March 2009).

Brown, D. H. and Lockett, N. (2004) 'Potential of Critical E-Applications for Engaging SMEs in E-Business: A Provider Perspective', *European Journal of Information Systems*, 13: 21–34.

China SME Informatization Development Report (2007) Online. Available at: http://www.sme.gov.cn/web/assembly/action/browsePage.do?channelID=1085017184454 (accessed 19 March 2009).

China SME Online (2007) SME Promotion Law of the People's Republic of China. Online. Available at: http://www.sme.gov.cn/web/assembly/action/browsePage.do?channelID=10852196511l (accessed 19 March 2009).

DiMaggio, P. J. and Powell, W. W. (1983) 'The Iron Cage Revisited: Institutional Isomorphism and Collective Rationality in Organizational Fields', *American Sociological Review*, 48(2): 147–160.

EU (2009) 'European Commission Facts and Figures – SMEs in Europe'. Online. Available at: http://ec.europa.eu/enterprise/ (accessed 19 March 2009).

Freeman, C. (1988) 'Japan: A New National System of Innovation?', *Technological Change and Economic Theory*, in G. Dosi, C. Freeman, R. Nelson and G. Silverberg (eds), London: Printer Publishers.

Galaxy Training (2004) Online. Available at: http://www.sme.gov.cn/web/assembly/action/browsePage.do?channelID=1085017184455&contentID=1090732817106 (accessed 5 June 2007).

Genhatharen, D., Craig, S. and Burn, J. (2005) 'Government Supported Community Portal, Regional Market Places for SMEs: Evidence to support a Staged Approach', *Electronic Markets* 15(4): 405–417.

Gibbs, J. L. and Kraemer, K. L. (2004) 'A Cross-Country Investigation of the Determinants of Scope of E-commerce Use: An Institutional Approach.', *Electronic Markets*, 14(2): 124–137.

Hall, P. and Løfgren, K. (2004) 'The Rise and Decline of a Visionary Policy: Swedish ICT-policy in Retrospect', *Information Polity*, 9(3): 149–165.

King, J. L., Gurbaxani, V., Kraemer, K. L., McFarlan, F. W., Raman, K. S. and Yap, C. S. (1994) 'Institutional Factors in Information Technology Innovation' *Information Systems Research*, 5(2): 139–169.

Kraemer, K. L. and Dedrick, J. (1995) 'National Technology Policy and Computer production in Asia Pacific Countries', *Centre for Research on Information Technology and Organizations*. Online. Available at: http://www.crito.uci.edu/git/publications/pdf/pac-023.PDF (accessed 3 March 2009).

Kraemer, K. L., Gurbaxani, V. and King, J. L. (1992) 'Economic Development, Government Policy and the Diffusion of Computing in Asia-Pacific Countries', *Public Administration Review*, 52 (2): 146–157.

Kroeber, A. (2007) 'China's Push to Innovate in Information Technology', *Innovation with Chinese Characteristics*, in L. Jakobson (ed), Basingstoke: Palgrave.

Land, F. (1990) 'Viewpoint: The Government Role in Relation to Information Technology', *International Journal of Information Management*, 10: 5–13.

Levy, M. and Powell, P. (2005) *Strategies for Growth in SMEs: The Role of Information and Information Systems*, Oxford: Elsevier.

Li, Y. (2007) 'Strengthen Technological Transformation to Support SMEs'. Online. Available at: http://www.sme.gov.cn/web/assembly/action/browsePage.do?channelID=12124855162 (accessed 20 March 2009).
Lipsky, M. (1980) *Street Level Bureacracy: Dilemmas of the Individual in Public Services*, New York: Russell Sage Foundation.
Locke, S. (2006) 'E-Local Government Strategies and Small Business', *The Journal of American Academy of Business* 10 (1): 21–30.
Lovelock, P., Clark, T. C. and Petrazzini, B. A. (1996) 'The Golden Projects': China's National Networking Initiatives', *Information Infrastructure and Policy*, 5 (4): 265–278.
National ICT Policies (2002) Online. Available at: http://www.american.edu/initeb/wl5521a/National%20ICT%20Policies.htm (accessed 5 June 2007).
Ping, C. (2008) 'Abstract, China SME Informatization Development Report 2007'. Online. Available at: http://www.sme.gov.cn/web/assembly/action/browsePage.do?channelID=1085637727977 (accessed 8 January 2009).
Scupola, A. (2003) 'Government Intervention in SMEs E-Commerce Adoption: An Institutional Approach', in 7th Pacific Asia Conference on Information Systems. Online. Available at: http://66.102.1.104/scholar?hl=en&lr=&q=cache:3y530THnWCEJ:www.pacis-net.org/file/2003/papers/e-business/28.pdf+Scupola,+2003 (accessed 5 August 2007).
Sichuan SME Bureau (2009) *Accelerating SME Development*. Online. Available at: http://www.sme.gov.cn/web/assembly/action/browsePage.do?channelID=11543066380, (accessed 20 March 2009).
Taylor, M. and Murphy, A. (2004) 'SMEs and the take up of E-Business', *Urban Geography*, 25 (4): 315–331.
'UNCTAD Information Economy Report: A Development Perspective 2006', in United Nation Conference on Trade and Development. Online. Available at: http://r0.unctad.org/ecommerce/ecommerce_en/ier06_en.htm (20 May 2007).
Vega, A., Chiasson, M. and Brown, D. (2008) 'Extending the Research Agenda on Diffusion: the Case of Public Program Interventions for the Adoption of E-Bbusiness Systems in SMEs', *Journal of Information Technology* 23: 109–117.
World Bank (2007) 'China's Information Revolution: Managing the Economic and Social Transformation', World Bank, Washington, DC.
World Bank (2009) 'China Quarterly Update', World Bank, Washington, DC.

8 Fiscal reform, ownership restructuring and corporate objectives in Chinese state-owned enterprises

Da Teng

Introduction

Despite extensive political and economic literature on State-Owned Enterprises (SOEs), the theoretical and empirical literature on managing different SOEs remains embryonic. The central problem facing those who attempt to construct a theory of SOE management is dealing with the multiple pressures acting on SOEs with regards to firms' objectives (Kornai 1992; Kornai *et al.* 2003). Governments have multiple socio-political and economic goals. SOEs may be expected to seek profit, to promote industrialization, to advance technology, to create jobs, and to reduce regional disparities. Research on critical managerial tasks is complicated by these objectives and research on effectiveness is hampered by disagreements on accountability and performance criteria (Aharoni 1981; Aharoni 1982; Jones 1982; Hafsi *et al.* 1987; Hafsi and Koenig 1988). The organizational life cycle literature (Chandler 1962) yields insight into this problem by proposing that the key variables of managerial priorities and effectiveness criteria change during stages in the life cycle (Hafsi *et al.* 1987). I argue that strategic orientation and managerial priorities in Chinese SOEs change not as reflections of the organizational life cycle, but rather as reflections of the politically structured restriction of resources after the Chinese economic reform.

The literature on SOE-government relationships displays great diversity (Hafsi *et al.* 1987). Some have described the SOE as an "obedient servant" of government, while others emphasize the market function and argue SOEs are autonomous (Hafsi 1985). Finally, the bulk of the literature contends that there is an adversarial relationship between SOE and government, where the government is trying to superimpose its socio-political goals on market-oriented SOEs (Hafsi *et al.* 1987; Kornai 1992). The discussion on corporate objectives of Chinese SOE may become clear when we take China's post-reform evolving political system into consideration. Like many countries in the world, China's experienced the tendency of economic decentralization. However, there are two key differences between China experience and the experiences of other countries. First, in many western countries, economic decentralization coexisted with political evolution or decentralization. In contrast, the Chinese economic decentralization took place under the control of the Chinese Communist Party. Therefore, central government still maintains a strong power over local officials and cadres, who are not elected directly by the people but are appointed or removed by the parties (Tan 2002; Li and Zhou 2003). Second, although central government tightly controls the local officials in terms of their promotion or demotion, local authorities enjoy great autonomy in terms of economic decisions for local development (Li 1997; Chung 2000). Such a circumstance is partly attributed to unclear duty-cutting between central and local governments (Qian 1996; Qian and Roland 1998), but more importantly, such a circumstance reflects a difference in cognisance, discretion and agendas between local and central authorities (Goodman 1994).

It therefore leads us to ask: (1) What are the different objectives of the state and its agencies in being block holders in listed enterprises? and (2) How are the various governmental institutions actually involved in the governance of such enterprises?

A study of state-owned organization's ownership and objectives, defined here as socio-political (Stiglitz and Weiss 1981; Greenwald and Stiglitz 1986; Boardman and Vining 1991), economic (Boardman *et al.* 1986; Boardman and Vining 1991) is important for several reasons. First, understanding relationships between ownership structure and objectives can help to reveal the underlying logic for organizations' activities and can help organization members evaluate strategies (Boardman and Vining 1991). It has long been hypothesized that the behaviour of a company is variable, depending on the relative degree of public/private ownership and the extent of concentration/dispersion of share holdings. Different ownership conditions affect the extent to which the company engages in profit maximization or socio-political goal maximization. They also affect the degree of conflict between large block holder and minority shareholders, and between an owner and management (Jensen and Meckling 1976). In particular, studying the relationship between ownership and corporate objectives can provide researchers and investors with multiple and integrative organization perspectives. A better understanding of the relationships can help investors evaluate the consistency of the firm's proposed strategies with resources, interests and the constraints underlying ownership; and can also help stockholders to understand and monitor managers' activities (Boardman *et al.* 1986). Second, researchers have often studied state-owned organizations reflecting one ownership type; their findings may have been implicitly over generalized to all organizations (Meyer 1982; Sapienza 2004). The first step to assessing the generalizability of diverse findings and integrating them is to identify how these broad classes of organizations differ. This chapter therefore argues that the behavioural consequences of different objectives of SOEs is likely to be variable and determined primarily by the nature of ownership. Different ownership conditions affect the extent to which SOEs engage in profit maximization and socio-political goal maximization.

Theoretical background

Corporate objective – the theoretical background

The ability and incentive of owners to control managers is related to the nature of ownership. Property rights theorists argue that since ownership of SOEs is generally less transferable than ownership of private companies, SOEs are less subject to the market for corporate control, resulting in inferior performance (Shleifer 1998). And there is much empirical evidence to suggest superior performance of private sector firms (Vining and Boardman 1992). However, there are two major problems with most of the empirical research.

Jensen (2001) argues that a firm must have a single objective in order to tell us what is a better performance criteria and what is worse; we then must face the issue of what that definition of better is. In other words, to judge the performance of a firm one has to consider how performance is defined and measured. Economists focus mainly on efficiency as a criterion for performance, but there are different definitions of efficiency. Financial efficiency, for example profitability, cannot be the sole criterion for judging performance because SOEs were created to achieve social or strategic objectives and reported profits often depend critically on the prices of both inputs and outputs set by the government (Boardman and Vining 1989).

Under such propositions, the objectives for state-owned enterprises can be first grouped into two main categories. First, there are socio-political agendas for SOEs (Kaldor 1980; Boardman *et al.* 1986; Boardman and Vining 1991). Since the 1950s in China, state ownership has played an important role in nationalization programs. Such nationalization programs were based on the belief that enlarging public properties and activities could open the way to a fundamental change in the distribution of power within society (Qi 1995; Qian 1996). Such motives may be linked to the promotion of economic growth and social transformation in underdeveloped regions (Vernon and Aharoni 1981; Jones 1982). Thus, an SOE should not be considered as a pure economic actor. It has many other functions beyond profit seeking. For instance, many Chinese SOEs, particularly large and medium sized ones, formed small societies in which all kinds of social welfare are provided by the firm (Qian 1996). Therefore, the argument in favor of SOEs can be summarized thus: "make its decisions on the basis of long-term considerations and these are not or cannot be profit minded" (Kaldor 1980, p. 5).

On the other hand, a SOE may also have profit-oriented objectives. The economic reform and fiscal reform fostered profit incentives for SOEs and turned SOEs from traditional institutions into modern companies. Therefore, these firms have independent relationships with the government and have profit oriented corporate objectives.

Chinese economic reform and corporate objectives of different Chinese state-owned enterprises

Three important but unequally studied types of governmental ownership are examined: state enterprises that are predominated by central government; state enterprises that are predominated by provincial government, and state enterprises that are owned by municipal government. Noting the institutional difference across counties, Shleifer and Vishny (1997) argue that the effectiveness of control by large shareholders is tied to the ability to exercise their control rights. Compared to the Soviet Union where the strong ministerial system transmitted economic plans directly to enterprises, the Chinese system decentralizes economic and administrative power to the localities (Qian 1996). At the local level (i.e. provincial and municipal government), the constraints of the state plan and fiscal system, however, provided localities with little inducement to generate additional revenues before the economic reform in the late 1970s. Localities were required to turn over most of the revenues generated within the locality to the upper levels, which in return provided budget allocations for expenditures.

The economic reform and institutional changes in the 1980s marketized the economy with the removal of constraints on local government autonomy and injected strong economic incentives for local government to be entrepreneurial. Two of the most influential institutional changes that promoted local government to become entrepreneurial were the "decollectivisation of agriculture production" and fiscal reform (Davis and Vogel 1990), which both affected fiscal flows and revenue retention. The "household responsibility system" for agricultural production stripped village government of the rights to income from the sale of agriculture produce. Fiscal reform clearly defines the localities' share of the tax revenues and grants them the rights to the fiscal surplus, or residual, which the literature on agency theory posits as the most important mechanism for facilitating hierarchic control (Wong 2000). The Chinese case illustrates the general point that "under a range of conditions, the principal's optimal incentive structure for the agent is one in which the latter receives some share of the residual in payment for his effort, thus giving him a direct stake in the outcome." The institutional changes therefore made local-level governments in China fully "economic actors" with their own interests, not just administrative service providers as they are in other counties (Qi 1995).

Central government and its agencies, namely the State-owned Asset Supervision and Administration Commission (SASAC), on the other hand, may seek to take advantage of block shareholding and to serve the long-term interests of their own. Because their obligations often extend over generations, central government may be concerned with long-term economic indicators and political issues. Instead of promoting individual enterprise, efficiency, and competition, central governments may influence corporate resource allocation to support social objectives such as regional development, or protecting employment (Vernon and Aharoni 1981).

The determinants of corporate objectives orientation

Fiscal reform – soft budget constraints view

The term "soft budget constraint" has been adopted to examine firms' and governments' behaviour in socialist economies. Kornai (1980 and 1986) observed the soft budget constraint phenomenon in the Eastern European countries and suggested that the state provides resources to the SOE, either in the form of necessary inputs or of various protection instruments. Subsidies, loans, tax exemptions, and legal barriers to entry are but few examples. Since then, this concept has been widely accepted to explain the inefficiency of socialist economies and insufficient profit-making incentive for SOEs. According to this analysis, as owners of enterprises, governments have other objectives besides profitability (Kornai 1992): maintenance of full employment, funding of pensions, medical insurance, and provision of housing and social services. SOEs' financial interests are further weakened by the ability of government to redistribute funds from profitable enterprises to subsidize those that are unprofitable. Analysts and scholars agree that soft budget constraint is pervasive in socialist economies and the government tends to bail out loss-making enterprises with financial subsidies or other instruments. Therefore, we suggest the strategic orientation of a SOE is actually based on hardness of the budget constraints. Passing policy requirements down to the SOE cannot be done by compulsion alone (Hafsi and Koenig 1988), rather the government tends to restrict resource availability to control SOEs' behaviour.

The government's non-profit interests in firms, and a dependence on government for bailouts and subsidies, create a mutual dependence between government and enterprise. There arises a regime in which budget constraints are softened and the firm's incentives to fulfil socio-political objectives are strong. In contrast, a firm's incentives to pursue profit are stronger if budget constraints are hardened (Qian and Roland 1998). Therefore, as demonstrated in Figure 8.1, moving along the political hierarchy from central to municipal government is equivalent to reducing exerted government owners' control and transferring a SOE from a social political orientated organization to a market oriented one.

Economic reform hardened the budget allowance for provincial and municipal governments, and fiscal reform strongly linked local expenditures with local revenues. Such a link aligns the interests of local governments to local economic prosperity and SOEs' success. Provincial and municipal government officials and SOEs' managers were aware of these constraints and understood that the bargaining with central government over more resources and more favorable financial terms had ended. From a resource dependency perspective, the lack of resources

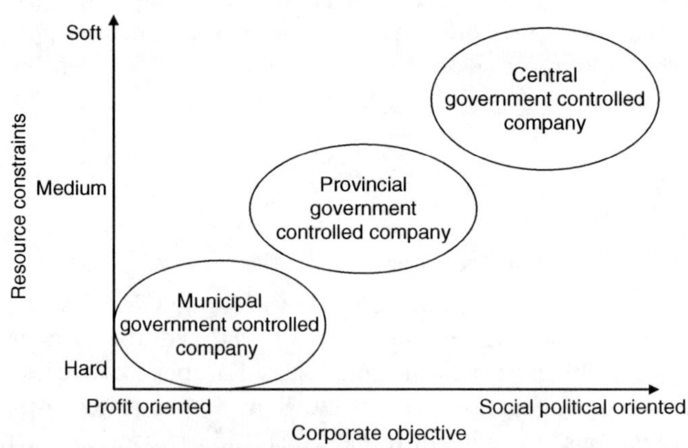

Figure 8.1 Theoretical framework.

and subsidies, on one hand, may be an obstacle to local welfare. Given limited resources, local government may engage in a concealment of resources, which do more harm than good for the creation of social welfare. On the other hand, lack of resources explicitly provides local government (and SOEs) with incentives to gather revenues. It is well known that privatization and corporate restructuring were largely driven by local government and were associated with the devolution of authority from the central to local levels of government (Qian and Weingast 1997). However, devolution of the supervisory power of state-owned enterprises from central to local government entails supply of resources to these firms in a hardening budget constraints environment. Therefore, municipal government had either privatized firms under their supervision or used SOE to pursue profit oriented objectives to supplement the financial resources for local development. For instance, local levels of government, in particular the municipal level, have initiated massive employee lay offs in the mid 1990s. Between 1995 and 1997, more than 25 million workers were laid off, and the majority were from municipal government. Furthermore, Li (1997) indicates that local governments are more likely to reduce employees' welfare than central government in case of the same poor performances that occurred in the late 1980s and early 1990s. These discussions indicate that local government supervision over state enterprises, as opposed to central government supervision, was impacted by the hardening budget constraints. Under these institutional conditions, any moves or intentions toward social political objectives in local government controlled companies will be restricted unless sufficient resource is compensated by the central government.

In contrast, the strategic orientation of central government controlled company with bureaucratic resource redistribution is more likely to be compatible with the benevolent government agenda. State-owned enterprises were designed to produce political goals. SOEs typically have heavy ideological and social burdens. A Chinese SOE is supposed to be responsible for many aspects of workers welfare: education, medical care, housing, and retirement services. In addition to providing employees' welfare, the central enterprise usually takes advantage of the central-made policy in domestic and international investment. The financial interests of central government controlled companies are weakened by the continuous supplement of resources. Needless to say, central government has easy access to more monetary and other types of resources than provincial and municipal government. The fiscal arrangement and monetary centralization have created a soft resource constraint where the national government had more control over banks and therefore could bail out their SOEs by extending credit (McMillan and Naughton 1992; Qian 1999). Behind the analysis of soft budget constraints facing central firms is an equally important assumption: the budget constraint upon central government controlled company is rather soft, and company's financial interests are weakened by competing non-financial interests.

PROPOSITION 1 Ceteris paribus, *state-owned enterprises with predominately central government ownership are more likely to adopt social political oriented corporate objectives.*

Proposition 2 Ceteris paribus, *state-owned enterprises with predominately municipal government ownership are more likely to adopt profit oriented corporate objectives.*

Research methodology

Multi-method research approach

This section discusses in detail the research methodology applied in this study. This study requires a deep knowledge of both the SOEs and the context in which it is embedded. This understanding can best be achieved by adopting multi-method approach. The multi-method approach is a current topic of debate in academia. Scholars from different disciplines recommend the use of multiple methods to study complex social phenomena (Brewer and Hunter 1989; Creswell 2003). Multi-method approaches refer to the use of multiple methods (typically quantitative and qualitative) in conducting research. Brewer and Hunter (1989) define multi-method projects as "either single studies or more complex programs of continuing research, which systematically employ various combinations of field, survey, experimental, and non-reactive methods to address their research questions" (p. 28). Combined with quantitative and qualitative methods, multi-method approaches help to obtain full answers and increase the robustness of our understanding (Mingers 2001). This approach can help to gain knowledge about different aspects of a particular phenomenon, and, therefore, can produce an overall better and more complete explanation. Adopting a multi-method approach to studying the SOE-government relationship therefore presents a variety of advantages.

This study first investigates the impact of state ownership on corporate objectives that are defined as economic and social political orientations in China. The sample is taken from listed companies on the national stock exchanges and, as such, they are subject to disclosure requirements. Therefore, modelling firm objectives are first approached using quantitative techniques because of availability of data.

To further test propositions 1 and 2, I employed a qualitative case study research methodology. The case study is the method of choice when the phenomenon under study is not readily distinguishable from its context (Adelamn *et al.* 1976; Yin 2003a, b). This research method recognizes the complexity and "embeddedness" of social truths. On the other hand, quantitative statistical analysis obscures an important question, which is how different state owners are actually involved in corporate governance to pursue their respected objective. Furthermore, it is difficult for statistical analysis to answer questions, such as: how should these enterprises deal with the tension between the different corporate objectives? As the reform proceeds, will different approaches appear as the enterprises deal with the relationship between different leaderships in their own ways or will there be a convergence to universal standards? Furthermore, privatization has brought large numbers of investors who have a stake and demand a voice in how SOEs are managed. How should these enterprises deal with the tension between the majority and minority shareholders? These questions request an in-depth investigation that can examine SOE corporate objectives, characteristics, and decision-making process.

Sampling, data sources and variables construction in statistical analysis

For the statistical analysis, I conduct a longitudinal panel data sampling. The longitudinal panel data sampling is on all listed firms since 2001. The sample includes all 1,329 corporations which have been listed on the stock exchanges of Shanghai and Shenzhen from 1998 to 2006. The sample consists of 9,149 firm-year observations. Data used in this study is collected from several sources. This first source is the Sinofin database. This information service was developed by Beijing University. I obtain companies' ownership structure from this database. Performance-related data (i.e. return on asset (ROA), sales, assets etc) and employment data are obtained from Thomson ONE banker (financial and worldscope datasets). Thomson ONE Banker is one of the most frequent used databases in the UK. I collected performance related data, number of employees, effective tax rate, and industrial code (i.e. global industry classification standard (GICS) code) from this database.

Dependent variables. In this study, I used employment growth rate, profitability, productivity, and effective tax rate to measure corporate objectives and compared these variables in three groups of SOEs. The need to maximize employment is an important policy issue for SOEs because unemployment threatens not only continued growth but social and political stability. This variable was measured as the change in the number of employees in a firm between year t and year $t + 1$ divided by the number of employees in the firm in year t. State enterprises with different owners may experience conflicting profit growth pressures. Maximizing employment would consequently decrease the productivity. Productivity and profitability are measured by sales per employee and profit per employee. Effective tax rate is measured as income tax paid divided by income.

Government ownership types. A critical series of measures in this dissertation are those relating to state ownership, as state ownership classification is central to the investigation of the impact on corporate objectives and corporate governance. So it is necessary to develop a measurement under which "state controlled company" can be defined. There is a precedent in the literature. La Porta *et al.* (1999) identify that an institution or individual that holds 20 percent of the equity is able to substantially control a publicly traded company. Following the spirit of La Porta and his colleagues' work, a state controlled company is defined as the governmental institution that holds the largest volume of shares, in excess of 20 percent of total shares issued (La Porta *et al.* 1999). Moreover, my research deals with the influence of the controlling shareholding on corporate policies. In order to ensure other shareholders have minimal effect on corporate objectives, I also control other shareholder's ownership. The sum of the top four largest shareholders' shareholding must not exceed the proportion of the largest state owners.

To further elaborate the ultimate ownership classification that is proposed by La Porta *et al.* (1999), I trace down the complex control chain of publicly listed

Chinese companies to their ultimate owners. A firm with its largest shareholder being the central government or its agencies (i.e. State-owned Assets Supervision and Administration Commission and ministries) is classified as a "central government controlled company." A firm with its largest shareholder being the provincial government or four provincial-level cities (i.e. Beijing, Shanghai, Tianjin, and Chongqing) is classified as "'provincial government controlled company". A firm with its largest shareholder being the municipal government is classified as "municipal government controlled company." With the methods described above, 627 samples were recognized as governmental controlled companies. Three dummy variables were used to present the effectiveness of government control.

Control variables. The effect of firm size is well-documented in the literature and the empirical results show that the firm size has an impact on firm outcomes. Djankov and Murrell (2002) also suggest that the larger SOEs may have been in a better position to receive various forms of state assistance because they carry out some social objectives for the state. We use the natural logarithm of asset (lnasset) as a proxy for firm size. Return on assets is the most widely used measure of firm performance and efficiency. In the privatization and corporate governance literature, ROA is widely adopted to measure performance (Chen *et al.* 1998; Dewenter and Malatesta 2001; Chang and Wong 2004; Chen *et al.* 2005a, b). ROA is profit after tax divided by the book value of total assets. At the firm level, the variability of employment can be influenced by the market. Market risk affects employment as changes in product demand affect output, prices, and the derived demand for labor for the firm. A given percentage change in sales may induce different changes in employment for one firm when compared with another. This variable was measured as the change in sales in a firm between year t and year $t+1$ divided by sales in year t. Industry is controlled to capture the heterogeneity of industrial effect on corporate objectives. Industry is measured based on Global Industry Classification Standard (GICS) measures. To control the industry effect I made ten industry dummies using the manufacturing industry as the reference category. The industry dummy is dichotomous in that it is noted as 1 if the firm is in the industry or 0 otherwise. Each firm is classified in one industry only.

Case study design for the quantitative approach

To test the above propositions, namely that the introduction of corporatization and partial privatization will be associated with the divergence of corporate objectives of Chinese SOEs, I employed a qualitative research methodology by looking at four prominent companies that represent sectors that have strategic value to China.[1] I analyzed a combination of secondary and primary data sources. For secondary sources, I collected and analyzed the company annual reports and other public information. For primary data, I first interviewed the senior managers of each company. Through these personal interviews, I collected information about comprehended (1) the company's main ownership characteristic and their governance approaches; (2) the roles that the governmental owners play, the major conflicts and communication between the owner and manager, and (3) the influence of preferences of the owners on corporate policy. To better comprehend the issues surrounding SOE objectives in China, I interviewed relevant government officials to provide greater richness and depth of understanding. I conducted interviews with government officials (two Mayors and two heads of the state asset administration bureau at provincial and municipal level) for each local government controlled company. Though semi-structured discussions with officials, I can better distinguish the objective approaches, the main characteristics, and the preferences of government owners. I surveyed many relevant literatures in order to make my semi-structured interviews with executives and governmental officials have a specific focus as well as to generate additional insights.

Statistical analysis results

Tables 8.1 and 8.2 provide the correlation matrix and descriptive statistics for all variables used in this research. It shows that, on average, municipal government controlled companies had a substantially higher level of productivity and profitability than central government controlled companies, measured in terms of sales per employee and profit per employee. In particular, the sales per employee at municipal government controlled companies are three times higher than central government ones, which is a reflection of a relatively smaller firm size in terms of numbers of employees. The average number of employees in central government controlled companies is 7,458, while municipal government companies on average employ 3,311 employees. In addition, the employment growth rate in central company is higher than other SOEs. Regardless of the employment issue, central government controlled companies had a higher level of financial performance than the other two groups of SOEs, measured by ROA. Return on assets shows how profitable a company's assets are in generating revenue. However, given the fact that our samples are in different industrial sectors, return on assets may not be an effective measurement for firm's performance. In terms of the control variables, central government owned company had the largest firm size (Lnasset = 7.89). Central government controlled companies also had the greatest sales. All the groups showed increased sales compared with the previous year, which is consistent with Chinese economic growth.

Results for hypothesis testing by "*t*-test" are provided in Table 8.3. My hypothesis, in general, predicts that companies controlled by central government are more socio-political oriented than municipal government companies. Specifically, I expect that the tax rate, productivity, and profitability in municipal companies are higher than in central and provincial companies. In contrast, the employment growth rate would be lower in municipal government controlled companies. The "*t*-test" shows that there are clearly differences among the three groups; and the results are statistically significant. There is a clear tendency for central government firms to be less profit oriented than municipal ones. For example, the average profit per employee for municipal firms is 0.50, while the value for central government firms is 0.35. Productivity displays the greatest difference. Average sales per employee for municipal firms are 6.74, nearly thrice the value for central

Table 8.1 Mean, standard deviation and correlation for variables in this study

		Mean	*SD*	*Min*	*Max*	*1*	*2*	*3*	*4*	*5*	*6*	*7*	*8*	*9*	*10*	*11*	*12*
1	Central government controlled company	0.24	0.43	0.00	1.00												
2	Provincial government controlled company	0.39	0.49	0.00	1.00	−0.45	1										
3	Municipal government controlled company	0.37	0.48	0.00	1.00	−0.43	−0.61	1									
4	Employment growth rate	0.06	0.30	−0.62	3.44	0.03	0.01	−0.03	1								
5	Sales per employee	3.99	37.54	0.03	729.58	−0.02	−0.04	0.05	−0.02	1							
6	Profit per employee	0.47	5.02	−0.50	134.28	−0.01	0.01	0.01	−0.02	0.70	1						
7	Effective tax rate	23.39	15.48	0.00	113.31	−0.12	−0.01	0.120	−0.02	0.05	0.05	1					
8	Lnassets	7.71	1.09	3.70	14.39	0.09	0.09	−0.17	0.07	0.38	0.31	0.01	1				
9	ROA	3.73	7.55	−152.54	138.93	0.03	−0.01	−0.03	0.07	−0.02	0.00	−0.26	0.08	1			
10	ROA $t-1$	4.07	7.62	−152.54	138.93	0.02	0.01	−0.03	0.10	−0.01	0.02	−0.08	0.09	−0.07	1		
11	Lnsales	7.12	1.35	3.93	13.61	0.13	0.06	−0.18	0.06	0.33	0.26	0.03	0.86	0.11	0.088	1	
12	Change in sales	0.22	0.57	−0.88	20.90	0.05	−0.02	−0.02	0.17	−0.02	−0.02	−0.07	0.02	0.12	−0.184	0.07	1

Notes: Pearson's correlation coefficients were used for continues variables, point biserial correlation coefficients were used for dichotomous variables. $N = 3,265$.

Table 8.2 Statistical description by state ownership types

Var.	*Controller*	*Total assets*	*Sales*	*Change in sales (%)*	*ROA*	*No. of employees*	*Employment growth (%)*	*Sales per employee*	*Profit per employee*	*Tax rate (%)*	*Control ratio (%)*
Obs	Central				748					653	748
Mean	government	12,925.2	9,925.7	0.28	4.32	7,753	0.08	2.57	0.32	20.01	57.07
SD	owned	59,002.9	47,464.7	0.91	6.14	33,331	0.31	16.26	2.16	13.83	13.92
Min	company	228.9	53.6	−0.66	−49.4	509	−0.61	0.05	−0.50	0.06	23.03
Max		611,995	799,115	20.90	31.72	443,808	2.75	210.1	33.14	100.49	85.00
Obs	Provincial				1,198					1,044	1,198
Mean	government	6,351.1	4,122.6	0.20	3.81	4,898	0.06	2.3	0.50	22.90	54.23
SD	owned	41,293.7	15,609.2	0.32	6.20	6,331	0.32	18.7	6.22	15.36	13.42
Min	company	174.6	50.8	−0.88	−45.5	504	−0.58	0.03	−0.13	0.01	20.95
Max		1,230,105	262,921	3.13	28.55	45,943	3.44	349.13	134.28	113.31	83.84
Obs	Municipal				1,101					937	1,011
Mean	government	5,284.8	4,037.3	0.21	3.64	3,353	0.04	6.8	0.54	26.02	49.13
SD	owned	38,227.2	29,014.1	0.47	9.47	3,831	0.24	38.9	5.30	16.03	14.57
Min	company	40.6	60.3	−0.58	−152.6	504	−0.62	0.03	−0.04	0.00	21.34
Max		760,020	497,858	10.51	138.9	29,711	3.44	543.5	83.52	109.16	81.32

Table 8.3 Univariate tests for corporate objective variables

	Central vs. provincial		*Central vs. municipal*		*Provincial vs. municipal*	
	mean	*t statistics*	*mean*	*t statistics*	*mean*	*t statistics*
Employment growth rate	0.08 0.06	1.19	0.08 0.04	2.74***	0.06 0.04	1.49
Tax rate	20.01 22.90	−3.92***	20.01 26.02	−7.77***	22.90 26.02	−4.42***
Sales per employee	2.57 2.26	0.38	2.57 6.74	−2.00***	2.25 6.74	−2.66***
Profit per employee	0.32 0.50	−0.74	0.32 0.54	−1.06	0.50 0.54	−0.18
ROA	4.32 3.81	1.76*	4.32 3.64	1.73*	3.81 3.64	0.53

Notes: *Denotes significant at a 10 percent level; **Denotes significant at a 5 percent level; ***Denotes significant at a 1 percent level; Central represents a Central government controlled company; Provincial is a Provincial government controlled company; Municipal is a Municipal government controlled company; all coefficients are standardized.

government firms. In addition, central government firms have statistically significant higher average employee growth rates than municipal firms do. They also have higher average employee growth rates than provincial firms, but the difference is statistically insignificant. The results also demonstrated great differences in terms of effective tax rate. Among the three categories, central government controlled companies pay the least tax, and municipal government taxes its SOEs with the highest tax rate.

Overall, the results are consistent with hypotheses predicting lower employment growth and greater employment intensity and tax rate for municipal government firms, but the results do not show there is significant difference in term of profitability. The univariate tests discussed above do not allow for several factors that may systematically affect employment growth and productivity. One obvious factor is a firm's (previous) performance. Others are industry membership and firm size.

The results of formal tests of the hypotheses are provided in Table 8.4. Table 8.4 includes the regression with controls only, and this helps to verify whether the main regressors contributed to the explanatory power of the models used. I allow for the factors mentioned above in a multivariate regression framework. Measures of employment growth, tax rate, and productivity are regressed on a dummy variable distinguishing government-owned firms, industry dummies (INDUSTRY), year dummies (YEAR), the natural log of firm assets (LNASSETS), firm's change in sales[2] (CHANGEINSALES), and previous year's ROA (ROA_{t-1}).

Table 8.4 first presents the results of regression analysis of the factors affecting the employment growth rate. Regressions with employment growth rate as the dependent variable consistently indicate that central government firms have higher employment growth rate than municipal firms. In model two, municipal

Table 8.4 Regression results for corporate objectives (random effects)

	Employment growth		*Tax rate*		*Sales per employee*		*ROA*		*Profit per employee*	
	Model 1	*Model 2*	*Model 1*	*Model 2*	*Model 1*	*Model 2*	*Model 1*	*Model 2*	*Model 1*	*Model 2*
Lnasset	0.017***	0.018***	−0.66	−0.532	1.508***	1.547***	−0.029	−0.093	0.345***	0.346***
	(0.005)	(0.006)	(0.79)	(0.791)	(0.318)	(0.319)	(0.379)	(0.376)	(0.096)	(0.096)
Chsales/Lnsales	0.106***	0.107***	1.22*	1.538**			1.390***	1.317***	−0.047	−0.047
	(0.009)	(0.009)	(0.64)	(0.642)			(0.307)	(0.306)	(0.076)	(0.076)
ROA_{t-1}/ROA	0.005***	0.005***	−0.72***	−0.716***	0.004	0.005		0.074***		−0.003
	(0.001)	(0.001)	(0.06)	(0.062)	(0.013)	(0.013)		(0.017)		(0.014)
Control ratio		−0.001**		−0.042		0.029				
		(0.000)		(0.036)		(0.066)				
Open sector	0.009	0.013	3.38***	2.403**	−0.071	−0.116	−1.297**	−1.268**	0.026	0.026
	(0.014)	(0.015)	(1.14)	(1.147)	(0.788)	(0.792)	(0.562)	(0.564)	(0.18)	(0.18)
Strategic sector	−0.016	−0.013	0.28	0.068	−0.352	−0.369	−1.177**	−1.310**	−0.080	−0.079
	(0.014)	(0.014)	(1.14)	(1.134)	(0.810)	(0.812)	(0.556)	(0.553)	(0.184)	(0.185)
Year dummy	YES	YES	YES	YES	YES	YES	YES	YES	YES	YES
PGD		−0.009		2.310*		0.258		−0.182		
		(0.015)		(1.266)		(2.191)		(0.621)		
MGD		−0.029*		5.353***		1.290		0.575		
		(0.015)		(1.326)		(1.647)		(0.645)		
Constant	−0.11***	−0.058	21.44***	18.114***	−7.85***	−10.21***	−4.369**	−7.395***	−1.771***	−1.640*
	(0.042)	(0.048)	(3.54)	(3.963)	(2.686)	(4.610)	(1.673)	(1.883)	(0.597)	(0.915)
Observations	3,046	3,046	2,634	2,634	3,046	3,046	3,046	3,046	3,046	3,046
Overall R^2	0.067	0.07	0.08	0.10	0.15	0.15	0.05	0.07	0.11	0.11
Wald χ^2	198.88	206.81	182.29	204.32	51.50	52.63	102.76	123.04	34.55	34.67
Prob > χ^2	0.0000	0.0000	0.0000	0.0000	0.0000	0.0000	0.0000	0.0000	0.0000	0.0000

government dummy variable's coefficient is negative and statistically significant, indicating that municipal government ownership type has negative impact on employment growth rate. I also found that provincial government ownership has a negative but not statistically significant effect on employment growth. Indeed, numerous scholars have compared state ownership and private ownership and confirmed that SOEs tend to employ more workers than they actual need. For example, Boycko *et al.* (1996) argue that state ownership cause firms to employ excess labor inputs. Moreover, government shareholding is thought to forgo maximum profit in the pursuit of social and political objectives. Therefore, *ceteris paribus*, the socio-political objective oriented central government controlled companies tend to increase their employment. The finding also shows that large firms are more likely to increase employment. This finding is consistent with employment literature that suggests large state firm tend to employ more labor due to their superior advantage in resource and socio-political obligation.

The above tests indicate that municipal government ownership is negatively associated with employment growth in Chinese SOEs, although the regression coefficients are weakly significant. In the next stage, the hypothesized relationship between government ownership and tax rate was verified. The regression provided positive and significant coefficients for both the provincial and municipal government variables, and these results support my hypothesis. For instance, the coefficient for provincial government type is positively related to tax payment compared to central government ownership and the results are statistically significant. The results in Tables 8.3 and 8.4 show that municipal government has the highest tax rate when comparing the three groups of SOEs, which is in line with my hypothesis. Firm size (lnasset) and sales have little explanatory power on tax rate and firm performance measurement (ROA) has negative and significant impact on effective tax rate.

The results support my hypothesis and suggest that municipal government controlled companies pay more tax to municipal government than central firms. Central government obviously has access to a large amount of resources and can even change policy in favor of central controlled companies. On the other hand, municipal government controlled companies operated in a hard budget environment. Their ultimate owners have limited resources and might not be able to/willing to bail these companies out if they face economic difficulties. In addition to that, economic reform hardened the budget allowance for provincial and municipal governments, and fiscal reform strongly linked local expenditures with local revenue. Such a link aligns the interests of local governments to local economic prosperity and SOEs' success. Provincial and municipal government officials and SOEs' managers were aware of these constraints and understand that the bargaining with central government over more resources and more favorable financial terms had ended. From a resource dependency perspective, lack of resources explicitly provides local government (and SOEs) with incentives to gather revenues. Under these institutional conditions, any moves or intentions toward social political objectives in local government controlled companies will be restricted unless sufficient resources are compensated by central government.

In contrast, the affinity of central government controlled companies with bureaucratic resource redistribution is so close that the company's strategic orientation is more likely to be compatible with the benevolent government agenda. The financial interests of central government controlled companies are weakened by the continuous supplement of resources. And in addition to providing employees' welfare, the central enterprise usually takes advantage of the central-made policy in domestic and international investment. Behind the analysis of soft budget constraints facing central firms is an equally important assumption: the budget constraint upon a central government controlled companies is rather soft, and a company's financial interests are weakened by competing non-financial interests.

Unsurprisingly, regression results in Table 8.4 indicate that government ownership has insignificant impact on productivity and profitability. In fact, the relationship between state ownerships and corporate performance remains controversial among economists (Tian 2001). On one hand, numerous scholars have found negative relationships between firm performance and state block shareholding. For instance, a study by Xu and Wang (1997) using data from 1993 to 1995 finds that there is a relationship between corporate ownership and performance, confirming the positive role of institutional investor with corporate performance and a negative role of the "state share."

I hypothesize that the lower the political level, the greater probability that a SOE should be profit oriented. I have tested the effects of government ownership dummies on four dependent variables by controlling corporate governance variables and other firm specific issues (i.e. firm size, firm performance). In results not reported in the chapter, I conducted additional tests on the choice of measures of profitability. I repeated my analysis using alternative empirical definitions of firms' performance with quantitatively similar results. In addition, there is a concern addressed in many corporate governance studies (Demsetz and Lehn 1985; Demsetz and Villalonga 2001) arguing ownership and ownership structure are endogenous variables and can produce multi-dimensional firm outcomes. In contrast, other researchers argue that corporate governance is the primary influence on corporate outcomes. The interactions between ownership and corporate governance could shape the corporate objective. In such cases, inferences from our model might be inefficient. To tackle these problems, we tested interactive variables in each regression test. Interactive variables are PD[3] * BOARD SIZE, PGD * SUPERVISORY BOARD SIZE, PGD * BOARD DEPENDENCY; and MGD * BOARD SIZE, MGD * SUPERVISORY BOARD SIZE, MGD * BOARD DEPENDENCY. However, our results show no evidence of significant impact from these interactive variables. It indicates state ownership itself has direct influence on corporate objectives. The results empirically provide a systematic confirmation on the important role of the government in Chinese SOEs from Qian (1996) and Oi (1995).

Case studies results

This section investigates how corporate objectives differ within the state ownership category at holding company level and examines whether the objectives might converge, or develop independently. I found that corporate objective had become much more profit oriented within the municipal government owned category than central government owned category.

Predominately central government ownership

Strong governmental control is expected in this category, usually in the direction of socio-political goals. Managerial efforts should primarily be concerned with socio-political goals. This is the group where one would be most likely to see corporate development decisions negotiated and discussed adequately with the government before getting permission to be implemented. The objective of the central government controlled companies in China must be understood in the context of the overall socio-political standing. While questions may be raised about how central government manages those large companies, there is no doubt about these companies are representing central government's interests. Managers in central government controlled companies are eager to partake in some political oriented affairs. Such alignment between management and the central government can be explained by path dependence as years of working under a command economy had sharply affected company's initiative. Moreover, the historical extensive and intensive government governing creates incentives for management to implement organizational strategic that take advantage of the political packing (Huang 2003).

The case of company *C* shows how central government can articulate, communicate to management, and press for political interests. The history of company *C* may be traced back to early days of the People's Republic of China. Along with the development and reform of China's social and economic system, Company *C*, formerly a governmental department, has developed into an international oil company. In the 1950s, the Chinese government formed the Ministry of Petroleum Industry and Ministry of Petroleum Chemical Industry to manage of fuel, petroleum exploration, mining, and other related sectors. In 1983, central government decided to disband the Petroleum Chemical Industry Ministry and create Sinopec Corporation. In 1988, the government dissolved the Ministry of Petroleum Industry and replaced it by a state-owned company, *C*. Such embeddedness produced overwhelmingly socio-political obligations for this company. Although central government restructured and corporatized company *C* and claimed that a modern enterprise system would be established within this company in 1998, company *C* has been an effective tool to fulfil central government's political policies.

The modern enterprise system has left very little imprint on the firm's operations. In fact, the party committee controls all kinds of activities in company *C*. The "co-operation" between the firm and central government are remarkable, as reported by one interviewee:

> Central enterprises provide unfailing support to (the country's) economic development and help to maintain the social stability. As a role model of central enterprises, it is a delight to contribute... The central council guides the

> strategic orientation of our company... on one hand, our company upholds the strategic decisions made by the government and implements such decisions thoroughly; on the other hand, the government offers helps to our company's development. So it is a win-win result... disagreements certainly exist. For instance, we met such situation when we carried out Sino-Russia Petroleum Conduit Project. This project was discussed with the central council and National Development and Reform Commission for more than one year before it was approved. Of course, such disagreements focused on technical details.

The company's growths are therefore nurtured by such a "co-operation." Indeed, managers appear to see themselves as fitting into fairly sharply defined, socio-politically specialized roles. Such a role can be observed in many instances. For example, the current senior executives of company *C* were high ranking civil servants, trusted by key civil servants and politicians, and promoted from other provinces and municipal cities. Since the 1980s, company *C* has played a key role in both formulating and implementing the government's oil strategy. It has been particularly sensitive and responsive to the demands of politicians and civil servants alike. One interviewee states that:

> As a central enterprise, we are obliged to shoulder and fulfil social responsibilities in order to promote the harmonious development of society. For instance, in response to the call of the Chinese government to build a "new socialist countryside", and to promote the economic development of poor areas and increase farmers' incomes, the company has offered RMB 38 million to promote trade in agricultural and associated products. Our company also donate several orphanages and hospitals in Sudan... we also funded many infrastructural projects in Africa, such as bridges, railways etc.

and also,

> (As a central enterprise), we are obliged to shoulder the duties in order to promote social stability and economic development. For example, now the international oil price has reached the highest point. But the company remains the oil price at a reasonable lower price. That is our contributions to our country and the society... of course, the oil price is guided by the central government... in order to ensure the development of whole Chinese economy, and our company has suffered a big loss.

These examples show that co-operation is a necessity, for both the firm and its master, in order to achieve common goals. Although the manager in company *C* stated to "maximise shareholder's benefits" is the primarily concern of the company, he also emphasized promoting economic development and ensuring social stability are important responsibilities and objectives because company *C* holds political obligations for the country. If we divide the decision process of the central government controlled firms into two sub processes, one internal to the firm and one external involving governmental actors (Hafsi and Koenig 1988), we can conclude that the company's objective can be considered as a political phenomenon. External actors guide the strategic orientation and objectives, while the internal process should make decisions on how to fulfil such objectives.

Low municipal government share of ownership with concentrated insider and foreign ownership

In this group we expect municipal government owned enterprises to behave in accordance with private shareholder goals: high incentive to maximize profit, high management discretion, and limited power of the government to achieve sociopolitical goals. One example is company *Z*, which is 12 percent owned by the city *Y* municipal government. The company *Z* is one of largest wine makers in China today. The history of this company can be tacked back to 1891, when Mr. Chang Bishi, an overseas-based Chinese, developed the industrialized production of wine in China. Since 1978, China has implemented a series of changes in the administration of its industrial enterprises aimed at improving productivity. Instead of privatizing state-owned enterprises en masse, China has concentrated on enterprise restructuring by adopting a new enterprise governance structure that stresses enterprise autonomy and managerial incentives. Thus, company *Z* as a solely state-owned enterprise started to progress a controlled but progressive reform since 1982. By 1985, this company had introduced the "managerial responsibility system," under which managers were delegated power to make many decisions. Managers under this system could make decisions on outputs, product mix, and prices on outside-of-the plan outputs. By 1986, the reform deepened significantly and company *Z* had adopted "contract responsibility system." Under the contract system, the municipal government signed contracts with managers specifying the responsibilities of each party and arranging the distribution of enterprise earnings.

Because the consequent reform centred on the establishment of a "socialist market economy with Chinese characteristics" by transforming the ownership system into a mixed structure with the public sector dominant and various types of ownership coexistent, the municipal government attempted to restructure company *Z* into a shareholding company. In 1997, the company started to offer B shares in ShenZhen stock exchange. In 2004, the company had become a state controlled company by selling its shares to employees and managers. Furthermore, the municipal government decided to sell shares to another two foreign investors in 2005 and company *Z* transferred to a mixed ownership enterprise.

The changed objectives of company *Z* was the consequence of an explicit change in ownership structure. Company *Z* was 100 percent owned by the municipal government and was a factory that produced wine under the central or provincial made plan. A consequence of its state-owned nature was that the corporate behaviour of company *Z* remained unified as many other SOEs. All kinds of resource (financial resources, labor etc.) were allocated by the government. During 1990s, the municipal government still retained the right to intervene in all company decisions, including both substantive and procedural issues, with the incentive to both improve firm performance and provide social welfare to employees on the behalf of the government. Although municipal government gave the management autonomy for operating the business, there were considerable disagreements among managers and government officials as to what should be the primary objective. In fact, this debate existed at two levels, with the municipal government and firm management. The result of this debate was that government replaced a few managers in 2001. And the company has performed variably since then (Figure 8.2). The municipal government realized that a SOE combines the economic objective with the socio-political objectives, which may not bring desirable results. Furthermore, "socio-political burdens" were facing challenges from managers of most SOEs and those managers tended to pursue a strategy that stressed economic objectives. Therefore, the fact that municipal government sold shares to managers and employees in 2004 can be considered as an indication that profit maximization has been settled as the primary objective of company *Z*. Thus, the government, by virtue of retaining 12 percent shares, is able to act more on the basis of rational block shareholder. The vice chairman of company *Z* stated that:

> The ownership restructure was initiated by the local government. In the year 2001, the local government intervened in our company's management; they changed some superior managers in our company. But such intervention was unsuccessful... they (the government) realized that one hundred percent state ownership could not bring the financial benefits that they expected... pursuing profit is the nature of modern companies, the government can provide social welfares through other ways. What is reform? Reform is about changing the objectives and consciousness.

The city *Y* government started to privatize Company *Z* in the year 2003. As mentioned, the government owns 12 percent of the company, and the manager, workers, and two foreign investors own 45 percent, 33 percent, and 10 percent respectively. Thus, the private and foreign shareholders dominate business decisions while the state has a diminished administrative role. The original intervention powers are weakened thereby forcing local government to abdicate their traditional functions. Local government appears to have little influence on the firm's activities, and there is no apparent conflict between *Z* and the government. The vice chairman affirmed that the economic goals are the primary objective of their company. He stated that commitments to profitability and cost-cutting are supported by the all owners, including the government. He confirmed that:

> The social and political goals were not our objectives for years . . . for instance; this problem (labor layoff) had been mitigated through employee shareholding. The primary objective of our company at his period is to expand our market share and hope to receive fruitful financial return in the future.

Table 8.5 Summary of corporate objectives of Chinese state-owned enterprises

Economic objective oriented SOEs	*Hybrid objective SOEs*		*Social-political objective oriented SOEs*
Strong economic incentive		*Strong social political incentive*	
I. Low municipal government ownership with concentrated insider and foreign ownership: Dispersed government ownership; Shareholders centred regime; Pressure to fulfil the rationale of the private owner; Possibly management control.	II. High municipal government ownership with concentrated insider and foreign ownership: Managed by entrepreneur; Strong profit maximizing 'incentives'; Joint owner control if consensus on goals; If not, conflict between owners may exhibit cognitive dissonance.	III. High provincial government ownership: Managed by experienced cadres; Relatively weaker profit maximizing 'pressure'; Strong pressure on fulfil social political objectives; Strong government monitoring; Company and government relation may become adversarial.	IV. High central government ownership: Concentrated central government owner control; Pressure to fulfil the rationale of the public owner; Weaker profit maximizing pressure.

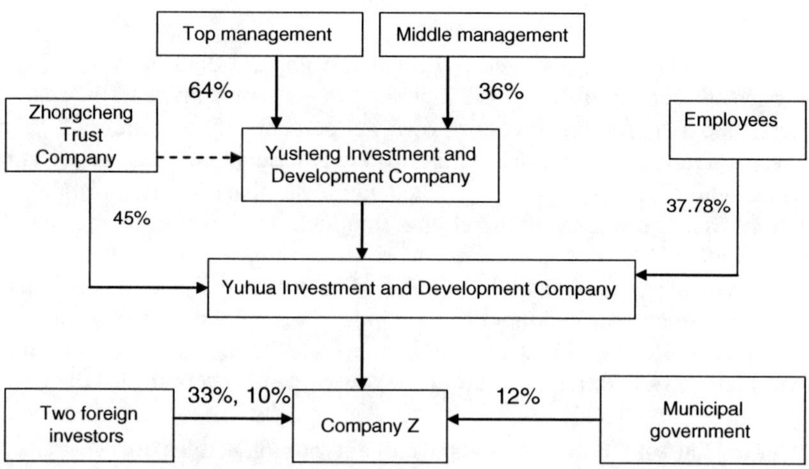

Figure 8.2 Ownership structure of company *Z*.

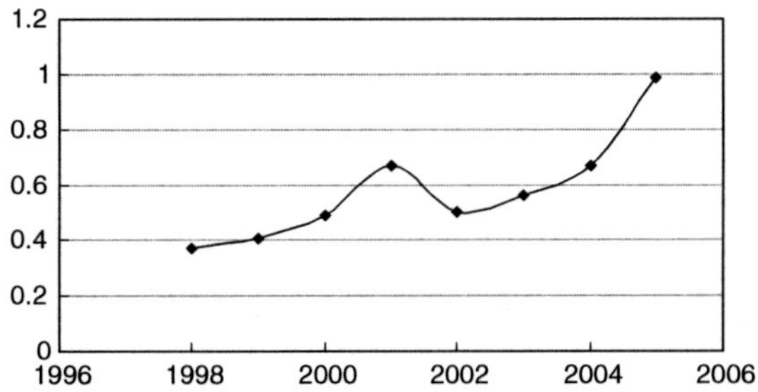

Figure 8.3 Performance of company Z before and after ownership restructure.

Concentrated municipal government ownership with concentrated insider ownership

The coexistence of various ownership types is a feature of China's market-oriented reforms. In this group, company insiders dominate business operations while the state continues to play an important political role as before. Hua *et al.* (2006) contend that state ownership can prevent managers from corruption via political education for the party members while insider ownership could help to retain employees and improve the cohesiveness of the entire enterprise with monetary rewards instead of the spiritual rewards derived from political education. Hua *et al.* (2006) agree with the Wedeman (2003) argument and assert "as state institutions became market-oriented actors, individual cadres also became 'bureaucratic entrepreneurs.'" However, private ownership and state ownership cannot always complement and supplement each other, although private and state shareholders' goals are congruent around profit maximization.

Normal group II case is illustrated by Company *M*. Company *M* was founded in 1956 to produce reciprocation refrigeration compressors. It is the first company in Chinese history that can produce the compressor and screw refrigeration compressors. Company *M* is 52 percent owned by the municipal government and the remainder owned by the company employees and managers. The ownership structure was the consequence of political deliberation. In fact, company *M* debated an alternative ownership pattern – like company *Z*, so the insiders dominate the business – but municipal government rejected company *M*'s plan. Although some officials believe that private or foreign ownership would bring better firm performance, two disadvantages are the facilitation of internal managerial entrenchment and shrinking resources that can be used by the government. The municipal government believes that a uniform SOE restructured approach (i.e. a reformed enterprise with dominate state ownership and minority private or foreign ownership) is needed to avoid the complete break-up between the government and the company.

One crucial question, which has special resonance because of the ownership change, is which strategic orientation would management enforce, economic

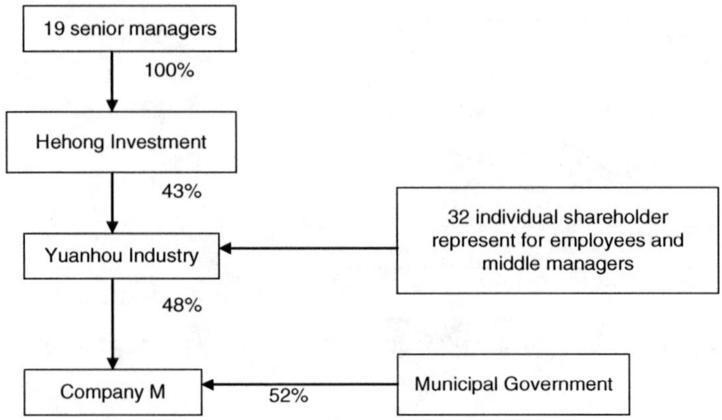

Figure 8.4 Ownership structure of company *M*.

or socio-political? There are dual pressures for the senior manager to choose the strategic orientation. In fact, partial privatization in China allows the "dual pressures" to prevail and creates socio-political restriction. The first pressure is manifested by the blurry relationship between the firm and government. The newly restructured mixed ownership enterprise had a history of very close relationships with the municipal government. Although the intention of such ownership transfer was to enhance profit incentives and competitive pressures in order to promote efficiency and establish a more professionally managed company, the government may not able to resist the political gains accruing from interference (Boardman and Vining 1991; Qian 1996). Instead of promoting enterprise efficiency and competition, local governments may influence corporate resource allocation to support social objectives such as local development, reducing fiscal deficits, or protecting employment. This contention is supported by the vice chairman of company *M*. He stated that

> we are facing the difficulties of disposing of surplus labors... we are not privately owned company, we cannot simply lay them off. The government wants to promote the social stability and the officials certainly do not want to see any demonstrations... in fact, we can grow even faster if we can get rid of those political pressures . . . although the government no longer intervening our daily operation, and social obligation has been kept at a reasonable low level... the government still need us (to fulfil some socio-political objectives).

The second pressure comes from inside the company. Much of the conceptual literature based on agency theory contains the argument that principals have two options for reducing agency costs arising from conflicts of interest and self-serving behaviours on the part of agents: generate information about the agents' efforts, or link incentives to the agents' outcomes. Managers of company *M* have administrative power over "their enterprises" and tend to adopt a strategy to fulfil economic objectives such as profit maximization because they have already invested all or most of all their financial and personal resources in that company. Furthermore, their managerial behaviour would be carefully monitored by other inside shareholders because middle managers and other employees also have bought some proportion of shares. The vice chairman of company *M* admitted the second sort of pressure comes from inside the company by stating that:

> (before the re-corporatisation) people who come to occupy managerial positions in our company tend to be motivated to enhance firm profitability if they wish to remain in their positions… there are different methods to measure a company's performance and managers' capability of running a company. But the simplest variable is the profit . . . after the ownership reform in 2003, managers and workers started to own shares; the "intra motivation" problem is thus solved out. In fact, there was not conflict on this primary corporate objective, as both the managers and the government's goal are congruent around profit maximization… everyone in our company has pressured for better performance… the chairman is under the greater pressure because SOE reform has created a responsibility system. If our company underperforms, the employee, middle managers and even the government have the person to blame on.

Furthermore, Jensen and Meckling (1976) suggest that linking a manager's shareholding closely to firm performance might lead to risk-avoiding behaviour on the part of the manager. The underlying assumption is that the manager, by owning shares either through incentive compensation or purchasing, has already invested most of his or her no diversifiable human capital and monetary capital in the firm and the agent is thus relatively risk averse. However, the interviews suggest that managerial shareholding may have desirable incentive and motivational properties and it does not necessarily produce undesirable risk-bearing behaviour. This issue is summarized succinctly by the vice chairman of company *M*:

> We are the first generation entrepreneurs in China… shareholding definitely motivates all managers, but the primary consideration of operation the business is not monetary rewards… I have been work at this company for more than 20 years. All managers want to see our achievement in terms of company growth. At the same time, we do not mind endure risk if there was a business opportunity. But the government officials are less likely to bear the same risk… even we had a successful risky investment, the officials would not benefit from this project. But if the risky investment failed, they could involve in trouble. In short, the government wants us to growth steadily.

Predominately provincial government ownership

As discussed above, the management agreed that the economic orientation would play an important role in shaping the process and outcomes of the company's operation. In contrast to many of their counterparts, managers in municipal government controlled companies have been able to develop a wide range of effective, innovative organizational structures and practices, sometimes with the participation of workers and municipal government and sometimes without. Insider shareholding as one kind of managerial innovation in company-government relations have become models of "best practice."[4] If the organizational structure and company-government relations produce "best practice" cases, why don't those provincial and central government owned companies follow municipal government's approach? After all, the performances of municipal government controlled companies have been improving since the late 1990s and provincial and central government owned companies were struggling to cope with a recession that was sharpened by unification and a host of new social and political problem. There are two main reasons to look to the state solely owned model. First, managers tend not to base their strategic decisions systematically on the long-term interests of multiple stakeholders, including non-state investors, employees, and society as a whole. What kind of role the government as the sole owner can play has become a question of deep concern to the private and public sectors. A possible answer to this question can certainly be illuminated through the comparison with municipal government ownership. Second, the central and province owned companies have begun to recover and promise significant new growth. The strength of the companies will be augmented by continuing business cooperation and merger and acquisitions that are led by the government. While municipal government controlled company firms will probably maintain a strong competitive edge in certain sectors – such as the high technology industry; better understanding of the provincial government and central government owned company that mainly operated in strategic important sectors would have important policy implications.

The key differences between corporate objectives in the central government controlled and provincial government controlled companies have less to do with the content of the objectives than with the negotiation processes. Management in provincial government owned companies resists government because they fear that the company would simply become the political instrument of the government again. In contrast, central government dominates the objective negotiating process and ensures organizational changes are well planned and thoroughly implemented. The interviewee in central control company believed that their counterparts in provincial government controlled companies felt less constrained by the bureaucracy and hierarchy in their organizations, and are granted broader scope for decision making. But the company owned by provincial government enjoys less political and financial support from the government (author's interview 2008).

Company *L* illustrates well the group III characteristics. The linkages between the government and the company may help us to understand the company's strategic orientation. Before 2003, company *L* was a bureau, which was governed by provincial government. Typically, officials in provincial government are less knowledgeable about operation and administration of a company due to informational asymmetry compared with municipal-level officials. In the early 2000s, the provincial government therefore appointed an official to be the chairman of the bureau, while promoting an insider to be the chief executive. The chairman's responsibility (who also is the party committee leader) focuses on the strategic orientation of the company, and the insider chief executive is responsible for the daily operations. Because company *L* is in the resource industry with historically strict government control, the government shareholder usually focuses on its owned interest while ignoring interests of the management. However, internal management, led by the forceful chief executive, is proactive and sometime confrontational. Indeed, relations between company *L* and its management and the provincial government have been conflicting.

The Chinese literature on state ownership is somewhat sceptical of solely state-owned companies' independence and effectiveness. During the interview, both top and middle management agreed that the company was thrown into chaos for a period of time when corporatization was introduced. And everyone also agreed that this had to do with the lack of clear corporate objectives and developmental guidance. In the transforming economies of the post-Soviet era, Chinese state-owned enterprises often found themselves with a significant stock of surplus labor and extensive welfare obligations (e.g. housing services) created by the full employment guarantees under the socialist system. Employment restructuring and social welfare devolvement thus became the major objective of enterprise reform at company *L* in the 1990s. However, the interviews showed that the company was still building new apartments for lower level managers and workers in 2004. Furthermore, the chairman of company *L* stated that:

> The corporatization helped us to abandon many social burdens, such as hospital, police station, schools etc. The corporatization changed us to a modern company... one objective of modern company surely is to pursue profit. However, corporatization cannot solve out all historical burdens, for instance, many labor cannot be simply laid off.

While many analysts hold that the government shareholder is overworked in fulfilling socio-political objectives, the chairman of company *L* confirmed that his company is developing a proactive strategy in countering rationalization. Such rationalization is projected in order to present the governmental shareholder's interest that may conflict with managers' and/or workers' short-term preferences and still keep in mind the long-term welfare of the company. For instance, as a part of the strategic process, starting in the 2005, to further SOE reform and gain competitive advantages, the provincial government decided to push strategic mergers among large state-owned firms.[5] Company *L* was one of the targeted firms. Such strategic adjustment was related primarily to the company *L*'s continuous, rapid development of "new" businesses. It employs mostly low-skilled, blue-collar workers. During the 1990s, middle and lower level managers had developed many small business related and unrelated to the core business of company *L*. The unrelated business diversification in company *L* makes it risky for the government to offer further financial and political support. The problem is that such support can be of use to the new businesses, and new businesses with these supports can be poached by free riders. Thus, the provincial government asked the company to release and privatize those businesses, either through employee buy-out or through foreign joint venture. The government first began to push for this strategy in 2005 but with limited success. Internal management had argued that the effects of rationalization cannot be optimal because the strategic merger and privatization of new businesses are not based on market competition, rather based on political commands. The management is unhappy to comply with this idea because privatization not only accompanies strict political constraints (e.g. the potential investors have to sign a contract that promises the new investors would lay any labor off for three to five years), but also would not be beneficial to the management. As one interviewee stated:

> such industrial association and merger is some kind of political issue... for managers, we have to abandon those (unrelated businesses) for nothing. The government would not consider how much efforts we had contributed... In 1990s, our company faced serious difficulties, and we would not survive without supports from these businesses. Now, the parent company starts to have a good day (i.e. make profits), we cannot just sell those businesses... the provincial government and SASAC have discussed this issue with senior managers of large SOEs for many times, and most mangers would not like to abandon these businesses. On one hand, these businesses have sentimental value; on the other hand, this activity would be beneficial for the corporation.

This case illustrates not only some of the strengths but also one of the generic weaknesses of the provincial government ownership. The internal management of company *L* was unable to realize and reject the rationalization scheme because the decision making process was highly centralized. Nonetheless, the case shows how management can anticipate organizational change. The most striking aspect of the company *L* case is the uncooperative management and the managers' ability to make their interests heard, although it appeared likely that the strategic merger and new businesses privatization would be introduced by the end of this research.

Reassessing the corporate objectives

The strong influence of the institutional context on management policies and styles is illustrated by the contrasts among central, provincial and municipal government owned companies. Is the difference between styles of managing – in particular managerial priorities – purely a difference in style, or does it reflect objective constraints imposed by the ownership? Do companies try to export policies and practices developed in the municipal level to provincial level and vice versa? To answer these questions it was necessarily to look at companies' governmental owners.

The basic points of the government – the willingness to provide a stable institutional infrastructure in order to promote economic development, and interest in participating in determining the terms of organisational change – have remained more or less unchanged in the 1990s and 2000s. However, both domestic and international circumstances have fundamentally changed. Intensified domestic and international competition demands frequent and subtle adjustments to products and services. And the government officials often failed to process effective adjustments due to asymmetric information and lack of professional competences. During the 1990s, many SOE had hard times and the government intervention model cannot continue to perform effectively under such circumstances. However, the SOE reform was carried out with the absence of many conventional institutions. In fact, such reform did not produce conventional "best practice institutions" with secured private property rights and complete separation between the government and the SOE. Rather SOE reform can be considered as complements to the existing institutions.

Qian (2002) states that "underlying China's reform is a series of institutional changes concerning the market, firms, and the government . . . The institutional reforms achieved two objectives at the same time: they are both efficiency enhancing and interest compatible." Qian's argument is well illustrated by municipal government's interests. As detailed above, municipal government controlled businesses have upheld that the economic objective is the "primary concern." In fact, municipal government has provided a stable institutional infrastructure, within which both business and government officials have found ample "incentives" to engage in collaborative relationships.

The business and mangers under municipal government control have taken full advantage of the supportive framework offered by the socialist market economy with Chinese characteristics, including a highly opened market for private investors and managerial autonomy. The head of the state asset supervision and administration commission in a municipal city stated that:

> The goal of SOE restructure is to enhance firm's productivity and profitability though introduces private and foreign investments... the state nature of the company can be expressed by the remaining state ownership. One hundred percent state ownership cannot produce desirable (financial) results. The private and foreign investors can be fresh blood for our city and companies. There are no political or any kinds of constraints for them at all; in the contrast, we can provide a stable intuitional infrastructure for their development, because we can benefit from their development as shareholders.

And also;

> We intend to resolve two intrinsic managerial problems in traditional SOE through the restructure. One problem is the governance problem due to absence of principal; another is the lack of managerial incentives... the reform brought us new companies with varied investment principals. The

> insider shareholding has indeed motivated management and employees' incentives for financial performance improvement... a good investment principal do not necessarily have to operate the business; rather, we can receive fruitful results though effective governance and active guidance.

Although local government lose the dominant position, it does not mean that the state owner becomes nominal. The vice chairman of company *Z* agrees with this argument by saying:

> The ownership reform is a prudence political decision. The 12 percent ownership likes the "golden share" and the government trends to use their shares to maximize their interests... on one hand, the remaining ownership brings the government with higher financial returns than before; on the other hand, the 12 percent ownership makes sure that the government would not loose complete control over the company... diminished state ownership would reduce the government intervention on company's operation and daily management, but it does not mean that the local government became a nominal owner. In fact, the foreign ownership and insiders own 43% and 45% of the company; you can see how important the 12% share would be. For example, the remaining share can be interpreted as an indication that any attempt to absolute control on our company is politically unfavorable.

In contrast, provincial government tend to balance the economic and socio-political goals by complementing the existing state-owned institutions. The SOE reform and restructuring is only an incremental adjustment. Such adjustment is generally divided into two respects, inside and outside. The first means the combinative-adjustment of a company's organizational structure and management; the second means the strategic merger and acquisition of large SOEs. Through these adjustments, the corporations should improve management and administration, gain cash income steadily, and provide considerable investment repayments to investors.

One interviewee stated that:

> The provincial government will not retreat from strategic important sectors, rather we need to increase the investment and supports... the state owned enterprises failed to adapt to the market economy and many problem of traditional state ownership have exposed, heavy historical burdens, backward managers selection system are but few examples... Thus, many people believe that private owned company outperforms state owned company. And without privatisation, we cannot improve the performance of the SOE. I do not agree with this opinion. The main problem of such contention is that those people overlook the essence of the SOE... in fact, maximising the social and enterprise benefits are our objectives. We have many SOE shoulder heavy social burdens, particular the surplus labor and welfare and pension provided to retired employees, it is a historical issue. We intend to remove such burdens gradually ... but we must

> consider the social consequences... the "large state owned corporation plan" can be considered an experiment for resolving those problems. We are going to combine large state owned corporation into groups, for example coal group, iron and steel group. But the premise is that SOEs should solve out their internal problems. Many SOEs have some small businesses apart from core business... if we can sale these businesses to managers and workers, we can clear up the social burdens without causing any trouble.

Conclusion

As discussed by Wang and Xia in Chapter One, China's economic reforms have changed the national economic system in many respects. Many scholars observed the changing institutional environment after the economic reform in 1978. However, a limited number of researchers have studied the effects of the changing institutional environment on SOEs. Even fewer studies discuss the divergence of SOEs' strategic orientations following the economic reform. In this chapter, I elaborated the strategic orientation of different state-owned enterprises. China's reform has set the direction for restructuring: its economic core must be dominated by public sectors with SOEs controlling the "commanding heights" of the national economy while allowing diverse types of ownership to develop. Therefore, understanding the governmental behaviour and interests in a changing institutional environment become important because a large amount of evidence has shown that the active players behind Chinese partial privatization are governmental institutions.

This study helps to understand the different strategic orientation of listed Chinese SOEs. Our large-sample comparisons reveal several empirical regularities. The findings have indicated that a SOE's sociopolitical ambition is positively associated with the softness of its budget constraints. These findings are consistent with a model of strategic selection of corporate objectives suggested in previous state ownership research (Hafsi *et al.* 1987; Hafsi and Koenig 1988; Boardman and Vining 1991; Qi 1995; Qian and Roland 1998). In addition, building on Kornai's (1980) emphasis on "conflicts between the government and managers in terms of resources redistribution," this research also makes a contribution to "soft budget constraints" research by linking resource aspects of the political hierarchy with the development of the corporate objectives and corporate monitoring. By taking advantage of the unique context of Chinese economic reform, this study suggests that tax sharing reform tightens the budget allowances and provides vital incentives to municipal government to pursue profit oriented objectives, which, in turn, can inform the corporate governance structure of the focal firm and help to build up a insider controlled board. Using employment growth rate as a measurement, for instance, I show that municipal government controlled firms are more economic objective oriented than central and provincial government controlled companies because they tend to employ less workers.

The diversity of corporate objectives among Chinese SOEs reflect the changing political and economic environment in China after the fiscal and SOE reform in the 1990s. In the central company case, the government's non-financial objectives, and the firm's dependence on government, create a mutual dependence between government and enterprise. On one hand, the government depends upon firms for financial outputs and the provision of political support. On the other hand, enterprises engage in constant bargaining with government officials over more resources and more favorable financial terms. The provincial government faced with a large number of firms to monitor therefore suffers from severe information problems. Even if its financial interests in firm profitability were very strong, a government is so constrained by non-financial considerations and information problems it would be unable to enforce financial discipline over firms. This could be one explanation why the government tends to combine the SOE into large groups. SOEs are overseen by local government and other stakeholders with an interest in maximizing financial returns. Therefore, it doesn't matter if the local government is the dominant owner; the company would be operated following the logic of private ownership. Criticism of management buyout state that managerial block shareholding would develop CEO entrenchment and consequently discourage long-term CEO commitments. But the "golden shares" owned by the government may be a good instrument to mitigate such costs.

The failure of empirical tests to confirm the hypothesized positive relationships between municipal government ownership, firm productivity, and profitability doesn't appear to be counterintuitive. The Chinese government encourages SOEs to issue shares and create Shareholding Company as a means to attract investment. Therefore, most state holding companies packaged their "profit-making assets" and formed new companies to list on the stock exchanges, while all social burdens (i.e. schools, educational institutes, hospitals, and other employee welfare providing institutions) have remained at the unlisted patents companies. Given the fact that all public traded companies are the "superior assets" of government controlled holding companies, insignificant differences in terms of the productivity among government controlled firms are not surprising results.

This study has several limitations that may suggest avenues for future research. First, by linking different government owners with corporate objective, it contributes to a better understanding of the strategic orientation in Chinese listed SOEs. However, this study did not make further inroads in identifying "how many actors are involved." It was beyond the ambition of this research to open the block box of state-owned organization research and analyze the context and content of how different state owners process, conduct, and perform. However, by developing and empirically supporting the theoretical framework of different aspects of state controlled firms, this study paves the way for further studies on corporate governance processes and dynamics that may use different research methods, such as interviews, case studies, and surveys.

Notes

1 Both the managers and governmental officials requested anonymity.
2 Change in sales refers to the growth rate in term of the firm's sales.

3 PGD refers to provincial government dummy; MGD refers to municipal government dummy.
4 The rise and development of MBO/EMO depend on the Chinese economy environment, in which the policies of "the reduction of state-owned stock" and "remain the key enterprises and release small and medium sized ones" provide the suitable economic base and developing chance to MBO/EMO. The key problem of SOE reform is how to account for the illegibility and the subject-lack of property right. MBO might be a better experiment. Many managers and scholars affirm MBO will become the major way of Chinese property right reform in the future.
5 Since early 2000s, Provincial government *S* started to implement a SOE restructure strategy. The purpose of such restructure is to unify government control and create competitive advantages in manufacturing, natural resources sectors (author's interview 2008). One example is the establishment of Shandong Iron and Steel Corporation in 2008. This corporation was formed by two large provincial owned companies, Jinan iron and steel corporation and Laiwu iron and steel corporation.

References

Adelamn, C., Jenkins, D. and Kemmis, S. (1976) 'Re-Thinking Case Study: Notes from the Second Cambridge Conference', *Cambridge Journal of Education*, 6 (3): 139–150.

Aharoni, Y. (1981) 'Performance Evaluation of State-owned Enterprises: A Process Perspective', *Management Science*, 27: 1340–1347.

Aharoni, Y. (1982) 'State-owned Enterprise: An Agent without a Principal', in L. P. Jones (ed.) *Public Enterprises in Less-Developed Countries*, Cambridge, New York: Cambridge University Press, 67–76.

Boardman, A., Eckel, C. and Vining, A. (1986) 'The Advantages and Disadvantages of Mixed Enterprises', *Research in International Business and International Relations*, 1.

Boardman, A. E. and Vining, A. R. (1989) 'Ownership and Performance in Competitive Environments: A Comparison of the Performance of Private, Mixed, and State-owned Enterprises', *Journal of Law and Economics*, 32: 1–33.

Boardman, A. E. and Vining, A. R. (1991) 'The Behavior of Mixed Enterprises', *Research in Law and Economics*, 14: 223–250.

Brewer, J. and Hunter, A. (1989) *Multimethod Research: A Synthesis of Styles*, Newbury Park, CA: Sage Publications.

Chandler, A. D. (1962) *Strategy and Structure*, Cambridge, MA: MIT Press.

Chang, E. C. and Wong, M. L. (2004) 'Political Control and Performance in China's Listed Firms', *Journal of Comparative Economics*, 32 (4): 617–636.

Chen, G., Firth, M. and Rui, O. (1998) *The Economic Performance of Privatized Firm in China*, The Hong Kong Polytechnic University.

Chen, G., Firth, M., Gao, D. and Rui, O. (2005a) 'Ownership Structure, Corporate Governance, and Fraud: Evidence from China', *Journal of Corporate Finance*.

Chen, G., Firth, M. and Rui, O. (2005b) 'Have China's Enterprise Reforms Led to Improved Efficiency and Profitability?', *Emerging Markets Review*, 123: 1–28.

Chung, J. H. (2000) *Central Control and Local Discretion in China-Leadership and Implementation During Post-Moa Decollectivization*, New York: Oxford University Press.

Creswell, J. W. (2003) *Research Design: Qualitative, Quantitative, and Mixed Methods Approaches*, Thousand Oaks, CA: Sage Publications.

Davis, D. and Vogel, E. F. (1990) *Chinese Society on the Eve of Tiananmen: The Impact of Reform*, Harvard University Asia Center.

Demsetz, H. and Lehn, K. (1985) 'The Structure of Corporate Ownership: Causes and Consequences', *The Journal of Political Economy*, 93 (6): 1155–1177.

Demsetz, H. and Villalonga, B. (2001) 'Ownership Structure and Corporate Performance', *Journal of Corporate Finance*, 7: 209–233.

Dewenter, K. and Malatesta, P. H. (2001) 'State-Owned and Privately-Owned Firms: An empirical Analysis of Profitability, Leverage, and Labor Intensity', *American Economic Review*, 91 (1): 320–334.

Goodman, D. S. G. (1994) 'The Politics of Regionalism: Economic Development, Conflict and Negotiation', in D. S. G. Goodman and G. Segal (eds) *China Deconstructs: Politics, Trade and Regionalism*, London: Routledge, 1–20.

Greenwald, B. and Stiglitz, J. E. (1986) 'Externalities in Economies with Imperfect Information and Incomplete Markets', *Quarterly Journal of Economics*, 101: 229–264.

Hafsi, T. (1985) 'The Dynamics of Government in Business', *Interfaces*, 15 (4): 62–69.

Hafsi, T. and Koenig, C. (1988) 'The State-SOE Relationship: Some Patterns', *Journal of Management Studies*, 25 (3): 235–249.

Hafsi, T., Kiggundu, M. N. and Jorgensen, J. J. (1987) 'Strategic Apex Configurations in State-Owned Enterprises', *The Academy of Management Review*, 12 (4): 714–730.

Jensen, M. and Meckling, W. (1976) 'Theory of the Firm: Managerial Behaviours, Agency Cost and Ownership Structure', *Journal of Financial Economics*, 3: 305–360.

Jones, L. P. (ed.) (1982) *Public Enterprises in Less developed Countries*, Cambridge: Cambridge University Press.

Kaldor, N. (1980) 'Public or Private Enterprises: The Issues to be Considered', in W. J. Baumol (ed.) *Public and Private Enterprises in a Mixed Economy*, New York: St. Martin's Press, 1–12.

Kornai, J. (1992) *The Socialist System: The Political Economy of Communism*, Princeton, NJ.: Princeton University Press.

Kornai, J., Maskin, E. and Roland, G. (2003) 'Understanding the Soft Budget Constraint', *Journal of Economic Literature*, 41 (4): 1095–1136.

La Porta, R., Lopez-de-Silanes, F. and Shleifer, A. (1999) 'Corporate Ownership Around the World', *The Journal of Finance*, 54 (2): 471–517.

Li, H. and Zhou, L.-A. (2003) 'Political Turnover and Economic Performance: The Disciplinary Role of Personnel Control in China', author manuscript, The Chinese University of Hong Kong.

Li, L. C. (1997) 'Provincial Discretion and National Power: Investment Policy in Guangdong and Shanghai, 1978–93', *The China Quarterly*, 778–804.

McMillan, J. and Naughton, B. (1992) 'How to Reform a Planned Economy: Lessons from China', *Oxford Review of Economic Policy*, 81: 130–143.

Meyer, A. D. (1982) 'Adapting to Environmental Jolts', *Administrative Science Quarterly*, 27: 515–537.

Mingers, J. (2001) 'Combining is Research Methods: Towards a Pluralist Methodology', *Information Systems Research*, 12 (3): 240–259.

Qi, J. C. (1995) 'The Role of the Local Government in China's Transitional Economy', *The China Quarterly*, 144 (Special Issue: China's Transitional Economy): 1132–1149.

Qian, Y. (1996) 'Enterprise Reform in China: Agency problem and Political Control', *The Economics of Transition*, 4 (2): 427–447.

Qian, Y. (1999) 'The Institutional Foundations of China's Market Transition', Annual Conference on Development Economics, Washington, DC.

Qian, Y. and Roland, G. (1998) 'Federalism and the Soft Budget Constraint', *American Economic Review*, 88 (5): 1143–1162.

Qian, Y. and Weingast, B. (1997) 'Federalism as a Commitment to Perserving Market Incentives', *The Journal of Economic Perspectives*, 11 (4): 83–92.

Sapienza, P. (2004) 'The Effects of Government Ownership on Bank Lending', *Journal of Financial Economics*, 72: 357–384.

Shleifer, A. (1998) 'State Versus Private Ownership', *Journal of Economic Perpectives*, 12 (4): 133–150.

Stiglitz, J. E. and Weiss, A. (1981) 'Credit Rationing in Markets with Imperfect Information', *American Economic Review*, 71: 393–410.

Tan, Q. (2002) 'Growth Disparity in China: Provincial Causes', *Journal of Contemporary China*, 11 (33): 735–759.

Tian, G. (2001) 'State Shareholding and the Value of China's Firms', working paper, London Business School.

Vernon, R. and Aharoni, Y. (eds) (1981) *State-Owned Enterprises in the Western Economies*, London: Croom Helm Ltd.

Vining, A. and Boardman, A. (1992) 'Ownership Versus Competition: Efficiency in Public Enterprise', *Public Choice*, 73 (2): 205–223.

Wong, C. P. W. (2000) 'Central-local Relations Revisited: the 1994 Tax Sharing Reform and Public Expenditure Management in China', International Conference on 'Central-Periphery Relations in China: Integration, Disintegration or Reshaping of an Empire?', Chinese University of Hong Kong: March 23–24.

Yin, R. K. (2003a) *Applications of Case Study Research*, Newbury Park, CA: Sage Publications.

Yin, R. K. (2003b) *Case Study Research: Design and Methods*, Newbury Park, CA: Sage Publications.

9 Cultural distance and cross-border mergers and acquisitions of China

Empirical evidence from the electricity industry of China

Lei Wang

Introduction

The Chinese economy grew dramatically after China's "open door" domestic economic reforms in 1978. After a couple of decades of development, Chinese firms acquired certain competencies and were keen to expand abroad to exploit international markets. China joined the World Trade Organization (WTO) in 2001, which stimulated a wave of Chinese firms' "going out." Statistics from a World Investment Report (2008) indicate that Chinese external Foreign Direct Investment (FDI) increased from around US$2 billion in 2000 to US$22 billion in 2007. China's outward investment includes Mergers and Acquisitions (M&As), which in 2006 was valued at US$15 billion, accounting for more than 70 percent of total FDI that year. The value of M&A activity is predicted by many economists to increase in 2009 as the Chinese economy is impacted by the current global financial crisis to a relatively lesser extent than many developed countries. This affords Chinese firms with the opportunity to seek potential investment targets abroad. Although China's outward investment is continuously expanding and cross-border M&As are broadly acknowledged by Chinese firms as the quickest and most convenient entry mode of investing abroad, historically about 70 percent of cases failed (Invest in China website). Therefore, it is critical for Chinese firms to understand what factors impact on the success of international investment. However, to date China's outward FDI has been rarely studied mainly due to its very recent development. Appropriate rigorous and quantitative analyses are even scarcer.

Researchers of international direct investment have examined relevant factors in broad domains, from economical, financial, political, institutional, and cultural perspectives, to identify issues influencing the success of overseas investment. Amongst these, the cultural distance between home and host countries is one of the most discussed and acknowledged forces influencing investment performance (Shenkar 2001). The literature suggests that, according to the resource-based view of the firm, success depends on "sustainable competitive advantage" and "the organizational routines and repertoires that lead to a firm's sustainable competitive advantage tend to be constrained by national culture" (Morosini *et al.* 1998: 140).

A wealth of empirical studies on the issue also provides evidence of a relationship between national culture and sustainable competitive advantage. Despite popular acceptance of the existence of this relationship, opinions on how cultural distance influences the M&A performance are rather varied, and findings from empirical studies are also mixed, leading to a "national cultural distance paradox" (Brouthers and Brouthers 2001).

In this chapter, I explore this issue by analyzing cross-border M&As transaction data in the Chinese electricity industry during a period of 13 years – from 1996 to 2008. My objective is to understand how the national cultural distance between Chinese firms and their investments abroad influences their performance following merger and acquisition activity, and to identify and elaborate the relationship between cultural distance and performance. I chose the electricity industry for my empirical setting mainly because it is an industry of prime importance and included some modern industrial sectors such as internet service providers and telecommunications (Granovetter 1998).

This chapter is organized into five sections, the first of which has already been covered. The next section provides a review of the literature on the effect of cultural distance on investment performance and develops my hypotheses. The data and variables are explained in the third section. In the fourth section I then test the hypotheses and outline the estimated results. My discussions and conclusions are the subject of the fifth, and final, section.

Literature review and hypotheses

Some researchers argue that greater cultural distance leads to lower performance in multinational firms (Li and Guisinger 1992). The theoretical argument for this view is that greater cultural distance is likely to cause to organizational conflict, less efficient communications, and poorer implementation of organizational actions (Tihanyi *et al.* 2005). Jemison and Sitkin (1986) contend that a high level of cultural distance between firms tends to result in "cultural ambiguity" and process losses during the post-acquisition period. Empirical studies have also found evidence to support this theory. Li and Guisinger (1991) found that firms in the United States were more likely to fail in cases where their foreign partners came from culturally dissimilar countries. Chang (1995) also discovered supportive evidence for this view by studying Japanese electronic manufacturing firms in the United States during the period 1976–1989. The phenomenon that cultural disparity results in difficulties for post-acquisition integration, and even the failure of overseas investment, has been observed in many cases. An example is China's Lenovo Group, which acquired IBM's personal computing division for US$1.25 billion in 2005. At the start of the post-acquisition phase the clash between American and Chinese cultures caused confusion for the corporation's management resulting in Lenovo missing some market and innovation opportunities. Lenovo then faced serious difficulties in the four years following their acquisition. The financial report of Lenovo in November 2008, indicates that the group's net profit decreased by 78 percent (SOHU website). Another example is when the CEO of a Chinese television producer – TCL Group which acquired Alcatel's mobile phone business in 2004 – complained his French managers refused to take phone-calls at the weekend.

My first hypothesis is:

HYPOTHESIS 1 *There is a negative linear relationship between cultural distance and the performance of cross-border mergers and acquisitions.*

Even though cultural distance has been popularly thought of as barrier to post-acquisition integration and viewed as having a negative impact on the performance of international M&As, arguments to the contrary have also emerged. For example, Shenkar (2001: 524) pointed out that

> the implicit assumption that differences in cultures produce lack of 'fit' and hence an obstacle to transaction is questionable. First, not every cultural gap is critical to performance... Second, cultural differences may be complementary and hence have a positive synergetic effect on investment and performance.

There is some evidence from empirical studies to support this view. Morosini and colleagues (1998) found a positive relationship between national cultural distance and cross-border acquisition performance by examining a sample of 52 cross-border acquisitions taking place between 1987 and 1992. Chakrabarti *et al.* (2008) found that cross-border acquisitions perform better when the acquirer and the target firms come from countries that are culturally more distant. Some cases of successful post-acquisition integration between two distant cultures can be found. For instance, in 2003 one of China's five largest electric power generation groups, Huaneng Power International, acquired the electric firm OzGen, an Australian subsidiary of InterGen of the United States. Before being acquired by Huaneng, OzGen had suffered losses for years. After the acquisition OzGen integrated well with Huaneng and began to achieve surpluses (China Trade News).

Therefore, I set up an alternative hypothesis for hypothesis 1 as follows:

HYPOTHESIS 1 ALTERNATIVE: *There is a positive linear relationship between cultural distance and performance of cross-border merger and acquisition.*

Because of the contrary views and mixed empirical results on this topic some researchers argue that the relationship between cultural distance and merger-acquisition performance should be non-linear. Shenkar (2001) suggested that the assumption of a linear impact of cultural distance on investment, entry mode, and performance is questionable. Wang and Schaan (2007) suggest an inverted U-shaped relationship between cultural distance and performance. They maintain that when cultural distance is low learning difficulties between two cultures may not be great. The benefits of cultural distance, such as complementarity and diversity may outweigh negative effects such as conflict. Therefore, cultural distance may benefit performance. However, when the cultural distance is great, the acquirer firms' routines are impossible to transfer directly. The learning difficulties between the acquirer's and target's cultures are either insurmountable or very time consuming, and the negative effects are greater than the benefits. In this case cultural distance may damage performance.

This leads to my second hypothesis

HYPOTHESIS 2 *There is an inverted U-shaped relationship between cultural distance and performance in cross-border mergers and acquisitions.*

Methodology

Data

The data used in this study derived from several sources. The cross-border merger and acquisition data from 1996 to 2006 were obtained from the Securities Data Company (SDC) Platinum Database – Merger & Acquisition. The 2007 and 2008 transaction data was taken from the website of PricewaterhouseCoopers. To be included in this study, transactions from both sources had to meet the following criteria:

(1) acquirers are firms operating in China's electricity sector (Hong Kong included);
(2) targets are from different countries;
(3) acquirers have to be quoted on the stock exchange.

Given these criteria, we ended up with 18 transactions.

The stock prices of the acquirer firms on the transaction effective date and two years after the transaction were collected from a stock website (stockstar), and matched to the merger and acquisition data. An increased ratio of the stock prices was calculated for each acquirer based on the two stock prices.

Table 9.1 contains the basic descriptive statistics report for the merger and acquisition data sample used to support the analysis discussed in this chapter.

The national cultural data was obtained from the Geert Hofstede website. The other data used for control purposes in the analysis are mainly from a few online websites and were matched to the merger and acquisition data. The total assets data of acquirers in the transaction effective year are taken from the acquirers' annual financial reports, downloaded from the websites of acquirer firms. The Standard Industrial Classification (SIC) codes of both acquirer and target firms with relevant transactions between 1996 and 2006 were taken from the SDC database, along with merger and acquisition data. The SIC codes for the firms that had transactions in 2007 and 2008 are verified against a business information source (Alacra Store). GDP and GDP per capita data were taken from the World Economic Outlook (WEO). The data of geographic distance between investment home and host countries were acquired from the Internet.

Table 9.1 Descriptive statistic report of the merger and acquisition data sample

Year	*Numbers of transactions?*	*Numbers of host member countries*	*Average transaction value ($mil)*	*Average performance of acquirers (percentage)*	*Average total assets of acquirers ($mil)*
1996	1	1	Missing	−38.40	450
1997	0	0	0	0	0
1998	1	1	235.38	−17.42	5,896.26
1999	1	1	102.08	−15.60	5,896.26
2000	2	1	13.16	−16.15	6,126.06
2001	3	2	115.84	−26.77	4,356.42
2002	2	2	690.52	−35.27	5,734.97
2003	1	1	85.71	30.50	12,566.97
2004	1	1	227.00	−27.72	9,700.06
2005	0	0	0	0	0
2006	0	0	0	0	0
2007	2	2	366.00	−24.72	3,553.65
2008	4	3	1,072.48	−18.20	18,829.80
Average	1.4	1.2	242.3	−14.6	5,623.88

Variables

Dependent variable

The performance of cross-border M&As is the dependent variable in this study. The increased ratios of stock prices of the acquirers over a two-year period following their acquisition were used to measure performance. The stock price movement of the acquirer firm is a market-based measure for performance, which has been frequently referred in the literature as a measure of post-acquisition performance (Chatterjee *et al.* 1992; Singh and Montgomery 1987). Two years was chosen as the measurement period as the first two years after an acquisition are critical to the acquirer's performance. This is suggested in a wealth of literature (Jemison and Sitkin 1986; Balloun and Gridley 1990). Morosini *et al.* (1998) provide another explanation for choosing a two-year period being that the process of amalgamation should generally be completed within two years and the results of the integration can be measured effectively within this time-frame.

Independent variable

The independent variable, national cultural distance, is measured using Kogut and Singh's (1988) index, compiled from Hofstede's (1980) national cultural dimensions. Hofstede's cultural indices use four cultural dimensions (uncertainty avoidance, individuality, masculinity, and power distance) to describe the collective "programming of the mind" of people in a nation. Kogut and Singh formed a composite index based on the deviation along each of the four cultural dimensions (Kogut and Singh 1988). Kogut and Singh's formula is broadly referred to in the literature as the best method of calculating cultural distance (Morosini 1998; Yu *et al.* 2009). It is shown as follows:

$$CD_{ck} = \sqrt{\sum_{i=1}^{4} (I_{ic} - I_{ik})^2}$$

where: CD_{ck}: cultural distance for the kth country; I_{ik}: Hofstede's score; ith cultural dimension and kth country; c: indicates China.

Using this formula, a multidimensional measure that estimates the cultural distance between China and its investment countries is created.

Control variables

While my focus is on the effect of cultural distance on performance, I also control for a list of other factors that have been found important in the literature. I have included three levels of control variables in this study.

FIRM LEVEL

I use the size of acquirer as a firm-level control variable. Tihanyi *et al.* (2004) argue that firm size is important for firms' performance and found that small firms are prone to fail in foreign operations. Gomez-Mejia and Palich (1997) suggested that firm size may help to reduce risk and boost the performance of multinational firms. The size of a firm indicates levels of competency. Large firms are able to inject more capital into their target firms during the process of post-acquisition integration, increasing the chance of survival. The impact of acquirer size on the performance success of international investment is empirically tested in the literature (Wang and Schaan 2008). The size of an acquirer in this study is measured by their total assets in the transaction effective year. The logarithm values are taken as the data for this variable.

INDUSTRY LEVEL

Same industry is the only control variable at industry level in this study and is defined according to whether or not the acquirer and target firms are from the same industry. Lubatkin (1983) has argued that when the acquirer and target firms are from the same industry, post-acquisition performance is better. His explanation is that firms in the same industry generate economies of scale and scope when they integrate (Lubatkin 1983). When the acquirer and target firms are from same industry, the acquirer firm possesses the necessary knowledge on the industry, which helps them to manage the target firm. Singh and Montgomery (1987) demonstrate that gains to shareholders were higher for acquisitions in the same industry. Same industry is measured based on the 4-digit SIC code of firms. It is a dummy variable. If the acquirer and the target firms have the same 4-digit SIC code, "1" is coded, otherwise "0" is coded.

COUNTRY LEVEL

There are five country-level control variables.

Economic conditions in the target firm's country and the economic difference between investment in home and host countries are considered by some researchers as important factors which influence the success of M&As. Slangen (2006) argues that acquisitions should perform better if economic conditions in the investment host country are favorable. Chakrabarti and his colleagues (2009) state that economic difference between the two countries might be expected to have a considerable effect on performance. Therefore, I include three economic variables as country-level controls in my models. They are the GDP of the host country, GDP per capita of the host country, and the economic difference. Economic difference takes the ratios of GDP per capita in the investment home country divided by that in the host country as its data. The logarithm values of the GDP of the host country and the GDP per capita of the host country were taken as the data for these two variables.

Uncertainty avoidance by the host may influence post-acquisition performance as well. Uncertainty avoidance is defined by Hofstede (2001: 161) as "the extent to which the members of a culture feel threatened by uncertain or unknown situations." In nations with a high uncertainty avoidance index, people feel that "what is different is dangerous" (Hofstede 1999: 41). This may create additional barriers that foreign investors have to overcome (Bhardwaj *et al.* 2007). Therefore, I argue that high uncertainty avoidance may have a negative impact on M&A performance. To control for this in the models Hofstede's (1980) national culture scores for the uncertainty avoidance index of the host country was adopted.

Geographic distance is another popularly addressed factor in the performance of international investment. Grant (1987: 82) noted, "The closer the international operations are, the easier it is to internationally integrate operations." Short geographic distance allows managers to more quickly, frequently, and less expensively, travel to the locations of target firms, making it is easier for acquirer firms to manage their foreign subsidiaries (Gomez-Mejia 1984). Thus, I assume that shorter geographic distance should help firms' integration and cross-border M&A performance. Geographic distance is measured as the shortest flying hours from the capital city of the investment home country to the capital city of the investment host country in the transaction effective year.

Models

The regression model that I used to test my hypotheses is in the following form:

$$\begin{aligned}\text{Performance} = {} & \text{Intercept} + \ln(\text{Size of acquirer}) + \text{Same industry}\\ & + \ln(\text{GDP of target's country}) + \ln(\text{GDP per capita of}\\ & \times \text{target's country}) + \text{Economic difference}\\ & + \text{Uncertainty avoidance of host} + \text{Geographic distance}\\ & + \text{Cultural distance} + \text{Cultural distance square} + \varepsilon\end{aligned}$$

where ln: natural logarithm; Performance: Chinese electric firms' cross-border M&As performance; Size of acquirer: the total assets of acquirer firm; Same industry: whether or not the acquirer firm and target firm are from the same industry; GDP of target's country: GDP of the country where the target firm is from; GDP per capita of target's country: GDP per capita of the country where the target firm is located; Economic difference: the ratio of GDP per capita of China against that of the target firm's country; Uncertainty avoidance of host: Hofstede's uncertainty avoidance in the target firm's country; Geographic distance: How distant the capital city of the acquirer firm's country from the capital city of the target firm's country is. Cultural distance: Kogut and Singh's cultural distance index linear term. Cultural distance square: Kogut and Singh's cultural distance index quadratic term.

Results and analyses

The descriptive statistics and correlation matrix for the independent variables and the dependent variable in this study are presented in Table 9.2. The table shows a few correlations larger than 0.5, therefore, in the regression process, I adopted a stepwise technique to select the variables and to avoid possible multicollinearity between the correlated ones.

Since the correlations among the first four variables – size of acquirer, same industry, GDP of target's country, and GDP per capita of target's country – are rather low, I started the stepwise regression with Model 1, which contains these four control variables. Next, the remaining control variables were entered one at a time into Model 2, Model 3, and Model 4. Cultural distance and its quadratic term were included in sequence in Model 5 and Model 6. The statistical results of Model 1 show the adjusted R-squared is 0.324 and the F-statistic is significant at a 10 percent significance level with the value 3.035. The model is successful in passing statistical tests. In Model 2, because the adjusted R-squared value is reduced to 0.276 and the F-statistic is no longer significant when including the economic relative ratio variable, I dropped this variable from the model. By repeating the stepwise, I arrived at the final model – Model 6 – with an adjusted R-squared of 0.546 and a significant F-statistic of 3.917 at the 5 percent significance level. All of the models and their statistics are presented in Table 9.3. The statistical results suggest that Model 6 is the best one to explain the dependent variable compared to other models presented.

The results of Model 5, which contains only control variables and the cultural distance linear term, show that the cultural distance linear term is not significant in the model. This suggests that a linear relationship between cultural distance and performance does not exist. Therefore, hypothesis 1 and its alternative were rejected. The results of Model 6 indicate that the cultural distance quadratic term is negative and significant at the 10 percent significance level and the cultural distance parameter is positive and significant at the 5 percent significance level, which indicates that the relationship between cultural distance and performance is of an inverted-U shaped quadratic curve. The results support the second

Table 9.2 Means, standard deviation and correlation matrix of the variables

Variables	*Mean*	*S.D.*	*1*	2	*3*	*4*	5	*6*	*7*	*8*
1 Size of acquiror	8.34	1.42								
2 Same industry	0.44	0.51	0.03							
3 GDP of target's country	6.91	1.37	0.19	−0.34						
4 GDP per capita of target's country	10.56	0.36	0.16	−0.06	−0.07					
5 Economic relative ratio	3.02	3.29	0.34	−0.19	0.25	−0.65				
6 Uncertainty avoidance of host	43.94	21.57	0.05	−0.32	0.67	0.00	0.25			
7 Geographic distance	8.26	6.30	−0.17	−0.09	−0.19	−0.07	−0.04	0.10		
8 Cultural distance	36.22	24.15	0.09	−0.35	0.17	−0.01	0.30	0.58	0.39	
9 Performance	−20.78	17.09	0.42	0.22	0.20	0.11	0.24	0.38	−0.01	0.28

Table 9.3 Results of regression analysis

	Model 1	*Model 2*	*Model 3*	*Model 4*	*Model 5*	*Model 6*
Intercept	−231.839*	−184.096	−199.565#	−222.069#	−190.233#	−223.660*
Control variables						
Firm-level variable						
1 Size of acquirer	6.096*	6.866#	5.589*	6.075*	6.657*	6.128*
Industry-level variable						
2 Same industry	8.957	7.763	11.034	9.342	13.009#	16.784*
Country-level variables						
3 GDP of target's country	−2.498	−2.210	−1.017	−0.881	−2.091	−4.856
4 GDP per capita of target's country	16.428	11.368	11.698	13.256	10.452	14.902
5 Economic difference		−0.725				
6 Uncertainty avoidance of host			0.245	0.181	0.065	−0.564
7 Geographic distance				0.561		
Independent variables						
8 Cultural distance					0.259	2.406*
9 Cultural distance squared						−0.022#
Adjusted R-squared:	0.324	0.276	0.353	0.348	0.409	0.546
F-statistic	3.035#	2.295	2.855#	2.514#	2.956#	3.917*

# $p < 0.1$; * $p < 0.05$; ** $p < 0.01$.

hypothesis, which means that the performance of cross-border M&As improves with cultural distance when that distance is relatively low and tends to decrease when the distance is greater than a certain point after accounting for a series of control variables. The shape of the relationship resembles an inverted U-shape. This suggests that Chinese firms need to consider both cultural diversification and cultural familiarity when they choose their investment partners in order to achieve an appropriate cultural distance.

One of the control variables in Model 6, namely size of the acquirer, is positive and significant in all models. This positive effect suggests that acquirer firms with larger assets perform better than those with fewer assets. As presented earlier, theoretically, firms with more assets have more competencies to operate effectively and therefore should perform better. The implicit assumption for Chinese firms is that they should develop a prominence in the domestic market and develop relevant capital capabilities and competencies to enable them to effectively conduct an international operation. M&As are usually accompanied by a high failure rate in international markets. For Chinese firms that developed only over the past 30 years, and still lack capital capability and international operation experience, a relatively cautious and conservative investment strategy is recommended.

The coefficient of another control variable, same industry, is also positive and significant in Model 5 and Model 6. It shows that Chinese firms' M&As occurring in the same industry perform better. When the acquirer and target firms are from same industry acquirer firms possesses the necessary knowledge to help them manage their foreign targets. It is also argued that two firms from the same industry can develop economies of scale and scope when they operate together. When they are from same industry the acquirer firms can concentrate on promoting their business instead of managing a pure capital operation. This is a typical characteristic of the initial investment stage.

Other control variables concerning economic conditions are not significant in all models, indicating that macro-economic conditions in the target firm's country do not play a significant role on the performance of M&As. Neither does the level of uncertainty avoidance in the investment host country nor geographic distance between China and the target country.

Conclusion, recommendations, and limitations

This chapter has developed a quantitative method to analyze the relationship between the performance of M&As in Chinese electric firms and the cultural distance of the investment home and host countries. It has two important contributions. First, it contributes to the area of "national cultural distance paradox" research by providing empirical evidence of a quadratic relationship between cultural distance and performance of international investments. Second, it indicates the impact on Chinese firms' international investment performance through the conduct of a quantitative analysis.

The main findings in this study and their implications for Chinese firms are:

First, I found an inverted U-shape relationship between the performance of cross-border mergers and acquisitions and the cultural distance between China and the country where the target firm is from. This suggests that Chinese firms should consider both cultural diversification and cultural familiarity when they choose their investment partners in order to achieve an appropriate balance in cultural distance.

Second, we found that performance is positively impacted by the size of the acquirer, which suggests that firms willing to exploit foreign markets through M&As need first to develop a prominence in domestic market, and in the process develop the capital strength to conduct international operations.

Third, I found that firms perform better when their target firms are in the same industry as them. This is a characteristic of the initial investment stage and suggests that Chinese firms should aim to promote their industrial business rather focus on their capital investment during the initial post-acquisition phase.

In summary, Chinese firms grew rapidly over the last 30 years and developed competencies to conduct international operations. Cross-border M&A is popularly considered by Chinese firms as the fastest and most efficient method of entering foreign markets. However, Chinese firms' M&As are still symbolized by their initial investment characteristics. The significant parameters on performance suggest a cautious and conservative investment strategy should be adopted taking account of a balance between cultural diversity and cultural familiarity, adequate capital capabilities, and the investment goal.

This study has two main limitations. First, I measured firms' performance with stock price changes over the two years post-acquisition. Some studies suggest a long-term measure to measure performance of firms (Chakrabarti *et al.* 2009). Future research could test the robustness of the models proposed in this study with other performance measurements. Second, the data sample that I adopted to test the hypotheses is taken from the Chinese electric industry. Whether or not the conclusions on the significant parameters argued in this chapter can be generalized to other industries or countries requires further study.

References

Alacra Store: http://www.alacrastore.com/ (accessed May 20, 2009).

Balloun, J. and Gridley, R. (1990) 'Post-merger management understanding the challenges', *The McKinsey Quarterly*, 4: 90–102.

Bhardwaj, A., Dietz, J. and Beamish, P. W. (2007) 'Host country cultural influences on foreign direct investment', *Management International Review*, 47 (1): 29–50.

Brouthers, K. D. and Brouthers, L. E. (2001) 'Explaining the national cultural distance paradox', *Journal of International Business Studies*, 32 (1): 177–189.

Chang, S. J. (1995) 'International expansion strategy of Japanese firms: capability building through sequential entry', *The Academy of Management Journal*, 38 (2): 383–407.

Chakrabarti, R., Gupta-Mukherjee, S. and Jayaraman, N. (2009) 'Mars–Venus marriages: culture and cross-border M&A', *Journal of International Business Studies*, 40: 216–236.

Chatterjee, S. (1992) 'Sources of value in take-overs: synergy or restructuring – implications for target and bidder firms', *Strategic Management Journal*, 13: 267–86.

China Trade News: http://www.chinaculture.org (accessed May 20, 2009).

Geert Hofstede website: http://www.geert-hofstede.com/ (accessed May 20, 2009).

Gomez-Mejia, L. R. (1984) 'Effects of occupation on task related, contextual and jobs involvement orientation: a cross-cultural perspective', *Academy of Management Journal*, 27: 706–20.

Gomez-Mejia, L. R. and Palich, L. E. (1997) 'Cultural diversity and the performance of multinational firms', *Journal of International Business Studies*, 28 (2): 309–335.

Granovetter, M. and Patrick, M. (1998) 'The making of an industry: electricity in the United States', in M. Callon (ed.) *The Law of Markets*, Oxford: Blackwell, 147–173.

Grant, R. M. (1987) 'Multinationality and performance among British manufacturing companies', *Journal of International Business Studies*, 18 (3): 79–89.

Hofstede, G. (1980) *Culture's Consequences: International Differences in Work-Related Values*, Beverly Hills, New York: Sage Publications.

Hofstede, G. (1999) 'Problems remain, but theories will change: the universal and the specific in 21st- Century global management', *organizational Dynamics*, 28 (1): 34–44.

Hofstede, G. (2001) *Cultural Consequences: Comparing Values, Behaviors, Institutions and Organizations Across Nations*, Beverly Hills, California: Sage Publications.

Jeminson, D. B. and Sitkin, S. B. (1986) 'Corporate acquisitions: a process perspective', *Academy of Management Review*, 11 (1): 145–163.

Kogut, B. and Singh, H. (1988) 'The effect of national culture on the choice of entry mode', *Journal of International Business Studies*, 19 (3): 411–430.

Li, J. and Guisinger, S. (1992) 'The globalization of service multinationals in the 'triad' regions: Japan, Western Europe and North America', *Journal of International Business Studies*, 23: 675–696.

Lubatkin, M. (1983) 'Merger and the performance of the acquiring firm', *Academy of Management Review*, 8 (2): 218–25.

Morosini, P., Shane, S. and Singh, H. (1998) 'National cultural distance and cross-border acquisition', *Journal of International Business Studies*, 29 (1): 137–158.

Shenkar, O. (2001) 'Cultural distance revisited: towards a more rigorous conceptualization and measurement of cultural differences', *Journal of International Business Studies*, 32 (3): 519–535.

Singh, H. and Montgomery, C. A. (1987) 'Corporate acquisition strategies and economic performance', *Strategic Management Journal*, 8: 377–86.

Slangen, A. H. L. (2006) 'National cultural distance and initial foreign acquisition performance: The moderating effect of integration', *Journal of World Business*, 41: 161–170.

SOHU website : www.sohu.com (accessed May 20, 2009).

Stockstar: http://quote.stockstar.com/stock/ (accessed May 20, 2009).

Tihanyi, L., Griffith, D. A. and Russell, C. J. (2005) 'The effect of cultural distance on entry mode choice, international diversification, and MNE performance: a meta-analysis', *Journal of International Business Studies*, 36: 270–283.

'The current situation of Chinese corporations' cross-border merger and acquisition', Ministry of Commerce of the People's Republic of China. Online. Available at: http://www.fdi.gov.cn/index.htm (accessed May 20, 2009).

UNCTAD (2008) *World Investment Report 2008: Transnational Corporations and the Infrastructure Challenge*, United Nations Publications.

Wang, H. and Schaan, J. L. (2008) 'How much distance do we need? revisiting the "National Cultural Distance Paradox"', *Management International Review*, 48: 263–277.

Yu, T., Subramaniam, M. and Cannella, A. A. (2009) 'Rivalry deterrence in international markets: contingencies governing the mutual forbearance hypothesis', *Academy of Management Journal*, 52 (1): 127–147.

10 R&D, direct technology transfer and productivity growth

Evidence from Chinese manufacturing industries

Yanbing Wu

Introduction

Technological change is an important determinant of long-run productivity growth and therefore of increases in living standards over time. Research and development (R&D), which leads to new products and processes that either increase firms' revenues or reduce firms' costs, is regarded as the fundamental driver of technological progress and endogenous growth. Therefore productivity growth should be amplified when R&D expenditures are also raised. Under the circumstance of economic globalization, another important way to achieve technological progress is to fully absorb and exploit the advanced technologies and experiences of the rest world. For developing countries in which few firms have well-established R&D operations, tapping into the existing world knowledge stock would seem to be a natural way of shortening the technology gap.

Since China's reform and opening up, the Chinese central government has been consistently emphasizing the importance of technology development and viewing it as an engine for the process of catching-up with advanced industrial economies and industrialization. Chinese central government has taken effective policy instruments to reform the mechanisms of science and technology and carried out preferential policy measures towards encouraging foreign technology introduction from developed countries. As a result, in-house R&D and direct foreign technology transfer have been steadily rising since 1978. For example, R&D expenditure in 2007 totaled 371 billion Yuan which was about 50 times R&D expenditure in 1987. The ratio of R&D spending to GDP reached 1.49 percent in 2007, a substantial increase relative to the level of 0.61 percent in 1987. Direct foreign technology transfer reached US$25 billion in 2007, while it was only US$2.5 billion in 1979 (Chinese National Bureau of Statistics 2008). Now technological progress has become a critical ingredient for sustained economic growth in China. It is believed that over the long term, China's economic performance will ultimately depend upon its ability to acquire and adapt new technologies.

Against this background, this research draws on previous studies to offer information on two questions related to R&D, technology transfer and productivity growth, which are also two important topics that have attracted considerable attention in research on technology issues in advanced industrial countries. First, are

R&D and technology transfer important factors in explaining the growth of Total Factor Productivity (TFP) at the industry level? Second, if R&D and technology transfer are important factors, how great are their impacts? In practice, the main evidence related to those questions consists of econometric estimates of the output elasticity and the rate of return to R&D and technology transfer. This research uses an industry-level data set of Chinese large- and medium-size manufacturing industries over the period of 1996–2006 to systematically investigate the contribution of each of these channels to industry-level performance. Through this empirical study, this research is expected to provide an explanation for Chinese economic growth and some suggestions for Chinese technological development.

In this chapter we find that R&D has a significant contribution to productivity growth in Chinese manufacturing industries, whereas direct technology transfer, whether foreign or domestic, has no significant impact on productivity growth. When the productivity growth is decomposed into technical efficiency change and technological progress, we find that the positive impact of R&D on productivity growth seems to work mainly through technical efficiency improvement. The remainder of the chapter is organized as follows. The second section reviews the related literature. The third section explains the conceptual and econometric framework. The fourth section describes the data. The empirical results are presented in the fifth section. The sixth section estimates the effects of R&D and technology transfer on the components of productivity decompositions. Finally, the seventh section provides conclusions and the policy implications.

Literature review

The interest in econometrically assessing R&D investments started in the early 1960s. The earliest research to investigate the effects of R&D on productivity centered on individual industries within manufacturing and particularly on the agricultural sector (Minasian 1962, 1969; Griliches 1964; Mansfield 1965). As time passed and more sources of data became available, later studies tended to broaden the samples by including more industries, many firms in a single industry, or many firms in many industries. These studies, by including the knowledge stock in the Cobb-Douglas production function, tried to identify the acceleration of productivity growth that occurs due to R&D investments. However, the conceptual framework was not satisfactorily developed until the late 1970s (Griliches 1979); from then on, a large number of empirical studies of estimating the effect of R&D investments on productivity growth have emerged in many countries. The estimated magnitudes of the R&D contribution to productivity growth span a wide range depending on the aggregation level of data, the methodology and the period being considered: some studies have found that R&D's effect on productivity is essentially zero, whereas others have found that its effect is substantial and that it exceeds that of other types of investment by a large margin. Most of the estimates, however, lie somewhere between the two extremes, and as a result a consensus has formed around the view that R&D spending has a significantly positive effect on productivity growth, with a rate of return that is about the same size as or perhaps slightly larger than the rate of return on conventional investments.

For studies on Chinese industries during the reform era, given the transitional nature of China's industrial economy, a particular focus is placed on the impact of institutional reform on the performance of China's industrial enterprises. Increasing interest has also been attached to R&D and innovation, as well as their impacts upon industry performance in the Chinese manufacturing sector. Among the existing empirical studies, the econometric evaluation of the impact of China's R&D on productivity has been a focus of analysis in recent years. Hu (2001) adopted a production function framework to analyze the impact of R&D on productivity using a cross-section of innovative enterprises from Beijing, China. He found that private R&D has a strong impact on firm productivity and government R&D contributes indirectly to productivity by promoting private R&D. Hu and Jefferson (2004) used a firm-level dataset of large and medium-size industrial enterprises during the period of 1991–97 in the Beijing area to find substantial and significant returns to R&D in the cross-section dimension. Based on a rich set of panel data covering the population of China's large and medium-size manufacturing enterprises during 1997–1999, Jefferson *et al.* (2006) found that the contributions of R&D expenditures to productivity are statistically significant and returns to industrial R&D appear to be at least three to four times the returns to fixed production assets.

In the context of China's opening up policy, a vast majority of the empirical literature has emerged about the impacts of technology spillovers through foreign direct investment upon manufacturing industries' performance. For example, Liu (2002) used industry-level data of 29 manufacturing industries over the period of 1993–1998 in the Shenzhen Special Economic Zone of China to find that foreign direct investment has large and significant spillover effects in that it raises both the level and growth rate of productivity of manufacturing industries. However, it is especially noticeable that very few studies have paid attention to the relationship between direct technology introduction and productivity growth. In the existing literature using China's data, only Hu *et al.* (2005) examined the contributions of domestic R&D, foreign technology transfer and domestic technology transfer, as well as their interactions to productivity, using a large data set for China's large and medium-size enterprises during 1995 to 1999. The central findings of this research are that domestic R&D and foreign technology transfer have strong impacts on the productivity of industrial enterprises and the impacts of both domestic and foreign technology transfer on productivity are largely conditional on their interactions with in-house R&D.

The above literature that assesses China's R&D and technology introduction econometrically mainly uses the firm-level dataset. Moreover, shortcomings of the available data and the difficulties associated with the estimating methods make it difficult to identify with any precision the size of contributions that R&D and technology introduction make. By using an industry-level data set of Chinese large and medium-size manufacturing enterprises during the period of 1996–2007, this research analyzes the contributions of three technology acquisition channels, i.e. R&D, foreign and domestic technology transfer, to improving China's industrial performance. Compared with the existing literature, some academic contributions in this research are as follows.

First, on the basis of the expansion of the Cobb-Douglas production function, not only the output elasticities but also the rates of return of R&D, and foreign and domestic technology transfer are estimated in this research. Meanwhile, Data Envelopment Analysis (DEA) is used to decompose productivity growth of Chinese manufacturing industries into technical efficiency change and technological progress, and then the effects of three technology acquisition channels on Malmquist productivity index and its components are re-estimated to verify the reliability of the production functions estimates.

Second, the available data concerning real R&D expenditures are bedeviled by the lack of a suitable price index for R&D inputs. Fortunately, the *China Statistical Yearbook on Science and Technology* provides detailed data about R&D expenditures which are composed of compensation for laborers, raw material expenditure, expenditure on the purchase of fixed assets and other expenditure for R&D. Based on these data, a more reliable R&D price index can be constructed to deflate the nominal R&D expenditures, which gives us an opportunity of calculating with more precision R&D's contribution to productivity growth.

Finally, a noteworthy issue in exploring the contribution of R&D to productivity is the so-called "double counting" problem. Given that a proportion of capital and labor belongs to the R&D department, R&D machinery and R&D employees should be subtracted from the ordinary capital and labor while calculating the output elasticity and rate of return to R&D. Nevertheless, the data used in the existing literature are not always detailed enough to allow such corrections. In this research, the data are corrected by subtracting the employees devoted to the R&D department from the total numbers of employees. With double counting for R&D employees corrected, the estimation results are more credible than those of ignoring this issue.

Conceptual and econometric framework

A common approach of innovation studies is to treat R&D within a production function framework as a factor of production, symmetric with physical capital, labor, and other inputs. The R&D input is most appropriately interpreted as a stock of knowledge constructed as the sum of discounted past R&D expenditures. The model used here is essentially the same as that employed by other scholars, except that the sources of knowledge are disaggregated into three parts: domestic R&D, foreign technology import and domestic technology transfer.

The Cobb-Douglas production function is usually regarded as a starting point for most econometric studies of assessing the contribution of knowledge to productivity. In a particular industry, after accounting for time and industry differences, the production function is assumed to be the following:

$$Q_{it} = AC_{it}^{\alpha}L_{it}^{\beta}(RS_{it})^{\gamma_R}(FS_{it})^{\gamma_F}(DS_{it})^{\gamma_D}e^{\lambda t+u_i+\varepsilon_{it}} \tag{10.1}$$

where Q is the industry's output, C is the industry's stock of physical capital, and L is the industry's labor input. *RS*, *FS* and *DS* represent the industry's stocks of

R&D, foreign technology import and domestic technology transfer respectively. The term A is a constant, t is a time trend, λ captures the disembodied technical change. α and β are the elasticities of output with respect to physical capital and labor respectively, and γ_R, γ_F and γ_D are the elasticities of output with respect to three knowledge stocks. u_i captures unobservable effects which are unchangeable with time, and ε_{it} is an error term.

As usual, to implement the estimation of the production function, Equation (10.1) can be rewritten in logs as:

$$q_{it} = a + \lambda t + u_i + \alpha c_{it} + \beta l_{it} + \gamma_R rs_{it} + \gamma_F fs_{it} + \gamma_D ds_{it} + \varepsilon_{it} \qquad (10.2)$$

Lower case letters denote the logarithms of variables. Under constant returns to scale with respect to the conventional measures of capital and labor, the sum of factor elasticities, $\mu = \alpha + \beta$, is unity. For interpretive reasons, the equation can be rewritten so that the deviation from constant returns is measured explicitly, by subtracting labor from both sides of Equation (10.2):

$$\begin{aligned}(q_{it} - l_{it}) = a + \lambda t + u_i + \alpha(c_{it} - l_{it}) + (\mu - 1)l_{it} + \gamma_R rs_{it} \\ + \gamma_F fs_{it} + \gamma_D ds_{it} + \varepsilon_{it} \qquad (10.3)\end{aligned}$$

The coefficient of the logarithm of labor $(\mu - 1)$ now measures the departure from constant returns. If this coefficient is significantly different from zero, constant returns to scale for capital and labor can be rejected. Accounting for the possible effects of the restriction of returns to scale on the estimates of γ_R, γ_F and γ_D, we shall report both the estimates obtained with and without imposing constant returns to scale.

Estimating Equation (10.3) requires very few assumptions about the production function and provides results that have a straightforward interpretation. Meanwhile, in the process of estimating the parameters of R&D and technology transfer, several econometric problems are worth noticing.

First, in estimating Equation (10.3), we face a possible econometric problem concerning the potential correlation between the independent variables and unobservable effects. In our panel data, u_i represents time-invariant industry specific characteristics which may be corresponded to permanent differences in production technology and economic environment. However, the unobservable industry specific characteristics may be quite likely to correlate with the production inputs on the right-hand side of Equation (10.3). For example, industries with high technologies may also sustain greater than average expenditure on R&D and technology purchases. The ordinary least square estimates of the coefficients would then be subject to omitted-variable misspecification and bias. Several methods exist to correct for this bias. The habitual and convenient way is to compute the within regression using the deviations of the observations from their specific industry means, which is equivalent to including industry dummy variables in the total regression. Another substitute way is to use the first difference estimation in which the industry specific characteristics can be eliminated from the right-hand side of Equation (10.3). The first difference regression is as follows:

$$\Delta(q_{it} - l_{it}) = \lambda + \alpha\Delta(c_{it} - l_{it}) + (\mu - 1)\Delta l_{it} + \gamma_R \Delta rs_{it} + \gamma_F \Delta fs_{it} + \gamma_D \Delta ds_{it} + \Delta\varepsilon_{it} \qquad (10.4)$$

Second, multicollinearity is another possible econometric problem associated with Equation (10.3). This problem is engendered by the fact that the variables of interest move together over time so that the estimates of the parameters tend to have large estimated variances and little statistical significance, thus it is difficult to identify accurately the contribution of each input. By contrast, since the first-difference of the logarithm of variable is approximately equivalent to the yearly growth rates of the variable, which can greatly reduce the correlations among independent variables[1] as well as control for permanent differences across industries, we are prone to use the first-differenced equation, i.e. Equation (10.4), to evaluate the contribution of R&D and technology transfer to productivity growth.

Third, the inputs in the production function may not be completely exogenously determined. Technical knowledge and productivity are likely to be mutually dependent – output is a function of, among other things, technical knowledge, and technical knowledge is a function of past output and expected future output, e.g. higher output leads to higher R&D expenditure and technology transfer. Under these circumstances, Ordinary Least Squares (OLS)-based estimates of the coefficients on knowledge may be biased. The solution to this simultaneity is the use of simultaneous-equation techniques or Instrumental Variables (IV) estimation. However, they are not always applied to explore the contribution of knowledge because the data required to use them do not always exist and the exogeneity of these instruments is then questioned, raising other problems (Griliches 1986). For this reason, we do not wipe out the possible bias induced by simultaneity.

Finally, when using Equations (10.2) to (10.4) to evaluate the output elasticities, one of the most difficult tasks is to measure the stocks of the three knowledge capitals. To avoid this problem, some authors have chosen to use an equation that yields an estimate of the Rate of Return (ROR) to knowledge instead of the knowledge elasticities. The specification is a transformation of Equation (10.4), which assumes that the marginal products of knowledge across industries are equal.

Since by definition the elasticity of R&D stock γ_R is equal to $(\Delta Q/\Delta RS)(RS/Q)$, term $\gamma_R \Delta rs$ can be rewritten as

$$\frac{\Delta Q}{\Delta RS}\frac{RS}{Q}\frac{\Delta RS}{RS} = \frac{\Delta Q}{\Delta RS}\frac{\Delta RS}{Q}$$

The fraction $\Delta Q/\Delta RS$ is the marginal product of R&D stock (termed as ρ_R) which is interpreted as the rate of return to R&D. In order to estimate ρ_R, the variable ΔRS (representing the change of R&D stock) is needed. Most of the previous studies have usually assumed that R&D capital does not depreciate so that the difference of R&D capital (ΔRS) is equal to the current R&D expenditures (termed as R),[2] i.e. $\Delta RS = R$, then the term $\gamma_R \Delta rs$ can be rewritten as $\rho_R(R/Q)$. Similarly, the terms $\gamma_F \Delta fs$ and $\gamma_D \Delta ds$ in Equation (10.4) can also be rewritten as $\rho_F(F/Q)$ and $\rho_D(D/Q)$ respectively, where F and D represent the expenditures on foreign and domestic technology transfer respectively, and ρ_F and ρ_D represent the rate of return to the corresponding variables. Therefore, Equation (10.4) can be transformed into the following form:

$$\Delta(q_{it} - l_{it}) = \lambda + \alpha\Delta(c_{it} - l_{it}) + (\mu - 1)\Delta l_{it} + \rho_R\left(\frac{R}{Q}\right)_{it} + \rho_F\left(\frac{F}{Q}\right)_{it} + \rho_D\left(\frac{D}{Q}\right)_{it} + \Delta\varepsilon_{it} \qquad (10.5)$$

Compared with Equation (10.4), the main advantage of Equation (10.5) is that the relevant variables on the right-hand side are the intensities of R&D and technology transfer to output which are easily measured. Meanwhile, it must be borne in mind that there are at least two potential problems with this rate of return approach (Hall and Mairesse 1995). First, the rate of return estimated using Equation (10.5) is a gross rate of return. To obtain the net rate of return we need to subtract the (unknown) depreciation rate for R&D and technology transfer; thus the problem of depreciating incurred when estimating the stocks of R&D and technology transfer is not really avoided. Second, the timing of the relationships among R&D, technology transfer and productivity growth is not clear, so applying various lag structures of variables in the regression seems to be appropriate. Fortunately, Mairesse and Sassenou (1991) in their survey point out that R&D expenditures by firms is very stable over time, most of the variation is in the cross-section. In this study we experiment with the timing of both the three-knowledge variables and sales revenue and confirm that it has little impact on the regression results and the intensity coefficients do indeed seem to be unbiased.

Taking the advantages and disadvantages of the output elasticity and the rate of return method into account, we use the two different methods to evaluate the effects of the three technology acquisition channels on productivity growth.

Data and variables

Data

The main data for this research, which span the population of Chinese large and medium-sized manufacturing enterprises,[3] are drawn from the *China Statistical Yearbook on Science and Technology* published by China Statistics Press. Large- and medium-sized enterprises dominate Chinese industry, accounting for 64 percent of China's total industrial value added in 2006. In addition, the correlative price indexes are necessary in order to eliminate the influence of price fluctuation on output and inputs. Price indexes are drawn from the *Chinese Statistical Yearbook* which the National Bureau of Statistics of China (NBS) reports each year. Our sample spans a period of 11 years from 1996 to 2006 and includes data for

29 two-digit manufacturing industries every year; therefore a balanced panel data, which is composed of 319 observations, is constructed.

R&D expenditure is measured by intramural expenditure on technical development which refers to the actual expenditure made for scientific and technological activities by the survey units during the reference period, including service expenses, professional expenses for scientific research, management expenses for scientific research, purchases of fixed assets with investment in non-capital construction, capital construction expenditure for scientific research, and others. Direct foreign (domestic) technology transfer is measured by an industry's expenditures on technology purchased from foreign (domestic) providers.

Variables

R&D stock and technology transfer stock

In order to estimate the elasticities of output with respect to R&D, foreign and domestic technology transfer, stock measures for each of the three technology variables are needed. Knowledge accumulated through these technological activities in the past generates benefits in the present and the future. However, knowledge depreciates and becomes obsolete not only because new knowledge replaces old knowledge but also because the appropriability of knowledge decreases as the diffusion of that knowledge takes place with the passage of time. Following the methods of Griliches (1979), by using a perpetual inventory model like that commonly used for physical capital, we construct the stocks of R&D, foreign and domestic technology transfer as the discounted sum of past expenditures on respective activity.

We first construct the R&D capital stock. R&D stock has been viewed as a measurement of the current state of technical knowledge, determined, in part, by current and past R&D expenditures. The perpetual inventory method defining R&D capital stock is the following:

$$RS_{it} = R_{it} + (1 - \delta)RS_{i,t-1} \tag{10.6}$$

where *RS* is the R&D stock for industry i in year t; δ is the depreciation rate of R&D capital, and R is industry i's gross R&D investments in year t. To implement the equation, we must first calculate the price index for R&D expenditures, the initial R&D stock and the depreciation rate.

As Mansfield (1984) points out, the available data concerning real R&D expenditures are bedeviled by the lack of a suitable price index for R&D inputs. The usual R&D price deflator used in the past literature is either the GNP deflator or a weighted average (with almost equal weights) of the consumer price index and assets price deflator. Fortunately, the *China Statistical Yearbook on Science and Technology* provides detailed data for R&D expenditures which are composed of compensation for laborers, raw material expenditure, expenditure on the purchase of fixed assets and other expenditure for R&D. Based on these data, we construct the R&D price index as the following:

R&D price index = (compensation for laborers/R&D expenditures)
× consumer price index
+ (raw material expenditure/R&D expenditures)
× raw material price index
+ (expenditure on the purchase of fixed assets
/R&D expenditures)
× fixed assets price index
+ (other expenditure for R&D/R&D expenditures)
× other expenditure price index.

The yearly price indices for consumer, raw material and fixed assets are from the *China Statistical Yearbook* (CSY), but the above price indices for each manufacturing are not available in the CSY. In addition, because the implication of other expenditure on R&D is not clear, we represent the price index of other expenditure by the arithmetical average of consumer price index, raw material price index and fixed assets price index. Using the constructed R&D price index to deflate the nominal R&D expenditures, we get the real R&D expenditures for 29 manufacturing industries during the years 1996–2006.

As for the initial R&D stock, with the assumption of pre-sample R&D expenditures growing at a rate of g, the R&D stock at the beginning of the year is defined by the following equation:

$$\begin{aligned} RS_{i1} &= R_{i1} + (1-\delta)R_{i0} + (1-\delta)^2 R_{i-1} + \cdots \\ &= R_{i1} + \frac{1-\delta}{1+g}R_{i1} + \left(\frac{1-\delta}{1+g}\right)^2 R_{i1} + \cdots \\ &= R_{i1}\sum_{S=0}^{\infty}\left(\frac{1-\delta}{1+g}\right)^S = R_{i1}\frac{1+g}{\delta+g} \end{aligned} \tag{10.7}$$

Assuming that a depreciation rate of 15 percent of R&D stock which has been most frequently used previously in this type of estimation and a pre-sample growth rate of 5 percent in real R&D expenditures,[4] the initial R&D stock is 5.25 times the R&D expenditures in 1996 ($(1+0.05)/(0.15+0.05) = 5.25$). On the basis of the initial R&D stock and Equation (10.6), we can compute the R&D stocks of the 29 manufacturing industries during 1996–2006.

Similarly, the stocks of foreign and domestic technology transfer can be computed by the same method as the measurement of the R&D stock. The difference is that the expenditures on the two technology transfers are deflated by the fixed assets price index because there is no detailed data on the compositions of technology transfers in the statistical yearbook. Besides this, with the assumption of the depreciation rate of 15 percent and the pre-sample growth rate of 5 percent in expenditures on technology transfers, the perpetual inventory method (Equation (10.6)) can be used in the same way to compute the stocks of the two technology transfers.

Output, labor and capital

The output at constant price is constructed by deflating the sales revenue of each manufacturing industry during 1996–2006 by ex-factory price index of industrial products. Although measuring value added instead of sales revenue is more appropriate, the required data are not available in our database. As Mairesse and Hall (1996) find, however, the elasticity of R&D is not seriously biased when sales revenue is used instead of value added. Another area of potential distortion is the immeasurable improvements of output, i.e. better quality, increased product variety, etc. Since the price indices of the Chinese statistical agencies fail to fully account for these intangible improvements, our output record may be underestimated and the R&D elasticity downward biased. Labor is measured simply by the total number of employees because there is no available information on the labor working hours of industry.

Our measure of physical capital (C) is the original value of equipment instead of fixed assets which are not available in our database, so the physical capital is underestimated and accordingly its elasticity may be downward biased. Growth theory suggests that capital input must be a measure of "productive stock," implying that its efficiency declines as it get old. The usual approach of measuring physical capital stock is the perpetual inventory method, which has already been used in the computation of knowledge stock, i.e. $C_{it} = I_{it} + (1 - \sigma)C_{i,t-1}$ and $C_{i1} = I_{i1}[(1 + d)/(\sigma + d)]$, where C is physical capital stock, I is the expenditure on physical capital, σ is the depreciation rate, and d is the pre-sample growth rate of physical capital. The key parameters of computing the equipment stock in this study are set in the following: the value of equipment is deflated by fixed assets price index, the depreciation rate of equipment is assumed as 15 percent which is computed by Zhang *et al.* (2008), and the pre-sample growth rate of equipment is set to 5 percent (i.e., the initial stock of equipment is 5.25 times the expenditure on equipment). Then equipment stock can be computed by using the perpetual inventory method described above.

Another noteworthy issue in exploring the contribution of R&D to productivity is the so-called "double counting" problem, which originated with Schankerman (1981) and echoed by Cuneo and Mairesse (1984) and Griliches and Mairesse (1984). Given that a proportion of capital and labor belongs to the R&D department, we should subtract R&D machinery and R&D employees from the ordinary capital and labor. Nevertheless, the data are not always detailed enough to allow such corrections. In our database, we have the data on R&D employees but no data on R&D machinery, so the data is corrected by subtracting the employees devoted to the R&D department from the total numbers of employees. After correcting double counting for R&D employees, it is usually believed that the estimation results are more credible than those of ignoring double counting of R&D, therefore we mainly report the results of data corrected in the following text.

Descriptive statistics

When calculating the average ratios of the expenditures on R&D, foreign and domestic technology transfer to sales revenue across 29 two-digit manufacturing industries during 1996–2006, as listed in Table 10.1, we find several patterns. As a whole, most manufacturing industries, other than the tobacco processing industry and the printing and record medium reproduction industry, invest far more in R&D than in technology transfer, which shows that R&D is the main foundation of innovation in Chinese industry. From the R&D intensity in Table 10.1, we also find huge differences of innovation capacity among manufacturing industries: R&D tends to be relatively more intensive in technologically advanced industries, such as machinery, electric equipment, medical and pharmaceutical products, electronic and telecommunications equipment, etc., in which the R&D intensities are more than 2 percent. Nevertheless, the R&D intensities in traditional industries, i.e. leather, food processing and tobacco, are less than 0.5 percent. We also find that foreign technical providers play a large role in shaping industry's innovation capacity; however, in sharp contrast to their foreign counterparts, domestic suppliers seem to be an insignificant source of technology transfer.

Table 10.1 also summarizes the results of the estimation of the three technology stocks per firm in 2006. The absolute size of R&D stock per firm is large in ferrous metals, transport equipment and tobacco processing industries, whereas it is very small in the furniture, leather and garments industries, which reflects the great differences in R&D investments of different industries. In addition, the stock of domestic technology transfer per firm is much less than that of foreign technology transfer per firm which in turn is less than R&D stock per firm for most industries.

Table 10.2 presents the time mode of three knowledge variables for the period of 1996–2006. R&D intensity in the Chinese manufacturing industry has a continually rising trend during 1996–2001, but decreases during 2001–2003, and then tends to increase after 2003. The intensity of direct foreign technology transfer tends to decline; meanwhile, the intensity of domestic technology transfer only has a little change during the period of 1996–2006. The time pattern of the three knowledge stocks per firm is basically the same as that of the three technical intensities. These changes reflect that in recent years the indigenous innovation capacity has increased gradually and dependence on foreign technologies tended to reduce.

Empirical results

This section analyzes the impacts of R&D and technology transfer on productivity growth. We first estimate the output elasticities of the three knowledge stocks using Equation (10.4), and then compute their rates of return using Equation (10.5).

Table 10.1 Technology intensity and technology stocks in manufacturing sectors

	Average 1996–2006 (%)			*2006 (million Yuan)*		
	R/Y	*F/Y*	*D/Y*	*RS/N*	*FS/N*	*DS/N*
Food processing	0.44	0.14	0.02	746.56	154.86	31.97
Food production	0.89	0.26	0.03	985.95	175.47	39.33
Beverage production	1.23	0.78	0.04	2,565.52	930.49	56.47
Tobacco processing	0.46	0.73	0.08	6,093.65	6,270.32	1,051.89
Textile industry	0.94	0.52	0.05	852.67	352.69	46.42
Garments and other fiber products	0.66	0.38	0.01	427.87	125.92	9.87
Leather, furs, down and related products	0.43	0.30	0.01	301.63	104.58	6.99
Timber, bamboo, cane, palm fiber and straw products	0.98	0.19	0.02	726.55	105.24	14.61
Furniture manufacturing	0.62	0.20	0.02	242.64	19.80	18.82
Papermaking and paper products	1.35	0.84	0.07	1,702.49	638.91	60.67
Printing and record medium reproduction	1.02	1.10	0.05	655.52	392.86	38.38
Culture, educational and sports goods	0.97	0.08	0.02	438.74	24.50	4.61
Petroleum processing and coking products	0.45	0.30	0.04	3,345.11	1,310.39	282.32
Raw chemical materials and chemical products	1.79	0.52	0.09	3,691.17	717.97	151.24
Medical and pharmaceutical products	2.36	0.27	0.22	3,337.44	286.01	254.68
Chemical fiber	1.70	1.09	0.13	5,627.13	2,327.93	298.19
Rubber products	1.57	0.36	0.04	2,512.10	374.82	53.23
Plastic products	1.57	0.62	0.04	962.57	256.32	15.80
Nonmetal mineral products	1.44	0.39	0.08	989.99	172.65	46.05
Smelting and pressing of ferrous metals	1.53	0.80	0.07	9,116.09	2,663.93	604.34
Smelting and pressing of nonferrous metals	1.30	0.46	0.08	3,764.41	862.96	174.15
Metal products	1.29	0.39	0.03	1,021.81	171.09	17.73
Ordinary machinery	2.74	0.57	0.06	2,689.55	397.83	55.01
Equipment for special purposes	2.68	0.31	0.07	3,178.25	279.27	104.54

Table 10.1 Continued

	Average 1996–2006 (%)			*2006 (million Yuan)*		
	R/Y	*F/Y*	*D/Y*	*RS/N*	*FS/N*	*DS/N*
Transport equipment	2.30	0.53	0.05	6,316.75	1,138.75	161.99
Electric equipment and machinery	2.70	0.72	0.11	3,692.59	534.36	99.05
Electronic and telecommunications equipment	2.22	0.66	0.02	5,935.06	1,334.83	39.25
Instruments, meters, cultural and office machinery	2.19	0.42	0.03	2,075.84	314.19	28.23
Other manufacturing	1.08	0.22	0.04	678.33	53.50	23.04

Notes: The intensities of the three technical inputs are calculated by current prices. The three technical capital stocks are constructed by perpetual inventory method with a depreciation rate of 15 percent and a pre-sample growth rate of 5 percent in technical expenditures. *N* denotes the number of firms in an industry.

Table 10.2 Time series of technology intensity and technology stocks (1996–2006)

	R/Y (%)	*F/Y (%)*	*D/Y (%)*	*RS/N (million Yuan)*	*FS/N (million Yuan)*	*DS/N (million Yuan)*
1996	1.17	1.00	0.08	954.87	1,206.62	66.54
1997	1.22	0.76	0.04	1,007.26	1,207.45	63.60
1998	1.31	0.60	0.05	1,069.26	1,182.55	66.46
1999	1.37	0.46	0.04	1,223.05	1,181.07	66.36
2000	1.53	0.51	0.06	1,452.89	1,146.30	70.24
2001	1.57	0.52	0.06	1,586.54	1,095.42	76.49
2002	1.56	0.59	0.06	1,826.51	1,141.11	88.59
2003	1.36	0.43	0.06	1,966.41	1,043.91	100.63
2004	1.43	0.24	0.06	1,929.52	880.51	108.42
2005	1.50	0.15	0.05	2,357.38	855.73	125.30
2006	1.49	0.12	0.04	2,574.97	775.60	130.65

Notes: The intensities of the three technical inputs are calculated by current prices. The three technical capital stocks are constructed by perpetual inventory method with a depreciation rate of 15 percent and a pre-sample growth rate of 5 percent in technical expenditures. *N* denotes the number of firms in an industry.

Elasticity estimates

Table 10.3 shows the results obtained for the production function estimates when constant returns to scale is not imposed by using different estimation techniques. In order to check the estimates' robustness, column (10.1), (10.2) and (10.3) of Table 10.3 report the regression estimates of R&D, foreign and domestic

Table 10.3 Estimates of the output elasticities (constant returns to scale not imposed)

	Stocks					*Expenditures*
	Correction				*No correction*	*Correction*
	(1)	*(2)*	*(3)*	*(4)*	*(5)*	*(6)*
Constant	0.0992	0.1154	0.1127	0.1016	0.1006	0.1067
	(6.72)***	(8.60)***	(8.41)***	(6.81)***	(6.75)***	(7.87)***
$\Delta \text{Ln}(C/L)$	0.4237	0.4764	0.5024	0.3983	0.4053	0.4463
	(2.87)***	(3.28)***	(3.49)***	(2.67)***	(2.72)***	(3.10)***
$\Delta \text{Ln}(L)$	0.0111	0.0872	0.1127	−0.0144	0.0035	0.0420
	(0.08)	(0.65)	(0.84)	(−0.10)	(0.02)	(0.31)
$\Delta \text{Ln}(RS)$	0.1503			0.1448	0.1391	0.0655
	(2.15)**			(2.02)**	(1.94)*	(2.91)***
$\Delta \text{Ln}(FS)$		0.0601		0.0542	0.0566	0.0044
		(1.31)		(1.18)	(1.23)	(0.67)
$\Delta \text{Ln}(DS)$			0.0109	0.0005	0.0004	−0.0016
			(0.55)	(0.02)	(0.02)	(−0.34)
Adj. R^2	0.2809	0.2736	0.2700	0.2794	0.2609	0.2869
F-value	38.6259	37.2865	36.6320	23.4091	21.4032	24.2597

Notes: The three technical capital stocks are constructed with a 15 percent depreciation rate. Numbers in brackets are t-statistics of the estimated parameters. ***indicates that the estimated parameter is significantly different from zero at the 1 percent level of significance, **at the 5 percent level, and *at the 10 percent level.

technology transfer respectively, and column (10.4) of Table 10.3 reports the estimates with the three knowledge stocks included in a regression. To avoid double counting of R&D employees we distinguish between the employees working with R&D production and other workers as two separate labor inputs. The R&D personnel have been subtracted from the total labor because the latter includes both R&D- and non-R&D personnel. Column (10.5) of Table 10.3 also gives the estimates with the measure of labor, which has not been corrected for double counting of R&D employees. In addition, to compare the effects of the stocks and expenditures of the knowledge variables on productivity growth, column (10.6) of Table 10.3 presents the estimates with the technical expenditures used as the independent variables. Table 10.4 shows the same estimates in format when constant returns to scale imposed. The key results reported in Tables 10.3 and 10.4 are summarized below.

The results for the capital to labor ratio for all estimation regressions are similar. The coefficient on the labor variable is not significantly different from zero for all the regressions in Table 10.3, which shows that the hypothesis of constant returns to scale is accepted for the first-differenced estimates. The corrections for double-counting of R&D employees tend to increase the R&D capital coefficients across the columns of Tables 10.3 and 10.4, which are consistent with the studies of Schankerman (1981), and Cuneo and Mairesse (1984) who find that the

Table 10.4 Estimates of the output elasticites (constant returns to scale imposed)

	Stocks					*Expenditures*
	Correction				*No correction*	*Correction*
	(1)	*(2)*	*(3)*	*(4)*	*(5)*	*(6)*
Constant	0.0999 (8.35)***	0.1231 (19.83)***	0.1225 (18.66)***	0.1007 (8.39)***	0.1009 (8.40)***	0.1102 (14.38)***
$\Delta\text{Ln}(C/L)$	0.4125 (10.71)***	0.3859 (10.53)***	0.3853 (10.45)***	0.4128 (10.71)***	0.4018 (10.23)***	0.4030 (10.88)***
$\Delta\text{Ln}(RS)$	0.1522 (2.34)**			0.1424 (2.11)**	0.1397 (2.07)**	0.0666 (3.01)***
$\Delta\text{Ln}(FS)$		0.0655 (1.45)		0.0535 (1.18)	0.0567 (1.25)	0.0045 (0.69)
$\Delta\text{Ln}(DS)$			0.0124 (0.63)	0.0005 (0.02)	0.0004 (0.02)	−0.0015 (−0.32)
Adj. R^2	0.2834	0.2751	0.2707	0.2819	0.2635	0.2892
F-value	58.1372	55.8353	54.6481	29.3608	26.8480	30.3968

Notes: The three technical capital stocks are constructed with a 15 percent depreciation rate. Numbers in brackets are t-statistics of the estimated parameters. ***indicates that the estimated parameter is significantly different from zero at the 1 percent level of significance, **at the 5 percent level, and *at the 10 percent level.

"double counting" corrections increase the R&D elasticity. We also find that the coefficients with the measured stocks used as dependent variables are obviously larger than those with the expenditures used as dependent variables. The most important finding from Tables 10.3 and 10.4, in any case, is that the R&D capital coefficients remain fairly high and statistically significant and the coefficients on foreign and domestic technology transfer are quite small and insignificant whether the constant returns to scale are imposed or not.

A common result across the regressions, i.e., column (10.1) and (10.4) of Table 10.3, is that the estimates on R&D are positive and quite significant, with the results indicating that R&D has a significant impact on productivity growth. Specifically, the estimate of R&D elasticity is about 0.15 when the R&D stock is separately included in the regression (column 1 of Table 10.3), while it decreases to 0.14 when the three knowledge variables are all included in the regression (column 4 of Table 10.3). The R&D coefficients have almost similar changes when constant returns to scale are imposed (Table 10.4). As a whole, the coefficients of R&D remain stable in magnitude. The findings are consistent with similar studies carried out in other countries confirming the positive and statistically significant correlation between R&D and output. Our findings are also consistent with the studies using Chinese firm data, which affirm the significant role of R&D for productivity (Hu 2001; Hu and Jefferson 2004; Hu *et al.* 2005; Jefferson *et al.* 2006). Although the estimates of the R&D elasticity from these studies vary according to the sample, the central tendency, which is cited frequently, ranges from about 0.10 to about 0.20 (Griliches 1988; Mairesse and Sassenou 1991). Our estimate of the R&D elasticity of around 0.15 lies in the range of central tendency. The organizational culture of R&D-intensive firms expedites the discovery of new knowledge, practices and innovations that favor productivity performance. As a result, productivity growth should be amplified when R&D expenditures are raised. At the same time, we should highlight once again a fact which has already been pointed out by other previous studies (Mairesse and Sassenou 1991): the estimates in the first-differenced, which control for permanent differences across industries, usually have an R&D output elasticity which is much smaller than that in the cross-section estimates. Because the cross-section estimates neglect the differences across industries that are correlated with the presence of R&D capital, we regard the first-differenced estimates as more reliable parameters.

Although the estimates on R&D are statistically significant, those on foreign technology transfer are statistically insignificant. From column (10.2) and (10.4) of Tables 10.3 and 10.4, we can see that the coefficients of the foreign technology transfer are positive but not significant, showing that the market-mediated technology imports have no significant impact on productivity growth. At first sight the insignificant contribution of foreign technology transfer to productivity may be surprising, because along with China's institutional reform and economic opening, many technologically lagging firms learn to innovate by first imitating technologies created in developed countries. For China, where few firms have well-established R&D operations, utilizing the advanced technologies of developed countries would seem to be a natural way of shortening the technology gap. However, technological market failures that compromise the ability to appropriate returns to technology transfer reduce the volume and sophistication of technologies that can be transferred through markets (Caves 1996). More importantly, Chinese firms usually pay much attention to hardware imports that do not match the skill level of this country and neglect software introduction. In the meantime the absorptive capacity of technology has been ignored by Chinese firms in the process of purchasing foreign technologies. For example, according to Gilboy (2004), Chinese firms tend to import technology by purchasing foreign manufacturing equipment, often in complete sets such as assembly lines. Throughout the 1980s and 1990s, such hardware accounted for more than 80 percent of China's technology imports, whereas licensing accounted for only 9 percent, "know-how" services 5 percent and consulting 3 percent. Over the last decade, large- and medium-sized Chinese industrial firms have spent less than 10 percent of the total cost of imported equipment on indigenizing technology, which is much lower than the average for industrial firms in Organization for Economic Co-operation and Development (OECD) countries (about 33 percent). The unreasonable structure of technology imports and absence of absorptive capacity in Chinese industrial firms substantially limit the contribution of foreign technology imports to productivity growth.

The estimated coefficients of domestic technology transfer are also statistically insignificant, whether we impose constant returns to scale in the production function and whether we correct the double counting of R&D employees in the labor input. This phenomenon can be explained as follows. Compared with the technologies in developed countries, the technological level in China, as a whole, is backward. The technologies are characterized by competition and exclusiveness among domestic industrial enterprises, which cause enterprises to take effective measures to protect their own core technologies. Due to the need for technological confidentiality, enterprises are unwilling to sell their technologies to other domestic enterprises. In addition, the immature and imperfect technology market in China also limits technology transfer among domestic enterprises. The above interpretations can be verified by the data reported in Tables 10.1 and 10.2 which show that the intensity of domestic technology transfer is much smaller than that of R&D and foreign technology transfer. In a word, both the technology competitiveness among domestic enterprises and the imperfect technology markets in China baffle the domestic technology exchanges, which results in an insignificant contribution of domestic technology transfer to productivity growth.

Rate of return estimates

Because of the difficulty of measuring knowledge stocks, an alternative approach to evaluating the productivity of technology, i.e. the rate of return method, is often used. The rate of return method actually estimates the correlation between the growth rate of labor productivity and the technical intensities (which are denoted as the ratio of contemporaneous knowledge variables to sales revenue). The results of the estimating Equation (10.5) are shown in Table 10.5 with constant returns to scale not imposed. Similar estimates in format are reported in Table 10.6 with constant returns to scale imposed.

As we can observe in the first column of Table 10.5, with constant returns to scale not imposed, the coefficient of the intensity of R&D expenditure is about 1.87 which is statistically significant at the 5 percent level of significance and it decreases to about 1.86 in column (10.4) where the intensities of technology transfer are included in the regression. When constant returns to scale are imposed in the production function (Table 10.6), the coefficient of the R&D intensity is around 1.78 whether other knowledge variables are included in the regression or not. Obviously, the estimated rate of return to R&D with CRS not imposed is higher than that with CRS imposed. Another finding, as can be observed in column (10.4) and (10.5) of both Tables 10.5 and 10.6, is that the magnitude of the rate of return to R&D is almost unchanged when the labor used to produce R&D is removed from the labor inputs in the production function.

Tables 10.5 and 10.6 also reveal that while the intensity of R&D is a significant determinant of productivity growth, the intensities of foreign and domestic technology transfer are not: the coefficients of those variables are insignificantly different from zero across the columns of Tables 10.5 and 10.6, which are consistent with the findings of the insignificant impacts of technology transfer stock on productivity growth contained in the aforementioned results. In a word, we do not find a significantly positive relationship between the productivity growth and technology transfers whether we use either the output elasticity or the rate of return method.

Table 10.5 Estimates of the rate of return (constant return to scale not imposed)

	Correction				*No correction*
	(1)	*(2)*	*(3)*	*(4)*	*(5)*
Constant	0.0844 (4.80)***	0.1129 (7.82)***	0.1086 (7.68)***	0.0856 (4.76)***	0.0842 (4.68)***
$\Delta\text{Ln}(C/L)$	0.5274 (3.71)***	0.5072 (3.53)***	0.5088 (3.55)***	0.5302 (3.71)***	0.5353 (3.75)***
$\Delta\text{Ln}(L)$	0.1506 (1.14)	0.1197 (0.90)	0.1256 (0.94)	0.1507 (1.13)	0.1663 (1.25)
R/Y	1.8662 (2.48)**			1.8570 (2.30)**	1.8571 (2.30)**
F/Y		0.0868 (0.07)		−0.5118 (−0.38)	−0.5239 (−0.39)
D/Y			8.3853 (0.98)	1.9278 (0.21)	1.6479 (0.18)
Adj. R^2	0.2847	0.2693	0.2717	0.2800	0.2620
F-value	39.3344	36.4962	36.9330	23.4823	21.5162

Notes: Numbers in brackets are t-statistics of the estimated parameters. ***indicates that the estimated parameter is significantly different from zero at the 1 percent level of significance, **at the 5 percent level, and *at the 10 percent level.

Table 10.6 Estimates of the rate of return (constant returns to scale imposed)

	Correction				*No correction*
	(1)	*(2)*	*(3)*	*(4)*	*(5)*
Constant	0.0989 (8.16)***	0.1236 (15.26)***	0.1200 (16.07)***	0.1002 (7.92)***	0.1002 (7.92)***
$\Delta\text{Ln}(C/L)$	0.3712 (10.10)***	0.3828 (10.04)***	0.3784 (10.20)***	0.3741 (9.82)***	0.3633 (9.37)***
R/Y	1.7853 (2.38)**			1.7813 (2.22)**	1.7729 (2.20)**
F/Y		0.0597 (0.05)		−0.5188 (−0.38)	−0.5346 (−0.40)
D/Y			8.0074 (0.93)	1.7801 (0.19)	1.4774 (0.16)
Adj. R^2	0.2839	0.2698	0.2720	0.2793	0.2605
F-value	58.2959	54.3779	54.9765	29.0027	26.4505

Notes: Numbers in brackets are t-statistics of the estimated parameters. ***indicates that the estimated parameter is significantly different from zero at the 1 percent level of significance, **at the 5 percent level, and *at the 10 percent level.

It is especially noticeable that the estimate of the rate of return of 1.78–1.87 to R&D expenditures is strikingly high. The range of the estimated rate of return to R&D in the previous literature runs from zero to nearly 0.60, with a central tendency between 0.20 and 0.30 (Griliches 1988; Mairesse and Sassenou 1991). Our estimate of the rate of return to R&D is much higher than that of the previous studies using the database in developed countries, but similar to Hu and Jefferson's (2004) estimates of 1.64 for the Chinese machinery industry and lower than 1.95 for the Chinese chemical industry. They are also similar to Mansfield's (1980) estimate of 1.78, but substantially lower than Link's (1981) estimate of 2.31 for the rate of return to basic research in the US manufacturing sector.

Why is the estimated rate of return to R&D in Chinese industry so high? We can provide some preliminary arguments responses to the possible econometric problems in the equation. First, we note that R&D intensity can be defined either as R&D over sales revenue or as R&D over value added. Since sales revenue is much higher than value added, the first ratio is considerably smaller than the latter which amplifies the estimated rate of return to R&D. Using value added, which is unfortunately unavailable to us, instead of sales revenue, may attenuate the rate of return to R&D. Second, there may be a problem of endogeneity of R&D intensity in Equation (10.5). In principle, we should use all of the predetermined variables in the estimation regression; however, few variables are likely to be truly exogenous given the available data to us. Failing to resolve the possible endogeneity issue may result in the upward bias of the estimates of R&D returns.

Another convictive explanation for the strikingly high estimates of R&D returns is that our estimates, by using the industry-level data, capture the social return to R&D which is defined as including both the return earned by the original innovator and any gains that spill over to other firms not involved in the R&D effort. Scherer (1982, 1984) believes that it is important to follow R&D from industry of origin to industry of use, as many firms "purchase" R&D from other firms implicitly when buying certain products and services. For each industry, R&D inputs from other industries are inputed through the use of a technology flow matrix based on information on industries of origin and use of inventions culled from patent data or input-output flows between industries. If spillovers to R&D exist within an industry, the estimated return to R&D may be higher when computed using industry-level rather than firm-level data. According to this view, our estimated return to R&D using industry-level data includes not only the impact of R&D from one's own industry on productivity growth but also the impact of "inter-industry technology flows" on productivity growth. Given that the estimates of the social return to R&D average more than 100 percent in the previous productivity literature, our estimates of return to R&D seem to be not too surprising.

Robust check

We can investigate the robustness of the above estimates by experimenting with various ways of measuring the knowledge stocks and physical capital stock. To test the sensitivity of the estimates of R&D and technology transfer to the different parameters assumption, we recalculate the regression using both the output elasticity and the rate of return method. To save space we only report the estimates with constant returns to scale imposed and the double counting of R&D employees corrected. The estimates for output elasticity and the rate of return are reported in Tables 10.7 and 10.8 respectively.

When the depreciation rate of R&D is set to 25 percent, which is the high end of the orders of magnitude obtained by Pakes and Schankerman (1984) using patent renewal data and applied by Hall and Mairesse (1995) in their empirical study, the output elasticity of R&D is about 0.14 (column 1 of Table 10.7). When the pre-sample growth rate in R&D expenditures is set to 15 percent, the elasticity of R&D is around 0.13 (column 2 of Table 10.7). While the depreciation rate and the pre-sample growth rate of expenditures are set to 25 percent and 15 percent respectively, the elasticity of R&D is slightly decreased to 0.12 (column 3 of Table 10.7). Although one may expect that the choice of the R&D depreciation rate would significantly affect the R&D elasticity, it does not. Many researchers, such as Griliches (1980) and Harhoff (1998), have tried different depreciation rates (10, 15, 20 and 30 percent) and find that R&D elasticity remains stable. In this study, using a higher depreciation rate when constructing R&D capital stocks makes little difference to the estimates. In the same way, the different choice of the pre-sample growth rate of R&D expenditures also does not affect the estimates significantly. In Table 10.7 we also find that with the assumption of the different parameters, the coefficients of technology transfer, whether purchased from foreign or domestic, are still statistically insignificant, showing the stability of our estimates.

Other parameters that may affect the results are the misspecification of the equipment stock variable. With the assumption of the 15 percent of depreciation rate of equipment, using a 15 percent of pre-sample growth rate for equipment instead of 5 percent, we recalculate the regression and find that the elasticity of R&D increases to 0.17 (column 4 of Table 10.7), which is higher than the above estimates but the difference is not large. In the assumption of 15 percent of pre-sample growth rate for equipment we also estimate the rates of return to R&D and technology transfer (Table 10.8). The estimated marginal product of R&D is 1.96, which is higher than the aforementioned estimate of 1.78 when constant returns to scale imposed. We also find that the estimated rates of return to technology transfer, whether foreign or domestic, are still insignificant.

As a matter of fact, using all the possible parameters, we have tried a number different ways of measuring these variables but to little effect. The various measures we tried turn out to be very good substitutes for each other and the choice between them has little practical import. The resulting differences in our estimates, even when they are statistically significant, are nonetheless quite small and not very meaningful. In particular, they do not substantially alter the order of magnitude and the significance of the coefficients of our interest, γ and ρ.

Table 10.7 The effects of different parameters on elasticity estimates

	$\sigma=0.15, d=0.05$			$\sigma=0.15, d=0.15$
	$\delta=0.25$ $g=0.05$	$\delta=0.15$ $g=0.15$	$\delta=0.25$ $g=0.15$	$\delta=0.15$ $g=0.05$
	(1)	*(2)*	*(3)*	*(4)*
Constant	0.1004 (9.01)***	0.0986 (7.19)***	0.0999 (8.30)***	0.0862 (6.72)***
$\Delta\text{Ln}(C/L)$	0.4147 (10.92)***	0.4018 (10.65)***	0.4050 (10.79)***	0.3886 (10.41)***
$\Delta\text{Ln}(RS)$	0.1360 (2.50)**	0.1282 (1.89)*	0.1223 (2.22)**	0.1726 (2.50)**
$\Delta\text{Ln}(FS)$	0.0483 (1.48)	0.0404 (0.99)	0.0412 (1.32)	0.0476 (1.04)
$\Delta\text{Ln}(DS)$	−0.0013 (−0.08)	0.0011 (0.06)	−0.0004 (−0.03)	0.0026 (0.13)
Adj. R^2	0.2890	0.2779	0.2839	0.2701
F-value	30.3743	28.8118	29.6416	27.7356

Notes: Numbers in brackets are t-statistics of the estimated parameters. ***indicates that the estimated parameter is significantly different from zero at the 1 percent level of significance, **at the 5 percent level, and *at the 10 percent level.

Table 10.8 The effects of different parameters on rate of return estimates

	$\sigma=0.15, d=0.15$
Constant	0.0900 (7.05)***
$\Delta\text{Ln}(C/L)$	0.3459 (9.48)***
R/Y	1.9630 (2.42)**
F/Y	−0.9145 (−0.67)
D/Y	3.1931 (0.34)
Adj. R^2	0.2668
F-value	27.2952

Notes: Numbers in brackets are t-statistics of the estimated parameters. ***indicates that the estimated parameter is significantly different from zero at the 1 percent level of significance, **at the 5 percent level, and *at the 10 percent level.

Estimating the effects of R&D and technology transfers on productivity decompositions

We have thus far examined the effects of R&D and technology transfer on the productivity growth of manufacturing industries using Cobb-Douglas production function estimation. Now we use DEA to decompose total factor productivity into technical efficiency change and technological progress, and then run regressions to examine the contributions of R&D and technology transfer to the Malmquist productivity index and its components.

The output-based Malmquist productivity change index is commonly expressed in the following form:

$$M_o^{t+1}(x^{t+1}, y^{t+1}, x^t, y^t) = \frac{D_o^{t+1}(x^{t+1}, y^{t+1})}{D_o^t(x^t, y^t)} \left[\frac{D_o^t(x^{t+1}, y^{t+1})}{D_o^{t+1}(x^{t+1}, y^{t+1})} \frac{D_o^t(x^t, y^t)}{D_o^{t+1}(x^t, y^t)} \right]^{\frac{1}{2}} \tag{10.8}$$

where y is the output and x is the input vector of the manufacturing being evaluated. D_o is an output distance function. The distance function is the inverse of the out-oriented efficiency score, which can be calculated by solving different linear programming problems (Fare *et al.* 1994). The superscripts on D_o indicate the time period within which the efficiency scores are calculated. The superscripts on x and y indicate the time period of the data used in the calculation of the efficiency scores. The ratio outside the brackets on the right-hand side of Equation (10.8) represents the change in technical efficiency from period t to $t + 1$, and the bracketed term in (10.8) captures the geometric mean of the shift in production frontier. As a result, the Malmquist index is decomposed into the technical efficiency change and the technological change of the industry. A Malmquist index of more than one signifies an improvement in productivity from t to $t + 1$.

To examine the effects of R&D and technology transfer on the Malmquist productivity index, we run the regression:

$$M_{it} = \lambda + \varphi_R \Delta rs_{it} + \varphi_F \Delta fs_{it} + \varphi_D \Delta ds_{it} + \Delta\omega_{it} \tag{10.9}$$

where M represents the Malmquist productivity index, and φ represents the coefficient estimates. Since the Malmquist index indicates the annual change of productivity growth, we transform the explanatory variables, i.e. R&D, foreign and domestic technology transfer, into first differences.

The regression results are reported in the first column of Table 10.9. It can be seen that R&D is the most statistically significant factor affecting the Malmquist productivity index, and that technology transfers (foreign and domestic) are not associated with productivity growth in a statistically significant manner, which are consistent with the estimation results obtained by using both the output elasticity and the rate of return methods described above.

Table 10.9 The effects of the knowledge variables on the Malmquist index and its components

	(1)	*(2)*	*(3)*
	Productivity growth	*Technical efficiency change*	*Technological progress*
Constant	0.0476	−0.0689	0.1242
	(2.57)***	(−4.95)***	(9.55)***
$\Delta \text{Ln}(RS)$	0.4749	0.5248	−0.0732
	(4.32)***	(6.36)***	(−0.95)
$\Delta \text{Ln}(FS)$	0.0913	−0.0323	0.1143
	(1.18)	(−0.55)	(2.10)**
$\Delta \text{Ln}(DS)$	0.0073	0.0305	−0.0279
	(0.21)	(1.17)	(−1.14)
Adj. R^2	0.0663	0.1352	0.0118
F-value	7.8420	16.0574	2.1501

Notes: Numbers in brackets are t-statistics of the estimated parameters. ***indicates that the estimated parameter is significantly different from zero at the 1 percent level of significance, **at the 5 percent level, and *at the 10 percent level.

The decomposition of the Malmquist index provides a way of measuring the channels of R&D and technology transfer affecting productivity growth. In column (10.2) and (10.3) of Table 10.9, we report the results of regressions on technical efficiency change and technological progress. It can be seen that R&D is highly statistically significant for technical efficiency change but not for technological progress. In contrast, foreign technology transfer has a statistically significant positive effect on technological progress but not on technical efficiency change. The estimate on domestic technology transfer is still not statistically significant in any of the regressions in Table 10.9.

From the above observation, we know that the significant role of R&D in improving productivity growth is mainly attributable to the contributions of R&D to technical efficiency. Given the relatively backward technology level in Chinese manufacturing, indigenous R&D can greatly improve the technical efficiency of each manufacturing industry; however, it cannot markedly shift the production frontier of the manufacturing sector upward. In addition, basic research in the Chinese manufacturing sector is relatively weak and as a result it cannot substantially support the development of applied research, which further hinders the shift of the production frontier of the manufacturing sector. The unreasonable structure of R&D investments in the manufacturing sector may be another complementary interpretation. As a whole, R&D still greatly facilitates the productivity growth of the manufacturing sector, which is consistent with the estimates obtained by using either the output elasticity or the rate of return method.

Although foreign technology transfer does not guarantee a higher rate of productivity growth and technical efficiency change, it significantly affects technological progress. Chinese manufacturing enterprises usually focus on large-scale introduction of foreign equipment and production lines, which may result in the upward shift of the production frontier. However, because of the lack of software support and technical absorptive capacity, the technical efficiency does not improve correspondingly. To integrate the two effects, we can find from column (10.1) of Table 10.9 that foreign technology transfer has no statistically significant impact on the Malmquist productivity index.

Conclusions

Using an industry-level data set of Chinese large- and medium-size manufacturing enterprises over the period of 1996–2006, we investigate the impacts of three technology acquisition channels (i.e. in-house R&D, direct foreign technology transfer, and domestic technology transfer) on the industry's productivity growth using both the output elasticity and the rate of return method. With the different assumptions (such as constant returns to scale in the production function, different depreciation rates for technical capital stock, and the choice of whether to include an adjustment for double counting of R&D employees in the labor inputs), we find that there is strong evidence for the significant contribution of R&D to productivity growth in Chinese manufacturing industries, whereas technology transfer, whether foreign or domestic, has no significant impact on productivity growth. When the productivity growth is decomposed into technical efficiency change and technological progress, we find that the significantly positive impact of R&D on productivity growth seems to work mainly through technical efficiency improvement rather than through technological progress.

The contribution of R&D to productivity growth means that creating a favorable innovation environment is of great significance for China's sustainable economic growth. China should further take effective measures to reform the mechanisms of science and technology, strengthen intellectual property protection, and improve legal system and innovative environment, which will substantially stimulate Chinese enterprises to invest in R&D. After all, it seems to be impossible to introduce the advanced and core technologies from developed countries by means of direct technology transactions. International experiences have also showed that the fundamental driving force of innovation stems from national enterprises. Only through domestic innovation can China initiatively adjust its economic structure and transform its economic growth pattern.

At the same time, under the circumstance of economic globalization, developing countries should also pay much attention to exploit and absorb the advanced technical achievements in developed countries. Over the past two decades, the Chinese government has carried out preferential policy measures towards encouraging foreign direct investments and the introduction of foreign technologies from developed countries. However, due to the absence of absorption capacity to imported technologies and ignorance of software support, direct introduction of foreign technology does not make corresponding contributions to productivity growth in Chinese manufacturing industries. The introduction of foreign technologies in the next step should conform to the features of resource endowments and the principle of comparative advantages in China. It is only appropriate technology introduction that will ultimately enhance China's productivity and economic performance.

Notes

1 In our database, the correlations between the corresponding variables are as follows: cor(LnRS, LnFS) = 0.81, cor(LnRS, LnDS) = 0.85, cor(LnFS, LnDS) = 0.78; and cor(ΔLnRS, ΔLnFS) = 0.13, cor(ΔLnRS, ΔLnDS) = 0.25, cor(ΔLnFS, ΔLnDS) = 0.09.

2 According to the Perpetual Inventory Method (PIM), which is described in the third section of this chapter, $\Delta RS_{it} = RS_{it} - RS_{it-1} = R_{it} + (1-\delta)RS_{it-1} - RS_{it-1} = R_{it} - \delta RS_{it-1}$. When the depreciation rate δ equals to zero, then $\Delta RS_{it} = R_{it}$.

3 To define large and medium-sized enterprises, China's National Bureau of Statistics (NBS) uses either of two industry specific criteria: annual production capacity or original vale of the productive fixed assets. For further elaboration of the criteria used to classify firm size, see the web site of the China's NBS (http://www.stats.gov.cn/english/statisticalstandards/).

4 To verify the stability of estimation results, the depreciation rate and the pre-sample growth rate of expenditures are changed and the results of experimentation with the assumption of different parameters are reported in the fourth section of this chapter.

References

Caves, R. E. (1996) *Multinational Enterprises and Economic Analysis*, 2nd edition, Cambridge: Cambridge University Press.

Chinese National Bureau of Statistics (2008) *China Statistical Yearbook on Science and Technology*, Beijing: China Statistics Press.

Cuneo, P. and Mairesse, J. (1984) 'Productivity and R&D at the Firm Level in French Manufacturing', in Z. Griliches (ed.) *R&D, Patents and Productivity*, Chicago: University of Chicago Press, 375–92.

Fare, R., Grosskopf, S. and Lovell, C. A. K. (1994) *Production Frontiers*, Cambridge: Cambridge University Press.

Gilboy, G. J. (2004) 'The Myth behind China's Miracle', *Foreign Affairs* 83 (4): 33–48.

Griliches, Z. (1964) 'Research Expenditures, Education, and the Aggregate Production Function', *American Economic Review*, 54 (6): 961–74.

Griliches, Z. (1979) 'Issues in Assessing the Contribution of Research and Development to Productivity Growth', *Bell Journal of Economics*, 10: 92–116.

Griliches, Z. (1980) 'R&D and the Productivity Slowdown', *American Economic Review*, 70 (2): 343–8.

Griliches, Z. (1986) 'Productivity, R&D and Basic Research at the Firm Level in the 1970s', *American Economic Review*, 76 (6): 141–54.

Griliches, Z. (1988) 'Productivity Puzzles and R&D: Another Nonexplanation', *Journal of Economic Perspectives*, 2 (4): 9–21.

Griliches, Z. and Mairesse, J. (1984) 'Productivity and R&D at the Firm Level', in Z. Griliches (ed.) *R&D, Patents and Productivity*, Chicago: University of Chicago Press, 339–74.

Hall, B. H. and Mairesse, J. (1995) 'Exploring the Relationship between R&D and Productivity in French Manufacturing Firms', *Journal of Econometrics*, 65: 263–93.

Harhoff, D. (1998) 'R&D and Productivity in German Manufacturing Firms', *Economics of Innovation and New Technology*, 6: 28–49.

Hu, A. G. Z. (2001) 'Ownership, Government R&D, Private R&D, and Productivity in Chinese Industry', *Journal of Comparative Economics*, 29 (1): 136–57.

Hu, A. G. Z. and Jefferson, G. H. (2004) 'Returns to Research and Development in Chinese Industry: Evidence From State-owned Enterprises in Beijing', *China Economic Review*, 15: 86–107.

Hu, A. G. Z., Jefferson, G. H. and Qian, J. C. (2005) 'R&D and Technology Transfer: Firm-level Evidence from Chinese Industry', *Review of Economics and Statistics*, 87 (4): 780–6.

Jefferson, G. H., Bai, H., Guan, X. and Yu, X. (2006) 'R&D Performance in Chinese Industry', *Economics of Innovation and New Technology*, 15 (4/5): 345–66.

Link, A. N. (1981) 'Basic Research and Productivity Increase in Manufacturing: Additional Evidence', *American Economic Review*, 71: 1111–2.

Liu, Z. Q. (2002) 'Foreign Direct Investment and Technology Spillover: Evidence from China', *Journal of Comparative Economics*, 30: 579–602.

Mairesse, J. and Sassenou, M. (1991) 'R&D and Productivity: A Survey of Econometric Studies at the Firm Level', *Science Technology and Industry Review*, 8: 317–48.

Mairesse, J. and Hall, B. H. (1996) 'Estimating the Productivity of Research and Development: An Exploration of GMM Methods Using Data on French and United States Manufacturing Firms', NBER working paper, No. W5501.

Mansfield, E. (1965) 'Rates of Return from Industrial Research and Development', *American Economic Review*, 55: 110–22.

Mansfield, E. (1980) 'Basic Research and Productivity Increase in Manufacturing', *American Economic Review*, 70 (5): 863–73.

Mansfield, E. (1984) 'R&D and Innovation: Some Empirical Findings', in Z. Griliches (ed.) *R&D, Patents and Productivity*, Chicago: University of Chicago Press, 127–48.

Minasian, J. R. (1962) 'The Economics of Research and Development', in R. Nelson (ed.) *The Rate and Direction of Inventive Activity: Economics and Social Factors*, Princeton University Press, 93–142.

Minasian, J. R. (1969) 'Research and Development, Production Functions and Rates of Return', *American Economic Review*, 55: 80–5.

Pakes, A. and Schankerman, M. (1984) 'The Rate of Obsolescence of Patents, Research Gestation Lags, and the Private Rate of Return to Research Resources', in Z. Griliches (ed.) *R&D, Patents and Productivity*, Chicago: University of Chicago Press, 73–88.

Schankerman, M. (1981) 'The Effects of Double-counting and Expensing on the Measured Returns to R&D', *Review of Economics and Statistics*, 63 (3): 454–8.

Scherer, F. M. (1982) 'Inter-industry Technology Flows and Productivity Growth', *Review of Economics and Statistics*, 64 (4): 627–34.

Scherer, F. M. (1984) 'Using Linked Patent and R&D Data to Measure Inter-industry Technology Flows', in Z. Griliches (ed.) *R&D, Patents and Productivity*, Chicago: University of Chicago Press, 417–64.

Zhang, J. (2008) 'Estimation of China's Provincial Capital Stock (1952–2004) with Applications', *Journal of Chinese Economic and Business Studies*, 6 (2): 177–96.

11 The distribution of income and well-being in rural China

A survey of panel data sets, studies and new directions

Xi Chen

Introduction and overview

China has been experiencing unprecedented growth over the past 30 years, with a commensurate increase in average living standards. However, the strategy of "*Let some people get rich first*" has resulted in a huge income gap between urban and rural, east and west, coastal and inland China. There are mounting concerns that the growing inequality hinders sharing of the fruits of economic development. In addition, social unrest that accompanies worsening inequality may slow down economic transition and hinder future growth.

Most poor people still live in rural China. According to the China National Bureau of Statistics (NBS), in 2009 the rural population of China was 0.72 billion, taking up 54 percent of the total population. The official ratio of urban–rural per capita income amounts to 3.33:1. Recent household-level data show that within-village inequality has grown from 0.22 in 1978 to 0.44 in 2009 (or even above 0.50 in some studies). Inequality seriously questions whether the impressive achievements in poverty reduction can equally benefit the general public in rural China. With unequal access to education, healthcare, the rural financial system, and non-farm work opportunities in rural China, retaining our focus on rural inequality and farmers' well-being are crucial in maintaining economic growth and social stability in contemporary China.

Rural and urban household surveys for China are largely independent. In this chapter, inequality and income distribution in rural China will be addressed. Two other sources of rising inequality in China, namely inequality between urban and rural areas and inequality within urban areas are not touched upon in this review. Nevertheless, it is worth emphasizing the importance of rural inequality in influencing the other two sources of rising inequality in China. For instance, it is found that much of the increase in the rural–urban gap appears to be the result of a growing difference in incomes between rural households in the coastal and interior provinces. Meanwhile, in standard datasets such as the Urban Household Survey (UHS) sponsored by the NBS, faster growing suburban areas are getting reclassified as urban areas and included in the urban inequality index. Massive migration from rural to urban areas caused by rural inequality might also influence urban inequality and the rural–urban gap.

Studies on rural inequality were initiated in the early 1990s when distributional snapshots with cross-sectional data became available. Extensive literature has been accumulated on the evolution of inequality in rural China since the onset of reforms in the late 1970s. The primary attention has been given to estimating the level of inequality and its changes over time, identifying the underlying sources of the inequality and its changes, and exploring aggregate- (disaggregate-) level effects of inequality. Since the late 1990s and the early 2000s, a second wave of inequality studies has begun to dominate the discussion as more and more panel datasets in China have become available. To our knowledge, this chapter is the first comprehensive review of studies on income distribution and well-being that use available longitudinal datasets from rural China.

Given the early focus of inequality studies using aggregate data and the fact that later available household survey datasets are not of a census type, research has largely been silent in exploring the mechanisms of inequality and evaluating its real welfare impacts. However, people do not live on an isolated island. Though important in grasping an overall picture of the inequality situation in China, the urban–rural, east–west, and coastal–inland framework does not address the community-level interactions between the rich and the poor and the resulting feeling of inequality and deprivation. It is especially the case when a rural community populated with the absolute poor is severely closed, both geographically and culturally. The rise of within-area inequality might increase the absolute poor residents' level of anxiety and hatred, as their happiness is largely anchored in comparisons to other members of their community. In addition, it has been well documented that both the poor and the rich may have been underrepresented in the official surveys. Fortunately, a newly initiated census-type household survey project might enable us to fundamentally change this situation.

The chapter is organized as follows. In part two, we begin by summarizing available panel datasets for rural China that can help explore issues on inequality and income distribution. In part three, comparisons among panel datasets are conducted. Major data issues that might act as obstacles to research and policy enforcement are then analyzed. Part four reviews the trend and spatial decompositions of rural income inequality, its major determinants, and its relationship with household welfare. Dimensions other than income inequality, such as income mobility and income polarization, are categorized and reviewed respectively. A newly established branch of discussions on inequality and health is summarized, which sheds light on our proposal for datasets of special features. On the basis of the review, Part five proposes new research areas with previous panel datasets and a new area with a new panel dataset. Part six is the conclusion.

Panel data sources for China

In China, five major household-level panel datasets are used to explore rural inequality and distribution, which include RCRE (Research Center for Rural

Economy), RHS (Rural Household Survey), CHNS (China Health and Nutrition Survey), CHIPS (Chinese Household Income Project Survey), and CAPM (Chinese Academy of Preventative Medicine). These panel data sets include both balanced and unbalanced panels, and the majority of them are unbalanced because of sample rotation or attrition.

To compare levels of inequality from a country as vast as China, it is crucial that the samples be representative of the same population, and, ideally, of all China. In principle, RHS and RCRE are the best datasets to meet this requirement, and both surveys are effectively implemented by sectors in the central government, which are the NBS and the Ministry of Agriculture (MOA) respectively. The RHS is an annual China rural household survey dating from the early 1980s. It is of high quality in many respects, including both sampling methods and the unusual effort made to minimize non-sampling errors. It covers 31 provinces, 7,100 villages, and 68,190 households. However, in-depth analysis of the RHS has been limited to selected sub-samples of provinces, and only for a few years (such as Ravallion and Chen 1999; Tsui 1998b). The full sample RHS data has not yet been publicly released and systematically analyzed. Similarly, the RCRE is an annual China rural household survey from the mid 1980s. It is also nationally representative, covering 31 provinces, 360 villages, and 24,000 households. Likewise, all households covered by the RCRE are asked to keep detailed diary records of household information.

Different from the RHS and RCRE, the CHNS, CHIPS, and CAPM are organized by research institutions with relatively limited geographic coverage and/or smaller samples. The CHNS is an ongoing international collaborative project between the University of North Carolina (UNC) and the Chinese Center for Disease Control and Prevention (CCDCP). It is designed to examine the effects of the health, nutrition, and family planning policies, and programs implemented by national and local governments, and to see how the social and economic transformation of Chinese society is affecting the health and nutritional status of its population. It covers a seven-year household panel dataset in nine provinces, 100 villages, and 2,000 households. Daily dietary intake is carefully measured in the dataset. The CHIPS covers around 20 provinces and 4,000–9,000 households, which is mainly sponsored by the Chinese Academy of Social Sciences (CASS). Three surveys have been conducted in 1988, 1995, and 2002, which include detailed current and retrospective information on households' income and consumption and their components. The CAPM is a two-year social survey of 25 provinces, 138 villages, and around 8,000 households in rural China between 1978 and 1989. The first survey focuses on the relationship between nutrition and cancer; the second wave also involves multilevel socioeconomic questionnaires.

Besides the above-mentioned data, some datasets are collected for special research purposes. For example, MORDUCH, used in a study by Morduch and Sicular (2002), is a small random sample survey of 259 farm households in 16 villages in an eastern China county. The survey follows households from 1990 to 1993. The survey was tailored to deliver consistent information on income and other economic, social, and political variables. Another census-type household panel survey, the IFPRI–CAAS, is collected by the International Food Policy Research Institute (IFPRI) and the Chinese Academy of Agricultural Sciences (CAAS). The dataset focuses on three administrative villages in a western China county. The survey reveals detailed information on household incomes and expenditures (including detailed information on social spending). Information is collected for each household member.

Given the limited availability of household panel data, macro-level panel datasets are a popular tool. For instance, the RSESS-NBS (Rural Social and Economic Survey Service of the NBS) includes time series (1985–2002) and cross provincial (28 provinces) data from rural China. The RSESS-NBS can be found in books such as *Poverty Monitoring Report of Rural China* and *China Yearbook of Rural Household Survey.* Compiled aggregate-level data can be found on the websites of some research institutions. For example, researchers in IFPRI compiled a dataset mainly from *China Statistical Yearbook*, *China Rural Statistical Yearbook*, *China Fixed Asset Investment Yearbook*, *China Education Expenditure Statistical Yearbook*, relevant World Bank publications, and *China Transportation Yearbook.* The dataset provides information on key economic indicators in 29 provinces from 1952 to 2001. Another convenient way to obtain a long-term aggregate panel data is through two statistical yearbooks, the *Comprehensive Statistical Data and Materials on 50 Years of China* and *Comprehensive Statistical Data and Materials on 55 Years of China.* Some long-term indicators in those two yearbooks have been adjusted to make them the most comparable over time.

Panel data assessment

Comparisons among major datasets

Before the 1990s, more aggregate-level panel datasets were available than household-level panel data. The overall household inequality was understated, since inequality *within* rural and urban areas of each province was suppressed. Analogously, when we analyze trends and the role of contributing factors to inequality such as township and village enterprises, conclusions are valid only insofar as most rural inequality arises from differences in mean incomes across these units. Moreover, they could not say anything about the evolution of household-level inequality within those areas.

Since then, a few household-level data sets have come on stream. Compared to aggregate datasets, household panel data can construct a rich, comparable panel of villages that might be used to address a host of econometric and empirical issues that trouble researchers (Benjamin *et al.* 2005a). Moreover, with access to household-level data over time, by exploiting the household dimension of the panel, we can link the evolution of household-level welfare to initial conditions in the village.

The first concern is on geographic representation. Among all panel datasets, the RHS–NBS covers the broadest areas over the longest time period. In investigating

Table 11.1 Major panel datasets for income distribution studies in rural China

Data source	*Category*	*Household*	*Village*	*Province*	*Sample period*	*Main characteristics*	*Literature*
Micro-level panel data							
RCRE	Planned panels	24,000	360	31	1986–present (except 1992, 1994)	Diary book + visiting; nationally representative; 1/3 sample attrition over the period 1986–1999; collected on an annual basis; from fixed rural survey sites	Benjamin *et al.* (2005a, 2006); Wan and Zhou (2005); Araar (2008); Brauw *et al.* (2008); Zhang *et al.* (2006)
RHS–NBS	Planned panels	68,190	7,100	31	1981–present (annually)	Sample rotation on a five-year basis; diary book + visiting; detailed household income and consumption; nationally representative; micro data publicly unavailable; collected on an annual basis; the only data source covering a reasonably long time period	Ravallion (1998) Chen and Ravallion (1996)
CHNS	Planned panels	1920/2160	96/108	9	1989, 1991, 1993, 1997, 2000, 2004, 2006	A three-day observations in each survey on detailed nutrition and health information; poor income and expenditure information; rural and urban samples; county names not revealed	Benjamin *et al.* (2002, 2005b); Ling (2008); Li *et al.* (2006); Wang (2005)
CHIPS	Retrospective panels	4178/7888/ 9200	–	18/22	1988, 1995, 2002	Recall data for income in years between nearest waves; detailed information on household income components; include a subsample of rural migrants; combine rural and urban samples	Khan and Riskin (1998); Yao *et al.* (2004); Chen (2005); Khor and Pencavel (2006); Ying *et al.* (2006); Brauw and Rozelle (2008); Brauw and Giles (2008)

Table 11.1 Continued

Data source	*Category*	*Household*	*Village*	*Province*	*Sample period*	*Main characteristics*	*Literature*
CAPM	Planned panels	7,950	130/138	25	1983, 1989	Detailed information on nutrition, health, and medical research	Nee (1994)
MORDUCH	Planned panels	259	16	1	1990–1993	Special attention to consistent definitions of income	Morduch and Sicular (2002)
IFPRI–CAAS	Planned panels	805/823	3	1	2004, 2006, 2009	Census-type household survey; detailed information on social spending, stigmatized behavior and health outcomes; three-day observation on food and nutrition intake; geographically isolated; multi-ethnic populated	Brown *et al.* (2010); Chen *et al.* (2010)
Macro-level panel data							
RSESS-NBS	Macro panels	–	–	28	1985–2002	Provincial-level panel data	Huang *et al.* (2008)
IFPRI	Macro panels	–	–	29	1952–2001	Longer provincial-level panel data	Fan *et al.* (2005)
RHS Statistic	Macro panels	–	–	28	1982–1998	Provincial-level panel data; detailed sub-categories of food consumption	Wan (2005)
CCPFSY	Macro panels	1860 counties			1993–2000	Detailed information on public sector at the county level	Zhang (2009)

Notes: There are no inadvertent or pseudo panels other than planned panels and retrospective panels. Only rural samples in each wave of the CHIPS are included.

the role of geographic factors for inequality, most of the panel datasets in Table 11.1 are able to track a panel of villages, even where there has been household attrition. This guarantees geographic comparability over the complete time period. However, discrepancies still exist between datasets, for example, in the rate of growth of farm income between the RCRE and the CHNS. It might reflect the kinds of villages that are selected, with more "suburban" villages possibly included in the CHNS. The CHNS villages may have more acreage in vegetables and other cash crops, and have been less exposed to a sharp drop in grain prices that occurred after 1995.

The second concern lies in the availability of historical household data. Ideally, to analyze the evolution of inequality in contemporary China we should have a nationally representative household survey over the entire period. Among all sets of panel data employed to analyze rural inequality and income distribution in China, the RHS–NBS can be ideally representative. Unfortunately, while such household surveys have been conducted throughout the second half of the last century, they are available to researchers only for the post reform period and in any case sporadically, for restricted years with varying but limited coverage. Only aggregate data is published and available for public use,[1] and details of the construction of the RHS–NBS income estimates and Gini coefficient is sketchy. As a result, inequality measures based on the full sample are not comparable with results derived from its sub-sample and other data sources. Besides, the publicly available aggregate RHS–NBS data does not include information on housing, subsidies, and income in kind.[2] In this sense, the major utilized household-level datasets such as the RCRE, CHNS, and CHIPS are good complements that provide the aforementioned information.

Third, each micro dataset has its own special focus. For example, the RCRE data has been collected from many fixed villages annually. The RHS–NBS data has an even longer time period and is nationally representative. The CHNS data is specialized to conduct nutrition and health research. The CHIPS data has more detailed information on household income. The CAMP data has gathered detailed information for nutrition, health, and medicare research.

Deficiencies of major data sets still exist. First, almost no panel datasets available (including the RHS–NBS and RCRE) contain detailed enough information at the individual level. However, since the 1990s, driven to some extent by growing policy concerns, considerable work on intra-household allocation has begun around the world. To catch up, we need to improve the quality of our panel data at the individual level and correct policy instruments that may have a gender differentiated impact. Second, refusal rates are likely to be higher among households with a high opportunity cost of time or many illiterates, but neither the RCRE nor the NBS report refusal rates. Further, by design the RHS–NBS, RCRE, and CHNS are not successful in accurately estimating household incomes from family-run business.[3] A richer set of questions should be included in the surveys to track this important source of income. Underestimation of this income source might induce a significant underestimate of income inequality due to non-agricultural income growth, especially at the top end of the distribution (Benjamin *et al.* 2005a).[4]

Finally, while the CHNS contains more details that can facilitate the exploration of the robustness of conclusions to definitions of "income," it does not have detailed expenditure data.

The fourth point relates to treatment of income. Income in the RCRE and RHS–NBS data are both defined as income earned from all enumerated sources, including both cash and imputed values for in-kind income from various sources.[5] Much of the difference between levels and trends of income among datasets can be explained by differences in the valuation of home-produced grain. For instance, relative to the RCRE, the NBS treatment of the in-kind component is likely to result in an underestimate of incomes and consumption prior to 1990, and an overestimate of the growth in incomes or consumption for 1987 to 1999 period. Given that grain income was valued at a price still systematically related to the quota price after 1990, Benjamin *et al.* (2005a) find a strong positive correlation between the size of the gap between the two income series and their estimate of the ratio of the market-to-quota price.[6] Two other differences in the income series lie in the treatment of taxes and fees and depreciation on fixed assets. Studies using the NBS usually subtract both, while typical studies applying the RCRE (e.g. Benjamin *et al.* 2005a) do not subtract taxes due to their focus on the earning ability of households. However, they depreciate assets themselves due to the arbitrariness of recorded depreciation expenses in the RCRE.

Furthermore, there has been concern expressed over the ability of respondents to recall past income. Records collected from the CHIPS data may rely on respondents' recall. The single-interview approach and respondents' recalling of past incomes may have errors, thus the correlation among incomes across years will embody errors in measurement. For instance, individuals may report the same incomes or the same proportion of incomes in different years, which will end up with more inertia in the income distribution data and understate the true income mobility. By contrast, the RHS–NBS data and the RCRE data are less likely to suffer from recall error, since each selected household maintains a diary over the entire year as well as two transaction books. The survey has been conducted on an annual basis. An assistant interviewer living in the county seat is supposed to visit each household every two weeks (or every month for the RCRE) to check the books. The unusual rigor applied to the collection, checking and processing of the RHS–NBS data and the RCRE data means that they are less likely to suffer from a variety of non-sampling errors common to household surveys in many other datasets.

Finally, the definition of household membership is important to note. For households in the RHS–NBS and the RCRE, household size is based on registration, but it excludes migrants. However, household membership in the CHNS data is defined more on the basis of economic attachment (residency) than registration. Household heads and family members who send remittances are included. An increasingly serious omission over time occurs as the number of people who work and live outside grows. To tackle this problem, the CHIPS 2002 included a subsample of rural migrants living in urban areas, while most datasets still exclude this increasingly important group.

In China where the market is imperfectly and unevenly developed, studies have discussed a variety of data and methodological issues for comparisons of inequality.

Relevant data issues

Measurement errors

Inequality measures, such as the level of inequality, factor decomposition of inequality, and its change over time, are seriously affected when income or consumption is measured with error (Ravallion and Chen 1999). Special attention should be paid to whether the underlying income concept includes income items such as imputed rents for owner-occupied dwellings, imputed incomes from home production, and in-kind income. Besides, allowing for inter-regional cost of living differences and evaluating consumption rather than expenditures (e.g. consumer durables) is important. When studying rural–urban inequality, attention should be paid to the reclassification of rural areas as urban. An adjustment of the NBS urban–rural inequality data and strictly follow a panel of rural villages over time is required.

VALUING CONSUMPTION OF OWN PRODUCTION

A significant portion of rural household activity is directed towards production for a household's own consumption, and it tends to account for a high share of income for the poor. Its undervaluation due to the downward price bias from the market-clearing level leads to an overestimate of inequality. Meanwhile, prices used by provincial statistics departments diverged progressively from market prices over time, which also lead to an overestimate of the rate of increase in inequality.

The process of imputed price adjustment for the RHS–NBS in the 1980s and 1990s serves as an example (World Bank 1992; Khan *et al.* 1993; Ravallion and Chen 1999).[7] Besides, Benjamin *et al.* (2005a) find that some localities used the same weighted average quota and above quota sales' price calculated in 1990 to value in-kind income between 1991 and 1995, which might give an additional source of downward bias in income and consumption growth between 1991 and 1995.

To correct these deficiencies, Chen and Ravallion (1996), Tsui (1998b), Ravallion and Chen (1999), and McCulloch and Calandrino (2003) apply sub-samples of the NBS data and show that all credible estimates of inequality in rural China should correct those biases. For instance, to reflect the increased marketization of the economy, following Chen and Ravallion (1996),[8] Tsui (1998b) and McCulloch and Calandrino (2003) revalue the grain kept for personal consumption. However, this revaluation can only be implemented for grain due to the lack of relevant information for other goods.

A similar adjustment is conducted in the RCRE data, where grain produced for self-consumption or stored was valued at prices reflecting the quota price. Because of lower than market quota prices through the mid-1990s, income from grain production and consumption out of home production are both likely to be biased downward. Benjamin *et al.* (2005a) revalue households' non-marketed grain at average village market prices.

PRICE DIFFERENCES

Inflation/deflation is adjusted for time-series data to convert income and consumption into constant dollars (Yuan). McCulloch and Calandrino (2003) use the CPI index from the *China Statistical Yearbook* to deflate nominal variables. However, the published CPI uses an (unknown) mix of market and official prices, rather than market prices, to value certain goods, which may underestimate the rate of increase of consumer prices and therefore overestimate the improvement in real terms.

Spatial differences may also be important. Prices in some parts of the country may be systematically different from those elsewhere, in which case estimates of inequality can be biased. However, most of the past literature has ignored spatial differences, for example, in the cost of living. Two exceptions include Chen and Ravallion (1996) and Tsui (1998b), who construct provincial-level spatial and inter-temporal spatial deflators for four and two provinces respectively. Recently, research interests have been extended to explore the rural–urban gap. However, it should be noted that adjusting for inflation over time using separate urban and rural consumer price indices does not incorporate the spatial difference at any one point in time. A constructed set of spatial price deflators documented by Holz and Brandt (2004) is widely used to adjust cross-sectional differences in urban and rural prices across provinces, and between rural and urban areas. Overall, adjusting spatial price differences might minimize the problem of overestimation of inequality and the exaggeration of the contribution of spatial disparity regarding price differences.

DURABLE CONSUMPTION AND INCOME

Housing services and durables are usually relatively equally distributed at the beginning, but more unequal with different rates of accumulation of housing and an increasing share of consumption as an economy develops. Especially as durables and housing reflect consumption decisions linking permanent income, it is important to consider how they are treated in the construction of consumption and income.

The impact of durables and housing on inequality is significant. The NBS data on consumption expenditure include one-off expenditure on durables in the year in which the purchase decision was made. However, durable goods, by definition, last for a number of years. Meanwhile, owing to the infrequent purchases of consumer durables, the estimated unit values of durable goods might be based on the records of a few households and the prices may not be representative. A similar problem is encountered in relation to housing expenditure as it is difficult to include imputed rental values. The NBS only include all housing expenditure in the year in which the spending takes place, as a result of the limited rental market for housing in rural China.

Scholars have made lots of efforts in calculating and adjusting consumptions of durable goods and housing. Khan and Riskin (1998) and Khan *et al.* (1999) construct a revised measure for urban and rural China based on the asset valuations available in the primary survey data. Chen and Ravallion (1996) include five percent of the recorded dwelling value for housing and 10 percent for durables in total consumption. Improving upon Chen and Ravallion (1996), Tsui (1998b) adopts the available NBS price data for consumer durables, which consist of average retail price information collected by the urban survey teams of the NBS.

Utilizing the RCRE, Benjamin *et al.* (2005a) and Brauw and Rozelle (2008) also consider inflating the value of the stock of housing and durables to reflect the increase in prices of durable goods. McCulloch and Calandrino (2003) approximate the rental value of the stock of durables in each year in rural Sichuan, and they also impute the rental value of housing expenditure using information about rents in the local area.

Sample attrition bias

Attrition bias is present in panel data collection for several reasons. First of all, in some data sets, such as the RCRE, RHS–NBS, and CHIPS, whole villages drop out because they are annexed into a city. In some other cases when panel datasets are based on written records collection, sample attrition may reflect the fact that maintaining diaries of their households' incomes and expenditures makes it difficult for illiterate households to participate and the opportunity cost of keeping records for the rich are high. Some rich residents might leave their villages for an entire year, some people might show unwillingness to make efforts, and some people do not want to reveal their personal information. To the poor, attrition may also be endogenous to shocks (Lokshin and Ravallion 2001). It is difficult to distinguish such households from those that change too much to keep in the panel or those who were replaced by the surveyors for certain reasons (Ravallion and Jalan 2001). However, to the poor endogenous attrition may be minimized, since sampled households in the RHS–NBS are paid to participate. Khor and Pencavel (2005) find that unmarried, younger and older people are less likely to be represented in the CHIPS 1995. Benjamin *et al.* (2005a) and Brauw and Giles (2008) compare cross sections of the RCRE and RHS–NBS with overlapping years of the CHNS and CCAP 2000 that are not based on diary record.

Comparing with other surveys in which households are known to be randomly sampled, a disproportionate number of households at both ends of the income distribution are excluded from the NBS, CHNS, and RCRE data, which might lead to an underestimate of income inequality (Benjamin *et al.* 2005a). Sometimes the numbering of the replacements is not properly handled, since a considerable amount of replacements are assigned the same ID number of the survey units as those that are replaced (Shen and Yao 2008). To check the accuracy of the original ID and the continuity of the RCRE, Hoken *et al.* (2006) develop data matching methods, construct new panel databases and test the sample attrition biases. They demonstrate that a large number of spurious continuities of panel survey appear to exist in the original ID. To compensate for sample attrition, the 1997 CHNS includes all newly-formed as well as additional households in original communities to replace households lost. Faced with more severe attrition such as a drop out of an entire community, a new community in the original province would be added (Chen 2005).

Units of measurement

In evaluating inequality, per capita estimates are usually imputed to all members within a given household. Higher levels of aggregate analyses base their units of measurement at the village, township, county, or provincial level, which underestimate inequality because it ignores the internal inequality arising from differences in welfare among households within these administrative units. This simplified treatment also forms a poor basis upon which to evaluate the contribution of cross-unit inequality to the total. This issue has not been effectively addressed in studying inequality in rural China as individual consumption or income data are rarely available.

To deal with the problem of equalizing all family members within each household, estimates of household income and consumption expenditure were divided by the number of adult equivalents in the households using the World Health Organization adult equivalence scale (McCulloch and Calandrino 2003). This scale is derived from detailed studies of the nutritional requirements of males and females of different ages in developing countries. Meanwhile, income or consumption should be adjusted by household size, as the relative need of different sized households is different. Chen and Ravallion (1996) provide an example of integrated adjustments.

The unit of measurement also affects the estimated effect of inequality on growth. The dependence of growth rate at household level on the initial log of indicators such as capital stock can induce spurious effects after aggregation process (Ravallion 1998). Even when the growth rate is linear in the initial capital stock, a term for the change in inequality will be found in the residual of the usual aggregate growth rate regression. More complex forms of nonlinearity and alternative functional forms for the inequality measure relevant to the micro-level externality can yield further spurious effects of measured inequality.

Adjustment for income volatility

The impact of income and consumption volatility on inequality has received limited attention in the literature. Compared to urban income, volatility of rural income is substantially higher in China. At present, poor rural households either have no access to capital markets or only have access at prohibitively high borrowing rates, which limits their ability to smooth income. Thus, it is vital to adjust for rural income volatility when constructing measures of inequality to obtain a more realistic inequality estimate and to build a more comparable basis for rural–urban inequality. Previous studies on income volatility in rural China (Jalan and Ravallion 1998; Li *et al.* 2005) do not make direct adjustments to welfare measures. Whalley and Yue (2006) use the CHIPS for rural residents to construct measures of certainty equivalent income and calculate summary distributional measures for the modified income data.

Main findings from panel data

Rising income inequality and economic development

From 1987 to 1999, income distribution improved by most measures during the early part of the period, as average incomes rose substantially with only a modest increase in inequality. However, the distribution worsened significantly over the late 1990s and the early 2000s, with rising inequality and falling absolute incomes, especially at the bottom end of the income distribution (Benjamin *et al.* 2005a). This situation was attributed to collapsed agricultural income and uneven growth of non-farm income due to the contribution of non-farm family businesses. Within the non-farm incomes category, local income was relatively disequalizing, while income from outside the village was relatively equalizing (Benjamin *et al.* 2005b). Almost no studies using household data show the recent trajectory of rural income inequality.

Determinants of income inequality

Studies on determinants of income inequality can be categorized into two major branches, inequality by income sources and assets and inequality by geography. The first category emphasizes declining agricultural income, disequalizing non-farm income (especially family businesses), egalitarian land distribution, and physical and human capital. Inequality determinants classified by geographic hypotheses are briefly summarized and followed by an extensive review of spatial decompositions. Besides the above-mentioned two branches, crucial events and development strategies in rural China can explain some of the inequality trend, including urban-biased development policy, rural industrialization, rural financial development, fiscal decentralization, market fragmentation, globalization processes, grassroots democracy, and the role of political power and connections.

DETERMINANTS OF RURAL INEQUALITY BY INCOME SOURCES AND ASSETS

In general, changing structure and composition of income generates higher inequality (Tsui 1998a), which recently has been followed by more specific studies on different components of income and their contributions to inequality. It is unclear whether equality of farm income due to the current egalitarian land distribution policy is necessarily good for overall income inequality, since more inequality of farm income might actually reduce overall income inequality

(Benjamin *et al.* 2006). However, Chen (2005) verifies the negative role that farm income plays in inequality. Within farm income, grain production plays the most important role in rising inequality, and non-farm income plays the secondary role, while other farm incomes have a decreasing effect on inequality (Ravallion and Chen 1999; Benjamin *et al.* 2005b). Wan and Zhou (2005) conclude that cropping pattern is more crucial than labor and human capital inputs based on disequalizing income from non-farm family businesses and the failure of non-farm labor markets in constituting rising income inequality.

Decomposing inequality into land category, farm assets and human capital shows several things: first, farm assets are inequality-reducing over the period because of their diminishing rate of return cross-section and over time (Ravallion and Chen 1999); and second, constraints on farm size implicit in the Chinese administrative allocation of land together with agricultural goods price change may ease its contribution to overall inequality (Wan and Zhou 2005; Benjamin *et al.* 2006). Although land inequality grew from 1987 to 2002, it is still low by developing country standards (Benjamin *et al.* 2005b). However, land area is a poor measure of land endowment, given the usual negative correlation between land capacity and farm size. Higher return over time to good quality farm land is inequality-increasing (Ravallion and Chen 1999). Thus, spatial decompositions based on cultivated area alone exaggerate differences in land across space. Third, education is found to have little effect on inequality (Wan and Zhou 2005) but is gaining importance (Wan 2007). The rising intra-regional and urban–rural differential distribution of education and entrepreneurial attributes leads to more intra-regional and urban–rural inequality (Benjamin *et al.* 2002; Guo 2007). Improving education and off-farm job market simultaneously leads to success in family businesses and labor markets (Benjamin *et al.* 2002).

DETERMINANTS OF RURAL INEQUALITY BY GEOGRAPHY

When encompassing weather, infrastructure, and other natural resources, geography would account for a very significant share of total rural inequality. Using provincial-level data, Wan (2007) finds that location and location-related factors comprise the largest contributor to total regional inequality, although its percentage contribution has decreased over time. Utilizing household survey data, Ravallion and Chen (1999) find that the differences in income between those living in mountainous rural areas and those on the plains have been an important source of rising inequality. However, Benjamin *et al.* (2005a) rule out geography as the most important factor for understanding the dispersion of incomes; rather, the prevailing inequality is due to inequality between neighbors within a village.

DETERMINANTS OF RURAL INEQUALITY BY DEVELOPMENTAL STRATEGY

First, urban-biased development policies help us understand the picture behind spatial rural inequality. Before the economic reform, the role of the state sector was important in the interior. However, since then growth of the non-state sector in the interior provinces has been much slower as more resources have gone to support a larger population tied to the state sector. It has handicapped the growth and labor demand in the rural secondary and tertiary industry. In contrast, much faster growth in the non-state sector in coastal provinces has helped provide a wide array of job opportunities for both rural and urban areas there. The unbalanced spatial job creation and fragmented capital market have significant negative effect on rural inequality (Zhang and Tan 2007). Due to the still fragmented factor markets, fast growing international trade and foreign capital investments have been concentrated in the more developed coastal region rather than vast inland areas, leading to further aggravating regional rural inequality (Zhang and Zhang 2009).

Evidence shows that most of the rising inequality in rural industrialization is spatial and has increasingly contributed to regional inequality (Wan 2007; Chen 2005). However, income from rural industry does not contribute to the rise in local inequality because wages from rural industry, mostly labor intensive sectors, were equalizing. Growing spatial inequality can also be attributed to uneven opportunities represented by the uneven development of TVEs and other markets (Guo 2007).

How does rural financial development influence income inequality? Theoretical predictions on the finance-inequality nexus are inconclusive and mixed, including an inverted U-shaped relationship (Greenwood and Jovanovic 1990) and a negative linear relationship (Banerjee and Newman 1993), both from provincial panel data (Liang 2006) and household panel data (Wan and Zhou 2005).

China's current fiscal system is largely decentralized compared to her centralized governance structure. Due to large differences in initial economic structures and revenue bases, the implicit tax rate and fiscal burden to support the functioning of local government vary significantly across jurisdictions. The regressive nature of the rural taxation system explains why the fiscal decentralization exacerbates the rural–urban gap and gaps among rural areas, and it has been confirmed by studies using *China County Public Finance Statistical Yearbook* (CCPFSY) (Zhang 2009) and rural household data (Khan and Riskin 1998; Benjamin *et al.* 2006).

Does grassroots democracy help mitigate income inequality in rural China? Shen and Yao (2008) utilize village- and household-level RCRE to find that village elections reduce inequality, and their role is not played through more income redistribution, but through more pro-poor public investment.

Political power and connections captured by party membership, presence of a past or present cadre, or the class labels given to families in the late 1940s and early 1950s are found to facilitate access to uneven opportunities and the resulting rural inequality (Morduch and Sicular 2002).

Rising inequality and household welfare

Rising income inequality might offset welfare gains in the economic reform. The relationship holds controlling for own resources in the household-level specification, which casts doubt on the effect of an imperfect credit market. At the village level, Benjamin *et al.* (2006) explore growth and its potential linkage to various initial conditions. First, low inequality enhances growth in non-farm incomes and tilts the village away from agriculture; second, higher inequality is associated with higher overall tax rates and more regressive taxes, lower levels of revenue and expenditures, insufficient provision of public goods, and poorly developed factor markets.

Asset and consumption inequality are sometimes employed to complement the measure of income inequality. Ravallion (1998) finds a significant harmful effect of asset inequality on consumption growth. However, the effect is lost in an aggregate growth regression. At the provincial level, rising income inequality is identified to be an obstacle to a steady-state level consumption. Wan (2005) finds slow conditional convergences for total grain, fine grain, edible oil, poultry, aquatic product, and sugar, and divergences for animal fat and red meat. Testing nonlinear dynamics of household incomes and expenditures simultaneously over time shows negative effect of inequality, especially on mean income (Ravallion and Jalan 2001).

Absolute poverty has fallen dramatically in China in the past 30 years' reform, and rural areas account for the bulk of the decline in poverty. However, rising inequality within the rural sector greatly slows poverty reduction (Yao *et al.* 2004; Ravallion and Chen 2007). Yao *et al.* (2004) provide a poverty reduction simulation under different inequality scenarios and growth rates. It shows that even under the most optimistic scenario, China will still have a large number of rural poor until 2015, but even under the pessimistic assumption of income and inequality growth, China can still manage to cut its impoverished population. However, Yao's combined data (the RCRE and CHIPS) are from different households. Employing the RSESS-NBS Data, Huang *et al.* (2008) find that changes in the incidence of poverty are not only related to overall economic growth, but also depend on the sources and distribution of income growth.

Spatial inequality and decompositions

Many key policy issues on inequality and income distribution show themselves in a disaggregated fashion, and the individualistic tendency in the inequality measurement is reinforced by the use of decomposable inequality measures (Kanbur, 2000). Spatial inequality and decomposition reflects one of the major concerns. Spatial inequality is often defined at regional, provincial, and county level. Some papers cover a single level, others two or three. Relevant studies use proxy variables such as per capita income, GDP per capita, gross value of industrial and agricultural output or one of its components, consumption, collective income, or even grain output as indicators of living standard. Most of the studies in this field limit their analyses to a snapshot, without a time profile (e.g. Cheng 1996; Gustafsson and Li 1998; Hussain *et al.* 1994; Knight and Song 1993; Lee 2000; Tsui 1993; Griffin and Zhao 1993; Hu 1997; Wu 2000), however, it is rarely seen after 2000.

Among those applying panel data, most of them use provincial-level data to decompose spatial inequality. The results include greater consumption equality between 1952 and 1987 (Lyons 1991), U-shaped inter-provincial income inequality between 1978 (or 1985) and 1993 (or 1994) (Duncan and Tian 1999; Fujita and Hu 2001), and increasing inter-regional inequality but decreasing intra-regional inequality between 1985 and 1994 (Fujita and Hu 2001). Concerning the contribution of inter-regional inequality to provincial inequality, the results show 14–35 percent between 1978 and 1993 (Jian *et al.* 1996; Kanbur and Zhang 1999), 38–41 percent between 1986 and 1992, and 50–60 percent between the mid 1980s and 1996 (Wan 2007).

Fewer studies employ county- or village-level panel data. Howes and Hussain (1994) and Peng (1999) use county data between 1985 and 1991 to find that inter-county inequality increased by 37 percent and 20–26 percent respectively. Rozelle (1994) employs one-province village panel data between 1983 and 1988 and concludes an increase in inequalities among villages, towns, and counties.

Meanwhile, even fewer studies (Tsui 1998a; Gustafsson and Li 2002; Gustafsson *et al.* 2007; Ravallion and Chen 1999; Chen 2005; Benjamin *et al.* 2005b; Morduch and Sicular 2002; Wan and Zhou 2005; Guo 2007) explore spatial inequality in China with household panel data. According to Gustafsson and Li (2002), only four in 16 papers summarized use household data, let alone household panel data.

Tsui (1998a) finds that inter-provincial inequality only accounts for 6–12 percent of total rural inequality between 1985 and 1990. Guo (2007) further finds that the major part of inequality has changed from inter- to intra-village level from 1986 to 2000. Benjamin *et al.* (2005b) confirm that the province and village respectively only explain 10 percent and 30–40 percent of rural inequality. Most inequality in rural China is *within* villages.

Overall, only a few studies use household panel data that cover most provinces in China over time, and no study summarized above simultaneously uses data at county level, provincial level, and regional level. As a special case, Gustafsson and Li (2002) provide a comprehensive study between 1988 and 1995. They show that in rural China inter-county inequality increased from 43 percent to 47 percent of total inequality. Among inter-county inequality, intra-provincial inequality stayed at 18 percent of total inequality, while inter-provincial inequality changed from 25 percent to 29 percent. Among inter-provincial inequality, intra-regional inequality dropped from 13 percent to 6 percent of total inequality, while inter-regional inequality increased greatly from 12 percent to 23 percent. While income inequality within rural counties increased from 1988 to 1995, the uneven income increase across counties was also important for the growth of rural inequality. However, in Gustafsson and Li (2002) the particular counties are not identical, which poses some problems for interpretation.

Two other points should be noted. First, robustness of decomposition should be addressed. Morduch and Sicular (2002) demonstrate how sharply different conclusions can emerge for different decomposition rules. Second, it is dangerous to use data of limited coverage to project the magnitude and change of income inequality in rural China as a whole (Gustafsson and Li 2002) as income has grown at noticeably different rates in different parts of rural China during the economic reform.

Income inequality and other dimensions

Income inequality and mobility

If a society is characterized by a great deal of income mobility, income inequality derived from the comparison of income in a single year may be misleading as an indicator of longer run income inequality. Studies on income mobility are crucial complements to the measure of income inequality, as more and more rural residents are moving from west to east and from inland to coastal regions. Even if people stay where they are, institutional transformation may still bring a drastic change to their relative positions.

There are two categories of income mobility: macro mobility answers how much income mobility exists in the economy and how has it changed over time;[9] micro mobility defines which individual or group experiences movements, of what magnitudes, and what these movements are correlated with.[10]

Very few studies are on the macro mobility in rural China. Wang (2005) and Ying *et al.* (2006) both find that major income mobility indicators (e.g. time independence, positional movement and income mobility as equalizers of longer-term incomes) fall over time in rural China. However, income mobility helped equalize longer-term incomes relative to initial incomes in rural China in the 1990s (Wang 2005). Nee (1994) finds that positional movement in rural China was higher in 1983–1989 than in 1978–1983, which he explains by "institutional change resulted in a dramatic shake-up of the rural stratification order."

The only study on micro mobility in rural China we are aware of is Zhang *et al.* (2006). Using the RCRE in rural China from 1987 to 2002, Zhang *et al.* (2006) finds the possibility for the poorest 25 percent to climb up to higher income status increased. However, the upward mobility of those of the middle-income has gradually become stagnant. The richest five percent and 10 percent are the biggest winners during the process. Zhang *et al.* (2006) also breakdown the change of income inequality between the wealthy and the poor into two parts: the income change of those remaining in the wealthy group and the poor group persistently, and the change due to the shift of income status of those who move upward to the wealthy group or downward to the poor group, the latter of which was accompanied by an increasing contribution of income mobility to inequality. To identify factors which may influence the probability of moving upward, downward, or holding position, they find that the household dependent population ratio, human capital endowment, land rental market participation, and party membership have significant effects on income mobility in rural China.

Inequality and polarization

While inequality measures are conceived to assess the expected divergence or disparity among incomes, polarization measures are sensitive to the level of identification of individuals by their income levels. Intuitively, a higher level of between-group inequality is related to the polarization phenomenon. This gives additional information that inequality measures fail to capture.

Concern over growing polarization has been prominent in policy discussions since the economic reform, when the rural–urban gap has been an important dimension in polarized China (Li 1996). Utilizing rural and urban components from 1983 to 1995, Zhang and Kanbur (2001) test three typical polarization indices against two standard measures of inequality, which do not show distinct results. An alternative polarization index is also developed to offer more insight. It is found that rural–urban polarization is more serious in levels but modestly decreasing compared with a dramatically increasing inland-coast polarization trend. Wan (2007) finds that the fast increase in regional inequality is accompanied by worsening polarization.

Araar (2008) breaks down the polarization index by population groups and income sources over the period 1986–2002. For policy purposes, those decompositions can help target the apparent poor groups of population and propose corrections on existing distributive policies. Araar's results show that even if inequality has increased sharply during the last two decades, the pure polarization component has remained constant or even decreased on average.

Income inequality and health

Public health studies find the relationship between income inequality and adult health outcomes in developed countries. Specifically, there seems to be a correlation between social hierarchy and mortality as well as a correlation between social hierarchy and morbidity. Existing evidence from China shows similar results.

Ling (2008) examines the role of relative income and income inequality on anthropometric health outcomes as well as health related behaviors. Reverse causation is dealt with by exogenously introducing statutory retirement age and employing retired samples. The elderly are rapidly aging and most vulnerable to the economic reform. Normally, the elderly in China have mainly relied on intergenerational transfers within families. Besides income shocks due to economic restructuring, the health outcome and status competition of the working people may reallocate resources from elderly dependants in households. In addition, the relative incomes of the elderly may be crucial in determining their health. The confluence of these trends and the Elderly Dependency Ratio (EDR) is found to affect their health outcomes such as high waist circumference, overweight or obese, and underweight. Meanwhile, it leads to unhealthy behavior, such as smoking cigarettes or pipes in the past, possibly to cope with stress.

Ling (2007) also conducts a separate study on the relationship between relative deprivation and anthropometric health outcomes for infants and children and still finds strong and consistent evidence of the effects of relative deprivation on health.

Both Ling (2007) and Ling (2008) predict that relative deprivation and unequal growth affect the "social gradient of health" in China by potentially increasing the prevalence of obesity among the rich, while concurrently being unable to reduce the prevalence of underweight among the poor.

Li and Zhu (2006) find an "inverted-U" relationship between Self-Reported Health Status (SRHS)[11] and community-level income inequality. They also confirm that high inequality increases the probability of health-compromising behaviors such as smoking and alcohol consumption. Meanwhile, Li and Zhu (2006) find that relative status has a strong positive effect on self-reported health status, but its protective effect decreases with inequality and is finally offset by extremely high inequality.

Summarizing health outcome indicators utilized, Ling (2007, 2008) attempts to circumvent biases and errors in the SRHS in Li and Zhu (2006) by anthropometric measures including self-reported dietary intake and other objective indicators. Errors in self-reported responses lead to imprecise measures. Li and Zhou (2006) adopt objective health measures such as Physical Functions (PF) and Activities of Daily Living (ADL). Their PF measures include indicators such as heart, lungs, and stomach conditions, and blood pressure. The ADL, only available for individuals over 50, measures whether the individual is physically restricted or unable to perform daily activities, such as taking a bath, eating and drinking alone, or putting on clothes. To capture health behavior, Ling (2008) uses self-reported measures of past and current smoking behavior, while Li and Zhou (2008) use current drinker and drinking frequency as well as past and current smoking behavior.

Areas for further research

The research on inequality and well-being starts the early twenty-first century in a vibrant state, with the new conditions raising new questions, and old questions anew. We will put forward important areas with existing panel data that are underdeveloped. A new data set is highlighted followed by a promising direction for future research.

New research areas with existing panel data sets

Factors influencing rural inequality

Is geography one of the most important factors for rural inequality? Existing provincial-level panel studies find this to be true, especially when weather, infrastructure, and other natural resources are encompassed. However, studies utilizing household survey data rule out geography as the most important factor and conclude that the prevailing inequality is within village. If within-village inequality is crucial, we should turn our attention to determinants of within-village inequality, such as village-level institutions, village produce and labor market development, rural industrialization, informal mutual insurance, and distribution of household endowments. One important avenue for future research is to assess causal linkages between village growth and inequality considering a comprehensive set of factors.

How does financial development influence income inequality? Theoretical predictions on the finance-inequality nexus are inconclusive. Empirical evidence with provincial panel data shows a negative role. However, if we believe that the financial market is not neutral to every rural resident, as poor residents own low amounts and types of collateral, the relationship between rural finance and inequality might be nonlinear. Meanwhile, there has been no household-level empirical test in rural China, the relationship is still undecided and awaits further exploration.

Education distribution is likely to improve at a slower pace than market institutions and opportunities, which might disproportionately benefit the better educated. Is education unequally distributed among generations (cohorts), or is there considerable inequality of education within age groups? The answers to these questions have crucial implications for how education and income distribution evolve.

Rural inequality decomposition

Most studies do not net out spatial dimensions of income composition other than confirming the significant contribution of non-farm income to inequality. For example, wage income from local and non-local sources are usually lumped together, while total wage income is sometimes combined with income from family-run businesses. Grouping imperfectly correlated incomes together conceals important aspects of emerging inequality and their links to household attributes and the external economic environment with which these households interact.

Effects of inequality on growth

In studying the link between inequality and growth, household-level estimation has been conducted and a set of instruments have been used to address measurement error. Explanations ruled out include imperfect credit market, artificial relationship due to the means to aggregate data, and measurement error. Although we observe a negative impact of higher village inequality on household economic growth, we cannot rule out the existence of an unobserved third factor correlated with both initial inequality and subsequent growth. Further, we do not know whether the link between inequality and growth is in the short run or long run.

Income inequality and mobility

Is more mobility always better than less mobility, no matter to what extent? As we know, rural China is now experiencing a rapid transformation with incomplete social security. Too much mobility may reduce welfare through making rural residents feel more at risk given their insufficient ability to smooth income and consumption.

To better understand macro income mobility in rural China, future studies might be directed to answering two questions: how much income mobility is there with different mobility measures, and how does macro mobility change over time for each of these measures? In parallel, to improve our knowledge of micro income mobility, further discussions are on two aspects. First, how do changes in income differ from changes in log-income and position concerning unconditional micro mobility? How has income mobility profile changed over time in the course of China's rapid economic growth? Second, what are the conditional determinants of income change and how do these determinants change over time?

Inequality and health

Studies have identified the impacts of income inequality on health outcomes and health related behaviors among older adults in rural China. Although reverse causation is dealt with by exogenously introducing statutory retirement age in urban China and employing sampled population above the statutory retirement age, scholars are still concerned about reverse causation in urban China, and that unhealthy behavior may cause subsequently lower socio-economic status.

New research areas with new panel data set

Can popular community-level inequality indices capture the large picture of rural inequality? A second thought on how to bridge the gap between inequality and the inequality spectrum will reveal an untouched area with far reaching implications.

Neoclassical utility and relative concern

A longstanding assumption in economics is that an agent's utility depends solely on the absolute level of well-being.[12] However, Smith implicitly put forward the idea in *The Wealth of Nations* in 1776 that people should be endowed with the ability to appear in public without shame. Since Veblen's seminal work in 1899, a few people started to argue that utility or happiness depends in part on the comparison of one's own consumption to that of others, and it was first formally modeled by Duesenberry (1949) in his relative income hypothesis. Since the 1970s, compelling evidence on relative concern has been accumulated (Easterlin 1974; Sen 1983; Frank 1985; Van de Stadt *et al.* 1985).

Most people have a highly localized reference group with which they compare themselves, and people tend to make comparisons with others similar to themselves but above them (Runciman 1966; Frank and Levine 2008). Among others, the comparisons are more saliently based on relative consumption as well as relative income.

Evidence from designer-label goods consumption in Bolivia (Kempen 2003), festivals' budgets in India (Banerjee and Duflo 2007), "splendid" funerals in Ghana (*The Economist* 2007), relative deprivation and migration in Mexico (Stark and Taylor 1991), bride-prices and dowries in south Asia and Africa (Rao 1993; Dekker and Hoogeveen 2002), marriage payments in Bangladesh (Anderson 2007), and community-level consumption in Nepal (Fafchamps and Shilpi 2008) show strong support for relative concern over consumption.

Relative income in the reference group also matters. Relative income is of greater importance in determining an individuals' access to local resources are scarce in a backward community. Moreover, unequal income distribution in a society may lead to instability in social capital,[13] poor health outcomes as well as health-compromising behaviors through rising mistrust and stress or declining social cohesion (Knack and Keefer 1997; Wilkinson 1997; Li and Zhu 2006; Ling 2009). Deaton (2001) even argues that relative deprivation defined in terms of the relative weight of all incomes of people within the reference group who are better off can be positively linked to mortality. Relative deprivation over the income dimension much better predicts the US states mortality rates than either the income or Gini coefficient.[14] The ordinary inequality measures do not explicitly distinguish idiosyncratic deprivation each agent perceives and inequality in a society, leaving out rich implications drawn from the agent level (Chen *et al.* 2010).

While Heffetz (2007) argues that relative concern over conspicuous spending is only relevant for the rich country context, the evidence above has clearly shown that it also matters in developing countries. Fafchamps and Shilpi (2008) further notice that isolation from market, typical for developing countries, is associated with a significant increase in relative concern. However, the empirical studies of an impoverished context, particularly in developing countries, are inadequate.

Relative concern in rural China and the proposed research data

Rural western China is an ideal region to observe relative concern, because the dense population guarantees close social contacts among local residents and facilitates a sound definition of reference group. Vast mountainous landscapes and thousands of years of rural culture lead to isolation from the market. Meanwhile, status seeking and face-saving have been centerpieces throughout Chinese history.

Recently, drastic socioeconomic transformation from a rural society to an industrialized one has spurred a great divergence in social classes, high-income mobility, and competitions for status. It becomes difficult to define clearly Chinese farmers' social reference groups, since they are now more and more divided by their diversified occupations as well as income sources, social networks, and entitlements.

The escalation in conspicuous consumption is particularly reflected in housing, gift exchange, and household ceremonies, but there are no salient increases in productive investment that would secure durable increases in welfare (Brauw and Rozelle 2008; Brauw and Giles 2008). Incomes allocated to gift giving, dowry, bride price, and funerals are thought of as vehicles for social prestige that might challenge social status (Yan 1996; Liu 2000). Such spending also facilitates social networks, which may be relied upon for mutual assistance, personal financing, or other forms of help.

On the other hand, the welfare consequences of "positional externalities" associated with status seeking are severe for Chinese households living close to subsistence. The highly ritualized practices of gift giving compel villagers to offer gifts to avoid isolation from local networks. Since farm income is limited and grows slowly and nonfarm income is highly unequal and favorable to the rich, for poor residents large portions of income facilitating gift exchange cannot be compensated with limited labor resources. For example, field records show oral evidence that inflows of remittances to some households set in motion status contests with adverse consequences to others through their engagement in blood sales over the long term (Brown *et al.* 2010). Worse still, more severe isolation from outside, combined with more unequal market access, usually lead to more pervasive status seeking activities.

Studies on the effect of relative deprivation need detailed information on household social spending in major events and other interested behaviors that previous data sets do not have. More importantly, social network information that helps identify reference groups is missing in the literature. In addition, most of the data sets do not have accurate factor market information, such as wage rate, interest rate, bride price, and land rental rate.

Further, household panel data is needed to capture dynamic behaviors of status competitors. Panel data might also alleviate the simultaneity issue and omitted variable bias that may arise in a cross-section. Considering the panel data sets available, only a small portion of households in each village are interviewed. Among the interviewed, households in the tails of income distribution are tended to be overlooked. Although such datasets are helpful for measuring overall rural inequality, they are less useful for discerning inequality in a village. More importantly, despite its high costs and the resulting limited coverage, conducting a census-type panel survey provides a feasible way through which we acquire a complete picture of relative deprivation without relying on sampling. An ideal dataset further requires relative isolation from the outside market.

Therefore, an extensive in-depth panel dataset for only a few communities complements and improves upon the previous panel data. The IFPRI–CAAS is an example that satisfies the aforementioned major requirements: (1) three waves of census-type panel survey; (2) detailed information on social network, social status, and social behavior; (3) a geographically isolated region; (4) a large share of ethnic minorities that diversify social norms under study. These data features help us go beyond the immediate explanations of many important behaviors that are labeled with poverty, as poverty cannot really answer why not all poor people engage in these behaviors. Facilitating identification of social interactions, these features aid in understanding the heterogeneous patterns in behaviors that might improve policy targeting.

Applying the first two waves of the IFPRI–CAAS, Chen and Zhang (2009) explore the causality between social norm, status seeking, and blood donation behavior. First, they find preliminary evidence that social status seeking, intensified through positional spending and relative deprivation, drives more blood donation. Relative deprivation complements the measure of income inequality. Second, social norms matter through social pressure and imitation in networks. Further, contrary to the well-received idea, shocks do not consistently induce blood donation, suggesting the link between blood income and other needs that deserves further research.

Following the first two waves (2005 and 2007) of the IFPRI–CAAS, we conducted the 2010 wave in which extensive data collection on long-term gift exchange and social network was also implemented. Employing two identification strategies, i.e. instrumental variable and network-based identification, to control for the effect of social interactions on stigma behavior, Chen *et al.* (2010) estimate the impact of concern for relative income using all three waves of the IFPRI–CAAS. Apart from the income effect, Chen *et al.* (2010) find that social influences and relative concern are two key determining factors. First, the poor are faced with more pressure to raise social status, thereby donating blood. The pressure to donate blood is especially salient for households with more unmarried sons, suggesting tightening tension in the unbalanced marriage market. Second, the disutility associated with blood donation drops as more people in a reference group participate. A person's preference on stigmatized behavior is largely shaped by the behavior of peers.

Conclusions

China's rapid economic growth over the last 30 years has equipped her with the world's second largest economy. China has also witnessed a huge increase in average living standards. However, resource distribution is getting more and more unequal between urban and rural, east and west, coastal and inland China. There are mounting concerns that the growing inequality might hinder sharing of the fruits of economic development, and the resulting social unrest may slow down economic transition.

However, it is first a miracle in human history that China has succeeded in sustaining fast growth and declining poverty for the last three decades. Meanwhile, it is also a miracle that China could successfully manage a stable society and smooth development when the Gini coefficient has already hit the widely accepted critical point in the early period. The study of income distribution and well-being in this fast transforming society is vital to understand this success, which might pave the way for improved policy-making and more harmonious growth, and substantially contribute to economics.

According to China's official statistics, the rural population of China still accounts for more than half of the total population. With unequal access to education, healthcare, the rural financial system, and non-farm opportunities, combined with low returns to agriculture, focusing on rural inequality and social class divergence are of utmost importance in maintaining economic growth and social stability in contemporary China.

Most previous studies of rural inequality and well-being in rural China use cross-sectional data, focusing on their levels, trends, and sources of inequality. The primary analyses have been built on macro data up until late 1990s. The last decade has witnessed a second wave of inequality studies dominated by micro panel datasets.

This chapter serves as one of the first comprehensive reviews of studies on those critical issues that use available longitudinal datasets from rural China. Most importantly, the fast but unequal economic growth suggests that relative concern based on resource distribution matters greatly to well-being for people of different backgrounds, albeit largely neglected in the current policy discourse and academia. Highlighting it as an urgent direction to be explored, our unique dataset and research project may initiate the third wave of upgraded studies on distribution and well-being.

Notes

1 The main aggregate results can be found in: *Statistical Yearbook of China*, *Rural Statistical Yearbook of China*, *Yearbook of Household Survey*, *Annual/quarterly Statistical Analysis Report*, and relevant research papers.
2 The RHS–NBS began to value in-kind components of income at approximate market prices since 1990.
3 Both the RCRE and CHNS surveys simply ask respondents for total revenue and expenditure from family businesses, while the distinction between fixed and variable costs is often lost in the enumeration process. In general, this is among the most difficult sources of income to enumerate accurately. Considerable efforts were placed in the CCAP 2000 survey by careful enumeration of balance sheets of family businesses. However, the CCAP 2000 is only a cross-sectional dataset.
4 Another interpretation for the underestimation of income inequality is that the much higher valuation of in-kind income in the RCRE data for the years 1993–1995 helped dampen the effect of dis-equalizing growth in wage and business incomes. The effect is temporary. However, once farm prices begin to fall, we see the sharp increase in inequality associated with falling farm incomes in the RCRE data.
5 For instance, income from farm-household production, forestry, animal husbandry, handicrafts, gifts as well as labor earnings and income received as a gift are included. Borrowings from (or loans to) informal and/or formal sources are excluded.
6 Benjamin *et al.* (2005a) estimate the ratio of the market-to-quota price, which was as high as 1.46 in 1995, and then fell below 1 by 1997. After 1997, the NBS series has been directly related to the market price, and they observe some convergence in the income and consumption series.
7 From 1991 to 1996 the NBS instructed survey teams to use an "average contract price" to value non-marketed grain from own production. This average contract price was the weighted average of the quota price and the above quota price for sales over quota to the local grain bureau. Both of these prices were administratively determined. Survey teams were further instructed to use weighted average market prices only if there were no local administrative prices (meaning no local crop procurement). It was not until 1997 that the NBS instructed survey teams to value all non-marketed agricultural commodities at market prices.
8 Chen and Ravallion (1996) find that after revaluation of income in kind from gain production, a much larger share of the (albeit smaller) increase in rural inequality was due to grain income than past data would have suggested.
9 Six concepts are quantified to measure macro income mobility: time-independence, positional movement, share movement, non-directional income movement, directional income movement, and income mobility as an equalizer of longer-term incomes (Fields 2007).
10 Two types of micro mobility studies have been conducted. Unconditional micro mobility examines individual correlates of income change as one of the correlates is controlled at

a time. Conditional micro mobility gauges the effect of one correlate controlling for the role of others.

11 The SRHS is a subjective measure of individual health, which suffers from measurement errors. However, studies show that the SRHS is highly correlated with subsequent mortality, even when more objective health measures are controlled (Deaton and Paxson 1998).

12 The permanent income hypothesis and the life cycle hypothesis are two typical examples.

13 Kawachi *et al.* (1997) summarize plausible mechanisms linking income inequality and outcomes, which include erosion of social capital and stressful social comparisons.

14 However, the analysis is based on the state level and needs to be improved.

References

Anderson, S. (2007) 'The Economics of Dowry and Bride Price', *Journal of Economic Perspectives*, 21 (4): 151–74.

Araar, A. (2008) 'On the Decomposition of Polarization Indices: Illustrations with Chinese and Nigerian Household Surveys', Cahier de recherché/working paper, 08–06.

Banerjee, A. V. and Duflo, E. (2007) 'The Economic Lives of the Poor', *Journal of Economic Perspectives*, 21 (1): 141–167.

Banerjee, A.V. and Newman, A. (1993) 'Occupational Choice and the Process of Development', *Journal of Political Economy*, 101 (2): 274–98.

Benjamin, D., Brandt, L., Glewwe, P. and Guo, L. (2002) 'Markets, Human Capital, and Inequality: Evidence from Rural China', in R. Freeman (ed.) *Inequality Around the World*, London: Palgrave, 87–127.

Benjamin, D., Brandt, L. and Giles, J. (2005a) 'The Evolution of Income Inequality in Rural China', *Economic Development and Cultural Change*, 53 (4): 769–824.

Benjamin, D., Brandt, L., Giles, J. and Wang, S. (2005b) 'Income Inequality during China's Economic Transition', working papers tecipa-238.

Benjamin, D., Brandt, L. and Giles, J. (2006) 'Inequality and Growth in Rural China: Does Higher Inequality Impede Growth?', IZA Discussion Paper No. 2344. Available at SSRN: http://ssrn.com/abstract=937877.

Brown, P., Bulte, E. and Zhang, X. (2010) 'Positional Spending and Status Seeking in Rural China', forthcoming in *Journal of Development Economics*.

Chen, Y. (2005) 'The impact of Agricultural and Industrial Development on Income inequality in Rural China', doctoral dissertation, Chapter 3, Boston College.

Chen, S. and Ravallion, M. (1996) 'Data in transition: Assessing rural living standards in southern China', *China Economic Review*, 7: 23–56.

Chen, X. and Zhang, X (2009) 'Blood for Social Status: A Tale of Three Villages in Rural China', paper presentation at AAEA 2009 Annual Meeting, Milwaukee.

Chen, X., Sahn, D. and Zhang, X. (2010) 'Relative Income, Network Interactions and Social Stigma', paper presentation at IAMO Forum 2010 in Halle, Germany.

Deaton, A. (2001) 'Relative Deprivation, Inequality, and Mortality', NBER working paper #8099, Cambridge, MA: National Bureau of Economics Research.

Deaton, A. and Paxson, C. (1998) 'Aging and Inequality in Income and Health', *American Economic Review*, 88 (2): 248–53.

De Brauw, A. and Giles, J. (2008) 'Migrant Labor Markets and the Welfare of Rural Households in the Developing World: Evidence from China', Policy Research Working Paper Series 4585, the World Bank.

De Brauw, A. and Rozelle, S. (2008) 'Migration and Household Investment in Rural China', *China Economic Review*, 19 (2): 320–335.

Dekker, M. and Hoogeveen, H. (2002) 'Bridewealth and Household Security in Rural Zimbabwe', *Journal of African Economies*, 11 (1): 114–145.

Duesenberry, J. (1949) *Income, Saving, and the Theory of Consumer Behavior*, Cambridge, Mass.: Harvard University Press.

Duncan, R. and Tian, X. (1999) 'China's Inter-provincial Disparities: an Explanation', *Communist and Post-Communist Studies*, 32: 211–224.

Easterlin, R. (1974) 'Does Economic Growth Improve the Human Lot? Some Empirical Evidence', in P. David and M. Reder (eds) *Nations and Households in Economic Growth*, New York: Academic Press, 89–126.

Fafchamps, M. and Shilpi, F. (2008) 'Subjective Welfare, Isolation, and Relative Consumption', *Journal of Development Economics*, 86 (1): 43–60.

Fields, G. (2007) 'Income Mobility', ILR working paper, Cornell University.

Frank, R. (1985) *Choosing the Right Pond*, New York: Oxford University Press.

Frank, R. and Levine, A. (2008) 'Expenditure Cascades', working paper, Cornell University.

Fujita, M. and Hu, D. (2001) 'Regional Disparity in China 1985–1994: the Effect of Globalization and Economic Liberalization', *Annals of Regional Science*, 35: 3–37.

Guo, J. (2007) 'Changing Income Inequality: Evidence from Rural China', working paper, Department of Economics, University of Warwick.

Gustafsson, B. and Li, S. (1998) 'Inequality in China at the End of the 1980s: Locational Aspects and Household Characteristics', *Asian Economic Journal*: 35–63.

Gustafsson, B. and Li, S. (2002) 'Income Inequality Within and Across Counties in Rural China 1988 and 1995', *Journal of Development Economics*, 69: 179–204.

Gustafsson, B., Li., S. and Sicualar, T. (2007) *Inequality and Public Policy in China*, New York: Cambridge University Press.

Heffetz, O. (2007) 'Conspicuous Consumption and the Visibility of Consumption Expenditures', working paper, Cornell University. Online. Available at: http://forum.johnson.cornell.edu/faculty/heffetz/papers/consp.pdf (accessed November 16, 2008).

Hoken, H., Senda, T., Matsuda, Y., Tsujii, H. and Cao, L. (2006) 'Statistical Matching for Longitudinal Data of Rural Households in China: Construction of MHTS Panel Data Set and Estimation of Attrition Bias', NO. E2006013, CCER working paper, Peking University.

Holz, C. and Brandt, L. (2004) 'Spatial Price Differences in China: Estimates and Implications', manuscript. University of Toronto. Online. Available at: http://ssrn.com/abstract=689224 (accessed March 18, 2009).

Howes, S. and Hussain, A. (1994) 'Regional Growth and Inequality in Rural China', working paper, London School of Economics.

Huang, J., Zhang, Q. and Rozelle, S. (2008) 'Economic growth, the nature of growth and poverty reduction in rural China', *China Economic Journal*, 1 (1): 107–122.

Jalan, J. and Ravallion, M. (1998) 'Transient Poverty in Post Reform Rural China', *Journal of Comparative Economics*, 26 (2): 338–57.

Jian, T., Sachs, J. and Warder, A. (1996) 'Trends in Regional Inequality in China', *China Economic Review*, 7 (1): 1–21.

Kanbur, R. (2000) 'Income Distribution and Development', in A. B. Atkinson and F. Bourguignon (eds) *Handbook of Income Distribution*, Vol. 1, North Holland.

Kanbur, R. and Zhang, X. (1999) 'Which Regional Inequality? The Evolution of Rural–Urban and Inland–Coastal Inequality in China from 1983 to 1995', *Journal of Comparative Economics*, 27: 686–701.

Kawachi, I., Kennedy, B. P., Lochner, K. and Prothrow-Stith, D. (1997) 'Social Capital, Income Inequality, and Mortality', *American Journal of Public Health*, 87 (9): 1491–1498.

Kempen, L. (2003) 'Status consumption and ethnicity in Bolivia: Evidence from Durables Ownership', *International Journal of Consumer Studies*, 31 (1): 76–89.

Khan, A. and Riskin, C. (1998) 'Income and Inequality in China: Composition, Distribution and Growth of Household Income 1988 to 1995', *China Quarterly*, No. 154: 221–53.

Khan, A., Griffin, K. and Riskin, C. (1999) 'Income Distribution in Urban China during the Period of Economic Reform and Globalization', *American Economic Review*, 89 (2): 296–300.

Khan, A., Griffin, K., Riskin, C. and Zhao, R. (1993) 'Sources of Income Inequality in Post-Reform China', *China Economic Review*, 4: 19–35.

Khor, N. and Pencavel, J. (2005) 'Income Disparities and Income Mobility in China', paper delivered at the Conference on China's Policy Reforms: Progress and Challenges, Stanford University Center for International Development, October 1.

Khor, N. and Pencavel, J. (2006) 'Income Mobility of Individuals in China and the United States', IZA research paper, No. 2003.

Knack, S. and Keefer, P. (1997) 'Does Social Capital Have an Economic Payoff? A Cross-Country Investigation', *Quarterly Journal of Economics*, 112 (4).

Li, H. and Zhu, Y. (2006) 'Income, Income Inequality, and Health: Evidence from China', *Journal of Comparative Economics*, 34 (4): 668–693.

Li, S., Wang, P. and Yue, X. (2005) 'The Causes of Chronic and Transient Poverty and Their Implication to Poverty Reduction Policy in Rural China', Final Report to Poverty and Economic Poverty (PEP) Network. Online. Available at: http://www.pep-net.org/ (accessed August 22, 2008).

Liang, Z. (2006) 'Financial Development and Income Inequality in Rural China 1991–2000', WIDER research paper, 2006/96.

Ling, D. (2007) 'Relative Deprivation and Children's Health in China', working paper, California State University, Fullerton.

Ling, D. (2008) 'Do the Chinese "Keep Up with the Joneses"? Implications of Growing Economic Disparities and Relative Deprivation on Health Outcomes among Older Adults in China', working paper, California State University, Fullerton.

Liu, X., *In One's Own Shadow: An Ethnographic Account of the Condition of Post-Reform China*, Berkeley: University of California Press.

Lokshin, M. and Ravallion, M. (2001) 'Nonlinear Household Income Dynamics in Transition Economies', Mimeo, Development Research Group, the World Bank.

Lyons, T. (1991) 'Interprovincial Disparities in China: Output and Consumption, 1952–1987', *Economic Development and Cultural Change*, 39: 471–506.

McCulloch, N. and Calandrino, M. (2003) 'Vulnerability and Chronic Poverty in Rural Sichuan', *World Development*, 31 (3): 611–628.

Morduch, J. and Sicular, T. (2002) 'Rethinking Inequality Decomposition, with Evidence from Rural China', *Economic Journal*, 112: 93–106.

NBS (various years). *China Statistical Yearbook*. Beijing: China Statistical Publishing House.

Nee, V. (1994) 'The Emergence of a Market Society: Changing Mechanisms of Stratification in China', *American Journal of Sociology*, 101 (4): 908–949.

Peng, Y. (1999) 'Agricultural and Nonagricultural Growth and Intercounty Inequality in China 1985–1991', *Modern China*, 25 (3): 235–263.

Rao, V. (1993) 'The Rising Price of Husbands: A Hedonic Analysis of Dowry Increases in Rural India', *Journal of Political Economy*, 101: 666–677.

Ravallion, M. (1998) 'Does Aggregation Hide the Harmful Effects of Inequality on Growth?', *Economics Letters*, 61: 73–77.

Ravallion, M. and Chen, S. (1999) 'When Economic Reform Is Faster Than Statistical Reform: Measuring and Explaining Income Inequality in Rural China', *Oxford Bulletin of Economics and Statistics*, 61 (1): 33–56.

Ravallion, M. and Chen, S. (2007) 'China's (Uneven) Progress Against Poverty', *Journal of Development Economics*, 82 (1): 1–42.

Ravallion, M. and Jalan, J. (2001) 'Household Income Dynamics in Rural China', Policy Research Working Paper Series 2706, the World Bank.

Rozelle, S. (1994) 'Rural Industrialization and Increasing Inequality: Emerging Patterns in China's Reforming Economy', *Journal of Comparative Economics*, 19: 362–391.

Runciman, W. G. (1966) *Relative Deprivation and Social Justice*, Routledge & Kegan Paul.

Sen, A. (1983) 'Poor, Relatively Speaking', *Oxford Economic Papers*. New Series, 35 (2): 153–169.

Shen, Y and Yao, Y. (2008) 'Does Grassroots Democracy Reduce Income Inequality in China?', *Journal of Public Economics*, 92 (10–11): 2182–98.

Stark, O. and Taylor, J. E. (1991) 'Migration Incentives, Migration Types: The Role of Relative Deprivation', *Economic Journal*, 101: 1163–1178.

The Economist (2007) 'Can Ghanaians Afford Such Splendid Funerals?', May 24.

Tsui, K.-Y. (1993) 'Decomposition of China's Regional Inequality', *Journal of Comparative Economics*, 17: 600–627.

Tsui, K.-Y. (1998a) 'Factor Decomposition of Chinese Rural Income Inequality: New Methodology, Empirical Findings, and Policy Implications', *Journal of Comparative Economics*, 26 (3): 502–528.

Tsui, K.-Y. (1998b) 'Trends and Inequality of Rural Welfare in China: Evidence from Rural Households in Guangdong and Sichuan', *Journal of Comparative Economics*, 26: 783–804.

Van de Stadt, H., Kapteyn, A. and Van de Geer, S. (1985) 'The Relativity of Utility: Evidence from Panel Data', *Review of Economics and Statistics*, 67 (2): 179–187.

Veblen, T. (1899) *The Theory of the Leisure Class*, MacMillan, New York.

Wan, G. (2005) 'Convergence in Food Consumption in Rural China: Evidence from Household Survey Data', *China Economic Review*, 16 (1): 90–102.

Wan, G. (2007) 'Regional Income Inequality in Rural China, 1985–2002: Trends, Causes and Policy Implications', WIDER research paper, 2007/05.

Wan, G. and Zhou, Z. (2005) 'Income Inequality in Rural China: Regression-based Decomposition Using Household Data', *Review of Development Economics*, 9 (1): 107–120.

Wang, H. (2005) 'The Household Income Mobility and its Equalizing Long-term Income in China', *Economic Research Journal*, No. 1: 56–66.

Whalley, J. and Yue, X. (2006) 'Rural Income Volatility and Inequality in China', NBER working paper No. W12779.

Wilkinson, R. G. (1997) 'Health Inequalities: Relative or Absolute Material Standards?' *British Medical Journal*, 314: 591–595.

World Bank (1992) 'China: Statistical System in Transition', Online. Available at: http://www.worldbank.org/research/1992/09/736924/china-statistical-system-transition (accessed March 2, 2009).

Yan, Y. (1996) *The Flow of Gifts: Reciprocity and Social Networks in a Chinese Village*, Stanford: Stanford University Press.

Yao, S., Zhang, Z. and Hanmer, L. (2004) 'Growing Inequality and Poverty in China', *China Economic Review*, 15 (2): 145–163.

Ying, H., Li, S. and Deng, Q. (2006) 'Income Mobility in Urban China', *Economic Research Journal*, 10: 30–43.

Zhang, Q., Huang, J. and Mi, J. (2006) 'Income Inequality and Economic Mobility in Rural China: Who Can Move up the Ladder of Success?', working paper, Northwestern University.

Zhang, X. (2009) 'Fiscal Decentralization and Political Centralization in China: Implications for Growth and Inequality', in S. Fan, R. Kanbur and X. Zhang (eds) *Regional Inequality in China: Trends, Explanations and Policy Responses*, London and New York: the Routledge.

Zhang, X. and Kanbur, R. (2001) 'What Difference Do Polarisation Measures Make? An Application to China', *Journal of Development Studies*, 37 (3): 85–98.

Zhang, X. and Tan, K. (2007) 'Incremental Reform and Distortions in China's Product and Factor Markets', *The World Bank Economic Review*, 21 (2): 279–299.

Zhang, X. and Zhang, K. (2009) 'How does Globalization Affect Regional Inequality within a Developing Country? Evidence from China', in S. Fan, R. Kanbur and X. Zhang (eds) *Regional Inequality in China: Trends, Explanations and Policy Responses*, London and New York: the Routledge.

12 Determinants of China's inter-regional equalization of basic public services

Xuebing Tang

Introduction

Since the Reform and Opening-up policies were implemented 30 years ago, local governments in China have played a minor role in the field of basic public services (BPS). This has led to a serious shortage of these services, with the welfare system not having developed as rapidly as economic growth as a result. Education, health, and housing have become the huge burden of Chinese people (Zhang 2005). At the same time, due to the inconsistency of China's regional economic development, the disparity in the economic development between the Eastern regions and the Central Western regions has been gradually increasing. This has led to a large deficiency the provision of regional BPS in a context of ambiguous goals and the non-standardized operation of an inter-governmental transfer payment system. Nowadays China's BPS typically has these characteristics: "overall low level, uneven development, low-level-convergence efficiency" (Chen and Cai 2007). However, inter-regional Equalization of Basic Public Services (EBPS) requires a service-oriented government, a harmonious society, and an increase in the capacity of society to reduce regional economic disparities, to co-operate in the implementation of the main functional areas, and to regional development. The current expansion of central government's financial capacity and the transformation of government functions provide a solid economic and political foundation for Chinese EBPS. Therefore, EBPS has an important practical and theoretical significance.

This chapter has two innovations. First, I have developed China's inter-provincial evaluation system of the EBPS by conducting interviews with experts and employing eigenvalue methods, and then analyzing the features of Chinese regional EBPS. Current literature places more emphasis on qualitative research on China's inter-provincial evaluation system of EBPS. Chen and Cai (2007) constructed the most comprehensive performance evaluation system of BPS for which they chose 165 indicators to research eight BPS. However, they focused on regional differences in the performance of China's BPS. An and Ren (2008) chose seven BPS and 16 single indicators to measure China's inter-provincial EBPS from 2000 to 2006. However, a limitation here was that they chose too few standard indicators, which indicated that superior regions strengthen their position of advantage. This was certain to draw the conclusion that the gap in China's inter-provincial BPS has been increasing, which contradicts the fact that inferior regions have improved their BPS level since 1994. Also, their research period is too short to draw reliable and scientific conclusions.

The evaluation system developed in this chapter is composed of 35 inter-provincial indicators from 1996 to 2006. These include Chinese inter-provincial BPS index as first-level indicators, and education, public health and medical care, public culture; scientific research, employment and social security, public infrastructure, and environmental protection as secondary indicators. It has been found that China's inter-provincial EBPS is low and has displayed a downward trend. The equalization level of all kinds of BPS varies significantly – the services for which the level of equalization is quite good are public cultural services, public infrastructure services, and ecological and environmental protection services. Services where equalization is not so strong are employment and social security, public health, and medical services. Services in urgent need of attention include education and research and development (R&D).

Second, I use panel data to analyze the determinants of inter-provincial EBPS in China. There are few papers utilizing qualitative analysis of the determinants of Chinese inter-provincial EBPS, and these papers mainly focus on transfer payments. Song and Yuan (2008) used China's inter-provincial panel data for the period 1998 to 2005 to analyse the role of transfer payments in China. They indicated that China's policy of transfer payments had been determined by the need to maintain national stability, reduce resistance to reform and consider the political equilibrium of central authorities. Therefore its role in EBPS is not significant. Liu (2008) suggests that transfer payments play a limited role in narrowing the regional gap in financial capability. Therefore, his research is relatively narrow in perspective, neglecting other factors affecting the EBPS.

Utilising econometric analysis, this study analyzed the reasons why Chinese regional EBPS has been declining. I found that regional disparities in economic development, differences in fiscal decentralization, the degree of inward investment, marketization, and the level of urbanization all indicate a significant positive correlation with the regional provision of BPS. Regional disparities in financial capacity and governmental preferences indicate a significant negative correlation with the level of regional provision of BPS; however, transfer payments from central government do not play a role in promoting the EBPS. This suggests that in order to improve regional EBPS in China, disparities in regional economic development should be controlled within an acceptable range and that a normative fiscal decentralization and an appropriate system of transfer payments should be established. At the same time, central government should reform the current rigid system of household registration management to ensure a rational flow of population and to induce local governments to improve the supply of BPS rather rely on the competition for regional economic growth.

The rest of the chapter is organized as follows: the first section outlines the dynamic evaluation system of China's EBPS which was developed during this research, and analyzes its characteristics from 1996 to 2006. The second section presents the main results concerning the determinants of China's inter-regional EBPS. The third section outlines the conclusions of this research.

Dynamic evaluation system and assessment results of China's inter-provincial equalization of BPS

Selection and design of the dynamic evaluation system

In this study, the dynamic evaluation system of China's inter-provincial EBPS is divided into a three-tier rating system:

- *Primary indicators:* inter-regional equalization index of BPS. In accordance with the connotation of inter-regional EBPS, this indicator was established to measure levels of inter-provincial equalization for all BPS in China. In fact, a primary indicator is a/the coefficient of variation, so the greater the value of the primary indicator, the lower the degree of China's inter-provincial EBPS.
- *Secondary indicators:* this study adopted basic education, public health and medical care, public culture, scientific research, employment and social security, public infrastructure, and environmental protection as secondary indicators of China's BPS. The selection of these indicators not only stresses the importance of basic public services as public goods, but also highlights the importance of current financial constraints and the requirements of central government's overall strategic objectives.
- *Tertiary indicators:* the selection of tertiary indicators considers the corresponding economic and social implications of secondary indicators and its availability. At the same time, per capita indicators are required to avoid the impact of population size. Finally, some of these tertiary indicators must be flow indicators and the others stock indicators.[1]

To summarize, each secondary indicator is made up of five to seven tertiary indicators. Therefore I selected 35 tertiary indicators to make up my dynamic evaluation system of China's inter-provincial EBPS, as shown in Table 12.1.

Assessment method

BPS can be divided into seven categories, so the equalization evaluation system of BPS is a multi-dynamic comprehensive evaluation method requiring a mathematical model which will translate multiple indicators into a holistic indicator. This study proposes a dynamic evaluation system of China's inter-provincial EBPS, utilizing an experts-questionnaire and employing eigenvalue methods. These are calculated as follows:

If X_{ijt} is an original indicator of region i at time t in service j, P_{it} is the population size of region i at time t.

A seven-step model is proposed:

Step I: involves a pre-treatment evaluation of indicators. First of all, aggregate indicators are converted into per capita indicators as follows:

$$\bar{X}_{ijt} = \frac{X_{ijt}}{P_{it}} \tag{12.1}$$

Table 12.1 China's inter-provincial equalization evaluation system of BPS

First indicator	*Secondary indicator*	*Third indicator*	*Units*
China's inter-provincial equalization index of BPS	Basic education	Budget expenditure on education for every student in primary school	Yuan/student
		Budget expenditure on education for every student in junior school	Yuan/student
		Budget expenditure on education for every student in high school	Yuan/student
		Full-time teachers for every student in ordinary primary school	Person/student
		Full-time teachers for every student in ordinary secondary school	Person/student
	Public health and basic medicine	Budget expenditures per capita health expenditure	Yuan per capita
		The number of beds per 10,000 people	Piece
		The number of doctors per 10,000 people	Number
		Water coverage in city	%
		The number of public toilets in city per 10,000 people	Number
	Public culture	Expenditure of culture and sports broadcasting per capita	Yuan per capita
		Broadcasting population coverage	%
		TV population coverage	%
		The number of public libraries per 10,000 people	Number
	Basic R&D	The fees of three items in technology per capita	Yuan per capita
		Technological spending per capita	Yuan per capita
		The number of domestic invention patents per 10,000 people	Item
		The number of domestic design patents per 10,000 people	Item
		The number of domestic patent applications per 10,000 people	Item
	Employment and social security services	The registered urban unemployment rate	%
		Per capita expenditure on social security	Yuan per capita
		The ratio of old-age insurance to total population	%

Table 12.1 Continued

First indicator	*Secondary indicator*	*Third indicator*	*Units*
		The ratio of medical insurance to total population	%
		The ratio of industrial injury insurance to total population	%
		The ratio of maternity insurance to total population	%
		The ratio of unemployment insurance to total population	%
	Public infrastructure	The number of owned mobile phones per 100 people	Number
		The capacity of owned telephone exchanges per 100 people	Number
		The number of owned local telephones per 100 people	Hu
		Highway mileage per capita	M
	Ecological services and environmental protection	Urban public green area per capita	m^2
		Integrated utilization rate of industrial solid waste	%
		Green area of the urban park per capita	m^2
		The ratio of nature reserve area to land area	Hectare/10,000 hectares
		The ratio of comprehensive utilization value of waste products of industry to industrial output value	%

Next is the uniformization of the indicators; and since there is only one minimum (the smaller the better) indicator, the registered urban unemployment rate, hence:

$$\bar{X}_{ijt} = 1 - X_{ijt} \tag{12.2}$$

This indicator has been translated into a maximum of one. As for the relative indicators, they remain unchanged $\bar{X}_{ijt} = X_{ijt}$.

Finally, dimension indicators must be translated into dimensionless ones. If M_{jt} and m_{jt} are the maximum and minimum values of $\bar{X}_{ijt}$, these are:

$$x_{ijt} = \frac{\bar{X}_{ijt} - m_{jt}}{M_{ij} - m_{jt}} \tag{12.3}$$

It is clear that the range of dimensionless indicators is [0, 1].

Step II: We sent a questionnaire to 10 experts and asked them for the relative importance of the indicators in Table 12.1. Then according to theses experts' opinions, we ranked the indictors and gave each a different weighted value (ranking the more heavily weighted higher) p_{ij}.

Step III: We determined the weighted value of tertiary indicators according to the eigenvalue method. If the seven sub-categories of services are a sub-system, and x_{ijt} is an indicator after pre-treatment of sub-system x in region i at time t item j, then transforming $x^*_{ijt} = p_{ij}x_{ijt}$, and this data then forms a matrix as indicated below:

$$A_t = \begin{vmatrix} x^*_{11} & x^*_{12} & \dots & x^*_{1m} \\ x^*_{21} & x^*_{22} & \dots & x^*_{2m} \\ \dots & \dots & \dots & \dots \\ x^*_{n1} & x^*_{n1} & \dots & x^*_{nm} \end{vmatrix} \tag{12.4}$$

We then structured the symmetric matrix $H_t = (A_t)^T A_t$, and calculated the maximum eigenvalue $\lambda_{\max}$ and the corresponding Eigenvector b_j of H_t. Finally, we normalized b_j $(j = 1, 2, \dots, m)$, to achieve the weighted coefficient of indicators x_{ijt}:

$$w_{jt} = \frac{b_j}{\sum_{j=1}^{m} b_j} \tag{12.5}$$

Step IV: Here we developed the comprehensive evaluation function of the secondary sub-system function region i at time t:

$$s_{it} = \sum_{j=1}^{n} w_{jt}x_{ijt} \tag{12.6}$$

s_{it} represents the relative developmental degree of different types of BPS.

Step V: We calculated the coefficient of variation (CV) to gain the equalization level of sub-BPS at time t:

$$cv_t = \frac{\sqrt{\frac{\sum_{j=1}^{n}(s_{it}-\bar{s}_t)^2}{n-1}}}{\bar{s}_t} \times 100\% \tag{12.7}$$

$\bar{s}_t$ is the average value of sub-BPS at time t in all regions. The greater cv_t is, the lower the degree of equalization of sub-BPS.

Step VI: The importance of sub-BPS varies. Based on the experts-questionnaire approach, we got weighted coefficients u_i of sub-BPS, and finally obtained a composite indicator of BPS for all regions S_{it}:

$$S_{it} = \sum_{i=1}^{7} u_i s_{it} \tag{12.8}$$

Then we calculated the coefficient of variation of S_{it}:

$$CV_t = \frac{\sqrt{\frac{\sum_{i=1}^{n}(S_{it}-\bar{S}_t)^2}{n-1}}}{\bar{S}_t} \times 100\% \tag{12.9}$$

$\bar{S}_t$ represents an average value of overall BPS at time t for all regions. The greater CV indicates a lower degree of EBPS.

Step VII: We repeated the above steps and calculated cv_t and CV_t at time t, hence we achieve an evolution process for EBPS in China.

Data sources and assessment results

Limited by the data's availability and integrity, I collected provincial data from 1996 to 2006, apart from Tibet. Most of the data came from the *China Statistical Yearbook* from 1997 to 2007, *China Compendium of Statistics* 1949–2004, *New China Fifty years' Government Finance Statistics*, *Finance Yearbook of China* from 1997 to 2007, *China Educational Finance Statistics Yearbook* from 1997 to 2007, and the *Provincial Statistics Yearbook* and *CEI Statistical Database*.

We derived China's inter-provincial EBPS as indicated in Table 12.2 by using calculation methods for the above indicators.

From the overall level and organic composition of China's inter-provincial EBPS, we can draw the following conclusions:

First, China's inter-provincial EBPS has been lower and had a downward trend. As can be seen from Table 12.2, this index has remained above 0.45, reaching a high of 0.54 in 2005, which basically validates the conclusion drawn by Chen and Cai (2007) – BPS in China is "uneven development, the overall level low." The overall equalization index presented an upward trend which peaked in 2005 and declined slightly in 2006. This indicates that the gap in the supply of BPS in China is gradually widening between provinces. Fortunately, the index in 2006 is less than the index in 2005, which shows that this deteriorating trend of EBPS may be improving. Owing to a greater emphasis on the implementation of BPS from central government and governments at all levels in recent times, inter-provincial EBPS may gradually increase in the future. In order to draw a comparison with inter-provincial economic gaps, I also calculated the inter-provincial weighted coefficient of variation of per capita GDP in China from 1996 to 2006. As can be seen from Figure 12.1, the coefficient of variation of per capita GDP has been

Table 12.2 China's inter-provincial equalization index of BPS (1996–2006)

Year	*BPS*	*Basic education*	*Public health and basic medicine*	*Public culture*	*Basis scientific research*	*Employment and social security*	*Public infrastructure*	*Environmental protection*
1996	0.466	0.71	0.545	0.386	1.242	0.525	0.496	0.402
1997	0.456	0.762	0.537	0.355	1.195	0.339	0.503	0.392
1998	0.495	0.77	0.538	0.328	1.135	0.6	0.492	0.398
1999	0.478	0.805	0.527	0.332	1.263	0.466	0.47	0.438
2000	0.487	0.834	0.627	0.3	1.203	0.465	0.435	0.358
2001	0.511	0.838	0.6	0.327	1.325	0.613	0.466	0.367
2002	0.513	0.856	0.632	0.33	1.328	0.49	0.451	0.405
2003	0.502	0.88	0.577	0.363	1.375	0.507	0.432	0.363
2004	0.499	0.896	0.555	0.364	1.36	0.534	0.454	0.355
2005	0.542	0.899	0.751	0.389	1.362	0.586	0.437	0.393
2006	0.523	0.94	0.563	0.374	1.386	0.666	0.379	0.403

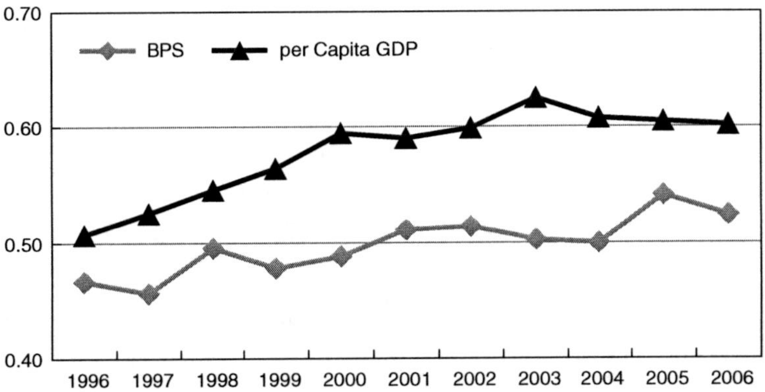

Figure 12.1 China's inter-provincial equalization index of overall BPS (1996–2006).

greater than the equalization index of BPS, which accounts for the fact that the inter-provincial gaps in BPS are less than the gap in economic development. It is noteworthy that the economic gap between China's provinces has gradually reduced since 2003, and the equalization index of BPS began to decline in 2006, lagging by three years.

Second, sub-BPS vary significantly in their degrees of equalization. Based on the average equalization level of sub-BPS in 2002–2006, seven sub-BPS can be divided into three categories: relatively acceptable, much-improved, and urgent-to-improve.

Relatively acceptable services in terms of equalization include public culture, public infrastructure, ecological services, and environmental protection. As can be seen from Figure 12.2, the equalization index for the three above-mentioned sub-services in the most recent five-year period were less than 0.45. This indicates that these sub-services had a relatively higher degree of equalization and the gap between them was controlled to a reasonable extent. However, the trajectories of these three sub-services are different. The equalization trajectory of public culture was "U-type," showing that the gap between provincial public cultural was initially wide and subsequently narrowed. The reason for this is because of the relative neglect of the public cultural projects until recently.

Much-improved services include employment, social security services, public health and medical services. The equalization index of these four sub-services was between 0.5 and 0.8, for seven sub-services, so their equalization degrees need improving. The trajectory of public health and basic medical services has been relatively stable (except in 2005), due to this service being a stock investment, mainly by local governments. Regional economic development determines the governments' input into public health and medical services, resulting in the regional economic disparity being the same as the gap in public health and basic medical services. The equalization index of employment and social security services

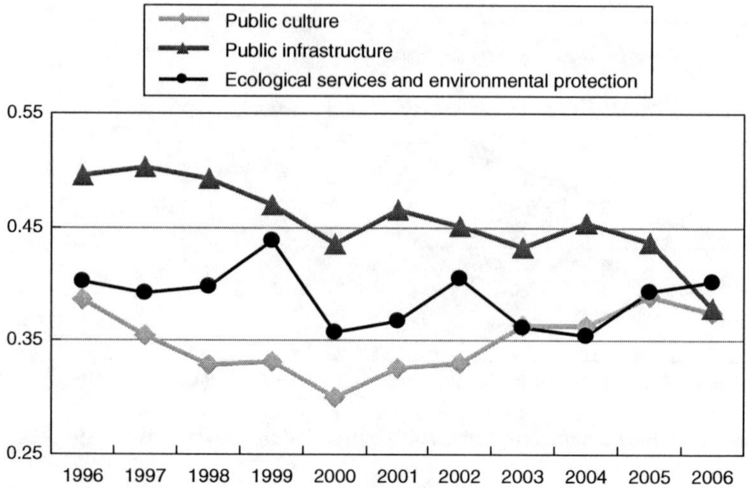

Figure 12.2 China's inter-provincial equalization index of public culture, public infrastructure, ecological services and environmental protection (1996–2006).

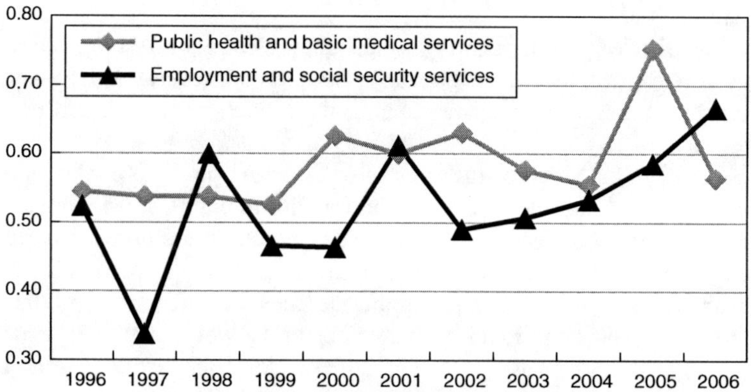

Figure 12.3 China's inter-provincial equalization index of employment and social security services, public health and basic medical services (1996–2006).

has tended to decrease recently, which shows that the regional gap in the provision of this service is gradually widening. This is mainly due to the increase of coverage and security standards being dependant on regional urbanization, living standards, and the size of the government's financial resources. In developed provinces and cities, the local increase in urbanization and living standards, combined with the increase in local governments' annual revenue being greater than GDP growth, contributes to an increase in fiscal expenditure on local job training

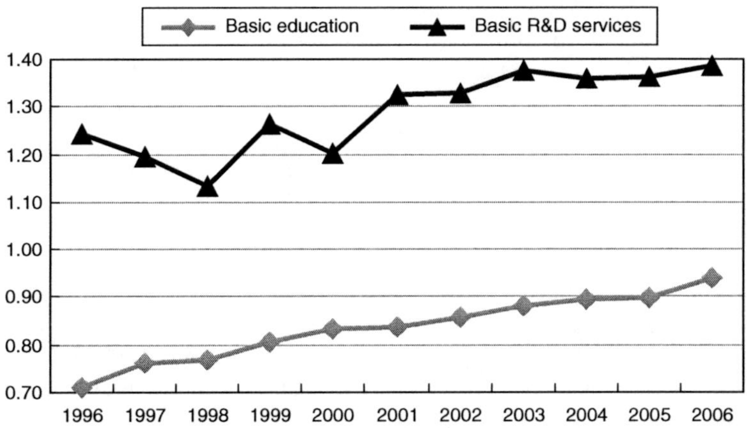

Figure 12.4 China's inter-provincial equalization index of basic education and basic R&D (1996–2006).

and social security standards. This has led to increasing inter-regional disparities for this BPS.

Basic education and R&D services are the ones which need most attention in terms of regional equalization. Here, the average equalization index has risen to 0.894 and 1.362 from 1996 to 2006, respectively, representing the highest differentials in the seven categories of basic services. As indicated in Figure 12.4, the equalization index for basic education increased from 0.71 in 1996 to 0.94 in 2006, indicating a rising disparity between regions in China in their provision of basic education services. Although the central government stressed the importance of basic education, the educational input mechanism of "one-province-one-entity" reinforced inter-provincial disparities. As education carries a greater weight in total BPS, a reduction in regional disparities for educational services will contribute to an improvement in overall inter-regional EBPS. The equalization index for R&D services has remained at 1.3 or above for the five years, indicating deteriorating inter-regional disparities, and this area requires urgent attention if this issue is to be addressed. In recent years, most of China's basic research funds have been allocated to developed regions – where most of the research institutes and universities are located. The lack of research funding in less developed regions results in a reluctance by high-quality talents in scientific research to work in these regions. This contributes to a vicious circle which leads to a mounting inter-regional gap in basic R&D services.

Determinants analyzing China's inter-regional equalization of BPS

Model settings

Determinants analyzing China's inter-provincial EBPS should begin with the supply- and demand-side factors. From the perspective of supply factors, regional economic development significantly impacts on the local supply-side capacity for BPS. If the tax rates between local governments' are the same then higher levels of local economic development in some regions will lead to greater income. Therefore, the gap between developed and developing regions will continue to increase. However, local residents in developed regions demand that their local government provides more and better quality basic services, and strongly reject foreign populations sharing local services. Local public goods tend to be used within its own region, with little crowding out by service providers in other regions and therefore can be seen as a national public goods. Therefore disparity in the level of economic development negatively correlates with the EBPS. That is, the greater the gap in per capita GDP, the greater the equalization degree of BPS is. What's more, transfer payments from central government to local government can compensate for an insufficient supply capacity in inter-regional BPS. Therefore, a rational transfer payment system could provide an appropriate tool in equalizing BPS. However, the transfer payment system in China is determined mainly by political considerations rather than economic ones, and includes inherent defects such as non-standard and non-transparent transfers. As a result, transfer payments in China play a minor role, or have a negative effect, in equalizing BPS. Another important supply factor for BPS is based on governments' bias, where decision-making at all levels of government in China follows the top-down model in relation to the provision of public goods such as education and infrastructure. Local governments' emphasis on GDP as a performance evaluator has resulted in a preference of supporting 'hard' public goods (such as roads and bridges) rather than 'soft' public goods (such as education, social security, public health, and basic medicine) to the extent that some local governments are currently in arrears with the payment of primary teachers' salaries. Therefore, the local preference for hard public goods also impacts on the supply level of BPS.

From the perspective of demand factors, the extent of marketization and inward investment, and the rate of urbanization and industrialization, significantly affect inter-regional demand for BPS. Domestic and foreign scholars generally believe that China's market-oriented reforms have put vitality into the Chinese economy, and improved the efficiency of resource allocation (Huang 2010). However, the degree of market-oriented progress in Eastern and Western regions are very clearly uneven. Higher levels of marketization require more efficient government functions, as local residents and businesses will progressively demand more and better quality BPS from local government. However, excessive marketization may also lead to certain basic services being privatized, resulting in a greater deficiencies in other BPS. Therefore, the relationship between the degree of marketization and EBPS is not clear. Rising levels of inward investment leads to an increase in foreign-funded local enterprises. Generally, the choice of location for foreign-funded enterprises tends to be the region with better quality BPS. Therefore, an increase in inward investment is often accompanied by an expansion of local BPS. In general, the growth in urbanization and industry require a high-quality development of BPS. The higher the rate of urbanization, the greater the concentration of demand for BPS per unit of land area. A consequence of this is a reduced per unit cost in supplying BPS due to economies of scale.

According to supply and demand factors for BPS, we can generally explain why China's inter-provincial EBPS continues to fall. As the gradual expansion in the reform of China's socialist market economy continues, the gap in economic development between China's various regions has intensified, and the corresponding financial gap between regions has also expanded. Therefore, if each region continues to rely solely on its own revenue for BPS, this gap will further increase. At the same time, China's reform and internationalization also relied on a process of gradual financial decentralization. As part of this process, the central government gradually acquired a much greater proportion of fiscal revenue, which led to inconsistencies relating to financial resources and responsibilities of governments at all levels. This requires central government to make transfer payments to local governments to compensate for the insufficient supply of BPS. However, due to deficiencies, transfer payments do not play a role in equalizing BPS. Moreover, local government's preference for hard public goods over soft public goods during this period of rapid industrialization and urbanization, has led to an inadequate supply of BPS. Local residents in developed regions demand higher quality and more BPS, which when added to the scale effects of supplying BPS, due to rapid urbanization and industrialization, ensure that local governments in developed regions have sufficient finance to provide basic services. Developing regions face lower rates of urbanization and industrialization, as well as migration of large numbers of surplus labor to developed regions. As a result, local government in developing regions is more preoccupied with economic development rather than the provision of basic services, leading to greater regional disparities. Therefore, China's inter-provincial EBPS has deteriorated.

China's inter-provincial equalization level of BPS is a function of the following factors:

$$E_p = f(PGDP, Finance, Prefer, Decentr, \\ Transfer, Open, Market, Urban) \quad (12.10)$$

In this function, *PGDP*, *Finance*, *Prefer*, *Decentr*, *Transfer*, *Open*, *Market*, *Urban*, refer, respectively, to inter-provincial differences in economic development, financial capacity, local governments' preferences, fiscal decentralization, size of transfer payments, inward investment, marketization, and urbanization.

In order to test the function, an empirical model was established as follows:

$$E_p = cons + a_1 gdp + a_2 finance + a_3 prefer + a_4 decentr + a_5 transfer \\ + a_6 open + a_7 market + a_8 urban + f_i + u_i \quad (12.11)$$

In this function, *cons* is a constant term, f_i regional effects, and u_i an error term.

Data description

Specific variables and data sources in the econometric model were described as follows:

The explained variable is s_{it} – China's inter-provincial equalization index of BPS, calculated in Equation (12.8). The indicators selected in this study considered all BPS by combining stock and flow indicators more objectively and comprehensively. At the same time, the indicators we obtained after weighting, reflecting the relative importance of different BPS.

- Inter-provincial disparities in economic development are the ratio of per capita GDP in one province compared to national per capita GDP. If the ratio is greater than 1, it indicates that the degree of economic development in that province is higher than the national average; if less than 1, it indicates that it is below the national average. Inter-provincial disparities in financial capacity are the ratio of per capita revenue in one province compared to national per capita revenue.
- Provincial governments' preference is the ratio of the investment in capital construction compared to total expenditure in local budgets.
- The degree of fiscal decentralization is the ratio of provincial per capita fiscal expenditure compared to the national figure.
- The size of transfer payments is the ratio of net per capita transfer payments in one province compared to the national figure.
- The level of internationalization is the ratio of total investments by foreign enterprises compared to per capita GDP in a particular province.
- The level of marketization is the ratio of the total number of employees employed by state-owned units compared to the total number of employees in a particular province.
- The level of urbanization is the ratio of the non-agricultural population compared to the total population in a particular province.

The data comes mainly from *Finance Yearbook of China* and *China Statistical Yearbook* from 1997 to 2007. Owing to the lack of relevant data in Chongqing in 1996, data was extracted by Linear Interpolation Methods of data from 1997 to 2006. Tibet was removed due to imperfect data, leaving 30 samples in panel data. Table 12.3 indicates the results of descriptive statistics for the panel data.

Empirical test

For model (12.11), it was necessary to control individual characteristics and timing of non-observed units to avoid deviations in the model setting and to improve parameter estimations as a result of the two-dimensional characteristics of the panel data. Using the weighted cross-section estimation method the effects of heteroscedasticity were eliminated. This study makes use of Generalized Least Squares estimates (GLS) to detect fixed or random effects. The results of the Lagrange Multiplier test (LM test) and the Hausman test require the use of a fixed

Table 12.3 Descriptive statistics of panel data

Variable	*Mean*	*Median*	*Maximum*	*Minimum*	*Std. dev.*
Provincial equalization index of BPS	0.282997	0.255023	0.757622	0.084830	0.139539
Inter-provincial gap of economic development	1.121767	0.823569	4.431607	0.335497	0.792429
Inter-provincial gap of financial capacity	0.590021	0.355655	3.293479	0.175730	0.633869
Provincial governments' preference	0.107031	0.093033	0.295092	0.031344	0.048288
The degree of fiscal decentralization	1.259577	0.964169	5.220658	0.517194	0.908842
The size of transfer payments	1.273534	1.037453	6.996580	0.437868	0.721578
The level of opening to the outside world	0.295612	0.107373	1.749675	0.032044	0.389794
The level of marketization	0.159462	0.133103	0.537298	0.054618	0.089476
The level of urbanization	31.88128	26.88000	85.76000	13.87000	15.62169

effects panel model for economic analysis. The regression results developed by software Eviews 5.1 are indicated in Table 12.4.

Model (1) in Table 12.4 shows regression results when all of the above supply and demand factors of BPS are brought into the regression function (12.11). Based on regression results for Model (1), Model (2) shows the impacts of location factors by setting up two dummy variables – Eastern regions and Central regions.[2] Based on regression results of Model (2), Model (3) shows regression results after removing variables that are not significant. Three econometric models show that most variables were significantly greater than the 0.01 level, while the adjusted R^2 is greater than 90 percent, apart from the size of transfer payments, indicating an ideal regression. I have mainly interpreted the results based on Model (3).

From Table 12.4 it can be seen for the inter-provincial gaps in economic development, fiscal decentralization, inward investment, marketization and urbanization, the dummy variable Eastern region correlates positively with China's inter-provincial EBPS, while the inter-provincial differences in financial capacity and provincial governments' preferences correlate negatively with EBPS.

An increase of 1 percent in the inter-provincial gap in economic development results in a decrease of 0.05 percent in inter-provincial EBPS. This suggests that local economic development is the base for the development of BPS. Therefore to implement an equalization strategy for BPS, differences in Chinese regional economic development cannot be too large, or it will result in a large disparity

Table 12.4 Regression results of determinants of China's inter-regional equalization of BPS

Variable	*(1)*	*(2)*	*(3)*
C	0.071089 (8.901954)***	0.069366 (8.212169)***	0.070235 (8.970144)***
Inter-provincial gap of economic development	0.066332 (7.016698)***	0.051825 (4.485683)***	0.053593 (4.717903)***
Inter-provincial gap of financial capacity	−0.157503 (−3.210544)***	−0.14202 (−2.892942)***	−0.105662 (−5.549391)***
Provincial governments' preference	−0.500252 (−7.479473)***	−0.482695 (−7.101497)***	−0.48486 (−7.348168)***
The degree of fiscal decentralization	0.164165 (4.149853)***	0.161611 (4.120417)***	0.130451 (11.00952)***
The size of transfer payments	−0.014848 (−0.961859)	−0.01182 (−0.768936)	
The level of opening to the outside world	0.068623 (7.133885)***	0.059684 (5.535991)***	0.058141 (5.433344)***
The level of marketization	0.292997 (6.380974)***	0.277873 (5.994997)***	0.267021 (5.925570)***
The level of urbanization	0.000913 (2.525643)**	0.001034 (2.696413)***	0.001173 (3.220761)***
Dummy variable – eastern regions		0.017335 (2.088673)**	0.014675 (2.055068)**
Dummy variable – central regions		0.004324 (0.715622)	
LM test	6.692121***	6.495541***	6.566219***
Adjusted R^2	0.937955	0.938595	0.938783

Notes: The figures in the parentheses represent the standard deviation, ***, **, * which represent significance levels of 1 percent, 5 percent, and 10 percent respectively.

between regional BPS. An increase of 1 percent in the degree of fiscal decentralization results in an increase of 0.13 percent in EBPS. This proves that fiscal decentralization in China helps to promote the local supply level of BPS. Therefore, it indicates that the incentive effects of fiscal decentralization have been significant, forcing the enhancement and improvement of local BPS to intensify regional competitiveness. An increase of 1 percent in the level of inward investment results in an increase of 0.058 percent in China's inter-provincial EBPS. This illustrates that China's internationalization is based on providing high-quality and efficient BPS and that Foreign Direct Investment (FDI) forces local governments to develop public infrastructure to attract more FDI. An increase of 1 percent in the level of marketization, results in an increase of 0.267 percent in China's inter-provincial EBPS. Increased marketization means a gradual improvement in the local market environment, and the improvement of BPS is a key element in the development of a market environment during China's transformation from a traditional planned economy to a socialist market economy. An increase of 1 percent in the level of urbanization results in an increase of 0.11 percent in China's inter-provincial EBPS. The rise in the rate of urbanization results in the concentration of population and industries, and economies of scale in the supply of BPS. The dummy variable eastern region has a significantly positive correlation with China's inter-provincial EBPS. However central regions do not indicate a significant correlation with EBPS, indicating that the disparity in BPS is mainly between eastern and central-western regions, while the gap in EBPS between central and western regions is not very significant. Eastern regions are relatively developed and it is likely that they will strengthen their advantages in BPS. In contrast the level of welfare for residents in the central and western regions is likely to lag behind eastern regions.

An increase of 1 percent in the inter-provincial gap in financial capacity results in a decrease of 0.105 percent in China's inter-provincial EBPS. This suggests that most of China's local finance relates to government expenditure on consumption and direct investment with little investment in local BPS. Therefore the gap in BPS does not reflect the gap in local finance, and many local governments hope for an increase in central government's fiscal transfer payments to assist local BPS. In general, the more local fiscal revenue generated the more is invested in local BPS. However, over recent years administrative expenses in many developed regions in China have increased dramatically, accounting for a far higher figure than the corresponding increases in expenditure relating to BPS. The fact that provincial governments' preferences correlate negatively with EBPS has ensured that developing the local economy has taken preference over improving local residents' welfare through greater BPS. Therefore, it is imperative that local governments restructure their operations and incorporate BPS into performance evaluation systems for government officials.

Models (1) and (2) demonstrate that the size of transfer payments is not significantly related to EBPS. Due to deficiencies in the current transfer payment system, this has not played a role in regional EBPS.

Conclusion

This article analyzes developing trends and determinants of inter-regional EBPS in China during the period 1996 to 2006, and the conclusions drawn are as follows:

First, based on development of China's economy and social characteristics, the inter-provincial equalization assessment system of BPS in China must include basic education, public health and basic medical care, public culture, basic scientific research, employment and social security, public infrastructure, and environmental protection, as well as set up different weight coefficients in accordance with their fundamental situation.

Second, China's inter-provincial EBPS follows a downward trend between 1996 and 2006. Relatively acceptable levels of equalization are evident in services such as public culture, public infrastructure, ecological services, and environmental protection, much-improved levels of equalization are evident in services such as employment and social security services, public health and basic medical services, while services requiring urgent improvement in terms in inter-regional equalization include basic education and R&D.

Third, it was found that inter-provincial disparities in economic development, fiscal decentralization, inward investment, marketization, and urbanization, the dummy variable eastern region is positively correlated with China's inter-provincial EBPS; while inter-provincial disparities in financial capacity and provincial governments' preferences were negatively correlated with regional EBPS, it was found that transfer payments have not contributed to regional EBPS.

It is recommended that all levels of government in China adopt the following measures based on the conclusions drawn in this chapter:

First, the government should focus on those sub-BPS which have larger weighting coefficients in the equalization assessment system and on services such as basic education, public health, and basic medical care, which require urgent attention, so that limited financial resources can achieve the most efficient results.

Second, as the inter-provincial disparity in economic development is positively correlated with China's inter-provincial EBPS this demands a narrowing of the gap in inter-provincial economic development. Through rational population flows support for developing regions by developed ones, and establishing aggregation economies in central and western regions, it should be possible to maintain the economic differentials between regions at an acceptable level.

Third, the degree of fiscal decentralization, inward investment, marketization, and urbanization are positively correlated with inter-provincial EBPS, which indicates that the government should improve the degree of fiscal decentralization, inward investment, marketization, and urbanization in central and western regions.

Finally, the fact that the inter-provincial differentials in financial capacity and provincial governments' preferences correlate negatively with equalization levels and transfer payments, indicates that they have not played a role in EBPS. This forces the central government to establish a scientific, rational, and equitable transfer payment system and to incorporate the development of BPS into performance evaluation systems for government officials.

Notes

1 As the largest developing country, China has gradually increased the size of basic public services spending and size. Therefore, flow indicators can reflect the improvement of basic public services and stock indicators can reflect the development level.

2 Using traditional trichotomy: eastern regions include Beijing, Tianjin, Hebei, Liaoning, Shanghai, Jiangsu, Zhejiang, Fujian, Shandong, Guangdong and Hainan (11 provinces); central regions include Shanxi, Jilin, Heilongjiang, Anhui, Jiangxi, Henan, Hubei, Hunan (eight provinces); western regions includes Inner Mongolia, Guangxi, Sichuan, Guizhou, Yunnan, Shaanxi, Gansu, Qinghai, Ningxia, Xinjiang, and another ten provinces (20 provinces).

References

An, T. and Ren, Q. (2008) 'The Construction of Equalization Indicator System of Public Services in China-based on a Quantitative Analysis Perspective of Regional Disparities', *Finance & Trade Economics*, 6: 79–82.

Chen, C. and Cai, Y. (2007) *The Chinese Government's Public Service: Institutional Change and Comprehensive Evaluation*, Beijing: China Social Sciences Press.

Huang, J. (2010) 'Six Years of China's Agricultural Development and the Miracle of Three Decades of Reform-Institutional Innovation, Technological Progress and Market Reform', *Economy of Agricultural Technology*, 1: 4–18.

Liu, Y. (2008) 'Empirical Analysis on Equalization Effects of China's Fiscal Transfer Payment', *Local Financial Research*, 2: 12–16.

Song X. and Yuan, D. (2008) 'Equalization of Public Services, Political Balance and Transfer Payments – Based on Experienced Analysis of Inter-provincial Panel Data in 1998–2005', *Financial Research*, 4: 92–97.

Zhang, R. (2005) ' "Unsuccessful" Medical Reform', *Outlook*, 25.

13 Does real effective exchange rate volatility affect foreign direct investment?

Evidence from China

Min Ye and Siyue Liu

Introduction

Research question

The growing trend of globalization facilitated a large amount of international capital flows among different currency areas. The issue of the impact of exchange rate on foreign direct investment (FDI), one of the most important ways of international capital flows, has caused widespread concern.

FDI has played a very important role in China's economic development since the reform and opening over the past 30 years. Since 1993, China has always been the second largest country for foreign capital inflows, second only to the United States. In 2003, China overtook the United States for the first time and became the largest attractor of FDI in the world. Up to now, FDI inflows to China have always ranked in the top three worldwide. With the growing importance of the Chinese economy to the world economy and the generally favoured potential for Chinese economic development, the FDI inflows to China are expected to increase further.

However, along with China's rapid economic development, the United States and western countries began to challenge the RMB exchange rate system and tried to influence and exert pressure for a revaluation of RMB with the comment that there is serious underestimation of the RMB exchange rate. Not only at the political level, but in academia, there are also a variety of perspectives on the issue of "whether the RMB is undervalued." Mondale, the Nobel Prize winner, disagreed with the statement that the RMB was undervalued and was in support of the current stable RMB policy; other foreign scholars hold the contrary view that the RMB should appreciate. Under the huge pressure of appreciation, the People's Bank of China (the country's central bank) promised that the RMB exchange rate system would become more flexible but the RMB exchange rate continued to drop. On July 21, 2005, the People's Bank of China announced the abolition of the single dollar-peg monetary policy and a managed floating exchange rate system with reference to a basket of currencies came into effect. Between July 2005 and mid-2008, the RMB gradually rose against the dollar by about 21 percent.

Does the RMB exchange rate and its volatility exert any impact on the FDI inflow to China? And if it does, what are the impacts? These are the questions we want to address in this research. And apparently, as China is one of the largest destinations for worldwide capital flows and one of the most important economies, addressing these questions can help understand the inter-relationship between the rising China and its integration with the world economy, from some specific aspects of the Chinese economy.

Literature review

A great many empirical studies on the role of FDI in host countries indicate that FDI is a transfer of capital, which can be interpreted in terms of comparison of expected returns on alternative investment decisions, while exchange rate is regarded as the relative price of the international capital. Hence, both the level and the variability of exchange rates can have an impact on the movement of FDI.

There has been a lot of empirical research on the impact of the level of exchange rate on FDI. Froot and Stein (1991) found the influx of large-scale FDI to the United States from 1970 to 1980 should be attributed to the weakness of dollar exchange rate in the same period. Goldberg and Klein (1997) analyzed the role of the exchange rate in the decision of FDI flowing from Japan and the United States into Southeast Asia and Latin America and their empirical studies showed that the appreciation of the yen and the dollar did increase Japan's and the United States' investment in these countries. Campa (1993) believed that the overseas investment decisions of transnational corporations are based on their expectation of future earnings. The stronger a country's currency, the higher the expectation of future earnings will encourage multinational corporations to enter such a market (i.e. the more FDI inflows will be attracted). In recent years some scholars, such as MacDermott (2008), found that some data from Western developed countries suggested a positive relationship between exchange rates and FDI.

The literature on both the theoretical and empirical effects of exchange rate volatility on FDI has come up with conflicting conclusions. Sercu and Vanhulle (1992) thought that the intensity of exchange rate volatility had reverse effects on foreign direct investment. In contrast, Cushman (1988) found a positive impact of exchange rate volatility on inward FDI. He showed that, in the presence of exchange rate volatility, producing in the destination market is a good substitute for exports. This holds as long as the production is not for export. Gorg and Wakelin (2001) studied the impact of exchange rate fluctuations on FDI to the United States and found that there was no data which could indicate any influence of exchange rate volatility and the expected FDI on the United States' inflow and outflow of FDI.

The above research about the impact of exchange rate changes on FDI are based on developed countries. With the continuous deepening of China's financial reform, the relaxation of China's capital control and the broadening of the RMB exchange rate flexibility, exchange rate movements will continue to greatly impact on China's economy and FDI. Some articles on the relationship between China's exchange rate changes and FDI have also appeared. Xing and Wu's (2003) study found that the depreciation/appreciation of the real exchange rate will bring on an increase/decrease of the introduction of foreign direct investment. Domestic scholars generally believe that the dramatic fluctuations in the exchange rate have reverse effects on foreign direct investment and the long-term stability of the RMB is an important factor to attract FDI. Additionally, Zhang (2003), Zhang (2005); Zhang and Yang (2006) analyzed and held that the uncertainty with respect to real exchange rate negatively impact on inflows of China's FDI. In general research in this area is still significantly deficient in China.

Background

The evolution of China's exchange rate regime[1]

Before 1994, the RMB exchange rate was strictly controlled by the Chinese government. From January 1, 1994, reform of the exchange rate regime involved the introduction of a single managed float and a new exchange rate of 8.72 RMB/USD saw the currency devalued by 33 percent (from the prior official exchange rate of 5.74 RMB/USD). As can be seen in Figure 13.1, which depicts the value of the RMB against the US dollar following a period of appreciation (of just over five percent) from 1994 to 1997 the RMB, was de facto pegged against the dollar until July 2005. This included the time of the 1997 Asian crisis when the Chinese authorities successfully defended the RMB against speculative attack. In fact, during the period 1997 to July 2005, the RMB remained within a narrow band of 8.27 to 8.28 RMB/USD and appreciated against the US dollar by only 0.25 percent.

On July 21, 2005, the People's Bank of China announced that the RMB official exchange rate would be adjusted to 8.11 USD/RMB; an appreciation of 2.1 percent. At the same time, the central bank announced that it would abandon the ten-year-old peg against the US dollar and move to a managed floating exchange rate system with reference to a basket of currencies. From July 2005 and mid-2008, the RMB gradually rose against the dollar by about 21 percent.

The evolving RMB/USD exchange rate, with indicated Chinese exchange rate regime, can be seen in Figure 13.1. The RMB exchange rate against other major currencies, such as the euro (EURO), the Japanese yen (JPY), the UK pound (GBP) and the Hong Kong dollar (HKD) are presented in Figure 13.2. As HKD is fixed to the US dollar in a currency board arrangement, the RMB/HKD exchange rate displays a similar trend to that of RMB/USD exchange rate, while the RMB/EURO, RMB/JPY and RMB/GBP maintain high volatility during the same period in a managed floating exchange rate regime.

The features of China's FDI inflows

Since reform and opening, foreign direct investment, which played a very important role in China's economic development, has become the main way for China to attract foreign capital. Since the beginning of foreign capital utilization in 1979, China's utilization of foreign capital has, in general, experienced five stages.

In the initial stage, from 1979 to 1986, foreign investment was primarily from Hong Kong and Macao, largely concentrating in coastal areas and in

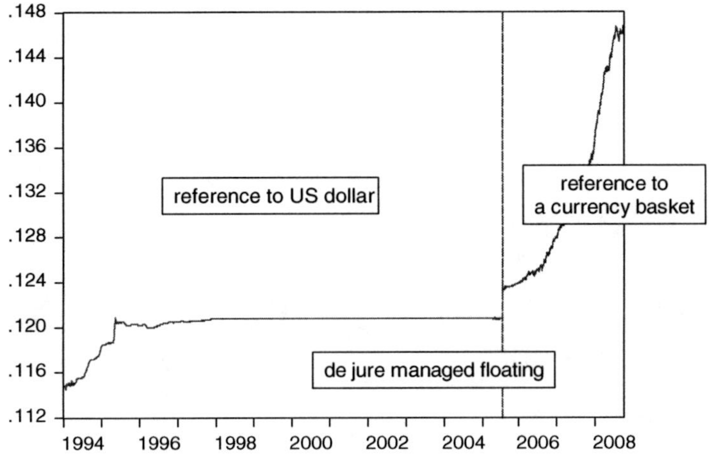

Figure 13.1 The RMB exchange rate against the US dollar (January 1994–September 2008).

Source: Datastream.

labor-intensive industries and services. The period 1987–1991 is a stage of steady development. Compared to the first stage, the investment from Taiwan increased, investment expanded to the eastern regions, and the investment industries focused on export-oriented production. The third stage, from 1992 to 1993, was called a rapid development stage. There was an adjustment period of development from 1994 to 2000, during which more multinational companies entered China's market, and more industries began to make use of foreign investment. Since 2001, the utilization of foreign capital has entered a mature and stable phase. From 2001 to 2008, the total amount of foreign capital utilization is US$512.16 billion, with an average annual amount of US$64.02 million.

The World Bank predicted, on September 28, 2007, in *Prospects and Strategic Research on China's Utilization of Foreign Investment*, that during the period from 2006 to 2010, about 30 percent of the estimated US$250 billion of FDI that flow to developing countries would flow into China.

The characteristics of China's utilization of FDI are as follows. First, China's abundant and cheap labor resources have facilitated a high proportion of processing trade. The costs of foreign-funded enterprises are mainly from importing raw materials, spare parts and machinery and equipment from abroad. The appreciation of the RMB will make them relatively cheaper, and thus reduce the costs of production significantly. Therefore, multinational companies investing in China mainly aim to take advantage of China as the "world factory," and their products are mostly exported to the world market after processing or assembly. Second, new investments comprise the majority of foreign direct investment, and cross-border mergers and acquisitions only take up a small proportion. In recent years, as the

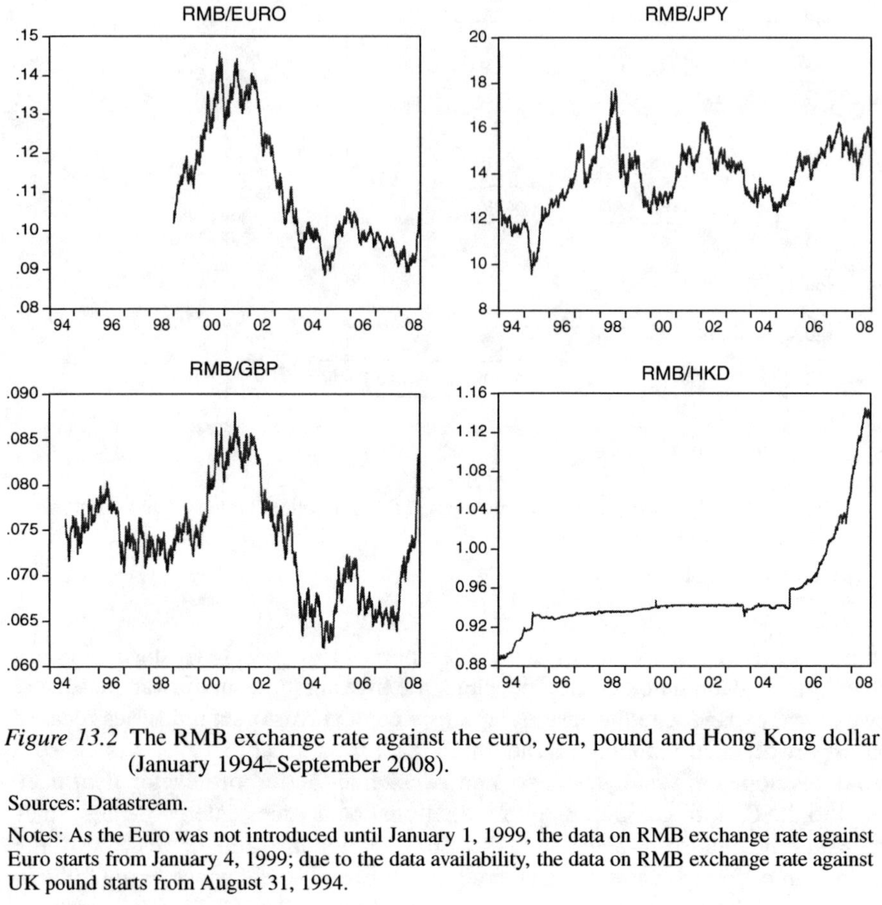

Figure 13.2 The RMB exchange rate against the euro, yen, pound and Hong Kong dollar (January 1994–September 2008).

Sources: Datastream.

Notes: As the Euro was not introduced until January 1, 1999, the data on RMB exchange rate against Euro starts from January 4, 1999; due to the data availability, the data on RMB exchange rate against UK pound starts from August 31, 1994.

policies were relaxed and the global transnational mergers and acquisitions greatly expanded, mergers and acquisitions of transnational corporations in China progressed steadily, but they still account for a very small proportion of the whole FDI.

Methodology and data

Model variables

The Vector Autoregression (VAR) model used in this study contains four endogenous variables. The main variable of interest is FDI. We use the actual foreign investment in China as our FDI variable. According to FDI theory, other things being equal, an increase of the size of an economy usually leads to an increase of the attractiveness to FDI, which is known as the market size effect. To control for

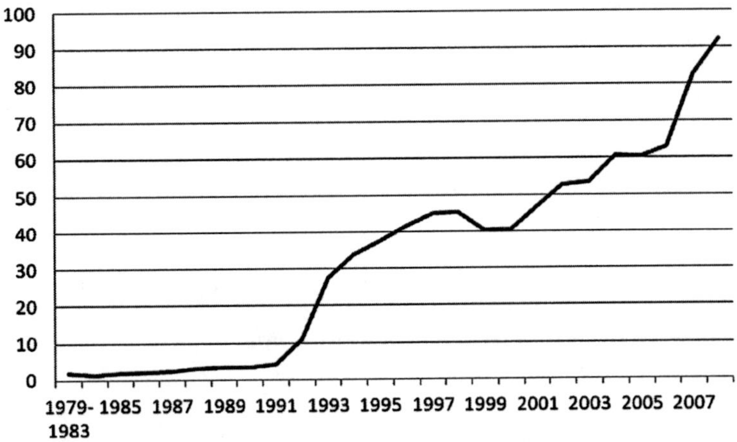

Figure 13.3 The actually utilized FDI in China (1979–2008) (unit: billion US dollar).

Source: Each period of *China Statistical Yearbook*.

Note: The amount of actually utilized FDI in China from 1979 to 1983 is cumulative.

market size, we scale nominal FDI by nominal GDP (FG).[2] We divide nominal FDI by nominal GDP.

Because the growth rate of GDP is greatly correlated with FDI, it is generally considered as a proxy of the average rate of return of capital, and there is no doubt that the long-term and high-speed growth of China's economy is an important factor to attract continuous inflow of FDI. Thus, the economic growth rate, which is measured by cumulative year-on-year growth of GDP (G), is thought to influence investment.

Our model also includes the International Monetary Fund's (IMF's) measure of the real effective exchange rate (REER)[3] and its volatility (VE). We use the conditional variance of the log of the real effective exchange rate as our measure of VE. With the exception of REER, all data is seasonally adjusted.[4] REER enters the VAR models in log difference (DLNREER), and G enter the model in first difference (DG), to ensure the stationarity of the time series. Quarterly data is used.

We restrict our estimation to the period after China began to implement a single managed floating exchange rate regime based on market supply and demand. Hence, we do not use data prior to 1994 in our study. The estimation period ends in the third quarter of 2008, as some of the latest data is not available yet. Most of the data comes from International Monetary Fund, the Bank for International Settlements, China's State Administration of Foreign Exchange, and the National Bureau of Statistics of China.

Measuring volatility

While various measures of exchange rate volatility have been used in empirical research, for example standard deviation, deviations from trend, and the difference

Table 13.1 Real exchange rate movement forecasts and their associated volatility, VE (absolute value of *z*-statistics in parentheses)

Estimation equation:
DLNREER = 0 + [AR(3) = 0.590764440189, MA(1) = 0.393671550815, MA(3) = −0.420916387361]
(4.2426) (3.5144) (3.2604)

GARCH = 1.81603758493e-05 + 0.196020967516 ∗ RESID(-1)^2 + 0.811179307959 ∗ GARCH(−1)
(0.5057) (2.7274) (12.3346)

Q-statistic (12) = 5.0314, Q^2-statistic (12) = 9.8904, estimation period: 1980:1–2008:3

Note: Q-statistic is the Ljung–Box Q-statistic for the residuals, while Q^2-statistic is the Ljung–Box Q-statistic for the squared residuals.

between previous forward and current spot rates, this study employs the conditional variance of the real effective exchange rate from Generalized Autoregressive Conditional Heteroscedastic (GARCH) models to proxy the VE.

In order to overcome the deficiency of quarterly data, we extend our estimation period from 1980 to 2008 when measuring the volatility of REER. And then we only select the quarterly volatility of REER from 1994 to 2008. Specifically, GARCH (1, 1) model is used to capture the time-varying conditional variance of REER. The model for the mean of REER is specified with an Autoregressive Moving Average (ARMA) (3, 3) model using traditional Box–Jenkins (1976) methodology. The ARMA model for the mean of REER series, together with the GARCH model for the conditional variance of REER, is reported in Table 13.1.

The Q-statistics in Table 13.1 show that autoregressive models of the first difference of REER produce white noise residuals, while an estimation of the Q^2-statistic indicates that the GARCH (1,1) model produces a white noise series for the squared residual series as well. As Table 13.1 shows, there are significant Autoregressive Conditional Heteroscedastic (ARCH) or GARCH effects in the REER series.

A plot of VE is shown in Figure 13.4. We restrict the plot of VE to the data used to estimate the corresponding VAR model. As Figure 13.4 shows, the conditional variance is not constant, and there is a particularly large decrease in VE at the beginning of our estimation period, and the VE spikes around 1999. And the VE is more stable in the later portion of our sample period than in the earlier portion. (The VE does become more stable following 2000.)

From Figure 13.4, we can see that since 1994, the RMB exchange rate fluctuations have a gradual stable trend, which is consistent with the objective facts. As introduced before in the second section, prior to 1994, the RMB has long been over-estimated. The reforms since January 1, 1994 made the RMB exchange rate devalue from 5.74 to 8.72 RMB/USD, in order to merge the official exchange rate with swap market exchange rate. Therefore, the exchange rate volatility demonstrates a slump in 1994.

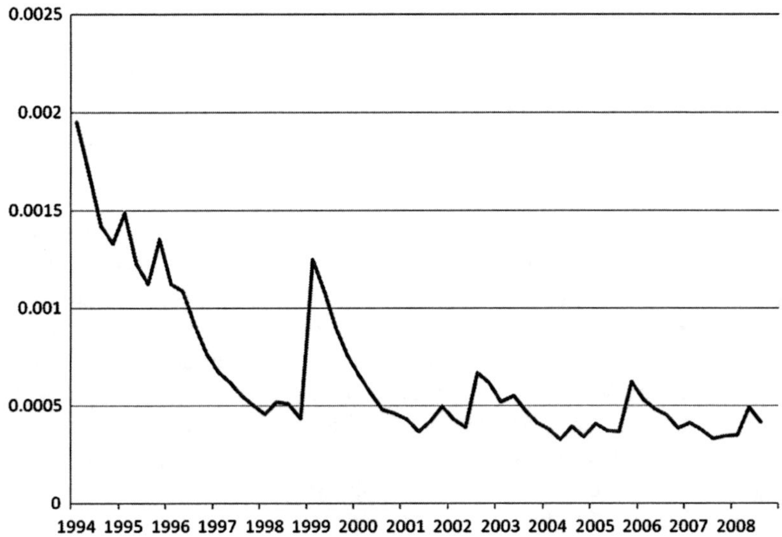

Figure 13.4 Volatility of real effective exchange rate (VE).

A single managed floating exchange rate system, based on market supply and demand, was implemented after the reform, and the RMB exchange rate tended to remain stable. During the period of the Asian financial crisis since 1997, the RMB faced tremendous pressure of devaluation. But on the whole, the Chinese government successfully resisted the pressure, and the RMB exchange rate did not significantly fluctuate.

Methodology

We employ a VAR model to examine the impact of a variety of macroeconomic influences on FDI. Specifically, we examine the relationships among system variables by looking at the response of the system to "typical" shocks to system variables. A typical shock is defined as a positive one-standard-deviation shock to the residual from a given VAR equation.

One way to examine the impact on system variables of typical shocks is to compute Variance Decompositions (VDCs). VDCs show the portion of the forecast error variance of each variable in the system that is attributable to its own shocks and to shocks to other system variables. Both direct and indirect effects are captured by VDCs. In this study we are most concerned with the portion of the forecast error variance in FDI explained by shocks to G, REER and VE. VDCs can show if shocks to one variable have significant impacts on another variable. However, they do not show the direction of these impacts. This question can be answered by using Impulse Response Functions (IRFs). IRFs can describe the effects of a shock to one variable in the system on the conditional forecast of another variable. We are most concerned with the reaction of FDI in response to shocks to REER and its VE.

As provided by Eviews6.0, five methods, such as Akaike's Information Criteria (AIC), Schwarz Information Criterion (SC), Hannan–Quinn Information Criterion, Final Prediction Error (FPE) and Sequential Modified LR Test Statistic (LR) can be used to determine the lag length for your VAR Model. The lag order selected by most of the criterion is determined as our best lag length. In our model all criterion points to a lag length of four quarters.

In order to compute VDCs and IRFs, the VAR residuals must be orthogonalized. We use a Cholesky Decomposition to produce these orthogonal residuals. The Cholesky Decomposition requires that the variables in the VAR be ordered in a particular fashion. Because of cross-equation residual correlation, when a variable higher in the ordering changes, all variables lower in the ordering are assumed to change.[5] The extent of the change depends of the degree of the residual correlation. Our results are based on the ordering DG, DLNREER, VE, and FG.

This ordering is consistent with the primary focus of our chapter. FG is placed last in the ordering. This allows shocks to all system variables to have contemporaneous impacts on FG, but shocks to FG have no impacts on other system variables.[6] This is consistent with past investment studies in which current values of explanatory variables have an impact on investment. Based on the efficient markets arguments of Gordon and Veitch (1986), we place financial variables, REER and VE, after G in the ordering. And as VE is derived from REER, we place REER above VE. This allows REER to have an impact on VE, the conditional variance of the exchange rate series.

Empirical results

The VDCs are reported in Figure 13.5 and Table 13.2, and the IRFs are reported in Figures 13.6 and 13.7. Because the focus of our study is the determination of FG, we only report the VDCs for FG. An analysis of Figure 13.5 reveals that, aside from shocks to FDI itself, shocks to REER and VE explain more of the forecast error variance in China's FDI than other system variable at each time horizon. And from Table 13.2 we can tell that, at longer time horizons, shocks to REER explain more than 13 percent and shocks to VE explain about 10 percent of the forecast error variance in China's FDI. Hence, among the variables in our model, the REER and VE are the most important determinants of China's FDI.

Given the focus of our study, we only report the IRFs for the response of FG to REER and VE in Figures 13.6 and 13.7. We have also calculated a two-standard deviation confidence interval for each IRF. Figure 13.6 reveals that a positive shock to REER has a positive impact on FG, and the impact lasts for longer time horizons, while Figure 13.7 shows that the response of FG to a VE is negative, for a modest range.

Discussion of the results

We have examined the impact of shocks to macroeconomic variables, and specifically to the economic growth rate (G), REER and its VE, and on FDI in China.

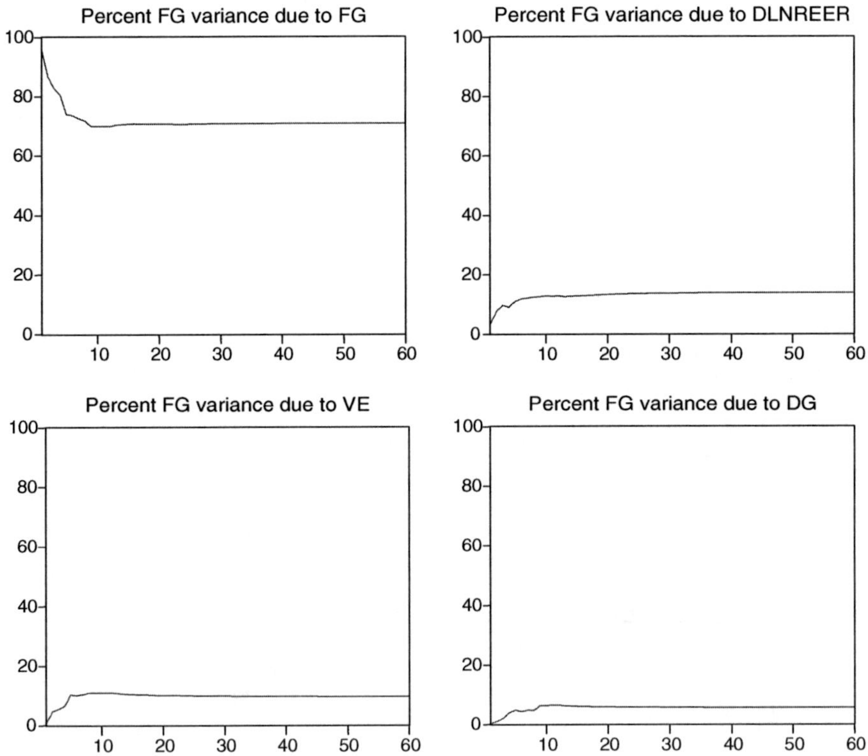

Figure 13.5 Variance decompositions.

Table 13.2 Variance decompositions of FG

Period	*S.E.*	*FG*	*DLNREER*	*VE*	*DG*
4	0.006036	80.51463	8.993762	6.584481	3.907128
8	0.007208	71.90305	12.35747	10.99928	4.740201
12	0.007618	69.96173	12.72032	10.93797	6.379982
16	0.007933	70.81097	12.84791	10.25948	6.081642
20	0.008136	70.72898	13.26074	10.13976	5.870517
24	0.008249	70.65804	13.53753	10.02773	5.776703
28	0.008316	70.79823	13.61443	9.886409	5.700928
32	0.008360	70.83552	13.70328	9.805414	5.655786
36	0.008388	70.84859	13.77464	9.752697	5.624070
40	0.008403	70.86527	13.80497	9.721388	5.608374
44	0.008412	70.87617	13.82630	9.700796	5.596736
48	0.008418	70.88025	13.84057	9.687555	5.591621
52	0.008421	70.88204	13.84896	9.680591	5.588406
56	0.008423	70.88372	13.85367	9.676316	5.586298
60	0.008424	70.88425	13.85638	9.673801	5.585566

Cholesky ordering: DG DLNREER VE FG.

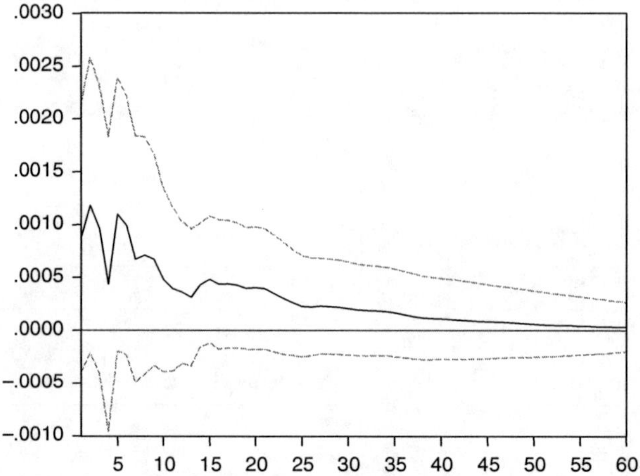

Figure 13.6 Response of FG to Cholesky One S.D. DLNREER Innovation.

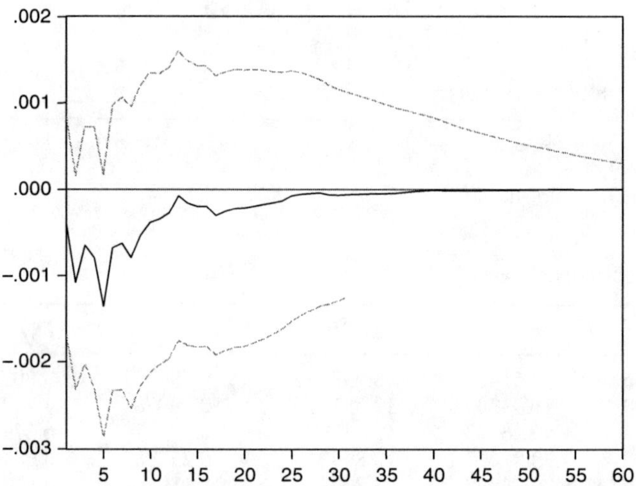

Figure 13.7 Response of FG to Cholesky One S.D. VE Innovation.

Our main interest lies in the impact of real effective exchange rate and its volatility on FDI.

Our VDCs reveal that innovations to exchange rate and its volatility explain significant portions of the forecast error variance in FDI at longer time horizons. Shocks to REER appear to have the largest impact on FDI. Therefore, it's reasonable for us to assume that more of China's inward FDI is strategic rather than speculative investment, as to a larger extent, it changes with the movement of the absolute level of exchange rate rather than exchange rate volatility. This result makes sense as China is well known for its competitive advantage in labor-intense manufacturing, and is forever considered as "world factory" for a long period of time. A great number of multinational enterprises outsource their productions to China because of the sufficient labor force and significant low labor costs. This foreign multinational enterprises' outsourcing is expected to continue, as Chinese competitive advantage in the labor force and costs will persists for a long time in the future, and the environment for foreign direct investment has continued to improve. Accordingly, more foreign capital is willing to invest in China based on long-term strategic planning decisions, rather than short-term speculative purposes.

Contrary to the results of most previous empirical research, the outcomes of our IRFs indicate that the impact of REER shocks on FDI is positive and lasts for a long-term time horizon. Considering the characteristics of China's utilization of FDI, as well as the "relative cost-effectiveness of production" theory advocated by Cushman (1985, 1988) and others, we believe that, the reasons why the impact of REER shocks on FDI is positive may boil down to the following two points. First, China's successful accession to the World Trade Organization (WTO) advanced the development of the level of China's opening up and the improvement the market environment, which further improved China's location advantages, and thus offset, to a large extent, the adverse effect of the appreciation of the RMB on attracting foreign direct investment. For developed countries, they attach more importance to the market of China. Take Germany and Japan as an example, in 2005 when the nominal exchange rate of RMB appreciated by 5.47 percent, the direct investment from Germany and Japan increased by 44.3 percent and 19.8 percent. These data show that the enhancement of China's location advantages after acceding to the WTO significantly reduced any negative impact resulting from appreciation of the RMB on introducing foreign direct investment. Second, the adverse effect of the appreciation of the RMB was partly offset by China's rapid economic growth as well. China's economy has maintained a more than nine percent growth rate since 2003, accompanied by the further expansion of economic scale and improvement of economic strength. Increase in foreign direct investment is more likely to benefit from such a good overall macroeconomic situation. That is, the appreciation of the RMB may not reduce the amount of foreign direct investment.

To the extent that shocks to VE have an impact on FDI, the impact is smaller and negative, which means that the decrease in long-term RMB exchange rate volatility could contribute to promoting the inflow of FDI. In other words, in order to attract more FDI inflows, we should stick to a stable exchange rate regime, and the exchange rate should be maintained at a smaller fluctuation range. This is consistent with the Chinese exchange rate policy, a managed float. As we know, the appreciation of RMB will offset the competitive advantages of China, as a host destination for foreign capital, resulting in a significant decrease in FDI inflows. On the other hand, the high volatility of the exchange rate will increase investment risk, and the uncertainty of investors' anticipated income, thus hindering FDI inflows. Actively promoting FDI inflows is still needed for China's economic development. Therefore, maintaining the relative stability of the RMB exchange rate is of important practical significance.

Conclusion

With the increasing integration of the Chinese economy with the world economy, the Chinese exchange rate is not only a domestic problem, but rather an issue that captures worldwide attention. Though there are hot disputes about whether the RMB is undervalued, what the real value of RMB should be, and which kind of exchange rate regime is best for China. Our results demonstrate that, at this stage, as well as in the future, a relative stable RMB exchange rate is a favorable and requisite choice for China, from the perspective of absorbing foreign capital. On the other hand, the relative stability of the RMB exchange rate is also beneficial to foreign investors, through decreasing the costs of their investment decision and the unpredictability of their investment risk.

Our results also indicate that the appreciation of the RMB may not reduce the amount of foreign direct investment because of China's location advantages, increasingly improved environment for FDI, and the attraction of China's great potential of economic development. That is to say, the huge amount of FDI inflows to China is not necessarily generated by the so-called undervaluation of the RMB exchange rate. This further demonstrates that the viewpoint held by a lot of people is untenable, that the vast foreign capital flows into China is due to the regulated RMB exchange rate, and hence the RMB should be re-valued. As analyzed before, more foreign capital is willing to invest in China for long-term strategic planning reasons, rather than short-term speculation on exchange rate movements.

However, it must be noted that, as exchange rate and FDI are certain aspects of the Chinese economy and because of the links relating Chinese economy to world economy, the relation between them should be dynamic and impacted by the dynamics of the inter-relationship between rising China and its integration with the world economy. To explore these impacts to help understand the changing relation between exchange rate and FDI involves more work to do in future.

Acknowledgements

The authors would like to thank Elaine Hutson and Xiaopo Qin for their valuable comments and suggestions, and Ping Ye for her assistance with data collection.

Notes

1 The information in this section was obtained from: (1) the website of The People's Bank of China (China's central bank) (www.pbc.gov.cn); (2) "The real effective exchange rate of RMB have continually dropped for 4 months", Xin Hua Net, July 20, 2009 and (3) Bloomberg.

2 Note that scaling nominal foreign direct investment by nominal GDP produces the same variable as scaling real foreign direct investment by real GDP.

3 The real effective exchange rate is a CPI-based, trade-weighted index that has been converted to an index (2000 = 100) and adjusted for relative price movements.
4 Foreign direct investment, GDP and cumulative year-on-year growth rate of GDP are all reported in seasonally unadjusted form. We seasonally adjust foreign direct investment, GDP and cumulative year-on-year growth rate of GDP using the X-11 procedure in Eviews6.0.
5 Variables lower in the ordering are not allowed to contemporaneously influence variables higher in the ordering.
6 FG does have an influence on other system variables through the lags in the VAR.

References

Box, G. E. P. and Jenkins, G. M. (1976) *Time Series Analysis: Forecasting and Control* (revised edition). San Francisco: Holden-Day.

Campa, J. M. (1993) 'Entry by Foreign Firms in the United States under Exchange Rate Uncertainty', *Review of Economics and Statistics*, 75 (4): 614–622.

Cushman, D. O. (1985) 'Real Exchange Rate Risk, Expectations, and the Level of Direct Investment', *Review of Economics and Statistics*, 67 (2): 297–308.

Cushman, D. O. (1988) 'Exchange Rate Uncertainty and Foreign Direct Investment in the United States', *Weltwirtschaftliches Archiv*, 322–336.

Froot, K. A. and Stein, J. C. (1991) 'Exchanges Rates and Foreign Direct Investment: An Imperfect Capital Markets Approach', *Quarterly Journal of Economics*, 106: 1191–1217.

Goldberg, L. S. and Klein, M. W. (1997) 'Foreign Direct Investment, Trade and Real Exchange Rate Linkages in Southeast Asia and Latin America', NBER working paper 6344, National Bureau of Economic Research, Inc.

Gordon, R. J. and Veitch, J. M. (1986) 'Fixed Investment in the American Business Cycle, 1919–83', in Gordon, R. J. (ed.) *The American Business Cycle: Continuity and Change*, Chicago: University of Chicago Press.

Gorg, H. and Wakelin, K. (2001) 'The Impact of Exchange Rate Variability on US Direct Investment', paper presented at the GDP Conference on FDI and Economics Integration, University of Nottingham.

MacDermott, R. (2008) 'Linking Exchange Rates to Foreign Direct Investment'. *The International Trade Journal*, 22 (1): 3–16.

Sercu, P. and Vanhulle, C. (1992) 'Exchange Rate Volatility, International Trade, and the Value of Exporting Firms', *Journal of Banking & Finance*, 16: 155–182.

Xing, Y. and Wu, G. (2003) 'Exchange Rate and Japan's Direct Investment in China', *Journal of World Economy*, 6.

Zhang, G. (2005) 'The Impact of Exchange Rate Fluctuations on Foreign Direct Investment', *International Economic Cooperation*, 9.

Zhang, W. and Yang, Z. (2006) 'The Impact of Exchange Rate Fluctuations on China's Foreign Direct Investment', *New Finance*, 2: 25–27.

Zhang, Y. (2003) 'The Current RMB Exchange Rate Facilitate the Introduction of Foreign Direct Investment', *Financial Science*, 201: 6–9.

14 Cost efficiency of banks in China

A stochastic frontier analysis

Yizhe Dong

Introduction

Over the past 30 years, China has been one of the world's fastest growing economies, with an average growth rate of almost 10 percent per year in real gross domestic product (GDP), and has been a major contributor to world economic growth. In 2007, China overtook the United States to become the world's second largest merchandise exporter after the European Union (EU). In 2009, China replaced Japan as the world's second-largest economy after the United States, and the country is leading the world out of recession. These remarkable achievements are largely linked to the Chinese market-oriented economy reforms and the globalization of trade. However, in contrast to economic success, the Chinese banking sector has been widely criticized for its low performance. Banks play a central role in both the financial system and the real economy, which was vividly illustrated again during the 2008 financial crisis. Thus, the performance and efficiency of its banking sector is becoming the one of most important issues for the Chinese government, and its health is very critical to the health of the general economy at large.

The Chinese banking sector has traditionally been characterized by high levels of government controls where regulatory authorities maintained a protected banking environment that inhibited competition. However, starting in 1979, with the opening up and reform policy, China's banking market environment has undergone significant changes. These drivers of change were particularly strong over the past 15 years, which were accompanied with remarkable economic growth. The deregulation reforms from 1994 to 2001 entailed a progressive move towards less administrative and more independent banking operations. In 1995, the *Commercial Banking Law* and the *Central Bank Law* were enacted to establish the legal underpinning for Chinese banking. Three specialist policy banks and four asset management companies were also established in this period to ameliorate the state-owned banks' performance. Since China joined the World Trade Organization (WTO) in December 2001, the banking sector reforms have moved towards a new phase. As the consequence of this deregulation, Chinese banks are put into a more competitive market. Internal pressure arises because of fierce competition among state-owned banks, joint-stock banks, and other regional banks, while external pressure comes from the free entry of foreign banks into the Chinese market. Thus, the Chinese government further injected financial capital into some big state-owned commercial banks and encouraged Chinese banks to partially privatize and take on minority foreign ownership. Therefore, it is interesting and valuable to know whether these institutional changes and deregulations have really enhanced the performance of the banks as expected by the Chinese government.

Efficiency (and/or productivity) indices can be used to assess the impact of major economic events such as deregulation, liberalization, or economic crisis on the performance of banking firms. Therefore, the objective of this chapter is twofold. First, we aim to explore the cost efficiency level in the Chinese banking sector and compare the performance of different types of banks operating in China. To do so, we employ the stochastic frontier analysis (SFA) to estimate the cost efficiency levels in the Chinese banking sector over the period 1994–2007, which cover both the pre-WTO and the post-WTO eras. In order to capture the heterogeneity across banks and lead to better estimates of the parameters describing the cost frontier and the cost inefficiency, we compare a number of different stochastic cost frontier model specifications to achieve a preferred one. The preferred model specification includes both the control variables (equity, asset quality, and time) in the cost function and the environmental variables in inefficiency term specification. Based on the results of the selected preferred model, we investigate the evolving pattern of cost efficiency in China' banking sector. We also compare the efficiency of the big four state-owned commercial banks, policy banks, joint stock commercial banks (JSCB), city commercial banks, and foreign banks. Second, we investigate the main determinants of the Chinese banking efficiency in order to find channels for improvement for policy purposes. The possible effect factors driving cost efficiency include the nature of ownership, bank size, corporate governance and deregulation reform, and market structure.

The remainder of the chapter is organized as follows. The second section provides a brief review of some key existing studies that investigate the Chinese banking efficiency. The third section explains the methodology to be used. The fourth section defines the variables, data and model specifications used in the study. The fifth section discusses the empirical results. The sixth section summarizes the findings.

Literature on Chinese banking efficiency

Over the past 20 years, substantial research effort has gone into measuring the efficiency of financial institutions, particularly commercial banks. A comprehensive review of efficiency studies has been provided by Berger and Humphrey (1997). They survey 130 studies that between them apply at least five major frontier efficiency analyses to financial institutions across 21 countries. Within this survey, applications of non-parametric (69 studies) and parametric approaches (60 studies) are split fairly evenly. Despite a very large literature on banking efficiency, very few papers have investigated Chinese banking efficiency. Fortunately, there is a growing appreciation of the importance of the Chinese banking industry and a steady stream of studies on Chinese banks has emerged in recent years that have used frontier efficiency analysis to measure relative efficiency.

Wang *et al.* (2005) apply several nonparametric models including various data envelopment analysis (DEA) models (i.e. CCR, BCC, Bilateral, Slack-Based Measure) and the free disposal hull (FDH) model to evaluate the efficiency of 16 commercial banks in China. Their analysis shows that the FDH seems to have difficulty in distinguishing efficient banks and inefficient banks when compared to other nonparametric models. Moreover, they find that private banks have higher efficiency than state-owned banks. Although the study reaches some useful conclusions, it only estimates different kinds of efficiencies (technical, pure technical, and scale efficiency) of the sampled banks and does not explore what might be the driving factors behind the efficiency scores obtained.

It is well known that the Chinese banking industry has undergone considerable deregulation since the 1990s. Several studies investigate the impact of deregulation on Chinese banking efficiency. In order to identify the changes of Chinese banking efficiency over the reform period, Chen *et al.* (2005) use DEA to estimate the cost, technical, and allocative efficiency of 43 Chinese banks over the period from 1993 to 2000. The results show that the big four state-owned commercial banks have higher technical efficiency and allocative efficiency than the joint stock commercial banks especially the nationwide joint stock commercial banks. This contradicts some previous studies, which find joint stock banks to be more efficient than state-owned banks (see for example, Karim 2001). Moreover, both large banks and small banks show a relatively high level of cost efficiency – again contradicting earlier work in the area. This finding may indicate that the Chinese banking sector does not follow a U-shaped average cost curve. Furthermore, Chen *et al.* (2005) find that the financial deregulation in 1995 was found to have improved both the technical and allocative efficiency in the early years after deregulation. However, they also find that the impetus towards higher efficiency fell away after 1997. This may be due to the impact of the Asian financial crisis, a huge increase in non-performing loans, or some other factors. Chen *et al.* (2005) also provide evidence that technical efficiency makes a greater contribution to cost efficiency than allocative efficiency, implying that Chinese banks need to improve their ability to minimize costs through input combinations.

Fu and Heffernan (2007) employ SFA to investigate cost X-efficiency in the Chinese banking sector over the period 1985–2002.[1] The results show that, on average, the X-efficiency of Chinese banks ranged from a low of 40 percent up to a high of 50 percent. The joint-stock banks are more efficient than the state-owned commercial banks, having X-efficiency scores which ranged from 41 percent to 49 percent. In order to analyze and explain the variation in the efficiency scores, the authors propose a two-stage regression procedure, which employs efficiency scores as the dependent variable regressed against a set of explanatory variables such as bank size, market structure, ownership, etc. The results suggest that Chinese banking cost efficiency could be improved if more state banks are converted to joint-stock ownership, and if the state-owned banks change their soft budgetary constraints to hard budgetary constraints. As Berger and Mester (1997) point out, the two-stage approach is legitimate only if the additional explanatory variables in the second stage are exogenous and are not correlated with the input and output variables in the first stage. Therefore, one serious problem for Fu and Heffernan's (2007) study is the variables chosen in the second stage. Some of the variables employed in the second stage are endogenous – for example, the ratio of purchased funds to total assets, total loans over total assets, and total investment over total assets – all of which are correlated with the input and output variables. This endogeneity problem that this engenders makes the conclusions reached by Fu and Heffernan (2007) about the direction of causation somewhat problematic.

Based on the agency theory and budgetary constraints theory, Yao *et al.* (2007) argue that the ownership reform and "hard" budget constrains may be important for raising Chinese banking efficiency levels. The study applies a single-stage SFA to investigate the effects of ownership structure and hard budget constraints on Chinese banks' efficiency over the period 1995 to 2001. The empirical results show that the mean level of technical efficiency over the sample is about 63 percent. Yao *et al.* (2007) find that Chinese joint-stock banks are more efficiency than their state-owned banks. In addition, the banks facing a harder budget tend to outperform banks that are heavily capitalized by the state or regional governments. Finally, Yao *et al.* (2007) suggest that the Chinese government should reduce the way that it interferes in banking operations and also allow recapitalization from private sources.

Kumbhakar and Wang (2007) employ an input distance function approach to examine the technical efficiency and total factor productivity changes of 14 national Chinese banks from 1993 until 2002. They adopt a one-step estimation procedure that incorporates explanatory variables into the efficiency analysis. Here it should be noted that this one-step estimation procedure is superior to a two-step estimation procedure.[2] Kumbhakar and Wang (2007) find that the big four state-owned commercial banks are less efficient than the joint stock commercial banks and that most Chinese banks are operating below the optimal scale. In addition, they find that small banks tend to be more efficient than large banks and that deregulation has not improved Chinese banking efficiency significantly. Their results also show an improvement in total factor growth, at the rate of 4.4 percent per annum, in the Chinese banking sector.

Ownership is always a "hot issue" in the discussion of financial sector reform. Generally, it is believed that ownership structure is an important factor that affects the level of banking efficiency. Berger *et al.* (2009) use the stochastic frontier approach to analyze the profit and cost efficiency of Chinese banks over the period from 1994 until 2003. They compare the efficiency of the big four state-owned banks, the non-big four state-owned banks, private banks, and foreign banks. With respect to cost efficiency, the average efficiency across all banks is 89.7 percent. Berger *et al.* (2009) find that foreign banks and non-big four state-owned banks are the most efficient Chinese banks, followed by the Big Four banks with private banks being the least efficient. With regard to the profit side, the mean profit efficiency level is 46.7 percent. Foreign banks are the most efficient, followed by private banks and non-big four state-owned banks, with big four state-owned banks being measured as the least efficient. Berger *et al.* (2009) argue that the inconsistency between the findings for profit efficiency and cost efficiency of state-owned banks may be explained by the "skimping hypothesis" and government cost subsidies, etc. To the author's knowledge, Berger *et al.* (2009) are also the first to study the efficiency effects of minority foreign ownership in the wider (that is, international) banking sector.[3] The results show that minority foreign ownership is associated with higher efficiency either for both efficiency concepts (profit and cost) or for both categories of majority domestic ownership (non-big four state-owned and private domestic banks). In other words, Chinese banks have benefited from minority foreign ownership during the transition deregulation period of 2002–06. Berger *et al.* (2009) also apply an additional set of robustness checks for "selection effects." The checks suggest that the effects of minority foreign ownership in most cases do reflect improvements above and beyond any selection effects. Because of the efficiency benefits to foreign ownership of Chinese banks, they recommend that the Chinese government should reduce ownership restrictions and encourage more foreign ownership into Chinese banks.

Methodology

This study utilized the SFA, as developed by Aigner *et al.* (1977), to estimate the cost efficiency of Chinese banks. The main advantages of this approach are the allowance for measurement error, and the generation of bank-specific efficiency estimates. Considering the characteristics of our data set and the purpose of this study, we decided to use this classical stochastic frontier model for the panel data. The single equation stochastic cost function for a panel data set can be written as:

$$\ln TC_{it} = f(Q_{it}, W_{it}; \beta) + v_{it} + u_{it} \quad i = 1, \ldots, I, t = 1, \ldots, T \tag{14.1}$$

where $\ln TC_{it}$ is the logarithm of the total cost of bank i at time t; $f(Q_{it}, W_{it}; \beta)$ is the deterministic kernel of the cost frontier; Q_{it} and W_{it} are a vector of outputs and of input prices in logarithmic form at time t; v_{it} is a two-sided normal disturbance term with zero mean and variance σ_v^2 representing the effects of noise; and u_{it} is a non-negative random disturbance term capturing the effects of cost inefficiency and is usually assumed as a half-normal distribution, $N^+(0, \sigma_u^2)$. Additionally, v_{it} and u_{it} are independently distributed from each other. Cost efficiency is measured relative to the efficient cost frontier, which is defined as the ratio of the minimum cost to the cost actually incurred. Because the cost frontier is specified as being stochastic, the appropriate measure of cost efficiency becomes:

$$CE_{it} = \frac{f(Q_{it}, W_{it}; \beta)\exp(v_{it})}{f(Q_{it}, W_{it}; \beta)\exp(v_{it} + u_{it})} = \exp(-u_{it}) \tag{14.2}$$

Note that the value of u_{it} cannot be observed directly from Equation (14.2), only the composite error term $\varepsilon_{it} = v_{it} + u_{it}$ can be observed. A solution to this problem is obtained by using the distribution of the inefficiency term conditional on the estimation of the composed error term. For the half-normal case, Battese and Coelli (1988) proposed an appropriate point estimator for the cost inefficiency that involves the conditional expectation of $\exp(-u_{it})$ given the entire error term.[4] They are given by:

$$CE_{it} = E[\exp(-u_{it}) \mid \varepsilon_{it}] = \left[\frac{1-\Phi(\sigma_* - \varepsilon_{it}\gamma/\sigma_*)}{1-\Phi(-\varepsilon_{it}\gamma/\sigma_*)}\right] \cdot \exp\left\{-\varepsilon_{it}\gamma + \frac{1}{2}\sigma_*\right\} \quad (14.3)$$

where $\Phi(\cdot)$ is the standard normal cumulative distribution function, $\sigma = \sqrt{\sigma_v^2 + \sigma_u^2}$, $\sigma_* = \sigma_v^2\sigma_u^2/\sigma^2$ and $\gamma = \sigma_u^2/\sigma^2$. The value of γ must lie between zero and one. A value of one indicates that the deviation from the frontier is due to inefficiency, while a value of zero indicates that the deviation is explained by noise. The estimates of efficiency are unbiased but inconsistent, because the variation associated with the distribution of the estimator $(u_i \mid \varepsilon_i)$ is independent of i and remains non-zero (Green 1990).[5] The efficiency measure from Equation (14.3) takes values over the interval $[1, \infty)$ and a value equal to one means fully efficient. Therefore, the cost efficiency score can be calculated as $1/CE_{it}$. In this study, we employ maximum likelihood techniques to obtain estimates of β and the parameters of the two error components (see Equation (14.2)). First, the likelihood function should be defined. Then the log likelihood function can be maximized with respect to the parameters in order to obtain maximum likelihood estimates of all parameters.[6]

In Aigner *et al.* (1977), the original model assumes efficiency and follows a half-normal distribution with mean zero. This specification implies that the likelihood of inefficient behaviour monotonically decreases for increasing levels of inefficiency and most units are likely to be concentrated close to the cost frontier causing artificially high efficiency levels. But there is no theoretical reason to support the ex ante monotonic assumption invoked by Aigner *et al.* (1977). Given this, Stevenson (1980) argues that inefficiency is not likely to be distributed with such a monotonically declining density function. The study also argues that the half-normal distribution assumption used by Aigner *et al.* (1977) is unnecessarily restrictive. Instead Stevenson (1980) introduces a normal-truncated formulation that assumes u to be normally distributed with a nonzero (constant) mean truncated at zero from above. Thus the truncated normal distribution introduced by Stevenson (1980) requires one more parameter μ (its mean) to be estimated and the point estimate of cost efficiency for each bank is given by the formula:

$$\begin{aligned} CE_{it} &= E[\exp(-u_{it}) \mid \varepsilon_{it}] \\ &= \left[\frac{1-\Phi(\sigma_* - (-\sigma_u^2\varepsilon_{it} + \mu\sigma_v^2)/\sigma\sigma_*)}{1-\Phi(-\sigma_u^2\varepsilon_{it} + \mu\sigma_v^2/\sigma\sigma_*)}\right] \\ &\quad \cdot \exp\left\{-\frac{-\sigma_u^2\varepsilon_{it} + \mu\sigma_v^2}{\sigma} + \frac{1}{2}\sigma_*\right\} \end{aligned} \quad (14.4)$$

We may prefer the truncated specification to the half-normal model, because the former provides a somewhat more flexible representation of the pattern of efficiency in the data. But both models face an important limitation that fails to account for heterogeneity across the banks, an issue we now develop.[7]

Theoretically, the bank is assumed to operate in perfectly competitive input-output markets. Thus, the bank's input prices are taken as exogenous. However, this assumption may not be valid when banks are heterogeneous. Some of the factors contributing to banks' heterogeneity could make their input prices as partially endogenous and thus influence the production process. Therefore, the potential endogeneity of the input price should be controlled in the measurement of the cost efficiency of banks. Additionally, under the conventional frontier model, different banks are assumed to produce equivalent quality in terms of output. However, there are likely to be differences across the banks in the quality of outputs. Because the traditional output variables do not fully capture heterogeneity in bank outputs differences in production quality may be incorrectly measured as differences in cost inefficiency (Berger and Mester 1997). Some banks might be incorrectly labelled as inefficient merely because they produce higher quality outputs than other banks. Thus, failure to recognize this heterogeneity in bank outputs may bias estimates of cost efficiency.

To overcome these problems, we try to incorporate these differences into the specification of the cost function. Formally, it is appropriate to include control variables, Z_{it}, along with the output and input price in a stochastic cost frontier, which can be written as:

$$\ln TC_{it} = f(Q_{it}, W_{it}, Z_{it}; \beta) + v_{it} + u_{it} \quad i = 1, \ldots, I, \ t = 1, \ldots, T \qquad (14.5)$$

Apart from including control variables in the deterministic kernel of the stochastic cost frontier, the model given by Equation (14.5) is structurally indistinguishable from the conventional stochastic cost frontier model given by Equation (14.1). In this formulation, Z_{it}, is assumed to directly influence the cost of production, and alter the shape of the cost frontier. However, the model still estimates a common benchmark. Although, this model may be more precise in its estimates of the parameters and cost efficiency, it does not account for heterogeneity due to the exogenous variables, which either change the position of the frontier or influence the inefficiency term.

Up to now, all the models we have presented assume that all the banks in an industry use the same production technology to convert inputs into outputs and face similar environmental conditions, i.e. the shape of the cost frontier is the same for all banks. We know, however, that some heterogeneous environmental variables (exogenous variables), which are neither inputs to the production process nor outputs of it, may influence the performance measures obtained. For example, variations in market structure, regulation, and ownership form, etc. may cause variations in bank performance. Thus, the omission of such heterogeneity leads to biased estimates of the parameters describing the cost frontier and misstates cost inefficiency as a consequence.

In the simplest case, if the environmental variables, which are not under the control of management, directly influence the structure of the production process itself, it is appropriate to incorporate these variables into the cost function as regressors (e.g., Good *et al.* 1993). In this case we write stochastic cost function as:

$$\ln TC_{it} = f(Q_{it}, W_{it}, Z_{it}, E_{it}; \beta) + v_{it} + u_{it} \quad i = 1, \ldots, I,\ t = 1, \ldots, T \quad (14.6)$$

where E_{it} is a vector of exogenous variables in the deterministic kernel of the stochastic production frontier accounting for systematic differences across the banks due to ownership structure, size and market structure etc. By including the additional variables, the cost frontier incurs a parallel shift. This is different from the influence of incorporating control variables, which changes the shape of frontier. In other words, each bank faces a different cost frontier, but we still assume that the shape of the frontier is the same for all banks. One limitation of this model is that the additional variables do not explicitly explain the variation in the efficiency of different banks.

Another way to account for heterogeneity and to achieve an explicit explanation of efficiency is to estimate the parameters of the stochastic frontier and inefficiency models simultaneously in one stage. This approach assumes that the environmental variables influence the degree of cost inefficiency (the distribution of inefficiency) and hence that cost efficiencies are expressed as a function of these factors and are integrated into the stochastic frontier model. By comparing this with the incorporation of exogenous variables into the cost function, this method allows adjusting the raw efficiency scores to reflect the nature of the operational environments which banks face (Kumhakar and Lovell 2000). This approach also avoids the omitted variables and independence problem, which plagues the two-stage estimation procedure (see Kumhakar and Lovell 2000; Wang and Schmidt 2002, for further discussion). Thus, we also employ the one-stage stochastic frontier model of Battese and Coelli (1995) to estimate bank efficiency. The general Battese and Coelli (1995) model is specified in the same way as Equation (14.5) with one exception, that the inefficiency term u_{it} expressed as an explicit function of a vector of exogenous variables E_{it} and a random error term. It can be expressed as follows:

$$\ln TC_{it} = f(Q_{it}, W_{it}, Z_{it}; \beta) + v_{it} + (\delta E_{it} + w_{it}) \quad i = 1, \ldots, I,\ t = 1, \ldots, T \quad (14.7)$$

where the random error term w_{it} captures the effect of the "unobserved" factors and is defined by a truncated normal distribution with zero mean and constant variance; E_{it} captures the observed factors which explain differences in cost efficiency across banks and δ is a vector of parameters to be estimated. Since the inefficiency term u_{it} is nonnegative, the truncation point is $-\delta E_{it}$.

In the above model, the truncated inefficiency term u_{it} is independently but not identically distributed and takes the form: $u_{it} \sim (\delta E_{it}, \sigma_u)$. The cost efficiency of the ith bank is then given by:

$$CE_{it} = \exp(-u_{it}) = \exp(-\delta E_{it} - w_{it}) \quad (14.8)$$

Table 14.1 Model specifications

Models	*Specification*	*Inefficiency u*	*Heterogeneity*
Baseline (M1)	$f(Q_{it}, W_{it}; \beta)$	$u_{it} \sim N^{+}(0, \sigma_u^2)$	None
Truncated (M2)	$f(Q_{it}, W_{it}; \beta)$	$u_{it} \sim N^{+}(\mu, \sigma_u^2)$	None
Controlled (M3)	$f(Q_{it}, W_{it}, Z_{it}; \beta)$	$u_{it} \sim N^{+}(\mu, \sigma_u^2)$	Bank specific observed factors in cost function
Kernel (M4)	$f(Q_{it}, W_{it}, Z_{it}, E_{it}; \beta)$	$u_{it} \sim N^{+}(\mu, \sigma_u^2)$	Bank specific observed factors in cost function
Error effects (M5)	$f(Q_{it}, W_{it}, Z_{it}; \beta)$	$u_{it} \sim N^{+}(\mu + \delta E_{it}, \sigma_u^2)$	Bank specific observed factors in cost function Heterogeneity in the mean of inefficiency distribution

Here, we also use maximum likelihood estimation to determine values of the unknown parameters in the above model. The expressions for the likelihood function and efficiency point estimator are presented in Battese and Coelli (1993).

When considering the different models summarized above we cannot find a convincing theoretical argument, which suggests that one particular specification for assessing efficiency is better than another. Hence, the choice of frontier models is "frequently a judgement call" (Kumhakar and Lovell 2000, p. 266). It thus turns out that the specification of inefficiency in frontier modelling is usually *ad hoc* and is based on tractability rather than on any optimal theoretical criteria for assessing efficiency (Kumbhakar *et al.* 1997). Given this, in this study, we employ the different stochastic cost frontier models briefly summarized in Table 14.1. These models use different assumptions for the distribution of (in) efficiency terms, and different ways to incorporate control and environmental variables. Importantly, however, we also compare the results obtained from each model in order to assess the reliability and robustness of our results and, in particular, to determine the most appropriate model with which to measure Chinese banking efficiency.

Data and specifications

Inputs and outputs variables

Following the discussion on the stochastic cost frontier models, which will be utilized to estimate efficiency levels for the Chinese banking sector, this section defines the output and input (price) variables which are used in our modelling procedures. This study follows the intermediation approach; due to the advantages of this approach and the availability of data, this suggests that operating expenses and total interest payments comprise total costs. Labor, total borrowed funds and physical capital are the bank's inputs; three outputs are total loans, other earning assets (e.g. investments, interbank assets), and non-interest income, which acts as a proxy for non-traditional activities (off balance items). Although off-balance sheet items are technically non-earning assets, they increase the bank's income and are an important component of banking business. Therefore, it should be included when modelling a bank's cost characteristics; otherwise, total output would be understated (Jagtiani and Khanthavit 1996; Rogers 1998; Clark and Siems 2002).

Control variables

In addition to the above input and output variables, our study also incorporate several control variables which have the potential to influence a bank's costs in a variety of ways. The control variables enter into the stochastic frontier model in the same way as the output (or input price) variables and these variables are fully interactive with the other parameters of the model. The control variables included in our model – namely, the level of equity, the amount of non-performing loans and the time trend – are used to help in addressing the omitted variables problem and the heterogeneity of our sample of banks. Omitting these control variables may result in some efficient elements of banking operations being incorrectly measured as differences in cost inefficiency.

The first control variable included in the banking cost function is the level of equity which is recognized as a quasi-fixed input in the cost function. The treatment of the level of equity is an important aspect of efficiency measurement. For example, Berger and Mester (1997) argue that a bank's insolvency risk depends on its financial capital which provides a cushion against portfolio losses and financial distress. Insolvency risk (non-performing loans) influences the bank's costs through the risk premium which the bank has to pay for its borrowings. This issue is particularly important in the Chinese banking sector where the insolvency risk of a bank could be great because of a large proportion of non-performing loans in the loan portfolio. Moreover, financial capital provides an alternative to deposits and other borrowed funds as a source of loan able funds, thus it also directly affects costs as an input into the production process.

Following Hughes and Mester (1993) and Mester (1996, 1997), another important control variable added to the cost function is nonperforming loans. This captures the quality of a bank's assets as well as the probability of bank failure, which can influence banks' costs in a number of ways. On the one hand, problem loans would be endogenous to the bank. A large proportion of nonperforming loans may be due to "bad management." Inefficient banks do not practice adequate loan underwriting and monitoring and hence will have higher losses due to non-performing loans. The low quality loans may also be caused by short-run cost savings on the initial credit evaluation and loan monitoring ("skimping"). This would produce cost efficiencies artificially higher than a bank which spends resources to ensure its loans are of higher quality. On the other hand, problem loans are likely to be exogenous to the bank due to negative economic shocks ("bad luck"). Exogenous events increase problem loans. As a consequence, the bank entails extra administrative expenses and managerial effort to resolve these bad loans. These extra operating costs lead to a reduction in cost efficiency. Controlling for non-performing loans in cost functions helps remove, by statistical means, the costs of dealing with problem loans.

Finally the time trend variable is included in the stochastic cost function in order to control for the effects of technical progress over time. The time trend is a "catch all" variable which captures the effect of technological factors, such as learning by doing and organizational changes allowing for the more efficient use of existing inputs.

Exogenous variables

In our study, the environmental variables are also incorporated in the model to account for heterogeneity and to investigate the determinants of the cost efficiency of banks. Environmental variables cannot generally be controlled by bank managers, or at least are partially exogenous. These variables fall into five broad categories: bank ownership type, bank size, banking deregulation, cooperate governance, and market structure characteristics.

The first category environmental variable include in our analysis is the ownership structures of banks in order that we might take account of the difference between state-owned, domestic, private and foreign banks. The second environmental variable included in our efficiency models is the size of banks. We do this in order to control for potential scale biases in the estimating process. Bank size maybe an important determinant of net interest margins and spreads if there are economies of scale in banking. One bank may be more efficient than another as a result of the economies of scale that arise from size rather than better management. We also include a dummy variable to capture the impact of bank deregulation on the Chinese banks' efficiency. A key objective of deregulation or reform is to improve resource allocation and banks' performance (Berger and Humphrey 1997). There have been two important banking reform time points in China during the last 20 years: 1994 and 2001. Before 1994, Chinese banks operated within the confines of a central economic plan and remained subject to administrative controls and the process of deregulation was slow. However, from 1994 Chinese regulation undertook a series of reforms that strengthened the legal status of commercial banks, and stipulated that banks operate independently so that there would be increased competition between banks. Since China's entry into the WTO at the end of 2001, the Chinese government has accelerated banking reform in order to modernize the banking system. The government accelerated the process of bank privatization, encouraged foreign share purchases, and enhanced corporate governance and so on. Therefore, it is useful to divide the sample into two sub-periods: the first covering the reform period from 1994–2001, and the second 2002–07, by which time China had joined the WTO.

The next environmental variable is a dummy variable to capture the fact that listed banks may improve efficiency from better corporate governance.[8] Once a bank goes public, it becomes subject to legal, regulatory, and disclosure requirements which usually lead to better corporate governance and which imposes additional external monitoring procedures on management. Therefore, it might be expected that banks with publicly traded shares might be more efficient, all else being equal. The final variable characterizes the competitive conditions of the market in which the banks operate. The degree of concentration of the banking industry is usually measured by the Herfindahl–Hirschman index (HHI) which proxies for the bank's market power or the intensity of the competition between banks. The degree of concentration and market share, as the indicators of the characteristics of market structure, may influence a bank's profitability and operational efficiency. We include both the HHI and market share in the estimating models because the HHI is an aggregate measure that only changes over time whereas the market share variable differs from bank to bank and over time.

Model specification

When parametric methods are used to estimate efficiency, we should first consider the choice of a functional form for the cost function. Thus, this study applies a transcendental logarithmic (translog) functional form to estimate cost function. Translog functional form developed by Christensen *et al.* (1973) is the most commonly used cost function in the bank efficiency literature. The translog functional form for our general empirical cost frontier model, which includes three outputs, three input prices, three control variables, and seven environmental variables, is specified as:[9]

$$\begin{aligned}
\ln\frac{TC}{W_3} &= \beta_0 + \sum_{i=1}^{3}\beta_i \ln(Q_i) + \sum_{m=1}^{2}\chi_i \ln\left(\frac{W_i}{W_3}\right) \\
&+ \sum_{i=1}^{3}\sum_{m=1}^{2}\iota_{im}\ln(Q_i)\ln\left(\frac{W_m}{W_3}\right) + \frac{1}{2}\sum_{i=1}^{3}\sum_{j=1}^{3}\varphi_{ij}\ln(Q_i)\ln(Q_j) \\
&+ \frac{1}{2}\sum_{m=1}^{3}\sum_{n=1}^{3}\eta_{mn}\ln\left(\frac{W_m}{W_3}\right)\ln\left(\frac{W_n}{W_3}\right) \\
&+ \sum_{k=1}^{3}\rho_k \ln Z_k + \frac{1}{2}\sum_{r=1}^{3}\sum_{s=1}^{3}\xi_{rs}\ln(Z_r)\ln(Z_s) \\
&+ \sum_{k=1}^{3}\sum_{m=1}^{2}\theta_{km}\ln(Z_k)\ln\left(\frac{W_m}{W_3}\right) \\
&+ \sum_{k=1}^{3}\sum_{i=1}^{3}\psi_{ki}\ln(Z_k)\ln(Q_i) + u_{it} + v_{it}
\end{aligned}$$

$$\begin{aligned}
u_{it} &= \delta_0 + \delta_1 STATE_{it} + \delta_2 FOREIGN_{it} + \delta_3 SIZE_{it} + \delta_4 LIST_{it} \\
&+ \delta_5 REFORM_t + \delta_6 HHI_t + \delta_7 MS_{it}
\end{aligned}$$

Here, ln*TC* is the natural logarithm of total (operating and financial) costs; Q_i *are* output quantities which are total loans, other earning assets, and non-interest income, respectively; W_2 is the price of labor, W_2 is the price of deposits and W_3 is the price of physical assets. The financial capital (Z_1), non-performing loans (Z_2) and a time trend (Z_3) are control variables. B, χ, ι, φ, η, ρ, ξ, θ, ψ, and δ are parameters to be estimated. The duality theorem requires that the cost function must be linearly homogeneous in input prices and continuity requires that the second order parameters must be symmetric. Thus, the total costs and input price terms are normalized by the last input price W_3, in order to impose a linear homogeneity restriction on the model. In addition, the standard symmetry restrictions $\varphi_{ij} = \varphi_{ji}$, $\eta_{mn} = \eta_{nm}$ and $\xi_{rs} = \xi_{sr}$ apply to the above cost function.

In addition, the inefficiency term u_{it} is obtained by truncation (at zero) of the normal distribution with mean, δE_{it}. $STATE_i$ is a dummy variable that takes a value of one if bank i is a state-owned bank, and zero otherwise. $FOREIGN_i$ is a dummy variable which has a value of one if bank i is a foreign bank, and zero otherwise. The dummy variable for domestic private banks is dropped from the regression (as a reference group) to avoid multicollinearity. The variable $SIZE_{it}$ represents the size of bank i in year t. $LIST_{it}$ is a dummy variable which takes a value of 1 if bank i was publicly listed in year t, and zero otherwise. Moreover, a reform dummy variable, *REFORM*, is equal to one for banks in the second reform stage (2002–2007) and zero for banks in the first reform stage (1994–2001). Finally, HHI_t is a proxy for market concentration in year t, and MS_{it} is the market share for each bank.

Data

Our sample is an unbalanced panel that covers 41 Chinese banks over the period from 1994 to 2007, and totals 397 observations. The sample comprises the big four state-owned banks, three policy banks, 12 national and regional joint-stock banks, 16 city commercial banks, and six foreign banks. At the end of 2007, these 41 banks owned almost 80 percent of total assets of the Chinese banking institutions. The 14-year period on which our study is based corresponds to the period over which China started vigorous banking reforms and was also post-WTO accession. These changes are expected to have a significant impact on Chinese bank performance. The data are mainly drawn from the *Almanac of China's Finance and Banking* issued by the China Finance Society (1994–2007) and *Bank Scope* – Fitch's International Bank Database. Additional data and double checks were made from other data sources, such as bank annual reports, the China Banking Regulatory Commission's database, the China Economic Information Network (www.cei.gov.cn), the *China Statistical Yearbook* and the *China Labour Statistical Yearbook*.

This study adopts the intermediation approach to define the inputs and outputs (price) of banking services (see Sealey and Lindley 1977). More specifically, Chinese banks collect deposits and use labor and fixed capital to transform these inputs into loans, investments, and non-interest income. Under this treatment, the outputs are specified as total loans (Q_1), which include: short-term customer loans, medium- and long-term customer loans, trade bills, bills discounted, entrusted loans and impaired loans, but exclude loan loss reserves. The other earning assets (Q_2) are comprised of balances due from the central bank and other depository institutions, inter-bank loans, short-term investments, long-term investments, trading securities, and securities held under Repo agreements, but exclude investment loss reserves. The non-interest income (Q_3) is comprised of net fees and commissions, gains on exchange, gains on investment and other operating income. The inputs are specified as: the total deposits plus other borrowed funds (X_1) which include short- and long-term deposits, short- and long-term saving deposits, deposits from the central bank, deposits from commercial banks and other depository institutions, inter-bank funds purchased, securities sold under agreement of repurchase, government deposits, and short- and long-term bonds. Total physical capital (X_2) is the book value of total fixed assets less accumulated depreciation and employees (X_3) is measured by the total number of employees.[10] Data for state-owned and most nationwide banks are complete. But about 15 percent of the data on the number of employees are missing for city commercial banks. Therefore, we assume the growth rate of the number of employees is the same as the growth rate of total assets for a given bank.[11]

The methods for measuring cost efficiency also require the total costs and the market prices of the inputs. The total costs include the costs of borrowed funds, – wages and salaries, and other operating expenses. A major problem concerning price data is that banks do not often record prices paid for the inputs purchased. Instead they normally record the total expenditure on each input category. However, it is normally possible to derive "unit values" which are essentially average prices of a broadly-defined group of inputs (Coelli *et al.* 2005). The input prices are defined as the following three variables. First is the price of deposits plus other borrowed funds (W_1), which is calculated by the ratio of total interest expenses on borrowed funds to total borrowed funds. Total interest expenses consist of interest paid on total deposits and interest on interbank borrowing. Second is the price of physical capital (W_2), also called the user cost of capital, which is defined as the ratio of other operating expenses to fixed assets. Other operating expenses are calculated as the operating expenses minus expenses on employees. Last is the price of labor (W_3). It is measured by the ratio of personnel expenses to the number of employees. Many sample banks follow Chinese Accounting Standards (CAS), which was developed only in recent years following the principles of the International Accounting Standards Board (IASB). Therefore, most banks did not disclose the personnel employee expense figures in the early years of the sample. We assume that the growth rate of the price of employees matches the growth rate of the average wage rate for the finance sector.[12] Based on this assumption, we can use the data for the available years to calculate the price of labor for missing years. Data relating to input price and output variables are summarized in Table 14.2.

Table 14.2 shows the mean, standard deviation and other statistics of the total costs across the 41 banks for the period from 1994 until 2007. Thus, the first element of the first row of the table gives the average (mean) total cost across the 41 banks for the period 1994–2007 (24,584 million RMB). The second element of the first row gives the standard deviation of the costs across the 41 banks, also for

Table 14.2 Descriptive statistics of input price and output variables 1994–1997. Unit: million RMB

	Mean	*St. dev.*	*Min*	*Max*
Total cost (*TC*)	24,584	65,577	13	633,080
Total loans (Q_1)	296,686	530,281	182	2,572,235
Total other earning assets (Q_2)	176,090	377,239	77	2,887,447
Non-interest income (Q_3)	2,270	4,863	1	43,680
Price of funds (W_1) (%)	0.0331	0.0311	0.2421	0.0052
Price of fixed assets (W_2) (%)	0.5612	0.5085	6.9303	0.08516
Price of labour (W_3)	0.0736	0.0441	0.2612	0.0114
Total assets	513,063	958,968	291	5,465,969

Notes: All data are in real 1994 terms and they have been converted using GDP deflator.

1994–2007 (65,577 million RMB). Finally the last two elements of the first row show minimum (13 million RMB) and maximum (633,080 million RMB) across all 41 banks for the period from 1994 until 2007. The other entries in this table are to be similarly interpreted.

In addition to the above input price and output variables, this thesis also employs a variety of control and environmental variables to account for heterogeneity in the sample and to explain differences across the cost efficiency estimates. The first of these is the total equity of the individual banks and this is used to control for different risk preferences across banks. The quality of output is proxied by the gross monetary value of non-performing loans (that is before any write-offs). The time trend is defined as follows: $T = 1$ for 1994, $T = 2$ for 1995, ..., $T = 14$ for 2007. These proxies for aggregate technical progress across time for the banks are included in our sample. As previously noted we also employ several environmental variables in our empirical analysis. Hence, we classify a bank as stated-owned when government agencies control at least 50 percent of its total capital. Domestic private banks are defined as those banks whose private domestic ownership is greater than 50 percent of total capital. Banks are classified as foreign banks if foreign institutions and/or shareholders control at least 50 percent of the affected bank's total capital. Moreover, the domestic private bank dummy is dropped from the regression equations employed in our analysis in which case the constant term in the affected regressions captures any domestic private bank effects. Bank size is measured by the natural logarithm of total assets. The HHI, the proxy for market concentration, is defined as the sum of the squared asset market shares of all banks. The HHI is slightly greater than zero for a perfectly competitive market and assumes a unit value for a monopoly. Market share is defined as the ratio of an individual bank's total assets to the total assets of all banks in a given year. Moreover, we define the period from 1994 until 2001 as the pre-deregulatory period (the first reform stage) and the period from 2002 until 2007 as the post-deregulatory period (the second reform stage). Table 14.3 summarizes descriptive statistics of all control and environmental variables across the 41 Chinese banks covering the period of our analysis from 1994 until 2007.

Table 14.3 Descriptive statistics of the bank's control and environmental variables

Variable	*Description*	*Mean*	*St. dev.*	*Min*	*Max*
The control variables					
Z_1	Equity	24,592	55,867	79	571,795
Z_2	Non-performing loans	52,723	128,523	0	644,503
$Z_3(T)$	Time trend	8.751	3.758	1	14
The environmental variables					
STATE	Dummy variable for state-owned banks	0.5202	0.5002	0	1
FOREIGN	Dummy variable for foreign banks	0.0682	0.2524	0	1
PRIVATE	Dummy variable for foreign banks (as a reference group)	0.4116	0.4931	0	1
SIZE	Log of total bank assets	5.7102	5.9818	2.4634	6.7377
REFORM	Dummy variable for second stage reform (2002–2007)	0.5592	0.4971	0	1
LIST	Dummy variable for listed banks	0.1607	0.3677	0	1
HHI	Herfindahl–Hirschman index (the sum of the squared asset market shares of all banks)	0.1489	0.0307	0.1133	0.2405
MS	Asset market share	0.0353	0.0664	0.00002	0.3460

Empirical results

Cost frontier estimates

The five models discussed in last section are used to estimate the cost stochastic frontier and cost efficiency of the 41 Chinese banks observed during 1994–2007. All the stochastic frontier models are estimated by maximum likelihood techniques, using the computer program FRONTIER 4.1 (Coelli 1996). The maximum likelihood estimates of parameters of the stochastic frontier cost functions are presented in Table 14.4. Model 1 contains parameter estimates of the translog model without control variables and environmental variables, and efficiency follows a half-normal distribution. In Model 2, efficiency is assumed to follow a truncated normal distribution. Model 3 incorporates three control variables in cost function. Model 4 includes environmental factors in the deterministic kernel of the cost frontier to affect the production technology and Model 5 introduces environmental factors as explanatory variables of cost efficiency.

The estimated individual coefficients in the stochastic frontier given by the translog functional form are due to many interrelations between the different explanatory variables difficultly direct interpretation as in the Cobb–Douglas function. Total costs and all the continuous explanatory variables are in logarithms

Table 14.4 Maximum likelihood parameter estimates for stochastic frontiers cost functions

Variables	*Parameter*	*Model 1*	*Model 2*	*Model 3*	*Model 4*	*Model 5*
Constant	β_0	−0.2289***	−0.1944***	−0.2515***	−3.6257***	−0.2173***
		(0.0347)	(0.0177)	(0.0239)	(0.9652)	(0.0253)
$\ln Q_1$	β_1	0.6431***	0.6419***	0.5484***	0.3429***	0.5526***
		(0.0218)	(0.0216)	(0.0261)	(0.0582)	(0.0264)
$\ln Q_2$	β_2	0.3101***	0.3117***	0.2693***	0.1600**	0.2941***
		(0.0253)	(0.0248)	(0.0246)	(0.0371)	(0.0250)
$\ln Q_3$	β_3	0.0524***	0.0536***	0.0385***	0.0316***	0.0314**
		(0.0148)	(0.0148)	(0.0140)	(0.0136)	(0.0140)
$\ln(W_1/W_3)$	χ_1	0.7903***	0.7919***	0.7073***	0.7022***	0.7259***
		(0.0156)	(0.0155)	(0.0207)	(0.0214)	(0.0211)
$\ln(W_2/W_3)$	χ_2	0.1074***	0.1075***	0.1298***	0.1413***	0.1246***
		(0.0206)	(0.0203)	(0.0190)	(0.0185)	(0.0195)
$0.5 \ln Q_1 \ln Q_1$	φ_{11}	0.1016***	0.1037***	0.1037	0.1072*	0.1013
		(0.0241)	(0.0238)	(0.0639)	(0.0629)	(0.0648)
$\ln Q_1 \ln Q_2$	φ_{12}	−0.0615**	−0.0640**	−0.1043***	−0.0789**	−0.1288***
		(0.0276)	(0.0267)	(0.0371)	(0.0365)	(0.0368)
$\ln Q_1 \ln Q_3$	φ_{13}	−0.0152	−0.0156*	0.0067	−0.0067	0.0148
		(0.0093)	(0.0092)	(0.0204)	(0.0197)	(0.0207)
$0.5 \ln Q_2 \ln Q_2$	φ_{22}	0.0664*	0.0689*	0.1108***	0.0784**	0.1067***
		(0.0400)	(0.0385)	(0.0381)	(0.0379)	(0.0370)
$\ln Q_2 \ln Q_3$	φ_{23}	−0.0021	−0.0022	−0.0206	−0.0145	−0.0098
		(0.0176)	(0.0174)	(0.0160)	(0.0155)	(0.0154)
$0.5 \ln Q_3 \ln Q_3$	φ_{33}	0.0141	0.0145	0.0112	0.0074	0.0070
		(0.0123)	(0.0121)	(0.0120)	(0.0117)	(0.0112)
$0.5 \ln(W_1/W_3)$	η_{11}	0.0412	0.0403*	0.0605*	0.0410	0.0656*
$\ln(W_1/W_3)$		(0.0240)	(0.0237)	(0.0337)	(0.0327)	(0.0345)
$\ln(W_1/W_3)$	η_{12}	−0.0359*	−0.0363	−0.0293	0.0057	−0.0253
$\ln(W_2/W_3)$		(0.0309)	(0.0305)	(0.0334)	(0.0324)	(0.0335)
$0.5 \ln(W_2/W_3)$	η_{22}	−0.0077	−0.0071	0.0184	−0.0288	0.0101
$\ln(W_2/W_3)$		(0.0377)	(0.0374)	(0.0338)	(0.0337)	(0.0343)
$\ln Q_1 \ln(W_1/W_3)$	ι_{11}	0.0223	0.0213	0.0584*	0.0468	0.0480
		(0.0208)	(0.0201)	(0.0347)	(0.0338)	(0.0344)
$\ln Q_1 \ln(W_2/W_3)$	ι_{12}	−0.0034	−0.0027	−0.0046	0.0199	0.0097
		(0.0216)	(0.0207)	(0.0304)	(0.0294)	(0.0313)
$\ln Q_2 \ln(W_1/W_3)$	ι_{21}	0.0118	0.0120	0.0431	0.0113	0.0238
		(0.0282)	(0.0272)	(0.0345)	(0.0326)	(0.0323)
$\ln Q_2 \ln(W_2/W_3)$	ι_{22}	−0.0304	−0.0281	−0.0684**	−0.0442	−0.0349
		(0.0338)	(0.0326)	(0.0329)	(0.0315)	(0.0323)
$\ln Q_3 \ln(W_1/W_3)$	ι_{31}	−0.0140	−0.0143	−0.0282	−0.0217	−0.0223
		(0.0135)	(0.0134)	(0.0176)	(0.0165)	(0.0167)
$\ln Q_3 \ln(W_2/W_3)$	ι_{32}	0.0095	0.0100	0.0221	0.0221	0.0155
		(0.0165)	(0.0163)	(0.0151)	(0.0143)	(0.0151)
Control variables						
$\ln Z_1$	ρ_1	–	–	0.0343	0.0384*	0.0361*
				(0.0213)	(0.0208)	(0.0211)

Table 14.4 Continued

Variables	*Parameter*	*Model 1*	*Model 2*	*Model 3*	*Model 4*	*Model 5*
$\ln Z_2$	ρ_2	–	–	0.0942*** (0.0120)	0.0796*** (0.0117)	0.0876*** (0.0121)
T	ρ_3	–	–	0.0032 (0.0043)	−0.0231*** (0.0117)	−0.0024 (0.0044)
$0.5 \ln Z_1 \ln Z_1$	ξ_{11}	–	–	0.0083 (0.0192)	0.0148 (0.0189)	0.0067 (0.0199)
$\ln Z_1 \ln Z_2$	ξ_{12}	–	–	0.0002 (0.0115)	−0.0030 (0.0111)	−0.0070 (0.0118)
$\ln Z_1\ T$	ξ_{13}	–	–	−0.0252*** (0.0076)	−0.0136* (0.0077)	−0.0206*** (0.0078)
$0.5 \ln Z_2 \ln Z_2$	ξ_{22}	–	–	0.0141*** (0.0025)	0.0109*** (0.0026)	0.0098*** (0.0028)
$\ln Z_2\ T$	ξ_{23}	–	–	0.0068** (0.0031)	0.0012 (0.0032)	0.0008 (0.0035)
$0.5\ TT$	ξ_{33}	–	–	0.0002 (0.0024)	0.0010 (0.0027)	−0.0004 (0.0024)
$\ln Z_1 \ln Q_1$	ψ_{11}	–	–	0.0092 (0.0366)	−0.0199 (0.0375)	0.0125 (0.0373)
$\ln Z_1 \ln Q_2$	ψ_{12}	–	–	0.0309 (0.0324)	0.0351 (0.0323)	0.0352 (0.0327)
$\ln Z_1 \ln Q_3$	ψ_{13}	–	–	−0.0114 (0.0200)	0.0002 (0.0194)	−0.0226 (0.0202)
$\ln Z_2 \ln Q_1$	ψ_{21}	–	–	−0.0179 (0.0138)	−0.0096 (0.0134)	−0.0086 (0.0145)
$\ln Z_2 \ln Q_2$	ψ_{22}	–	–	−0.0020 (0.0115)	−0.0027 (0.0112)	0.0066 (0.0120)
$\ln Z_2 \ln Q_3$	ψ_{23}	–	–	0.0027 (0.0065)	0.0068 (0.0061)	0.0010 (0.0066)
$T \ln Q_1$	ψ_{31}			0.0073 (0.0084)	0.0088 (0.0081)	0.0132 (0.0088)
$T \ln Q_2$	ψ_{32}			0.0077 (0.0078)	0.0006 (0.0074)	0.0074 (0.0079)
$T \ln Q_3$	ψ_{33}	–	–	−0.0017 (0.0053)	0.0000 (0.0049)	−0.0012 (0.0053)
$\ln Z_1 \ln(W_1/W_3)$	θ_{11}	–	–	−0.0784*** (0.0293)	−0.0500* (0.0283)	−0.0616** (0.0298)
$\ln Z_1 \ln(W_2/W_3)$	θ_{12}	–	–	0.0390 (0.0301)	0.0194 (0.0293)	0.0266 (0.0305)
$\ln Z_2 \ln(W_1/W_3)$	θ_{21}	–	–	0.0106 (0.0104)	0.0098 (0.0101)	0.0099 (0.0110)
$\ln Z_2 \ln(W_2/W_3)$	θ_{22}	–	–	0.0014 (0.0092)	−0.0134 (0.0094)	−0.0066 (0.0097)

Table14.4 Continued

Variables	*Parameter*	*Model 1*	*Model 2*	*Model 3*	*Model 4*	*Model 5*
$T\ \ln(W_1/W_3)$	θ_{31}	–	–	0.0005	0.0020	0.0032
				(0.0069)	(0.0067)	(0.0074)
$T\ \ln(W_2/W_3)$	θ_{32}	–	–	0.0030	0.0056	0.0023
				(0.0063)	(0.0063)	(0.0066)
Environmental variables						
STATE	δ'_1	–	–	–	−0.0209	–
					(0.0257)	
FOREIGN	δ'_2	–	–	–	−0.2591***	–
					(0.0732)	
SIZE	δ'_3	–	–	–	0.3156***	–
					(0.0861)	
LIST	δ'_4	–	–	–	−0.0116	–
					(0.0299)	
REFORM	δ'_5	–	–	–	0.1114***	–
					(0.0340)	
HHI	δ'_6	–	–	–	−1.8682	–
					(1.2535)	
MS	δ'_7	–	–	–	−3.6257	–
					(0.9652)	
Intercept	δ_0	–	–	–	–	2.2074***
						(0.5199)
STATE	δ_1	–	–	–	–	−0.2516**
						(0.1065)
FOREIGN	δ_2	–	–	–	–	−0.1061***
						(0.2899)
SIZE	δ_3	–	–	–	–	−0.3563***
						(0.1031)
LIST	δ_4	–	–	–	–	−0.0066
						(0.0857)
REFORM	δ_5	–	–	–	–	1.2117**
						(0.5284)
HHI	δ_6	–	–	–	–	−1.5270
						(1.2195)
MS	δ_7	–	–	–	–	−7.2047***
						(2.4588)

Notes:

1. ***, **, and * indicate 1 percent, 5 percent and 10 percent significance levels, respectively.
2. Asymptotic standard errors are in parentheses.

and divided by their respective sample means. This normalization of variables permits the first-order parameters of the translog function to be interpreted as the respective cost elasticities evaluated at the sample mean. Table 14.4 shows that the parameter estimates of output quantities and input prices terms are positive and highly significantly different from zero across all five model specifications. Therefore, the estimated cost functions fulfil the theoretical requirement (i.e. non-decreasing in outputs and in input prices). For example, the coefficient estimate of the total loans (Q_1) in Model 5 suggests that, on average, a one percent increases in the amount of loans will increase the costs by about 0.55 percent. Similarly, the cost elasticity with respect to other earning assets (Q_2) is 0.29 in Model 5, suggesting that a one percent increase in other earning assets will raise total cost by 0.29 percent. Also, we observe that the magnitude of coefficient of non-interest income (Q_3) is significantly smaller than for the other two outputs, implying that the amount of non-interest income does not have a large impact on total costs. This may be because off-balance activities (represented by the non-interest income) account for a small part of the output portfolio in the Chinese banking sector. The estimated elasticity of cost with respect to total borrowed funds (W_1) is relatively higher than for the other two input prices, in the range 0.7022 to 0.7919 across five models. The results indicate the total costs are most responsive to price of borrowed funds and suggest that on average a one percent increase in price of borrowed funds will raise total costs about 0.7 percent to 0.8 percent depending on the model. The coefficient of price of physical capital (W_2) indicates the share of costs attributed to physical capital, which ranges between 0.1413 percent and 0.1075 percent depending on the specification adopted.[13] Moreover, we observe that the coefficient of non-performing loans (Z_2) has a positive sign and is significantly different from zero in Models 3, 4, and 5, implying that larger non-performing loans are related to higher cost. Regarding Model 4 which includes all environmental factors in the deterministic kernel, most parameter estimates associated with environmental factors are not statistically significant, implying that those variables may not be shifting the cost curve.

Key estimation results

Except for the parameter estimates of cost functions, it is also interesting to note that Table 14.5 reports some other key estimation results for all five specifications of cost frontiers, respectively. The parameters that determine the shape and location of the inefficiency distribution are shown in the first three columns. The inefficiency location parameter μ is significantly different from zero for environmental factors in error specification (M5). This may be explained by the fact that we introduce heterogeneity in the efficiency distribution in this model. However, estimate of μ in alternative models are not significant at the five percent level. The γ parameters that correspond to the estimated proportion of bank inefficiency in the composed total error term are significantly different from zero for in both the baseline model (M1) and all alternative models. This parameter shows high value (close 1) in the models that account for heterogeneity, revealing that most

Table 14.5 Key estimation results

Model specification	μ	γ	σ^2	*Log likelihood*	*LR test of one-sided error*
Baseline (M1)	0	0.5115***	0.0557***	88.8902	2.4076 (3.841)
Truncated (M2)	−6.9109*	0.9637***	0.7414*	91.6750	7.977 (5.991)
Controlled (M3)	−7.4554*	0.9821***	0.8376*	164.3368	26.2449 (5.991)
Kernel (M4)	−0.8215	0.9888***	0.1001	185.0729	36.2558 (5.991)
Error effects (M5)	2.2074***	0.8639***	0.1237***	175.1729	47.9171 (16.919)

Notes:
1. $\sigma^2 = \sigma_u^2 + \sigma_v^2$; $\gamma = \sigma_u^2/(\sigma_u^2 + \sigma_v^2)$.
2. χ^2 critical values for 5 percent significance level are in the parentheses.
3. ***, ** and * indicate 1 percent, 5 percent and 10 percent significance levels, respectively.

of the variation in observed cost from the frontier is due to bank inefficiency. The difference of γ coefficients between Models 4 and 5 is most likely explained by the way in which the environmental factors are included in these models. At the same time, the magnitude of the variance parameter σ^2 in alternative models is larger compared to the baseline specification.

The logarithmic values of the likelihood function, a frequently used criterion of better statistical properties of an econometric model estimated through the maximum likelihood function, are presented in the fourth column of Table 14.5. We find that the log-likelihood value for Models 3, 4, and 5 are higher than the baseline and truncated specifications, suggesting that including a set of explanatory variables in specification to account for heterogeneity improves the fit significantly. The last column in Table 14.5 reports the results of log-likelihood ratio tests (one side) of the standard response function (ordinary least squares (OLS)) versus full frontier model. The null hypothesis in this test is $\gamma = 0$ versus the alternative $\gamma > 0$. If the null hypothesis is accepted, this could indicated that σ^2 and δ_i are zero and hence that the inefficiency effects in the cost function are not present, leaving a specification with parameters that can be appropriately estimated using OLS (Coelii 1996). If the null hypothesis is rejected, this could suggest that a standard mean response function is not an adequate representation of the data. In the case of the baseline model, the null hypothesis is accepted at the 5 percent level of significance, suggesting that the SFA is an inappropriate specification of the cost model. However, in the case of alternative models, the null hypothesis is significantly rejected in favor of the stochastic frontier cost function. Therefore, the results of the baseline model should be viewed with caution or discarded and the results of alternative models accounting for heterogeneity seem more reliable for empirical analysis.

Model specification tests

We turn now to the formal tests to compare all considered models, which we discussed in the methodology. In order to reach the best-specified cost frontier model, we have conducted the generalized likelihood ratio test that is a convenient way to check whether a reduced (restricted) model provides the same fit as a general (unrestricted) model. Table 14.6 presents the steps and results of the log-likelihood tests. The first column of the table lists the specifications tested. The second column presents the restriction imposed or the null hypotheses. The next column reports the log likelihood value for the specification. The fourth column shows the calculated log likelihood test statistic. The fifth column gives the critical value for test statistic. The last column reports the testing decision, i.e. whether the null hypothesis is rejected or accepted or the imposed restriction is valid or not.

In Table 14.6, the first step is to test the half normal model (M1) against the truncated normal model (M2). The null hypothesis is that the model assuming the inefficiency term following a half normal distribution is better than the model assuming the inefficiency term following a truncated normal distribution. It is equivalent to test the restriction $\delta_0 = 0$ is valid or not. When this restriction is imposed on the truncated normal model, the log likelihood value reduces to 88.890 (M1) from 91.675 (M2). The generalized likelihood ratio test statistic turns out to be 5.57, which is greater than the χ^2 critical value at the 5 percent level. Therefore, we reject the null hypothesis of $\delta_0 = 0$, suggesting the truncated-normal distribution model is more compatible than the half-normal distribution model for the data under analysis.

The second step is to compare the model specifications including different combinations of control variables to reach the most appropriate specification in this step. The unrestricted model in this step includes all three control variables in cost function (financial capital, asset quality, and time). Based on first step decision, this model is estimated assuming the inefficiency term follows a truncated normal distribution.

First, we test the model specifications that drops only one control variable against the unrestricted model. At this point, there are three null hypotheses to be tested. The first null hypothesis is that the specification of cost function without time parameters gives better fit than that of the cost function including all control variables, i.e. imposing all the coefficients associated with the time trend equal to zero. The second null hypothesis is that the cost function specification without the non-performing loans parameters is more appropriate than the unrestricted model. The third null hypothesis states that the specification of the model without equity parameters is better than that of the unrestricted model.

As Table 14.6 shows, the value of the generalized likelihood ratio statistics for above three cases is larger than the critical value. Thus, the all three null hypotheses are rejected at the five percent level of significance. This means that model including all three control variables again is the dominant specification compared to the models including two control variables. Second, the unrestricted model will be compared with some alternative models that include only one control variable. Again, three null hypotheses will be assumed here. The first null hypothesis is that the model including only equity level is more appropriate than the unrestricted model. The next null hypothesis is that the model including only non-performing loans is more appropriate than the unrestricted model. The third null hypothesis

Table 14.6 Hypotheses testing of the cost function

Model description	*Restriction* (H_0)	*Log likelihood*	*LR test of the one-side error*	*Critical value* $\alpha = 5\%$	*Decision* H_0*: restricted model is better than unrestricted model*
Step 1: Half normal vs truncated normal					
– Truncated normal distribution (M2) distribution (M2)	Unrestricted	91.675			
– Normal distribution (M1)	H_0: $\delta_0 = 0$	88.890	5.57	3.841 (1)	Reject H_0
Step 2: Model without control variables vs model with control variables					
– Truncated normal with all control variables	Unrestricted	164.337			
– Without time trend parameters	H_0: $\rho_3 = \xi_{31} = \xi_{32} = \xi_{33} = \theta_{31} = \theta_{32} = \psi_{31} = \psi_{32} = \psi_{33} = 0$	151.230	26.214	15.507 (8)	Reject H_0
– Without NPL parameters	H_0: $\rho_2 = \xi_{21} = \xi_{22} = \xi_{23} = \theta_{21} = \theta_{22} = \psi_{21} = \psi_{22} = \psi_{23} = 0$	123.404	81.866		Reject H_0
– Without equity parameters	H_0: $\rho_1 = \xi_{11} = \xi_{12} = \xi_{13} = \theta_{21} = \theta_{22} = \psi_{21} = \psi_{22} = \psi_{23} = 0$	148.219	32.236		Reject H_0
– Without NPL and time trend parameters	H_0: $\rho_2 = \rho_3 = \xi_{21} = \xi_{22} = \xi_{31} = \xi_{32} = \xi_{33} = \theta_{21} = \theta_{22} = \theta_{31} = \theta_{32} = \psi_{21} = \psi_{22} = \psi_{23} = \psi_{31} = \psi_{32} = \psi_{33} = 0$	103.762	121.15	27.59 (17)	Reject H_0
– Without equity and time trend parameters	H_0: $\rho_1 = \rho_3 = \xi_{11} = \xi_{12} = \xi_{31} = \xi_{32} = \xi_{33} = \theta_{11} = \theta_{12} = \theta_{31} = \theta_{32} = \psi_{11} = \psi_{12} = \psi_{13} = \psi_{31} = \psi_{32} = \psi_{33} = 0$	142.023	44.628		Reject H_0

Table 14.6 Continued

Model description	*Restriction* (H_0)	*Log likelihood*	*LR test of the one-side error*	*Critical value* $\alpha = 5\%$	*Decision* H_0*: restricted model is better than unrestricted model*
– Without equity and NPL trend parameters	H_0: $\rho_1 = \rho_2 = \xi_{11} = \xi_{12} = \xi_{13} = \xi_{22} = \xi_{23} = \theta_{11} = \theta_{12} = \theta_{21} = \theta_{22} = \psi_{11} = \psi_{12} = \psi_{13} = \psi_{21} = \psi_{22} = \psi_{23} = 0$	107.994	112.686		Reject H_0
– Without all control variable parameters	H_0: $\rho_1 = \rho_2 = \rho_3 = \xi_{11} = \xi_{12} = \xi_{13} = \xi_{22} = \xi_{23} = \xi_{33} = \theta_{11} = \theta_{12} = \theta_{13} = \theta_{21} = \theta_{22} = \theta_{23} = \psi_{11} = \psi_{12} = \psi_{13} = \psi_{21} = \psi_{22} = \psi_{23} = \psi_{31} = \psi_{32} = \psi_{33} = 0$	91.675	145.324	36.415 (24)	Reject H_0
Step 3: Models without environmental variables vs models with environmental variables					
– Including environmental variables in cost function	Unrestricted	185.073			
– Not including environmental variables in cost function	H_0: $\delta'_1 = \delta'_2 = \delta'_3 = \delta'_4 = \delta'_5 = \delta'_6 = \delta'_7$	164.337	41.472	14.067 (7)	Reject H_0
– Including environmental variables in error effects	Unrestricted	175.172			
– Not including environmental variables in error effects	H_0: $\delta_1 = \delta_2 = \delta_3 = \delta_4 = \delta_5 = \delta_6 = \delta_7$	164.337	27.67	14.067 (7)	Reject H_0

Notes:

1. Degrees of freedom are in parentheses.
2. Log-likelihood test statistic = 2 (unrestricted log-likelihood function (ULLF)–restricted log-likelihood function (RLLF)).

states that the model including only the time trend is better than the unrestricted model. Similarly, all above null hypotheses are rejected at the five percent level of significance according to the log likelihood ratio statistic. So the unrestricted model is still the best model. Last, we compare the unrestricted model with the model excluding all three variables, which is identical with the Model 2. In this case, the null hypothesis states that the truncated model without any control variables is better than the unrestricted model, i.e. all the coefficients associated with the equity, non-performing loans and time trend to equal zero. The log likelihood test rejects the null hypothesis in favour of the unrestricted model again. Based on the above results, we find the control variables have significant effects on the total cost and should be included in the cost function. Therefore, the most appropriate specified model up to this step is the truncated model including all three control variables.

The third step is to examine whether including the environmental variables in model specification has any significant explanatory power. The tests are made by comparing the model including the environmental variables in the deterministic kernel of the frontier (M4) and/or in the distribution of the inefficiency term (M5) with the truncated model including all control variables (M3). The Model 3 excludes the environmental factors from the analysis and thus becomes a special case of Model 4 or Model 5 in which all the coefficients associated with the environmental variables equal to zero. The null hypotheses are that the specified truncated model including control variables but excluding the environmental variables is more appropriate than the models that include the environmental variables. In the above cases, the log-likelihood ratio test statistics are 41.472 and 27.67 respectively, which are both larger than the critical value of χ^2 at the 5 percent level of significance. Thus we reject both the null hypotheses and conclude that the environmental factors should not be ignored in the study of Chinese bank efficiency.

The question of whether the environmental variables should be treated as explanatory variables in cost function (M4) or as determinants of cost inefficiency (M5) is not directly answered by the generalized log likelihood ratio test. These two model specifications are not nested and hence no set of restrictions can be imposed which allow a test of one specification against the other. Therefore, it is difficult to provide an unequivocal assessment as to whether the stochastic cost function specification M4 or the stochastic cost function specification M5 is more compatible with the Chinese banking data that is available to us.

On the basis of the above empirical results, however, we do find that sample heterogeneity significantly influences the stochastic cost frontier estimation. Thus, any model of Chinese banking efficiency that is used for policy purposes should explicitly account for sample heterogeneity by introducing control variables and/or environmental variables as part of its arguments. Otherwise it would be misspecified, leading to inappropriate parameter and efficiency estimates and, more importantly, potentially flawed policy decisions. However, the selection between a model considering the environmental variables as a part of the deterministic kernel of the frontier and a model considering the environmental variables as determinants of cost efficiency is a difficult issue. Here, we prefer the model that treats environmental variables as explanatory variables of cost efficiency. The reasons for this are, first, the improved significance of the critical parameters $\mu\gamma$ and σ^2 in Model 5 and the insignificance of coefficients for most of the environmental variables in Model 4. Second, we also believe that the estimated frontier represents the outer boundary of the cost possibility set, irrespective of environmental issues (Coelli *et al.* 1999). Moreover, in our study, we are interested not only in the efficiency level but also wish to know the sources or determinants of the cost inefficiencies. Thus, the Model 5 specification would appear to be the most useful of all the models we examine here.

Efficiency level

Turning our attention to the cost efficiency scores, these scores have been predicted by using the well known Battese and Coelli (1982) result. Table 14.7 provides a statistical summary of the estimated efficiency scores of all banks for the various models. Thus, the mean, median, and the lowest and highest efficiencies for the models are presented in the Table 14.7. Regarding the overall mean values of cost efficiency scores for the entire period, we find a relative small range, from 87.26 percent to 91.14 percent, indicating that the average bank in the sample could reduce its cost by approximately 13 percent to 9 percent matching its performance with the best practice bank. Model 5 (heterogeneity in inefficiency term) yields the highest mean and medium, while the baseline model (half-normal) generates the lowest. Compared to the other alternative specifications, the efficiency estimates in the baseline half normal specification are lower. This result indicates that neglecting the heterogeneity across banks may create a downward bias in efficiency scores. Moreover, explicitly accounting for the heterogeneity in terms of ownerships, size, market structure, etc. in the distribution of the inefficiency component leads to a mean cost efficiency that is approximately two percent to four percent points high than other specifications. However, the mean efficiency scores in Models 2, 3 and 4 are a similar, suggesting that accounting for the heterogeneity in the efficiency frontier did not influence efficiency estimates very much.

Table 14.7 Summary statistics of the average efficiency estimates

	Model 1 Baseline	*Model 2 Truncated*	*Model 3 Controlled*	*Model 4 Kernel*	*Model 5 Error*
Mean	0.8726	0.9029	0.8983	0.8900	0.9114
Median	0.8795	0.9149	0.9166	0.9139	0.9379
Standard deviation	0.0480	0.0527	0.0668	0.0777	0.0789
Maximum	0.9581	0.9685	0.9752	0.9755	0.9808
Minimum	0.6179	0.5217	0.4802	0.4595	0.3625

Notes: The efficiencies are calculated using 14 years of data for 44 banks (397 observations), and the numbers in the table are based on the average efficiency for each bank over the sample period.

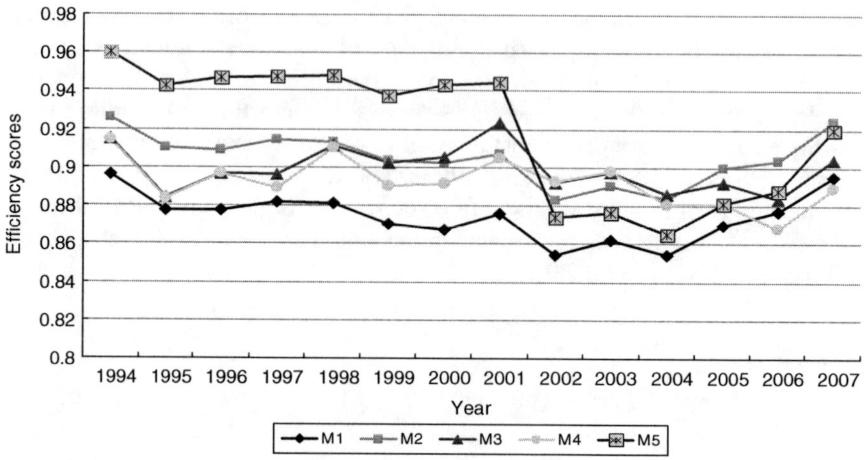

Figure 14.1 Average cost efficiency scores over time.

Regarding the maximum value in those models, we found that these are quite high in Models 3, 4, and 5, suggesting that the heterogeneity across companies is an important driver of cost differences. In sum, it is clear that controlling for heterogeneity is necessary. However, the results show that efficiency estimates may be sensitive to the way in which we account for sample heterogeneity.

The yearly average cost efficiency of all banks for the five different models is plotted in Figure 14.1. The trends or patterns of efficiency levels obtained from five different specifications are broadly similar over time, specially the Model 3 and Model 4. In general, most of banks were relatively efficient early on (before 2002) but less efficient later (after 2002). In addition, the significant decrease of efficiency level appeared between 2001 and 2002 across all the models. These emerging patterns may provide evidence that the 2001–2002 calendar year appeared to be associated with a structural change in the trend of cost efficiency and that this is associated with China's entry into the WTO that occurred around about this time.

Spearman's correlation for different models

Another potentially interesting comparison is whether the ranks obtained for the efficiencies scores across the different specifications show any compatibility. The ranking of banks according to cost efficiency scores can provide some information on the impact of structural change on bank efficiency. If different models rank banks completely differently, then the generalized conclusions may be cautious and as such depend on which frontier efficiency specification is employed (Abdulai and Tietje 2007). The Spearman rank correlation matrix of the efficiency estimates are presented in Table 14.8. These coefficients show how close the ordering of the banks are among each other, using the full sample of banks. In general,

Table 14.8 Spearman rank correlation between efficiency estimates

	Model 1 *Baseline*	*Model 2* *Truncated*	*Model 3* *Controlled*	*Model 4* *Kernel*	*Model 5* *Error*
Half-normal (M1)	1.0000				
Truncated (M2)	0.9994	1.0000			
Controlled (M3)	0.8148	0.8150	1.0000		
Kernel (M4)	0.7623	0.7626	0.9433	1.0000	
Error (M5)	0.5778	0.5901	0.6360	0.5664	1.0000

Note: All correlations significant at the 1 percent level.

the rank correlation according to the efficiency scores among the first three models (i.e. Models 1, 2, and 3) are lower than between them and the last two models (i.e. Models 4 and 5). The near perfect correlation of efficiency ranking between the half-normal model and truncated model suggests that these models indentify the same banks as best and worst performers. This shift of the inefficacy distribution seems to influence all banks in the sample to a very similar degree. The inclusion of control variables in efficiency estimation leads to a decline of rank correlation to around 0.8, indicating that this inclusion not only absorbs some heterogeneity but also affects some banks' ranking order. However, Models 3 and 4 show a very high correlation (0.94) in the estimated efficiency. This may suggest that introducing the environmental factors in the kernel specification leads to only minor changes in the ranking order. The results also show that the rank order correlations between Model 5 with other alternative models are lower than others, ranging from 56 percent to 63 percent. These results suggest that Model five which include environmental factors (heterogeneity) in inefficiency term specification ranks bank efficiency in a markedly different way when compared to other alternative models.

In sum, these results further improve our understanding of the effect of heterogeneity on efficiency estimates. It seems that accounting for the heterogeneity is an important issue which, when not taken into account, may lead to biased results.

Chinese banking cost efficiency and analysis

Cost efficiency estimates are derived from the preferred stochastic frontier model which includes all control variables in cost function and allow environmental variables to affect the distribution of inefficiency term. The statistics of estimated efficiency scores are reported in Table 14.9.

Generally, the results in Table 14.9 show relatively high average cost efficiency in the Chinese banks, with efficiency scores that range from 86.5 percent to 96 percent. This result is consistent with the results reported in the literature, such as Berger *et al.* (2009). The average cost efficiency for the sample period is 91.14 percent, meaning that, on average, the sample could potentially save inputs costs

Table 14.9 Average cost efficiency scores for the Chinese banking sector (1994–2007)

	Mean	*St. dev.*	*Min*	*Max*	*Observation*
1994	0.9601	0.0070	0.9501	0.9728	11
1995	0.9425	0.0286	0.8579	0.9735	18
1996	0.9467	0.0271	0.8610	0.9729	19
1997	0.9477	0.0254	0.8881	0.9741	20
1998	0.9482	0.0317	0.8388	0.9747	20
1999	0.9374	0.0361	0.8333	0.9767	26
2000	0.9432	0.0198	0.8997	0.9741	29
2001	0.9445	0.0288	0.8519	0.9808	32
2002	0.8741	0.1128	0.3625	0.9543	34
2003	0.8765	0.1155	0.4697	0.9686	35
2004	0.8653	0.0933	0.6095	0.95867	36
2005	0.8812	0.0841	0.6158	0.9751	38
2006	0.8881	0.1005	0.5150	0.9663	39
2007	0.9200	0.0477	0.7620	0.9689	40
Overall	0.9114	0.0790	0.3625	0.9808	397

by approximately 10 percent by using its inputs more efficiently without changing the level of output. We find that mean cost efficiency is significantly higher (about 7 percent) in 2001 (before China's WTO entry) than that in 2002 (after WTO entry). This decline could be a consequence of deregulation and liberalization reforms. It is also worthy of note that the standard deviations of the average efficiency prior to WTO accession (1994–2001) are quite low, implying that the cost efficiency levels of the sample banks are very close to each other. But, interestingly, the average cost efficiency rises after China's admission to the WTO (2002–07). There are two possible explanations for this change in the dispersion of efficiency scores. First, the sample data before 2002 mainly include the nationwide banks that have similar characteristics in terms of inputs and outputs, while later period data also include many other types of banks, such as city commercial banks. Hence it is this which may cause the low variation of cost efficiency across different banks in the early period but which rises in later periods. Second, the significant external environmental changes due to WTO entry may have created winners and losers amongst the Chinese banks.

The temporal performance (efficiency) pattern for the Chinese banking sector is also of interest. Figure 14.2 illustrates the trend of average cost efficiency changes over the sample period. Note how the Chinese banking sector shows an overall decreasing trend in cost efficiency over the study period. The mean cost efficiency remains at a relatively high level and varies very little during the period from 1994 until 2001. This may indicate the reforms implemented by the Chinese government may have enhanced the performance of Chinese banks over this period. Moreover, banking competition was relatively weak throughout this period. Banks enjoyed large interest margins – probably because of this. It is worth noting however, that average efficiency declined sharply after China's admission to the WTO,

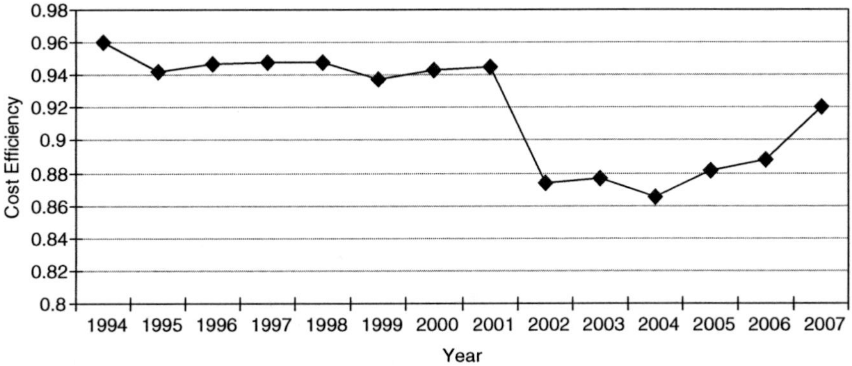

Figure 14.2 Average cost efficiency scores for Chinese banking sector (1994–2007).

particularly in 2002. This may suggest that the external environmental changes introduced in 2002 may have had a negative impact on Chinese banking efficiency. Banks may have had to incur additional costs in order to prepare for the intensive competition and other environmental changes which arose from China's admission to the WTO. Moreover, the new loan classification system was formally applied to all banks from 2002. Along with this new system, banks are allowed to carry out more aggressive provisioning against non-performing loans resulting in a significant decline in the book value of bank loans. This will thus be reflected in declining efficiency because of the output reduction caused by loan write-offs without any changes in the input usage. However, we find that the negative impact on efficiency disappeared in 2005 and that the mean efficiency increased significantly in 2005–07. This finding implies that banking reforms implemented in this period may have improved Chinese banking efficiency.

Having examined the cost efficiency of the aggregate Chinese banking sector over time, we now further analyze cost efficiency level in more details by different banking categories. Figure 14.3 displays the average value of the cost efficiency scores according to their origin and ownership: specifically Big Four, state-owned policy banks, nationwide JSCBs, city commercial banks (CCBs), and foreign banks. Although these groups of banks operate in the same market, each group faces a different set of regulations. In light of this uneven and changing regulatory environment, we expect to find performance variation, both across groups of banks and over time. We seek to quantify and also to explain this anticipated performance variation.

During the period 1994–2001, all bank subcategories show relatively low variation in efficiency scores and also remain at a relatively high level of efficiency. However, they exhibit greater variability in mean efficiency over the period 2002–2007. All bank groups show a significant decline in average efficiency. As shown in Figure 14.3, the Big Four and policy banks have tended to exhibit higher mean

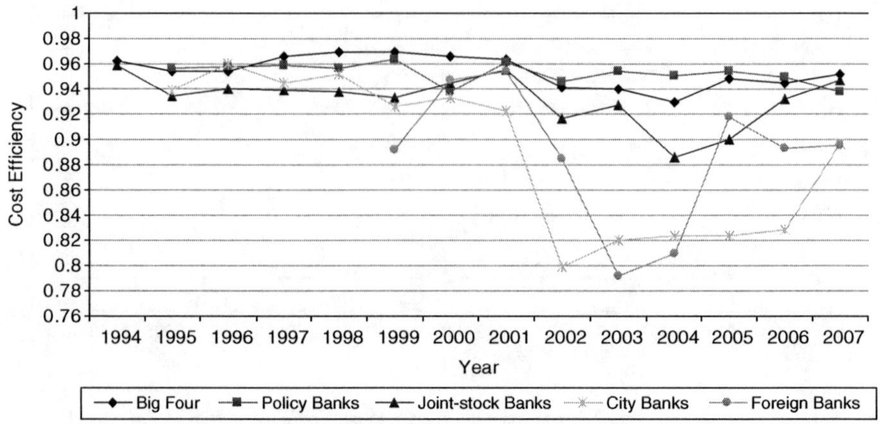

Figure 14.3 Average cost efficiency by different bank types.

cost efficiency than other subcategories. The average cost efficiency score for the big four state-owned banks and state-owned policy banks are 95.43 percent and 95.25 percent respectively. It is observed that amongst the rest of the subcategories, no bank group has a clearly dominant position over the sample period. These findings contradict a common perception in the literature and the results of some previous studies. For example, Fu and Heffernan (2008) found that the JSCB were more X-efficient than the Big Four over the period 1985–2002. Berger *et al.* (2009) showed that the foreign banks were more efficient than other banks types. Differences in such finding may be due to different modelling methods, such as different model specification and sample period.

Big four state-owned commercial banks

Overall, the Big Four exhibit quite good performance in cost efficiency relative to other bank types. The results can possibly be explained by the Big Four having an extensive branch network which assures a stable retail banking business. It may also reflect in part continual government subsidies on the cost side. The Big Four show an improving trend in efficiency during the period from 1997–99, indicating that they took advantage of the early reforms which the Chinese government focused almost exclusively on them. For example, the Chinese government recapitalized the Big Four with RMB 270 billion in 1998. Then in 1999 the government established four asset management corporations (AMCs) to buy RMB 1.4 trillion of non-performing loans from the Big Four. From 1998, the Big Four also started to improve organizational management efficiency by reducing the number of redundant branches and employees. Up to 2002, they reduced the number of branches by nearly 30 percent and employees by 10 percent. Following China's admission to the WTO at the end of 2001, we observe however that the cost efficiency of the Big Four deteriorated. This may have occurred because of the under capitalization of the Big Four and a large amount of non-performing loans on the Big Four's balance sheets. But beginning in 2005, the Big Four's cost efficiency began to improve again. After a few years of intense debate, the Chinese government also launched a new series of reforms for the Big Four. The government injected RMB 499.6 billion into state-owned banks at the end of 2003 and allowed the four banks to transfer their non-performing loans to AMCs in 2004 and 2005. More recently, the government has encouraged the big state-owned banks to introduce foreign capital and to list on one or more of the Chinese stock exchanges. All these measures appear to have enhanced the banks' performance and could provide an explanation for the improvement in the cost efficiency that has occurred in the Big Four in the period beginning in 2005.

State-owned policy banks

The state-owned policy banks tend to show relatively little variation in their efficiency scores over time, and, unexpectedly, exhibit high cost efficiency levels. There are several possible explanations for these results. First, the policy banks are mainly engaged in the government policy-oriented finance business and, as a result, could be receiving favourable treatment from the government that improves their cost efficiency. Second, the policy banks only focus on policy lending and they may possess more experienced and specialized teams that enable them to evaluate and monitor their lending in an efficient way. Third, the policy banks, compared with commercial banks, do not necessarily have a strong network of branches, and the higher staff levels associated with this and other factors result in considerable savings in their operating expenses.

Joint stock commercial banks

This study is based on 12 JSCBs.[14] Each of these banks operates on a nationwide basis. Referring to Figure 14.3, we find that JSCBs show less efficiency when compared with their counterparts – the Big Four. This result is similar to that reported by Chen (2005). However, the efficiency levels for the JSCBs and the Big Four have tended to converge over the last few years. There are several possible explanations for these results. First, the JSCBs' branch networks are much more limited than those of the Big Four. This constrains their competitiveness and leads to relatively small market shares. Another possible explanation is that JSCBs do not enjoy an implicit government guarantee of their debts and they also do not receive the subsidies from government that are received by the state-owned banks. This may increase the cost of their borrowed funds and this in turn influences their cost efficiency levels. However, JSCBs have shown a considerable improvement in average cost efficiency in the last three years (2005–2007). This trend may indicate that JSCBs have gained efficiency benefits from foreign strategic investments, which are expected to result in new management systems and techniques and better corporate governance.

City commercial banks

Generally, CCBs show a relatively low level of cost efficiency when compared to the efficiency scores of the other types of bank. The most likely reason for this is that city commercial banks are restricted to opening branches within their own city boundaries. This regulation may impact on their cost efficiency scores relative to nationwide banks, particularly for those located in smaller, less prosperous cities, because they are less able to achieve economies of scale and spread risk (Laurenceson and Qin 2008). It is noteworthy that the mean efficiency levels of CCBs shows a significant difference between the period before and after 2001. This may be due in part to our sample choice. Before 2001 the sample data are only available for several big CCBs and most of these have characteristics that are similar to JSCBs. However, in the later sample period, we include more varied CCBs, of different sizes, and which are located widely across China. The changing nature of the CCBs over our sample period may be one of the reasons for the decline in cost efficiency in the later period.

Foreign banks

Figure 14.3 shows that foreign banks exhibit less average cost efficiency than do nationwide domestic banks. This finding may be interpreted as evidence that foreign banks are managed less efficiently, but this is not necessarily the case. It can also reflect less familiarity with the regulatory system and a greater restriction on business scope and geographic range. The foreign banks' efficiency estimates are available only after 1999 and do not indicate a consistent trend over the study period. In the initial three years, they show increasing efficiency. In the first two years after China's admission to the WTO, we observe a significant decline in efficiency in foreign banks. However, this decline may simply reflect the costs of setting up business and branch expansion in order to facilitate competition with China's domestic banks. This is reflected in the fact that the cost efficiency of foreign banks improves significantly after 2003. The greater variability in the efficiency of foreign banks may be due to their dependence on less stable wholesale or corporate resources, interbank market borrowings, and the refinancing of assets.

The determinants of cost efficiency

In the previous section, we present and discuss the cost efficiency results obtained from the Battese and Coelii (1995) model. It should be noted that another advantage of their model is allowing the single-step estimation of (in) efficiency in which bank effects are directly influenced by a number of environmental (exogenous) variables. Thus in this section we will focus on the results of the inefficiency term equation in the Battese and Coelii (1995) model to investigate how the environmental factors affect banks' performance, i.e. the determinants of cost efficiency. According to the theory and literature, we hypothesize that the determinants of bank inefficiency are the nature of ownership, size, corporate governance, deregulation, and market structure. Those factors are at least partially exogenous. The estimation results of the influence of the environmental variables on bank inefficiency are reported at the bottom of the Table 14.4.

First, it is interesting to investigate the observed variation in cost efficiency is determined by their ownership structure. This study divides Chinese banks into three categories, namely, state-owned banks, domestic private banks, and foreign banks. The domestic private banks are omitted from the regression, so other bank ownership efficiencies are measured relative to this category. The negative sign on the coefficients of the state-owned ownership dummy (−0.2516) suggests that state-owned banks were operating less inefficiently than domestic private banks. This result is consistent with the findings of Berger *et al.* (2009). A much more possible explanation is the "skimping" behaviour in which banks might economize the loan underwriting and monitoring costs to achieve higher cost efficiency in the short run, but yield poor loan revenues in the long run (Berger and DeYong 1997).[15] Moreover, the government subsidies for state-owned banks on the cost side also increase their efficiency level. Similarly, the sign of coefficient on foreign ownership is negative (−0.1061) and significant at the one percent level. Hence, foreign banks are more efficient than domestic private banks, the omitted category. This result partially support the global advantage hypothesis which asserts that foreign ownership is associated with more efficient management and thus foreign banks are able to outperform the domestic banks. However, we also found that the foreign banks are less efficient than state-owned banks. The reason for this could be that foreign banks hire high-skilled workers, which leads to huge expenditure on high salaries. Moreover, foreign banks also incurred large costs in attempting to provide superior quality of services with the expectation of higher revenues. But our efficiency measure does not take into account those factors, thus foreign banks may be wrongly considered as less cost efficient.

Size can also be an important factor that drives the variation in efficiency across banks. In our case, the logarithm of the total asset variable, a proxy for bank size, is negatively (−0.3563) related to cost inefficiency. It reflects that bigger banks tend to be more efficient and if increasing total assets by 1 percent will help reduce the cost inefficiency by 0.36 percent. This result is consistent with other banking studies (e.g., Hasan and Marton 2003). Bigger banks may have experienced some economies of scale and scope from growth and joint production resulting in lower inefficiency. Furthermore, larger banks may have a more professional or specialized management team that can better control bank costs.

The coefficient of listed banks dummy is negative (−0.0066) but not significant. This suggests public listing has no impact on efficiency. The market discipline hypothesis implies that banks whose shares are publicly traded should exhibit higher efficiency, but our findings indicated that the Chinese capital market exerts no discipline over bank management. This could also be due to the fact that stock markets responding more strongly to profit measures rather than to cost efficiencies (Chu and Lim 1998).

Unexpected, there is a significant positive correlation between deregulation (China's WTO accession) and bank inefficiency. This result indicates that China's WTO accession did not improve banks' performance imminently. This effect may be attributed to competition that stemmed from the relaxation of barriers to entry. Intuitively, the competitive pressure forced the banks to increase their borrowing rate and narrow down their net interest margins. The deterioration of bank efficiency may also be due to the lagged banking reforms. Most recent banking reforms were effective after 2003, two years after WTO accession. The banks' efficiency had improved in later years of the sample period and this is confirmed by early analysis.

The extensive theory and empirical research reveal that the market structure could affect the bank performance or efficiency. In this case, we find that the coefficient of Herfindahl–Hirschman index (market concentration variable) is negative but not significant and the coefficient of market share is negative and statistically significant. These results do not support the quiet life hypothesis. The quiet life hypothesis states that the banks with more market power or in less competitive market environments might feel less pressure to control their cost and then lead to less efficiency. The significant positive relationship with market share and cost efficiency which we observed indicates that banks with a dominant share of banking assets could facilitate their operations more efficiently and thus lead to lower average total cost. Alternatively, this result may be explained by the efficiency structure hypothesis. It asserts that relatively efficient banks might have competed more aggressively and ultimately gained larger market shares. Thus it also suggests that market share is positively related to efficiency.

Conclusion

China's economy has held up remarkably well during the recent global recession. It expanded by 8.7 percent in 2009, substantially above the global average growth rate. However, the future growth of China's economy may depend on the performance and reforms of its banking sector. Since the late 1970s, the Chinese government has gradually implemented a series of reforms aimed at improving the stability and efficiency of its banking sector, and the Chinese banking sector has experienced significant structural transformations and fundamental changes. Therefore, this study investigated the cost efficiency and main determinates of the Chinese banking sector over its reform period, 1994–2007. The study provides a more recent and comprehensive evidence on the impact of the Chinese government's reform program on the efficiency of the Chinese banking sector.

This study estimated the cost efficiency of Chinese banks using the stochastic cost frontier approach. We followed the recent efficiency methodologies that proceed by applying various model specifications to take into account the heterogeneity in the sample of Chinese banks. We compared the estimated parameters from different specifications, conducted a specification test, and discussed the effect of accounting for the heterogeneity on efficiency scores. As a result, we found a preferred model specification for our sample, i.e. the translog cost function form that includes the control variables (capital adequacy, asset quality and the time trend) and all the environmental variables. Thus the preferred model gave us estimates of cost efficiency and its determinants.

Based on the chosen preferred model, cost efficiency averaged around 91.14 percent over the period 1994–2007. We found average cost efficiency sharply declined after China's WTO accession. This result indicates that the significant external environmental changes due to WTO entry have an impact on the cost efficiency score. However, interestingly, the banking deregulation and other banking reforms implemented in 1995 and 2004 appeared to have enhanced the cost efficiency of Chinese banks. When breaking sample banks into Big Four, policy banks, JSCBs, CCBs and foreign banks), the Big Four and policy banks show a relatively higher mean efficiency score then other groups. This is consistent with Chen *et al.* (2005). Moreover, amongst the rest of the subcategories, no bank group gains a clear dominant position over the sample period.

We also examined the environmental factors in explaining or determining Chinese banking cost efficiency. State-owned banks and foreign banks are more efficient than domestic private banks. Similarly, larger banks tend to be more efficient. In order to examine whether the deregulation had a significant impact on the performance of these banks, we separated the sample period into two sub-periods, viz., pre-WTO accession period (1994–2001) and post-deregulatory period (2002–2007). We found that deregulation (WTO accession) deteriorated cost efficiency. Moreover, we found that the banks with larger market share are more cost efficient and there is no evidence to support the quiet life hypothesis.

Notes

1 The sample has 187 observations collected from four state-owned and ten joint stock banks.
2 The two-step estimation procedure suffers from some serious biases. See Wang and Schmidt (2002) for details.
3 We know only of prior studies of majority foreign ownership in other nations (e.g. Fries and Taci 2005).
4 An alternative point estimator for efficiency is given by Jondrow *et al.* (1982) (JLMS). Battese and Coelli (1988) and Kumbhakar and Lovell (2000) point out that the Battese and Coelli (1988)'s estimator is to be preferred, particularly when u_i is not close to zero. This is the JLMS estimator includes only the first term in the power-series expansion of $\exp(-u)$.
5 An estimator is consistent if its values approach the true parameter value and if its variances get smaller as the sample size increases indefinitely.
6 See Kumbhakar and Lovell (2000) for the derivation of the likelihood function and its partial derivatives with respect to the parameters of the model.
7 These models absorb all unmeasured heterogeneity through the inefficiency term (u_{it}).
8 The listed bank is a common governance indicator. Berger *et al.* (2005) also list some other types of governance indicators such as CEO-Chairman affiliation, and governance change.
9 Here, we only present the Battese and Coelli (1995) cost frontier specification for reasons of space. All other model specifications which were discussed in previous section can easily derive from this general model.

10 The measurement of the quantity of physical capital (assets) is quite difficult, because, unlike labor input, capital assets are a durable input used in the production process through the life of the asset. It is typically assumed that the productive capital stock reflects the quantity of capital services used in production. Therefore, it is feasible to use the capital stock as a proxy for the capital input.

11 This assumption is widely accepted in banking efficiency studies. See Altunbas *et al.* (2001), Vannet (2002), Rezvanian and Mehdian (2002) and Fu and Heffernan (2007).

12 Other studies such as Fu and Heffernan (2007), Ariff and Can (2007) adopt the average wage paid by financial institutions as a proxy for the price of labor.

13 The labor price coefficient (W_3) can be recovered by using the linear homogeneity restriction. It is calculated by $1 - \chi_1 - \chi_2$ and is similar in magnitude to physical capital price.

14 They are Bank of Communications, CITIC Bank, China Everbright Bank, China Merchants Bank, Huaxia Bank, China Mingsheng Bank, Shenzhen Development Bank, Shanghai Pudong Development Bank, Guangdong Development Bank, Industrial Bank, Evergrowing Bank, and China Zheshang Bank.

15 Further examination confirms this explanation. The state-owned banks, particularly the big four- have much higher rates of non-performing loan than other banks.

References

Abdulai, A. and Tietje, H. (2007) 'Estimating technical efficiency under unobserved heterogeneity with stochastic frontier models: application to Northern German dairy farms', *European Review of Agricultural Economics*, 34: 393–416.

Aigner, D., Lovell, C. A. K. and Schmidt, P. (1977) 'Formulation and estimation of stochastic frontier production function models', *Journal of Econometrics*, 6: 21–37.

Altunbas, Y., Gardener, E. P. M., Molyneux, P. and Moore, B. (2001) 'Efficiency in European banking', *European Economic Review*, 45: 1931–1955.

Ariff, M. and Can, L. (2008) 'Cost and profit efficiency of Chinese banks: A non-parametric analysis', *China Economic Review*, 19: 260–273.

Baradwaj, B. G., Flaherty, S. and Li, J. (2008) 'Are chinese banks positioned to compete in the post-WTO environment?', *Chinese Economy*, 41: 56–75.

Battese, G. E. and Coelli, T. J. (1988) 'Prediction of firm-level technical efficiencies with a generalized frontier production function and panel data', *Journal of Econometrics*, 38: 387–399.

Battese, G. E. and Coelli, T. J. (1993) 'A stochastic frontier production function incorporating a model for technical inefficiency effects', working paper, Department of Econometrics, University of New England.

Battese, G. E. and Coelli, T. J. (1995) 'A model for technical inefficiency effects in a stochastic frontier production function for panel data', *Empirical Economics*, 20: 325–332.

Berger, A. N. (1995) 'The profit-structure relationship in banking – tests of market-power and efficient-structure hypotheses', *Journal of Money, Credit and Banking*, 27: 404–431.

Berger, A. N. and Bonaccorsi di Patti, E. (2006) 'Capital structure and firm performance: A new approach to testing agency theory and an application to the banking industry', *Journal of Banking and Finance*, 30: 1065–1102.

Berger, A. N. and De Young, R. (1997) 'Problem loans and cost efficiency in commercial banks', *Journal of Banking & Finance*, 21: 849–870.

Berger, A. N. and Hannan, T. H. (1998) 'The efficiency cost of market power in the banking industry: a test of the quiet life and related hypotheses', *Review of Economics and Statistics*, 80: 454–465.

Berger, A. N. and Humphrey, D. B. (1990) '*Measurement and Efficiency Issues in Commercial Banking*', Board of Governors of the Federal Reserve System (U.S.).

Berger, A. N. and Humphrey, D. B. (1997) 'Efficiency of financial institutions: International survey and directions for future research', *European Journal of Operational Research*, 98: 175–212.

Berger, A. N. and Mester, L. J. (1997) 'Inside the black box: What explains differences in the efficiencies of financial institutions?', *Journal of Banking and Finance*, 21: 895–947.

Berger, A. N., Clarke, G. R. G., Cull, R., Klapper, L. and Udell, G. F. (2005) 'Corporate governance and bank performance: A joint analysis of the static, selection, and dynamic effects of domestic, foreign, and state ownership', *Journal of Banking and Finance*, 29: 2179–2221.

Berger, A. N., Demirgüç-Kunt, A., Levine, R. and Haubrich, J. G. (2004) 'Introduction: Bank concentration and competition: an evolution in the making', *Journal of Money, Credit and Banking*, 36 (3): 433–451.

Berger, A. N., DeYoung, R., Genay, H. and Udell, G. F. (2000) '*Globalization of Financial Institutions: Evidence from Cross-Border Banking Performance*', Board of Governors of the Federal Reserve System (U.S.).

Berger, A. N., Hasan, I. and Zhou, M. (2009) 'Bank ownership and efficiency in China: What will happen in the world's largest nation?', *Journal of Banking and Finance*, 33: 113–130.

Berger, A. N., Hunter, W. C. and Timme, S. G. (1993) 'The efficiency of financial institutions: A review and preview of research past, present and future', *Journal of Banking and Finance*, 17: 221–249.

Berger, A. N., Leusner, J. H. and Mingo, J. J. (1997) 'The efficiency of bank branches', *Journal of Monetary Economics*, 40: 141–162.

Bhattacharyya, A., Lovell, C. A. K. and Sahay, P. (1997) 'The impact of liberalization on the productive efficiency of Indian commercial banks', *European Journal of Operational Research*, 98: 332–345.

Bonin, J. P., Hasan, I. and Wachtel, P. (2005) 'Bank performance, efficiency and ownership in transition countries', *Journal of Banking and Finance*, 29: 31–53.

Bos, J. W. B. and Schmiedel, H. (2007) 'Is there a single frontier in a single European banking market?', *Journal of Banking and Finance*, 31: 2081–2102.

Bos, J. W. B., Koetter, M., Kolari, J. W. and Kool, C. J. M. (2009) 'Effects of heterogeneity on bank efficiency scores', *European Journal of Operational Research*, 195 (1): 251–261.

Chen, T. (2002) 'A comparison of chance-constrained DEA and stochastic frontier analysis: bank efficiency in Taiwan', *Journal of the Operational Research Society*, 53: 429–500.

Chen, X., Skully, M. and Brown, K. (2005) 'Banking efficiency in China: Application of DEA to pre- and post-deregulation eras: 1993–2000', *China Economic Review*, 16: 229–245.

Chu, S. F. and Lim, G. H. (1998) 'Share performance and profit efficiency of banks in an oligopolistic market: evidence from Singapore', *Journal of Multinational Financial Management*, 8: 155–168.

Christensen, L. R., Jorgenson, D. W. and Lau, L. J. (1973) 'Transcendental logarithmic production frontiers', *The Review of Economics and Statistics*, 55: 28–45.

Clark, J. A. and Siems, T. F. (2002) 'X-Efficiency in banking: Looking beyond the balance sheet', *Journal of Money, Credit, and Banking*, 34: 987–1013.

Coelli, T. J. (1995) 'Estimators and hypothesis tests for a stochastic frontier function: A Monte Carlo analysis', *Journal of Productivity Analysis*, 6: 247–268.

Coelli, T. J. (1996) '*A Guide to Frontier Version 4.1: A Computer Program for Stochastic Frontier Production and Cost Function Estimation*', CEPA working paper, Department of Econometrics, University of New England, Armidale NSW Australia.

Coelli, T. J., Perelman, S. and Romano, E. (1999) 'Accounting for environmental influences in. Stochastic frontier models: With application to international airlines', *Journal of Productivity Analysis*, 11: 251–273.

Coelli, T. J., Prasada Rao, D. S., O'Donnell, C. J. and Battese, G. E. (2005) *An Introduction to Efficiency and Productivity Analysis*, 2nd edn, Springer.

Cole, R. A. and Gunther, J. W. (1995) 'Separating the likelihood and timing of bank failure', *Journal of Banking and Finance*, 19: 1073–1089.

Demsetz, H. (1995) *The Economics of the Business Firm: Seven Critical Commentaries*, Cambridge, New York and Melbourne: Cambridge University Press.

Denizer, C. A., Dinc, M. and Tarimcilar, M. (2000) *Measuring Banking Efficiency in the Pre- and Post-Liberalization Environment: Evidence from the Turkish Banking System*, The World Bank.

Dietsch, M. and Lozano-Vivas, A. (2000) 'How the environment determines banking efficiency: A comparison between French and Spanish industries', *Journal of Banking and Finance*, 24: 985–1004.

Drake, L. and Hall, M. J. B. (2003) 'Efficiency in Japanese banking: An empirical analysis', *Journal of Banking and Finance*, 27: 891–917.

Farrell, M. J. (1957) 'The measurement of productive efficiency', *Journal of the Royal Statistical Society. Series A (General)*, 120: 253–290.

Farsi, M., Filippini, M. and Kuenzle, M. (2007) 'Cost efficiency in the Swiss gas distribution sector', *Energy Economics*, 29: 64–78.

Fu, X. (2004) *Efficiency and Competition in China's Banking Sector*, PHD thesis, Cass Business School, City Univeristy, London, UK.

Fu, X. and Heffernan, S. (2007) 'Cost X-efficiency in China's banking sector', *China Economic Review*, 18: 35–53.

Fu, X. and Heffernan, S. (2009) 'The effects of reform on China's bank structure and performance', *Journal of Banking and Finance*, 33: 39–52.

García Herrero, A. and Santabárbara, D. (2008) *Does the Chinese Banking System Benefit from Foreign Investors?*, Bank of Finland, Institute for Economies in Transition.

Good, D. H., Nadiri, M. I. and Sickles, R. C. (1993) 'Efficiency and productivity growth comparisons of European and U.S. air carriers: A first look at the data', *Journal of Productivity Analysis*, 4: 115–125.

Greene, W. H. (1990) 'A Gamma-distributed stochastic frontier model', *Journal of Econometrics'*, 46: 141–163.

Grifell-Tatjé, E. and Lovell, C. A. K. (1996) 'Deregulation and productivity decline: the case of Spanish savings banks', *European Economic Review*, 40: 1281–1303.

Grigorian, D. A. and Manole, V. (2002) *Determinants of Commercial Bank Performance in Transition – An Application of Data Envelopment Analysis*, The World Bank.

Gujarati, D. N. (2003) *Basic Econometrics*, 4th edn, Gary Burke.

Hasan, I. and Marton, K. (2003) 'Development and efficiency of the banking sector in a transitional economy: Hungarian experience', *Journal of Banking and Financ*e, 27: 2249–2271.

Havrylchyk, O. (2006) 'Efficiency of the Polish banking industry: Foreign versus domestic banks', *Journal of Banking and Finance*, 30: 1975–1996.

Humphrey, D. B. and Pulley, L. B. (1997) 'Banks' responses to deregulation: Profits, technology, and efficiency', *Journal of Money, Credit and Banking*, 29: 73–93.

Hughes, J. P. and Mester, L. J. (1993) 'A quality and risk-adjusted cost function for banks: Evidence on the 'too-big-to-fail' doctrine', *Journal of Productivity Analysis*, 4: 293–315.

Isik, I. (2003) 'Efficiency, ownership and market structure, corporate control and governance in the Turkish banking industry', *Journal of Business Finance and Accounting*, 30: 1363–1421.

Isik, I. and Hassan, M. K. (2002) 'Efficiency, ownership and market structure, corporate control and governance in the Turkish banking industry', *The Financial Review*, 37: 257–279.

Jagtiani, J. and Khanthavit, A. (1996) 'Scale and scope economies at large banks: Including off-balance sheet products and regulatory effects 1984–1991', *Journal of Banking and Finance*, 20: 1271–1287.

James, L. and Fengming, Q. (2008) 'Has minority foreign investment in China's banks improved their cost efficiency?', *China and World Economy*, 16: 57–74.

Jondrow, J., Knox Lovell, C. A., Materov, I. S. and Schmidt, P. (1982) 'On the estimation of technical inefficiency in the stochastic frontier production function model', *Journal of Econometrics*, 19: 233–238.

Karim, M. Z. A. (2001) 'Comparative bank efficiency across select ASEAN countries', *ASEAN Economic Bulletin*, 18: 289–304.

Koetter, M. (2005) *Measurement Matters – Alternative Input Price Proxies for Bank Efficiency Analyses*, Deutsche Bundesbank, Research Centre.

Kumbhakar, S. C. and Lovell, C. A. K. (2000) *Stochastic Frontier Analysis*, Cambridge: Cambridge University Press.

Kumbhakar, S. C. and Sarkar, S. (2003) 'Deregulation, ownership, and productivity growth in the banking industry: Evidence from India', *Journal of Money, Credit and Banking*, 35: 403–424.

Kumbhakar, S. C. and Wang, D. (2007) 'Economic reforms, efficiency and productivity in Chinese banking', *Journal of Regulatory Economics*, 32: 105–129.

Kumbhakar, S. C., Heshmati, A. and Hjalmarsson, L. (1997) 'Temporal patterns of technical efficiency: results from competing models', *International Journal of Industrial Organization*, 15: 597–616

Kyj, L. and Isik, I. (2008) 'Bank x-efficiency in Ukraine: An analysis of service characteristics and ownership', *Journal of Economics and Business*, 60: 369–393

Laurenceson, J. and Qin, F. (2008) 'Has minority foreign investment in China's banks improved their cost efficiency?', *China and World Economy*, 16: 57–74

Meeusen, W. and van Den Broeck, J. (1977) 'Efficiency estimation from Cobb–Douglas production functions with composed error', *International Economic Review*, 18: 435–444.

Mester, L. J. (1993) 'Efficiency in the savings and loan industry', *Journal of Banking and Finance*, 17: 267–286.

Mester, L. J. (1996) 'A study of bank efficiency taking into account risk-preferences', *Journal of Banking and Finance*, 20: 1025–1045.

Mester, L. J. (1997) 'Measuring efficiency at U.S. banks: Accounting for heterogeneity is important', *European Journal of Operational Research*, 98: 230–242.

Moreno, R. (2002) 'Reforming China's banking system', *FRBSF Economic Letter*, May 31.

Resti, A. (1997) 'Evaluating the cost-efficiency of the Italian banking system: What can be learned from the joint application of parametric and non-parametric techniques', *Journal of Banking and Finance*, 21: 221–250.

Rezvanian, R. and Mehdian, S. (2002) 'An examination of cost structure and production performance of commercial banks in Singapore', *Journal of Banking and Finance*, 26: 79–98.

Rogers, K. E. (1998) 'Nontraditional activities and the efficiency of US commercial banks', *Journal of Banking and Finance*, 22: 467–482.

Sealey, C. W. J. and Lindley, J. T. (1977) 'Inputs, outputs, and a theory of production and cost at depository financial institutions', *Journal of Finance*, 32 (4): 1251–66.

Shepherd, W. G. (1972) 'The elements of market structure', *The Review of Economics and Statistic*', 54: 25–37

Shepherd, W. G. (1982) 'Economies of scale and monopoly profits', *Industrial Organization, Antitrust, and Public Policy*, Boston: Kluwer Nijhoff.

Stevenson, R. E. (1980) 'Likelihood functions for generalized stochastic frontier estimation', *Journal of Econometrics*, 13: 57–66.

Syetarm, H. (2004) *China's Financial Sector: Institutional Framework and Main Challenges China Special*, Deutsche Bank AG, DB Research.

Valverde, S. C., Humphrey, D. and Paso, R. L. D. (2007) 'Opening the black box: Finding the source of cost inefficiency', *Journal of Productivity Analysis*, 27: 209–220.

Vander Vennet, R. (2002) 'Cost and profit efficiency of financial conglomerates and universal banks in Europe', *Journal of Money, Credit and Banking*, 34: 254–82.
Wang, H. and Schmidt, P. (2002) 'One-step and two-step estimation of the effects of exogenous variables on technical efficiency levels', *Journal of Productivity Analysis*, 18: 129–144.
Wang, W., Huang, H. and Lai, M. (2005) 'Measuring the relative efficiency of commercial banks: A comparative study on different ownership modes in China', *Journal of American Academy of Business*, 7 (12.5): 219–223.
Yao, S., Jiang, C., Feng, G. and Willenbockel, D. (2007) 'WTO challenges and efficiency of Chinese banks', *Applied Economics*, 39: 629–643.

15 The effect of historical events on the speed of price evolution indexed by an operational time for China's futures market

Ren Zhang, Youwei Li and Donal McKillop

Introduction

The non-normality of security price returns has attracted a large number of studies. The observed distributions are commonly called leptokurtic because of the narrower body of the distribution and fatter tails. One explanation suggested for the leptokurtosis in speculative market prices is the serial correlation in the time series of absolute or squared returns. This assertion, however, cannot explain the determinants behind these dynamic dependencies. An approach for rationalizing the strong contemporaneous correlation in price series is provided by the MDH (mixture of distributions hypothesis) developed by Clark (1973), in which a stochastic time variable (operational time) as opposed to calendar time was subordinated to the price process, and this operational time can be approximated by a physically observed variable: trading volume (or number of trades). According to the MDH theory, price changes and trading volumes are driven by the same underlying latent information flow that influences the expectations of market practitioners to result in price volatilities.

The MDH has been modified by researchers in recent decades including Tauchen and Pitts (1983), which refined Clark's specification by including trading volume as an endogenous variable. Lamoureux and Lastrapes (1990) put the information arrival variable into autoregressive conditional heteroskedasticity (ARCH)/generalized autoregressive conditional heteroskedasticity (GARCH) models to find the source of the autocorrelation in price change variance. Andersen (1996) divided trading activities into two parts: one part was related to information arrivals whereas another one was not. Other research tended to discover if the dynamic of price volatility and volume share long run or short run behaviour (Bollerslev and Jubinski 1999; Ane and Rangau 2008). These studies are all based on the assumption that the price change variance and trading activity are simultaneously directed by the information arrival process.

The aforementioned literature gives an explanation about how information arrivals actually affect price evolution and trading activity. Clark (1973) suggested that price evolved at a different rate each day (or other identical calendar time intervals such as two days, one week and so on) because the accumulations of the number of information arrivals are different each day. In other words, different speeds of price evolution each day is due to the fact that information is available to traders at a varying rate. On a day when a large volume of information is available, it may violate previous expectations of traders, trading is brisk, and the price evolves faster. On a day when a small volume of information is available, trading is slow and price evolves slowly. In futures markets, a large number of traders are at any time waiting for more profitable opportunities with their own expectations about a futures contract's price. When new information arrives, traders' expectations and the futures price change. Those inside traders may have the information earlier and then change their trading behaviour. Other traders may only learn of uncertain information or obtain the information slower than inside traders. Thus, different expectations among traders cause traders to buy or sell assets in different directions, which results in significant trading activity and price changes. On the other hand, new information may be perceived by all traders to change their expectations in the same way, and then move price in the same direction. Under this situation, high price changes go with low volume (but above average trading volume).

Therefore, market price volatilities are caused by the new information flow arrivals which also lead to great variations on trading volume, and the changes on price and volume should be positively correlated. Volume of trading thus can be an operational clock to measure the speed of price evolution. For modelling price movement on operational time, Clark (1973) introduced a subordinated stochastic process (SP), and its test results displayed that the SP outperformed the stable paretian hypotheses developed by Mandelbrot (1963) by providing higher likelihoods, and it considers the leptokurtosis in the distribution of price change series, therefore surpasses the normal distribution.

The speed of price changes sometimes could slow down or become faster due to the effect of historical events such as policy changing or economic shocks. When "good" or "bad" events occur, the accumulation of the number of information arrivals increase, asset prices thus appear to sharply increase or decline and price evolves at a faster rate with active trading behaviour; whereas during less eventful periods, prices evolve slowly with dull trading activities. The effects of historical events on the speed of price changes can be investigated by estimating possible structural breaks and then comparing the price evolution in different segments divided by those breaks in a time series. Kim (2003) investigated the effect of historical events on the price change of Korea Composite Stock Price Index (KOSPI). He estimated multiple structural breaks on the SP linear regression models developed by Clark (1973). His empirical results are robust in supporting Clark's conclusion and showed that the estimated breakpoints were very well related to the real historical events.

For the method of estimating structural breaks, a large number of studies focus on testing a single change point or a known number of breaks. Some studies, however, estimate multiple structural changes and develop the methodologies to investigate the structural change at unknown time or unknown number of break points (Andrews *et al.* 1996; Grcia and Perron 1996; Liu *et al.* 1997; Bai and Perron 1998, 2003). A popular methodology is that by Bai and Perron (1998, 2003) where they estimated multiple structural shifts employing less restrictions compared to previous approaches. Their approach accommodates the serial correlation and heteroskedasticity in the errors. They also allowed for different distributions for the errors and the regressors across segments. Due to these advantages, the method developed by Bai and Perron (1998, 2003) is used to estimate structural breaks in this chapter. Based on Kim's idea, we investigate the structural breaks on the SP linear regression model where operational time is approximated by the cumulative volume of trading. Eight main futures products related to agriculture, metal and energy in China's three dominant futures exchanges are examined in this chapter. As most of the past studies associated with the MDH or the relationship between price volatility and trading activity focus primarily on the markets of western industrial nations, little evidence has been reported for the eastern emerging markets, especially for China's developing futures market. We initiate this study to attempt filling in the gap. The number of breakpoints is selected by using Bayesian information criterion (BIC) suggested by Yao (1988). Our findings provide evidence of whether estimated structural breakpoints are close to real historical events. In addition, the Shanghai Futures Exchange (SHFE)'s data covers the period to June 2009, enabling the impact of the recent economic crisis to be assessed.

The remainder of the study is organized as follows. The second section introduces the data used. Eight futures contracts are investigated with delivery month, contract period and the number of observation detailed. The third section gives details of the methodology. The content of this section includes the subordinated stochastic process and the models developed by Clark (1973), the sequential method developed by Bai and Perron (1998, 2003) for identifying breakpoints, and the criterion of specifying the minimum number of observations per segment while estimating structural breaks. The fourth section presents empirical findings and the discussion related to each contract. Finally, the fifth section summarizes the article and provides the conclusions.

Data

Eight futures return series selected from three dominant Chinese futures exchanges are investigated in this study. Futures contracts are hard wheat and the cotton selected from the China Zhengzhou Commodity Exchange (CZCE); soybean meal, soybean No. 1, and corn selected from the Dalian Commodity Exchange (DCE); copper, aluminum, and fuel oil selected from the SHFE. The number of observations, delivery month, and the duration of contracts are displayed in Table 15.1.

Table 15.1 shows that there are six delivery months: January, March, May, July, September, and November for the hard wheat futures contract, the soybean No. 1 contract and the corn contract. The delivery months of the cotton futures

Table 15.1 Products, delivery month and sample period for China's futures contracts

Series	*Delivery month*	*Contract period*	*No. of Daily obs*
CZCE			
Hard wheat	Jan, Mar, May, July, Sep, Nov	July 1993–June 2008	3,012
Cotton	Jan, Mar–Dec	June 2004–June 2008	1,000
DCE			
Soybean meal	Jan, Mar, May, July, Aug, Sep, Nov, Dec	July 2000–June 2007	1,662
Soybean No. 1	Jan, Mar, May, July, Sep, Nov	Mar 2003–June 2007	1,264
Corn	Jan, Mar, May, July, Sep, Nov	Sep 2004–Sep 2007	728
SHFE			
Copper	Jan–Dec	Jan 1999–June 2009	2,395
Aluminium	Jan–Dec	Jan 1999–June 2009	2,546
Fuel oil	Jan–Dec	Apr 2004–June 2009	1,177

Notes: This investigation originally includes ten futures contracts. Two additional contracts are: white sugar selected from the CZCE, and soybean oil selected from the DCE. However, due to their short sample spans (they were both first introduced in 2006), we do not report the results in this paper.

contract are from January to December. There is no delivery in February when the Chinese New Year occurs. The delivery month of the soybean meal contract are January, March, May, July, August, September, November, and December. The three futures products in the SHFE all have the same delivery months from January through to December.

The sample period for each contract is different because each product began at a different date and data availability differs across exchanges. Because the data used is not readily available, the sample period for the DCE's contracts end in 2007. The CZCE data ends on 30 June 2008, one year longer than that of the DCE's data. The sample series' lengths of the SHFE's contracts are available until 30 June 2009. The time series of daily observations for each product are obtained by rolling over the compounded continued returns consecutively between each nearest delivery contract of the product. It should be noted that the number of observations in these time series are less than the real trading days after removing jumps and gaps in price data especially for the hard wheat contract.

Methodology

The subordinated stochastic process (SP)

Now we suppose that discrete stochastic processes are usually indexed by a calendar time in a straightforward form: $X_0, X_1, \ldots, X_t, X_{t+1}, \ldots$. Instead of indexing by the integers $0, 1, 2, \ldots, t,\ t+1, \ldots,$ the process could be indexed by a set of numbers $t_1, t_2, t_3, \ldots,$ where these numbers are themselves a realization of a stochastic process with positive increments, so that $t_1 \leq t_2 \leq t_3 \ldots$ This means that if $T(t)$ is a positive stochastic process, a newly formed process $X(T(t))$ is thought to be subordinated to the parent process $X(t)$. $T(t)$ is called the directing process (operational time). The distribution of $\Delta X(T(t))$ is deemed to be subordinate to the distribution of $\Delta X(t)$, where $\Delta X(t)$ presents the individual effects in the price evolution process, and $T(t)$ is a operational clock measuring the speed of price evolution. $X(T(t))$ is the price process itself.

Using the MDH process, Clark (1973) developed a contemporaneous relation between speculative asset price volatility and trading activity. Three regression models are proposed to construct the relationship between these two variables. After adjusting price changes by "volume clock," the best estimate can be obtained by utilizing the model in which original price change series can be better adjusted to the normal distribution.

Three models developed by Clark (1973) are as follows:

$$\Delta X_t^2 = \alpha + \beta v_t + \varepsilon_t \tag{15.3.1}$$

$$\log(\Delta X_t^2) = \alpha + \beta v_t + \varepsilon_t \tag{15.3.2}$$

$$\log(\Delta X_t^2) = \alpha + \beta \log(v_t) + \varepsilon_t \tag{15.3.3}$$

where v_t denotes trading volume. Test results in Clark (1973) suggested that both model (2) and model (3) were good in explaining price changes. However, the linear specification in model (1) was the worst with a low F statistic for the correlation of two variables. Our empirical test also shows an inferior result for model (1). Therefore, it is not considered or reported in this chapter.

It should be noted that model (3) presents a lognormal-normal distribution for price changes. The "lognormal-normal" describes a process, $X(t)$ whose independent increments $\Delta X(t)$ are normally distributed, directed by a process $T(t)$, whose independent increments are lognormally distributed. This process was strongly supported by the empirical tests in Clark's paper to be the best obtainable regression. The kurtosis of the price changes had been reduced by a very significant amount after adjusting returns by the logarithm of volume data.

To adjust price changes by operational time, the distribution of the adjusted return series can be found in the following way: If the estimated volume clocks, $\Delta T(t) = f(v_t)$, are given as $e^{\widehat{a}+\widehat{\beta} v_t}$ by model (2), and $e^{\widehat{\alpha}} v_t^{\widehat{\beta}}$ by model (3), then $\Delta X(T(t))/\sqrt{f(v_t)}$, the price returns adjusted by the estimated volume clocks should be distributed as $\Delta X(t)$. Based on Clark's theory, it should be normally distributed or lognormal-normally distributed.

Multiple structural breaks

We use Bai and Perron's multiple linear regression models with m breaks. Observations then are partitioned into $m+1$ regimes:

$$y_t = z_t' \delta_j + u_t, \quad t = T_{j-1}+1, \ldots, T_j \tag{15.3.4}$$

where y_t denotes the observed dependent variable at time t; z_t are vectors of the independent variable, and $\delta_j (j = 1, \ldots, m+1)$ are the corresponding vectors of coefficients; u_t is the disturbance at time t. The break points $(T_1, \ldots, T_m)$ are unknown. We now change the linear regression model (15.3.4) into matrix form:

$$Y = \bar{Z}\delta + U \tag{15.3.5}$$

where $Y = (y_1, \ldots, y_T)'$, $\bar{Z}$ is the matrix which diagonally partitions Z at $(T_1, \ldots, T_m)$, $\delta = (\delta_1', \delta_2', \ldots, \delta_{m+1}')'$, $U = (u_1, \ldots, u_T)'$. The estimation process is based on the least-squares principle. Thus, for each m-partition $(T_1, \ldots, T_m)$, δ_j are the associated least-squares estimates, which obtained by minimizing the sum of squared residuals $(Y - \bar{Z}\delta)'(Y - \bar{Z}\delta) = \sum_{i=1}^{m+1} \sum_{t=T_{i-1}} +1^{T_i} [y_t - z_t'\delta_i]^2$. Now we assume $\widehat{\delta}(\{T_j\})$ as the estimated matrixes of coefficient based on the given m-partition $(T_1, \ldots, T_m)$. In other words, the estimated regression parameters are the estimates associated with the m-partition $\{\widehat{T}_j\}$. If we substitute these $\widehat{\delta}(\{T_j\})$ in the objective function and denote the resulting sum of squared residuals as $S_T(T_1, \ldots, T_m)$, the estimated break points $(\widehat{T}_1, \ldots, \widehat{T}_m)$ are such that $(\widehat{T}_1, \ldots, \widehat{T}_m) = \arg\min_{T_1, \ldots, T_m} S_T(T_1, \ldots, T_m)$, where the minimization is taken over all partitions $(T_1, \ldots, T_m)$. Therefore the break point estimators are global minimizers of the objective function.

The idea of estimating break points presented above is based on calculating the global minimizers of the sum of squared residuals. Now consider the piecewise linear regression method suggested by Guthery (1974) to compute the global minimizers of the objective function. The piecewise linear function begins with an ordering of the observations and applies a dynamic program. With a sample of size T, the total number of possible segments is at most $T(T+1)/2$. The global sum of squared residuals for any m-partition and for any value of m must be a particular linear combination of these $T(T+1)/2$ sums of squared residuals. The estimates of the break dates, the m-partition $(\widehat{T}_1, \ldots, \widehat{T}_m)$, correspond to this linear combination, which must have a minimal value of sum of squared residuals, so that an optimal partition can be selected over all possible m-partitions.

The computation of the estimates $\hat{\delta}$, $\hat{u}_t$ and $S_T(T_1, \ldots, T_m)$ can be carried out by applying standard response function (ordinary least squares) segment by segment without constraints among them. Once the sums of squared residuals of the relevant partitions have been computed, a dynamic program algorithm can be used to compare possible combinations, and then find a partition, which achieves a global minimization over the entire sum of squared residuals. This method essentially proceeds through a sequential examination of optimal one-break partitions. The optimal partition resolves the following recursive problem:

$$SSR(\{T_{m,T}\}) = \min_{mh \leq j \leq T-h} [SSR(\{T_{m-1,j}\}) + SSR(j+1, T)] \tag{15.3.6}$$

It simply minimizes $S_T(T_1, \ldots, T_m)$ over the set of possibilities obtained by assuming the first j elements have been optimally partitioned in $m - 1 + 1$ parts and that $m+1$ part consists of the last $T-j+1$ elements. The optimal partitions can be obtained by iteratively using this dynamic program.

Before estimating structural breaks, it is very important to pre-specify a further parameter ε, the minimum fraction of observations allocated to any one segment, or the minimum number of observations per segment h, where $\varepsilon = h/T$. It may be considered as a bandwidth or trimming parameter imposed by researchers, and hence affects the asymptotic distribution. Results of the estimation are quite sensitive to the different choices of this parameter as a small bandwidth may results in the considerable size distortion when different variances in the errors across segments or serial correlation are allowed. When allowing different variances across segments or serial correlation is taken into account, a higher value of ε or h should be used, the minimum fraction of observations allocated to one segment may be imposed by $\varepsilon = 0.10$, $\varepsilon = 0.15$, $\varepsilon = 0.20$, $\varepsilon = 0.25$. Let λ symbolizes the break fractions and $\lambda_0 = 0$, $\lambda_{m+1} = 1$; $\hat{\lambda}_m$ denotes the fractions of the estimates of the break points. The maximum number of breaks considered should be eight rather than nine when $\varepsilon = 0.10$, because allowing nine break points results in the estimates to be exactly $\hat{\lambda}_1 = 0.1$, $\hat{\lambda}_2 = 0.2$, $\hat{\lambda}_9 = 0.9$. Similarly, the maximum number of breaks estimated should be five when $\varepsilon = 0.15$; when $\varepsilon = 0.20$, this number is considered to be three, and should be two when $\varepsilon = 0.25$ (Bai and Perron 2003: 14). Due to the consideration of larger observations (greater than 100) for each segment, and simultaneously considering a not small number of breaks, we estimate structural breaks to selected time series with $\varepsilon = 0.15$ (the maximum number of breaks is five).

Empirical findings

Empirical findings for the CZCE

The hard wheat contract

Table 15.2 displays the preliminary statistics of the daily returns of the CZCE's contracts. The results show that the kurtosis and the Jarque–Bera statistics are significantly reduced for the returns adjusted by operational time. However, they are still far from the normal distribution. The hard wheat returns exhibit a positive skewness of 0.689, and the value of the kurtosis, 10.641, is significantly different from normality. The Jarque–Bera statistic is too large and the corresponding P-value indicates that returns are significantly different from the normal distribution. The moments of hard wheat returns adjusted by Clark's model (2) and model (3) show both the skewness and the kurtosis have decreased. Values of the kurtosis for returns adjusted by model (2) and model (3) are reduced to 2.363 and 2.366 respectively which are both lower than three. However, although the Jarque–Bera statistics are reduced from 6886.016 to 46.302 after adjusting returns by model (2) and to 45.989 after adjusting returns by model (3), they are still too high to accept normality.

To investigate the effect of historical events on the asset returns adjusted by volume clocks, we apply the sequential methods to estimate multiple structural breaks

Table 15.2 Moments of the CZCE's returns

	Mean	*St. dev.*	*Skewness*	*Kurtosis*	*Jarque–Bera*	*P-value*
Hard Wheat	-6.060×10^{-4}	1.174×10^{-2}	6.891×10^{-1}	10.641	6,886.016	0.000
Adjusted by						
Model 2	2.120×10^{-15}	2.072	-5.796×10^{-3}	2.363	46.302	0.000
Model 3	3.260×10^{-15}	2.077	-1.213×10^{-2}	2.366	45.989	0.000
Cotton	-6.000×10^{-4}	6.829×10^{-3}	-4.188×10^{-1}	7.995	1,055.027	0.000
Adjusted by						
Model 2	6.020×10^{-16}	1.987	-4.538×10^{-1}	2.823	35.157	0.000
Model 3	4.769×10^{-16}	1.956	-4.424×10^{-1}	2.819	33.482	0.000

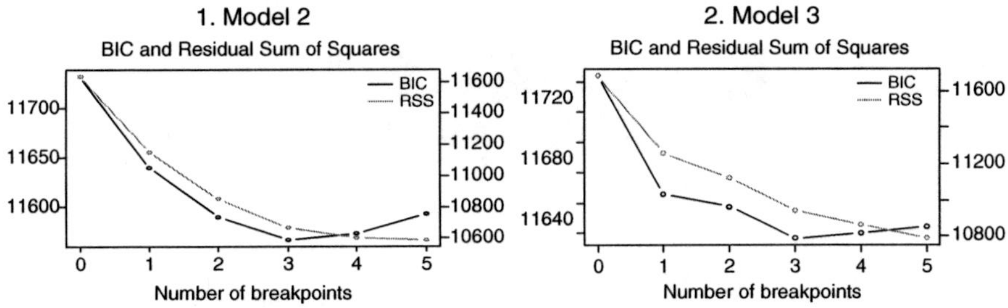

Figure 15.1 RSS (residuals of squared sum) and BIC for hard wheat models with up to five breaks.

Table 15.3 Estimated breakpoints for CZCE's contracts

	Model 2	*Model 3*
Hard wheat breakpoints ($h=0.15$)		
$\hat{T}_1$	08/07/1998	09/08/1998
$\hat{T}_2$	05/11/2001	12/09/2001
$\hat{T}_3$	24/09/2003	01/08/2003
$\hat{T}_4$	20/10/2005	14/12/2005
Cotton breakpoints ($h=0.15$)		
$\hat{T}_1$	15/03/2006	28/10/2005
$\hat{T}_2$	05/07/2007	22/10/2007

in two models. Figure 15.1 shows the RSS and BIC for the hard wheat returns adjusted by two models. The information criterion (BIC) selects three breaks for the returns adjusted by model (2). However, because of the well-known fact that information criteria are often downward-biased (Zeileis and Kleiber 2005a), Bai and Perron argue in favor of the presence of an additional break. Moreover, the decrease of the RSS when passing from a three breaks model to a four breaks model is not very small. These results may be summarized as pointing to a four breaks model. Similar to returns adjusted by model (2), Figures 15.1 and 15.2 reveal that the BIC selects three breaks for the returns adjusted by model (3). However, due to the possibility of downward bias of the BIC and a nontrivial decrease on the RSS when passing from a three break model to a four break model, we chose the model with four breakpoints.

Breakpoints estimates for the CZCE's returns adjusted by model (2) and model (3) are given in Table 15.3. We investigate the speed of futures price evolution by allowing for these structural breaks. The moments of the CZCE's returns adjusted by model (2) and model (3) with estimated multiple structural breaks are exhibited in Table 15.3. The Jarque–Bera statistics show that the null hypothesis that returns are normally distributed cannot be rejected at one percent significance level for the

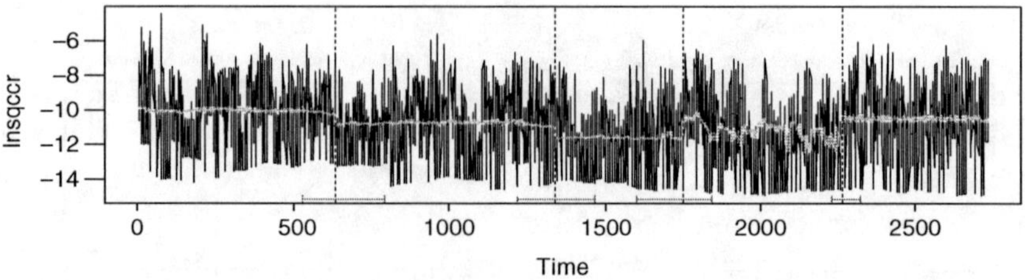

Figure 15.2 Conditional means of operational time for the hard wheat returns adjusted by model (3).

third regime and the fifth regime for the hard wheat returns adjusted by model (2); whereas the null hypothesis cannot be rejected at one percent significance level for the third, fourth and fifth regimes for returns adjusted by model (3). These results suggest that model (3) can be chosen as the best obtainable regression for operational time for the hard wheat contract as more regimes of returns adjusted by this model are normally distributed. Accordingly, we chose the four breakpoints estimated by model (3) as the best estimation.

Figure 15.2 shows the conditional mean of the hard wheat returns adjusted by model (3) (the middle line). The effect of historical events on the speed of price evolution can be revealed by observing the conditional means of model (3) with four breaks. The return series is divided by four breakpoints into five sections, and in each section it progresses at different levels. The first segment shows a relatively higher level of returns, which indicates a faster rate of price evolution for the hard wheat contract. Price evolves at a slow rate in the second segment and then becomes slower in the third section as lower levels of returns are displayed in these two regimes. Conditional mean shows more volatility in the fourth section with return level being slightly higher than that of in the third section. The fifth section shows a faster rate of evolution compared with the second, third, and the fourth section. However, it is still slower than the first.

To reveal the effect of historical events on the speed of price evolution, it is necessarily to investigate if the estimated breakpoints are intimately related to the real historical events. Zhang *et al.* (2008) pointed out that there is a structural break on August 31, 1998 for the hard wheat contract. They described that China's futures market experienced a strong growth (with a chaos) from 1993 to 1995. Chinese government adopted measures to rectify the market during this period. In August 1998, an order enacted by government came into force to cut down the number of futures exchange from 15 to three, and the number of products from 35 to 12. This event had a strong influence on the history of China's futures market, and therefore a structural break occurred. Figure 15.3 shows a peak in price series during 1995 (please note that all futures prices in this chapter are calculated in the Chinese currency RMB) and then prices gradually going down before the first

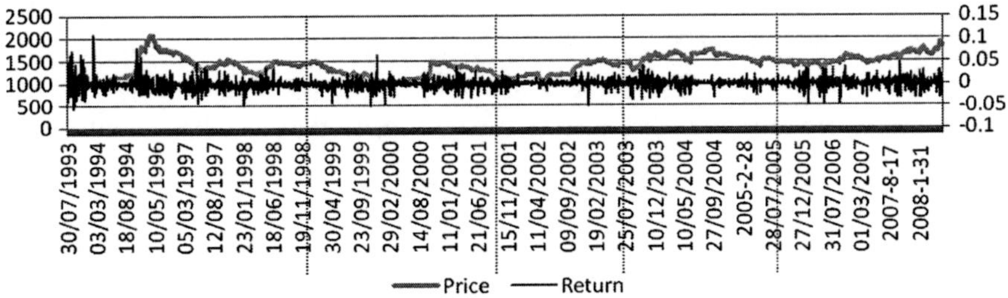

Figure 15.3 Price and return series of the hard wheat contract.

breakpoint on August 9, 1998. Returns series displays bigger clusters with more and higher extreme values in the first regime.

After 1998, China's economy was affected by the Asian financial crisis. Futures market, on the one hand, developed through encouraging government's policy; on the other hand, cracking down severely on futures exchanges and products resulted in a 30 percent to 40 percent yearly decline of trading volume until 2003. Price evolved at a very low rate during this period. Figure 15.3 exhibits a relatively lower price level and narrower returns from the first breakpoint to the second breakpoint on September 12, 2001. After the second breakpoints, price evolves slower than that of in the last regime with very narrow returns oscillating around zero. Wheat prices during this period were low because of the weak demand and oversupply. The "9.11 Event" may affect the CZCE since it seriously impacted on the Chicago Board Of Trade (CBOT). China formal joining of the WTO in December 2001 is supposed as a breakpoint since it brought about an increase in wheat imports. Although the hard wheat price rose after November 2002 to July 2003 due to lower yields, it did not lead to much increase on the speed of price evolution. From the third breakpoint to the fourth breakpoint, December 14, 2005, China's economy prospered as it walked out of the Asian financial crisis. Lots of papers and reports focused on its high economic growth and remarkable GDP. A large number of investors began buying long which resulted in an increase of futures market price. Figure 15.3 exhibits an increase on the hard wheat price after the third break. However, return series does not appear much fluctuated or extremely high. This might have happened because although a larger number of investors during this period had similar expectations of markets to move price in one direction, some of investors were still waiting and holding on the fence, so that prices kept at a relatively stable level (slightly going down) and evolved at a moderate speed. After the fourth breakpoint, against the backdrop of the highly increasing economy in China in 2006 (10.7 percent GDP growth rate), commodity trading in futures markets was brisk. In addition, many reports introduced higher grain and crops price and downward stocks throughout the world during this year (global spot grain price increase 12.83 percent and futures price increase 30.48 percent in 2006 compared with 2005, Zhu (2007)). The Commodity Research Bureau (CRB) Index reveals that globally the Continuous Commodity Index (CCI) reached 365.25 point in 2006, rising to 100 percent compared with the lowest point of 183.52 in 2002. Figure 15.3 exhibits a significant climb in hard wheat's price and strong volatilities of returns. In spite of the global financial crisis in August 2007, price evolution keeps a higher rate in the fifth regime compared with the last three regimes, but slightly slower than that of the first regimes.

The cotton contract

Raw cotton returns in Table 15.2 display a negative skewness of −0.4188 and a kurtosis of 7.995, significantly greater than three. The Jarque–Bera statistic and the *P*-value indicate that the null hypothesis of normality is rejected. After adjusting the cotton returns by model (2) and model (3), the values of kurtosis fall to 2.823 and 2.819 respectively. However, due to greater absolute values of skewness, the Jarque–Bera statistics are still too high at 35.157 and 33.482, and the *P*-values are almost zero, which indicates the rejections of normality.

The RSS and BIC for the cotton returns are shown in Figure 15.4. The BIC selects one break for the returns adjusted by model (2). The RSS rapidly decreases from a one break model to a two break model, and there is only a small decrease thereafter. We chose the model with two breaks. The BIC also chooses one break for the returns adjusted by model (3). However, due to the possibility of the downward-bias of the BIC, and there is a significant decline on the RSS from a one break model to a two break model, we choose two breaks for returns adjusted by model (3).

The moments of the adjusted cotton's returns for model (2) and model (3) with an estimated two structural break are displayed in Table 15.4. The kurtosis of returns in all regimes for both model (2) and model (3) are very close to that of the normal distribution, and values of the kurtosis in each regime of model (3) are lower than those of model (2). Owing to high absolute values of the skewness for model (2), the Jarque–Bera statistics are high and *P*-values show that returns are significantly different from normality. The absolute values of the skewness of the first and the third regimes for model (3) are also high, the Jarque–Bera statistics

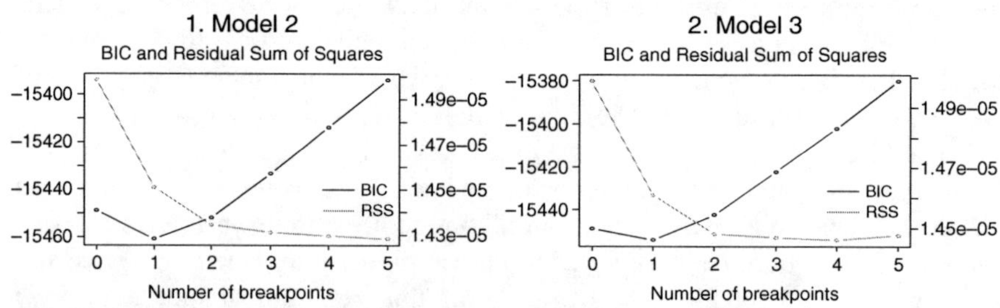

Figure 15.4 RSS and BIC for cotton models with up to five breaks.

Table 15.4 Moments of adjusted CZCE returns

Model	*Regime*	*Mean*	*St. dev.*	*Skewness*	*Kurtosis*	*Jarque–Bera*	*P-value*
Hard wheat							
Model 2	Reg1	6.930×10^{-16}	2.054	-4.049×10^{-2}	2.233	15.256	0.000
(Breaks = 4)	Reg2	-7.140×10^{-16}	1.903	2.000×10^{-2}	2.319	14.658	0.001
	Reg3	1.450×10^{-15}	1.818	2.029×10^{-1}	2.571	6.069	0.048*
	Reg4	3.420×10^{-15}	2.036	-1.439×10^{-2}	2.255	10.866	0.004
	Reg5	1.990×10^{-16}	2.104	-1.954×10^{-1}	2.466	8.781	0.012*
Model 3	Reg1	1.980×10^{-16}	2.044	-7.849×10^{-2}	2.233	16.296	0.000
(Break = 4)	Reg2	5.280×10^{-16}	1.918	-1.133×10^{-2}	2.309	13.972	0.001
	Reg3	3.230×10^{-16}	1.872	1.726×10^{-1}	2.392	8.389	0.016*
	Reg4	1.262×10^{-16}	1.988	-3.218×10^{-2}	2.359	8.767	0.013*
	Reg5	-1.050×10^{-15}	2.101	-2.024×10^{-1}	2.487	8.552	0.015*
Cotton							
Model 2	Reg1	-3.370×10^{-15}	2.091	-3.639×10^{-1}	2.718	10.771	0.005
(Breaks = 2)	Reg2	-3.680×10^{-16}	1.819	-4.002×10^{-1}	2.382	10.529	0.005
	Reg3	-8.710×10^{-4}	1.877	-6.918×10^{-1}	3.215	25.816	0.000
Model 3	Reg1	-7.800×10^{-16}	2.163	-4.162×10^{-1}	2.569	12.344	0.002
(Break = 2)	Reg2	-1.872×10^{-15}	2.010	-9.520×10^{-2}	2.341	8.057	0.020*
	Reg3	-1.640×10^{-15}	1.887	-6.252×10^{-1}	3.204	16.125	0.000

Notes: *Insignificant at 0.01; **Insignificant at 0.5; ***Insignificant at 0.1.

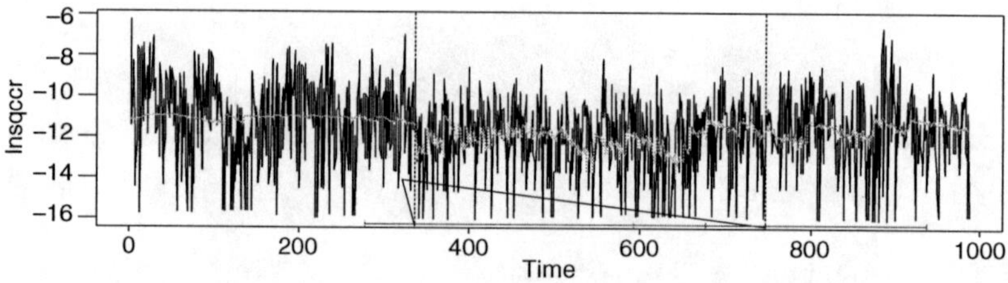

Figure 15.5 Conditional means of operational time for the cotton's returns adjusted by model (3).

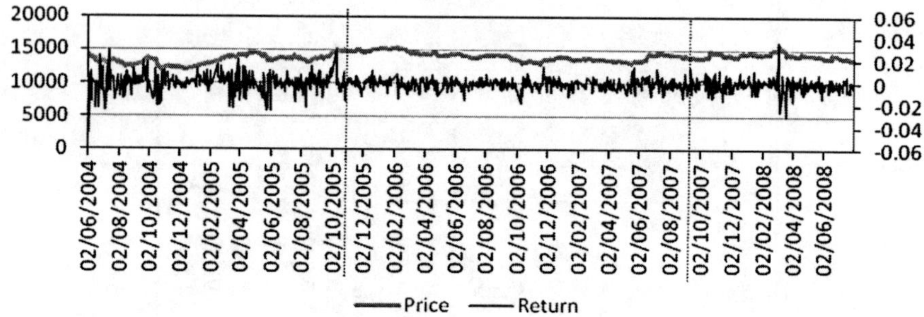

Figure 15.6 Price and return series of the cotton contract.

and the *P*-values of returns in these regimes reject normal distribution. However, the absolute value of the skewness in the second regime is very low which results in a lower Jarque–Bera statistic at 8.057. The null hypothesis cannot be rejected at the one percent significance level. The results suggest that model (3) and the corresponding estimated two breakpoints shown in Table 15.3 are the best for the cotton returns indexed by operational time.

Figure 15.5 displays the conditional mean of the cotton returns adjusted by model (3) with two breaks. The first regime shows a relatively higher level of returns, which indicates a faster rate of price evolution for the cotton contract. Price evolves at a slower rate in the second regime. In the third regime, there is a very small increase of the conditional mean, which indicates a slightly faster rate compared to the second regime.

Figure 15.6 exhibits price movement of the cotton contract in three regimes divided by two structural breaks. The first breakpoint, October 28, 2005, is very close to the fourth breakpoint of the hard wheat series, December 14, 2005. During 2003 and 2005, China's economy gradually walked away from the Asian financial crisis and grew very fast. Traders tended to buy long in futures market rather than sell short. These led to a significant increase of commodities price. Figure 15.6 shows a growth trend and higher volatilities on returns on the cotton's futures price before the first break. It should be noted that cotton price plunged with lowered returns during the second half of 2004 due to a good harvest and a large amount of cotton imports. However, they climbed up in 2005 (Changjiang Futures 2006). Changjiang Futures (2006) point out that there was a surge around the end of 2005 on cotton's price and returns when investors shifted their expectations optimistically. This might result in the appearance of the first structural break in return series. From the first break to the second break, October 22, 2007, although there is a significant upward movement on the grain and crops' prices in both domestic and international markets, cotton futures price did not show big volatilities. It moved stably. Cotton price series in Figure 15.6 displays a relative smooth trend with a rise at the beginning of the second regime. Returns in this regime keep oscillating within a narrow range from −0.01 to 0.01, which indicates a slower rate of price evolution. After the second breakpoint, cotton price rose due to increasing demand by textiles industry and the gloom expectation for yields. Returns began more fluctuated. However, due to the global economic recession, there is a downward movement on cotton's price after March 2008.

Empirical findings for the DCE

The soybean meal contract

Table 15.5 exhibits the preliminary statistics of returns of the selected DCE's contracts. Values of the kurtosis and the Jarque–Bera statistics are significantly reduced after adjusting returns by operational time. But they are still too high to normality. The soybean meal series shows a positive value of the skewness 0.07116 and the kurtosis 5.327 which are much higher than that of the normal distribution. The Jarque–Bera statistics and the P-value indicate that the normal distribution is rejected. After adjusting returns by model (2) and model (3), values of the kurtosis are much lower than that of the raw return. Both of them are lower than three. However, the absolute values of the skewness increase for the adjusted returns, so that the Jarque–Bera statistics are still at high levels of 38.500 and 42.706 respectively which are too far from the normal distribution.

Figure 15.7 displays the RSS and the BIC for the soybean meal returns adjusted by two models. The BIC for model (2) selects three breakpoints (see Figures 15.7 and 15.8) and there is no a rapid decrease on the RSS from a three break model to a four break model, the results may point to a three break model. Figures 15.7 and 15.8 give the RSS and the BIC for the soybean meal returns adjusted by model (3). Both the RSS and the BIC select a four breakpoint model.

The moments of the soybean meal returns adjusted by model (2) and model (3) with estimated multiple structural breaks are displayed in Table 15.7. The Jarque–Bera statistic for the second regime is very close to that of normal distribution at 5.067 with the P-value insignificantly different from the normal distribution at five percent for model (2). The Jarque–Bera statistics for returns adjusted by model (3) in the second regime, the third regime and the fifth regime are close to that of normality, and the P-values are insignificantly different from the normal

Table 15.5 Moments of the DCE's returns

	Mean	*St. dev.*	*Skewness*	*Kurtosis*	*Jarque–Bera*	*P-value*
Soybean meal	3.740×10^{-5}	1.158×10^{-2}	7.116×10^{-2}	5.327	323.268	0.000
Adjusted by						
Model 2	3.320×10^{-5}	2.129	-3.389×10^{-1}	2.627	38.500	0.000
Model 3	1.960×10^{-5}	2.147	-3.428×10^{-1}	2.559	42.706	0.000
Soybean No. 1	2.210×10^{-4}	8.697×10^{-3}	-1.256×10^{-1}	5.968	462.957	0.000
Adjusted by						
Model 2	4.970×10^{-16}	2.037	-4.425×10^{-1}	2.944	39.853	0.000
Model 3	1.310×10^{-16}	2.043	-4.429×10^{-1}	2.939	39.772	0.000
Corn	-1.100×10^{-4}	6.093×10^{-3}	6.302×10^{-1}	7.935	712.433	0.000
Adjusted by						
Model 2	1.810×10^{-15}	1.765	2.062×10^{-1}	2.316	17.518	0.000
Model 3	9.520×10^{-16}	1.779	2.012×10^{1}	2.329	16.786	0.000

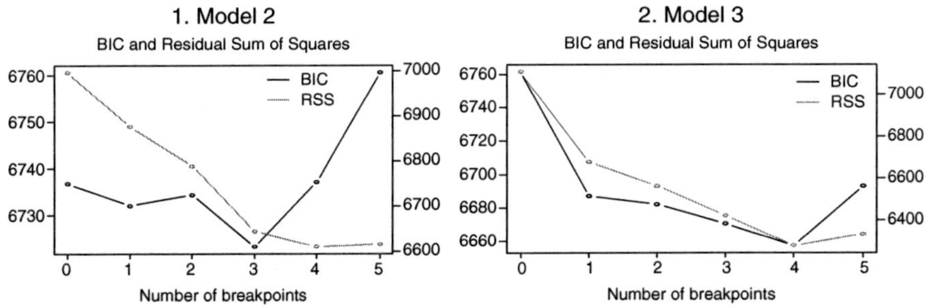

Figure 15.7 RSS and BIC for soybean meal models with up to five breaks.

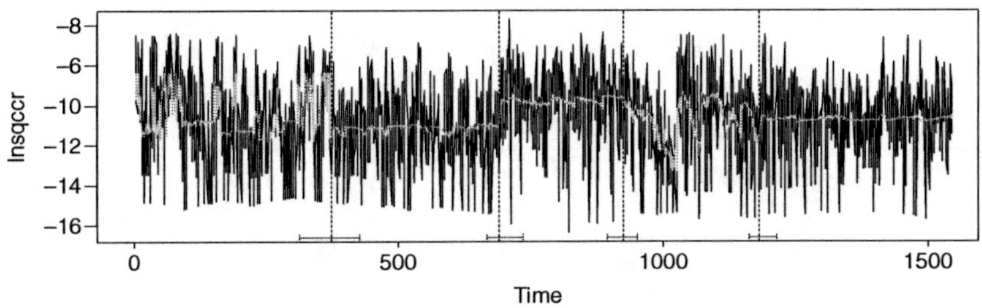

Figure 15.8 Conditional means of operational time for the soybean meal's returns adjusted by model (3).

distribution at five percent, and one percent significance levels. These results indicate that model (3) can be selected as the best obtainable regression for operational time, and we chose corresponding four estimated breaks shown in Table 15.6 as the best estimation.

Figure 15.8 shows the conditional mean of the soybean meal returns adjusted by model (3) with four breakpoints. In the first regime, price evolves fast but oscillated. After evolving at a slow rate in the second regime, price moves at the fastest rate in the third regime until a plunge appears in the fourth regime. The fifth regime shows a slower rate of price evolution than that of the third and fourth regime. However, it is faster than that of the second regime.

Figure 15.9 displays price and return time series of the soybean meal contract in different regimes divided by four breakpoints for model (3). The first break point, February 21, 2002, is estimated where Chinese government promulgated a measure to differentiate between the genetic modified soybean and the non-genetic modified soybean. Decreased imports of the genetic modified soybean and active trading of the non-genetic modified soybean in China's domestic market resulted in an increase on soybean meal's price after the first breakpoint. However, return series does not significantly rise until the second breakpoint September 11,

Table 15.6 Estimated breakpoints for DCE's contracts

	Model 2	*Model 3*
Soybean meal breakpoints ($h = 0.15$)		
$\hat{T}_1$	08/08/2001	21/02/2002
$\hat{T}_2$	11/09/2003	11/09/2003
$\hat{T}_3$	01/04/2005	31/08/2004
$\hat{T}_4$	–	20/10/2005
Soybean No.1 breakpoints ($h = 0.15$)		
$\hat{T}_1$	11/09/2003	12/09/2003
$\hat{T}_2$	24/06/2004	25/06/2004
$\hat{T}_3$	06/07/2005	16/08/2005
Corn breakpoints ($h = 0.15$)		
$\hat{T}_1$	10/06/2005	10/06/2005
$\hat{T}_2$	23/12/2005	23/12/2005
$\hat{T}_3$	29/08/2006	26/01/2007
$\hat{T}_4$	30/01/2007	–

2003. From the second breakpoint to the third breakpoint, August 31, 2004, due to the falling yields worldwide and strong demand in China's domestic market, soybean meal's price jumped rapidly with a peak in March 2004. Returns highly oscillate during this period and trading is brisk. From the third breakpoint to the fourth breakpoint, October 20, 2005, soybean meal's price appears significant volatilities with a big fall and then a following rebound. Due to the expectation of market downturn and the breakout of "bird flu" in July 2004, market went down sharply until February 2005. Thereafter, it strongly fluctuated by different investors' expectations. After four years increase and a short-term oscillation, soybean meal's price displays a relative stability at a lower level after the fourth breakpoint. Global soybean and soybean meal's price decreased during this period.

The soybean No. 1 contract

Table 15.5 shows a negative value of the skewness, −0.1256, for the soybean No. 1 returns. Value of the kurtosis 5.968 is much higher than that of the normal distribution. The Jarque–Bera statistic and the P-value indicate that the null hypothesis is rejected. After adjusting returns by model (2) and model (3), values of the kurtosis are substantially reduced and they are very close to normality. However, the absolute values of skewness are increased which may result in high values of the Jarque–Bera. The P-values indicate that the null hypothesis is rejected.

Figure 15.10 displays the RSS and BIC for the soybean No. 1 returns adjusted by model (2) and model (3). The BIC selects two structural breaks for returns, whereas the RSS suggests a minimum value of a four break model. Because of the downward-biased estimation of the BIC, and after a two break model, the RSS

Table 15.7 Moments of adjusted DCE returns

Model	*Regime*	*Mean*	*St. dev.*	*Skewness*	*Kurtosis*	*Jarque–Bera*	*P-value*
Soybean meal							
Model 2	Reg1	1.920×10^{-16}	2.284	-3.222×10^{-1}	2.282	14.539	0.001
(Breaks = 3)	Reg2	-1.840×10^{-15}	1.945	-2.564×10^{-1}	2.649	5.067	0.078**
	Reg3	6.800×10^{-16}	2.044	-8.789×10^{-1}	3.799	36.055	0.000
	Reg4	-4.870×10^{-16}	2.023	-4.279×10^{-1}	2.807	19.946	0.000
Model 3	Reg1	-1.360×10^{-15}	2.131	-3.621×10^{-1}	2.604	10.640	0.005
(Break = 4)	Reg2	-3.550×10^{-15}	1.964	-2.593×10^{-1}	2.599	5.636	0.060**
	Reg3	1.180×10^{-15}	2.046	-8.955×10^{-2}	3.848	7.286	0.036*
	Reg4	1.800×10^{-15}	2.018	-4.735×10^{-1}	2.895	9.834	0.007
	Reg5	1.980×10^{-15}	1.930	-3.665×10^{-1}	2.899	8.277	0.020*
Soybean No.1							
Model 2	Reg1	-3.020×10^{-15}	1.896	-5.529×10^{-1}	2.972	17.847	0.000
(Breaks = 3)	Reg2	-1.470×10^{-15}	2.011	-5.534×10^{-1}	2.967	9.298	0.010*
	Reg3	1.920×10^{-16}	2.023	-6.695×10^{-1}	3.530	21.322	0.000
	Reg4	-1.550×10^{-15}	1.966	-4.616×10^{-1}	2.997	15.445	0.001

Table 15.7 Continued.

Model	*Regime*	*Mean*	*St. dev.*	*Skewness*	*Kurtosis*	*Jarque–Bera*	*P-value*
Model 3	Reg1	-3.010×10^{-15}	1.882	-6.563×10^{-1}	3.147	25.440	0.000
(Breaks = 3)	Reg2	-1.350×10^{-15}	1.997	-5.558×10^{-1}	3.306	9.304	0.010*
	Reg3	2.960×10^{-16}	2.003	-7.246×10^{-1}	3.649	27.615	0.000
	Reg4	1.880×10^{-16}	2.016	-4.066×10^{-1}	2.811	11.850	0.003
Corn							
Model 2	Reg1	9.450×10^{-16}	1.457	2.571×10^{-1}	2.590	2.827	0.243***
(Breaks = 4)	Reg2	-2.080×10^{-15}	1.376	7.648×10^{-1}	3.259	11.232	0.004
	Reg3	-9.330×10^{-16}	1.773	7.269×10^{-2}	2.296	3.145	0.208***
	Reg4	5.660×10^{-15}	1.697	-2.925×10^{-1}	2.494	2.443	0.295***
	Reg5	-1.190×10^{-15}	1.757	-8.778×10^{-2}	2.203	4.048	0.132***
Model 3	Reg1	1.380×10^{-15}	1.433	3.589×10^{-2}	2.601	1.074	0.584***
(Breaks = 3)	Reg2	-4.280×10^{-16}	1.376	6.999×10^{-1}	3.217	9.332	0.010*
	Reg3	-4.140×10^{-16}	1.822	-5.177×10^{-2}	2.342	4.469	0.107***
	Reg4	9.510×10^{-16}	1.829	-1.101×10^{-1}	1.995	6.528	0.038*

Notes: *Insignificant at 0.01; **Insignificant at 0.05; ***Insignificant at 0.1.

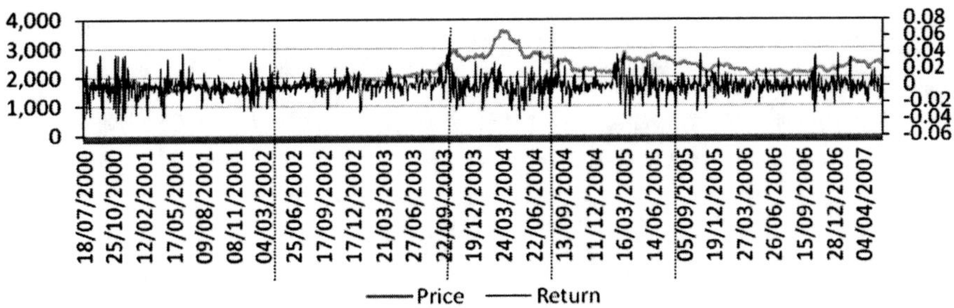

Figure 15.9 Price and return series of the soybean meal contract.

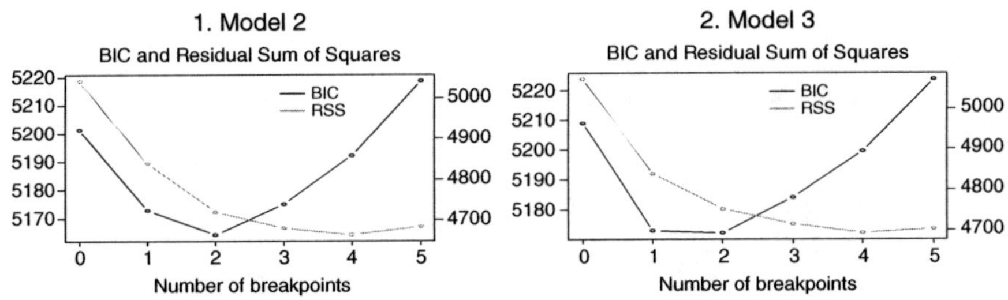

Figure 15.10 RSS and BIC for soybean No. 1 models with up to five breaks.

shows a considerable slide. These results may suggest a three break model for returns adjusted by model (2). The BIC suggests the selection of two breaks for returns adjusted by model (3). However, the RSS shows a rapid decrease after a two break model. We choose three as the estimated number of breaks.

Table 15.7 shows the moments of the soybean No. 1 returns adjusted by model (2) and model (3) with estimated multiple structural breaks. The Jarque–Bera statistics and the P-values show that returns are normally distributed cannot be rejected at one percent significance level for returns in the second regimes for both model (2) and model (3). However, compared with model (2), the absolute value of the skewness and Jarque–Bera statistic for model (3) are higher, although values of the kurtosis are very close to three, Moreover, there are two estimated coefficients for different regimes being insignificantly different from zero for model (3), but there is only one for model (2). Therefore, we choose model (2) as the best obtainable estimation for operational time for the soybean No. 1 contract. The estimated breakpoints for returns adjusted by model (2) (see Table 15.6) are the best estimation.

The conditional mean of the soybean No. 1 returns adjusted by model (2) is shown in Figure 15.11. The first regime displays the slowest rate of price evolution. Price evolves at the fastest rate in the second regime and then gradually slows

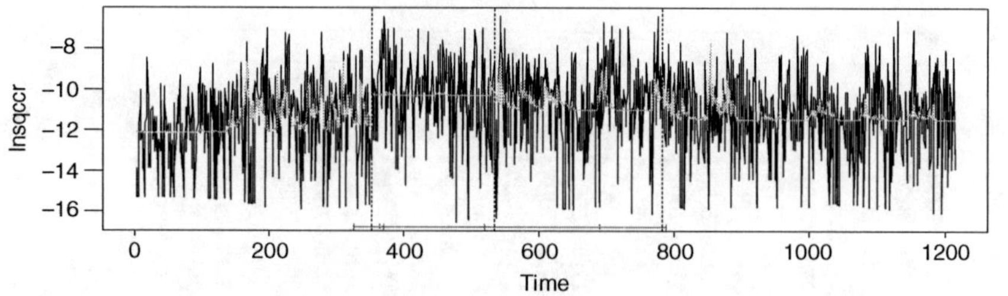

Figure 15.11 Conditional means of operational time for the soybean No. 1's returns adjusted by model (2).

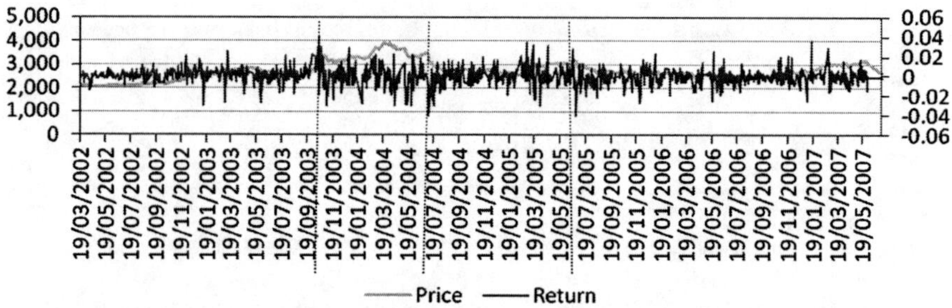

Figure 15.12 Price and return series of the soybean No. 1 contract.

down in the third regime and fourth regime. However, they are both faster than that of in the first regime.

Figure 15.12 exhibits price and return time series of the soybean No. 1 contract. Price movement is very similar to that of the soybean meal contract. The first breakpoint is exactly the same as that of the soybean meal contract at September 11, 2003. The second breakpoint is close to that of the soybean meal contract at June 24, 2004, and the third breakpoint, July 6, 2005, is not far from that of the soybean meal contract (October 20, 2005). From the first breakpoint to the second, price surges and returns strongly oscillate in a wide range due to the increasing demand of soybean and reduction of the supply. From the second breakpoint to the third breakpoint, price and returns are very unstable with alternate fall and rise until the third breakpoint where both price and returns drop down afterwards.

The corn contract

The preliminary statistics of corn returns are given in Table 15.5. Results show a positive value of the skewness, 0.6302, and a value of the kurtosis, 7.935, which are much higher than that of the normal distribution. The Jarque–Bera statistic is

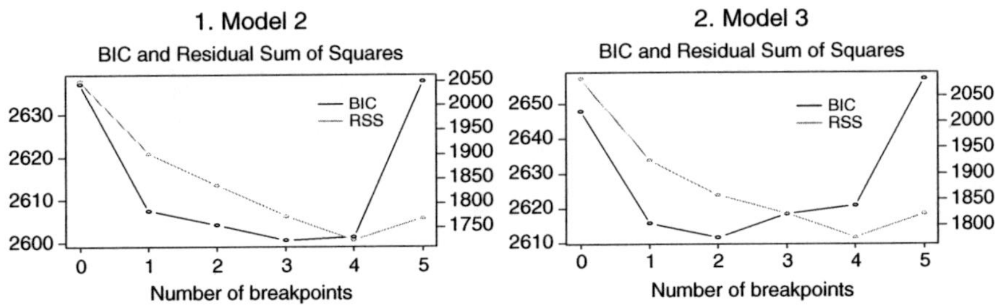

Figure 15.13 RSS and BIC for corn models with up to five breaks.

very high at 712.433. The null hypothesis that returns are normally distributed is rejected. The skewness and the kurtosis are significantly reduced after adjusting returns by model (2) and model (3). However the null hypotheses are rejected as the Jarque–Bera statistics are still too high to normality and the P-values are almost zero.

The RSS and the BIC for corn returns are shown in Figure 15.13. Both the RSS and BIC indicate four breaks for the returns adjusted by model (2). The BIC indicates two breakpoints for returns adjusted by model (3), whereas the RSS suggests a four break model. We choose three as the estimated number of breaks.

The moments of the adjusted corn returns for model (2) and model (3) with estimated multiple structural breaks are given in Table 15.7. Results are very robust for this contract: only returns adjusted by model (2) in the second regime are significantly different from normality. The Jarque–Bera statistics of model (3) with three breaks show that the null hypothesis cannot be rejected by returns in all regimes, which may indicate that model (3) can be chosen as the best obtainable regression for operational time.

The conditional mean of the corn returns adjusted by model (3) is shown in Figure 15.14. Returns in the first regime and the second regime display a slower rate of price evolution compared with the third regime where price evolves at the fastest rate. Returns in the fourth regime shows a slower rate than that of in the third regime; however, it is slightly faster than that of in the first and in the second regime.

Figure 15.15 exhibits price and return time series of the corn contract. Because the Chinese government promulgated measures to reduce the agricultural tax and decrease corn's export, corn's supply and storage increased in 2004. Before that, planting and yields of corn had been reduced for some years. An equilibrium between supply and demand appeared during 2004 and the first half year of 2005 (Yiming 2007). Corn's price became very stable with a slight upward trend until the appearance of the first break, June 10, 2005. Return series during this period oscillate in a narrow range except for a jump at the beginning of 2005. From the first breakpoint to the second breakpoint, December 23, 2005, Corn's price shows

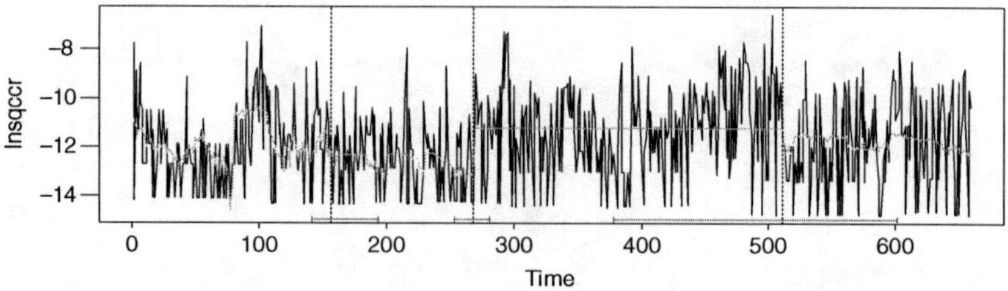

Figure 15.14 Conditional means of operational time for the corn's returns adjusted by model (3).

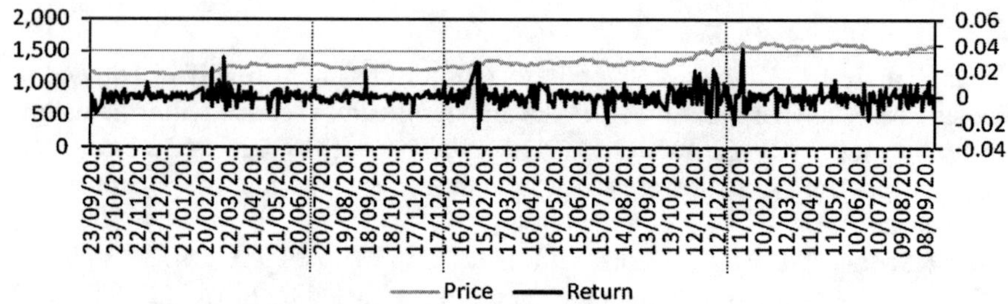

Figure 15.15 Price and return series of the corn contract.

a downward trend due to the RMB appreciation and outbreak of the "bird flu" (Da An 2005; Gaobo 2005). Returns during this period oscillate in a narrower range compared to the first regime. From the second breakpoint to the third breakpoint, January 26, 2007, agricultural commodity prices and oil's price significantly increased in the global market. Corn's price climbed up due to optimistic expectation of the export and the demand of fuel industry. Returns during this period exhibit strong volatilities and oscillations in a wider range. Although corn's price jumps in the fourth quarter of 2006 and keeps a high level throughout the fourth regime due to falling yields and soaring grain price in global market, there are no strong volatilities on returns.

Empirical findings for the SHFE

The aluminum contract

Table 15.8 exhibits the preliminary statistics of returns of the selected SHFE's contracts. Values of the kurtosis and the Jarque–Bera statistics are considerably reduced after adjusting returns by operational time except the fuel oil contract whose Jarque–Bera statistics of the adjusted returns are higher than that of the raw returns. The aluminum contract shows a negative value of the skewness −0.4350

Table 15.8 Moments of the SHFE's returns

	Mean	*St. dev.*	*Skewness*	*Kurtosis*	*Jarque–Bera*	*P-value*
Aluminium	-2.910×10^{-6}	9.192×10^{-3}	-4.350×10^{-1}	7.624	2,171.649	0.000
Adjusted by						
Model 2	6.250×10^{-16}	2.079	-7.269×10^{-2}	2.528	23.907	0.000
Model 3	-2.330×10^{-15}	2.034	-1.277×10^{-1}	2.483	32.534	0.000
Copper	6.120×10^{-4}	1.431×10^{-2}	-1.658×10^{-1}	5.255	532.931	0.000
Adjusted by						
Model 2	-2.280×10^{-15}	2.201	-4.012×10^{-1}	2.878	67.584	0.000
Model 3	1.830×10^{-16}	2.159	-3.774×10^{-1}	3.239	64.279	0.000
Fuel oil	4.290×10^{-4}	1.641×10^{-2}	-3.986×10^{-1}	4.261	106.212	0.000
Adjusted by						
Model 2	-1.220×10^{-15}	2.082	-8.025×10^{-1}	3.597	140.052	0.000
Model 3	-1.710×10^{-15}	2.091	-7.760×10^{-1}	3.552	129.644	0.000

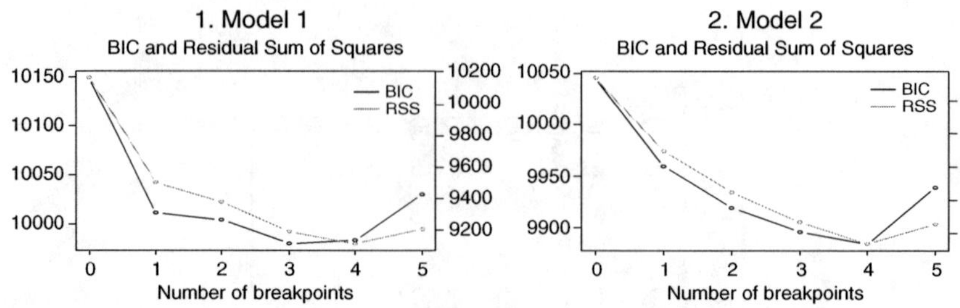

Figure 15.16 RSS and BIC for aluminum models with up to five breaks.

and a value of the kurtosis 7.624. They are much higher than that of the normal distribution. The Jarque–Bera statistic is very high at 2171.649. The *P*-value rejects the null hypothesis that returns are normally distributed. Both the absolute values of the skewness and values of the kurtosis are much smaller after adjusting returns by model (2) and model (3). However, the Jarque–Bera statistics are still too high to normality. The null hypotheses are rejected, as the *P*-values are almost zero.

Figure 15.16 shows the RSS and the BIC for aluminum returns adjusted by model (2) and model (3). The BIC selects three breaks for returns adjusted by model (2), whereas the RSS displays the lowest values at a four break model. We choose four breaks for the aluminum returns adjusted by model (2). Both the BIC and the RSS choose a four break models for returns adjusted by model (3).

The moments of the aluminum returns adjusted by model (2) and model (3) with estimated structural breaks are shown in Table 15.10. The Jarque–Bera statistics show that the null hypotheses that returns are normally distributed cannot be rejected at one percent significance level for the second regime of returns adjusted by model (2), whereas the null hypotheses cannot be rejected at one percent significance level for the second regime and the third regime of returns adjusted by model (3). These results suggested that model (3) can be selected as the best obtainable regression for operational time. The corresponding four breaks estimated by model (3) are chosen as the best estimation (see Table 15.9).

In Figure 15.17, the conditional mean of the aluminum returns adjusted by model (3) show that price evolves faster in the first regime than that of in the second regime where price evolves at the slowest rate. Price evolves at a faster rate in the third regime compared to the first regime and the second regime, but is slower compared to the fourth regime. The fourth regime displays the fastest rate of the price evolution among five regimes. Price evolves slower in the fifth regime compared to the fourth regime, but still faster than that of in the first, second and third regimes.

Figure 15.18 displays price and return time series of the aluminum contract in different regimes divided by four breakpoints for model (3). The first break, December 10, 2001, is estimated where the price of aluminum was the lowest since March 1999. This may be due to the gloomy global economy in 2001 and

Table 15.9 Estimated breakpoints for SHFE's contracts

	Model 2	*Model 3*
Aluminium breakpoints ($h = 0.15$)		
$\hat{T}_1$	10/12/2001	10/12/2001
$\hat{T}_2$	08/10/2003	08/10/2003
$\hat{T}_3$	30/12/2005	23/01/2006
$\hat{T}_4$	06/12/2007	16/02/2008
Copper breakpoints ($h = 0.15$)		
$\hat{T}_1$	22/02/2002	22/02/2002
$\hat{T}_2$	26/05/2003	26/05/2003
$\hat{T}_3$	09/12/2005	09/02/2006
$\hat{T}_4$	19/11/2007	08/11/2007
Fuel oil breakpoints ($h = 0.15$)		
$\hat{T}_1$	15/10/2007	02/04/2007
$\hat{T}_2$	–	17/07/2008

weak demand for aluminum, as well as the impact of the "9/11 Event" (Lin 2006). Returns oscillate in a narrow range before the first breakpoint. From the first breakpoint to the second breakpoint, October 8, 2003, the global economy had not completely recovered. At the same time, aluminum's yields in China significantly increased. These might influence the aluminum price moving stably at a low level. Returns in this regime are narrower than that of in the first regime. From the second breakpoint to the third breakpoint, the economy in Europe and America grew faster. Economy in Asia emerged from the Asian financial crisis. A bull market appeared during this period. Returns show strong volatilities as price increase during the period from the third breakpoint to the fourth breakpoint, February 16, 2008. This may be due to a surge in commodity prices in global markets, and supply could not meet the demand of the aluminum; the price soared with very strong return volatilities and the briskest volume of trading. However, the price and return, as well as trading volume, decreased during the second half of 2007 (especially after October 2007) where global economy was affected by a deteriorating financial situation. After a short rebound at the beginning of 2008, the price slumped with the economic downturn until November 2008, where the lowest point appeared. Returns oscillated narrower during this period. The price climbed up in 2009 because the Chinese government turned to adopt the easy monetary policy and injected a large amount of money to stimulate the economy and to activate domestic consumption, demand and employment.

The copper contract

The moments of the copper returns and the moments of returns adjusted by model (2) and model (3) are shown in Table 15.8. Raw returns show a negative

Table 15.10 Moments of adjusted SHFE returns

Model	*Regime*	*Mean*	*St. dev.*	*Skewness*	*Kurtosis*	*Jarque–Bera*	*P-value*
Aluminium							
Model 2	Reg1	-7.510×10^{-16}	1.735	-1.399×10^{-1}	2.242	18.001	0.000
(Breaks = 4)	Reg2	-1.290×10^{-15}	1.741	2.220×10^{-1}	2.410	8.596	0.017*
	Reg3	1.460×10^{-15}	2.035	-1.058×10^{-1}	2.258	12.286	0.002
	Reg4	1.880×10^{-16}	2.189	-5.699×10^{-1}	2.806	19.667	0.000
	Reg5	-3.410×10^{-15}	2.255	-3.609×10^{-1}	2.508	15.349	0.001
Model 3	Reg1	-1.190×10^{-15}	1.727	-1.451×10^{-1}	2.231	17.985	0.000
(Breaks = 4)	Reg2	-3.529×10^{-15}	1.987	-2.308×10^{-1}	2.397	9.076	0.010*
	Reg3	2.054×10^{-15}	1.862	-1.279×10^{-1}	2.388	8.980	0.011*
	Reg4	1.140×10^{-15}	2.199	-5.728×10^{-1}	2.792	19.941	0.000
	Reg5	8.850×10^{-16}	2.093	-3.443×10^{-1}	3.416	13.154	0.001
Copper							
Model 2	Reg1	-4.238×10^{-15}	1.962	-4.040×10^{-1}	3.010	19.678	0.000
(Breaks = 4)	Reg2	-3.548×10^{-15}	1.876	-2.792×10^{-1}	2.704	6.358	0.047*
	Reg3	1.987×10^{-16}	2.034	-3.077×10^{-1}	3.044	8.067	0.020*
	Reg4	-2.960×10^{-15}	2.112	2.964×10^{-1}	4.052	22.698	0.000
	Reg5	-4.550×10^{-15}	2.004	2.670×10^{-1}	3.565	12.010	0.003

Table 15.10 Continued.

Model	*Regime*	*Mean*	*St. dev.*	*Skewness*	*Kurtosis*	*Jarque–Bera*	*P-value*
Model 3	Reg1	-4.928×10^{-15}	2.015	-2.822×10^{-1}	2.898	9.905	0.007
(Break = 4)	Reg2	-2.670×10^{-16}	1.958	-2.556×10^{-1}	2.690	5.690	0.053**
	Reg3	2.856×10^{-16}	2.126	-1.950×10^{-1}	3.204	4.109	0.147**
	Reg4	-4.472×10^{-15}	1.929	3.895×10^{-1}	3.262	10.376	0.005
	Reg5	-4.420×10^{-15}	2.108	-1.927×10^{-1}	3.500	7.992	0.022
Fuel oil							
Model 2	Reg1	-2.920×10^{-15}	1.915	-7.834×10^{-1}	3.619	88.343	0.000
(Breaks = 2)	Reg2	2.260×10^{-15}	2.319	-9.050×10^{-1}	3.558	50.642	0.000
Model 3	Reg1	-1.530×10^{-15}	1.930	-7.685×10^{-1}	3.591	69.836	0.000
(Breaks = 2)	Reg2	7.850×10^{-16}	2.046	-9.104×10^{-1}	3.863	40.921	0.000
	Reg3	-5.040×10^{-16}	2.392	-8.862×10^{-1}	3.270	30.407	0.000

Notes: *Insignificant at 0.01; **Insignificant at 0.05; ***Insignificant at 0.1.

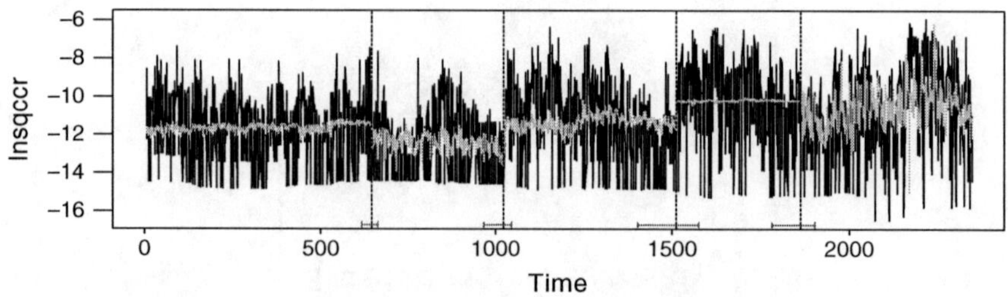

Figure 15.17 Conditional means of operational time for the aluminum's returns adjusted by model (3).

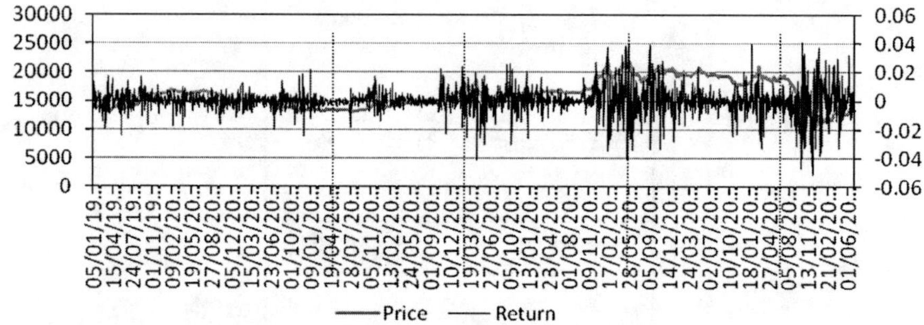

Figure 15.18 Price and return series of the aluminum contract.

value of skewness −0.1658 and a higher value of the kurtosis, 5.255, compared with that of the normal distribution. The Jarque–Bera statistic and the P-value reject the null hypothesis that returns are normally distributed. After adjusting returns by model (2) and model (3), values of the kurtosis are reduced to 2.878 and 3.239 respectively. However, the absolute values of the skewness are increased after adjusting returns by the two models to −0.4012 and −0.3774 respectively. The Jarque–Bera statistics are still too high at 67.584 and 64.269. The null hypotheses are rejected, as the P-value is almost zero.

The RSS and the BIC for copper returns are shown in Figure 15.19. The BIC indicates three breaks for the returns adjusted by model (2). However, there is only a very slight increase when moving from three breaks to four breaks. Additionally, because of the downward-biased estimation of the BIC, and the RSS indicate a four break model, we choose four as the estimated number of breaks for returns adjusted by model (2). Both the BIC and the RSS select four as the estimated number of the structural breaks for returns adjusted by model (3).

The moments of the copper returns adjusted by model (2) and model (3) with estimated four breaks are displayed in Table 15.10. The Jarque–Bera statistics show that the null hypothesis that returns are normally distributed cannot be

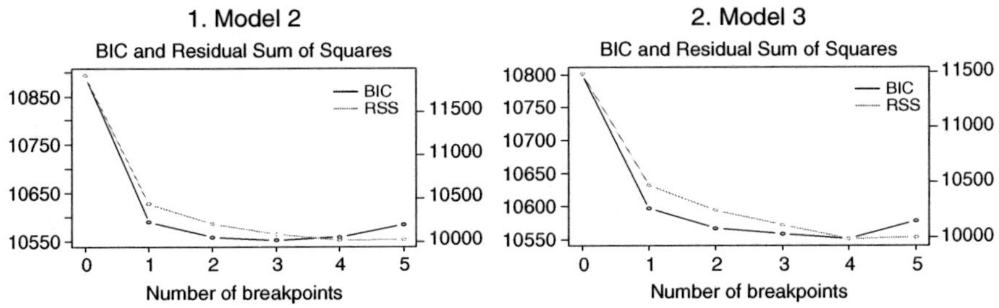

Figure 15.19 RSS and BIC for copper models with up to five breaks.

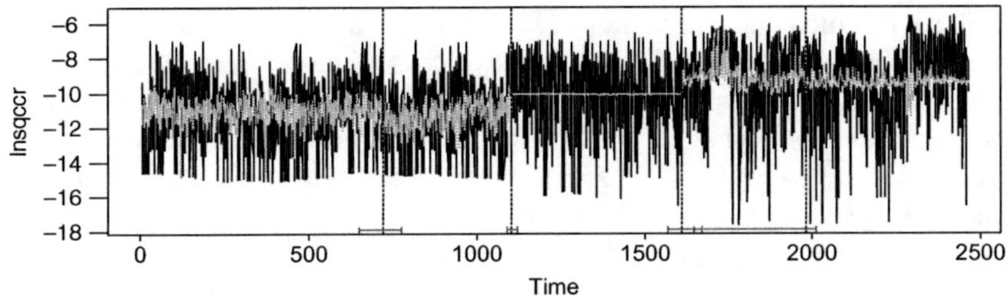

Figure 15.20 Conditional means of operational time for the copper's returns adjusted by model (3).

rejected at one percent significance level for the second regime and the third regime of returns adjusted by model (2). The null hypothesis cannot be rejected at five percent and one percent for the second regime, the third regime and the fifth regime of returns adjusted by model (3). Results suggest that model (3) can be selected as the best regression for operational time. The corresponding four breakpoint estimated by model (3) shown in Table 15.9 are chosen as the best estimation of structural breaks.

Figure 15.20 shows the conditional mean of the copper returns adjusted by model (3). Similar to the aluminum returns, the copper price evolves at the slowest rate in the second regime. In the third regime, price evolves faster than that of the first regime and the second regime, but it is still slower than that of the fourth regime where price evolves at the fastest rate. Price evolution is slightly slower compared to the fourth regime. However, it is still faster than that of the first, second, and third regime.

Figure 15.21 exhibits price and return time series of the copper contract in different regimes divided by four breakpoints for model (3). In the first and second regimes, price moves at low levels with small volatilities on returns. Around the first structural break, February 22, 2002, copper's price displays the lowest point due to the bleak markets in America, Europe, and Japan. From the first breakpoint to the second breakpoint, May 26, 2003, global economy was growing with

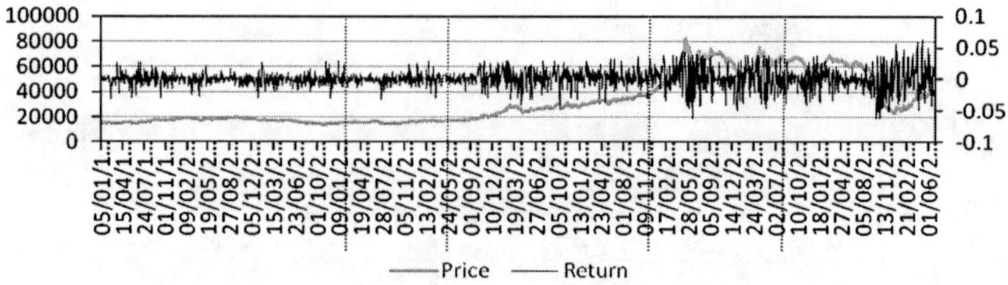

Figure 15.21 Price and return series of the copper contract.

a stable pace. China had a high demand on copper. These result in a small growth on the copper price with continuous small volatilities on returns and trading volumes. From the second break to the third break, February 9, 2006, copper's price climbs significantly due to the economic boom. Returns oscillate in a wider range. There is a soar on copper's price from the third break to the fourth break, November 8, 2007, due to significant increase of commodity prices in global markets and strong demand. Returns show strong volatilities during this period. After the fourth break, the price slumped until the end of 2008 due to the global financial crisis and economic downturn. The price has climbed since 2009 due to the Chinese government's easy monetary policy and strong investment. Returns and trading volume in this period significantly fluctuate.

The fuel oil contract

The moments of the fuel oil returns in Table 15.8 exhibit a negative value of skewness −0.3986 for the fuel oil's raw returns. The Jarque–Bera statistic is too high and the P-value is almost zero which result in a rejection of the null hypothesis that returns are normally distributed. After adjusting returns by model (2) and model (3), values of the kurtosis are reduced from 4.26 to 3.597 and 3.552 respectively. However, the absolute values of skewness increase significantly to 0.8025 and 0.7760 from 0.3986. The Jarque–Bera statistics are not reduced but raised from 106.212 to 140.052 and 129.644 after adjusting returns by model (2) and model (3). The P-values reject the null hypotheses.

The RSS and the BIC for fuel oil returns adjusted by model (2) and model (3) are shown in Figure 15.22. The BIC indicates zero breaks for returns adjusted by model (2) whereas the RSS suggests the minimum values of a four break model. We choose a one break model. The BIC chooses one break for returns adjusted by model (3). However, the RSS suggests a four break model. We select two as the estimated number of structural breaks.

Table 15.10 displays the moments of the fuel oil returns adjusted by model (2) and model (3) with estimated structural breaks. Results show that values of the kurtosis for returns adjusted by model (2) and model (3) in each regime are not

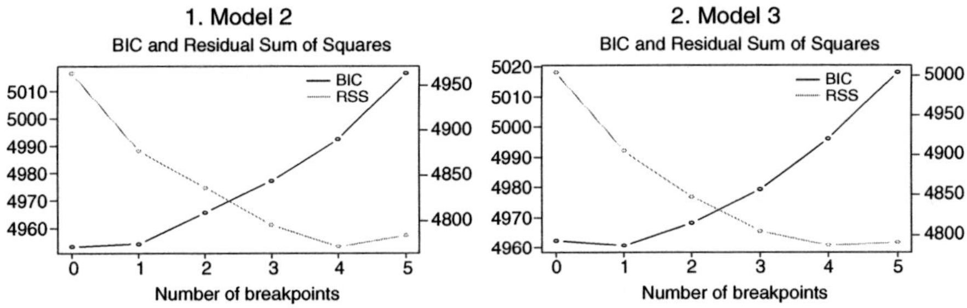

Figure 15.22 RSS and BIC for fuel oil models with up to five breaks.

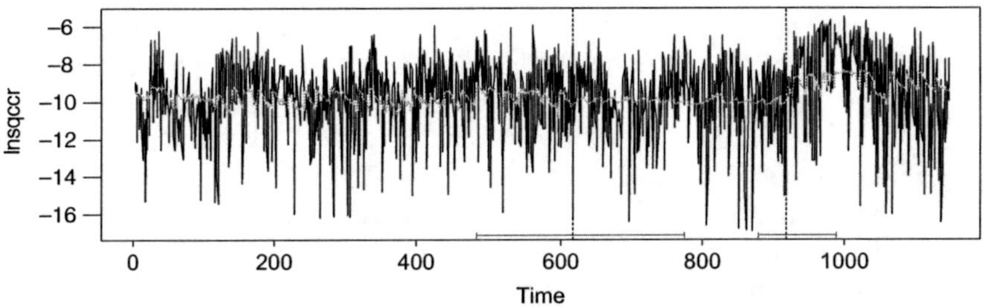

Figure 15.23 Conditional means of operational time for the fuel oil's returns adjusted by model (3).

too far from normality. However, the absolute values of skewness are much higher than that of the raw return. All the Jarque–Bera statistics are still very high (but lower than the returns without dividing by breaks) and all the *P*-values are almost zero, which indicates rejection of the null hypothesis that returns are normally distributed. It is difficult to decide which model is better for operational time given the results shown in the table. We compare the multiple R-squared and adjusted R-squared between two models. The multiple R-squared for model (2) is 0.9566, which is slightly less than that of model (3) at 0.9569. The adjusted R-squared for model (2) is 0.9564, which is slightly less than that of model (3) at 0.9566. Therefore, we select model (3) as the better obtainable regression for operational time. Two estimated breakpoints shown in Table 15.9 are the better estimations of the structural breaks.

The conditional mean of the fuel oil returns adjusted by model (3) is exhibited in Figure 15.23. The second regime shows the slowest rate of price evolution compared to the first regime (only slightly slower than that of in the first regime) and the third regime. Price evolves at the fastest rate in the third regime.

Figure 15.24 displays price and return time series of the fuel oil contract in different regimes divided by two breakpoints for model (3). Although results provided in Table 15.10 show that returns in all regimes reject the normality, the

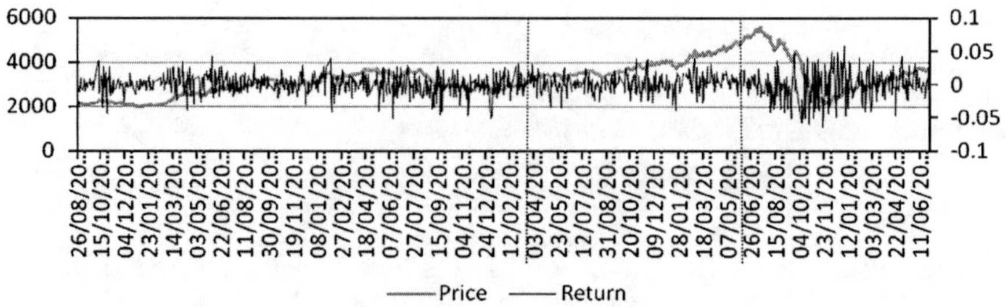

Figure 15.24 Price and return series of the fuel oil contract.

estimated breakpoints are very close to the real events. The first breakpoint, April 2, 2007, is very close to the point (January 2007) where a valley bottom appears after fuel oil price had kept moving at a high level for two years since 2005. From the first breakpoint to the second breakpoint, July 17, 2008, crude oil price in global market soar to the historically highest point US$147 per barrel in July 2008 due to strong demand and scarce supply, as well as buying long by the international hedge funds. Fuel oil price on the Shanghai futures exchange also surged to the highest point in history in the same month. Return series and volume of trading are less fluctuated during this period. After the second breakpoint, fuel oil plunged to the lowest point in November 2008 due to the global economic recession, and then climbed up again in 2009 when many countries injected huge amounts of money into banks and made policies to stimulate their economy. Returns and volume of trading strongly oscillate during this period, which may because of the uncertain expectations and speculations.

Conclusion

This chapter analyzes the effect of historical events on the speed of price evolution of futures products selected from China's futures market. The effects of historical events are investigated by allowing multiple structural breaks. We use models where price processes are indexed by trading volume as an operational time instead of calendar time. There are two competing models employed in this chapter. We choose the one which adjust returns to be closer to the normal distribution as the best obtainable regression. Those breaks estimated by the best model are selected as the pertinent breakpoints. Based on the empirical results, we obtain the following conclusions:

Allowing structural breaks in the models for operational time can be a practical method to measure the speed of price evolution

Empirical results show that those structural breaks estimated by models for operational time are very close to the real historical events. These historical events significantly influence the speed of price evolution: most of the estimated structural breaks appear in 2003, 2005–06 and 2008. In 2003, China's economy emerged from the Asian financial crisis, American and European economies gradually revived from recession, futures prices increased, and price evolution quickened. During 2005–06, commodity prices in global markets grew rapidly due to an economic boom. Most of the contracts examined in this study show that prices evolved at fast rates during this period. During the second half of 2007 and in 2008, the global economy went into recession due to the impact of the subprime crisis and problems among financial institutions. Product prices in futures markets (particularly cotton, sugar, aluminum, copper, and fuel oil) were affected by the crisis and slumped in 2008, but then quickly recovered in 2009 due to the Chinese government's stimulating actions. Although during the economic downturn in 2008, some futures contracts' prices (such as cotton, aluminum and copper) show short-term decreases or fluctuations, our findings suggest that the current global recession does not slow down the speed of price evolution of Chinese futures products.

Returns adjusted by model (3) are closer to the normal distribution compared with model (2)

Seven selected futures contracts suggest model (3) as the best obtainable regression for operational time. The corn contract is the most robust as returns in all regimes cannot reject normality. Model (2) is only supported in the case of soybean No. 1 contract. The fuel oil contract is a special case where there is no regime being normally distributed for adjusted fuel oil returns. We select model (3) as the best regression due to higher values of the multiple R-squared and the adjusted R-squared for this contract.

Price evolves slowly during the less eventful period, whereas it evolves at a faster rate as more information arrives

Our results to some extent support the MDH theory that price changes and trading volumes are driven by the same underlying latent information. When an historical event brings new information arrivals (especially when the information is uncertain or traders have different expectations for markets), price changes and trading volumes are active and result in a fast price evolution. Empirical findings suggest that prices evolve at fast rates during 2005 to 2006 and 2007 to 2008 when commodity prices surged and the financial crisis spread worldwide. Futures prices evolved at slower rates from 2000 to 2002. During that period the Chinese economy was recovering from the Asian financial crisis and worldwide economic inactivity. It was a less eventful period.

In summary, this study gives a full picture of price movement from the 1990s to the present, for the main futures products traded in China. With the Chinese economy growing rapidly in recent decades, there has been increased international attention focused on its influence in the global economy. As one of the most important financial instruments and an emblem of mature capital market, futures trading possess the irreplaceable power for price discovery and minimization of the transaction risk.

China's futures market was established in 1992. It has grown from a "toddler" to a modern derivatives market. In 2009, there were 2.16 billion lots (trading units) of commodity futures contracts traded in China's futures market, and total turnover amounted to ¥130.5 trillion. Trading volume accounted for 43 percent of the total commodity futures volume in global futures markets. New futures products have also increased in recent years from 18 in 2007 to 23 in 2009, and now encompass most of the essential commodities. At present, DCE is one of the top two soybean futures markets and the biggest non-genetically modified soybean futures market in the world. Copper's price on the SHFE has become one of the preferred reference prices for top international copper companies. More recently, in spring 2010, we saw the introduction of stock index futures in China, which has broadened futures trading into financial instruments. This represents a progress both to globalization and maturity.

In the "post-crisis era," there are expectations of a "new world order" and a possible "market reshuffling." China as a new growth engine of the world economy will attract a significant international investment, business, and commercial activities. China's futures market, therefore, can be expected to play a significant and ever expanding role in providing reliable price information and risk protection for international traders.

References

Admati, A. R. and Pfleiferer, P. (1988) 'A Theory of Intraday Patterns: Volume and Price Variability', *Review of Financial Studies*, 1: 3–40.

Aiolfi, M. and Timmermann, A. (2004) 'Structural Breaks and the Performance of Forecast Combinations', research working paper, Bocconi University and UCSD.

Andersen, T. G. (1996) 'Return Volatility and Trading Volume: an Information Flow Interpretation of Stochastic Volatility', *Journal of Finance*, 51: 169–204.

Andrews, D. W. K. (1991) 'Heteroscedasticity and Autocorrelation Consistent Covariance Matrix Estimation', *Econometrica*, 59: 817–56.

Andrews, D. W. K. (1993) 'Tests for Parameter Instability and Structural Change with Unknown Change Point', *Econometrica*, 61: 821–56.

Andrews, D. W. K. and Monahan, J. C. (1992) 'An Improved Heteroscedasticity and Autocorrelation Consistent Covariance Matrix Estimator', *Econometrica*, 60: 953–66.

Andrews, D. W. K. and Ploberger, W. (1994) 'Optimal Tests when a Nuisance Parameter is Present Only under the Alternative', *Econometrica*, 62: 1383–414.

Andrews, D. W. K., Lee, I. and Ploberger, W. (1996) 'Optimal Changepoint Tests for Normal Linear Regression', *Journal of Econometrics*, 70: 9–38.

Ane, T. and Geman, H. (2000) 'Order Flow, Transaction Clock, and Normality of Asset Returns', *Journal of Finance*, 55: 2259–84.

Ane, T. and Rangau, L. U. (2008) 'Does Trading Volume Really Explain Stock Returns Volatility?', *Journal of International Financial Markets, Institutions and Money*, 18: 216–35.

Bai, J. (1994) 'Least Squares Estimation of a Shift in Linear Processes', *Journal of Time Series Analysis*, 15: 453–72.

Bai, J. (1997) 'Estimation of a Change Point in Multiple Regression Models', *Review of Economic and Statistics*, 79: 551–63.
Bai, J. and Perron, P. (1998) 'Testing For and Estimation of Multiple Structural Changes', *Econometrica*, 66: 47–79.
Bai, J. and Perron, P. (2003) 'Computation and Analysis of Multiple Structural Change Models', *Journal of Applied Econometrics*, 18: 1–22.
Bellman, R. and Roth, R. (1969) 'Curve Fitting by Segmented Straight Lines', *Journal of the American Statistical Association*, 64: 1079–84.
Bollerslev, T. and Jubinski, D. (1999) 'Equity Trading Volume and Volatility: Latent Information Arrivals and Common Long-run Dependence', *Journal of Business and Economic Statistics,* 17: 9–21.
Callaway, R. E. (1989) 'Evidence of the Nonstationary of the Variance Rate of Return of New York Stock Exchange Listed Common Stock', *Financial Review*, 24: 199–214.
Chang, C. W. and Chang, J. S. K. (1996) 'Pricing Catastrophe Insurance Futures Call Spreads: A Randomized Operational Time Approach', *Journal of Risk and Insurance*, 63: 599–617.
Changjiang Futures (2006) 'Summarizing Cotton Futures Market for 2005 and the expectation for 2006'. Online. Available at: http://cjfo.com.cn/admin/ (accessed January 11, 2006).
Clark, P. K. (1973) 'A Subordinated Stochastic Process with Finite Variance for Speculative Prices', *Econometrica*, 41: 135–56.
Clark, T. E. and McCracken, M. W. (2002) 'Forecast-Based Model Selection in the Presence of Structural Breaks', research working paper, Federal Reserve Bank of Kansas City.
Da An (2005) 'Corn Domestic Price Stop Increase, Futures Price Continuously Fall', Online. Available at: http://daan.jlagri.gov.cn/info.asp?id=1583 (accessed August 1, 2005).
Downing, C. and Zhang, F. (2004) 'Trading Activity and Price Volatility in the Municipal Bond Market', *Journal of Finance*, 59: 899–931.
Edelman, D. and Gillespie, T. (2000) 'The Stochastically Subordinated Poisson Normal Process for Modeling Financial Assets', *Annals of Operations Research*, 100: 133–64.
Epps, T. W. and Epps, M. L. (1976) 'The Stochastic Dependence of Security Price Changes and Transaction Volumes: Implication for the Mixture-of-Distributions Hypothesis', *Econometrica*, 44: 305–21.
Fisher, W. D. (1958) 'On Grouping for Maximum Homogeneity', *Journal of the American Statistical Association*, 53: 789–98.
Gaobo (2005) 'Monthly Comment on Corn'. Online. Available at: http://www.sdny.gov.cn/art/2005/12/5 (accessed December 5, 2005).
Garcia, R. and Perron, P. (1996) 'An Analysis of the Real Interest Rate under Regime Shifts', *Review of Economics and Statistics*, 78: 111–25.
Glosten, L. R. and Milgrom, P. R. (1985) 'Bid, Ask, and Transaction Prices in a Specialist Market with Heterogeneously Informed Traders', *Journal of Financial Economics*, 14: 71–100.
Gnednenko, B. V. and Kolmogorov, A. N. (1954) *Limit Distributions for Sums of Independent Random Variables*, Cambridge, Mass: Addison-Wesley Publishing Company.
Guthery, S. B. (1974) 'Partition Regression', *Journal of the American Statistical Association*, 69: 945–47.
Hall, J. A., Brorsen, B. W. and Irwin, S. H. (1989) 'The Distribution of Futures Prices: A Test of the Stable Paretain and the Mixture of Normals Hypotheses', *Journal of Financial and Quantitative Analysis*, 24: 105–16.
Harris, L. (1986) 'Cross-Security Tests of the Mixture of Distributions Hypothesis', *Journal of Financial and Quantitative Analysis*, 21: 39–46.
Harris, L. (1987) 'Transaction Data Test of the Mixtures of Distributions Hypothesis', *Journal of Financial and Quantitative Analysis*, 22: 127–41.

Harris, M. and Raviv, A. (1993) 'Differences of Opinions Make a Horse Race', *The Review of Financial Studies*, 6: 473–506.

Hendry, D. F. and Mizon, G. E. (2001) 'Forecasting in the Presence of Structural Breaks and Policy Regime Shifts', working paper, Oxford University.

Holden, C.W. and Subrahmanyam, A. (1992) 'Long-Lived Private Information and Imperfect Competition', *Journal of Finance*, 47: 247–70.

Howison, S. and Lamper, D. (2001) 'Trading Volume in Models of Financial Derivatives', *Applied Mathematical Finance*, 8: 119–35.

Karpoff, J. M. (1987) 'The Relationship Between Price Changes and Trading Volume: A Survey', *Journal of Financial and Quantitative Analysis*, 22: 109–26.

Kendall, M. G. (1953) 'The Analysis of Economic Time Series: Part I, Prices', *Journal of the Royal Statistical Society*, 96: 11–25.

Kim, I. M. (1997) 'Detecting the Number of Structural Breaks', *Economics Letters*, 57: 145–8.

Kim, I. M. (2003) 'Operational Time of the Korea Stock Markets', *Economics Letters*, 78: 181–5.

Lamoureux, C. G. and Lastrapes, W. D. (1990) 'Heteroskedasticity in Stock Return Data: Volume Versus GARCH Effects', *Journal of Finance*, 45: 221–9.

Lamoureux, C. G. and Lastrapes, W. D. (1994) 'Endogenous Trading Volume and Momentum In Stock Return Volatility', *Journal of Business & Economic Statistics*, 12: 253–60.

Levy, P. (1925) *Calcul des Probabilites*, Paris: Gauthier-Villars.

Liangmao Futures (2006) 'White Sugar Futures Report 2006 (The First half Year of 2006)'. Online. Available at: http://www.51qh.com.

Liangmao Futures (2007) 'White Sugar Futures Report 2007 (The First half Year of 2007)'. Online. Available at: http://www.51qh.com.

Liesenfeld, R. (1998) 'Dynamic Bivariate Mixture Models: Modeling the Behavior of Prices and Trading Volume', *Journal of Business & Economic Statistics*, 16: 101–9.

Liesenfeld, R. (2001) 'A Generalized Bivariate Mixture Model for Stock Price Volatility and Trading Volume', *Journal of Econometrics*, 104: 141–78.

Lin, Y. (2006) 'The Factor That Affect Aluminum Price'. Online. Available at: http://www.dlqh.net.

Liu, J., Wu, S. and Zidek, J. V. (1997) 'On Segmented Multivariate Regressions', *Statistica Sinica*, 7: 497–525.

Lobato, I. and Velasco, C. (2000) 'Long Memory in Stock Market Trading Volume', *Journal of Business and Economic Statistics*, 18: 410–27.

Mandelbrot, B. (1963) 'The Variation of Certain Speculative Prices', *Journal of Business*, 36: 394–419.

Mandelbrot, B. and Taylor, H. (1967) 'On the Distribution of Stock Price Difference', *Operations Research*, 15: 1057–62.

O'Hara, M. (1995) 'Market Microstructure Theory', Cambridge, MA: Basil Blackwell.

Perron, P. (1989) 'The Great Crash, the Oil Price Shock and the Unit Root Hypothesis', *Econometrica*, 57: 1361–1401.

Perron, P. (2005) 'Dealing with Structural Breaks', working paper, Boston University.

Rice, J. (1995) *Mathematical Statistics and Data Analysis*, North Scituate: Duxbury Press.

Schwarz, G. (1978) 'Estimation the Dimension of a Model', *Annals of Statistics*, 6: 461–4.

Shalen, C. T. (1993) 'Volume, Volatility, and the Dispersion of Beliefs', *Review of Financial Studies*, 6: 405–34.

Tauchen, G. and Pitts, M. (1983) 'The Price Variability–Volume Relationship on Speculative Markets', *Econometrica*, 51: 485–505.

Upton, D. E. and Shannon, D. S. (1979) 'The Stable Paretian Distribution, Subordinated Stochastic Processes, and Asymptotic Lognormality: An Empirical Investigation', *Journal of Finance*, 34: 1031–9.

Watanabe, T. (2000) 'Bayesian Analysis of Dynamic Bivariate Mixture Models: Can They Explain the Behaviour of Returns and Trading Volume?' *Journal of Business & Economic Statistics*, 18: 199–210.

Westerfield, R. (1977) 'The Distribution of Common Stock Price Changes: An Application of Transactions Time and Subordinated Stochastic Models', *Journal of Financial and Quantitative Analysis*, 12: 743–65.

Wilkinson, G. N. and Roger, C. E. (1973) 'Symbolic Description of Factorial Model For Analysis of Variance', *Applied Statistic*, 22: 392–9.

Yao, Y.-C. (1988) 'Estimating the Number of Change–Point via Schwarz' Criterion', *Statistics and Probability Letters*, 6: 181–9.

Yiming (2007) 'Review of Domestic Corn Market (2006)'. Online. Available at: http://sh.shuangliao.gov.cn.

Zeileis, A., and Kleiber, C. (2005a) 'Validating Multiple Structural Change Models – An Extended Case Study', unpublished thesis. Online. Available at: http://epub.wu-wien.ac.at.

Zeileis, A. and Kleiber, C. (2005b) 'Validating Multiple Structural Change Models – A Case Study', *Journal of Applied Econometrics*, 20: 685–90.

Zhang, R., Mckillop, D. and Li, Y. (2008) 'The Distributional Properties of the Selected Contracts Traded on the China's Futures Market', working paper, Management School of Queen's University Belfast.

Zhu, X. (2007) 'Global Grain Price Rose Rapidly in 2006', *China Grain Economy*, 3: 45–7.

16 Poverty in Shenzhen

Stefan Gravemeyer, Thomas Gries and Jinjun Xue

Introduction

Poverty remains an urgent issue all over the globe, as stressed by the World Bank's recent poverty estimates in 2008. After the World Bank International Comparison Project published its updated purchasing power parity prices (PPP) a new global poverty line was set at US$ 1.25 a day. The new report once again stresses that developing countries, in particular, often have to tackle poverty reduction as part of their development process so that the poor can participate in the income gains resulting from accelerated development. Even if Bourguignon (2004) states that economic growth tends to reduce absolute poverty in a country, and although China has been remarkably successful in diminishing severe poverty, there are still enormous differences between highly developed urban settlements and rural areas (Knight and Song 1999). As a result, poverty has often been regarded (mainly) as a rural problem (Khan 1998). Having been neglected for a long time, urban poverty and inequality, in particular, have been of growing concern in recent years (Knight and Song 2003). Li (2006) stresses that even though poverty may not be as severe in Chinese urban agglomerations as in other developing countries it is still a problem that cannot be neglected. This is especially true if the subjective impression of relative poverty, which varies between cities, is accounted for (Gustafsson *et al.* 2006). The problem is amplified by migration, since migrants relocating from rural regions to urban centers are generally expected to be poorer than urban registered inhabitants (Appleton 2008).

The estimates of the extent of poverty in urban China vary widely due to different data sources, definitions of income, and poverty lines. Using two different approaches to calculate the cost of basic needs Meng *et al.* (2008) found that both the urban poverty rate, as well as the severity of poverty, rose significantly between 1986 and 2000. They estimate poverty in 2000 to have been between 0.3 percent and 0.4 percent for the income measure, depending on the definition of the cost of basic needs. Ravallion and Chen (2004) use a different method to calculate the cost of basic needs and arrive at a poverty rate of 0.54 percent for urban China in 2002. Appleton *et al.* (2008) employ a different dataset that includes governmental transfers, imputed rents, and a more broadly defined poverty line, and state that absolute poverty declined between 1988 and 2002. They estimate the poverty rate in 2002 to have been 2.88 percent (with a poverty line of US$2 a day) and 8.52 percent (US$3 a day), using a 1985 PPP exchange rate.

In the studies that cover this issue the migrant population has not been adequately considered on a micro level because many datasets only account for urban registered inhabitants (Meng *et al.* 2008), or have only insufficient data on migrants (Hussain 2003). Appleton *et al.* (2008) stress the importance of including migrants due to high migration growth and the general assumption that rural–urban migrants are generally poorer than urban residents, since rural-to-urban migration to the cities is generally perceived as a means to escape rural poverty (Park, Du and Wang 2004). Because of this lack of data it is not possible to analyze the effect that migratory status has on poverty or obtain unbiased estimates of poverty incidence. Neither it is possible to analyze the different determinants of poverty and income for both groups. Since the design of the 2005 Shenzhen household survey allows us to analyze the effects of the various poverty determining factors with respect to migrants, we are able to investigate these urgent issues, obtain an unbiased view of poverty in this city, and unravel the general connections between poverty and migration. Shenzhen is one of the most advanced, fastest growing and capitalist cities in China. It can be regarded not only as an example of one of the most successful agglomerations in mainland China, but also as a general example of one of the fastest transformation processes in the world. Uncovering the determinants of poverty in Shenzhen allows us to obtain a deeper insight into the circumstances facing other Chinese urban agglomerations.

When calculating poverty incidence in Shenzhen we are able to take the migrant population into account and to explore how various factors interrelate with poverty and migratory status. Is migratory status connected with poverty? Are migrants poorer? Are there differences in the forces that drag households into poverty for migrants and non-migrants? Has everyone benefited from the dramatic growth process, or were some left behind? To what extent do the poor differ from the non-poor? After calculating poverty measures to describe poverty incidence we use limited dependent variable regressions as well as OLS welfare regressions to answer these questions. We also use a generalized Oaxaca-Blinder decomposition to decompose the non-linear regressions and examine to what extent migrants are subject to income discrimination, thereby increasing their poverty risk.

Using our new data on migrants we can clearly see that migrants are far more vulnerable to poverty and earn significantly lower incomes than non-migrants. The determinants of poverty differ significantly between both groups and shed light on the causes of more pronounced migrant poverty.

Describing poverty in Shenzhen

Measurement issues

For our analysis of poverty in Shenzhen, we employed indices of the popular *P-Alpha class* of poverty measures which were introduced by Foster, Greer, and Thorbecke (1984). The general class of these indices is defined by

Deaton (1997):

$$P_\alpha = n^{-1} \sum_{i=1}^{n} \left(\frac{1 - x_i}{z} \right)^{\alpha} 1(x_i \leq z)$$

where α is a positive poverty aversion parameter, n denotes the size of the population, z defines the poverty line, x_i the welfare measure and $1(\cdot)$ is an indicator function that is one if the argument within the parentheses is true. The larger the poverty aversion parameter α, the more weight is given to the people farthest below the poverty line. This means that more importance is attributed to the depth of the poverty gap. For our further analysis of poverty in Shenzhen two specific sub-indices of the P-Alpha class are of interest:

Poverty headcount

The poverty headcount refers to the number of people who live in poverty as a fraction of the whole population. We obtained the *poverty headcount* by setting $\alpha = 1$ and attain:

$$P_0 = \frac{1}{n} \sum_{i=1}^{n} 1(x_i \leq z)$$

One disadvantage of this measure is that it does not take the depth of poverty into account. Whether most of the poor live slightly below the poverty line or at subsistence level is not reflected in the index. The same is true for policy measures that may make the poor better off while still not lifting them above the poverty line.

Since we are interested in more than the simple poverty headcount, and want to take the depth of poverty into account, one possibility is the *poverty gap ratio* which we obtained by setting the poverty aversion parameter α to one:

Depth of poverty

$$P_1 = \frac{1}{n} \sum_{i=1}^{n} \left(\frac{1 - x_i}{z} \right) 1(x_i \leq z)$$

Here, the contribution of the individual to the poverty index is larger the poorer they are. The index is a sum of all these shortfalls below the poverty line divided by the number of people and expressed as a fraction of the poverty line.

We will limit ourselves to these two measures in our discussion since they allow the greatest comparability due to their popularity. For a fuller discussion of these and other measures see Deaton (1997) or Ravallion (1993).

The correct definition of the poverty line is another issue. Either the cost of basic needs approach or a purchasing power parity price approach could be used.

We decided against the cost of basic needs approach, which is commonly used to assess poverty, and instead employed purchasing power parity prices for greater comparability with different dollar levels as well as local measures such as the minimum wage for urban Shenzhen. We used these broader definitions of poverty since the adoption of very low poverty lines – such as US$1 a day – equates to presuming that no urban poverty exists in China (Khan 1998). Furthermore, not only do we want to analyze extreme absolute poverty, which seems rare in Chinese cities, but also relative deprivation and poverty more generally, which is of equal importance for policy makers (Li 2006).

Dataset

For our analysis we used household data from the 2005 Shenzhen household survey (Xue and Gries 2008). Contrary to many other datasets like the National Bureau of Statistics of China (NBS) or early the China Household Income Project (CHIP) surveys, the household survey includes very detailed information on the migrant population on a micro level, which allows us to take this specific subgroup into account. The dataset comprises 1,056 households and 3,256 individuals. The survey was conducted using random sampling and considered residents' registration status. According to official data taken from the *Shenzhen Statistical Yearbook* 2005, one third of all inhabitants had a rural registration (hukou), while two thirds held an urban registration. This structure is reflected in the sample which was drawn from three of the six districts of Shenzhen: Luohu, Nanshan and Baoan. For a full description of the dataset see Xue and Gries (2008).

Poverty incidence in Shenzhen

First we calculated the poverty headcount ratio based on multiple broadly defined absolute and relative poverty lines. We employed the new Purchasing Power Parity exchange rates for 2005 from the 2008 World Bank International Comparison Program (ICP) to generate our absolute poverty lines. Furthermore, we considered the differences in needs across different household sizes and compositions and calculated household income per equivalent adult (Deaton 1997). This resulted in a far more realistic assessment of poverty. Without this correction a large household size would dramatically decrease average household income and increase poverty incidence without accounting for actual circumstances. The most sensible choice in this situation was to opt for the Organization for Economic Co-operation and Development (OECD) equivalence scale to adjust total household income for economies of scale, but not for gender (Grootaert and Braithwaite 1998),

$$x_i^{adj} = \frac{x_i}{N^{0.7}}$$

which is the welfare measure x_i (in our case, income) adjusted by the number of household members N to the power of 0.7.

Table 16.1 Poverty incidence by poverty line and adjustment

	Poverty rate in %		*Poverty gap ratio in %*	
	With equivalence scales	*Without equivalence scales*	*With equivalence scales*	*Without equivalence scales*
Unadjusted income				
Relative poverty (1/2 median[1])	24.8	22.8	8.41	7.77
Relative poverty (2/3 median)	35.8	33.5	13.98	13.07
Shenzhen min. wage (RMB 9,600) (Yearly value. Source: *Inequality in China*)	15.9	26.23	4.4	9.26
Dollars a day in PPP terms US$1	0	0	0	0
Dollars a day in PPP terms US$1.25	0	0.28	0	0.03
Dollars a day in PPP terms US$2	0.34	0.97	0.02	0.2
Dollars a day in PPP terms US$3	0.81	4.41	0.18	0.98
Regional CPI-adjusted income				
Relative poverty (1/2 median)	23.2	22.1	6.9	6.7
Relative poverty (2/3 median)	34.7	33	12.4	12.1
Dollars a day in PPP terms US$1	0	0.19	0	0.03
Dollars a day in PPP terms US$1.25	0.09	0.38	0.01	0.07
Dollars a day in PPP terms US$2	0.48	2.59	0.12	0.52
Dollars a day in PPP terms US$3	2.69	7.47	0.6	1.76

Notes:

1 Median incomes are: RMB 17,040 for unadjusted income and RMB 12,580 for the CPI-adjusted income. If corrections are made for equivalence scales, too, the values are RMB 23,391 for unadjusted income and RMB 17,309 for CPI-adjusted incomes. The mean and standard deviation (in parentheses) of the three types of income are RMB 31,878 (RMB 40,764), RMB 23,273 (RMB 29,794) and RMB 32,144 (RMB 40,420).

To measure poverty we used the old World Bank poverty line of US$1 as well as the new measure of US$1.25 that was proposed after the 2008 ICP was published. We also used the US$2 and US$3 a day levels as more broadly defined poverty lines, as in Appleton *et al.* (2008), to obtain a more differentiated view of poverty incidence.

To take account of the fact that Shenzhen is one of the most developed cities in China we corrected the PPP exchange rate of the 2008 ICP for the whole of China with a regional price deflator. The urban Shenzhen price expenditure basket by Brandt and Holz (2006) provided the best information about local prices in Shenzhen. We updated it with regional urban Consumer Price Index (CPI) data from the Chinese National Bureau of Statistics for the period 2000 to 2005 to arrive at the best correction factor for our 2005 data. With this correction our estimates became comparable to poverty estimates in real terms for other cities and regions in 2005 and allow us to measure absolute poverty in PPP terms much more accurately.

Table 16.2 Poverty incidence by hukou

Adjusted income	*Poverty rate in %*	
	Migrant	*Non-migrant*
Shenzhen minimum wage	27.6	6.1
Dollars a day in PPP terms US$1	0	0
Dollars a day in PPP terms US$1.25	0.21	0
Dollars a day in PPP terms US$2	0.86	0.17
Dollars a day in PPP terms US$3	4.92	0.87

*PPP values adjusted by regional CPI and equivalence scales/minimum wage adjusted by equivalence scales.

To picture relative and absolute poverty we calculated the poverty headcount ratios for relative poverty lines (the standard half as well as two thirds of median income). For a broader view of poverty we also considered the official minimum wage for Shenzhen as a poverty line.

Based on the different poverty lines we calculated the poverty gap to gain a descriptive overview of the depth of poverty in Shenzhen in 2005.

To get a visual impression of the differences between the migrant and non migrant population we calculated the poverty incidence separately for both population subgroups as displayed in Table 16.2.

It is evident that the rate of severe poverty is very low in Shenzhen even when specifically accounting for migrants. Measured by the new 2008 World Bank standard very few people live on less than US$1.25 a day in Shenzhen. A look at the broader poverty lines of US$2 and US$3 a day reveals a fair incidence of poverty. The depth of poverty proves to be very low no matter what poverty line is chosen. Adjusting income by equivalent scales very significantly reduces the poverty incidence on every level, reflecting the importance of household size in the poverty calculations. The same is true for the correction of household income by the regional urban CPI. If we take the higher living costs in Shenzhen city into account the poverty incidence in Shenzhen increases drastically. Our poverty estimates with CPI corrections, but without equivalence scale adjustment, come close to the results of Appleton *et al.* (2008) for urban China as a whole. The poverty incidence calculated by adjusting with equivalence scales and correcting income with the appropriate CPI is, in our opinion, the best estimate of poverty incidence in Shenzhen.

We used this adjusted income to calculate poverty incidence separately for migrants and non-migrants, which revealed that poverty incidence is much higher in the migrant subgroup. Using the three-dollar-a-day poverty line, the incidence is around five times higher than for migrants. Also, more than four times as many migrants earn less than the local minimum wage.

If we look at the relative poverty measures, and specifically the poverty incidence below the minimum wage, it appears significant and deeper. Nearly one third of the households earn less than the minimum wage, a figure that drops to around 15 percent if adjusted by equivalence scales. This proves the rather high income inequalities within the city. In our empirical analysis we will take a closer look at the factors determining relative poverty in Shenzhen. This is appropriate since Shenzhen's severe poverty rate is rather low and the city is so highly developed that the relative poverty approach that is often used in industrialized Western countries yields more interesting results. We will examine the role of migratory status in determining poverty, and investigate the differences between the migrant and non-migrant population and the extent to which migrants are discriminated against. Since migrants make up an ever-growing part of the urban workforce in China, answering these questions appears essential for poverty analysis.

Determinants of urban poverty in Shenzhen

The World Bank defines urban poverty as a multidimensional and dynamic phenomenon with close ties to vulnerability and asset ownership (World Bank Poverty Reduction Strategy Paper). In our analysis we will focus on the income dimension of poverty. The risk of income poverty is part of a dynamic framework comprising a variety of assets such as labor, human capital, other productive assets, and household composition, as well as social capital and social factors. Productive assets are all accumulated factors, immaterial or material, which allow households to generate income by utilizing these assets. We selected variables that generally belong to these categories as well as China-specific factors that are assumed to have an impact on the poverty status of a household.

For China it is generally agreed that the increase in inequality, the abolishment of the food coupon system, the restructuring of state-owned enterprises, and social welfare reforms had a strong impact on (urban) poverty (Meng *et al.* 2008). At the household level they identify the main contributing factors as: demographic structure, labor market involvement, and human capital. Furthermore, occupational sector, migratory (hukou) status, and self-employment greatly influence the risk of poverty (Khan 2008). Khan also stresses the connections between poverty, migration, and self-employment since a much higher proportion of migrants are self-employed compared to residents with an urban registration. Migrant poverty has also been identified as one of the major causes of urban poverty by Xue and Zhong (2003). Taking these findings and the World Bank classification as a starting point, we used the following variables in our analysis:

Household composition

Household composition summarizes all characteristics which describe the structure and size of the household. The composition of the household often has an impact on its poverty status in China (Meng *et al.* 2008). Average household age is included as a proxy for potential experience and the age structure of the household. This variable may also be a productive asset. We also included the dependency ratio between non-working age and working-age members, and household size.

Productive assets

We included average years of schooling and informal education to account for human capital within the household. We also accounted for the length of residence in Shenzhen since a longer residence may lead to higher income through acquired local knowledge, skills and social capital (Fan 2001). Since men consistently earn more than women in similar jobs, due to gender discrimination as stated by Shu (2005), we included a dummy variable where the head of household was male.

Social and China-specific factors

Migratory status is generally seen as a major explanation for income differences. Since people from rather poor rural areas migrate to cities in hope of higher income, large migrant populations are present in Chinese cities (Chen and Coulson 2002). Lu and Song (2006) point to the existence of major income differences between urban residents and rural migrants. Since registration status can be expected to have an impact we included rural hukou (registration) in our regression to identify the migrants. Since the introduction of special economic zones in Shenzhen triggered its rapid growth process, we included a dummy variable for residence status in a Special Economic Zone (SEZ) district.

Sector of occupation

Another factor which needs to be accounted for is the sector of occupation since it may have a significant influence on household income. As pointed out by Knight and Song (2003) this is also indicative in the case of China. State-owned enterprises may pay better than private-sector enterprises, and normally employ only urban registered inhabitants. Therefore, we included dummy variables for state ownership of the company, for self-employment, and for full or partly foreign ownership. The ownership status of the company may also correlate with migratory status.

We also considered implementing variables for health and medical expenditure as a proxy for the health status of the household. However, due to the endogeneity problem between health expenditure and income, and because the variable is insignificant, we decided to remove it from our model. Also, job provision for the household head by a friend or family member as a measure of the impact of social networking, marital status, and communist party membership of the household head proved insignificant in this model and were removed. Table 16.3 summarizes the variables in our model.

Model specification

We used the standard Probit model to analyze the impact of several household and household head characteristics on the poverty status of the household. The use of Logit and Probit regressions to analyze poverty is common in the literature and these have been used by Appleton (1996), Grootaert (1997) and Grootaert and

Table 16.3 Variable descriptions for all models

Variable	*Description*
Household composition	
av_age	Average age of the household members
Dpr	Dependency ratio
family_size	Number of people living in the household
Productive assets	
av_schooling	Number of non-working members
Infedu	Individual has had informal education (i.e. on-the-job training etc.)
Male	Household head is male
Stay	Years spent in Shenzhen
Social and China specific factors	
Rural	Individual has a rural hukou (registration)
Sez	Individual lives in the special economic zone within Shenzhen
Sector of occupation	
Foreignshare	Individual is employed by a company which is partly or fully foreign-owned
Soe	Individual is employed by a state-owned enterprise

Braithwaite (1998). One of the main benefits of using these methods is the avoidance of possible bias found in standard OLS welfare regressions due to increasing measurement error, as outlined by Grootaert and Braithwaite (1998). This bias may be caused by a correlation of the error term with income due to increasing measurement error when income increases. Collapsing the whole income distribution into a binary variable circumvents this problem, but comes at the cost of losing information about income distribution.

Our Probit model is specified as follows

$$PR(Y = 1 \mid X) = \Phi(\alpha + \beta X)$$

$Y \triangleq$ binary variable of poverty incidence
$\Phi \triangleq$ cumulative standard normal distribution
$\alpha \triangleq$ intercept
$\beta \triangleq$ vector of coefficients
$X \triangleq$ vector of variables

Vector X captures household characteristics and assets as well as the characteristics of the household head with an expected impact on the poverty status of the household. After evaluating different poverty lines for our analysis we came to the conclusion that the 50 percent of the median is most appropriate for our model, although the results remained robust for different poverty lines. We used

50 percent median income adjusted by the regional CPI and equivalence scales as the poverty line.

We also used a Tobit estimation to model the poverty gap and choose poverty line z as the censoring point:

$$Y = z, \text{ if } Y^* \geq z \quad \text{and} \quad Y = Y^*, \text{ if } Y^* < z$$

$$Y^* = \alpha + \beta X + e$$

$Y \triangleq$ logarithm of adjusted income
$\alpha \triangleq$ intercept
$\beta \triangleq$ vector of coefficients
$X \triangleq$ vector of variables
$e \triangleq$ error term

The Tobit model allows the estimates to differ between poor and non-poor population groups which enabled us to identify the differences between the two. To check the robustness of our estimates and to calculate parameters for the poor and non-poor population groups as a whole we also estimated a standard continuous OLS welfare equation using the same variables as in the Probit and Tobit regressions, a widely used method for poverty analysis (Grootaert and Braithwaite 1998). The OLS equation can be estimated under weaker assumptions concerning the error term, as pointed out by Ravallion (1996). Contrary to the Probit model the income variable is not transformed into a binary variable for poor and non-poor and then regressed on to access the variables that determine poverty. Rather, we estimated the influence of the various variables on income in general. Since this prevents a loss of information in the course of transforming income into a binary variable, this model serves as a good check for our Probit estimation. We anticipated that the sign and significance levels of the coefficients match the ones from our Tobit estimation and that the coefficients have the opposite sign than in our Probit regression:

$$Y = \alpha + \beta X + e$$

$Y \triangleq$ logarithm of adjusted income
$\alpha \triangleq$ intercept
$\beta \triangleq$ vector of coefficients
$X \triangleq$ vector of variables
$e \triangleq$ error term

To be able to judge the relative importance of the different variables we computed the marginal effects $\frac{dy}{dx}$ of the coefficient estimates for our Probit model, yielding the (*ceteris paribus*) increase in the probability of poverty for a marginal increase in the corresponding variable. In the case of dummy variables the increase in probability corresponds to a shift from zero to one in the binary dummy variable. We reported only the marginal effects in our result table since they are much more informative than the raw coefficients. From our Tobit estimation we reported the marginal effect of the explanatory variable on income if the household is below the poverty line. For all our models we also carried out separate regressions for the rural registered (migrant) and urban registered population groups to investigate the differences in parameters between both groups. This seemed appropriate after a Chow test revealed that the parameters of the migrant and non-migrant subgroups differ significantly. It thus became apparent that the factors that generate income and cause poverty differ between both population subgroups.

Estimation results

The results of our estimations are summed up in Table 16.4.

The standard OLS regression largely confirms the results of the Probit estimation. The Tobit estimation shows significantly different parameter estimates for the poor population. The same remains true for the separate regressions for the migrant and non-migrant sub-populations. The estimations appear robust with a relatively strong goodness of fit.

To estimate the degree of wage discrimination against migrants we also carried out an Oaxaca-Blinder decomposition of our Probit and Tobit regressions. We wanted to decompose the Probit and Tobit regressions into an endowment and return component. The return component is generally interpreted as the extent of discrimination. Since the standard Oaxaca-Blinder decomposition can only be used for the linear case we had to employ a generalization of this method as described for the non-linear case by Bauer and Sinning (2006). We provided the results for the migrants as reference group (Omega = 1) and for the non-migrants as reference group (Omega = 0).

Evidence of poverty causes and implications

The estimation results underline the multidimensional nature of poverty. Household composition, productive household assets, social factors and sector of occupation have a significant influence on poverty incidence, the income of the poor and the income of the total population. Most of the variables within these categories are significant and remain robust concerning the different estimation methods and population subgroups. Our main results are:

- Migrants are more likely to be poor than non-migrants.
- Poverty determinants differ substantially between migrants and non-migrants. Productive assets in particular are more important for migrants.
- Migrants face substantial income discrimination.

It is clear that migrants have a substantially lower income than their non-migrant counterparts and that their registration status drastically increases their probability of being poor (Table 16.4 AI and AIII). From our separate regressions it is evident that the factors that determine poverty status (Table 16.4 AI–III)

Table 16.4 Estimation results

Variable	*All observations (A)*		*Non-migrants (B)*		*Migrants (C)*	
	coef/effect	*se*	*coef/effect*	*se*	*coef/effect*	*se*
Probit estimations (I)						
av_age	0.002*	0.001	0.001	0.001	0.007**	0.003
family_size	−0.038***	0.013	−0.031***	0.010	−0.015	0.025
dpr	0.043***	0.014	0.016**	0.008	0.087***	0.033
av_schooling	−0.032***	0.005	−0.013***	0.003	−0.048***	0.010
infedu	−0.122***	0.026	−0.034**	0.013	−0.258***	0.080
stay	−0.004**	0.002	−0.002**	0.001	−0.004	0.004
male	−0.233**	0.102	−0.117	0.081	−0.268*	0.158
rural	0.164***	0.029				
sez	−0.099***	0.028	−0.047**	0.023	−0.107**	0.051
soe	0.049	0.045	0.014	0.025	0.135	0.103
foreignshare	−0.108***	0.028	−0.034***	0.012	−0.180**	0.087
self_employed	0.037	0.029	0.049*	0.030	0.007	0.052
Pseudo R2	0.252		0.262		0.105	
Tobit estimations (II)						
av_age	−0.001**	0.001	−0.001	0.001	−0.003***	0.001
family_size	0.009	0.006	0.030***	0.009	−0.010	0.010
dpr	−0.026***	0.006	−0.020***	0.008	−0.048***	0.012
av_schooling	0.012***	0.002	0.013***	0.003	0.016***	0.003
infedu	0.062***	0.017	0.040**	0.020	0.101***	0.031
stay	0.003***	0.001	0.002***	0.001	0.003*	0.002
male	0.105***	0.041	0.089**	0.041	0.126	0.087
rural	−0.076***	0.012				
sez	0.046***	0.011	0.041**	0.017	0.048**	0.019
soe	−0.018	0.019	−0.008	0.021	−0.060	0.044
foreignshare	0.063***	0.020	0.050*	0.030	0.080**	0.036
self_employed	−0.010	0.011	−0.036*	0.019	0.007	0.018
Pseudo R2	0.250		0.267		0.127	
OLS estimations (III)						
av_age	−0.006**	0.003	−0.009**	0.004	−0.010***	0.003
family_size	0.110***	0.027	0.203***	0.044	−0.001	0.034
dpr	−0.078**	0.031	−0.080*	0.043	−0.081*	0.044
av_schooling	0.084***	0.009	0.097***	0.014	0.071***	0.011
infedu	0.211***	0.066	0.166**	0.079	0.329***	0.111
stay	0.013***	0.003	0.014***	0.003	0.006	0.005
male	0.343**	0.141	0.293	0.187	0.414***	0.136
rural	−0.688***	0.059				
sez	0.283***	0.049	0.386***	0.080	0.119**	0.059
soe	−0.072	0.075	−0.108	0.095	−0.109	0.111
foreignshare	0.388***	0.080	0.330***	0.102	0.432***	0.123
self_employed	−0.104*	0.056	−0.314***	0.105	0.065	0.061
_cons	8.620***	0.207	8.276***	0.272	8.501***	0.225
Adjusted R2	0.461		0.253		0.186	
Number of observations	1.026		559		467	

Notes: $^{***}p < 0.01$, $^{**}p < 0.05$, $^{*}p < 0.1$.

Table 16.5 Decomposition results

Omega	*1*	*0*
Probit		
Endowment	48.3%	50.8%
Return	51.7%	49.2%
Tobit		
Endowment	32.2%	48.8%
Return	67.8%	51.2%

and income for the poor and non-poor vary widely between migrants and non-migrants (Table 16.4 BII and CII). Poverty incidence among migrants is much more influenced by productive assets and sector of occupation than among non-migrants (Table 16.4 CI). The same is true for the influence of productive assets on the income of the poor (Table 16.4 CII). By contrast, it is obvious from the decomposition that it is much harder for them to capitalize on their assets since the income gap between migrants and non-migrants is largely due to income and wage discrimination (Table 16.4). This fact is especially worrying since our analysis showed that poverty incidence and the income of the poor are more influenced by a household's productive assets in the case of migrant households.

If we take a closer look at the categories and single variables it can be seen that *household composition* proves to be of great importance. Here, family size as well as the ratio of non-workers to workers has a similar albeit expected contrary influence on the probability of falling below the poverty line. A large family with fewer working members will find it harder to earn an income that prevents its descent into poverty. If we distinguish between migrant and non-migrant households it is clear that the average age of the household and the dependency ratio influence the probability of poverty far more in migrant households than in non-migrant households, for whom family size is more important. The same is true for the income of the poor households. If we look at the income of the poor and non-poor as a whole, family size remains the only strongly distinguishing factor.

It is evident that *household assets* such as human capital defined by years of schooling and informal education have a high impact on poverty status. The existence of human capital allows the household to generate income from this asset and reduces its likelihood of being poor. Major differences appear between the different subgroups. The impact on poverty status of human capital for the migrant population is much higher and represents the strongest factor. If we look at returns to schooling it is clear that the poor earn a far lower return than the average population and no matter if poor or not the migrants have a lower return to schooling but a higher return to informal education than their non-migrant counterparts. The influence of duration of residence of the household head, which is an indicator of social networking and accumulation of region-specific knowledge and skills that can be capitalized on, has a negative influence on poverty incidence. The effect, though, is rather small. The effect of the household head's gender is mixed. It has a large influence on the probability of being poor mainly for the migrant subgroup, on the income of poor non-migrants and on the income of the average migrant, but not for the average non-migrant.

In general, our results – where they consider gender, age, and schooling – are largely in line with the results of Meng *et al.* (2008). Unlike their results, the positive impact of household size in our model is due to our different definition of the ratio of dependants to workers. Also, the results of Li (2006) stress the importance of gender, education, and household size. Appleton (2008) confirms the negative influences of female gender, dependency ratio, number of adult household members, and the positive impact of education. In our chapter, more detailed and interesting results are yielded by the social and China-specific factors and by the comprehensive comparison between the migrant and non-migrant subgroups, which we were able to include due to the specific design of the survey.

All of these *social and China-specific* variables are significant for the whole sample. Rural registration of the household head has a very negative influence on income and poverty incidence. Discrimination of rural registered workers, as well as the potential lack of good schooling etc. in rural areas, which negatively affects human capital, leads to a significantly higher probability of poverty for households with a rural registered family head. It is apparent that migrants who try to escape severe poverty though migration are at far greater risk of being poor than urban registered inhabitants. It should be noted that the negative influence of rural registration on income is less drastic for the poor subgroup. The policy effect of special economic zones is also important. If the household is located in the special economic zone in Shenzhen it is less likely to be poor which may imply that employment opportunities in this area are better than outside the SEZ. This policy has the largest influence on the income of the non-migrant population.

The results for the dummy variables that capture the *sector of occupation* are mixed. Employment by a state-owned enterprise is insignificant. This is a rather surprising result since we expected positive correlation of poverty with self-employment and a negative correlation with affiliation to a state-owned enterprise. It seems that neither the stabilizing nor the selection effect of state-owned enterprises is of any importance. Self-employment, which commonly implies low-income, one-man enterprises, is not relevant for migrants but is relevant for non-migrants. It negatively impacts on the income of the poor and the average urban registered inhabitants, increasing their probability of falling below the poverty line. If the household head works for a company that is fully or partly owned by a foreign investor they are less likely to be poor. This may be because foreign or sino-foreign joint ventures offer better pay, but may also be due to the fact that a greater number of better-qualified people work for those companies. Working for this type of company is especially positive for migrants, be they poor or non-poor. It also greatly diminishes their probability of being poor.

It is evident from our Oaxaca–Blinder decomposition results for the Probit estimation that depending on what group is chosen as a reference, 49 to 68 percent of the income of migrants is lower than that of non-migrants due to discrimination, not to differences in factor accumulation. This value rises to between 51 and 68 percent if we decompose the Tobit estimation results for the poor population (Table 16.4).

All these results underline the difficult situation migrants are in, as well as the differences in poverty determining factors between them and their non-migrant counterparts. Migrants have not been able to participate in the major prosperity gains as much as others, and continue to face serious income discrimination. Policy measures to increase the factor accumulation, particularly that of human capital, and to lessen income discrimination seem appropriate to alleviate poverty especially among the migrant population. But the hukou system, one of the primary causes of lower income and greater poverty among migrants, may also weaken the other negative effects of migration. An implication of this system is that it increases the opportunity costs for people considering migration to the cities by imposing higher costs on them. To this extent the existing discrimination of migrants also creates a barrier against excess migration and could hence help to keep in check the negative effects of excess migration as observed in many other developing countries. Thus careful judgment is needed to weigh the costs and benefits of poverty alleviation policies against each other. Furthermore, it should be noted that many rural–urban migrants can still move back to their villages in case the expected benefits fail to materialize. To this extent, this option serves as a safety net where available.

Conclusion

The extent of poverty in urban China varies greatly due to different definitions of poverty lines and welfare measures. We chose a broader definition of the poverty line to analyze poverty incidence in Shenzhen, one of the most developed cities in mainland China. We explored whether migratory status was connected with poverty and if migrants are poorer than non-migrants. Furthermore, it was our goal to highlight the different forces that drag migrant and non-migrant households into poverty, and to discover the extent to which the poor differ from the non-poor in this respect.

To estimate general poverty incidence in Shenzhen we had to adjust for local prices in this booming city. We corrected household income using a local expense basket by Brandt and Holz (2006), updated with the regional urban CPI from the Chinese National Bureau of Statistics. To take economies of scale into account we used the Organization for Economic Co-operation and Development's equivalence scale to correct household income. The poverty estimates we arrived at were low yet varied greatly depending on the adjustments made. This led us to the conclusion that a relative poverty approach seems suitable to analyze the determinants of poverty for Shenzhen. Shenzhen appears to be so highly developed that the approach commonly used for Western industrialized economies, where extreme poverty is largely absent, is reasonable.

To look deeper into the causes of poverty in Shenzhen we conducted multiple regressions. We used a Probit model to identify the factors influencing the probability of falling below the poverty line. A Tobit model was employed to analyze the income of the poor. To check the robustness of our estimations we also conducted standard continuous ordinary least squares welfare regressions. We conducted separate regressions for the migrant and non-migrant population subgroups to identify differences in income and poverty generating factors. The variables we chose for our analysis can be categorized as social factors, productive assets, sector of occupation and household composition. A non-linear decomposition analysis was conducted to inspect the extent of discrimination between both groups.

It became evident that migrant status of the household head greatly increases the probability of poverty and negatively influences household income. Migrants not only have a lower income and face a higher probability of being poor, but they are also discriminated against since a large part of the income gap between migrants and non-migrants is due to income and wage discrimination. This is especially grave since our analysis indicated that poverty incidence and the income of the poor are far more influenced by a household's productive assets in the case of migrant households.

These results highlight the serious problems rural–urban migrants face. It can be concluded that even though Shenzhen is an outstanding example of a very rapid development process, careful judgment will be necessary to tackle the income discrimination of migrants and support their accumulation of assets to further eradicate poverty.

References

Appleton, S. (1996) 'Women Headed Households and Household Welfare: An Empirical Deconstruction for Uganda', *World Development*, 24 (12): 1811–1827.

Appleton, S., Song, L. and Xia, Q. (2008) 'Growing out of Poverty: Trends and Patterns of Urban Poverty in China 1988–2002', IZA working paper No. 3459.

Bauer, K. and Sinning, M. (2006) 'An Extension to the Blinder-Oaxaca Decomposition to Non-Linear Models', RWI discussion paper No. 49.

Bourguignon, F. (2004) 'The Poverty-Growth-Inequality Triangle', working paper presented at the Indian Council for Research on International Economic Relations, New Delhi.

Brandt, L. and Holtz, A. (2006) 'Spatial Price Differences in China: Estimates and Implications, Economic Development and Cultural Change', University of Chicago, Chicago.

Chen, A. and Coulson, N. E. (2002) 'Determinants of Urban Migration: Evidence from Chinese Cities', *Urban Studies*, 39 (12): 2189–2197.

Deaton, A. (1997) 'The Analysis of Household Surveys', The World Bank, Washington.

Fan, C. (2001) 'Migration and Labor-market Returns in Urban China: Results from a Recent Survey in Guangzhou', *Environment and Planning*, 33: 479–508.

Grootaert, C. (1997) 'The Determinants of Poverty in Cote d'Ivoire in the 1980s', *Journal of African Economics*, 6 (2): 169–196.

Grootaert, C. and Braithwaite, J. (1998) 'Poverty Correlates and Indicator based Targeting in Eastern Europe and the Former Soviet Union', policy research working paper 1942, The World Bank, Washington.

Gustafsson, G., Shig, L. and Sato, H. (2006) 'Can a Subjective Poverty Line be Applied to Urban China? Assessing Poverty Among Urban Residents in 1999', in Shi, L. and Sato, H. (eds), *Unemployment, Inequality and Poverty in Urban China*, New York: Routledge.

Hussain, A. (2003) 'Urban Poverty in China: Measurement, Patterns and Policies', International Labour Organization, Geneva.

Khan, A. (1998) 'Poverty in China in the Era of Globalization', issues in *Development Discussion Paper 22*, International Labour Organization, Geneva.

Khan, A. (2008) 'Growth, Inequality and Poverty A Comparative Study of China's Experience before and after the Asian Crisis', *Inequality and Public Policy in China*, Cambridge: Cambridge University Press, 145–181.

Knight, J. and Song, L. (1999) *The Rural–Urban Divide: Economic Disparities and Interactions in China*, Oxford: Oxford University Press.

Knight, J. and Song, L. (2003) 'Increasing Urban Wage Inequality in China. Extent, elements and evaluation', *Economics of Transition*, 11 (4): 597–619.

Li, S. (2006) *Rising Poverty and Its Causes in Urban China, Unemployment, Inequality and Poverty in Urban China*, New York: Routledge.

Lu, Z. and Song, S. (2006) 'Rural–urban Migration and Wage Determination the Case of Tianjin, China', *China Economic Review,* 17: 337–345.

Meng, X., Gregory R. and Wan, G. (2008) 'China's Urban Poverty and it's Contributing Factors 1986–2000', *Understanding Inequality and Poverty in China Methods and Applications*, Helsinki: Palgrave Macmillan, 219–249.

Park, A., Yang, D. and Sagui, W. (2004) 'Is Migration Helping China's Poor?', paper presented at the conference on Poverty, Inequality, Labour Market and Welfare Reform in China, Australian National University, Canberra, 25–27.

Ravallion, M. (1993) 'Poverty Comparisons: A Guide to Concepts and Methods', LSMS working paper 88, The World Bank, Washington, DC.

Ravallion, M. (1996) 'Issues in Modelling Poverty', *The Economic Journal*, 106: 1328–1343.

Ravallion, M. (2004) 'China's (uneven) Progress against Poverty', World Bank Policy research paper No. 3408.

Shu, X. (2005) 'Market Transition and Gender Segregation in Urban China', *Social Science Quarterly*, 86: 1299–1323.

Xue, J. and Gries, T. (2008) 'Human Capital Accumulation and Income Distribution in Urban China : The Case of Shenzhen', *The Economic Science*, 2007 (12): 101–115.

Xue, J. and Zhong, W. (2003) 'Unemployment, Poverty and Income Disparity in Urban China', *Asian Economic Journal*, 17 (4): 383–405.

Index

Printed by Publishers' Graphics Kentucky